Limits to Globalization

έπάμεροι· τί δέ τις; τί δ' οϋ τις; σκιάς όναρ
άνθρωπος. άλλ' όταν ϊγλα διόσδοτος έλθη,
λαμπόν φέγγος έπεοτιν άνδρών καί μείλιχος αίών.

Pindar, *Pythian Ode* 8, 95–8

For Magic Mini and Walerie, and to the memory of the days in Everswinkel.

Limits to Globalization

Welfare States and the World Economy

Elmar Rieger and Stephan Leibfried

Translated by Benjamin W. Veghte
with the assistance of Elmar Rieger

polity

First published in 2003 by Polity Press in association with Blackwell Publishing Ltd

Editorial office:
Polity Press
65 Bridge Street
Cambridge CB2 1UR, UK

Marketing and production:
Blackwell Publishing Ltd
108 Cowley Road
Oxford OX4 1JF, UK

Distributed in the USA by
Blackwell Publishing Inc.
350 Main Street
Malden, MA 02148, USA

A catalogue record for this book is available from the British Library.

Library of Congress Cataloging-in-Publication Data
Rieger, Elmar.
Limits to globalization : welfare states and the world economy / Elmar Rieger and Stephan Leibfried ; translated by Benjamin W. Veghte with the assistance of Elmar Rieger.
p. cm.
Includes bibliographical references and index.
ISBN 0-7456-2850-8 – ISBN 0-7456-2851-6 (pbk) 1. Public welfare – Cross-cultural studies. 2. Public welfare – Economic aspects – Cross-cultural studies. 3. Globalization. I. Leibfried, Stephan, 1944– II. Title.
HV40 .R528 2003
361.6 – dc21
2002013977

Typeset in 10.5 on 12pt Sabon
by SNP Best-set Typesetter Ltd., Hong Kong
Printed and bound in Great Britain by TJ International, Padstow, Cornwall

For further information on Polity, visit our website: http://www.polity.co.uk

Contents

List of Tables, Figures and Boxes

TABLES

FIGURES

BOXES

List of Abbreviations

AAD	Agreement on Antidumping under GATT/WTO of 1994 (full title: Agreement on the Implementation of Art. VI of the GATT 1994)
ADC	Aid to Dependent Children of 1935 (part of the Social Security Act of 1935)
AFDC	Aid to Families with Dependent Children of 1962 (renamed TANF)
AFL-CIO	American Federation of Labor – Congress of Industrial Organizations; national umbrella organization of all US labour unions (http://www.aflcio.org/)
AS	Agreement on Safeguards under GATT/WTO of 1994
BIS	Bank for International Settlement, Basel, Switzerland, founded 1930 (http://www.bis.org)
BVerfGE	Decisions of the German Constitutional Court. Official Collection (*Entscheidungen des Bundesverfassungsgerichtes. Amtliche Sammlung*) (http://www.bvlrfg.de)
CFDA	Catalog of Federal Domestic Assistance
CFIUS	Committee on Foreign Investments in the United States
CPF	Central Provident Fund (Singapore)
CSSA	Comprehensive Social Security Assistance (Hong Kong)
EA	Emergency Assistance for Needy Families
EITC	Earned Income Tax Credit, a US tax welfare programme starting from 1974
EMU	European Economic and Monetary Union in the context of the European Community (EC) dating to 1999 and implemented since 1 January 2001 and 2002 respectively
FAZ	*Frankfurter Allgemeine Zeitung*
FDI	Foreign Direct Investment
G7 (8)	'Group of 7' (8); 'summit' of the larger and more important industrialized nations
GATT	General Agreement on Trade and Tariffs of 1947, in force as of 1 January 1948 (http://www.gatt.org)
GDP	Gross Domestic Product
GKV	German Public Health Insurance or *Gesetzliche Krankenversicherung* (http://www.g-k-v.com; http://www.bmgesundheit.de)
HERMES	The Hermes Kreditversicherung-AG in Hamburg, Germany; processes the state guarantees for German exports (http://www.hermeskredit.com)
ILO	International Labour Organization, Geneva, Switzerland, founded in 1919; also the first UN suborganization in 1946 (http://www.ilo.org)
IMF	International Monetary Fund (IMF), founded – together with the World Bank – in 1944 at the UN international economic conference at Bretton Woods, New Hampshire, 1–22 July (http://www.imf.org)

IRS	Internal Revenue Service, federal tax agency of the USA
ISSA	International Social Security Association, founded in 1927 (http://www.issa.int)
ITC	US International Trade Commission (http://www.usitc.gov)
ITO	International Trade Organization, planned for in the Havanna Charter of 1947
JOBS	Job Opportunities and Basic Skills Development, a US social policy programme
NAFTA	North American Free Trade Agreement of 1992 (USA, Canada, Mexico) (http://nafta.net)
NGO	Non-Governmental Organization
OECD	Organization for Economic Cooperation and Development, Paris, since 1961; the OECD is a successor organization to the Organization for European Economic Co-operation of 1948 and of the European Recovery Programme (ERP), in short, of the Marshall Plan (http://www.oecd.org)
OPS	Old-Age Pension Scheme (Hong Kong)
PFI	Portfolio Investment
PKV	German Private Health Insurance or *Private Krankenversicherung* (http://www.pkv.verband.de)
PRWORA	Personal Responsibility and Work Reconciliation Act of 1996 ('Clinton's Welfare Reform')
ROA	Return on Assets
RTAA	US Reciprocal Trade Agreement Act of 1934
SSA	Social Security Allowance (Hong Kong)
SIPP	US Survey of Income and Program Participation (http://www.sipp.census.gov/sipp)
TAA	US Trade Adjustment Act of 1962
TAA	US Trade Adjustment Assistance – welfare benefits for job losses attributed to free trade
TANF	Temporary Assistance for Needy Families, 1996 (successor programme to AFDC)
UNCTAD	United Nations Conference on Trade and Development, founded in 1964 (http://www.unctad.org)
UNDP	United Nations Development Program, 1965 – several earlier programmes were consolidated into the then UNDP (http://www.undp.org)
USTR	[Office of the] US Trade Representative (http://www.ustr.gov/)
WTO	World Trade Organization, founded in 1993, effective as of 1 January 1995 (http://www.wto.org)

Acknowledgements

For substantial support of our work, we are grateful to the Institute for Advanced Studies in Berlin (Wissenschaftskolleg zu Berlin), the Hanse Institute for Advanced Studies (Hanse Wissenschaftskolleg) in Delmenhorst, Germany (as well as to our patient and helpful co-fellows at these institutes during 1997–8), the Center for Advanced Study in the Behavioral Sciences in Stanford, California, the Department of Political Science at Stanford University, the American Institute for Contemporary German Studies in Washington, DC, Brown University – in particular its Department of Sociology and its Watson Institute for International Studies – the (now transubstantiated) German-American Academic Council (Bonn), which supported two summer schools at the Center for European Studies (CES) of Harvard University and at the Centre for Social Policy Research (CeS) at Bremen University, as well as a transatlantic research project on globalization, the German National Science Foundation (Deutsche Forschungsgemeinschaft), which supported our research on welfare reform in the USA and Germany in one phase of its globalization programme, the Fritz Thyssen Foundation and Die Sparkasse Bremen for their help in revising and publishing this volume and (almost) last but not least, the CeS and the Special Research Unit (Sonderforschungsbereich) 'Status Passages and Risk in the Life Course' (1988–2001), and, finally, Bremen University *in toto*, especially its Chancellor Gerd-Rüdiger Kück and its Rector Jürgen Timm, who supported both of us at critical junctures in this extended and arduous endeavour.

Work on this book went on in so many places over the last ten years – Mannheim, Cambridge (MA), Delmenhorst, Bremen, Heidelberg, Gaishardt (Suavia) and Providence (RI) for Elmar Rieger; Stanford, Berlin and Bremen for Stephan Leibfried – that we would not have finished without the continuing support and guidance of Suhrkamp Publishers in Frankfurt, especially Raimund Fellinger and Winfried Hörning, which led to the first German-language publication in 2001 (chapter 5 will be published as a separate volume there); of Polity Press, especially David Held; and of Cambridge University Press, especially John Haslam. Last and by no means least, we want to thank Benjamin W. Veghte, who helped us through all these years in effecting and amending diverse German–English transubstantiations of this text. And also, special thanks to the Schiele family for providing computer access in the final stage, and to the Rieger family for giving shelter to books and papers.

Thanks also to Jutta and Holger Viebrok for coping with our ever different versions of figures and tables, to Gitta Klein for fulfilling the complex and enduring task of editing this manuscript in two languages, to the Library of the Berlin Institute for Advanced Studies for satisfying our insatiable appetite for ever more books and journals, to Stefanie Hennecke, Zuzana Krell-Laluhová, Barbara Rexilius, Karolina Milewicz, and also Stefanie Weigman of the Harvard Law School International Legal Studies Library for their assistance, and also to Torsten Jarks for checking our literature and for proofreading – and to the many others whom we cannot list here. For advice, critique and constructive support we are grateful to Birgitta Wolff, Herbert Obinger, Josef Falke, Franz-Xaver Kaufmann, Robert O. Keohane, Achim Schmid, Waltraud Schelkle, Martin Seeleib-Kaiser, Benjamin W. Veghte, Uwe Wagschal, Michael Wiseman, Bernhard Zangl and Michael Zürn – and to the many others who have accompanied us through the 1990s with their suggestions and critical comments.

Most of the chapters in the book started life in a quite different form. Chapter 1 is an original contribution by both of us. Chapter 2 is based on a lecture given by Elmar Rieger at the Hanse Institute for Advanced Studies in Delmenhorst, Germany on 27 February 1997; it has been substantially revised. For a short version, see Rieger and Leibfried (2000). Chapter 3 is a version of Rieger (1999a), which we have revised. Chapter 4 is a revised and substantially expanded version of Rieger and Leibfried (1998b) and of 'The Social Politics of Trade', a lecture given by Elmar Rieger at a conference of the Social Policy Association in Lincoln, UK in June 1998. Chapter 5 is a somewhat revised version of Rieger and Leibfried (1999).

In addition, the editors and the publisher gratefully acknowledge the permission granted to reproduce the following copyright material in this book:

Tables 2.9 and 2.11 reproduced from Bernard M. Hoekman and Michel M. Kostecki, *The Political Economy of the World Trading System. The WTO and Beyond*, 2nd edn, pp. 303 f., 307. Copyright © 2001, Oxford University Press, Oxford, UK.

Table 2.10 reproduced from Richard Blackhurst, 'The Capacity of the WTO to Fulfill its Mandate'. In Anne O. Krueger, ed., *The WTO as an International Organization*, p. 40. Copyright © 1998 by the University of Chicago Press, Chicago, IL.

Table 2.13 reproduced from J. Michael Finger, Francis Ng and Sonam Wangchuk, 'Antidumping as Safeguard Policy', World Bank (WP 2730), p. 13. Copyright © 2001 J. Michael Finger, Francis Ng and Sonam Wangchuk. Also in Robert M. Stern, ed., *Issues and Options for US-Japan Trade Policies*, p. 148. Copyright © University of Michigan Press, Studies in International Economics, 2002.

Table 2.14 reproduced from Magnus Henrekson and Ulf Jakobsson, 'Where Schumpeter was Nearly Right – the Swedish Model and Capitalism, Socialism and Democracy'. *Journal of Evolutionary Economics* 11, p. 351. Copyright © 2000 by Magnus Henrekson and Ulf Jakobsson; and from Walter Korpi, 'Eurosclerosis and the Sclerosis of Objectivity: On the Role of Values Among Economic Policy Experts'. *Economic Journal* 106/439 (November), p. 1737. Copyright © 1996 Walter Korpi and *Economic Journal*, Blackwell, Cambridge, UK.

Table 3.3 reproduced from Alfred E. Eckes, *Opening America's Market: US Foreign Trade Policy Since 1776*, p. 245. Copyright © 1995 by the University of North Carolina Press, Chapel Hill, NC.

Table 3.4 reproduced from Paul T. Decker and Walter Corson, 'International Trade and Worker Displacement: Evaluation of the Trade Adjustment Assistance Program'. *Industrial and Labor Relations Review* 48/4 (July), p. 762. Copyright © 1995 by ILR Review, Cornell University, Ithaca, NY.

Table 3.5 reproduced from Lars Osberg, 'Long Run Trends in Economic Inequality in Five Countries: A Birth Cohort View'. Luxembourg: Luxembourg Income Study, p. 13 (WP 222). Copyright © 2000 Lars Osberg.

Tables 3.6–3.8 reproduced from Robert William Fogel, *The Fourth Great Awakening and the Future of Egalitarianism*, pp. 277 f., 279, 280 f. Copyright © 2000 by the University of Chicago Press, Chicago, IL.

Table 4.2 reproduced from United Nations Conference on Trade and Development (UNCTAD), *World Investment Report 2000: Cross-Border Mergers and Acquisitions and Development*, New York: United Nations, p. 2, table I.1. Copyright © 2001 by UNCTAD.

Table 4.8 reproduced from Frank Levy, *The New Dollars and Dreams: American Incomes and Economic Change*, p. 199. Copyright © 1999 by Russell Sage Foundation, 112 East 64th Street, New York, NY 10021.

Tables 5.3 and 5.4 rely strongly on Didier Jacobs, 'Social Welfare Systems in East Asia: A Comparative Analysis Including Private Welfare', London: LSE, Centre for Analysis of Social Exclusion (CASE paper 10). Copyright © 1998 Didier Jacobs.

Table 5.5 reproduced from Kym Anderson, Yujiro Hayami and Masayoshi Honma 'The Growth of Agricultural Protection'. In Kym Anderson and Yujiro Hayami, eds,

The Political Economy of Agricultural Protection. East Asia in International Perspective, p. 22. Copyright © 1986 by Allen & Unwin, Sydney, Australia.

Figure 3.6 reproduced from Hwanjoon Kim, 'Anti-Poverty Effectiveness of Taxes and Income Transfers in Welfare States', Luxembourg: Luxembourg Income Study. Copyright © 2000 by Hwanjoon Kim, also © 1979 by ILO Wilfred Beckermann.

Figure 4.1 reproduced from Kai-Uwe Schanz, *Export. Lizenzvergabe oder Direktinvestition? Eine wirtschaftstheoretische Analyse unternehmerischer Internationalisierungsstrategien vor dem Hintergrund der neuen WTO-Welthandelsordnung*, p. 16. Copyright © 1995 Rüegger Verlag, Chur/Zürich, Switzerland.

Figure 5.1 reproduced from Didier Jacobs, 'Social Welfare Systems in East Asia: A Comparative Analysis Including Private Welfare', London: LSE, Centre for Analysis of Social Exclusion (CASE Paper 10), p. 90. Copyright © 1998 Didier Jacobs.

Several quotes reproduced from Huck-ju Kwon's 'Democracy and the Politics of Social Welfare: A Comparative Analysis of Welfare Systems in East Asia', in Robert Goodman, Gordon White and Huck-ju Kwon, eds, *The East Asian Welfare Model. Welfare Orientalism and the State*, pp. 27–74. Copyright © 1998 by Routledge, London.

Several quotes reproduced from Max Weber, *Economy and Society*, ed. Guenther Roth and Claus Wittlich, trans. Ephraim Fischoff. Copyright © 1978 by the University of California Press, Berkeley, CA.

We are grateful to all those institutions which have provided us with material from their regular reports, yearbooks, working papers etc., among them: the German Council of Economic Experts, the International Labour Organization, the International Monetary Fund, the OECD, UNCTAD, US Congress (incl. the Green Book), the US Internal Revenue Service, the US Trade Commission, the US Census Bureau, the World Bank and the WTO.

Every effort has been made to trace copyright holders and to obtain their permission for the use of copyright material. The publisher apologizes for any errors or omissions in the above list and would be grateful if notified of any corrections that should be incorporated in future reprints or editions of this book.

Introduction

Facts and events are infinitely more fragile things than axioms, discoveries, theories – even the most wildly speculative ones – produced by the human mind.

Hannah Arendt 1967: 548

'Limits to Globalization' in the title of this book refers, first, to certain conditions of globalization that are regularly overlooked in discussions of its scope and impact on the social and political order of the nation-state as we know it. These conditions – for example, international exchange grounded in *national* economic and trade law, or the omnipresence of *domestic* trade policy regulation – are rarely given sufficient consideration in globalization discourse. Why not? Because this discourse focuses almost exclusively on what the *future* will bring – which in most cases is identical with what the future is *supposed* to bring. The latter differs according to one's taste – which, as is well known, is not subject to debate. In any case, in the shadow of usually grand normative narrative, justice is rarely done to the *causal* analysis of *empirical* conditions.

This book deals primarily with socio-political facts about welfare states placed in the world economy. Social policy concerns us here neither as an order of values and norms nor as 'theory', but as a complex of empirical facts conditioning real political and economic action. When actors orient their behaviour to certain values, norms or theories, or behave in a certain way because they believe in their validity, then this concerns us here solely as an empirical fact, and not as evidence of any kind of 'objective' correctness of this normative point of departure. However, the more a topic is subject to intense political debate, the more important it becomes to state as clearly as possible one's understanding of what social science should and can do. Thus, in all the chapters that follow we will treat problems of social science explanation in some detail.

At the end of the day, though, our goal is to educate judgement about practical social problems. In doing so, we try to remain within the sphere of *scientific* discussion. Just because there is a demand for conclusions that can be presented as 'solutions' does not mean that there is any solid *scientific* basis for them. Our investigations are not concerned with solving the problems that globalization supposedly poses for social and economic policy. All the chapters can be read separately, since each chapter proceeds from an *empirical* research question rooted in the *actual* problems which concrete actors in the fields of government, economics and society face with regard to globalization and social policy and with which they, *nolens volens*, are compelled to contend. We are concerned with the substance of the related policy conflicts. What lies at their core? How did they come to be? What effects on social and political reality do they, in turn, have? Such an approach, by necessity, includes some debunking of popular myths. Any decent explanation must explain *what is in fact the case* by showing what distinguishes it from *what is in fact not the case.*

To repeat, this volume does not offer any solutions, any 'how to' wisdoms, but instead points to *explanatory* problems in the globalization/welfare state conundrum. Our analysis is not concerned with doing justice to the *political* challenge that globalization and the welfare state pose or appear to pose. Rather, it seeks to do justice to the *social science* challenge of conceptually ordering empirical reality such that the conclusions reached pass the test of an empirical science. We are concerned with the facts.

As the epigraph to this introduction tries to indicate, facts are important because they can give power to truth. The politically most relevant truths are factual, and in consequence independent of opinion. Since, as James Madison noted, 'all governments rest on opinion',[1] such a claim on truth must necessarily strike at the very roots of all politics and all government. It is only in retrospect that every occurrence looks as if it could not have happened otherwise, but this is just a convenient illusion: 'nothing could ever happen if reality did not kill, by definition, all other potentialities originally inherent in any given situation' (Arendt 1967: 557). Facts are distinct from opinion or 'theory', but this does not make them transparent, 'for facts have no conclusive reason whatever for being what they are; they could always have been otherwise, and this annoying contingency is literally unlimited' (ibid.). Facts are neither self-evident nor do they speak for themselves. They reveal their meaning – including political significance – through the context in which they are consciously placed, and this 'placing' is what we call 'theory'.

In this volume, the facts that make up globalization are seen in relation to social policy, and the facts constituting social policy are placed in the context of globalization. As Weber (1904: 68) succinctly formulated it, the scope of the social sciences is not defined by 'the "actual" interconnections of "things" but the *conceptual* interconnections of *problems*'.

Social science arguments do not solve any public policy problem. That is the task of politics. Political struggles are power struggles, not the disinterested weighing of scientific arguments. Economics and social philosophy equip political actors with arguments, but they do not decide the outcome of political struggles. To criticize theoretical statements, i.e. the results of some *analytical* ordering of reality, because of their probable political-ideological implications is not exactly a contribution to the better understanding of this reality, despite the fact that such business has become a growth industry. In Plato's cave, the ranks are well filled, and torches pass from hand to hand.

[1] Federalist Paper No. 49 (Hamilton/Madison/Jay 1999 [1787–8]: 282).

It is this that gives rise to the shouting contest as to the true meaning of the shadows. For social science, the task must be to understand what *in fact* happened, i.e. that which takes place *outside* of the cave: why are things as they are? How did they become as they now are? Why do some want to change them and others try to maintain them as they are? We need more light, and we need more distance from quotidian politics: 'Theorists of international relations suffer from being too close to the events they discuss' (Keohane and Nye 1989: ix) – and this is true of other theorists as well.

The world is more than simply will and imagination. Every social action, particularly in politics, is dependent on conditions that it did not itself create, which can only be influenced to a limited extent and which have become so entwined with the interests of others that attempts to change them are very likely to meet resistance. This, in a nutshell, is the starting point of all social sciences. In this volume we study the determining *circumstances* of politics in the context of globalization. The focus of our social science interest is thus the constraints, typical conflicts and unavoidable dilemmas that condition political decision-making and action. In pursuing these problems, we may put ourselves and our readers in a somewhat uncomfortable position: 'It is precisely the vocation of our science to say things people do not like to hear' (Weber 1895: 23).

What issues and questions in particular do we explore in this volume? The following theses can be understood as the cornerstones of the analysis presented in the individual chapters.

1 For the majority of its actors and the mass public, the foundations of globalization remain unclear. Related to this is a serious political problem: how can globalization's gains, particularly in efficiency and welfare, be secured?
2 The welfare state and foreign trade are systematically interrelated. There are certain regularities that characterize their historical and contemporary relations, just as certain regularities describe the relations between policy-making in these two fields. Here, we argue the existence of a direct relationship only with regard to the policy-making sphere, i.e. with regard to the political-institutional interchangeability of trade policy and social policy. We do not argue that such a direct relationship exists with regard to the *outcomes* of these policies, i.e. for the effective security levels or actual changes in the level of risk faced by social groups. And it is a different question altogether what consequences, if any, welfare state protection has for a nation's business community or for its actual level of global market integration.
3 If one examines contemporary socio-political conditions, it appears unlikely that the positive economic effects of globalization are of an enduring nature. The new spatial conditions of economy and society indeed increase both within and among nations the prospects of cooperative and productive solutions to the long-standing problems of managing scarce resources. But they also encourage uncooperative behaviour. Virtually all governments nowadays are dependent on a democratic and thus exclusively national mass public. They may attempt to solve the mainly economic policy problems of global governance, but at the same time they face far different, essentially socio-political demands. Moreover, they lack an ongoing or even adequate executive capability to independently determine the direction and contents of their international action.
4 Governments do not grapple with 'globalization' itself, but with its effects – which governments directly encounter when dealing with the needs whose satisfaction

they have promised to their national electorate. With regard to international politics, only to a very limited extent does a national agenda for the political control of globalization exist which in actual fact is compatible with the functional requirements of a world market order.

5 Concomitant with the revolutionizing of the spatial scale of economic, social and political action, international interdependence increases. This gives rise to far-reaching expectations of an objectively necessitated radical reconstruction of the existing foundations of state, economy and society: that welfare state income guarantees must be reduced, social regulation of firms dismantled and the fiscal burden on 'productive' capital diminished. Despite the noise, these expectations have yet to be realized, and it is unlikely that they ever will be. Still, contrary to what an exuberant reform discussion would lead us to believe, governments, parliaments and courts have not remained passive, but have struggled to come to terms with globalization. Yet this struggle occurs primarily in national arenas. There, the instruments of *national* governance are reformed, and are often given a new, extra-territorial dimension. In some policy areas, the outcome turns out to be very different from what is expected. Increasingly, freedom of international movement has been restricted, for example, and borders have been reinforced. An aggressive mercantilism dominates trade policy. Moreover, the distributive effects of globalization give the still deeply entrenched welfare state response patterns more, not less weight. This predominantly domestic, not international, battle, which furthermore often unfolds quite differently in different national contexts, is hardly perceived, much less described and explained with regard to its true causes, various forms and consequences.

6 For national governments, the significance of international interdependence is twofold. On the one hand, its foreseeable repercussions bring about a loss of government autonomy, and state sovereignty is constrained by the juridification of international relations. On the other hand, some national governments experience increased possibilities to influence and put pressure on other societies, i.e. a gain in power. Moreover, governments intervene in other societies already by virtue of simply *how* they attempt to regulate their *own* society's social and economic conditions. For example, US economic policy-making – often motivated by purely partisan considerations or determined by particular domestic conditions – like reforms of US federal income protection programmes, has direct and often very significant effects on the members of societies in distant parts of the world.

7 Just as government freedom of action is dependent on 'globalization', the fate of globalization itself is decided by government action. Yet from this observation alone one can deduce neither a conclusive social science 'theory' nor any unambiguous political lesson. Similarly, the rapidly increasing interdependence of national economies and governments does not automatically lead to social and economic convergence or to a coordination of economic and social policy.

8 Globalization does not operate outside of and against local conditions, but rather always through them. For this reason, it is at all times of the utmost importance to understand local conditions in their particularity, as well as the consequences these particularities have for societal and individual fates respectively in the era of globalization. For the same reason it appears nonsensical to pit globalization against culture. Globalization is contested exactly because it *is* culture, albeit a very peculiar one. The core of globalization is an agonistic as well as imperialistic

economic 'rationalism' (Max Weber), with strong *eschatological* undertones. This 'commodity' is the most important Occidental product, and as such it is – sometimes enthusiastically and sometimes *bon gré mal gré* – imported by nearly all people of the world.

9 Limits to globalization as a cultural complex emerge not only from other cultures but also, and perhaps much more consequentially, from within. Democratic controls can drastically reduce the *political* mandate of the market mechanism. The more globalization as an impersonal, technical economic 'rationalism' evolves, the more a fundamentally negative attitude towards the essentially amoral market mechanism applies principled, *moral* demands to political governance of the economic realm. Grand social and political engineering will be back – because it never left us. Globalization is just its latest incarnation. It is part of the Western culture that it never accepts the institutions of the world as given. Rather, it creates strong and principled counter-images of some 'good society', which particularly in democratic polities can shatter the established order of things. Because of its unique transcendental qualities, Western culture is in essence a 'grammar of creation' (Steiner 2001). It is by no means true, and the remarkable stamina of social policy structures attests to it, that the 'utopian energies' of the welfare state (Habermas 1989) are being depleted – though they may take on a different form.

1

The Non-economic Preconditions of Globalization

Motorcars are travelling faster than they otherwise would *because* they are provided with brakes.

Joseph A. Schumpeter 1950 [1942]: 88

1 Globalization Issues and the Task of Social Theory

As globalization has reminded us most forcefully, problems of territoriality and space are too important to be left exclusively to geographers. Anything that eases the spatial movement of ideas, goods and persons also accelerates the course of history – and causes political problems in the process. Since the state is a combination of territory, people and government, every increase in the effective utilization and mastery of spatial distances made possible by technological progress has an initially negative and destructive impact on established forms of social order.

People establish a territorial basis because many critical issues of social order – including issues of distributive justice, such as security, recognition, welfare, education, and so on – can best be resolved *within* geographical units (Walzer 1983: 42–51; Elazar 1999). To think geographically about the political organization of space forces us to acknowledge that territory has its own *social* significance. The problems of space cannot be severed from concern with specific social processes.[1] The ability to move from one place to another and to physically evade political pressure – facilitated as much by technological as by organizational changes – has become a primary and thus also a contested means of power, for the members of different social groups depend to a different extent on public benefits and thus on the efficiency of territorial authority. In this situation, conflicts are inevitable, for changed spatial conditions have *institutional* repercussions.

In this book we argue that 'globalization' – described below in more detail – is largely a coincidental by-product of the welfare-democratic revolution in the institutional order in the most advanced post-war societies. Yet it also impacts back upon this geographically fixed socio-political order, removing its veil of naturalness and thus making its costs and restrictive effects visible. Indeed, this order's origins and development were shaped by very different spatial conditions which have long since been overtaken by the course of history. Spatial conditions and their significance as a determinant of social order are rarely perceived and even more seldom understood (Ruggie 1993; Jim Glassman 1999). The reason for this is that changes in spatial

[1] Cf. Robert Sack (1986) who pleads for *human* territoriality as a key concept in the social sciences and defines it as 'the attempt by an individual or group to affect, influence, or control people, phenomena, and relationships, by delimiting and asserting control over a geographic area' (19).

conditions are typically protracted and continuous, perceptible only retrospectively as great leaps and characterized by prolonged phases of suspension and slow adaptation, during which their political significance is easily overlooked. Nonetheless, time–space relations are constitutive for social, economic and political systems.[2] After all, under the 'reign of the spatio-temporal' (Friedrich Ratzel), conflict occurs not only over the appropriate reorientation and restructuration of political action, but also over the politics necessary to implement it – the latter being a problem in its own right.[3]

However, technical progress in the mastery of space, together with the resulting organizational possibilities for utilizing these new spatial conditions, are a necessary, but not a sufficient condition of the newly emerging global economy and information society. Welfare state structures of the developed post-war societies were and remain a critical variable for the timing, the form and the content of globalization. Conditions of emergence, though, are not identical with the existing or functional conditions, and clearly cannot be equated with conditions of rational further advancement. The mere demand for global governance – or its increased 'functional' necessity – by no means guarantees a corresponding supply of institutional solutions (Keohane 1982; Axelrod and Keohane 1985). The existing international organizations are 'powerless by design' (Feher 2000). They are not instruments for collective action, and none of them has a mandate to provide government. The now extant international governance of economic affairs involves no usurpation of the distinctive responsibilities of the separate national governments. The international apparatus is not an external organization based on delegated authority. It is made up of *national* organizations linked together for international work, and themselves forming the instruments of that work. In consequence, and not just by default, even under conditions of dramatically increased levels of interdependence, international economic policy is at its core a function of welfare-democratic and thus nation-state power relations. Moreover, globalization itself is an at first *unintended* effect of essentially domestic political developments, and it makes itself felt mostly in the national, apparently totally self-regarding politics of welfare states. In the following chapters, the focus is on the social and institutional repercussions of globalization in the most developed societies, the varying effects of these repercussions on national trade policy and on international economic policy, and finally, in turn, on the secondary consequences of these for the conditioning factors and the horizons of possibility for national social policy.

2 It is not quite true, as Harvey (1985: xii) claimed, that in the classical works of social theory there is an almost overwhelming predisposition to give time and history priority over space and geography. Weber (1978) described the locational competition of nation-states induced by the mobility of capital; Simmel's monumental *Soziologie* (1992 [1908]) includes a fascinating chapter simply titled 'Space'; Durkheim (1964 [1902]) foresaw a European integration brought about by an 'organic solidarity due to the division of labour'; and Marx and Engels (1998 [1848]: 39) described how the new cosmopolitan character of production and consumption has 'drawn from under the feet of industry the national ground on which it stood'. More recently, Giddens (1981) was one of the first in social theory to insist that time–space relations are determining features of social systems.

3 Still today, Ratzel's (1923, 1940) analyses of the relationship among spatial conditions, social order and political conflicts are illuminating. On Ratzel's geopolitical thought, see Weigert (1942a, b), Farinelli (2000), and Parker (2000). For two more recent overviews of a political geography see Burnett and Taylor (1981) and P. J. Taylor (1993).

The two fundamental problems of global governance

Since the claims of the 'theory' of globalization centre on the relationship between political organization and territoriality, which thus sees the nation-state as its number one victim, a first central political difficulty in effectively dealing with globalization issues under the new condition of 'complex interdependence' (Keohane and Nye 1989) is the absence of *legislative* international governance structures.[4] The latter is to a large degree the inadvertent side-effect of government action in societies in which critical changes in domestic conditions – in income, employment, distributional patterns, relations between individuals and between social groups – enjoy absolute priority over any type of problem-solving coordination at the level of international politics. The foundation of the national *de*regulation of foreign trade and its international liberal *re*regulation in the framework of GATT – which paved the way for economic globalization – was provided by the welfare state. What the welfare state revolution has done is to make material well-being the basis of citizens' *rights*. In the immediate post-war period, the welfare state was fashioned as a central propaganda tool in the Cold War competition between political and economic systems. Under the conditions of representative democracy, the only answer capitalism could give to the challenge of socialism was the proof that the material benefits it could secure were definitely greater than those of any alternative system. Thus welfare capitalism was born. But much more importantly, in the 1950s and 1960s, fuelled by the political rights of citizenship social policy's rise – from a series of makeshift interventionist measures to a systematic, formative power in people's lives and a primary symbol of societal modernity – represented a rejection of a free-market economy, or at least 'an insurance against revolt by the disinherited' (Laski 1933: 21).[5] It is thus one of the more ironic twists of world history that thereafter social policy became a pivotal precondition for the establishment of a free-market economy on an international scale.

4 As just one example for this line of thinking, see Ohmae (1995). For an introduction to the 'theory' of globalization, see Waters (1995). On the issue of 'complex interdependence' the work of Keohane and Nye and others is worthy of mention in many respects, and in particular for its demonstration that this condition is by no means new. Already in the 1950s and 1960s, a debate on 'transnational integration' occurred – one that easily could be confused with today's. Yet after the neo-mercantilist withdrawal from free trade and from world market integration in connection with the consequences of the oil crisis of 1971, the subject of 'complex interdependence' nearly disappeared from the theory of international relations once again. The concept was used as early as 1900 by Small (p. 628) in his discussion of sociological methods. Rothschild (1947: 306) pointed out in his study of oligopolistic price formation that von Neumann's and Morgenstern's *Theory of Games and Economic Behavior* (1990 [1944]) represented a pathbreaking attempt to understand problems of complex interdependence. Knorr (1947a: 36; 1947b: 556) introduced this concept into the study of international relations: 'Only if teaching practice focuses on the complex interdependence of domestic and international politics can the International Relations student understand the flux of national foreign policies in juxtaposition, their diverse elements of insistence, vacillation and contradiction, and their capacity for adaptive response' (1947b: 556). Keohane and Nye used the concept first in 1974 (p. 56), and endowed it with a central analytical and theoretical significance in their textbook *Power and Independence*, which appeared first in 1977 and, most recently, in a third and revised edition, in 2001. See also Keohane (2002: 1–114).

5 Cf. Marshall (1949) and Harold Laski, who anticipated a central point in Marshall's seminal analysis: 'Universal suffrage has meant the constant expansion of the functions of the state. It has enabled things to be achieved for the individual by the exercise of a corporate faculty of compulsion which are unattainable when they remain in the sphere of private and voluntary initiative' (Laski 1933: 201–2).

But if that which is termed globalization not only is an unintended consequence of developments that were pursued for quite different reasons and with very different objectives, and if it also seems to have turned against that which decisively contributed to its development, what then are the implications of this for the prospects of a 'global governance' called for in so many quarters today? What interests come into play here, and how strong is their respective influence? How may the advantages of globalization, above all the new degree of freedom in economic and social action and the welfare-producing effects of transnational interdependence, be put on a secure footing, and how can their negative side-effects be brought under control? How can welfare states master the challenges of globalization if that which helped to produce them is also that which threatens to undermine their own foundation? If one takes a closer look at the welfare state points-of-departure and the foundations of globalization – the subject of this and the next chapter – it becomes clear that *it is not so much the welfare state, but globalization which is endangered.*[6]

A second difficulty – again, an essentially political one – in dealing with globalization is that even when the institutional preconditions for effective global governance are thought to obtain (which is by no means assured), this still does not guarantee that 'correct' decisions will be made. And 'correct' refers at first only to a policy that would secure those increases in welfare and economic efficiency which globalization as an engine of growth also entails. To the extent that international politics is subjected to democratic standards, i.e. that form prevails over substance, chances increase that the predictability of the outcomes of international politics declines.[7] In national politics, checks and balances are inherent in the separation of powers and in the accountability, disclosure and publicity obligations of democratic governance, as in constitutionally inscribed counter-majority instruments of political obstruction and the duplicative and federally subdivided structure of the legislative branch.

In international politics, such institutional checks and balances do not exist as counterweights to a 'democratic' input into government action and thus to the latter's tendencies to expand and render itself perpetual. Moreover, in this particular arena, governments are to a large extent among themselves – and governments are, according to Robert Hudec (1987: 212), 'complex institutions known the world over for their inability to behave like rational beings'. The norms of international regimes and organizations – with the exception of those of the European Union – are addressed exclu-

6 As formulated here, this proposition applies to the developed welfare states of Western Europe and North America. For the other countries of the world the situation is somewhat different. This is primarily because globalization – in the form of capital inflows, access to technological know-how and new expert prospects – can provide them with more benefits than harm.

7 Constitutionalism, or *controlling* the power to coerce by establishing 'a government of laws and not of men' (Hume 1953: 106), is the essence of republicanism, not democracy. Where 'the people' rule, constitutional restraints are not only unnecessary, but positively injurious (S. Gordon 1999; Cooter 2000). Constitutionalism as 'rules against rules' will check the popular demand that is persistently for more government action rather than less. On the prevalence of form over content as the essence of democracy, see Schumpeter (1950 [1942]: 269): 'The democratic method is that institutional arrangement for arriving at political decisions in which individuals acquire the power to decide by means of a competitive struggle for the people's vote.' For a summary account, see Ricci (1970). On economic indeterminacy and the prospects of a democratic foundation of politics, see Reynolds (1995) and Wollheim's (1958: 242) 'anything goes' notion of modern democratic politics: 'It may be maintained that it is irrelevant whether Democracy does in fact maximise welfare, safeguard rights, accord with natural law, etc., for the fact is that under modern conditions it is the only working possibility.'

sively at governments. They have no 'direct effect' vis-à-vis private entities – be they firms, consumers or the advocates of some kind of 'public' interest worthy of protection, and therefore they cannot be invoked by such entities against governments, even in the case of egregious violations of norms (Berkey 1998; Kessie 2000). If we were to assume for a moment that non-governmental organizations truly did exercise an independent influence on international politics (Keck and Sikkin 1998), then the problem would arise, 'Who is the principal of these agents?'. Located beyond the market *and* the democratic framework of national governance structures, there is no authority effectively controlling their behaviour – they are thus unaccountable (Brody 1996; Jordan and van Tuijl 2000).

Because the need for and demands upon international politics have dramatically increased as a result of intensified interstate contacts brought about by globalization, the latter has exacerbated – not mitigated – the problems of international politics. The disproportion in global affairs between actual economic, social and environmental control and formal political power is quite fantastic. Let us examine the means for the resolution of global problems effectively available, i.e. in essence the institutional coordination and legal standardization of interstate cooperation. Here, the enormous gap between individuals' contemporary degree of reciprocal dependency regarding their welfare, on the one hand, and the legal-institutional solutions hitherto achieved by these individuals' state representatives, on the other, is plainly arresting (Elazar 1998; Perrez 1998). The technological and economic development associated with the revolution in spatial relations has called forth a range of new problems in all realms of social cooperation. Yet only very few of these problems have been coped with sufficiently by international politics and international law – and those that have been dealt with have been the less rather than the more important ones.[8] On the contrary, it is becoming more and more clear that this condition of complex interdependence has increased the potential for reciprocal – and often unintended – harm to unprecedented levels. For this reason, complex interdependence has become the point of departure in international power politics and for the various forms of coercive diplomacy.

Since private entities, including firms, have neither a seat nor a formally recognized voice in the arenas of international politics, they have to rely on their governments to represent their interests. Whether governments do so, under what conditions and under the influence of what kind of pressure, are both domestic and foreign policy questions, just as are the different forms this access to government will take depending on the specific characteristics of each group and political situation. And even when governments become active, the outcome is uncertain, because international law, which aims at supporting and institutionalizing cooperative solutions, is the weakest kind of law.

[8] For this reason, it is no coincidence that the principal political achievement of supranational institutional politics in the European Union is in the field of agricultural policy. The unquestionable high-point of a new approach to international politics represented by the Schuman Plan establishing the European Coal and Steel Community and by the European Economic Community at the end of the 1950s could not allay Claude's (1958: 51) scepticism vis-à-vis multilateral trade diplomacy: 'The role of the spokesman for the international interest is still too marginal, too exceptional, too poorly defined, too grudgingly accepted.' This judgement still applies today; consider in this regard the following definition of international law by a US judge: 'A theoretical body of precepts and propositions, *honored only in the breach*, that has little to do with the "real world"' (D. Wood 1999: 97; emphasis in the original). For a brief introduction to the practical problems of international law, see D. Wood (2000).

It consists neither of central legislative nor of central executive organs.[9] On the other hand, this is not the first time that states, confronted with interdependence and acting unilaterally, have expanded their legal instruments in order to achieve control over economic interreliance – including its unintended consequences – thus compensating for the weakness of international governance structures:

> There may be agreements made beyond our borders not intended to affect imports, which do affect them, or which affect exports. Almost any limitation of the supply of goods in Europe, for example, or in South America, may have repercussions in the United States if there is trade between the two. . . . (I)t is settled law . . . that any state may impose liabilities, even upon persons not within its allegiance, for conduct outside its borders that has consequences within its borders which the state reprehends; and these liabilities other states will ordinarily recognize.[10]

Globalization and interdependence have neither created a legal 'no man's land' nor condemned national legal systems – and with them, national politics – to impotence. On the contrary, the overwhelming share of new transnational and international conflicts are resolved in a national legal framework, in national courts. The legal literature on these developments demonstrates that national courts, governments and legislatures react to changed spatial relations – above all concerning relocation, physical absence and bridging distances – with new conceptions concerning the extraterritorial reach of national law. Legal practice is changing accordingly, albeit in a halting, uncoordinated manner and with uneven results. Nonetheless, it is clear that developments have begun in which the new, globalization-induced 'exit' opportunities of the

9 Whether the most recent advances in the juridification of international economic relations – for example the institutionalization of the new arbitration proceedings in the framework of the WTO – actually render international norms more binding, or whether they have the opposite effect as a result of the higher costs this development occasions when governments deviate from or change these norms, is still an open question. See the contributions in Issue 3 (2000) of *International Organization*, above all those by Goldstein and Martin (2000) and by Kahler (2000). On the cultural contradictions of transnational juridification, cf. Lawrence Friedman (1996) and Peng (2000).

10 *United States* v. *Aluminium Co. of America et al.* (148 F.2d 416 [1944], here p. 443). At issue in this ruling was the extraterritorial effect of the Sherman Antitrust Act. The author of this ruling, Judge Learned Hand, also maintained, however, that 'when one considers the international complications likely to arise from an effort in this country to treat such agreements as unlawful, it is safe to assume that Congress certainly did not intend the Act to cover them' (ibid.). On this conflict between legislative and political considerations in the extraterritorial application of national law, see Maier (1982). As long as no global cartel or global competition law exists, national economic law and cooperation among national antitrust authorities assume an importance that cannot be overestimated. What use do agreements on market opening and the dismantling of boundaries to trade, production and investment have if the market-closing activities of *private* entities in turn undermine these advances (D. Wood 1989, 1994, 1996, 2000)? For this reason, competition law is of central importance for the Internal Market of the European Union as well (Goyder 1993; Lennart Ritter et al. 2000). Diane Wood (1999: 109) summarizes the status quo in the politics of international competition rules through national means as follows: 'Currently, most major antitrust agencies around the world agree that they have jurisdiction to combat any practices, anywhere in the world, that have a direct, substantial, and reasonable forseeable effect on their domestic markets. Some refer to practices that are being "implemented" within their own markets; some refer to practices that target their domestic markets. The terminology does not matter. The key point is that this level of agreement on the proper scope of national regulation could, if it were acknowledged everywhere, resolve most competitive problems of an international scope by using exclusively national mechanisms.'

more mobile groups and actors are being matched by an internationally coordinated expansion of the domestic 'voice' of immobile groups (Benvenisti 1999). Margulis-Ohnuma (1999) thus speaks of an 'unavoidable correlation' between nation-statehood and the extraterritorial rule of welfare in the wake of changed spatial relations.[11] This does not mean, however, that the problem of international political coordination is settled. Rather, it poses itself in a more profound way, for, increasingly, disputes can entail a conflict between different socio-legal systems.

States' original and initially unlimited capacity to act is the greatest threat to international cooperation, for in the absence of a central authority every consciously instituted order is dependent on the action of every participating state.[12] The unique social structure of international law has always been characterized by a lack of a central authority equipped with coercive means that can enforce agreed commitments on reluctant members.[13] An international order can only come into being on the basis of explicit declarations of intent among equal and sovereign states. For maintaining this order, all members depend on the corresponding behaviour of each individual member. In principle, every state, as a sovereign community, is legally free from control by any other state. Yet the unorganized freedom of all leads to the effective dependency of all states on the state that is least interested in cooperation – or, what amounts to the same, which behaves uncooperatively – and thus is able to dictate the rules of the game to all others (Gilpin 1984; Axelrod and Keohane 1985; Kindleberger 1986b). As a result, transnational and international interdependence will unavoidably be associated with national power politics. This threat, which can stem from individual governments, suffices to force the others to pursue defensive measures, thus complicating the effective normative ordering of international politics. An international order can be created only by costly collective action, yet it can always be destroyed by any individual member which disposes of a certain degree of power. Ultimately, as long as there is no world government or international executive institution with an autonomous legisla-

11 Incidents that have occurred outside of the United States – in particular, human rights abuses or violations of environmental or worker protection standards by US firms – are being challenged by private parties before US courts with increasing frequency (Chibundu 1999; Kieserman 1999; Rosencranz and Campbell 1999). The globalization of financial markets was accompanied by a corresponding extraterritorial expansion of US jurisdiction (Bensen 1999; Calhoun 1999). In some areas, this practice is predicated on an explicit, not merely tacitly assumed, legal foundation: 'The recent prosecution of an Italian corporation, Montedison, S.p.A. by the U.S. Securities and Exchange Commission for violation of the Foreign Corrupt Practices Act based on conduct that occurred entirely in Italy, once again brings into sharp focus Congress' assertion of extraterritorial jurisdiction over foreign commercial activity' (H. L. Brown 1999: 407). In US judicial practice, there also seem to be no major difficulties about protecting consumers in the rapidly expanding field of e-commerce. This is partly the case because in the shadow of the extraterritorial application of the law, effective self-regulation has emerged (Puurunen 2000). National jurisdiction also seems to be getting a grip on the problem of internet 'virtual casinos', for it is established case law that the medium itself produces no change in legal status: 'There is nothing about the connecting medium itself that matters here or that differs from other communication means' (Keller 1999: 1609; see also Bak-Boychuk 1999). These developments constitute the exact opposite of the hollowing-out of the nation-state that Zürn (1998) sees as the main consequence of globalization.

12 On this and what follows, see M. Huber (1910), Brierly (1924), Schindler (1948), Jenks (1963), Claude (1981), and Boyle (1985: 3–74).

13 But note that this perhaps overstresses the difference between domestic and international law. Judith Shklar (1986: 55) observed that the 'monopoly of violence hardly explains anything about the actual conduct of government in a constitutional democracy. No monopoly of power ever got a single bill through Congress or Parliament.'

ture, the foundation of every international organization is the common interest of its members in cooperative solutions (M. Huber 1910; Waltz 1959, 1962). And thus it is of decisive importance to know where the commonalities of the newest incarnation of the international society of states lie, what the conditions of emergence of globalization were, and what consequences for the subsequent fate of globalization follow from these very particular conditions of emergence.

Social policy as a determinant of globalization

Because welfare statism marks the apogee of national autonomy, globalization is a key term above all for social policy. By all accounts, it not only seems to determine the socio-political agenda of the developed welfare states. It also, in the interest of greater national competitiveness, appears to dictate cuts in social expenditure as well as the implementation of market-oriented welfare state reforms, and thus ultimately gives the impression of unleashing and sustaining a 'race to the bottom'. A more careful examination of the discourse on the theory and practice of free trade reveals, however, the critical importance of the social – and thus nation-state based – foundations of open foreign trade relations. There is considerable evidence to support the contention – a primary thesis of this volume – that the universal transformation from industrial society to the welfare state played a critical role in shaping the conditions of the emergence of stable, sustained world market integration. As we will argue in more detail in chapter 2, in the period after World War II the welfare state was able to assume the social functions of protectionism – the defence of employment and incomes via tariffs, import quotas, licensing and restrictions on capital flows – and thereby paved the way for trade policy to take advantage of an international division of labour. The deep economic integration of the post-World War II period is much less the result of conscious international institution-building than of a fundamental shift from external methods of adjustment which differentiate between transactions with foreigners and domestic transactions to internal measures which do not rely on such discrimination.

Their institutional set-up enables welfare states to cope with the volatility of an internationalized economy on their own terms, without resort to protectionist trade measures, through income maintenance programmes, corporatist wage-setting, and regional fiscal redistribution. The welfare states themselves, by virtue of their domestic policies, are the major providers of order in the world economy.[14] Welfare statism, however, is only a necessary, but not a sufficient condition for order in international economic affairs. A statement about the roles welfare states can – and sometimes do – play in sustaining the deep integration achieved at the end of the twentieth century is not the same as a description of what they actually do.

Since the middle of the 1980s evidence has been mounting that an inner transformation has occurred in welfare states through the formation and consolidation – via political parties or lobbies – of manifest and latent privileging structures. These structures, in turn, have created a constellation in which the positive effects of welfare state institutions on trade liberalization threaten to turn into negative ones. When therefore,

14 The ensuing dilemma was already noted by Laski (1933: 245): 'The state-power cannot, for international purposes, be regarded as something distinct from the system of privilege which gives it its whole colour and complexion. Those who resist the settlement of problems at home in parliamentary terms are unlikely to utilise an international machinery for that end in which even the effectiveness of majority-rule does not apply.'

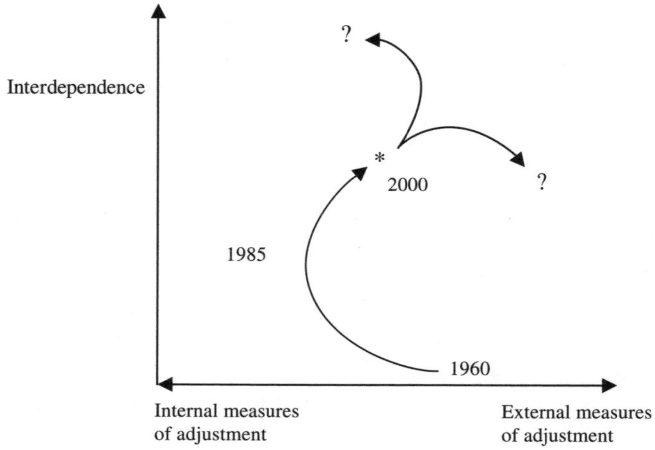

Figure 1.1 Coming full circle?

one tries to answer the question of what tasks social policy serves, one is tempted to analogize Abbe Siéyès' famous reply and to say that it is sufficient if it has survived the problems it is supposed to solve. Figure 1.1 can be used to illustrate the increased danger of a reversal to the *status quo ante* and thus a return to a much more disintegrated world economy. The most significant expression of this precarious constellation is, first, the difficulty of achieving socio-political reform precisely in those states in which the economy is most integrated into world markets; and, second, the increase in neo-protectionist tendencies in countries in which social policy was reformed in such a way that it no longer constitutes an alternative – or makes up only an inadequate alternative – to market income. The *raison d'être* of the welfare state is its use of political power to supplant, complement or modify operations of the market system in order to achieve discrete results which the market would not achieve on its own, and that in doing so it is guided by values other than those determined by open market forces (Marshall 1985 [1965]: 15). States differ greatly in the extent to which they follow such a course of action. In this volume, Germany and the USA will be examined as two paradigmatic examples of these opposing reactions to the same challenges of globalization, and in chapter 5 we discuss the East Asian forms of social policy. Figure 1.2 indicates the relative position of the three economically dominant countries with regard to their predominant reliance on means of adjustment and economic interdependence.

As something to be analysed on its own terms, globalization is not a topic of the investigations assembled here.[15] Also, we do not claim that the major features and main

[15] For a wide-ranging set of selections on concepts of globalization and the role of globalization in the transformation of intra- and international structures, see Held and McGrew (2000). Introductory discussions with directly opposed points of departure and conclusions are offered by Beck (1997, 1998), Frieden and Lake (2000) and Burtless et al. (1998) and continued in Burtless and Litan (2001). For a description of the domestic functioning of globalization, see Frieden and Rogowski (1996). On the political dimension see Strange (1996). On the historical economic perspective, see Bordo et al. (1999), Eichengreen (1996a, b) and James (2001).

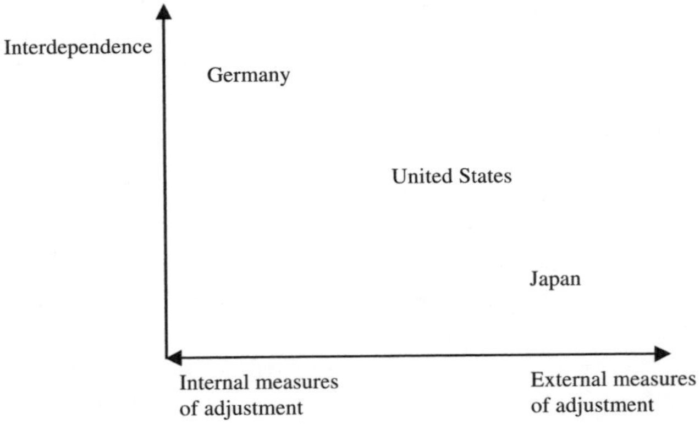

Figure 1.2 The relative position of welfare states in the institutional matrix of globalization

trends in the international economy or in national terms of trade can be explained solely with recourse to welfare state structures and variations in socio-political processes. Likewise, the trade policy decisions of individual governments are only one determinant – and often a relatively weak one – of global trade and investment flows. Conversely, we cannot draw or infer from these large-scale transformations of the international economy any unambiguous conclusions about what they might imply, or should imply, for national economic and social policy. With regard to the first point, Franz Eulenburg noted as early as the late 1920s:

> [T]he development of foreign trade policy differs from that of foreign trade itself, which is only one component of international economic relations. This policy thus provides no conclusive insight into the content and course of foreign trade. Also, from the perspective of individual countries, foreign trade development often proceeds in directions which are independent of, or even contrary to, the direction of their trade policy. These are targets, ambitions, preferences, which appear important enough in themselves, even if success follows only partially or not at all. (1929: 201)

In short, there is no assured *direct* linkage between the policies of governments and resulting trade flows, except in the negative sense that severe restrictions can definitely lead to lower trade flows, and in the positive sense that any move towards freer trade needs a specifically organized domestic *social* foundation. As the history of the second half of the twentieth century shows, structures of social policy and the policies pursued with or through them constitute a variable that strongly influences governments' foreign trade policy and, therefore, also firms' prospects of internationalization. Other variables are international regimes and collective organizations that regulate the global economy and establish norms, but these governance structures also depend in large measure on the policies and politics of welfare states. Welfare state institutions can lower the risks of national communities' dependency on and vulnerability to world markets and increase the security of international commercial transactions.[16]

16 On such international regimes, see the volume edited by Krasner (1983), Keohane's collection of essays (1989) and Young (1994). On the relevant functional changes in the international monetary system in the wake of the systematic welfare state transformation of the post-WWII era, see Eichengreen (1996a: 188–91).

Regulatory frameworks like GATT or the WTO, institutions such as the IMF or the BIS and consultative mechanisms like the G7 meetings increase the transparency and predictability of global economic interdependencies and to some extent 'domesticate' the world market.[17] These regulatory frameworks, however, can only complement, not replace, the domestic functions of public policy in coming to terms with the social consequences of a dynamic and fundamentally self-regulating world economy.[18] The ordering structure of the WTO, including its mechanisms of dispute settlement, is a response to the problems faced by *governments* with regard to economic and above all economic-political and socio-political interdependence, not a response to the problems of citizens or firms. The rules of GATT are substantially determined by welfare state structures, and they build on these. Governments seek to use international economic policy coordination and its established institutions to increase – or at least to secure the integrity of – their national scope for action in coming to terms with the social externalities of global economic integration and the international economic division of labour.[19] Possibilities within this context to *legally* contravene the rules of GATT or the WTO thus assume great importance:

> It is not the legal bond per se that holds GATT law together. It is, rather, *the convergence between what GATT law does and what governments need*. The viability of the GATT legal system ultimately rests on maintaining that convergence. (Hudec 1999b: 174; emphasis added)

The problem of globalization is not exhausted, however, with these preliminary references to its socio-political foundations and conditions. Rather, the questions must be posed anew and, above all, differently. Depending on the matter at hand, different aspects or dimensions of globalization become relevant. Globalization as such does not exist. In the discussion below, then, we will specify what is meant in the various analytical contexts by the term 'globalization'. In social science discussions and in political debates, the concept of globalization is often employed without a precise definition. Usually, one of the following developments is intended:

- Quantum leaps in the development of communication and transport technologies continually lowered the costs of transnational trade, or sharply increased their rewards, as opposed to domestic economic activity.
- Together with these technological advancements, a series of institutional-organizational changes in firms provided them with new opportunities to radically restructure their value chain and to broaden their range of instruments for strategic action. Politically, this meant most of all new *exit* opportunities for firms and thus a spectacular revaluation of *voice* power, i.e. a fundamental change in their relation to state authorities.

[17] On the abbreviations used here and below, see the list on pp. ix–x.

[18] For an introduction to the approaches, institutional actors and problems of a 'global' social policy, see Deacon et al. (1997) and Deacon (2000a, b). For an overview of the socio-political problems of 'fair trade' and a discussion of social clauses in trade policy, see Leary (1996), D. K. Brown et al. (1996) and Elliott (2000).

[19] For this reason, 'safeguard clauses' play a central role in GATT and in the WTO. Cf. Deardorff (1987), Hizon (1994) and Romero (1999). On the social safeguards in NAFTA see Gal-Or (1998), and on the critical significance of safeguards in China's negotiations on WTO entry, see Bhala (2000).

- As early as the 1980s, with the Thatcher and Reagan governments in Great Britain and the USA respectively, a renaissance of the market and of open competition as the guiding ideas in economic policy began. Neither conservative nor social-democratic governments in other countries could elude the revaluation of 'state', 'market' and 'society' as the quintessential political-economic ordering concepts associated with this watershed.
- With the dissolution of the Soviet Union and the transition to parliamentary democracy and a liberal market economy during the 1990s, the bipolar world order of the post-war period also disappeared. With the disappearance of the socialist alternative to liberal democracy the international society of states achieved a much more homogeneous social structure, permitting a more complex and productive division of labour to take place and thus a sufficient degree of solidarity in recognizing common objectives and acting to promote them.
- In part influenced by this development, the countries of the Third World – only East Asia had already led the way in the 1970s – proceeded on a broad front beginning in the 1980s from their traditional policy of protectionist import substitution to one of emphatic world market integration.
- In the wake of the transition from GATT to the WTO in the 1990s, the genuinely international regulation of the global economy was deepened and broadened.

All of these developments – and more – flow into the concept of globalization. As a result, the diverse aspects of globalization can generate the impression of being a strong independent force. Hence 'globalization' appears discursively above all as an autonomous entity vis-à-vis the national welfare state – as a force that influences it from without and determines government policy.[20] This view is misleading.

2 The New Economics of Globalization

In all political-economic discussions in which the term globalization is used as more than simply a fashionable phrase, it is intended to express a simple state of affairs: the circulation of economic goods no longer proceeds largely within the confines of distinct communities organized as territorial entities, but rather transcends state boundaries in a multitude of ways. The effective decision-making domain of business enterprises exceeds the jurisdiction of single governments. No country – no matter how territorially expansive – is in a position to meet its population's needs solely with domestic production. Further, every country must export a more or less sizeable portion of its goods, capital, labour and intelligence to foreign populations and in turn has an explicit interest in the production and consumption that occur in other countries. In short, its own welfare depends on events taking place in foreign economies.

Since some mismatch of economics and politics is a constant feature of world history, it is, at first glance, not clear why this obvious state of affairs which comprises globalization has led to such heated debate. The term describes not only an institutional normalcy but forms the backdrop to a trade policy norm which is evidently compelling: free trade, and not trade restriction, is conducive to the welfare of a political community. But it is equally true that throughout world history this precept has hardly

20 The most extreme position in this regard, portraying globalization as a totalitarian project, is expressed by Hardt and Negri (2000).

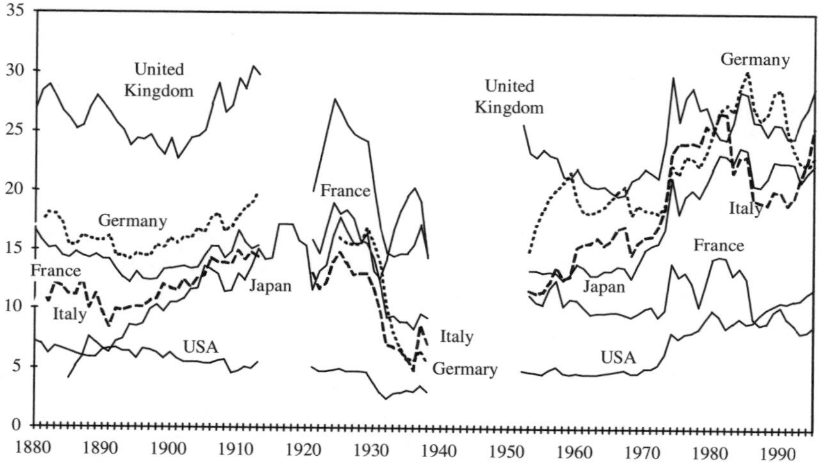

Figure 1.3 Foreign trade of selected industrial states, 1890–1995[1]

[1] Average of exports and imports (goods and services) as % of GDP.

Source: Own calculation based on EUROSTAT (1968, 1983, 1997); OECD (1983, 1995); Mitchell (1993, 1995, 1998)

ever been followed. Countries may have acquiesced to economic interdependence, but they have never welcomed it, much less actively promoted it. The current debates on so-called globalization have their precursors. In fact, the present-day discussion of the forms and consequences of globalization occurs, with regard to Western societies, in an environment – namely democratic welfare states – which was created as a response to the internationalization of the economy of the time and thus an attempt to contain interdependence.

However, the way in which the debate on globalization is conducted gives the impression that it constitutes a completely new constellation and challenge.[21] Yet internationalization tendencies in the economy, just as national counter-movements, are regularly recurring phenomena. First, as figure 1.3 shows, in the decade prior to the outbreak of World War I, some states were integrated in world markets to an extent that is entirely comparable with that of today. In his famous treatise, *The Economic Consequences of the Peace*, John Maynard Keynes in 1920 described eloquently the 'extraordinary episode in the economic progress of man' that came to an abrupt end in 1914:

> [Before 1914] the inhabitant of London could order by telephone, sipping his morning tea in bed, the various products of the whole earth, in such quantity as he might see fit, and reasonably expect their early delivery upon his doorstep; he could at the same moment and by the same means venture his wealth in the natural resources and new enterprises of any quarter of the world, and share, without execution or even trouble, in their prospective fruits and advantages. . . . He could secure forthwith, if he wished it, cheap and comfortable means of transit to any country or climate, without passport or other formality,

[21] Cf. Held and McGrew (2000), and for an empirically rich account which gives equal treatment to historical continuities and discontinuities Held et al. (1999).

> could despatch his servant to the neighbouring office of a bank for such supply of the precious metals as might seem convenient, and could then proceed abroad to foreign quarters without knowledge of their religion, language or customs, bearing coined wealth upon his person, and would consider himself greatly aggrieved and much surprised at the least interference. *But, most important of all, he regarded this state of affairs as normal, certain and permanent, except in the direction of further improvements, and any deviation from it as aberrant, scandalous, and avoidable.* (Keynes 1988 [1920]: 10; emphasis added)[22]

Second, the graph in figure 1.3 shows that, measured in terms of this indicator, the globalization process had already peaked in the mid-1980s. Clearly, one cause of this stagnation is the increase in 'grey' protectionism in the form of voluntary export limitation and non-tariff trade barriers, representing the exhaustion of welfare state institutions to protect the levels achieved in the international division of labour against the domestic pressures of social democracy (Salvatore 1993; Kaufmann 1997a, b).

The decisively new aspect of the current constellation of complex and deep economic interdependence is the development of the welfare state and its inner transformation. This transformation brought a change, first of all, in the perception and evaluation of the consequences of economic globalization in the domestic relations of developed societies, and, secondly, in the institutions and organizations which regulate the international economy. A higher rate of growth in international trade relative to production itself and consequently a rapidly advancing interdependence characterized the world economy as early as the late nineteenth century (Deutsch and Eckstein 1961; H. James 1996: 1–26; 2001). The same is true of the degree of integration and interdependence of financial markets.[23] In historical perspective it is striking, however, that previous globalization and internationalization tendencies in the economy were of a relatively short duration, and were very quickly followed by long periods of general foreign trade closure (Bairoch 1993: 16-33; Bhagwati 1998; H. James 1996: 1–26; 2001; Kindleberger 1996; Rogowski 1989).[24] This leads us in the present situation to

22 Then as now there are many fundamental questions implicit in Keynes's account: which inhabitants of London behaved or could behave in this way? Why did large parts of the world remain outside this happy state of affairs? However, it is only fair to note that Keynes did note the social asymmetries involved and stressed the 'intensively unusual, unreliable, temporary nature of the economic organization' which afforded some citizens the fruits of the globalization of his days. As Asa Briggs (1968: 39) also noted, the international economy before 1914 was 'a product of nineteenth-century experience: it was unique as well as mortal'. In essence, this book makes the same point about the contemporary incarnation of globalization.

23 The mere degree of the globalization of financial transactions is regularly adduced as evidence of an unprecedented development. In historical perspective, this assessment is untenable: 'Some measurements of the degree of financial integration in the world economy indicate that at the beginning of the twentieth century the world was more interconnected than at any subsequent time (including the 1990s, despite the trillions of dollars of daily currency movements). These measurements examine the behaviour of saving and investment levels. Investment and savings were coordinated on a global level, with the result that a surplus of investment in one area or state (that is, a balance of payments current account deficit) could be smoothly financed by the export of surplus savings from another area. Even in the highly integrated 1980s and 1990s, such transfers were much more difficult and raised many more political eyebrows than in the golden era that preceded the First World War' (H. James 1996: 12).

24 See the comment by Eugen Staley (1939: 52), reflecting on the raging economic nationalism of his day, which destroyed the world economy as a integrated system in spite of all technological progress: 'In the "Dark Ages" following the collapse of the Roman Empire, technology adjusted itself to politics. The magnificent Roman roads fell into disrepair, the baths and aqueducts and amphitheatres and villas into ruins. Society lapsed back to localism in production and distribution, forgot much of the learning and the technology and governmental systems of earlier days.'

pose two questions. First, what is the contribution of the development of the welfare state, which has occurred in the meantime, to the most recent wave of globalization, i.e. that of the late twentieth century? Second, what role does the inner transformation of developed welfare states play in the internationalization of trade, production and investment?

The present-day welfare state is essentially a product of the Great Depression of the interwar period and of the experience of the Second World War. Comprehensive social policy and activist economic policy and planning were thought to be solutions to the problems that threatened to tear apart European societies: economic and social insecurities caused by mass unemployment, large-scale sectoral upheaval, downward occupational mobility for large segments of the labour force, falling wages and short-term employment relations. Until then, these societies had reacted to such problems with protective tariffs and other autarchic policies. Indeed, in light of the preceding economic and political catastrophies, political scientists and economists such as Karl Deutsch (1979), Deutsch and Eckstein (1961), Edward Hallett Carr (1945), Wilhelm Röpke (1942), John Maynard Keynes (1933) and Gunnar Myrdal (1957) assumed that the breakthrough and rise of the welfare state as a new social order for developed, democratic nation-states would preclude any return to previous levels of world economic integration.[25] Against this empirically and theoretically well-founded horizon of expectations, it is the near simultaneity of the expansion of the welfare state and the growth of the international economic system that calls for further explanation, not the globalization process itself.

Globalization or internationally interdependent national economies?

Has some integral, effectively global capitalism replaced the mere summation of national economies? This is precisely what the concept of globalization suggests. It characterizes an independent entity which is sharply distinguished from what has hitherto been characterized as a mere assemblage of national economies.

The existence of international economic relations itself is not contested. If one takes a metaphorical approach, one can imagine the various individual national economies as interlocking circles. The interfaces represent the scope of international economic relations. Further, globalization means, to continue with this image, that the number of economies that participate in this international economy has increased considerably and that the shared interface of the individual states has grown in size. The exchange relations were intensified, the relations expanded and the interdependence between the national economies became increasingly complex and thus also more prone to surprises.

Yet the concept of globalization claims more than this. National economies, the argument goes, have become mere provinces of the international economy. Their partial character precludes their capacity to survive without a connection to all other provinces – or to the hegemonic core country, the USA. The term 'globalized economy' refers to the collaboration between individual national economies based on a division

[25] In 1909 Winston Churchill, then a 'new', or 'social', Liberal, declared that if he had to sum up the immediate future of democratic politics in a single word, he would choose 'insurance'. See Briggs (1968: 44), who also notes that in the period from 1890 to 1914 demands for protection were already universal and came from both the underprivileged and the business circles (ibid.: 45).

of labour, in which each individual economy has lost its economic independence. In a globalized economy, therefore, welfare is indivisible. But this view of things is false.

In the past as well, the concept of the national economy has encompassed international economic relations – and the latter were controlled by the long arm of the law. The capital inflows of German citizens from investments in US equity markets are included in German national accounts, just as is the cruiseship *Deutschland* – even if it only carries US citizens from New York to the Caribbean. If these transactions had not been taken into account, the concept of the national economy since the mid-nineteenth century would have been a mere torso without arms or legs. Far more important, still, is that the global economy is an aggregate and composite, yet not a unified, entity. It does not have its own foundations or form which would make it truly independent of national economies. Every economic relationship or market transaction is predicated on a quintessentially domestic legal order and makes use of unavoidably domestic legal forms. Both of these are products of national legislation in a fragmented world of territorial states. It is this national connection that makes a milieu of welfare states a critical conditioning factor of national and international politics in the process of globalization. But if the structures of an interdependent world economy and transnational society presuppose national welfare state systems, such systems do not presuppose them in the same way. In terms of individual life chances and citizenship rights, the economic world is not a seamless web. Welfare is, thanks to national systems of economic regulation and national social policies, territorially divisible. For this reason, all accounts of economic interdependence, from Richard Cooper (1968) to Robert Keohane and Joseph Nye (2001), are not on target if they assume an incontestable connection between the rise of international interdependence and a decline in domestic autonomy. The more important causation runs in the opposite direction.

Globalization, then, is not a process involving two somehow equivalent economic forms, where one dominates or even replaces the other. Instead of speaking of an independent, globalized economy, it makes more sense to proceed from the assumption of an international system of interdependent national economies. Globalized conditions are made up of processes that develop out of individual national economies. From this perspective, we can also see that the significance of governments and politics has increased, not decreased, as a result of international economic integration. As early as 1970, Kenneth Waltz called attention to the fact that economic interrelations rooted in *intra-industrial* trade, and increasingly also in *intra-firm* trade, do not generate *political* dependency:

> States are mutually dependent if they rely on each other for goods and services that cannot easily be produced at home. That kind of interdependence is difficult (costly) to break. The other kind of interdependence – sensitivity of response to variations in factor prices – may be economically more interesting; it is also politically less important. (1970: 210)

In light of the enormous increase in recent years in economic inequality among nations (Gylfason 2000), one point – which Waltz calls an 'iron law' – deserves more attention:

> The political elements of a state are formally differentiated according to the degrees of their authority, and their distinct functions are specified. Specification of roles and differentiation of functions characterize any state, the more fully so as the state is more highly

> developed. The parts of a highly developed polity are closely interdependent. . . . The domestic order is composed of heterogeneous elements; the international order is composed of homogeneous units. Each state regulates its own affairs and supplies largely out of its own resources the food, clothing, housing, transportation, and amenities consumed and used by its citizens. The international order is characterized by the coaction of like units. Since the functions of all states are highly similar, differentiation among them is principally according to their varied capabilities. Because the units that populate the international arena are the same in type, interdependence among them is low even if those units are of approximately equal size. Interdependence is further reduced by the immense disparity in the capabilities of states. This last point can be stated as an iron law: high inequality among like units *is* low interdependence. (Waltz 1970: 207; emphasis in original)

Given the increase in international inequality which was already beginning to become apparent at the time, Waltz proceeded from the assumption of decreasing interdependence (ibid.: 206). Yet it remains essential to transnational or global business activities – unrelated to the degree of national economic interdependence – that they are extended over different state territories and thus accessible to the intervention of at least two national governments. This constitutes its eminently political character.

Further, no one disputes that globalization has national political foundations to the extent that multilateral international regimes and bilateral treaties and agreements permit or prohibit, complicate or ease transnational flows of goods, services and persons. Through these agreements, international areas have been created within which goods and persons can circulate in similarly uninhibited fashion as in the territory of a single state. The international area to which this description best applies is the internal market of the European Union. It is, however, not only based on a common legal order to an extent unparalleled in other internal markets, customs unions or free trade spheres, but it is also distinguished by a supranational constitution with quasi-governmental character. Nonetheless, it is true of the European Union – contrary, for example, to the US 'internal' market – that the area's 'national' economy cannot (yet) be considered alongside the national economies of the member states as an independent entity.

Decisive, however, is that with the multiplication of the points of contact between government intervention and economic circuits, governments have not stopped acting pig-headedly or unilaterally. In terms of political action, the progress made in a more *rational* division of international labour did not produce more *reasonable* actors. The overwhelming share of foreign trade is not regulated by an internationally coordinated trade agreement policy or by the norms of the international economic regime of GATT and the IMF, but is instead shaped by unilateral actions – often not by legislatures, but by administrative agencies.[26] The economy of the European Union, too, is not the somehow exclusive object of a European economic policy, but is influenced and shaped

[26] In consequence, the results of this policy often, viewed on their own, make little sense. Hudec (1996: 15) describes the situation in the USA as follows: 'U.S. trade legislation is replete with protean concepts like "subsidy", "cause", and "injury", that leave room for widely varying interpretations. The government officials who administer these laws have been left free to devise all sorts of inconsistent definitions for their loosely defined concepts, and they have done so. Although Congress occasionally corrects a result here and there, *its overall approach has been to leave its trade laws in chaos, in confusion, everyone wins now and then*' (emphasis in original).

now as then by the myriad of uncoordinated activities of member states. Further, historically, increases in the volume of economic transactions, expansions of market freedom and increases in the number of marketable products have always been accompanied by increases in market regulation (Weber 1978: 82–5). This development is inevitable to the extent that goods and services are not 'objects' or 'things' but, at their core, social relations which depend, to be valid and to achieve the *appearance* of 'objects', on some kind of order (Böhm-Bawerk 1881; O. Williamson 1985; Braithwaite and Drahos 2000).[27]

There is thus nothing more misleading than associating the concept of 'free' trade with the new globalized economic conditions. Contemporary transnational trade is to all intents and purposes *political* economy. For business, this point has always been a hard fact. A textbook on corporate foreign trade states that for firms participating in foreign trade, particular functions and risks emerge from the fact that the boundaries of the national economic area are being traversed. These functions and risks are either not present in domestic economic activity at all, or not in similar fashion, or at the very least not in comparable intensity:

> National foreign trade policy measures bring about artificial conditions of competition which must be taken into account as points of departure in firm planning (subsidies, import quotas, tariffs, non-tariff trade barriers, development aid). Further, governments' monetary and finance policy measures distort international competition, and – due to the perpetual eventuality of changes in these measures – burden it with specific risks. The globalization of the economy has the additional effect that government foreign trade policy is recast as an instrument of inter-state competition, with the help of which the national site is to be given an advantageous position in international competition. (Grafers 1999: 9)

Alongside national legislative provisions concerning foreign trade, the network of internationally legally binding multilateral and bilateral trade agreements, as well as habitual or customary international commercial practices,[28] yield a very particular framework of action. This framework determines both the degree of freedom in corporate foreign trade – its 'autonomy interval' – and also the types and degree of risk that a firm takes upon itself when it engages in foreign trade (ibid.: 29).

Thus, when one looks at globalization processes in trade, production and investment from the perspective of their actual agents, i.e. of firms, it becomes clear that they are highly conditioned developments. The lack of a central international ordering power means that the institutional fit which actually allows an international division of labour is a largely uncoordinated result of the interplay of numerous

[27] Thus some normative framework *precedes* any kind of 'economy': 'In the strict sense of utility, it is not a "horse" or a "bar of iron" which is an economic "good", but the specific ways in which they can be put to desirable and practical uses; for instance the power to haul loads or to carry weights, or something of that sort' (Weber 1978: 69). Markets do not evolve 'naturally'. They are constituted by regulation. This is true of both formal and informal (black) markets.

[28] The most important of these are the International Regulations for the Interpretation of Trade Terms (Incoterms, first developed in 1936 and updated numerous times since), the *Wiener Kaufrecht* (which regulates the merchandise trade of virtually all internationally commercially significant states), the Hamburg Rules and Institute Cargo Clauses for shipping, and the various agreements aimed at organizing an international legal framework for commercial patents (Grafers 1999: 50–73).

factors.[29] Attendantly precarious is the stability of the institutional foundations of globalization, namely the reciprocal advantages resulting from the increasing international division of labour. It was the latter that brought forth the vast international goods exchange and the even more vast global monetary flows. Yet this implies neither that the achieved levels of international economic integration are independently sustainable nor that they are politically defensible. Neither supposedly functional constraints nor ideas and programmes of coordinated reaction amount by themselves to policy.[30]

This is not to deny that the expansion of the international division of labour is accompanied by certain reciprocal dependency relations. When a country produces only those goods for which it is particularly suited, while importing the others, this does not imply that it can satisfy its need for the latter only through imports. It merely means that it obtains these goods more cheaply when it imports them. It can, but does not have to, follow these price signals. As earlier with 'free trade', today with globalization it is a matter of obtaining the highest possible productivity for national capital. Then as now it revolved around the double insight that, first, the production costs of the same good in the same country can differ because of companies' differential economies of scale, and, second, that no country has more favourable conditions of production than its neighbouring countries for all goods. This double circumstance generates an interest in economic exchange.

The international division of labour does not eliminate national economies; rather, this 'division of labour' results from a division of production due to divergent productivity rates of capital and labour, as well as of organizational diversity. International exchange is determined by cost advantages, but not by any kind of economic laws which can no longer be influenced by state policy. These cost advantages constitute *incentives* for a certain behaviour, but they do not determine it. Up to now,

29 We differ here from important earlier studies on the systemic relationship between domestic conditions and the prospects of foreign trade liberalization, in particular from the works of Katzenstein (1984, 1985) on the fate of 'small' states in the international economy. He comes to the same conclusion as we do in underscoring, in line with Richard Blackhurst and other liberal economists (1977), that 'the link between the case for [international] free trade and the case for [domestic] laissez-faire has been broken' (1985: 47f.) and in observing already in 1980 (p. 533) that: 'Switzerland and the other small European states are clear exceptions to the generalization that liberalism in the international economy and interventionism in the domestic economy are incompatible.' In contrast to him, however, we proceed from the assumption that this compatibility can obtain in 'large' countries as well. Further, we argue that this is not some kind of 'necessary' connection, but rather an *elective affinity* of external and internal structural conditions which is largely beyond the strategic calculations of domestic political actors. As the fate of Sweden and Austria during the 1990s showed, 'cooperative corporatism' is not a guarantee that the 'correct', or functionally productive, answers to the difficulties of world market integration will be found. Finally, in a subsequent, and for our purposes equally central, point, Katzenstein, using the example of Switzerland, points out that functional equivalents do exist to socio-political instruments of state income security beyond the labour market: Switzerland reduced the foreign economic pressure on its labour force in that the temporarily very high share of guest workers more or less independently expanded or shrank depending on the labour market situation: 'The Swiss appear to have found their (im)moral equivalent of the welfare state' (1984: 104).

30 'Policy requires politics. Ideas for solving economic problems are plentiful, but if an idea is to prevail as the actual policy of a particular government, it must obtain support from those who have political power' (Gourevitch 1986: 17). Robert Hudec (1999a: 283) objects in the same way to the critique of the meagre achievements of international economic law: 'Before any more criticism is written, there first needs to be a careful examination of why the volumes of criticism already written have had so little influence.'

countries have been very quick to sacrifice these cost advantages for social, ethical, religious, military or other reasons.[31] The often cited international economic interdependence thus rests on a weak footing. In social science jargon, it is a dependent, not an independent, variable. Globalization is not something that can only increase in scale – it can also subside. Moreover, it has different dimensions, in which contradictory developments can be observed.[32]

If today's globalization – notwithstanding the relative cost advantages that endow the new international economic conditions with their particular dynamic and the fact that national politics largely adopts this rationality as well – is basically the unexpected outcome of a very peculiar constellation, then the empirical question arises how this outcome can be explained. How has it come about that the new realities of the global market economy appear to correspond to the teachings of foreign trade theory? And why did the economic rationality of the free trade idea prevail so late? Could economic theory be the cause of globalization?

This seems to be what critics of globalization believe. Yet it is one thing to observe that the new international conditions largely correspond to the theoretical tenets of foreign trade theory, but another to contend that the latter are the cause of the former. Max Weber, in 1908, characterized a very similar constellation as just a *cultural* artefact. The heuristic merit of economic theory rests on *cultural-historical* facts, not on its supposed foundation in some objective 'law':

> The historical peculiarity of the capitalist epoch, and thereby also the significance of . . . every economic theory of value for the understanding of this epoch, rests on the circumstances that – while the economic history of some epochs of the past has not without reason been designated as 'history of non-economic conditions' – under today's conditions of existence the approximation of reality to the theoretical propositions of economics has been a *constantly increasing* one. It is an approximation to reality that has implicated the destiny of ever-wider layers of humanity. (Weber 1908: 257; emphasis in the original)

Similarly today, the power of economics as positive analysis, concentrating on particular problems of empirical research, and not on its predilection to find general laws, probably produces this correspondence. And then as now there is evidence to support the contention that international conditions are not the product of a superior economic policy programme, but instead have completely different foundations and thus have a rather coincidental character. Globalization was not planned, and it is extremely doubtful that globalization as such can be managed in any meaningful sense, despite heightened efforts to build international governance structures.

31 As the dispute between the European Union and the USA concerning hormone-treated beef shows, potentially costly 'grounds of faith' have increased rather than decreased. See Berkey (1998: 46), who cites a report in the *Los Angeles Times* from 12 May 1997: 'French Agriculture Minister Vasseur went so far as to state that "France is entirely prepared to pay penalties if that is what is needed to prevent hormone-treated American meat from gaining entry to our territory".'

32 Keohane and Nye (2000, 2001) distinguish between an economic, military, ecological and socio-cultural 'globalism'. Economic globalism, which prevailed from 1850 to 1914, declined again sharply until 1945, during which time military globalism was on the rise. The worldwide influenza epidemic, which took 30 million lives in 1918/19, can be attributed not only to the large transcontinental troop movements of the time, but also to the far more extensive international mobility of workers, which in the ensuing period was largely brought to a halt. The religious fundamentalism which marks the end of the twentieth century can be seen as a decline in socio-cultural globalism.

The welfare-democratic roots of globalization

As discussed at the outset, two sets of relationships are essential to the conditions of emergence of globalization. In addition to the precarious relationship between the institutionalization of welfare states and their foreign trade liberalization, and the new micro-economics of the technologically advanced firm, a third one obtains. All these developments – the internationalization of the economy, the expansion of welfare state interventions and the growth of firms – have a fixed common point in the bureaucratization of social life. One fails to penetrate the surface of reality if one believes that globalization is the opposite of all of this, that it even constitutes the promise of less bureaucratic conditions, or an unholy anarchy of production – depending on the perspective. This is not the case – and the historical experiences with earlier globalization processes prove this convincingly. The pace of global firm mergers, the size of the new firms and, above all, the scale of their legal divisions speak a clear language. Focusing on today's ostensibly very 'free' trade and on the new mobility of capital, goods and services and information leads one to overlook that many of these transactions, while indeed transcending national boundaries, actually take place within units of one and the same firm and thus have an essentially bureaucratic and not at all a market character (Dunning 1993, 1997a; Doremus et al. 1998).

In the second half of the nineteenth century, when, through the gold standard, free trade in the form of the exchange of goods in the market shaped foreign trade relations far more than it does today, the market economy and democracy did not achieve a stable balance. This first test of power was won by democracy, confirming that once economics became the controlling factor in a democratic society, economies will be controlled.[33] And at the end of the twentieth century it was not the democratic but the autocratic states that enjoyed the strongest economic growth – e.g. South Korea, Taiwan, Singapore, Malaysia, Chile and, also, China. Social policy, which – as an independent, third pillar of modern society beside democracy and the market economy – was supposed to achieve an equilibrium, was ultimately turned against economic and political freedom by fascism and National Socialism. The thesis of globalization as 'divesting statism' (Zürn 1992, 1998) overlooks that *statism* is a side-effect, and not the foundation, of social policy. Social policy has an infinite number of modalities, due to its basically *negative* definition: to grant the individual citizen or social groups something markets presumably do not provide for. Its content, therefore, can only be determined empirically, but not a priori in some principled manner.[34] With regard to *welfare* democracy, the more fundamental point of departure for social policy, one can speak at most of a change in its manifestations, yet hardly of a waning of its driving forces. Rather, the opposite is the case.

33 Charles Lindblom (1982: 332) stated the same point as a general proposition: 'For minimal democracy, we require a market system. For fuller democracy, we require its elimination.'

34 Since social policy is closely bound up with highly diverse and fast-changing circumstances of concrete and often very vociferous individuals, it forms an area of compromise and contradiction in which both general principles of organized action and grand theories of all kinds are tested – usually to destruction. For the very same reason, the whirlwind of quite diverse empirical situations with which social policy is confronted implies almost by necessity that both the application of 'bad' theory and the misapplication of 'good' theory will have disastrous consequences for real people. Thus one of the reasons for the turn to the market is simply intellectual despair.

As early as 1905, Jacob Burckhardt observed that national sovereignty is the 'eternally fluctuating ferment of the modern world' (1982 [1905]: 323). By democracy, he understood the 'unbounded penetration of the public sphere'; everything becomes 'debatable', and the state is expected to carry out a 'social power programme' which threatens to overwhelm it (ibid.: 193, 262).

> *Democracy* . . . is a world-view which flows together out of a thousand different streams, and differs markedly according to the social stratum of its adherents. It is consistent in only one respect, however: namely, in that the power of the state can never be sufficiently large, extinguishing any boundary between state and society, so that it expects of the state all that which society will presumably no longer be able to do, while [at the same time] leaving everything continuously debatable [and in flux] and providing select casts with a special right to employment and subsistence. (Ibid.: 371; emphasis in original)

Jacob Burckhardt already perceived that which would not occur on a large scale until after his time: the expansion of the welfare state as a result of the democratization of society, the systemic excesses in regulating economy and society and, ultimately, the crystallization of grantee classes in the welfare state: 'Step by step we will arrive, relatively soon, at a point where the state is considered to be absolutely responsible for sustaining the population' (ibid.: 137). He viewed democracy as a specific culture and less as a form of politics: 'The breakthrough of democracy as the overpowering of the state by culture' – 'the exterior shape of government is secondary to this' (ibid.: 318, 137). Hence, for him, there was no countervailing power in sight, only 'here and there a whimpering for decentralization, self-government, North-American simplification etc.' (ibid.: 324). For him, even the market economy did not constitute a counterforce to this cultural revolution: 'Profit-making and commerce are continuously admonished in the harshest manner that they are not the most important thing in life' (ibid.: 326).

In the second half of the nineteenth century in Basel, however, Burckhardt had already experienced the globalization of his day: 'the cosmopolitan traffic, [the] world exhibitions; the dying out of the local with its pros and cons; the marked decline even of the national' (ibid.: 375). And he posed the question whether 'indeed everything will just become "business" as in America?' (ibid.). He clearly saw the 'collisions' of these democratic 'fermentations' with the desire for profit-making. The latter is 'ultimately the stronger of the two; the masses want tranquillity and income; if a republic or monarchy can provide them with these, they remain loyal; if not, without searching for long, they will rally behind the first form of government which promises them these privileges' (ibid.: 375). This insight provides a decisive clue to the understanding of present-day economic globalization. It has essentially democratic foundations, and in the future as well it will be forced to comply with democratic demands. This process is already under way.[35]

That which makes globalization seem threatening – the impression of a loss of control – is most likely a mere intermediate stage like the apprentice sorcerer, 'who is no longer able to control the powers of the nether world whom he has called up by

[35] A small but telling example from the autumn of 2000 was the occasionally violent and in part successful 'consumer' reactions by lorry drivers in Europe and North America to increases in petrol prices (Ayres 2000; Came 2000; Josey 2000; Morton 2000).

his spells' and cries for the master to his rescue.[36] When one compares the present condition of the welfare state with its so-called golden age of the 1950s and 1960s, in which grand reform projects such as Lyndon B. Johnson's War on Poverty and Konrad Adenauer's pension reform of 1957 were undertaken, one is using the wrong yardstick.[37]

The deregulation of the economy and trade which paved the way for globalization was a reaction to the conditions in which an highly regulated economy was no longer able to fulfil its promise of prosperity. It was an attempt to find an answer to the failure of regulatory welfare state politics. High rates of inflation and rising unemployment defined the era after the oil crisis in all developed economies. It was populist figures such as Ronald Reagan and Margaret Thatcher who campaigned under the banner of freeing their societies from the web of regulations. Their economic and social policies were anything but directed 'against the people'; on the contrary, they were expressly predicated on a democratic mandate. It was these special conditions which endowed their anti-regulatory policy with legitimacy and support, not the form of the policy itself. And these conditions are decisive. In a democratic environment, these conditions alone determine the substance of government policies. In short, in the highly organized political contexts of welfare democracies, markets are a tool of social policy, not a substitute for it.[38] Globalization is not so much market driven as state driven. For this reason, the important thing about globalization is not its allegedly autonomy-reducing form, but its democratic scope and above all its welfare-enhancing effects. World markets, too, are judged by their results, and the judgement is given by the broad masses, not by theologies of some elite.

In any case, there is no evidence to support the case that the economic interests which ostensibly prevail today indeed have the power widely attributed to them to erode the bureaucratic conditions in which social policy is rooted and which in turn it feeds. On the contrary, after the First and above all the Second World War, it was precisely society's economic structures – undergoing perpetual transformation – which called for new governance structures.[39] It would be equally errant to assume that these new, now global profit-making and financial interests would themselves somehow provide for 'freedom'. Max Weber described the conditions at the turn of the nineteenth century, which are strikingly similar to those of today:

> If the *only* things that mattered were 'material' conditions and the constellations of interests directly or indirectly 'created' by them, any sober observer would be bound to conclude that all *economic* auguries point in the direction of a growing *loss* of freedom. It is quite ridiculous to attribute to today's high capitalism, as it exists in America and is being imported into Russia, to this 'inevitability' of our economic development, any 'elec-

36 The quote is from Marx and Engel (1998 [1948]: 41). They make use of a poem by Goethe ('The Apprentice Sorcerer'), but leave out the return of the Master Sorcerer.

37 'Golden ages' are always like an optical deception in the rear-view mirror. If one takes a closer look at these periods, then one ascertains very quickly that at the time, everyone was complaining that there was too much yellow.

38 In some way this only repeats a basic idea of T. H. Marshall (1981: 133): 'It is legitimate, and also profitable, to regard [politically organized] welfare and the market as embodying two different ways of performing the same task, that of satisfying the needs and wants of the population.'

39 This is also demonstrated by the rapid growth in international organizations after the Second World War; cf. Rittberger with Zangl (1995: 72), Zürn (1998: Part B, 171ff.), and Shanks et al. (1996).

tive affinity' with 'democracy' or indeed 'freedom' (in *any* sense of the word), when the only question one can ask is how all these things can 'possibly' survive at all in the long run under the rule of capitalism. (Weber 1906: 69)

They are in fact only possible

if they are supported by the permanent determined *will* of a nation not to be governed like a flock of sheep. We are 'individualists' and partisans of 'democratic' institutions 'against the tide' of material constellations. Anyone who wishes to be the weather-vane of a 'developmental trend' should abandon these old-fashioned ideals as quickly as possible. The genesis of modern 'freedom' presupposed certain unique, never-to-be-repeated historical constellations. (Ibid.)

Bureaucratic politics as a means, and bureaucracy as an outcome are essential to the welfare-democratic answers to economic change. The more fundamental such change is, the more probable is its welfare-democratic result.[40] For precisely this reason, democratic structures can lead to 'more market' as a response to welfare state dilemmas and the exhaustion of the 'utopian potential' of welfare statism.

Political power or economic law?

One facet of globalization is that theoretical arguments for its economic rationality are adduced as irrefutable advice. This is supposed to neutralize the political struggle essential to every democracy and replace it with 'theoretical' truth. However, the truth claims of every 'theory' – including most religious world-views – are anathema to democratic politics. 'Truth' is not accessible to the weighing of different perspectives and thus to political compromise. Put differently, there is a general impression that political leaders seem to subordinate themselves to the views of business leaders. In some quarters this is bemoaned as a loss of the influence of democracy in the shaping of societal conditions; in others it is celebrated as the return of economic rationality to its proper domain. Both of these contribute little to clarifying the problems. Globalization was not created by economics. It arose as a result of completely different, essentially political forces. For this reason, one can justifiably object that, first, with regard to the point of departure, the ostensible 'terror of economics' poses no problem whatsoever, but, rather, pointed significant groups of the population to the way out of a self-made cul-de-sac. Three points, which usually receive at best cursory discussion, support the assessment that the globalization tendencies of the economy are political – and not theoretical – answers by welfare democracy to the seemingly unstoppable growth of the welfare state that is at the same time unable to deliver on its promises anymore.

First, beginning in the early 1980s ever greater spheres that were hitherto under the control of politics have been subjected to the ordering force of the market. This development is to be attributed less, however, to an intrinsic superiority of this form of coordination of needs than to the perception of those who hold power in democracy, namely the voters, that government and politics have reached the limits of what they

40 One of the few commentators to call attention to the increase in authoritarian elements in the era of globalization is Dahrendorf (1999).

had promised to provide. The difficulty here lies less in the technical capabilities of the political-administrative system than in the fact that in the competitive struggle for political power, incumbents and those fighting to replace them discovered social policy.[41] It is the welfare state itself which in the twentieth century systematically produced needs and built up expectations which it was increasingly unable to fulfil.

The welfare state has developed its own battalions, which now rally to its defence. Its clientele of insured persons and risk groups amount to – at least in Europe – essentially the entire population, and at the very least make up relevant majorities (Lepsius 1979; Alber 1984; Flora 1989; Rieger 1998). The problem today consists not in the welfare state being too weak to defend its socio-political benefit standards, but in its inflexibility precisely because of its strength. Social policy can become a victim of its own success. The institutionalized and dynamic expectations of the social risk society overpower both the welfare state bureaucracy and party politics.[42] It is mainly the quasi-corporatively organized, insured clientele which determines the socio-political status quo. The democratic welfare state still exists as a socio-political system designed to fulfil exclusively nationally defined needs, and its future lies precisely in this promise.

It is thus by no means clear that the individualization of expectations and the pluralization of needs, which are fundamental to economic globalization, will also lead to forms of social policy that are oriented towards individual needs and not to collective need satisfaction, as has hitherto been the case. The globalized economy is indeed driven by consumer wishes and customer satisfaction. Yet this does not necessarily or automatically imply a socio-political shift towards social security according to private choice and thus a turn away from social security as welfare state need fulfilment. Every case of individual responsibility involves costs. Under strict market conditions, these costs tend to fall upon the individual. This is *by definition* not the case in social policy. The collectivized help of others through the welfare state entails the

[41] As Weber (1978: 1128) was one of the first to note, such a development threatens to turn democracy into its opposite: 'Both the pragmatic interest in the flexibility of the parliamentary apparatus and the power interest of the representatives and party functionaries converge on one point: They tend to treat the representative not as the servant but as the chosen "master" of his voters.' For Weber, the criterion of formally voluntary solicitation as the focal point of party competition in a democratic regime was of major sociological significance since it produces a fundamental analogy between parties and firms. Both try to become independent of the sovereign consumer citizen by advertisement and the conscious creation of wants. In the same way as business managers *fashion* markets for their merchandise and services, the political entrepreneurs of all parties, regardless of whether they are on the left or on the right, invent markets for their social policy goods. The fact that voters are eager to take them does not mean that they in actual fact *need* them (ibid.: 284–8).

[42] In Germany this line of critique has a long tradition (A. Weber 1913; Bernhard 1914). For a neutral analysis, see Achinger (1971 [1958]) and Kaufmann (1997b) as well as Kaufmann's conceptual history (2001b). In the Anglo-Saxon world, this critique was even more pronounced and found its classical expression in T. H. Marshall's analysis, 'Value Problems of Welfare Capitalism' (1972). In this analysis he noted that in contrast to the economic process it is 'a fundamental principle of the welfare state that the market value of an individual cannot be the measure of his right to welfare' (ibid.: 107). However, since in the sphere of organized welfare, provision is made at the expense of one set of people for the immediate needs of others, the democratic political process is prone to introduce a perverse and ultimately self-defeating dynamic of its own: 'Democratic voting is egotistic; most voters voice what they believe to be their own interest' (ibid.). It was the great concern of traditional liberals that if pensioners and others who depend on the public purse were allowed to vote – i.e. the beneficiaries could put pressure on their benefactors – government would be corrupted and the foundations of democracy undermined.

promise of being able to lower or even completely avoid some of the costs of individual responsibility. The market antipathy of social welfare organizations, in terms of both their form and effects – characterized by Esping-Andersen (1985) as 'politics against markets' – is not coincidental, but systematic.[43] Similarly, the fashionable proposals to introduce the logic of the market into social policy – i.e. proceeding from the idea of the customer, the free consumer with his or her own needs and demands, and shaping the production and consumption relations of the welfare state accordingly – overlook that, historically, social policy was implemented against the market and that it derived and continues to derive its legitimacy from the fact that it is a quintessentially collective undertaking. Thus one has to stress the fundamental difference as well as the complementarity between welfare state institutions and market institutions.

The second point is necessarily related to the first one. That which today is termed globalization is not a fate that somehow came from above to befall the populations of the world and their political representatives. Globalization attained its political-economic form not under democratic parliamentary conditions alone – e.g. as deregulation in economic policy, liberalization in trade policy and multilateralism in an international free trade regime. The path to globalization was paved as well – above all with regard to the Second (socialist) World – by democratic revolutions in which consumer interests played an essential role. To bemoan the fate of democracy in globalization, or to call for *more* democracy to control a seemingly unleashed economy, is to ignore an important point: the conditions that are currently described as globalization were created and advanced both in terms of their institutional foundations and their dynamic by parliamentary, democratically legitimated decisions. Globalization was and is subject to an ongoing plebiscite of consumers and voters and is shaped by this perpetual *plebiscitum*. Even when the thesis of the 'McDonaldization of society' (Ritzer 2000) is clothed in social scientific garb, its core is the moralizing denunciation of mass consumers by the representatives of an elite culture. It is thus beside the point to want to pit 'democracy' against globalization, voters against consumers (Ritzer 2000; Alfino et al. 1998; Smart 1999). In some sense, and for better or for worse, globalization *is* the new form of *social* democracy.

Third, globalization losers and globalization winners are hardly distinct groups or classes pitted against one another. Even those low-skilled workers who are most threatened and most strongly impacted by unemployment can profit from globalization as consumers. This is not only due to the low rate of inflation, but also to the easier access to a larger range of goods, the emergence of new occupations and jobs, and, above all, to new forms of employment. In this respect, the functional capacity of the welfare state has been evident. The new poverty risks and the phenomenon of social exclusion are by no means meant to be understated here. Yet in contrast to widespread contentions, these groups have hardly been left in the lurch by social policy in either Western Europe or North America. On the contrary, the full spectrum of social problems resulting from globalization is dealt with in public policy on a daily basis (Leisering and Leibfried 1999). Welfare state benefit claims – the 'new property' (Charles A. Reich 1964) – have by no means disappeared. Thanks to welfare state

43 The *locus classicus* of this argument is Marshall (1949), who in this exemplary study noted that 'in the twentieth century, citizenship and the capitalist class system', the natural outgrowth of the market economy, 'have been at war' (p. 84). Marshall also observed that 'the wars of religion have been succeeded by the wars of social doctrine' (1962: 61).

institutions, low-income consumers in 'developed' or 'mature' countries, some of them unemployed for a very long time, could convert their wants into effective demand.[44] Politically decisive, in contrast to the social question of the nineteenth century, is thus that globalization has not, until now, divided populations. The new social conflict is individualized and diffuse (Dahrendorf 2002). Hence no broad political foundation exists which would allow the new social conflicts, which clearly exist, not least in the form of the so-called underclass, from being resolved by an authoritarian dictate of new distributional criteria.

3 The Politics of Globalization

'The philosophers have only interpreted the world, in various ways; the point, however, is to change it.' This is Marx's famous eleventh thesis on Feuerbach. Today, the reverse problem seems to present itself: Those who seek to change the world do not waste too much time beforehand on trying to understand it. Its reality appears to be beyond question. Nearly every social science study of ostensibly indubitable and 'necessary' connections between the welfare state and globalization seeks to engage in politics. Upon closer examination, however, it quickly becomes clear that the argument is always designed in such a way that the scientific findings reached perfectly match the political change desired. Regardless of the direction of the political change sought, the dramaturgy is always the same: more or less identical observations on the sole true nature of globalization are followed without much ado by ostensibly compelling but – small surprise – opposite conclusions on the future fate of social policy: 'Statistics and economics are an arsenal from which everyone chooses his weapon' (Burckhardt 1982 [1905]: 193).

For one camp, globalization proves that contemporary welfare state arrangements are no longer tenable and that they ultimately must be trimmed to their appropriate size. Economic laws, it is argued, prevail not only to the extent that free trade obtains. They enforce themselves, for as territorially bounded national economies have disappeared, so has the autonomy of the nation-state. Any resistance, regardless of whether it be of protectionist or social-conservative nature, is futile, it is contended, and harms itself by leading to a waste of resources. Hence adaptation is the order of the day.[45]

[44] For a graphic description of the extremely different fate of the unemployed in Germany, the United States and Hong Kong see the *International Herald Tribune* of 21 February 2002, p. 6 ('Testing the Safety Nets'). The German jobless worker cited had been unemployed since 1990, and the article pointed out that despite a jobless benefit of $529 per month, thanks to extra housing benefits, he could hold on to a three-room, 69 square metre (743 square foot) apartment costing more than the jobless benefit. This man lived for almost three decades in that same flat, and refused to move because he wanted to stay close to his divorced wife and children.

[45] This is the core of the argument presented for example by Siebert (1996a, b; 1999a, b) or Berthold (1997) as well as by Scharpf (2000a, b). In an international and popular form, this argument can be found in Thurow (1992) and Rifkin (1995). Scharpf and Schmidt (2000) have a similar point of departure, but a different political focus. 'The [economic] laws confirm themselves to the degree that free trade becomes dominant' and opposition, 'whether protectionist (tariffs) or social-conservative, is futile' – this is an excerpt from the speech 'On the Question of Free Trade', given in 1848 by Karl Marx (1848: 454 ff.). Marx favoured free trade because it was seen as speeding up the socialist revolution.

For the other camp, the same welfare state arrangements amount to a necessary precondition to a national economy opening itself up to globalization. Precisely under conditions of economic globalization, it is maintained, there is no alternative to politically organized existential provision. The latter is the only acceptable reaction to the social ruptures produced by capitalist economies. The goal, then, should be to protect the levels of welfare state provision hitherto attained in order not to undermine this necessary foundation which the main actors in world markets – firms – cannot procure by themselves.[46]

Both of these lines of argument are intellectually equivalent to short circuits. In so far as they depart from non-normative research, they represent social science reasoning. These two variants of capitulation demonstrate each in their own way, however, how violent and radical the contemporary ruptures have been. Thus it should not surprise us that in their descriptions both sides can take recourse to the brilliant passages from the Communist Manifesto and its formula of a 'constant revolutionising':

> All fixed, fast-frozen relations, with their train of ancient and venerable prejudices and opinions, are swept away, all new-formed ones become antiquated before they can ossify. All that is solid melts into air, all that is holy is profaned, and man is at last compelled to face with sober senses, his real conditions of life, and his relations with his kind.
>
> The need of a constantly expanding market for its products chases the bourgeoisie over the whole surface of the globe. It must nestle everywhere, settle everywhere, establish connections everywhere.
>
> The bourgeoisie has through its exploitation of the world-market given a cosmopolitan character to production and consumption in every country. To the great chagrin of reactionists, it has drawn from under the feet of industry the national ground on which it stood. All old-established national industries have been destroyed or are daily being destroyed. They are dislodged by new industries, whose introduction becomes a life and death question for all civilised nations, by industries that no longer work up indigenous raw material, but raw material drawn from the remotest zones; industries whose products are consumed, not only at home, but in every quarter of the globe. In place of the old wants, satisfied by the productions of the country, we find new wants, requiring for their satisfaction the products of distant lands and climes. In place of the old local and national seclusion and self-sufficiency, we have intercourse in every direction, universal interdependence of nations. And as in material, so also in intellectual production. The intellectual creations of individual nations become common property. National one-sidedness and narrow-mindedness become more and more impossible, and from the numerous national and local literatures, there arises a world literature.
>
> The bourgeoisie, by the rapid improvement of all instruments of production, by the immensely facilitated means of communication, draws all, even the most barbarian, nations into civilisation. The cheap prices of its commodities are the heavy artillery with which it batters down all Chinese walls, with which it forces the barbarians' intensely obstinate hatred of foreigners to capitulate. It compels all nations, on pain of extinction, to adopt the bourgeois mode of production, it compels them to introduce what it calls civilisation into their midst, i.e., to become bourgeois themselves. In one word, it creates a world after its own image. (Marx and Engels 1998 [1848]: 39–40)

[46] This argument is made by Ganßmann (2000). A social science version of this approach is offered by Rodrik (1997, 1998), and by Garrett (1997, 1998).

As this description shows, Joseph Schumpeter had good reason to come to the defence of Marx the sociologist against Marx the politician (1950: 9–20). Schumpeter owes his formulation of 'creative destruction' as the core and motor of market economic development to the Marxian insight into the constant 'revolt of modern production forces against modern conditions of production' (Marx and Engels 1998 [1848]: 41). He acknowledges Marx's superior capacity to 'pierce through the random irregularities of the surface down to the grandiose logic of things historical' (1950 [1942]: 10).

This capacity is critical again today. Then, as now, the motor of globalization is the combination of technological progress and sinking transport costs, which put production and communication on a new footing. Between 1830 and 1880, too, the share of transport costs in the value of goods shrank by half for the entire range of goods.[47] This created the foundations for world markets in which, in contrast to today, not only capital became mobile, but also – and to an equal extent – labour. Economists who did not lose their historical senses thus see present-day economic integration processes as a return to a normalcy which had abruptly ended with the outbreak of the First World War.[48] Yet now as then, it is not technology alone that endows economic activity with a new dynamism and which gives the latter its new forms. The development of the world economy in the interwar period and in the first decade after the Second World War shows that even a high degree of integration among national economies can give way to sudden, radical economic disintegration and political fragmentation. What causes such abrupt reversals of policy directions?

The ostensibly so compelling logic of globalization appears to be rooted less in its economic technical core than in a fast-paced social change which in many of its aspects is only feebly related to 'that single, unconscionable freedom – free trade' (Marx and Engels 1998 [1848]: 38). In fact, there is much more political control in international trade than in domestic economics. International economics was and remains a matter of an extremely reluctantly implemented and even more carefully guarded trade policy made by governments for governments through governments. In addition, these governments are solely responsible to a *national* electorate and thus to the members of a jealously shielded *exclusive* association. Elected officials gauge each and every foreign economic policy measure for their potentially negative effects on this target group – if only for reasons of enlightened self-interest alone. These essentially *domestic* political aspects of national and foreign economic policy are less obvious than the much more

47 Bairoch (1999: 164) has compiled some figures on this. The table below depicts the share of transport costs expressed as a percentage of the value of the respective good:

	around 1830	around 1880
Iron ore	115–20	60–65
Iron products	32–38	16–20
Cotton products	8–11	4–5

48 Cf. Thomson and Krasner (1989), J. G. Williamson (1995), Eichengreen (1996b), H. James (1996: chs 1 and 17) and Timmer and J. G. Williamson (1998). The apparent decoupling of financial from goods markets and the volume of international financial flows are often adduced as arguments for the position that present-day globalization cannot be compared with that of the nineteenth century (Beisheim et al. 1999; Walter et al. 1999). Yet management and finance experts regularly point out that the overwhelming share of financial globalization is caused by the new instruments for hedging 'real' transactions against the higher risks of international trade.

autonomous changes in production techniques, consumption habits and lifestyles. A retrospective comparison, however, can help render perceptible a general pattern in the political reactions to economic globalization processes. This pattern consists in a twofold change in the equilibrium among social groups, and precisely for this reason creates much more political tensions in societies with the most developed economies than in so-called underdeveloped countries. Under the transformed framework conditions of national politics, the social changes that produce globalization winners and losers can be followed by a revision in the distribution of the costs and benefits of preserving the community. The problem is the interconnection between economics and politics.

Precisely for this reason, in his speech 'On the Question of Free Trade', Marx declared himself in favour of free trade: the system of free trade would accelerate, he argued, the social revolution (Marx 1848: 458). The contradiction between classes would become sharpened and more palpable. Free trade makes 'the secondary conditions' disappear which 'workers up to now could believe to be responsible for their plight' (ibid.: 456). What Marx perceived in its early stages, but whose significance he radically underestimated – namely the emergence of social policy as a 'conscious and deliberated response of society on the anarchic form of the production process' (1977 [1867]: 504) – will, perhaps, prove again today to be the main reason why the latest economic revolution will most likely not have the effects that are desired or feared. The welfare state did not come into being as a one-time equilibration of opposing interests; social policy is an ongoing concern of an effectively democratized nation-state. The welfare state as such is not threatened. Rather, the welfare state and its social policy *are* this equilibration in the form of an incessant political process which regularly reinvents itself. The only way it can work is to incorporate ever more interests and needs into its transfer and regulatory systems in such a way that these interest groups get their money's worth out of the process. Ultimately, every welfare state will systematically link the material fate of each politically significant group with its own (Rieger 1998a).

The first of the two domestic societal changes which accompany globalization is indeed essentially economic in nature. At its core is the phenomenon that in the more developed economies low-skilled labour is in part due to technical progress which is no longer in demand and which in part has become comparatively expensive. Low-skilled labour becomes redundant, for the new information and communications technologies generate hitherto unimaginable rationalization effects in ever more realms of goods production as well as in the service sector. It also becomes more expensive, because as a result of the new transportation and communications infrastructure the costs of domestic economic production rise relative to those of international and foreign-based production. This appears to be the recurrence of a constellation which in the past has been repeatedly perceived as a societal challenge and which has provoked enormous social struggles.

Marx redivivus?

Ever since the foundation of the modern 'work society' (Dahrendorf) by industrialization and capitalism, causing the creation of jobs to become the alpha and the omega of all politics, the same question presents itself again and again: in managing scarce resources and attempting somehow to fairly distribute income and goods according to need, is technological progress a solution or a problem? What happens to the workers who are 'set free', or 'down-sized', by such progress? The answer of the classical economists amounted to the following: 'that all machinery that displaces workers simultaneously, and necessarily, sets free an amount of capital adequate to employ precisely those workers displaced' (Marx 1977 [1867]: 565). Marx contradicted this contention, and his argumentation – today just as in earlier periods of accelerated change – appears to mirror at least those segments of public opinion in which populist critique and 'leftist' or 'critical' social scientific explanations seem to meet:

> The workers, when driven out of the workshop by the machinery, are thrown onto the labour-market. Their presence in the labour-market increases the number of labour-powers which are at the disposal of capitalist exploitation. In Part VII we shall see that this effect of machinery, which has been represented as a compensation for the working class, is, on the contrary, a most frightful scourge. For the present I will only say this: workers who have been thrown out of work in a given branch of industry can no doubt look for employment in another branch. If they find it, and thus renew the bond between them and the means of subsistence, this takes place only through the agency of a new, additional capital which is seeking investment, and in no way through the agency of the capital that was already functioning previously and was then converted into machinery. And even if they do find employment, what a miserable prospect they face! Crippled as they are by the division of labour, these poor devils are worth so little outside their old trade that they cannot find admission into any industries except a few inferior and therefore over-supplied and under-paid branches. (Ibid.: 567–8)

For a large share of the labour force, rapid technical progress initially means a devaluation of their occupational qualifications. This devaluation can take two forms: either the price for their occupational labour sinks – wages are cut or are no longer adjusted to inflation, so that their real value declines – or, when this adjustment of the price of low-skilled labour is not possible, a lesser amount of this labour is demanded and the remainder of these workers are dismissed into unemployment. In essence, each of these forms of adaptation can be observed in both the USA and Germany. Starting in the mid-1970s, the USA experienced a decline in real wages which affected ever-greater segments of the labour force.[49] In the Federal Republic of Germany, on the other hand, contrary to the international trend, a relative stability of real wages was maintained at the expense of mass unemployment. For low-skilled workers in particular, this turned into long-term unemployment.[50] However, this differential impact of technological progress on the labour market chiefly has institutional causes, and it is above all for the macro-organizational setting that in the two countries job creation, in particular the creation of 'good' jobs, is not, or at least not to a sufficient degree, accompanied by job destruction. In Germany the combined effects of a centralized, corporatively organized collective bargaining system and a broadly cast and yet differentiated system of social protection, and in the USA precisely the lack of such arrangements, are mainly responsible for the different labour market outcomes. With regard to this reshuffling of labour markets, welfare state institutions themselves are initially of only secondary importance. Much like the Red Cross, but a good deal more

[49] Cf. F. Levy (1998), Mishel et al. (1999, 2001) and Blank (2000: 10 ff.).

[50] An economist at the IMF thus speaks of the 'unbearable stability of the German wage structure' (Prasad 2000).

unevenly due to differing national regimes, they provide for those who are no longer capable of labour market participation.

The institutions of the welfare state can play a substantial role, however, in the shaping of the future of individual workers or of the labour force as a whole. Particularly interesting here is the relationship between social and educational policy, or the question of how *productive*, or resourceful, social policy is. Do its institutions function as holding tanks for the unemployed and others who no longer participate in the labour market, or do they themselves improve the chances of the affected individuals to succeed under changed labour market conditions?[51] The coordination of social and educational policy is of central importance in this regard.[52] At issue here is thus what happens in social policy after the effects of radical economic change become apparent.

As the German case makes clear, social policy can be a cause of mass unemployment to the extent that it abets a 'cartel' made up of unions and employer associations, or of employees in firms and their management. It can open up strategic possibilities for corporatist and firm actors to preserve existing wage levels and levels of labour law and social protection for those workers who are still employed. In other words, it can help privilege the 'job holders' at the expense of the general public or the unemployed. Such an institutionally mediated outcome is only to a limited degree the result of the new economics of globalization and thus, at least in theory, much more open to political reform, since it is a purely domestic affair.

Globalization losers in welfare democracy

The social explosiveness of globalization, and in particular the conflicts surrounding welfare state institutions, is due to a second aspect of globalization: the new *political* deal it involves. Since the middle of the 1970s, an ever-expanding group of countries has gradually repealed controls on capital flows and other such restrictions. As a result, it became nearly impossible for any country to withstand this pressure to liberalize its capital markets (Helleiner 1994; Kapstein 1994, 1999, 2000). Capital thus became not only more mobile, but also – in today's solely relevant global dimensions – more scarce in relation to labour. The main cause of this has been the rapid growth in the global population over recent decades.[53] Thus, not only did capital become more mobile; its mobility also became more profitable. The new scarcity of capital and its greater mobility pose a far more direct challenge to the welfare state than do the economic conse-

51 In comparative welfare state analysis, Heidenheimer (1981) was one of the first to call attention to the critical importance of a conjunction or disjunction between educational and social policy (see also Katznelson and Weir 1985; Allmendinger 1999; Leibfried and Obinger 2001; Allmendinger and Leibfried 2003).

52 The Japanese government, in an attempt to help the unemployed, introduced in 1998 a grant system under which it subsidizes up to 80 per cent of the tuition for a career-training programme including classes for those qualifying exams that regulate access to well-paying jobs. Toyohiko Narikawa, the founder and president of Waseda Seminar K. K., a provider of private classes that prepare people for qualifying exams, which attract more than 100,000 students, said: 'Companies are protecting themselves, so workers are protecting themselves' (Tanikawa 2002: 13).

53 The ILO (2001) estimated that in the year 2000 there were 160 million unemployed persons in the world, 50 million of whom live in developed industrial societies. Alongside these unemployed are 500 million persons who earn less than 1 $US per day – the global poverty line. It is estimated that over the next decade there will be 460 million new labour market entrants.

quences of globalization. Globalization causes a systemic crisis in the welfare state not because it presents it with problems regarding benefits and their financing. Rather, it does so by calling into question the distribution of the fiscal burden of social policies. In the wake of globalization, the new institutional politics – the politics of defining the rules of the game – consists mostly in the struggle to adapt institutions suited to one set of objects and their attendant means to conditions in which those sets cannot freely operate. The result is necessarily serious strain, but there is no clear line upon which the large-scale reorganization should proceed that is not vetoed by one or the other group in society able to do so.

We mentioned above that the core of economic globalization consists in a shift in factor price relations from which no part of the economy is exempt. This systematic shift is a *political* problem due to the fact that it has *exogenous* causes: the revaluation and devaluation of labour market qualifications – just like the relative increase in the costs of social control by means of social policy rather than through market coordination – brings about an abrupt redistribution not only of individual life chances, but also of 'power', or 'influence' chances. Shifts in the latter are only seldom attributable to changes in *individual* performance. Thus it is one thing when certain social groups see themselves as globalization losers. For initially it is indeed not only the blind, but also the anonymous forces of the market that cause such socio-economic change. The *subsequent* fate of these individuals – how fast and under what conditions they find their next job – depends, however, to a great extent on institutional arrangements and the capability of the national political system.

It is another thing altogether, though, when the redistribution of political power associated with globalization also translates into a redistribution of fiscal burdens within a community. This development occurs in a system of *politically* – and thus *consciously* – created responsibilities. Hence these secondary – in contrast to the primary – shifts caused by globalization can also have dynamic effects, i.e. lead to a targeted, articulable dissatisfaction which can have consequences. The greater mobility of capital seems to make it more costly for any given state to retain capital within its borders – without its societal value having increased. This higher political price for capital to stay is the real reason why in all developed societies, tax cuts for corporations and for the affluent social strata have been and continue to be on the political agenda. If, under these conditions, the scope of welfare state benefits is not to be diminished, the financing burden must ultimately be shifted to those groups that are not mobile, i.e. the bulk of the workforce whose labour power is easily replaceable and who do not have to be specially wooed by employers.

Two processes thus overlap here: a new economic differentiation among individuals and groups in the wake of shifts in factor price relations, and an essentially socio-political or fiscal redistribution of the public burdens of the polity. For some individuals and groups, this can mean that they are at once doubly affected. First, the probability increases that they will become unemployed, earn less money and find their career prospects diminished. And second, their tax and social insurance contribution burden increases – without a corresponding increase in their social rights. In fact, they must reckon with the opposite, i.e. with *rising* fiscal burdens and *dwindling* social rights. Conversely, the new globalized markets not only provide the owners of capital as well as highly skilled workers with higher profits and incomes respectively; government compounds this effect by striving to relieve the tax burden on these individuals' incomes.

In the course of this twofold displacement in distributional relations among social groups, a socio-political dimension becomes more clearly visible than heretofore – and makes it more difficult to come to terms with the new political responsibilities and to pursue a rational social policy. The welfare state itself creates its own system of social inequality – additional to that of the market (Marshall 1949; Janowitz 1976). Just as social inequalities can persist without continuing to fulfil any economic function, such as offering mobility and performance incentives, differences among welfare state clients can also lose their social *raison d'être*. In developed welfare states, it is not only the clients' social rights that are at war with the capitalist class system; the same is true of the relations between the various producers and consumers of socio-political goods (Marshall 1949). The institutions of the welfare state allocate benefits according to their own rules and thereby create new and independent distinctions between privileged and burdened groups, between those with secure and those with insecure claims – i.e. between members of corporatively organized social insurance funds on the one hand and social assistance recipients on the other, who are left to a far greater extent to fend for themselves. It is expected from democratic social policy, however, that it creates distributional effects which the market economy, left to itself, would not have achieved. Yet when social and fiscal policy merely pays homage to the Matthew principle – giving more to those who already have – the problem of socio-political justice is exacerbated.

Now it is not only, and often not at all, the impact of a globalized market economy that puts pressure on welfare state arrangements. At least as important is the condition that social policy – as it currently exists as the sum of a multitude of institutions as well as a certain mode of dealing with problems – has difficulties legitimizing itself by its own standards. Every one of these institutions has its own interest group or party political justification, and every institution has a politically potent clientele. The 'good reason' for each such institution is indeed essentially historical to the extent that its once perhaps rational core probably no longer exists today. This notwithstanding, the institution continues to be defended – with considerable prospects of success – but not as much for social as for electoral and party political reasons. With regard to the efficiency of social policy, majoritarian democracy is afflicted with the problem that its point of departure is the self-interest of the voter. At issue in decisions on welfare, however, is provision for others as well as reciprocal provision. At the expense of one segment of society, measures are taken to provide for the risks and immediate needs of another. From the standpoint of those who pay, however, these needs are very distant or mere hypothetical eventualities (Marshall 1972: 108).

A basic problem in the entire globalization discussion consists in the failure to differentiate sufficiently between objective problems and political liability for them. Much of that which is causally attributed to economic globalization is actually a product of welfare state conditions themselves. At the same time it must be noted, however, that the interrelation between globalization and the welfare state can assume very different forms, and political decisions can play a critical role in its shaping. What role do nation-state socio-political arrangements play here?

The fate of national social policy

At first glance, the defining of socio-political trajectories and the shaping of welfare state institutions appear to have been decisively determined by the fact that they occurred within the more or less protected shell of the nation-state. This protected environment is no longer a given today. As a result, in the future, only those national specifics in social policy which are compatible with or appropriate to the market appear to have a chance of survival, or, expressed conversely, global capitalism will create the socio-political institutions that suit it.

This outcome need by no means be willed or planned, yet it is becoming increasingly probable as a result of the new *political* deal that globalization entails. If one follows the logic of a certain line of thinking in economic theory, the new national politics of the welfare state, too, is subject to the imperative of a now ineluctable international interdependence of all (socio-)political decision-making. As long as social policy resided in a more or less exclusive national economic framework and was shaped there, its anti-market, populist, electoral-strategic and ideological tendencies were able to assert themselves because they could be imposed on geographically imprisoned companies at a relatively low political cost. Only those firms that could adapt to the welfare state conditions of mass democracy survived. The welfare state created a world of production after its own image.

In the meantime, this constellation has turned into its opposite, at least to the extent that globalization has provided firms with new 'exit' options and has thus enhanced their political power – their 'voice' – to undermine the existent welfare state structures. Thus the demand that social policy should now orient itself towards economic conditions, that its structures should be compatible with and appropriate to the market (e.g. Homann and Pies 1996). If political units – whether local, regional or national – find themselves in a relatively similar position with regard to their largely *man-made* suitability as a home to economic activity, then even comparatively 'small' decisions in social and fiscal policy can have large effects on a company's decision-making concerning location and investment. Under the artificially created competitive conditions of *organized* locational advantage to which territorial units are subject, differences among the latter are systematically ground away. 'We do everything everyone else does' – this is how a Senator from Arkansas once described his state's budget policy (cited in Case et al. 1993: 285). Will global capitalism now create a welfare state world after its own image?

The fiscal federalism of the USA, including its independently limiting effects on the socio-political ambitions of state actors, apparently demonstrates on a small scale what can be expected on a large scale in global site competition. However, this view is totally misleading.

State governments in the USA do not behave the way they do – i.e. take the utmost care not to become 'welfare magnets' – as a result of some natural state of being, or of a Hobbesian non-order, but because of the US Constitution, which comprises a carefully designed political will. The much greater hurdle that social policy initiatives have to overcome in a locational competition environment framed by fiscal federalism, compared to one in which this mechanism does not obtain, is a constitutional device: US state governments simply do not have the legal powers necessary to build welfare states of their own. If they had had their way, they would have opted for 'welfare democracy', which in fact they did after the War of Independence, and which was stopped by a federalizing counter-movement (Beard 2000 [1913]; Jensen 1940).

In the preface to his 'Notes of Debates in the Federal Convention of 1787' James Madison counted among the main vices of the Articles of Confederation, soon to be replaced by the new Constitution which went into force in 1789, 'the animosity kindled among the States by their conflicting regulations' (Madison 1987 [1787]: 8). In their original position the American states behaved just like modern welfare states:

> The want of a general power over Commerce led to an exercise of the power separately, by the States, which not only proved abortive, but engendered rival, conflicting and angry regulations. Besides the vain attempts to supply their respective treasuries by imposts, which turned their commerce into the neighbouring ports . . . taxed & irritated the adjoining States . . . and treated the Citizens of other states as aliens. (Ibid.: 14)

As this remark makes clear, welfare statism depends on territorial closure, and that is not a 'state right' in the United States.[54] In other words, there is a Commerce Clause which effectively binds the behaviour of US state governments, and, at the same time, *empowers a national* government – but there is nothing that comes even close to this norm in the governance of the global economy.[55]

As the view on the United States shows, it must not be forgotten that the interdependence of national economies and the mobility of capital are hardly new phenomena, whose probable consequences are not anticipated and thus reflected in welfare state structures. The historical parallels suggest that, even under conditions of fully developed competition among states, the reciprocal relationship between the economy and social policy is by no means as close and compelling as, for example, the theory of fiscal federalism would lead one to expect – *pace* the absence of an international Commerce Clause.[56] Max Weber noted that it was not until the onset of a competitive nation-state system that modern rational capitalism received a guarantee for its survival. Constitutionally protected property rights only came into being 'wherever several political communities competed with one another by enlarging their tax base and by promoting capital formation for the sake of obtaining private loans' (Weber 1978: 353). Earlier beginnings of a capitalist, market-based development in the economy, for example during the Roman principate, failed because of the inability of

[54] As early as the turn of the nineteenth century Max Weber observed that the USA – compared to Europe which was turning increasingly away from free-market, profit-making capitalism towards a socio-politically domesticated capitalism of controlled consumption – constituted the 'exception from the general welfare-state trend'. He saw in the 'particularistic independence' of the individual states in the American union the reason for the 'failure of all serious efforts at unifying consumer interests' and thus of all the groups with an interest in a capitalism of controlled consumption (1978: 352). However, it is not federalism as such that constrains social policy in favour of market-based capitalism, but merely those forms consisting in autonomous sub-units – here, states – largely unrestricted in their legislative powers and enjoying neither a system of fiscal equalization nor an institutionalized participation of state *governments* in the federal legislative process. Only under these conditions can a locational competition emerge which has the effect of furthering a decline or at least a defensive stabilization in tax and social insurance burdens, while thwarting the social ambitions of democratic welfare states (Peterson and Rom 1990; Peterson 1995; Pierson 1995; Obinger 1998; Oates 1999).

[55] Up to the New Deal the Commerce Clause was mostly used by the Supreme Court to enforce *negative* freedom, i.e. *not giving Congress a general power of legislation*; thereafter, however, marking a fundamental constitutional transformation, it was and is actively used to *grant*, not to *deny* federal powers: 'Once the Commerce Clause is taken to authorize Congress to control whatever has an indirect effect on commerce, the national government may do almost anything a majority in Congress thinks proper' (Easterbrook 1992: 368). The same point was made most forcefully by Ackerman (1992: 322–5).

[56] On the limits of fiscal federalism to understand international locational competition, see S. Sinn (1992).

the civic protagonists of a free economy to defend themselves against the state, for they did not have the possibility of territorial 'exit' and thus had only a limited domestic political 'voice' (Weber 1896).

Moreover, a glance at the late nineteenth century shows not only that an expansionist social policy was pursued in the face of a comparatively much stronger process of world market integration of national economies, against the resistance of the business community, but also that this social policy assumed very different forms in different countries. The major, and until today still structurally defining distinctions in social policy – tax-financed versus contribution-financed systems, social insurance for selected employment groups versus general provision for the whole of the citizenry, uniform systems versus decentralized systems, self-administered versus state-bureaucratic systems – crystallized under conditions of international economics that would have led one to expect a convergence of socio-political solutions, not the divergence which actually occurred (Marshall 1961a).

These historical references cannot be brushed aside with the argument that at the time it was simply the compelling imperatives of the social question which dictated a social policy that ran counter to the market. The last major socio-political act of Germany's Second Empire was not in the realm of poverty or some other ameliorative policy. It was a social policy measure provoked exclusively by factional political pressure by the most privileged group in the labour force at the time: white-collar workers – then still called 'corporate civil servants' (*Betriebsbeamte*) because of the security of their jobs. The white-collar pension insurance introduced in 1911 is thus exemplary of an opportunistic distributional policy which operated beyond the scope of market-rational social policy (Zwiedineck-Südenhorst 1924, 1925). Interdependence and locational competition do not lead automatically to specific socio-political outcomes, just as one cannot compellingly deduce from this constellation a 'race to the bottom'.

The metaphor of a race to the bottom refers to a development which – if it is indeed more than a pseudo-fact – requires closer examination. More analytical attention needs to be devoted to specific policy contexts. Further, consideration should be given to the political reaction that such a process – to the extent that it indeed exists – generally triggers.

The *locus classicus* for the thesis of locational competition with predominantly negative consequences for the public interest is the dissenting vote of Louis Brandeis in a decision of the US Supreme Court on 13 March 1933:

> The removal by the leading industrial States of the limitations upon the size and powers of business corporations appears to have been due, not to their conviction that maintenance of the restrictions was undesirable in itself, but to the conviction that it was futile to insist upon them; because local restriction would be circumvented by foreign incorporation. Indeed, local restriction seemed worse than futile. Lesser States, eager for revenue derived from the traffic in charters, had removed safeguards from their own incorporation laws. Companies were early formed to provide charters for corporations in states where the cost was lowest and the laws least restrictive. The states joined in advertising their wares. The race was one not of diligence but of laxity.[57]

[57] 288 US 517, p. 557.

Before 'Delaware' became proverbial for domestic locational competition in the USA, New Jersey was the strongest magnet for the transfer of an incorporation – until this state's newly elected governor Woodrow Wilson put an end to it:

> A corporation exists, not of natural right, but only by license of law, and the law, if we look at the matter in good conscience, is responsible for what it creates. . . . If law is at liberty to adjust the general conditions of society itself, it is at liberty to control these great instrumentalities which nowadays, in so large part, determine the character of society. (Wilson 1911: 273, 275)

Governments are anything but impotent handmaidens to business in a race to the bottom. To the contrary, as a rule, exponents of this thesis expect it to spark political resistance. What matters to them is not its truth content or explanatory value, but its political impact, and the latter – when one sees its public echo – appears to be considerable.[58]

4 An Old Conflict Assumes New Forms

One can thus safely assume that the welfare state can fend very well for itself – as this book suggests, perhaps too well. In any case, it is not dependent on its social science advocates for its continued survival. The extent to which welfare state bureaucracies together with their organized clientele succeed in defending their interests can hardly be overestimated. Also, globalization needs no 'theory' to support it. Under conditions of welfare democracy, every crisis that government has experienced has ultimately led to more government. Politics and bureaucracy differ, however. Welfare state administrative apparatuses have not only remained mostly untouched by changes in political power, they have even acquired ever more responsibilities in the process.

This is true not only of the nation-state: international conditions, too, are increasingly subject to political control, as the scope and above all the growing intensity of efforts at international coordination of hitherto largely fragmented nation-state regulatory frameworks demonstrate (Slaughter 2000a).[59] The allegation that these regula-

[58] The argument of a welfare-reducing race to the bottom was initially grounded in the development of corporate law in the United States. It was articulated in an article by Cary (1974) that was pathbreaking also for the interpretation of US labour, social and environmental law. Yet this seemingly paradigmatic case in point did not remain uncontested. The counter-argument is predicated on the independent controlling effect that a market has on firms: market forces independently of legal regimes oblige managers to orient their behaviour towards the interests of investors, even when the latter no longer have any direct influence on firm decisions (Manne 1965; Dodd and Leftwich 1980; Easterbrook 1984; Romano 1987). For a differentiated treatment of the race to the bottom thesis in the field of corporate law, see Kostel (1993) and Bebchuk and Ferrell (1999). In the field of social and environmental law, Drezner (2000) similarly comes to the conclusion that the thesis of a race to the bottom is a myth. This does not mean, though, that the thesis is without consequences: 'Descriptive uses of language are themselves events *in* the world, which commonly have causal effects. Descriptions or assertions can have the effect of persuading hearers of their contents, which can lead to small-scale or large-scale world changes. . . . Even in such cases, however, the linguistic act does not directly confer truth on its content. It is still the portion of the world predicted that directly confers truth or falsity on the prediction's propositional content' (Goldman 1999: 21).

[59] In the wake of the oil crises of the early 1970s, the seemingly unstoppable victory march of US corporations – for which Vernon (1971) coined the phrase 'Sovereignty at Bay: The Multinational Spread of

tory orders have a predominantly economically liberal orientation overlooks a central aspect in all these developments. The technical means of such control – the formal authority to set norms, the material resources, including a bureaucratic apparatus and enforcement mechanisms – can also be used for goals that differ thoroughly from the original ones. What is decisive about the regulatory substance of international governance structures is, firstly, that for governments it actually pays off in the form of sustained economic growth that enables them to continue the policy of social concessions to those groups of their societies which feel left behind and, an important proviso, are politically significant, and, secondly, that they are able to control interdependence. Underlying all the WTO agreements and thus the mainstay of international economic governance is an elementary compact of coexistence between states which implies, to use an expression coined by Hedley Bull (1977: 83), '*a conspiracy of silence* entered into by governments about the rights and duties of their respective citizens'. This 'conspiracy of silence' includes their *corporate* citizens; neither individual nor corporate citizens can claim any rights from WTO agreements, since they are binding only on governments. The international economic treaties are much more designed to protect the integrity of nation-states and much less individual rights and private transactions. Also, domestic implementation legislation does not provide for any actionable right to private interests. A federal court in the United States formulated this as a general rule: 'No one has a protectable interest to engage in international trade'.[60]

The best example for a creeping social democratic usurpation of international governance structures is the European Union. What was created as a counter-project to the traditional nation-state and launched with the promise to create a 'government-free' space (Hallstein 1962) has now itself become an object of some kind of state building (Moravscik 1998a; Weiler 1999; Wallace and Wallace 2000). The parliamentarization and democratization of the Union are the most powerful levers for this development. The European internal market, with its four freedoms – free movement of goods and of capital, freedom to provide services and freedom of movement – is

---

U.S. Enterprises' – came to a very sudden halt. There followed a 'Storm Over the Multinationals' (Vernon 1977). Gourevitch (1978: 894) summarizes a study by Gilpin (1975) that investigates the political power relations in the new world economy as follows: 'When the state chooses to act, its power is greater than that of any subunit, including such transnational actors as multinational corporations. In general, whenever states assert their views they are able to prevail over international organizations. Interdependence derives from state policy, not the other way around; that is, it exists because states allow it to exist. Should states refuse to do so, the constraining quality of that interdependence would be broken. All of these propositions are truer of some states than of others and vary according to the historical period.'

60 *American Association of Exporters & Importers* v. *USA*, 751 F.2d 1239 (Fed. Cir. 1985). This ruling is no aberration. Ernst-Ulrich Petersmann (1993: 15) described this state of affairs in the following way: 'According to a recent decision by the Court of Appeals for the Federal Circuit, there has apparently not been one single court decision over the past 200 years which has upheld a right of importers to overturn a congressional exclusion of any product from importation. The reason given by the court for this absence of a "right to trade" is the following: "When the people granted Congress the power 'to regulate Commerce with foreign Nations' . . . they thereupon relinquished at least whatever right they, as individuals, may have had to insist upon the importation of any product" ' (*Arjay Associates Inc.* v. *Bush*, 891 F.2d 891, 898 Fed. Cir. 1989). Not only the United States, but all other countries view the individual freedom to import and export as a privilege rather than as an individual right which could be invoked as a cause of action against discriminatory or disproportionate governmental foreign trade restrictions. For a comparative review of national constitutions and international economic law with regard to individual rights, see the collection of Hilf and Petersmann (1993).

slowly but surely being overtaken by socially oriented political regulation (Leibfried and Pierson 1995, 2000; Falkner 1998; Geyer 2000).

The roots of this development are to a certain extent inherent in the nature of the institution, for two reasons. First, because in national economies, a parliament based on equal voting rights amounts to the political representation of the needs of the masses – and a person's needs are *not* based on his or her position in the machinery of goods-production (Weber 1917b: 105). Thus, a European Parliament of *direct suffrage*, notwithstanding the complex formulas of inter-institutional power-sharing, cannot but behave *as if* sovereign in its power, and for this reason can and will take an independent stand in relation to the economics of the European Union. Moreover, and representing in a similar way the outgrowth of welfare-democratic sentiments, we cannot expect these economically *and* politically sovereign consumers to make sacrifices in the interest of the future productivity of the market economy.[61]

Second, parliamentarization can be an answer to the concentration of *executive* powers and especially to the often extensive bureaucratization of European Union rule. Parliaments have always been institutions which primarily represent those who are ruled by the bureaucracy. '*What organ would democracy have*,' asks Max Weber (ibid.: 126), '*with which to control the administration by officials in turn,* if one imagines that parliamentary power did not exist?' (emphasis in original). Weber knew no answer to this question, except a negative one.[62] In the behaviour of the European Parliament and in the progressive expansion of its competencies, one can see the real political content of European integration and of supranational institution-building to the extent that European government is no longer limited to the mere administration of a framework for a free internal market. As a truly *independent* public power, the European Parliament now needs to gain more support among its constituents if it does not want to be considered illegitimate – and precisely for that reason a social democratic agenda became its going concern.

The change in the political form and structure of the European Union also entails a lesson concerning global governance structures. European integration along liberal economic lines was carried out and further enhanced by strong supranational bodies, above all by the European Commission and the European Court of Justice. Yet the more the Union was able to gain a profile as an independent political actor directly affecting the lives and work of European citizens, the stronger became the efforts to bring its institutions under democratic control, as well as to utilize them for non-economic purposes.

61 Tocqueville was one of the first to note 'the propensity that induces democracy to obey impulse rather than prudence, and to abandon a mature design for the gratification of a momentary passion' (1994 [1835–45]: I.235).

62 Despite the unrenouncable function of parliamentary control of bureaucracy, it is a nearly universal phenomenon that parliaments have de facto undergone an institutional debilitation. If one merely looks at the magnitude of public administrations in terms of the personnel, responsibilities and resources at their disposal, and then compares this with the number of parliamentarians, a massive deterioration of the control ratio between politics and the machinery of government becomes apparent in the history of parliament (Jänicke 1990: 27). Judicial control of the machineries of the state is similarly unable to keep pace with their growth. There is a simple reason for this: for their clients – and in welfare democracies they constitute an overwhelming majority of the electorate – these apparatuses fulfil immediate material needs and are hence corruption machines *par excellence*. On those grounds there exists a close relationship between the rise of mass democracy and the bureaucratization of the public sphere (Weber 1978: 226).

First, 'democracy' has become the universal standard of nearly all conditions of rule – including in the economic sphere. It is not only the economy that has now attained a global scale. Under democratic conditions and confronted with the forms and outcomes of a global economic society, politics is essentially oriented to the collective reduction of material vulnerability. The particular function of democratic politics in modern societies consists in coming to terms with the social risks of capitalist market building and rebuilding, influencing both their scale and their distribution and thus reducing – by means of what can be called 'income from social rights' – individuals' fear for their achieved levels of status and for their existential security in the wake of an ongoing economic-technical revolution (Zolo 1991).

Independent of the type of wealth – the publicly created and guaranteed as well as the private – the following maxim seems to apply: the 'wealthier' a society is, the more the need for security will gain political ground. A century ago, Jacob Burckhardt observed that the political redress of the need for security does not – at least primarily – protect those who are concerned with preserving the little that they have, but is, rather, a quintessential striving of the propertied classes. Security as a 'precondition of any happiness' demands:

> The subordination of arbitrariness to the rule of law, the treatment of all matters relating to property according to objective statutory law, and the provision of secure framework for profit-making and commerce on a large scale. All our contemporary morality is essentially predicated on this security, that is, the individual is spared from having to make the most critical decisions on matters relating to the defence of house and hearth, at least as a rule. And all that the state cannot perform is provided by insurance, that is, the purchase of protection from certain types of unhappiness through a specified annual sacrifice. As soon as existence or its yield has become sufficiently valuable, foregoing insurance even invites moral reproach. (1982 [1905]: 237).

Were Burckhardt alive today, he would see 'hedge funds' and 'futures' as the capitalist equivalents to social assistance and social insurance institutions.[63]

Second, every concentration of power provokes counter-movements – some of which attempt to control it, and others of which attempt to marshal it for other purposes. No matter what shape democracy might take on a European level, its effects will have a very specific, namely social character. When in international politics institutional actors with independent powers emerge – be it to create a 'new financial architecture' or to draft new rules of the game for global capitalism – then sooner or later the 'social democratic' counter-interests will attempt to take control of these new commanding heights. That this movement is borne mainly by so-called non-governmental organizations (NGOs) merely demonstrates how far the process of national de-parliamentarization has progressed – and that, as a result, resistance against the loss of democratic control of living conditions is expressed in non-parliamentary forms. Even small and tentative attempts at formally placing NGOs in international organizations such as the WTO have unavoidably changed their agendas. Globalization, and

[63] These 'protective devices which most economists accept as normal elements of rational management' were also noted by Schumpeter: 'Practically any investment entails, *as a necessary complement of entrepreneurial action*, certain safeguarding activities such as insuring or hedging' (1950 [1942]: 88; emphasis added). On the utopian impulses for the development of insurance, i.e. the desire for 'total security', see P. Bernstein (1996) and Weisbrod (1999/2000).

above all its attendant social and ecological phenomena, has dramatically reduced the legitimacy of international politics. Two years before the Seattle demonstrations against the WTO Ministerial Conference in December 1999, the WTO had already issued Guidelines for Arrangements on Relationships with Non-Governmental Organizations; yet these did not, one must add, significantly increase the transparency of such arrangements (Esty 1998: 125).

The fundamental conflict in modern society is that between profit-making and need – and not between labour and capital. The main forms of this need are societal recognition, maintenance of cultural identity, minimum social standards and ecological considerations. Business groups together with employees in private enterprises make up one camp, and the parties with a material stake in the welfare state and in welfare democracy – i.e. public service and social administration employees together with those who manage to scrape out a living as producers and consumers of socio-political goods – constitute the other. Conflicts over globalization and the welfare state abound between these two camps, but both agree that there are conspicuous deficits in the number of jobs available, the level of wages necessary for the consumption needs of families, the scale and scope of social services and in the protection of natural resources. The basic social conflict is less about the objects than about the ways and means to achieve them.[64]

Crudely formulated, the key question is as follows: should the future direction of economic policy follow the need interest, i.e. *directly* provisioning the citizens with social policy goods, or rely on the profit-making interest to produce welfare also for the uncompetitive groups and to take care of non-economic objectives? In a way, to formulate the question is to answer it. The welfare state as we know it today can also be understood as the organization and mobilization of the interests of *consumers*. The ubiquitous regulation of markets in the welfare state is geared to the satisfaction of the *needs* of consumers rather than to an interest in *profit-making*. Once the well-being of democratically empowered and thus politically sovereign consumers had become the going concern of welfare state systems, Keynesian demand policies were less a blueprint for a rational economic policy than the genuinely sociological perception by political actors of an immediate consequence of the essentially *social* quality of democratic politics in mass society. Strengthening mass purchasing power is to some degree an alternative to social insurance policy, *not* to market-based policies. In effect, the monetarist alternative to Keynesian policies is accepted as long as and to the

[64] That these deficiencies can be caused by the dynamics of autonomous markets does not mean, theoretically speaking, that market mechanisms cannot bring about modifications which correct them. From the perspective of economic theory, these needs, as Coase (1988) has shown, are negative externalities which, as long as transaction costs do not prohibit it, a renegotiation of property rights can correct in the sense that they provide incentives for mutual gain. 'International organizations' or 'supranational institution building' are not the only – and above all not inevitable – answers to the transnational problems of the modern world (Conybeare 1980). Yet the 'natural tendency' of democratic politics regularly takes a different direction: 'The political response [to market failure] all too often fails to match the policy instrument to the specific nature of the failure. . . . Non-economists have an almost universal desire to deal with market failures through carefully drafted regulation rather than a change in incentive structures. Drafting such regulation is the natural function of lawyers, and the legal profession continues to dominate Congress. When government intervenes in the marketplace, our political leaders typically rule out the manipulation of economic incentives to deter undesirable actions because reliance on market responses injects an uncertain, partially random, and therefore "unfair" set of forces into the picture' (Schultze 1996: 27).

degree that it is able to increase the wealth of *all* politically significant groups in a society, or that it does at least entail the credible *promise* of such increase. This is a sine qua non for all market-strengthening policies in a representative democracy, as Laski (1933: 25) pointed out:

> [A] policy of economy [i.e. strengthening the rights of property against social rights] may succeed as a temporary measure, amid the drama of crisis; it cannot succeed as a permanent policy. Its acceptance depends upon the clear proof that it is intended only as an expedient which is to be a prelude to further generosity. Otherwise, it is rapidly and deeply resented.[65]

Politically assured and protected consumption is the going concern of welfare state policies and constitutes their competitive advantage relative to market-based production of life chances precisely because of this distinctive organizational capacity and the promise of secure living conditions and status positions *independent* of market income. It is for this reason that T. H. Marshall could insist that social rights – the rights to welfare in the broadest sense of the word – are 'not designed for the exercise of power at all' (Marshall 1969: 141). To rely in social politics on the multiplication of social rights soon makes a farce out of what it multiplies. Social rights refer to individuals as consumers, and 'there is little consumers can do except to imitate Oliver Twist and "ask for more", and the influence politicians can exert over the public by promising to give it is generally greater than the influence the citizens – or those who care about these things – can exercise over politicians by demanding it' (ibid.).

Put pointedly and from the perspective of the maintenance of global *market* conditions, it would be better if there were no strong WTO and no autonomous bodies endowed with the legal power to create a multilateral agreement on investment and more of the like resembling an international commerce clause.[66] Even if these supranational organizations were empowered to achieve common – and not merely hegemonic – ends, which aimed at the creation of a liberal political-economic framework, or initially corresponded solely to the interests of multinational corporations, which is not necessarily the case, its political foundation would probably soon be conquered by 'socio-political' and other 'protection', 'solidarity' and 'ordering' interests engaged in a continual search for an Archimedean point for the realization of *their* conceptions.[67] The most important vehicle for this is bureaucracy, and it always entails the

[65] For a description of the main trust in US economic policy-making corresponding to this fundamental notion, see Krugman (2001).

[66] That in international arenas the concept 'state' is not used to characterize the new organizations does not mean that functionally equivalent decision-making instances are not being created. Power emerges through the cumulation of political functions. Using exactly this notion, Hermann Heller has described state-building in this way: 'If a scheme of functional centralization, cumulation and activation is developed for the purposes of making perpetual a new normative order, then we have before us a type of organization universally featured in large human associations' (1983 [1934]: 6).

[67] In *The Wealth of Man*, Peter Jay comes to very similar conclusions: every increase in economic welfare and opportunities 'generates predatory reflexes. These threaten both from within and without the societies enjoying the new opportunities, and the management of those challenges by government – through lawmaking and law enforcement, military action and political and diplomatic negotiation – determines how much, if any, of the original enlargement of opportunity is successfully cashed in improving living standards (or rising population) and how much is squandered in conflict. . . . Can the threat be managed in a way that preserves at least most of the original gain in economic opportunity to be enjoyed by

thwarting of hitherto free initiative. Heretofore diffuse, highly diverse opposing interests find in powerful international and supranational economic organizations a single point on which they can focus their coordinated efforts and from which they can demand new accountability. The actions against the WTO in Seattle in December 1999 (see Gantz 2000; Tiefenbrunner 2000) and against the IMF in April 2000 consisted merely of an uprising of a political will which lacked a leader or a conceptual orientation. It found its limits in the weakness, not in the strength of its opponent.[68] The lack of centralized institutional structure and focused political orientation among the instances of international economic regulation have until now been their best protection against the welfare-democratic demands that have been expressed.

Max Weber had already pointed out that it is precisely the fragmented nature of the community of states and thus inter-state competition for mobile capital that preserve both the market economy's political-economic foundations and the citizens' personal freedom. Of course, personal freedom is not the only value in relation to which both national and international conduct may be shaped, and it is not necessarily an overriding value. Nevertheless, and perhaps more by default than design, down to the present day an essentially transnational market economy on the one hand and a multitude of welfare-democratically closed nation-states on the other have been mutually stable. A world government would mean the end of globalization and would rob the world society of one of its most important guarantors of personal freedom. Without a credible threat of territorial exit, corporations – or the bearers of valuable 'capital' of any kind, and today this includes large segments of the labour force – would have no influential domestic political voice. The '*housing of the new serfdom*' would then assume global dimensions. This would mean that Max Weber's prophecies at the end of the nineteenth century – regarding 'good', i.e. rational, administration as the solution to the contradiction between globalization and the welfare state of his day – would finally have come true: making bureaucracy *inescapable* (Weber 1918a: 158–9).

5 Conclusion

As this chapter has tried to point out, one decisive detail is almost never mentioned in the globalization discussion: the twofold phenomenon that in the post-war period the most advanced industrial societies turned away from protectionism, and that freer trade as a revived 'engine of growth' is concentrated for the most part in the developed national economies. This was by no means inevitable, even when one accepts the

someone?' (2000: 286). The point that is politically critical for globalization is summarized by Jay as follows: 'Direct government action is prey to too many pressures other than those of the problem to be solved ever to be relied upon to adopt and implement strategies that may well require changes in private behavior by people who do not recognize or understand the need for such change' (ibid.: 302).

68 See here the comments of Lori Wallach, one of the main organizers of the resistance to the WTO and to the other bearers of the 'trade status quo': 'All of these crushing defeats of the trade status quo are brought to you mainly by the arrogance and inability to bend of those enjoying the trade status quo. The inability to bend has caused several major things to be smashed. But it's getting extremely tedious, because it's really boring to stop things. What would be interesting is to talk about the second phase. Not stopping a bunch of stuff, but rather, what would replace the status quo with' (Foreign Policy 2000: 37).

classical explanation – prominent in all textbook presentations of classical foreign trade theory – that free trade is beneficial overall and welfare-enhancing for every country. The fundamental *political* problem for trade policy consists, however, less in the ability to export than in the willingness to allow imports. Market access and import competition were and are the pivotal realms of national and international foreign trade policy. This problem does not lose but, rather, gains political significance to the extent that national economies reach higher and more sophisticated stages of economic development. It is the interdependence of the most advanced economies multifariously bound up with the social regulation of self-regarding welfare states that brings about a situation in which one nation's sovereignty is another nation's uncertainty. In a welfare state perspective, the technologically facilitated all-embracing *economic* community of nations made it more *difficult*, but did not render it impossible, to define and to defend the complex formulas of social justice that the democratic struggle revolves around. Welfare democracies are dominated by a communal psychology which thinks essentially in terms of the *national* state.

Because of the overwhelming presence of welfare states, the conflicts that mark international economic policy-making are more about *fair* than about *free* trade – 'fair' meaning the terms on which governments can defend the achievements of domestic public policy. The consequences and conditions of import competition form the core of the entire scientific and political discussion on foreign trade: 'levelling' the playing field and outlawing social dumping on the one hand, prescribing rules of origin and measures of local content etc. to protect exclusively national conceptions of employment structures on the other. *These* issues, and not some international laissez-faire, determine the greater part of the rules of the WTO agreements. What is striking about the period after the Second World War is that the Western industrial countries, either unilaterally or in the context of the various GATT rounds, gradually lowered the trade barriers with which they had attempted – if not to block import competition – at least to control the market access of foreign countries.

This dismantling cannot be explained away with the argument that these governments increasingly viewed free trade as more beneficial than protectionism. In economic theory, the benefits of free trade have occasionally, but never convincingly, been called into question. Yet, as history regularly demonstrates, the superiority of free trade doctrine rarely affects policy practice. British policy in the second half of the nineteenth century remains a striking exception. The British case can be attributed, however, to the country's twofold exceptionalism in terms of its hegemonic industrial *and* political position. The central question thus runs: why was free trade not able to become the prevailing doctrine in trade policy? And the admittedly cursory answer, which in the following chapters will be analysed in more detail, is: the ostensible or real negative effects of import competition on domestic wage levels, income distribution, the structure of industry and the quality of employment positions are widely attributed to foreign countries' unlimited market access. They thus constitute significant impediments to the realization of the ideals of free trade. Conflicts regarding trade policy have always revolved around these domestic societal frictions, and for this reason the fate of globalization was and is determined domestically.

One goal of this book consists in underscoring the critical significance of the institutionalization of social policy for trade policy. The main thesis of this volume is that not until the expansion of the welfare state in the first three decades following the Second World War were the governments of the most advanced industrial societies in a position to lower, lessen or eliminate import barriers. Not until the universalization of the right to market access could global market integration attain dynamism and autonomy.

This means neither that governments pursued social policy with this goal in mind, nor that they were always in a position to do so. Social policy has its own motive forces: political ones in the nation-state's striving for integration and legitimation, social ones in responding to the impact of the market on the distribution of life chances, and economic ones in improving the performance of labour markets and increasing the returns of human capital. In a government's decision-making on social policy, effects on its latitude in trade policy are seldom, if ever, an overriding concern. Once income security was guaranteed by the welfare state, however, governments had more flexibility in drafting their foreign trade policy. Here lies one of the reasons for the extraordinary growth of the global economy during the final third of the twentieth century. And here, too, lies the reason for globalization's dependency on *social* politics. Krugman (1995) called attention to this dependency when he argued against conceptions of a technological determinism and of an unstoppable global market dynamic. Globalization is not an irreversible process, above all because the parameters of welfare state intervention – the widespread experience of social insecurity and economic scarcity – have not disappeared in the new international economic world. On the contrary, they have become even more pronounced. As a result, in terms of rational economic policy, *socially* insufficient national preconditions of increased world market integration can easily translate into protectionist policies.[69]

Which tendency will actually prevail in which countries is, however, not yet clear. There is considerable evidence that governments increasingly become aware of the reciprocal dependency of national social policy, on the one hand, and the functional preconditions of a free global economy on the other. Whether national governments will indeed be in a position to deal adequately with the threefold challenge this poses – reforming welfare state policies, managing the globalization-induced ruptures in their social orders and institutionally securing global market conditions – is an open question. This is so because welfare state institutions represent privileges – and one thing that social groups are particularly good at defending is privilege.

Our emphasis on problems and herewith also opportunities in social policy decision-making is justified not only by the facts of the case, but also by the tendency in social science discourse on globalization to declare findings and then, without much ado, to jump to 'solutions' that cannot be substantiated by this branch of science. As David Hume was the first to point out, and as Max Weber repeatedly stressed, it is not possible without violating simple logic to derive from the empirical observed unequivocally binding norms and ideals (Weber 1904). It is not only of social scientific interest, but also of fundamental political significance that the conditions of human action are only to a limited extent explicable through theory, for they have a non-necessary character. Strangely enough, the history of the new science of politics is an ever-recurring attempt to repudiate or circumvent precisely this Aristotelian insight (Meier 1980; Hennis 2000 [1963]). In the natural sciences, theory is based on neither probability nor chance; rather, strict necessity prevails. As Einstein put it, the Lord doesn't roll the dice.

Rules and regularities can, but need not, apply to human conditions. Human behaviour and the realm of politics are not determined. Every problem presents the actor

69 On the instruments and general tendency of neo-protectionism, see Bhagwati (1988; revisited 2001) and Salvatore (1993). The now classical analysis is Corden (1997 [1974]).

with alternative possibilities. Every action, every decision is a realization of a possibility. There are no social scientific theories, trivial ones aside, of necessary truths. This leaves social science with two sources of knowledge: history and common-sense reasoning oriented towards set goals. What to globalization theorists as diverse as Melvyn Krauss (1997), Wolfgang Reinicke (1998) and Geoffrey Garrett (1998, 1997) seem to be 'necessary' developments and ineluctable relationships may at first glance appear to be deductions from ostensibly manifest premises.[70] Yet in fact, and this is easily demonstrated, these are nothing other than well-worn and ideologically familiar normative demands and apodictic statements. They argue *de more geometrico* and thereby conceal the contingent and discretionary nature of social action. That which they portray as a true image and objective investigation of a reality which exists independent of the observer and seems untinged by any subjective conceptions is actually a model – a normative design. This, of course, they would never concede. Their premises are not scientifically compelling and cannot be. In order to be operative, they must be voluntarily acknowledged. The first precondition for this is the admission that premises are always preliminary and debatable. Yet certain conceptions of social science contradict precisely this standard. To clothe argumentation in theoretical truth following the model of physical laws is monological, not dialogical – i.e. it reasons exclusively within one frame of reference – and to this extent is the antithesis and a rejection of any politics pursued as the art of the possible, and expressly seeks to exclude compromise.[71]

To repeat, the series of enquiries that constitute this volume should not be read as a set of prescriptions or recommendations. We do not attempt to offer solutions but rather to disclose problems. If our argument is an implicit defence of the welfare state, then this is so because it is more derived from a descriptive-historical than a prescriptive-functional reading of the complex interplay of welfare democracy and international economics. Both the domestic and the international order are dealt with in terms of actual or possible states of affairs; we do not *judge* their underlying and motivating values, goals or objectives, but try to gauge their *empirical* significance. If we canvass the merits of a particular perspective, it is for purely intellectual, not political, reasons. Scientific enquiry has its own morality, and the search for conclusions that can be presented as 'solutions' or 'practical advice' is a corrupting element in the contemporary study of welfare state politics, which, properly understood, is primarily an intellectual activity and not a practical one.

[70] Hence Richard Feynman, Nobel prizewinner in physics, is in some cases not totally off target when he refers to social science as 'cargo cult science': 'Because of the success of science, there is, I think, a kind of pseudoscience. Social science is an example of a science which is not a science; they don't do [things] scientifically, they follow the forms – or you gather data, you do so-and-so and so forth but you don't get any laws, they haven't found out anything. . . . We get experts on everything that sound like they're sort of scientific experts. They sit at a typewriter, they make up something. . . . There's all kinds of myths and pseudoscience all over the place' (1999: 22). 'Because science which is done carefully has been successful; by doing something like that, they think that they get some honor. . . . So I call these things Cargo Cult Science, because they follow the apparent precepts and forms of scientific investigation, but they're missing something essential, because the planes don't land' (ibid.: 209). On the distinction between theoretical truth and factual truth, see Heinemann (1948). On the apolitical character of argumentation *de more geometrico,* see McClure (1918), and on the emergence and developmental history of the idea of physical laws, see Zilsel (1942).

[71] Arendt, in particular, has called attention to this (1967).

2

Welfare State Mercantilism

Social problems are not only hard but finally insoluble. Yet many of them will inevitably get some kind of 'treatment'; it is a question of better or worse, or of making things better, more or less, or making them worse than before, even to downright disaster.

Frank H. Knight 1951: 19

I The Problem

Ever since the writings of David Hume, Adam Smith and David Ricardo, free trade and a transnational division of labour have constituted the guiding principles of international economics. Paul Samuelson called the law of comparative advantage – the foundation of free trade theory – the most beautiful idea in economic theory.[1] It is in a country's own national economic interest, the theory argues, for governments to abstain from intervention in transnational commercial transactions. Even if no other state follows their example, the country still benefits from not relying on tariff and non-tariff barriers to the import of foreign goods. As the brilliant French writer and economist Frederick Bastiat observed more than 150 years ago, the fact that other countries have a rocky and hence inaccessible coast is no reason to fill one's own harbours with rocks.[2]

Nevertheless, present-day forms of foreign trade hardly conform, if they correspond at all, to the logic of international economics. Free trade as the guiding principle of economic and trade policy, and its pendant, the international division of labour, have always been controversial, and in the political battles, protectionism nearly always had public opinion on its side – and won.[3] Also, the institutional foundations of the global economy, which until the post-World War II era were almost exclusively shaped by national foreign trade law and bilateral trade agreements, have never corresponded to principled conceptions of the unhindered mobility of goods, people and services. The

1 Cited in Gilpin (2000: 49f.). For an account of the origins and turbulent history of the idea of free trade, see Irwin (1996a).

2 On the intellectual history of the social critique of free trade, see Rieger and Leibfried (1998a).

3 Bastiat also drafted a mock petition 'from the Manufacturers of Candles, Tapers, Lanterns, Sticks, Street Lamps, Snuffers, and Extinguishers, and from Producers of Tallow, Oil, Resin, Alcohol, and Generally of E'thing Connected with Lighting': 'We are suffering from the ruinous competition of a rival who apparently works under conditions so far superior to our own for the production of light that he is *flooding* the *domestic market* with it at an incredible low price; for the moment he appears, our sales cease, all the consumers turn to him, and a branch of French industry whose ramifications are inumerable is all at once reduced to complete stagnation. . . . We ask you to be so good as to pass a law requiring the closing of all windows, dormers, skylights, inside and outside shutters, curtains, casements, bull's eyes, deadlights, and blinds – in short, all openings, holes, chinks, and fissures through which the light of the sun is wont to enter houses, to the detriment of the fair industries with which, we are proud to say, we have endowed the country, a country that cannot, without betraying ingratitude, abandon us today to so unequal a combat' (http://www.newaus.com.au/econ12.html).

industrial revolution paved the way for a market economy whose, according to Adam Smith, unavoidably cosmopolitan participants viewed national borders as arbitrary and hence irrational givens that ought to be done away with.[4] However, alongside the industrial revolution, a democratic revolution fashioned sovereign nation-states for which territorial closure, especially with regard to the economy, was essential (Krasner 2001).

That parliamentary representatives and government officials are obliged to provide welfare that is understood exclusively in terms of territory, and hence nationally, seems to condemn the economic rationality of the unhindered international division of labour to political irrelevance. As early as 1832, Henry Clay expressed the utopian character of free trade doctrine in the US Senate: 'The call for free trade is as unavailing as the cry of a spoiled child, in its nurse's arms, for the moon, or the stars that glitter in the firmament of heaven. It never existed, it never will exist' (cited in Voigt 1992: 193). The sole historical exception are the twenty years after the repeal of the British Corn Laws in 1846, which shifted the course of trade policy for all of Europe towards free trade (Kindleberger 1951, 1975). Indeed, one could argue that it is precisely the highly compromise-laden character of actual trade policy-making, and thus the compromised nature of trade policy practice, that furnishes the ideals of free trade and the unconstrained international division of labour with its characteristic and enduring allure.

But does not the level of global economic integration hitherto achieved, the dynamic of globalization and the existence of an independent world trade order above and beyond national economies demonstrate that sound economic reasoning ultimately and finally held sway? And have the democratic revolutions since 1989 not proven the superiority of an unlimited market economy vis-à-vis a socialist, centralized command economy which may be organized 'in one country' only?

Without a doubt, the international economy since the 1970s has economically become more liberal and open. Customs duties, at least in OECD countries, are very low and thus no longer regularly constrain trade. Other instruments habitually used by governments to regulate transnational trade, chiefly quota systems and import licences, have been employed decreasingly. Through the WTO, an independently organized system of economic law with its own sets of sanctions now clearly limits the ability of governments and legislatures to shape their foreign economic relations independently and according to their own discretion. Realms which hitherto were beyond the reach of free trade policies – such as government procurement, trade in services, intellectual property rights, investment measures and even agriculture – have now been subordinated to an international regulatory system of at least 'freer' trade, and are thus much more exposed to the dynamic of transnational competition (Maskus 2000). We may therefore expect that in the three principal areas of foreign economic policy – traditional tariff law, non-tariff trade barriers and international regulation of the conditions of production and investment – further progress will be made in liberalizing national economies and in subjugating them to the rules of the international economic order.

[4] 'For business purposes', said Jacques Maisonrouge, then president of IBM, in an address to the American Foreign Service Association in Washington DC on 29 May 1969, 'the boundaries that separate one nation from another are no more real than the equator. They are merely convenient demarcations of ethnic, linguistic, and cultural entities. They do not define business requirements or consumer trends' (quoted in Barnet and Müller 1974: 14).

How can this development be explained when the element that was supposed to condemn national free trade policy to a utopian status, namely the absolutely self-regarding responsibility of the national polity for social matters, has not receded, but has, rather, grown stronger with the constitutional grounding and institutionalization of democratic welfare states?

In the second section of this chapter we will provide a quick overview on the long-term movements in the level of international trade over the past 150 years. Furthermore, we will discuss explanations advanced to make sense of globalization and its reversion, international economic disintegration, introducing the argument that politics is the decisive factor for the development of world trade.

In the third section we present the concept of a conservative welfare function to bring out the political logic underlying domestic trade policy-making. We suggest that this notion is particularly helpful in explaining the rise of a free trade regime after the Second World War, and we detail this hypothesis in the fourth section by describing the large-scale transformation of welfare states as a precondition for a fundamental change in the perception of foreign trade.

In section 5 we discuss the social regulation of international trade. The principal conception developed here is that in the GATT/WTO system, under the specifiable domestic conditions of welfare democracy, *institutionalized ambivalence* is generated as state officials have to live up to the double requirements of national social security broadly understood and of freer trade. In the perspective of institutional ambivalence, we see the WTO legal system as a dynamic organization of norms and counter-norms, not as the expression of one dominant value. We suggest that major norms created to uphold open economy policies and the minor counter-norms allowing trade restrictions alternatively govern national trade policy, depending on the domestic situation as shaped by its foreign trade relations.

In section 6 we argue that markets as much as welfare state policies are all pieces of a highly differentiated social machinery for marshalling the nation's resources in response to the needs of domestic constituents. As private interests are effectively disenfranchised in the making of global economic governance, the most important single point of departure for understanding the political control of globalization is the following fact: the creation and regulation of markets is the carefully maintained right of sovereign states. The implication is that globalization is very much a deliberate political construction.

2 Economic Globalization in Perspective

Global economic integration, measured as the sum of exports and imports as a percentage of a country's Gross National Product, did not return to the level of 1913 until the mid-1970s, after the deep collapse of the Great Depression and after the general transition to more autarchic economic policy in the first two post-war decades had been slowly overcome (cf. figure 1.1, p. 14). In any case, since the mid-1990s the growth of world trade has subsided, in part due to the Asian crisis of 1997 onward and also to strong political forces that have fought, with some success, against free trade policy and its consequences. We will first and foremost describe the surprising growth in world trade after the Second World War, especially since the 1970s. Thereafter, we will discuss developments over the last decade of the twentieth century.

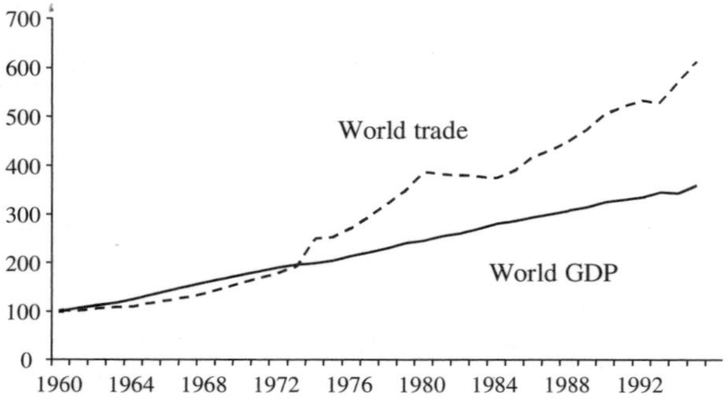

Figure 2.1 Growth in gross world product and world trade (1960 = 100)
Source: Council of Economic Advisers (1996: 224)

Figure 2.1 not only reveals the dynamics of globalization, but also clarifies the mechanism that leads to globalization. The engine of globalization is the persistently stronger growth of transnational trade compared to the growth of the economy itself. This results in a growing integration of national economies and the deepening of the international division of labour. In any case, we should keep in mind the absolute size of the volume of trade relative to that of production. At the end of the 1990s, world exports amounted to 21 per cent of the Gross World Product. In the 1970s, this figure was 17 per cent (UNDP 1999: 25).

Table 2.1 Growth in the value of world merchandise trade by region, 1990–1998

Exports				*Region*	*Imports*			
Value ($USbn)	*Annual % change*				*Value ($USbn)*	*Annual % change*		
	1990–8	*1997*	*1998*			*1990–8*	*1997*	*1998*
5,270	6	3	−2	World	5,465	6	3	−1
897	7	9	−1	North America	1,152	8	10	5
2,181	5	−1	3	European Union	2,172	4	−1	5
214	6	4	−5	Central and Eastern Europe	242	9	6	−2
276	8	10	−2	Latin America	340	14	19	5
1,293	7	5	−6	Asia	1,086	5	0	−18
388	4	2	−8	Japan	280	2	−3	−17
504	8	3	−8	East Asia	437	6	−1	−25
184	15	21	1	China	140	13	3	−2
107	1	2	−15	Africa	134	5	6	3

Source: http://www.WTO.org/WTO/statis/ae.htm (01.06.2000)

In Table 2.1 we describe the major changes in the composition of world trade. It shows that the rise of the East Asian countries constitutes a key difference vis-à-vis the first wave of globalization, which ended with the First World War. The world economy at the end of the twentieth century, though, is no longer dominated by a few select Western countries. Table 2.1 also makes clear, however, that despite this development, world trade has been a largely closed shop of the developed economies, i.e. remained within the OECD world: in 1998, nearly 60 per cent of world exports originated from North America and the European Union.This table further shows that the dynamic of world trade has weakened, and that the so-called Asian crisis, which began in 1997 with the collapse of the Thai Bhat, had ripple effects on all national economies, including the most developed ones in Europe and North America (Gough 1998; McLeod and Garnaut 1998; W. Woo et al. 2000). This constitutes further evidence of the new 'complex interdependence' (Keohane and Nye 2001). Even more disastrous was the dramatic global decline in the expenditure on information technology products in the wake of the rapid destruction of large portions of the so-called New Economy. In 2001, for the first time in more than three decades, world trade grew much less than output.[5] This stunning episode shows that world trade, and thus one of the main features of globalization, is very much a dependent variable and thus tightly bound to developments occurring outside the sphere that can be controlled by trade law and trade politics.

How can the return in world trade to pre-World War I levels and the acceleration of the growth in world trade since the mid-1970s be explained? Oddly enough, this question is hardly discussed in the literature, for its answer seems to be as obvious and compelling as the existence of the *new* and globalized *economy* itself.[6] Instead, the debate has concentrated on the actual or supposed consequences of globalization on the domestic societal and political conditions in developed national economies in the West. More to the point, since the mid-1980s nearly all domestic societal and above all political changes are used as evidence for the existence of 'globalization' as a *force majeure*. Regardless of which causes are actually held to be responsible, the decisive fact is that inequality and distributional problems again dominate the national and international political agenda (Aghion 1998; Fishlow and Parker 1999; Fogel 2000).

The development of an open and economically more liberal world economy as one of the consequences of economic globalization in recent decades was, however, by no means as self-evident as has been generally assumed. Also, underlying the different positions in this debate are specific, usually unarticulated and therefore all the more influential assumptions concerning the causes, workings and effects of globalization. These assumptions, suppositions and postulates, in turn, independently affect – regardless of their truth content – the interpretation of globalization and the national reactions to globalization itself. An example of this spectacle, performed by would-be engineers of self-fulfilling prophecies, is the supposed existence of a race to the bottom (Drezner 2000).

Most studies of the recent increase in international economic transactions do not directly or systematically enquire into its causes, thus no theory or empirical data on this question exist. Yet, upon closer examination of the literature, two explanations seem plausible.[7] The first explanation revolves around technical progress. The volume

5 See WTO News/Press Release 249, 19 October 2001: 'World trade slows sharply in 2001 amid the uncertain international situation.'

6 Rodrik (1995), too, calls attention to the lack of explanations both for the general liberalization wave since the mid-1980s and for the continued existence of protectionist practices in the trade policy of every nation. Particularly neglected in empirical research are differences in the causes, forms and effects of these policies.

7 For overviews of the literature and a discussion of research findings, see Odell (1990), Held and McGrew (2000), and the introductory chapter in Keohane and Milner (1996).

of international economic transactions here is merely a function of the dramatic decline in the costs of such transactions. In this view, advances in transportation and communications technologies are the overwhelming forces which render national borders more porous and make it possible for firms to slice up their chains of production. Businesses are then able to link company-specific competitive advantages with specific locational advantages in every single operational sphere – management, research and development, investments and their financing, and, finally, production and sales. In such an explanation, geography – location – becomes less consequential for the organization of economic activity. As the significance of spatial distances and of national boundaries for company decisions decline, the factors of production are becoming more mobile. Locational and competitive advantages shift rapidly and are increasingly becoming institutional-organizational and thus to a large extent political matters. In the process, a highly integrated and volatile global economy is taking shape, replacing the old, decidedly fragmented structure of international economic activity.[8]

The second explanation is based on the learning capacity of governments as the decisive factor in the crystallization of a more liberal system of international trade. According to this argument, ever more governments perceived that limits on international trade also limited national prosperity, and that policies oriented towards achieving autarchy and towards thwarting or substituting imports were self-destructive, for they were not only very costly but also an easy prey for interest groups concerned only with protecting their own advantage (A.O. Krueger 1997).

Both explanations are problematic and of limited explanatory value. Technical progress and the decline in international transaction costs are both continuous as well as cumulative processes. No one doubts that in 1970, as opposed to 1913, transportation and communications technologies were far more advanced and far less costly. Nevertheless, in the years prior to the First World War, the developed national economies were not only far more integrated into world markets than in 1960, but this integration extended to labour markets as well (J. Williamson 1998a). The volume and growth rates of international trade are markedly discontinuous, and these discontinuities are even stronger if one focuses on the fate of individual countries in the world market (Maddison 1991, 1995).[9] Put differently, national and international

[8] Bergeijk and Mensink (1997) show that the historical time series which are usually used to measure the globalization of the economy, i.e. the averages of exports and imports in percentage of national income, underestimate the current state of national economic integration compared with the decade prior to the outbreak of the First World War. This is because the costs of transportation, communication and insurance previously made up a much larger share of the value of exports and imports. In international trade statistics, exports are measured 'f.o.b.' (free-on-board) and imports 'c.i.f.' (cost-insurance-freight). A second cause of the systematic underestimation of the true extent of globalization is rooted in the fact that these time series as a rule measure values in current prices and thus do not account for the more rapid rise in prices for services relative to goods. In the course of the structural transformation of the economy, services – many of which are outside the market, e.g. the entire public sector as well as social insurance schemes – make up an ever larger share of Gross Domestic Product (GDP). For this reason, the ratio of exports and imports to GDP underrates the actual degree of economic integration.

[9] Figure 3 in Bergeijk and Mensink (1997: 166) shows, in terms of the volume of all exports (in constant prices) from 1820 to 1992, a continuous and – since 1960 – rising trajectory. The thesis of the technological causality and determinacy of the globalization trajectory appears to hold for global conditions. Still, it must be observed in opposition to this view that new technologies ultimately represent only opportunities of which social actors must take advantage if they are to become reality. Between social actors and the pure potential of a given technology stand the institutional prescriptions and the societal conditions of their mediation.

Table 2.2 Export and import dependency of German industry, 1875–1959 (1913 = 100)

Years	*Export dependency*[a]	*Import dependency*[b]	*Years*	*Export dependency*[a]	*Import dependency*[b]
1875–9	70		1929–30	88	79
1880–4	81	90	1931–2	91	87
1885–9	81	100	1933–4	57	79
1890–4	71	106	1935–6	46	54
1895–9	71	108	1937–8	41	49
1900–4	77	102	1950–1	42	37
1905–9	85	107	1952–3	50	43
1910–13	95	102	1954–5	55	44
1925–6	77	71	1956–7	61	48
1927–8	72	82	1958–9	60	42

[a] Weighted volume index of raw material, semi-finished and finished goods divided by volume index of state industry (weights are based on volume for 1913)
[b] Import volume index divided by index of total industry

Source: Hoffmann (1965: 159f., 163)

politics – i.e. institutions and public decisions that are accountable to a mass public – determine the volume and growth of world trade, not the state of technology. For world trade as for global economic growth, technical progress is a necessary, not a sufficient condition.[10] The political sphere can block globalization processes – as it resolutely did in the twentieth century during the interwar period. As Table 2.2 shows, both the import and export dependency of German industry rose until the outbreak of the First World War, then continuously declined vis-à-vis 1910–13 during the Weimar and even more during the National Socialist periods, only to rise again very slowly after the Second World War. The evidence of marked discontinuities in the development of the global economy and foreign trade can also be held against explanations that emphasize political learning. If there is an unchallenged message of economic science since the days of Adam Smith and David Ricardo, and particularly since those of the dazzling polemicist Bastiat, then it is that of the advantageous nature of free trade (Frey et al. 1984; McCulloch 1993; A. O. Sykes 1998).[11]

10 The American historian Robert G. Albion argued in 1932 for the concept of 'communication revolution' as something independent from the transformation of production and industry and far more effective in 'knitting the world closer together'. The communication revolution as something which enabled large-scale *organizational* transformations dates back to the beginning of the twentieth century: 'Admirals, diplomats, colonial governors, and supercargos in distant parts of the world formerly had to be trusted with wide discretionary powers to meet emergencies. Now, as one of them exclaimed in disgust, they have become little more than agents at the end of a telegraph wire' (1932: 719). In that respect, the World Wide Web and email did nothing but perfect an already existing organizational reality.

11 The practical problems of trade policy concerned neither the 'pure' nor the normative theories of free trade: 'The lesson we must keep in mind is that the problems that trade issues deal with are not analytically complex, though they might be politically difficult. The complication that is associated with them is not analysis; it is alibi – the product of an instinct to avoid the political difficulty' (Finger 1983: 750).

Why, then, did most countries in the course of the last third of the nineteenth century increasingly turn away from free trade towards protectionism? And why could governments be convinced of the advantages of liberal trade policy only after the Second World War – and even then only with great effort and subject to the permanent risk that what they thought of as trade concessions might be swiftly revoked?

Again, politics appears to be the decisive variable. The decision whether the arguments about free trade's benefits for a nation's foreign economic relations are accepted and implemented in trade policy is and was an essentially political one, which hinges upon a specific institutional context. For this reason, economists such as Paul Krugman and Jagdish Bhagwati, who have specialized in the theory and practice of international economics, tend to assume that growth in world trade has primarily political causes.[12] They also imply that the development in world trade towards greater economic integration is potentially reversible. Thus, Paul Krugman (1997) turns to political scientists after he discerns that the 'compelling logic of economics in favour of . . . free trade' plays only a minimal role in the deliberations of 'those individuals, who actually make decisions' and asks them: what is the source of the persistent political impulses – strengthening in recent years – against free trade policy?

The question must thus be turned on its head: how may we explain the proliferation first and foremost of forms of trade policy that close borders to imports in spite of the continuous revolutionary advances in transportation and communications technologies? Until the outbreak of the Second World War, protectionism increased steadily – even in Great Britain, which had taken free trade the farthest and whose government had been loyal to free trade policy for the longest time. Two opposing approaches have been proposed to explain this development. The first interprets protectionism as a politically mediated movement which develops in opposition to capitalism and which, as a social force, threatens to radically rebuild society as a whole in its own image. The second sees protectionism as the product of the mobilization of factional against general interests – the latter being better served by free trade.

The most important exponent of the first approach was Karl Polanyi (1957 [1944]). His seminal work, *The Great Transformation*, was written during the 1940s. Protectionism for Polanyi is an inevitable and quasi-automatic response by society; it represents the latter's attempt to prevent the expansion of a self-regulating market which subjects the living conditions of an ever-increasing segment of the population exclusively to an anarchic play of supply and demand. In essence, then, protectionism in foreign trade can be understood in the same way as, for example, the political and legal recognition of unions, as a compensatory counter-instrument to the market power of firms, in line with protective factory legislation and social policy designed to provide income security through social insurance schemes. These measures are all about limiting the 'commodification' of labour and curbing the degree of the market's laissez-faire in the areas of employment, wages and working conditions.

[12] In 1950 Frank Knight voiced germane despair in his presidental address delivered at the Sixty-third Annual Meeting of the American Economic Association in Chicago. After observing that 'the free traders . . . win the debates but the protectionists win the election', he continues: 'The serious fact is that the bulk of the really important things that economics have to teach are things that people would see for themselves if they were willing to see. And it is hard to believe in the utility of trying to teach what men refuse to learn or even seriously listen to. What point is there in propagating sound economic principles if the electorate is set to have the country run on the principle that the objective in trade is to get rid of as much as possible and get as little as possible in return?' (1951: 4).

Karl Polanyi argues that with the establishment of the market economy, ever more governments proceeded to intervene in the free movement of goods, capital and persons in order to secure their society's social and political stability. From this perspective, economic protectionism is a defensive strategy adopted by all governments under the pressure of market and particularly international economic conditions. Governments pursue protectionist strategies to fulfil their obligations concerning the social (re)integration of their societies facing foreign economic interdependency which renders the nation-state powerless:

> The pattern of international trade which was now spreading at an accelerated rate was crossed by the introduction of protectionist institutions designed to check the all-round action of the market. The agrarian crisis and the Great Depression of 1873–86 had shaken confidence in economic self-healing. From now onward the typical institutions of market economy could usually be introduced only if accompanied by protectionist measures, all the more so because since the late 1870s and early 1880s nations were forming themselves into organized units which were apt to suffer grievously from the dislocations involved in any sudden adjustment to the needs of foreign trade or foreign exchanges. The supreme vehicle of the expansion of market economy, the gold standard, was thus usually accompanied by the simultaneous introduction of the typical protectionist policies of the age such as social legislation and customs tariffs. (K. Polanyi 1957 [1944]: 214)

In a second explanatory approach, protectionism is seen to result from the successful pursuit of special interests by members of certain branches of the economy. Selected industries band together and exert pressure on governments to limit import competition. These demands are justified with the argument that they will help secure national employment and wage levels. Or, conversely, such groups argue that the 'unfair' competition of foreign competitors allows them to reap improper advantages, for example, from state subsidies or lower fiscal or regulatory burdens on production.[13] Such rent-seeking – i.e. 'ill-gotten gains' – has been described in many studies.[14] This interest group behaviour is represented as a highly contagious and dynamically upward-spiralling process, for interest group gains appear in concentrated form for the cartelized individual producers, while the fiscal and economic costs are widely spread among a vast number of consumers and taxpayers and are thus less visible. The economic history of the USA through the middle of the 1930s supplies ample evidence of such interest group-driven protectionism.[15]

The main problem with these explanations, just as with the two earlier explanations of the emergence of a more open world economy, is their excessive generality. The considerable differences both in the forms and in the political casting which pro-

[13] For an earlier formulation of the thesis that international competitive disadvantage results from the advanced state of social policy in certain countries, see Weber (1894).

[14] The core of this explanatory approach is the interest group theory of Mancur Olson (1971). In a lecture, he applied it to trade policy (1987). For an overview of empirical research, see Rodrik (1995) and Alt et al. (1996) who, however, call attention to the difficulties and limits of this approach as well.

[15] Cf. Schattschneider (1935), Taussig (1966 [1931]), Pincus (1977) and Baldwin (1985a). After the Civil War, this protectionism not only took the place that in other countries was assumed by centralized social policy, in that it appeared to guarantee employment security and high wages on a national scale; it also financed, via considerable federal customs receipts, the first large-scale, albeit very peculiar institutionalization of, US welfare state in the form of pensions for Civil War veterans and their kin (Amenta and Skocpol 1989; Skocpol 1995).

tectionism has assumed – divergences that cannot be explained with reference to the degree and pace of industrialization (Lotz 1902) – contradict Polanyi's interpretation. In Wilhelmine Germany, for example, protectionism was pushed through from above against the (consumption) interests of the working classes – a fact that the Social Democrats and unions repeatedly bemoaned. In the USA, by contrast, protectionism found widespread support precisely among workers (Eckes 1995; Etges 1999). Great Britain, where industrialization began and where the market economy determined the living conditions of the majority of the population far sooner and much more decisively than elsewhere, did not adopt free trade until after it had already achieved a comparatively high level of industrialization *and* attained higher living standards for the majority of the population.[16] And even after all other major economic powers in Europe had returned to protectionism, Great Britain stayed the course of free trade (P. M. Kennedy 1998 [1980]; Mock 1982). Even more critical is the fact that Polanyi gives no indication of why, after the Second World War, it was precisely in the most developed and thus – in his view – most vulnerable national economies that an initially cautious but then rapid reorientation towards free trade occurred.[17]

The substantial differences among countries in the form and degree of protectionism and in the fluctuations and watersheds in trade policy history do not fit any general pattern. They can also be held against the interest group explanation. The problem is not so much that trade policy rent-seeking cannot be observed in all relevant cases as that it describes a *general mechanism* of collective action for private benefit, rather than identifying the *specific*, and truly relevant causes of historically distinctive protectionist tendencies.[18] The public choice-informed general theory of rent-seeking fails conspicuously when it comes to explaining anti-protectionist interest group politics, or the success of a free trade regime and the collapse of protectionist countermovements (Destler and Odell 1987; Milner 1988).[19] There are, first of all, additional factors – such as constitutional constraints and the distinctive rules of the welfare-democratic game, or deep-seated cultural dispositions towards the market as a key entity in the distribution of income – as well as the particular political-institutional context

[16] 'It was the peculiar good fortune of Great Britain that its transformation from a society predominantly controlled in the interest of a landed interest to one controlled predominantly in the interest of an industrial middle class was accomplished in a specially favourable economic environment. That explains why we had 1832 instead of 1789, why the threat of the Chartist Movement was so easily answered by the rising standard of life among the masses after the repeal of the Corn Laws' (Laski 1933: 217).

[17] To be fair, it must be mentioned here, of course, that Polanyi's work was published in 1944. This notwithstanding, as will be substantiated below, Polanyi shows himself to be peculiarly blind to the significance of social policy as a framing condition, and not just an adjunct, of a market economy. Yet here too he finds himself in good company, for example with Joseph Schumpeter and his negative assessment of capitalism's prospects of survival in *Capitalism, Socialism and Democracy* (1950).

[18] For this reason, one of the 'inventors' of the 'law' of rent-seeking, Gordon Tullock, was sceptical concerning its explanatory power for both positive and normative analysis (Tullock 1988). The point of departure – which unfortunately often is also proffered as the conclusion – of public choice explanations was summarized in 1848 by Frederick Bastiat in his article '*L'Etat*' in the *Journal des debats*: 'The STATE is a great FICTION, by means of which EVERYONE tries to live at the expense of EVERYONE else' (see http://www.newaus.com.au/econ12.html).

[19] Of particular interest still today is the failure of the mass movement for the introduction of tariffs in the United Kingdom during the three decades prior to the First World War (B. H. Brown 1943).

which may play a decisive role in the explanation of the differences in the timing, frequency and quality of protectionist practice.[20]

3 The Thesis of the 'Conservative Welfare Function'

Karl Polanyi's description of the politically effective arguments in favour of protectionism and other forms of economic nationalism may indeed be accurate in terms of capturing the intended effects of such policies in the minds of its proponents. For the latter, tariffs stood for, 'ultimately, security against unemployment, stabilization of regional conditions, assurance against liquidations of industries, and, perhaps most of all, the avoidance of that painful loss of status which inevitably accompanies transference to a job at which man is less skilled and experienced than at his own' (K. Polanyi 1957 [1944]: 154). His assenting view of protectionism is to a large extent a product of his time, attributable to the Second World War and to the social devastations which helped to bring it about.[21]

Nonetheless, he correctly identifies two points as essential for trade protectionism. These are, first, incomes – their level, security and distribution among various groups and strata –- and, second, the essentially societal nature of trade policy debates. These fundamentally *political* conflicts concerning the shaping of foreign economic relations revolve not only around purely economic issues and mere material concerns, but also around social status and its imperilment: the *social* interests of groups, he observes, often are oriented primarily towards public recognition and social rank, towards status and its defence relative to other groups.[22] Trade policy measures have been employed not merely to respond to needs of industrial society which could not be satisfied through market mechanisms. On the contrary, Polanyi argues, the overwhelming majority of social and trade policy interventions have no direct and hardly any indirect impact on incomes. Yet, even when monetary issues were at stake, he notes, these were subordinated to other interests: 'Almost invariably professional status, safety and security, the form of a man's life, the breadth of his existence, the stability of his environment were in question' (ibid.). For social groups, in other words, of primary concern is how foreign economic relations and trade policy decisions impact on their place in society and, probably far more important, what impact they might have in the future.

20 This interest in discrepancy and divergence also implies a rejection of a general theory of protectionism. Instead, we are enquiring here into the *context* of protectionism and free trade: which conditions and constellations of government, economy and society make trade policy decisions more or less likely? The same question is asked, from a longer-term perspective, with regard to foreign and global economic structures as well.

21 Karl Polanyi assesses the impact of the expansion of market conditions of production in a thoroughly negative way and in this sense he is situated within the framework of the Marxist theory of the relative impoverishment of workers under capitalism. He differs from Karl Marx, as he attributes far greater importance to the state in terms of its autonomous capacity to regulate markets and to compensate for market outcomes, and above all as he emphasizes the autonomy of state policy.

22 The same social relativism of status positions can also be observed among individuals: employees of an identical occupation – e.g. cleaning women – earn more in successful companies whose employees have high average incomes than they do in companies whose employees have low average incomes (Mullainathan and Thaler 2000).

In order to explain, first, why economic nationalism rapidly spread in the form of protectionist trade policy, and second, why, after the Second World War, a successful and enduring policy of tariff reduction and ultimately abolition – i.e. the opening of national markets – occurred, the concept of the 'conservative welfare function' (Corden 1997 [1974]: 74–6) is most useful. It contributes to an understanding of actual trade policy-making in many countries by denoting a logic which guides the actions of government decision-makers. The conservative welfare function is at the foundation of the first part of our thesis explaining the emergence of a much more liberal trade regime after the Second World War, and in particular the emergence of economic globalization since the beginning of the 1980s. This thesis also helps us to understand why, before the First World War and during the interwar period, freer trade had only limited chances to be implemented, survive and develop.[23]

Put simply, the conservative welfare function proceeds from the assumption that government decision-makers will always attempt to avoid 'any significant absolute reductions in real incomes of any significant section of the community' (ibid.: 74). Such an orientation vis-à-vis income distribution not only leads to the phenomenon that politicians nearly always consider the existing distribution of income as being optimal. It also leads them to attribute more weight to the risk of negative developments than they do to opportunities for growth and improvement. As a result, Max Corden characterizes the welfare function as 'conservative'.[24] He seeks to convey the notion that changes in income are subjectively perceived to be greater when they take the form of a loss, and as less significant when they take the form of a gain, and that politicians react accordingly.[25]

Figure 2.2 represents this value function. It reflects the likelihood that decisions have varied impacts. Seen from a neutral reference point, impacts may be positive or negative deviations, gains or losses. Although valuations differ by person and case, experiments consistently reveal an S-shaped value function. Above the reference point it is concave, below its shape is convex. For example, the value of an improvement from $20 to $40 is greater than that of one from $160 to $180. The same is true when losses are appraised. Moreover, a further constant observed is that people react to losses far more intensely than they do to gains. The dissatisfaction associated with a loss of a certain magnitude is consistently greater than the satisfaction regarding a gain of the same magnitude (Tversky and Kahneman 1981: 454).

The reasons why governments act this way in practice can vary. First, government decision-makers, being politicians, have an interest in getting re-elected and thus are receptive to the critical signals which job losses and wage declines among core elec-

23 In this study, we are concerned primarily with the *social* foundation of foreign economic closure, i.e. with those factors that, as a result of political democratization, endowed worker interests with greater political power. There are also 'economic' grounds for protectionism, e.g. when a cartelization of domestic industries must be accompanied by a corresponding protectionist trade policy if it is to achieve its intended effect.

24 Gerhard Lenski, too, proceeds in his 'theory of social stratification' from the general thesis that the coordinated action of societies is oriented 'first and foremost' towards the 'maintenance of the political status quo': 'Since perfect stability or equilibrium is impossible, this goal might better be described as *the minimization of the rate of internal political change*. This manifests itself in various ways, but particularly in the development of the machinery of state and other agencies and instruments of social control, in the great concern for law and order which every society's leaders express, and the cultivation of political ideologies which justify the *status quo*' (1966: 41f.).

25 In economics this differential assessment of changes of equal size is termed the *endowment effect*. The *locus classicus* is Kahneman and Tversky (1979).

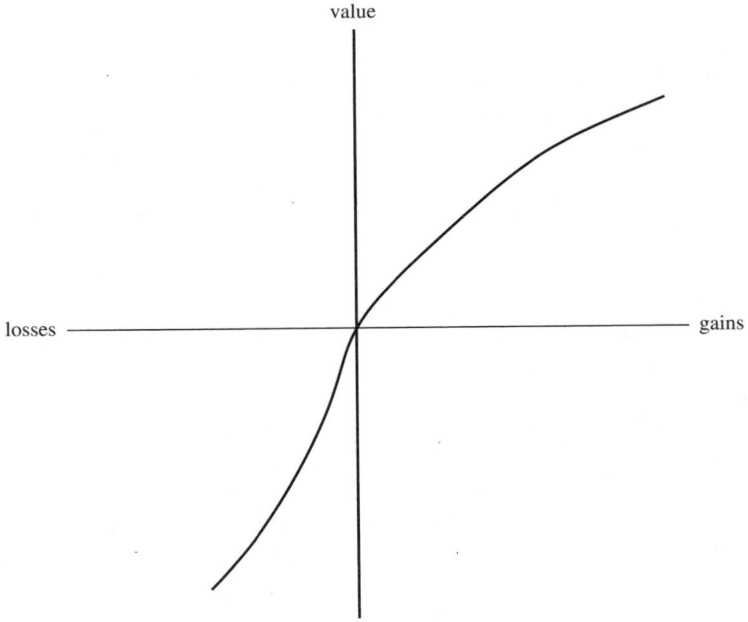

Figure 2.2 A conservative welfare function

toral groups mean for them. Further, a government orientation towards values of domestic protection and national defence can lead to foreign economic closure. It is hoped that through protective policies, threats can be warded off, be they posed by import competition to existing status positions or by the risk that such foreign competition might erode the economic foundations of the domestic social order. And finally, the domestic 'losers' from import competition can compel governments to adopt protectionist measures.[26] One thus need not assume with Polanyi that governments function either as neutral instances which perceive foreign economic closure as a societal obligation or as some kind of self-enforced objective necessity.[27] There are also no empirically convincing grounds for the opposite assumption that a market economy per se leads to societally intolerable outcomes, as some authors, with reference to Polanyi, have claimed, arguing further that globalization is *necessarily* condemned to failure (Greider 1997; Gray 1998: 1–21; Soros 1998).

The national part of the thesis

The political considerations captured by Max Corden in his notion of a conservative welfare function lead us to the following thesis with regard to domestic policy in

[26] For a description and discussion of the separate causes which protectionism can have and of the various paths it can take, see Hillman (1989).

[27] Since Polanyi is vague on how in reality this is achieved, his admonition that we have to get 'rid of the obsession that only sectional, never general, interests can become effective' remains unconvincing (1957 [1944]: 154). For example, he claims that 'precisely because not the economic but the social interests of different cross sections of the population were threatened by the market, persons belonging to various economic strata unconsciously [*sic*!] joined forces to meet the danger' (ibid.: 154f.).

welfare democracies in the realm of trade policy: to the degree to which governments effectively protect incomes through functionally differentiated socio-political institutions and redistribute income so as to maintain existing levels of social status, they can abstain from protectionist interventions in trade and from strict regulation of foreign economic relations. Provided that a sufficiently large number of countries pursue income and status protection through social policy, and no longer through protective trade policy, international trade can develop more freely in the framework of a collectively agreed upon and coordinated dismantling of trade barriers. Given that politicians introduced import tariffs and quotas chiefly to block international competition to domestic goods and to limit or completely forestall – in the wake of developments whose causes lie beyond the country's borders, and thus beyond the reach of unilateral political regulation and intervention – sudden or substantial, unexpected income losses among population groups exposed to foreign competition, their trade policies always amount to an attempt to erect a system of social protection.[28]

Social policy and trade policy, then, as premeditated reactions to the effects of an open national economy on occupational structures – and above all to the occasionally massive negative impact of imports on employment and incomes – are functionally equivalent. In both arenas, the maintenance of the extant levels and the distribution of incomes stand at the motivational centre of the political process, pitted against the income chances, employment conditions and distributional outcomes which a strictly competitive market environment would produce on its own.[29] Through both trade and social policy, government attempts to provide workers with an income that is not subject to the fluctuations in the value of their productive power, or effort, as determined by market conditions. Governments try to address fluctuations beyond the influence of the individual worker, at least with regard to potential income losses. This deliberate attempt to forestall actual or even only feared market outcomes is the intended, subjective meaning of both protectionist trade and social policy.[30]

This thesis can be broadened. If, all other factors being equal, the capacity of social policy to protect status positions and living standards against sudden, unexpected shocks to the occupational structure expands, then this might lead to adjustments in the political assessment of the risks of open markets and especially of the role of import competition and thus, ultimately, might direct politics to a decrease in the level of protectionism engineered by trade policy. Following the same logic, curtailments of

28 For a detailed discussion of the thesis of a conservative welfare function and its power to explain actual trade policy development, see Deardorff (1987) and Hillman (1989: 103–21).

29 Frank H. Knight remarks on the limits of *social* justice in market capitalism (1966: 164f.): 'Society does not consist entirely of producers, nor are real producers "economic men". And productive contribution depends on economic capacity, labor power, and managerial ability or property owned, plus a large influence of "luck". And an individual's production is due much more to biological and social inheritance, for which the individual is not responsible, than to the individual's past effort. An infant has no direct productive capacity at all, and he has neither freedom nor incentive; but as a consumer he has rights which any society must define, protect, and support. . . . In any population a majority of individuals, and a large proportion of families – much more the real unit – have no productive power worth employing, or not enough to suport life, or life at a socially tolerable level.'

30 For an 'asset theory of social policy preferences', see Iversen and Soskice (2001). They found strong empirical evidence for their key argument that individuals who have made valuable investments in human capital will demand insurance from the government against the possible future loss of income from those investments.

the welfare state which heighten the levels of socio-economic and status insecurity of politically important groups might generate increasing pressure to limit imports and to control foreign trade. Conversely, one can assume that expansions of the welfare state which lead to higher levels of income and status security among electorally significant groups enlarge politicians' room for manoeuvre in trade policy and lower the domestic political costs of openness to foreign economies.

Decisive, then, for the fate of an open economy, are the instruments at the disposal of social and trade policy-makers. Thus a fundamental welfare state orientation lies at the heart of both trade and social policy, with the crucial difference that the latter might imply a capacity to open up markets. Given the endemic volatility of occupational structures, social stability and economic security are goals that lie at the centre of all democratic politics. It is this supreme interest in safeguarding achieved income and security levels harboured by a majority of the workforce and of the economically vulnerable population which sets the tone and direction of social and economic policy in a democratic state.[31]

The thesis that a conservative welfare function guides democratic politics rests on the assumption that certain motives and principles guide the behaviour of social groups and politicians and lead to particular institutional structures on the national and international level. This leaves, however, two questions unanswered. First, are tariffs and other instruments of protectionist trade policy in actual fact, and not merely in theory, effective means of efficiently achieving social goals?[32] Second, can social policy *in the real world* alter income distribution and organize income protection in such a way that the *general* interest of economy and society in *future* productivity – including its social conditioning factors – are not compromised?[33]

Unfortunately, these questions cannot be treated here. The truth and substantive content of economic or even sociological theories of public policy as such is not the subject of this chapter – rather, it is the explanation of historical developments. We want to understand how trade and social policy actually unfolded and why, and also why this development did not take different pathways from those it actually did.

And, not to forget, we are not interested here in making policy recommendations. In other words, we do not seek to use the thesis of a conservative welfare function to

31 For more on this, see Joseph Schumpeter's commentary on Friedrich August von Hayek's lamenting of the decline of liberal values and the 'road to serfdom': 'The principles of individual initiative and self-reliance are the principles of a very limited class. They mean nothing to the mass of people who – no matter for what reason – are not up to the standard they imply. It is this majority that the economic achievement and the liberal policy of the capitalist age have invested with dominant power. Excepting intellectuals and politicians, nobody has changed his ideas. It is the people whose ideas count politically that have changed' (1946: 270).

32 In the context of foreign trade theory, attempts have been made time and again to specify the conditions under which tariffs or other means of political regulation of foreign economic relations and trade are in fact, and not just apparently, advantageous. The oldest and most renowned argument was formulated by both Friedrich List (1930 [1841]) and Alexander Hamilton (1817, 1928), namely the need to (temporarily) protect the development of domestic industry against the superior productivity of more developed national economies. The most recent attempt is Paul Krugman's formulation of a 'new' or 'strategic trade policy' (1987; 1990: 1–3). For a critique, particularly with regard to the (theoretically achieved) claim that free trade is *passé*, see Bhagwati (1988, 1998). With regard to the prospects of effectively implementing the 'new' theory of international trade Krugman (1996) became increasingly skeptical.

33 The issue and problems of social policy's market or incentive compatibility are discussed, for example, by Snower (1994), Homann and Pies (1996) and Lindbeck and Snower (1996).

derive statements concerning which economic and social policy, in light of objective social indicators, is in fact the best. The thesis merely describes the underlying motivations behind institutional developments in social and foreign trade policy, i.e. those ideas which, in competition with others, have justified and legitimized political action and which thus constitute potential causal factors in the explanation of events.

Ultimately, the thesis may also let us comprehend why it is predominantly groups in countries with the most developed economies, all sharing a democratic constitutional order, that perceive globalization as a threat. The peculiar shape of the conservative welfare function points to the power of status quo bias in democratic politics. Concern for safe property and secure income – and for the status associated with these – always outpaces advances in material prosperity.[34]

In one further respect as well, the thesis needs additional clarification. From a strictly economic point of view, one may consider it pointless to seek to determine whether changes in wage levels, employment and income distribution are caused by national or international competition, by a historic process of structural economic change which sooner or later affects all national economies, or by specific trade policies. Yet, the decisive point here too is that precisely such distinctions – be they theoretically convincing or not – have always been *politically* consequential.[35] This *empirical* state of affairs is reflected in the development of the institutions of trade and social policy and in the ways in which they are utilized by politicians.

In the United States, for example, when the International Trade Commission (ITC), following the initiation of an investigation, finds that an employee lost his or her job as a result of import competition, and not simply due to general structural economic change, this person may claim extra benefits from the former employer or the public – claims going far beyond normal income replacement through unemployment insurance. A worker with identical qualifications and work responsibilities in a neighbouring firm has no right to extended receipt of unemployment benefits or to publicly financed retraining measures if the closing of his company cannot be linked sufficiently to foreign competition, i.e. is found to be due to purely domestic circumstances – or if the lawyers representing this firm before the ITC are not convincing or sufficiently competent. Citizens and governments alike apparently consider it to be 'unfair' when, as a result of forces located beyond the nation's borders, jobs and income are lost. Economic arguments then fall on deaf ears.[36] Shifts in employment alleged to be internationally induced are viewed as exceptions to the normal risk of income loss which, it is generally agreed, an average employee must accept as natural.

It seems to be a customary feature of political economy that the functioning, rules and ultimately also the outcomes of a self-regulating market economy are accepted as fair only if they occur within a closed, national framework. For the outside forces of the international market economy, the accepted standards of fairness are different: 'Being foreign itself seems unfair' (Hudec 1999a: 242). The perception prevails that domestic jobs and incomes could be threatened and destroyed on a large scale by

[34] Hence Bhagwati (1998: 29–71) characterizes the developed societies of the North as 'fearful'.

[35] Also Weber (1895: 15) stressed the crucial difference between political economy – as an explanatory and analytic science it is *international* – and the typically *nationally* conceived criteria of value informing behaviour in concrete political economies.

[36] Cf. also Hudec (1999a: 278): 'As long as trade policy continues to worship at the shrine of fairness, trade policy advocates will find it necessary to try to satisfy the relentless demands for proof that trade is fair. The fact that fairness concepts make no sense in international trade matters will not excuse the need to employ them.'

foreign competition. Since foreign competition transcends national boundaries, the public believes that their government makes a determined political decision whether to open the nation's borders and voters hold it accountable in elections based on whether and to what extent it has permitted harmful import competition. Political responsibility for the results of international competition is thus clearly assigned to national authorities. Yet, within a national framework, it seems, market forces are allowed – under certain conditions – to function autonomously and to determine employment opportunities and income levels outside the sphere of politics.

The underlying assumption apparently is that what happens within the boundaries of a 'national economy' occurs framed by previously agreed upon, democratically approved rules. For this reason, the initial negative consequences – e.g. unemployment or a worsening of working conditions – must be accepted by those affected as part of a legitimate risk. The international economic order clearly lacks any direct democratic legitimacy and is not subject to direct democratic control which could force political accountability for the course of events. The foundation of every political order is effective territorial control. Political power is essentially territorial self-government and is ultimately authorized and legitimized by its success in protecting territory and inhabitants.[37]

International organizations not only lack this territorial dimension, they are also, with the exception of the European Union, as a rule unable to address individuals directly and forcefully. As NGOs' persistent and increasingly intense criticism of GATT, the WTO and the IMF shows, the always merely indirect parliamentary and democratic legitimation of GATT negotiations and of a country's entry into such international economic organizations by simply ratifying a *fait accompli* does not suffice to carry the full burden of the expected negative changes in employment and incomes.[38] Rather, the latter are perceived as a society's loss of democratic and thus political control. With the exception of the United States, individual governments as a rule have no means of influencing the policy of other governments towards their country's firms, or of intervening effectively in the global economy. From this doubly deficient nature of an international market economy one can arrive at the politically often very powerful normative position that the negative effects of the global economy must be politically corrected, or that they should be forestalled altogether by building a national economic firewall.[39]

37 'To tear down the walls of the state is not', as Walzer (1983: 39) points out in a more general context, 'to create a world without walls, but rather to create a thousand petty fortresses.' 'Hence', he explains, 'if states ever become large neighborhoods, it is likely that neighborhoods will become little states. Their members will organize to defend the local politics and culture against strangers. Historically, neighborhoods have turned into closed or parochial communities . . . whenever the state was open: in the cosmopolitan cities of multinational empires, for example, where state officials don't foster institutional structures (as in ancient Alexandria), or in the receiving centers of mass immigration movements (early twentieth-century New York) where the country is an open but alien world – or, alternatively, a world full of aliens. The case is similar where the state doesn't exist at all or in areas where it doesn't function. Where welfare monies are raised and spent locally, for example, as in a seventeenth century English parish, the local people will seek to exclude newcomers who are likely welfare recipients. It is only the nationalization of welfare (or the nationalization of culture and politics) that opens the neighborhood communities to whoever chooses to come in' (ibid.: 38).

38 On contesting international governance and the sovereign limits to global civil society, see Charnovitz (1997), A. Clark et al. (1998), and O'Brien et al. (2000).

39 On the latter, see the telling remark of George Washington in his Farewell Address, where he directly tackles the interaction of national stability, domestic government, and exterior vulnerability: 'If we remain one people, under one efficient government, the period is not far off when we may defy material injury from external annoyance' (quoted in Tocqueville 1994 [1835–45]: I.233).

With this undoubtedly highly simplified picture, we can now proceed to describe how citizens perceive the nation-state in regard to their central economic concerns. Without recourse to the perennial distinction society makes between that which is 'inside' and 'outside' of their national economies or to their typical self-conception as unique cultural achievements warranting protection, one cannot understand either the driving forces of national trade policy or the ways in which the world trade system is internationally regulated. Yet this observation of the significance of economic nationalism is not meant to be a normative statement, but a description of a fundamental aspect of economic policy-making (Berlin 1998). Explaining states of affairs is not the same as justifying them – and from the facts themselves we cannot scientifically derive proper action or policy.[40] The economic policy schizophrenia so essential to the actual shaping of foreign economic relations not only seems highly irrational seen from the perspective of economic theory, but has also, in all probability, led repeatedly to massive misallocations of the factors of production and encouraged widespread, endemic rent-seeking at the expense of consumers. This part of the thesis cannot, however, be further elaborated here.[41]

The international part of the thesis

The second, now international part of the thesis focuses on the institutional structure of the system of world trade, in particular on GATT and the WTO. These institutions are not merely part of the foundations of a more liberal economic order which binds all member states equally; they also make available instruments and procedures to governments with which they can legitimately counteract particular problems that they perceive themselves to be exposed to *after* having committed themselves to the course of a freer trade policy.

Individual norms and specialized procedures tailored to them – general exceptions, renegotiation rights, escape and safeguard clauses, but also procedural rights in international dispute settlement – (re)introduce elements of *managed* trade and thus give international economic relations a specifically ambivalent structure. These protectionist elements of the WTO system are supposed to help governments pursue their non-economic, i.e. predominantly welfare state, objectives in an orderly and – for other governments – predictable manner. The less governments are able to fulfil their protective function through functionally differentiated social policies and the more they then have to rely on trade-restricting means, the more important such international sanctions or channellings of the violation of national commitments to open market policies become. This legalized and thus disciplined resort to protectionism is intended to forestall the development of disastrous situations as they occurred, in extreme form, during the interwar years, when ever-higher tariffs and trade barriers – as parts of a crisis-exacerbating trade policy – wrought tragic social and political consequences in all of the societies concerned (Kindleberger 1986a; Oye 1992; Simmons 1994).

Stated as simply as possible, the second part of the thesis is this: the more the norms and procedures of the international economic order accommodate national govern-

40 For a more detailed discussion of this position in the philosophy of science, see Weber (1904).

41 Detailed studies and a balanced discussion can be found in the collection of essays edited by Bhagwati (1998).

ments' essentially welfare state constraints, the better governments will be able to observe the general rules of a free trade regime and to guarantee open markets in principle. If the world trade and world economic orders acknowledge that politicians' democratic obligation to pursue the social goals of a secure and levelling distribution of income can clash with their commitments to a freer trade regime, and that national interests can claim priority, then this increases the legitimacy and thus the stability of world markets. The significance of such a policy of international economic governance can hardly be overrated because in effect it allows countries with a low degree of institutionalized welfare statism to engage in free trade policies. This feature of the world trade system can explain why globalization could spread to developing countries. Before exploring this international part of the thesis in greater detail, we will examine more closely which kind of justification of foreign economic liberalization is at issue here, and which kind is not.

The realpolitik of the conservative welfare function

The first part of the overall thesis, relating to the functional equivalence between social and (import-restricting) trade policy, does not claim that governments intentionally designed social policy so as to remove tariffs and other barriers to transnational trade and to the transnational organization of firms. Welfare states were not built to encourage free trade policy. There is no historical evidence to support the proposition that governments had such a salutary secondary effect of social policy in mind and acted as they did for this reason. On the contrary, governments and industry representatives repeatedly fought demands for an expansion of welfare state institutions, stating that the social contributions or higher taxes needed to finance such an expansion would worsen the competitive situation of the export as well as the import sectors of the national economy. In some cases, industry has even demanded tit-for-tat protection from government in the form of compensatory tariffs and export-easing provisions in order to meet the additional costs occasioned by new social protection programmes or labour laws such as those restricting child or female labour – costs which foreign competitors, it was argued, did not have to bear.[42] The case was made that free trade under these unequal conditions of competition was self-destructive and that 'fair trade' must take its place (Zebel 1940).

In general, and viewed over longer time spans, social policies are primarily introduced, expanded and deepened on domestic grounds in the broadest sense (Goodin 1985). Foreign economic relations and the facts of trade policy played virtually no role in the normative theories of social policy underlying actual decision-making. Despite sometimes acknowledging an international dimension, the point of departure for modern state social policy-building was the 'social question' purely domestically conceived, as is brought into sharp relief by Max Weber in his view of the social politics of his time: 'The aim of our socio-political activity is not to make everybody happy but the *social unification* of the nation, which has been split apart by modern economic development, and to prepare it for the strenuous struggles of the future' (Weber

[42] This aspect of the history of social policy in Germany is treated extensively by Büren (1934). On the social politics of US trade policy, see Goldstein (1988, 1993) and Eckes (1995).

1895: 26f.).[43] Also, the international differences in the timing and the substantive content of political reactions to the social consequences of industrialization are not related to foreign economic or trade issues.[44] It is, rather, the other way around. Foreign economic relations and their implications for trade policy seldom played any explicit, significant role in decision-making about whether social policy should be pursued or what shape welfare state institutions should take. Authors ranging from Otto von Zwiedineck-Südenhorst (1911, 1924) to T. H. Marshall (1985 [1965], 1949) and to Gøsta Esping-Andersen (1985, 1990) have emphasized that as a general feature social policy represents politics *against* markets. This is particularly true with regard to foreign, or international economics: the foreign economic interests of domestic firms carry little weight in social policy formation, and the export interests of foreign firms carry no weight whatsoever.

Not until the two decades after the Second World War, as the governments of the developed countries faced the challenge of developing a new regulatory framework for international economic relations, did it become increasingly clear that they could progressively forgo tariffs. This became a realistic alternative to protectionism because welfare states were by then so comprehensive in scale and scope that they had already assumed – or could easily do so – the social protection functions hitherto shouldered by trade policy.

The institutionalization of the welfare state, which uses its own bureaucracy and resources to pursue social objectives, meant that trade policy lost its instantaneous societal significance and also its strategic status in domestic policy. Social policy rose from being short-term makeshift protection for a few to an independent determining factor of the living conditions of the entire population.

In contrast to the situation at the end of the nineteenth century and in the interwar period, trade policy and its social consequences no longer stood at the centre of public interest. Trade policy became a matter for specialists and disappeared from election campaigns.[45] The framework conditions of trade policy-making were thus completely transformed. Governments gained new latitude in this area. They now oriented their policies more towards long-term goals and pursued foreign economic and trade policies whose yield depended on the interdependent actions of a large number of very different actors – governments, firms and consumers – each of which had their own respective interests. The fruits of these policies were not easily appraised and could not be harvested until some day in the distant future. These are key features of the decisive change in international economic relations after the Second World War. Trade

43 Weber went so far as to claim that the primary object of social science is 'the present significance and the historical development of certain conflicts and constellations of interests which have arisen through *the dominant role of investment-seeking capital in modern societies*' (1904: 66; emphasis added). For him, the term 'social science' stands for 'the historical and theoretical treatment of the same problems, the practical solution of which constitutes "social policy" in the widest sense of the word' (ibid.: 67).

44 The best comparative study of the politics of the social question is still Tönnies (1926).

45 As a result of precisely this development, *very* special interests such as those of the speedily declining rural and agrarian economy, textile producers or the entire mining sector were able to develop into enclaves of tenacious protectionism. First, the light of publicity dimmed and, second, the costs for these pockets of protectionism could be distributed onto many more shoulders and thus were less perceptible. In Europe, the supranational organization of these political domains at the European Union level provided additional protection (Rieger 2000), whereas in Japan and the USA it is primarily the rural bias of parliamentary representation which accounts for the stickiness of some forms of protectionism (Fukui 1970; Reischauer and Jansen 1995: 20f.; F. E. Lee and Oppenheimer 1999; Schiller 2000).

policy was relieved of the burden of being a central feature of power and party competition within the state and in the social legitimation of autocratic regimes. In place of a national and interventionist trade policy order characterized by many particularities designed to do justice to actual or perceived problems of individual groups and industries by manipulating foreign economic entities, an international framework emerged which established general rules that held equally for all participants.

Despite this indisputably very slow, unequal 'discovery' – always threatened by setbacks – of the positive effects of the welfare state and its liberalizing effects on the ordering of international economic relations, the shaping of social policy in advanced Western welfare states remained strictly domestically oriented and was exclusively determined by national forces. The decisive point here is that within the framework of the developed welfare state, the state could pursue its social tasks separately from those related to foreign economic relations. Whether this is still the case and how the relationship between 'inside' and 'outside' is shaped in practice are empirical questions.

The relationship between social and trade policy – between the structures of the welfare state and those of foreign economic relations – can best be understood as one of an elective affinity. These coexisting interventionist orders are related in terms of their outcomes, not their intentions. Their economic rationality and social legitimation criteria differ enormously. Without having to be consciously taken into consideration by decision-makers in the respective realms, the institutional foundations of social policy also determine the horizon of possibility and the interval of autonomy for trade policy, and vice versa. Thus we may expect that, as the welfare state develops, typical patterned relationships come about between social and trade policy; specific structural forms of social and trade policy, respectively, can either reinforce and support, or inhibit and rule out one another.[46]

We should emphasize again that assuming an elective affinity between developed welfare state practice and a liberally framed foreign economic policy does not imply

46 A pattern already evident is one in which trade policy is supposed to fulfil social objectives and thus delays the introduction of social insurance schemes. This is the case, for example, in the United States. Protectionism, the argument goes, results in high wages and thus also in individuals' ability to bridge times of need with savings and to provide for their old age. Where a high degree of protectionism obtains, a paternalistic state policy that guarantees a minimum standard of living for low-income workers becomes unnecessary. Such protectionism also means that additional public monies are taken from levies that would otherwise have financed social programmes (Eckes 1995).

Another pattern can be observed in the Wilhelmine Reich. Here, Bismarck's decision to introduce social insurance as a means of domestic social integration also led to increasing protectionism. Citing the unfairness of their competition's lower socio-political burden, firms that felt threatened by imports demanded and received higher, compensatory protective tariffs. Without that socio-political context, the demands of industry would have carried far less weight (Rothfels 1927).

A third pattern is represented by British development. Here, the pre-eminence of free trade doctrine in foreign and domestic trade policy until shortly before the First World War seemed to rule out any social policy that burdened firms with higher taxes or contributions. Lloyd George attempted to make free trade compatible with redistributive social policy by not relying on (mobile) finance capital, but on (immobile) landowners for financing (Mock 1982: 306–25; P. Kennedy 1998 [1980] offers a comparative study of the German and British reactions to the twofold challenge of the social question and world-market dependency).

Elective affinities, then, characterize particular *relationships*, not lawlike, fixed patterns. This conceptual model helps to explain the interaction between institutional realms and the resulting effects for their further development. Elective affinities are thus the opposite of unambiguous or one-sided relationships of casual dependency between structures or institutional realms (Weber 1978: 341).

that governments must or do pursue a comprehensive social policy so they can open their economies. The German debate on competitiveness since 1993 appears to show exactly the opposite, in that German governments hold fast to the established institutions of social policy despite there being obvious drawbacks to the German economy's international position (Siebert 1996a). But Germany is by no means alone in this respect. In all developed welfare states the arenas in which social policy decisions are made are controlled by interests and ideas other than those which prevail in the forums in which decisions about foreign economic policy are made. Both welfare statism and international economics are distinct forms of social action following laws of their own and each of them to a large degree is independent of the forces driving and shaping the other realm. For this reason, there is no reason to assume that a liberal foreign economic policy and a specific social policy framework reciprocally condition each other unambiguously and independently of spatial and temporal conditions.

Our claim that decision-makers do not face politically compelling incentives to take into account the functional interrelations of social policy and free trade, though, does not hold for the second, the international part, of the thesis. In the negotiations on the original GATT, the contracting parties – and especially their governmental representatives – were particularly anxious to find solutions that guaranteed at once the integrity of their welfare state provisions and their interest in freer trade.[47] Every regulation in GATT was scrutinized with an eye to its impact on future government latitude in *unilaterally* securing and enhancing national welfare. At the time, the primary goal of every participating government was to *domestically* guarantee full employment; this was the lesson that governments drew from the Great Depression and the ensuing anti-democratic revolutions of National Socialism and fascism.[48] For this reason, each country's politically induced welfare state obligations ultimately determined the degree to which it was willing to concede tariff levels and national government control, or to forgo certain trade policy instruments. The two leading economic powers of the time, the United States and Great Britain, did not seriously consider

[47] The first draft of GATT was written in Lake Success, New York in the spring of 1947. It was then signed in Geneva on 30 October 1947 and went into effect on 1 January 1948. At the time, one had to make do with a provisional agreement, because the negotiating authority of the US government, which expired at the end of 1947, was restricted to a treaty, whereas entry into an international organization required congressional approval. In late 1947 and early 1948, a commission was created in Havana to lay the groundwork for an International Trade Organization (ITO). This commission elaborated the Havana Charter. After the US Congress failed to ratify this Charter, meaning that the USA could not become a member of the ITO, the administration of GATT was transferred to the preparatory committee of the ITO, out of which the GATT Secretariat in Geneva emerged. For this reason, the further development of GATT did not occur within the framework of an international organization, but rather in so-called trade rounds and in the framework of individual meetings. The original signatory states of GATT from 1947 were Australia, Belgium, Burma, Ceylon, France, India, Canada, Cuba, Luxembourg, New Zealand, the Netherlands, Norway, Pakistan, Rhodesia, the South African Union, Czechoslovakia, Great Britain and the United States (Diebold 1952; Senti 1986: 16–18; Aaronson 1996).

[48] This is also and especially true of the USA. The political expression of this full-employment obligation was the Employment Act of 1946: 'In this Act, Congress declared that it is the *responsibility of the Federal Government* to use all practicable means, with the *assistance and cooperation* of private industry and local government to achieve the goals set forth with respect to employment, production, and purchasing power' (Hansen and Viner 1947: 70; emphasis in original). On the subsequent political fate of this US, 'Pennsylvania Avenue style' Keynesianism, see De Long (1996).

introducing 'free trade' *in toto* (Hoover 1945; M. Polanyi 1945). In the final analysis, it was the conservative welfare function suggested by a welfare-democratic framework that shaped – and continues to shape – the thought and action of the lawyers, economists and politicians who developed and continue to develop international trade regulations and arbitration mechanisms. This conclusion becomes clear to anyone who inspects the chronicles of the various GATT rounds.

Up to this point we have fashioned a general ideal type which will enable us to recognize the more interesting particularities of historical and current developments in social and trade policy and to identify and explain crucial deviations from expected outcomes. Explanations based on ideal types do not aim at a general theory, but at understanding phenomena in terms of their respective particular significance. The conservative welfare function is precisely such a concept. It is a theoretical instrument that leads us to a deeper understanding of particular states of affairs. The concept is not an end in itself or a theory, but a tool for understanding these phenomena. An ideal type should not be confused or blended with historical reality.

In the section that follows, we present and elucidate various states of affairs which support the thesis of a conservative welfare function and discuss two complexes:

1 The first complex concerns the *national* determinants of the conservative welfare function, that is, the *first* part of the thesis. At first, we address the concurrence of the expansion of the welfare state and of the reduction in tariffs. We then proceed to examine the history and outcomes of the international economic negotiations following the Second World War, take a closer look at the statistical relationships between welfare state expansion and openness to foreign trade and, finally, enquire into the significance of systems of social protection for the success and sustainability of free trade policy in developing and transition countries. In conclusion, we will consider exceptions that prove the rule of the conservative welfare function: the rural and agrarian economic sectors, on the one hand, and US trade laws on the other.
2 The second complex comprises the forms and procedures of the management of *international* trade relations, i.e. the *second* part of the thesis. Here we will show how certain precautions are taken which serve governments as safety valves. Specifically, we will discuss exemption and escape clauses as well as other mechanisms which buy time for processes of adaptation, particularly for those governments that cannot rely on sufficiently developed income maintenance and insurance schemes.

4 National Determinants and Consequences of the Conservative Welfare Function

In this section we will show that the ideal-typical concept of the conservative welfare function suggests developments which correspond broadly to how social and trade policy in their reciprocal relationship actually progressed. Which institutional changes in these two policy domains of modern society concern us here specifically? And what is the mechanism through which the reciprocal relationship between these domains is established?

The concurrence of welfare state expansion and tariff reductions

Four factors drive the general movement towards an expansion of social policy, and are thus pivotal to an understanding of trade policy development:

1. The development of a full-income society.
2. The extension of social policy to all societal groups.
3. The growing role of the welfare state as employer.
4. The shrinking duration of employment over the life course due to later or incomplete entry into (education) and to earlier exit from (retirement) the labour market.

The income guarantee of the welfare state Put succinctly, social policy in developed welfare states can be described as the capacity to guarantee a 'full-income society' (Josef Joffe). The position in life and the life chances of citizens in general have become the object of directed, specifically organized state influence designed to achieve purposive change. The material living conditions of a country's entire population have become, in essence, *public* conditions to be altered with the aim of achieving greater social justice and a level of citizen participation in economic growth that is as inclusive as possible.[49] Characteristic of the welfare state reforms in Western Europe and North America in the first two decades after the Second World War was the leap from policies that provided protection against poverty to those that defended the social standing attained in competitive labour markets (Flora 1986–7), i.e. towards a welfare state that *dynamically* guaranteed the status quo.

Since the 1950s, broadly cast systems of income protection extending well into the middle classes, together with high income replacement ratios, defended individually achieved living standards against income loss due to illness, unemployment, invalidity and old age – and also against the costs of long-term care (Flora and Alber 1981; Schmähl and Rothgang 1996; Rothgang 1997, 2001). The pension reform enacted in the Federal Republic of Germany in 1957 is paradigmatic for this far-reaching transformation of social policy. It not only eliminated the risk of poverty in old age for the vast majority of pensioners, but also – by introducing a 'dynamic' element in the pension formula – tied pensioners' levels of living to the rising incomes of the workforce (Hockerts 1980). In all developed industrial countries, provisions with similar effects, such as indexing of pensions or an automatic cost-of-living adjustment, were introduced into social policy (Weaver 1988; Leisering 1992, 1995). Such measures served to strengthen the relationship between generations as well as between social groups by guaranteeing the equality of their material living conditions, their consumption prospects and their lifestyles *independently* of an individual's employment or labour market fate.[50]

[49] To describe the historical process through which the welfare state acquired its developed form, Ernst Forsthoff coined the term 'social realization' (1971: 30–3). On the changes in life situations and life courses associated with this, see Mayer and Müller (1986, 1989), Allmendinger and Hinz (1997) and Mayer (2001b).

[50] The US sociologist Lee Rainwater answers the question of 'What money buys' with 'membership in industrial society', i.e. citizenship (1974: xiii). The British sociologist T. H. Marshall (1949: 80) identified the adjustment of real income to the social needs and status of the citizen as the main trust of welfare statism. In this essay Marshall also identified the dynamic element in the new ameliorative social policies: 'The diminution of inequality strengthened the demand for its abolition, at least with regard to the essentials of social welfare.'

Security and continuity are essential moments of democratic citizenship primarily because membership in the community is enduring and cannot tolerate any kind of rupture. In a private and market setting, however, income and employment security cannot be as far-reaching as is the security inherent in citizenship status. In democratic welfare states, therefore, the insecurity of a particular employment position is paired with a vaguely formulated, yet nonetheless politically consequential, 'right to work' in the sense of a public obligation to ensure adequate labour market conditions (Marshall 1945: 221).[51] How this mandate is implemented, however, is indeed an open question, and is thus a decisive variable for trade policy decisions as well.

The growth in the role played by social benefits in securing individual living standards was accompanied by their progressive juridification: claims to social benefits became 'new property' (C. A. Reich 1964; Heinze 1984; Sunstein 1990). In divorce proceedings, for example, pension benefits can be as much an issue as other forms of property, and can be sliced up and reallocated among the parties. The more pronounced the property character of social benefits became, the more the higher courts restricted the scope of administrative discretion available to welfare state institutions in times of tight public budgets.[52] Yet, it was not only decisions of the high courts that made large realms of social policy taboo in electoral and government politics. The incorporation of very large population groups at considerable benefit levels into welfare state social programmes also fortified this taboo zone. Politicians refrain from policy interventions that would lead to benefit cuts or benefit denial for larger segments of the population, as those affected would punish those responsible the next time around at the polls.[53]

Starting from the inarticulate but nonetheless highly consequential major premise of an institutionally rich welfare statism, national trade representatives in the GATT rounds no longer needed to extensively consider the potential negative changes in incomes, employment patterns or regional distribution of industry which could result from stronger import competition and the protectionist reactions of the affected indus-

51 Here, too, we point to the country and the time period which one normally relies on to prove the opposite: in 1978 US Congress passed the Humphrey-Hawkins Act, which obligated the federal government to a set of goals which included lowering the unemployment rate to 4 per cent by 1978 ('and to maintaining it thereafter'), bringing inflation to 0 per cent by 1988, lowering federal expenditures as far as was macro-economically responsible – and providing greater subsidies for agricultural price supports (De Long 1996: 41f.). This law was not simply 'symbolic politics', but had very real teeth – and produced some hard facts. Technically speaking, it was an amendment to the Federal Reserve Bill Act and altered the prescribed objectives of federal reserve policy (M. Friedman 1982: 109; Brimmer 1983: 1; Goodhart 1989: 300). US monetarism which took shape in the late 1970s thus had welfare state roots and is measured de facto primarily in terms of its welfare democratic results.

52 For this reason, the US Supreme Court was loath to extend the strong constitutional protection enjoyed by property rights to advantageous individual circumstances dispensed via social policy and regulatory provisions. Social policy and social regulation are a product of the fundamentally discretionary police power of the state and hence enjoy no special constitutional protection (Epstein 1985). For an interpretation of social insurance claims in the Federal Republic from the perspective of constitutional law, see Heinze (1984). Guaranteeing the property character of social rights is, however, not necessarily decisive for their political protection. The greater the role social benefits play in securing the living standards of significant groups in the electorate, the higher the probability that they are politically inviolable (Skocpol 1991; Pierson 1994).

53 In the USA, social insurance programmes – in contrast to the various social assistance programmes – are referred to as the 'third rail' of electoral politics. The third rail in subway systems carries the electrical current. It immediately kills anyone who touches it.

Table 2.3 Long-term trends in real output per capita in selected industrial countries (average annual % change)

	Gold standard (1880–1913)		*Interwar period (1919–38)*		*Post World War II (1950–90)*	
	%	σ	%	σ	%	σ
Germany	1.9	1.6	4.2	8.0	3.7	3.0
USA	1.6	4.2	0.6	7.2	1.9	2.7
France	1.3	3.0	2.7	6.7	3.1	2.0
Italy	1.6	4.3	0.9	4.4	3.9	2.7
UK	1.1	2.3	1.1	4.3	2.4	2.5
Japan	1.9	5.9	1.7	4.7	6.0	3.6

σ = standard deviations of growth rates

Source: IMF (1994: 87)

tries and their employees. Instead, they could concentrate on the positive effects of a broadened and deepened international division of labour. The fundamental socio-political problem of an open economy – the much greater volatility of employment and incomes – takes on a different significance in welfare states than it does in societies lacking economic protection schemes (Katzenstein 1984, 1985). In macro-economic terms, the new dynamic features of welfare statism take the form of an 'automatic' stabilization of an economy: first, because even in times of sudden structural change or economic recession, welfare state transfers continue to flow steadily; and second, because the income losses due to unemployment are compensated for by publicly provided income from social rights. As is shown in Table 2.3, in the post-war period not only has economic growth per capita accelerated; also the ups and downs of national economies – measured as standard deviations of annual growth rates – have considerably diminished.

Welfare state institutions do not only provide a kind of indemnity against economic risks. Even if free trade's promise were fulfilled – that the international division of labour will lead to greater national prosperity – this does not mean that precisely those persons made redundant in industries that are in decline and no longer competitive will receive the new jobs in the expanding sectors. For large segments of the population social insurance schemes and government budgets now represent not only additional, but also alternative sources of income. These schemes limit the dependency of recipients on the labour market and increase the potential for intra-firm, occupational and regional mobility. The welfare state income guarantee liberates firms from social obligations which would otherwise, under conditions of welfare democracy, inevitably belong to the regulatory core of the employment contract.[54] This increases the

[54] The Japanese example of the institutionalization of life-long employment rights at the company level shows that weak public welfare may well mean strong occupational, company-provided welfare (A. Gordon 1985; Weiss 1993; Thelen and Kume 1999). In this context we read Nivola (1997) as placing the USA halfway between Japan and Continental European countries. With the term 'welfare democracy' we restate an issue that Titmuss (1956) already raised with his 'social division of welfare'.

Table 2.4 General government expenditure of selected OECD countries, 1880–1998 (as % of GDP)

	1880	*1913*	*1938*	*1950*	*1973*	*1980*	*1990*	*1998*
Germany	10.0	17.7	42.4	30.4	42.0	47.9	45.1	46.9
USA	—	8.0	19.8	21.4	31.1	31.4	35.2	32.8
France	11.2	8.9	23.2	27.6	38.8	46.1	49.8	54.3
Netherlands	—	8.2	21.7	26.8	45.5	55.8	54.1	47.2
UK	9.9	13.3	28.8	34.2	41.5	—	41.8	40.2
Japan	0.0	14.2	30.3	19.8	22.9	32.0	31.3	36.9

Sources: Maddison (1995: 65); US Census Bureau (1999: 847)

economic rationality of personnel politics and the allocative efficiency of labour markets.[55]

In Table 2.4 we present the growth in public expenditures in developed economies and, thus, the enormously increased potential of secondary income generation and (re)distribution. In short, governments' means of dealing with the risks of free trade have expanded considerably in both scale and scope. The benefit packages of social assistance programmes striving no longer to discriminate against or stigmatize their claimants can be understood as toleration bonuses. Such handouts are granted to persons who, due, for example, to their low skills, are most exposed to the risk of becoming a victim of drastically accelerated economic change, yet who in democracies can register their objection through the ballot box (Iversen and Soskice 2001).

The expansion of the welfare state The transition to status assurance was associated with a complete or at least near universalization of welfare state benefit schemes and services. In social insurance schemes, the income ceilings for participation in mandatory insurance were continually raised and social rights became integral to citizenship status (Alber 1987 [1982]; Marshall 1949). Social policy was not only no longer characterized by class politics; it also – for example, in terms of family benefits – became completely divorced from employee status. The prime example of this is the German practice of spousal tax class splitting (*Ehegattensplitting*): *fiscal* welfare essentially frees the spouse from the need to offer his or (usually) her services on the labour market, because the spouse's lack of income reduces the tax of the wage-earner. Other social elements in German tax law have the same objective of keeping women from entering the labour market. Primarily through tax deductions for educational expenses and home ownership, the middle classes therefore became clients of the welfare state, which thereby acquired a more democratic character. As a result of this universalization of social rights, nearly every citizen in the industrialized world was incorporated in one way or another into the labyrinthine systems of secondary income distribution (Huber

55 According to Marshall (1949: 84, 110), this change in basic business conditions explains how both social rights and the market economy could 'grow and flourish side by side in the same soil', even though social rights of citizenship and civil liberties are seen to be 'at war with each other'.

and Stephens 2001).[56] As a result, equalizing effects across social classes were achieved, running in opposition to the tendency of market processes to produce and enhance difference.[57]

This has two implications for trade policy. First, increased effectiveness of social policy enhances flexibility in foreign trade policy – even in areas that are decisive for the socio-economic fate of the middle classes. In the European Union, as a result of the liberalization of the service sector, the privatization of the utility industries and the opening of previously sheltered transportation and communication infrastructures to foreign competition, the incomes and the working conditions in these traditionally secure sectors have become driven essentially by transnational market developments.[58] Occupations that require high skill and training levels, and workers whose professions were once perceived as closed and self-governing, such as lawyers, doctors and engineers, have been subjected to competition and hence experience greater insecurity. One precondition for the successful incorporation of the service sector into the GATT system is the fact that the welfare state is no longer concerned merely with caring for the poor (Flora 1986–7; Goodin and LeGrand 1987). Further, the electorally induced political security of welfare state benefit programmes intensifies proportionally with the size of the group privileged by these programmes, which indirectly also protects advances in trade policy.[59]

The welfare state as employer The expansion of welfare state services – public health care and educational institutions but also social work, nursing and other public facilities including labour exchange services and communal or other authorities as producers of basic utilities – created not only a wide range of new, but also highly organized, groups of employees who, virtually residing in nation-state reservations, were well protected from international competition.[60] In Table 2.5 this development is shown in historical and comparative perspective. It demonstrates clearly the extent to which direct public production and provision of services has diminished the role of largely private-sector and thus market-driven job creation. This structural change in

[56] This short account does not imply that the expansion of welfare state institutions was based on a broad social consensus and thus was an uncontested development. Laski's admonition (1933: 223) is still valid today: 'The very fact that every concession to social decency in legislation, in housing, in schemes for miners' welfare, in the limitation of the hours of labour, even in maternity and child welfare provision, has been granted only after a profound, and often passionate, struggle, is evidence enough of the degree to which the claim to an equal commonwealth is resisted.'

[57] The panel data of Goodin et al. (1999: 183) show that even if family benefits and pensions are left aside, over a 10-year period 100 per cent of Dutch and nearly 60 per cent of German residents receive state benefits. The corresponding US percentage is only slightly below the German one. To understand the US–German contrast, we must keep in mind here, though, that the level and quality of benefits – above all in terms of statutory and bureaucratic eligibility hurdles – differ widely among countries. In the USA, the share of selective, i.e. means-tested, benefits in total public income-maintenance expenditures has hovered around 20 per cent since the 1960s (Myles and Pierson 1997: 448).

[58] Because of the long and very strong European tradition of public ownership of basic infrastructures and utility industries, which position the state as a provider of basic wants (Haverkate and Huster 1999: 287–98), this turnaround marks a revolution of sorts. For the very different – regulatory – approach to critical markets in the USA, see McCraw (1984).

[59] Theda Skocpol (1991), for example, argues that the universalization of welfare state benefits provides greater political protection against ideological fluctuations and forestalls a taxpayer revolt against social policy, since taxpayers benefit directly from it.

[60] For comparative statistics on the size of welfare state clienteles, see Pierson (2001: 413).

Table 2.5 The structure of employment in five economies, 1900–1995

	USA	*UK*	*Germany*[a]	*France*	*Japan*
			– 1900 –		
Goods[b]	66.8	56.7	78.9	74.7	79.3
• agriculture	38.3	13.0	39.9	43.4	64.8
• manufacturing	21.0	32.1	28.5	26.0	12.4
Market services	27.2	36.4	15.7	19.5	16.6
Non-market services	6.0	6.9	5.4	5.8	4.1
			– 1950 –		
Goods	43.7	50.9	66.3	61.6	68.9
• agriculture	10.5	6.4	23.9	28.0	43.6
• manufacturing	24.8	33.9	32.6	25.8	18.3
Market services	40.1	36.6	24.2	21.9	26.0
Non-market services	16.2	12.5	9.5	16.5	5.1
			– 1973 –		
Goods	32.4	44.8	54.5	48.0	53.3
• agriculture	3.2	3.2	7.2	10.2	16.1
• manufacturing	21.9	32.2	36.5	26.9	27.1
Market services	43.9	38.5	30.8	29.6	38.9
Non-market services	23.7	16.7	14.7	22.4	7.8
			– 1995 –		
Goods	21.8	26.7	38.4	30.3	41.1
• agriculture	1.6	2.1	2.8	4.6	7.3
• manufacturing	13.9	18.7	27.2	18.1	22.5
Market services	52.6	53.1	41.7	38.4	50.1
Non-market services	25.6	20.2	19.9	31.3	8.8

[a] Except for 1900, Germany refers to West Germany

[b] Goods comprise agriculture, manufacturing, construction, mining and public utilities; market services include transport and communication, distributive trades, financial services, personal and domestic services; non-market services are government employment plus education and medical services

Source: Crafts (2000: 36)

employment and occupational patterns has also caused a drop in the share of workers for whom import competition or export-dependency are central determinants of their economic well-being.

The shorter working life The growth of the welfare state leads to an increase in the portion of life spent outside gainful employment, whether in educational institutions or in old age. These metamorphoses of transition phases into independent, protracted life stages reduce the vulnerability of a society to major and unexpected economic changes which can emanate from highly interdependent world markets. Welfare state expansion has increasingly shrunk the window of social vulnerability in a life span.

Table 2.6 Years of education per person aged 15–64 for six countries, 1820–1992[a]

	1820	*1870*	*1913*	*1950*	*1973*	*1992*
USA	1.8	3.9	7.9	11.3	14.6	18.0
UK	2.0	4.4	8.8	10.6	11.7	14.1
Germany	—	—	8.4	10.4	11.6	12.2
France	—	—	7.0	9.6	11.7	16.0
Netherlands	—	—	6.4	8.1	10.3	13.3
Japan	1.5	1.5	5.4	9.1	12.1	14.9

[a] Average for both sexes

Source: Maddison (1995: 37)

Transition phases have become independent and distinct segments of life (Heinz 1991) in which individuals spend resources that they might not have acquired directly through the labour market.

In Table 2.6 we present the general increase (across countries) in the period of time spent in the educational system. It should be noted that the years cited here refer not to life years but to a weighted indicator. Years spent in primary and secondary educational systems are multiplied by the factors 1 and 1.4 respectively, periods in higher educational institutions by the factor 2. The table thus also indicates the increase in the value of human capital over the course of the last two centuries. Human capital formation is directly relevant to trade policy because one can assume that a greater stock of human capital means a greater capacity to adapt to changed and particularly to drastically increased demands on workers and thus to make productive use of economic progress. Moreover, individual investments into one's own human capital increase one's chances of benefiting from the competition among employers for scarce human capital. In the absence of domestic closed shop policies of trade unions, the less sought-after and the more specific human capital is, the more political pressure evolves to secure it from foreign competition.[61] The mere size of the labour force is itself a factor for trade policy of primary importance. For example, less than half of all Germans numbered among the economically active population in 1999 – 40.5 million out of 82 million – and for 36.4 million of these 40.5 million, gainful employment was their primary means of support (Statistisches Bundesamt 2000: 101). In Table 2.7 we compare the volume of gainful employment in Germany with that in the USA and clarify the different extent to which labour power can be kept away from the labour market. In Germany, the number of the employable population aged 15–64 that are gainfully employed is roughly 10 per cent lower than in the US, whereas the difference among men in the core period of their employment biography at age 25–54 is not as pronounced (3 per cent). The explanation for this lies in the different labour force participation rates of women generally as well as of men under the age of 24 and over the age of 54. Compared to Germany, the USA draws on 20 per cent more

61 Already in 1874 the English economist John E. Cairnes, in connection with his observation of a consciously designed hierarchical pyramid of closely protected occupational positions, spoke of 'non-competing industrial groups as a feature of our social economy' (1874: 73). On the politics of artificially creating both domestically and internationally non-competing groups, see Ohlin (1931).

Table 2.7 Potential labour power and its use in Germany and the USA, 1997 (%)

	Germany	*USA*
Employed/population: all aged 15–64 year olds	63.5	73.5
Employed/population: only men, aged 25–54	85.1	88.4
Utilization of societal work potential	48.1	69.5
Unemployment rate, standardized	9.7	4.9

Source: Kohli (2000: 370)

of its work potential. In Germany this potential is channelled not into gainful employment but – via legal and educational institutions and the marriage contract – into other social activities for the family or self.

In addition to protracted educational periods, the retirement age is the second major factor that has reshaped labour markets and, most significantly, shrunk their size and their role in the overall economic fate of the population. In Germany, until the outbreak of the First World War, the labour force participation rate of individuals aged 60 and over was very high. In 1895, among men it was 67.9 (women 21.9) per cent. By 1994, the male rate was 12.3 (women 3.4) per cent. In the span of one century, then, old age had developed into an independent phase in the life course which was more or less completely separate from the earlier period of gainful employment. And this happened despite the fact that today far more people can reach this phase of life and thus place heavy demands on the welfare state. On average, during the years 1881–90, the share of men (women) who reached their sixtieth year was 33.5 (39.3) per cent; the average during the period 1994–6, however, was 84.9 (92.3) per cent. At the same time, the expected duration of pension receipt has increased markedly. The mean life expectancy at the age of 60 for men (women) during the years 1881–90 averaged 12.4 (13.1) years. During the period 1994–6 it was 18.3 (22.7) years (all data from Kohli 2000: 364). This demographic movement occurred in all developed industrial societies, though it is far less pronounced in the Anglo-Saxon world, particularly in the USA, than in Continental and especially Northern Europe.

Summary The institutionalization of the welfare state has thus had a decisive, if indirect, impact on trade policy. This relationship is, as mentioned above, not the result of conscious planning by governments attempting to increase the space for the political manoeuvres necessary to pursue a more liberal trade policy and to subordinate national sovereignty to a multilateral regime of international regulations. There is no evidence of such intentions in the sources relevant to the path-breaking decisions on social policy in Western countries after the Second World War.

Moreover, socio-political institutions in all likelihood would look different from how they do today if their economic function – particularly with regard to foreign trade – had been the central rationality criterion in their development.[62] If social

[62] This is true above all for the decision as to whether social policy should be financed through general revenues, particularly general excise taxes, or via taxes on labour, i.e. social insurance contributions. Tax-financed social protection systems give policy-makers more flexibility than systems financed by payroll taxes, especially in economies that are deeply integrated into world markets. Social protection systems relying on employment are chronically confronted with the problem that social policy depends on labour market developments, and vice versa.

policy's normal developmental pattern can already be described as an irrational overstretching of the economically feasible (Zwiedineck-Südenhorst 1924) – that is, forcing companies operating at their margin out of business because of the extra costs piled on them by public policy – then this systemic disregard of economic rationality is especially true of foreign and international trade policy.[63] There is no politically powerful organized interest base linked to the latter, quite in contrast to national economic policy, where the Madisonian factions, for better or for worse, notoriously try to exert a direct influence on politics.

In addition, social inequalities among groups that public policy itself creates – e.g., among blue-collar workers, white-collar employees and civil servants, or between workers who are privileged by occupational welfare systems (e.g., miners or steel workers) and those who are not – represent monopolistic status appropriations which function as barriers to social mobility and fetter free labour markets.

In sum, the actually observable relationship between domestic social policy formation and a trade policy to install freer international markets is anything but some metaphysically prefigured harmony.

The outcome of the negotiations on international economic relations

The initial GATT rounds of the 1950s and 1960s were relatively limited and arduous bilateral negotiations between individual governments over the level of duties on specific goods. In a tit-for-tat-like manner, and item for item, each country sought to keep the potential negative employment effects of its duty concessions and compromises to a minimum. In later rounds, in particular the Kennedy and Tokyo Rounds, general, much more effective across-the-board tariff reductions found consensus, and thus duties on specific goods no longer stood in the foreground.[64] This progress in the economic yield of GATT negotiations could be due to the fact that in the 1970s and 1980s the governments of developed countries, given their by now quite comprehensive social policies, were in a much better position to ignore potential negative income and employment effects than they had been in earlier rounds. In Table 2.8 the quantum leaps in the scope of a more liberal world trade order are documented.

The findings of quantitative research

Quantitative, comparative welfare state research has demonstrated that trade openness and state expenditure levels exhibit a strong positive correlation. As is shown in figure 2.3, public expenditures on social protection and welfare tend to be higher in

63 Also Max Weber (1978: 83f.) noted that welfare policies are marked by the unavoidable fact that 'the dominant interests [are] not primarily concerned with maximising the opportunities of acquisition and economic provision of the participants in the market themselves; have, indeed, often been in conflict with them.' For Weber, *every* social policy will *diminish* the formal rationality of economic action and thus *block* markets from achieving productive and distributive maxima, since it implies the application of criteria of ultimate ends – ethical, political, egalitarian, and so on – 'and measure the results of economic action, however formally "rational" in the sense of correct calculation they may be, against these scales of "value rationality" or *substantive* goal rationality' (ibid.: 85).

64 For an historical account of the origins of GATT and how it developed through the Kennedy Round, see Dam (1970). On the Kennedy Round, see J. W. Evans (1971) and on the Tokyo Round, see Winham (1986).

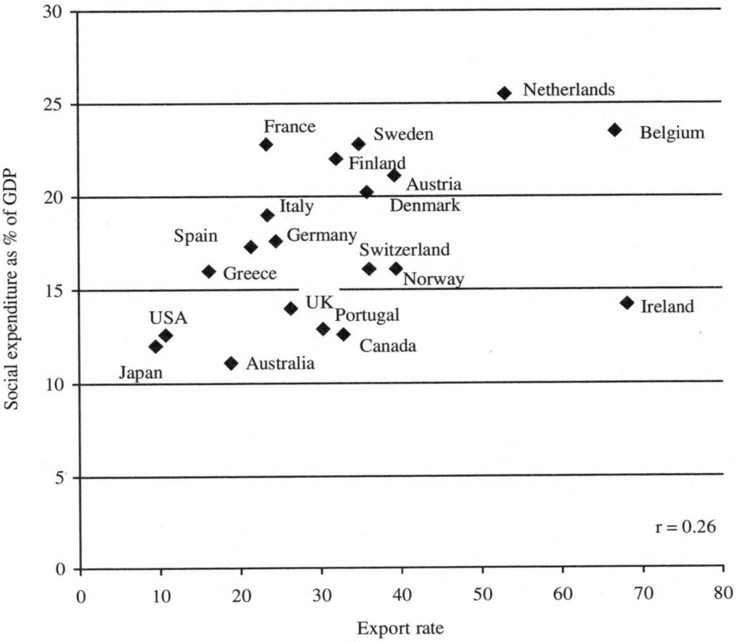

Figure 2.3 Export rate and social expenditure in OECD countries, 1990–1997
Source: OECD (1999a: tables 6.3 and 6.12)

Table 2.8 Tariff-reducing activity of GATT, 1947–1994

Round	*Date*	*Number of countries*	*Value of trade covered ($USbn)*	*Average tariff cut (%)*	*Average tariffs afterwards (%)*
Geneva	1947	23	10.0	35	—
Annecy	1949	33	—	35	—
Torquay	1950	34	—	35	—
Geneva	1956	22	2.5	35	—
Dillon	1960–1	45	4.9	35	—
Kennedy	1962–7	48	40.0	35	8.7
Tokyo	1973–9	99	155.0	34	6.3
Uruguay	1986–94	125	3,700.0	38	3.9

Note: Tariff averages refer to tariffs on non-primary products of industrial countries

Source: Jackson (1997a: 74)

countries more exposed to foreign economic risks – as measured by import and export shares. Open economies are confronted with the problem that effectively independent world economic conditions can cause structural and cyclical economic downturns at home. The reactions of such countries' businesses and governments to the challenges arising from this situation must stand the test of undeniably sovereign world markets.

There is reason to assume that such countries take extra organizational and institutional precautions to make up for the greater insecurities faced by their workforce and businesses. One such comprehensive institutional solution is welfare state structures, which offer an alternative source of life chances and provide income guarantees. The statistical relationship between the level of a country's social expenditures and its foreign economic openness was first demonstrated by D. Cameron (1978), and was recently thrust to the forefront of debates on the relationship between the welfare state and globalization by Rodrik (1996, 1997, 1998), Hicks (1999) and Iversen (2001).[65] The central problem of these studies is of course their inability to provide insight into the causal mechanism producing these relationships. For this reason, one can use the same data to argue that openness in foreign trade leads to greater economic growth, or that higher social expenditures are a growth dividend which these national economies have earned and which is then given back to or passed on to society in the form of more generous social benefits.

A further drawback of this descriptive statistical perspective on the relationship between foreign trade and social policy is its silence regarding the political mechanisms through which the alleged relationships are said to work. In which manner, and to what extent, does a certain commitment in trade policy, by means of the 'normative force of the factual', compel a certain type of welfare state engagement? Or is it welfare state decisions themselves that independently create hard facts and thereby set the terms and limits of substantive trade policy-making? Exactly which actors – businesses, unions, parties and governments – represent in exactly which socio-political arenas which trade policy interests? And which actors in trade policy arenas represent which socio-political interests? By their very nature, these questions cannot be answered through quantitative research. Nevertheless, it is fair to ask practitioners of the latter – as they very often claim that their results point to undeniable political 'solutions' for the trade and social policy challenge – how in their opinion these relationships have come about, i.e. which political phenomena underlie them.[66]

The role of social protection systems in developing countries

Quantitative studies by economists at the World Bank have found that in particular those countries in Latin America, Africa and Eastern Europe that have cast a social net for the poor and operated it efficiently have been more successful in replacing their previous autarchic policy of import substitution with a liberal, export-oriented trade policy.[67] The determination of governments to provide social security in often difficult

[65] One alternative explanation of this correlation is that a country's size is the decisive factor, because larger countries have less foreign trade as a share of their GNP and dispose, moreover, of economies of scale in public services. In his studies, Dani Rodrik has not found sufficient evidence to support this alternative interpretation. Rodrik also discusses broadly and in a balanced way the empirical findings of other investigations into the relationship between the welfare state features of national economies and their foreign trade policy.

[66] For paradigmatic explanatory approaches that do address the societal and domestic political conditions of trade policy, see Gourevitch (1977), Rogowski (1987), Milner (1988), Goldstein (1993) and Lake (1998a, b).

[67] Cf. C. Graham (1994) for a summary account as well as detailed case studies. On the IMF and *social* conditionality as part of the new Washington consensus, see Holla (2001). In September 2000, Michael Camdessus, who had been managing director of the IMF for thirteen years before retiring in February of that year, told the *Bangkok Post*, 'social policy is now at the heart of our strategies' (ibid.: 3).

and insecure transition periods of national economic adaptation to greater foreign economic openness was thus decisive for their ability to implement such economic reforms with more durable results. At least in terms of descriptive statistics, this relationship has been confirmed again and again.[68]

Social safety nets are of pivotal importance to the public support of a government which seeks to open its country to international trade over the long term. Such nets help forestall and counter the resistance of organized groups which have profited from the old economic order. Security nets also counter the common tendency in economic reform campaigns, in which members of groups who found themselves above the poverty level prior to the market opening see their jobs and relative prosperity threatened by import competition, and experience a drop to or below the poverty line. These 'new' poor are, as a rule, better organized than the 'old' poor, and hence, with regard to their voice, much more powerful, and politically far more easily mobilized against trade liberalization efforts. To make them the first beneficiaries of improved social security nets is very often a sine qua non for any successful transition towards freer trade (C. Graham 1994: 8). The more such security nets facilitate and support new coalitions for reforms in the domestic economy and foreign trade, and the more these nets help convince larger segments of the population that these economic reforms are advantageous to them, the greater the chances that the government will be able to carry out and sustain a national economic opening.

Exceptions that prove the rule: agriculture and US trade law

There are still some sectors that have been largely exempted from the now generalized free trade regime of GATT. Further, there is clear evidence that, despite the expansion of the world trade order, trade policy conceived in purely national terms in some countries has increased rather than decreased in importance. The causes of this can be found in recent trends in social policy and in the characteristics of particular social policy institutions. Yet these exceptions, as will be shown, prove the rule of the conservative welfare function.

The rural and agrarian economic sectors The rural economy is the largest sector to have been shielded on an enduring basis since the Second World War from the general move towards a liberal world trade system. This development began in 1955 with the US government's demand and receipt of a waiver for its agricultural policy (J. H. Jackson 1997a: 58). Since the then highly protectionist agricultural policy of the USA was exempted from the general rules of GATT, it was easy for European countries in the 1950s to attain special exceptions for their rural economies as well (Rieger 2000).

After the European Community institutionalized its Common Agricultural Policy in the 1960s, it became finally clear that the normal GATT rules would not apply to the rural economic sector. Farmers resisted trade liberalization primarily because – especially in bigger countries like the USA, Germany, France and Italy – no effective social protection existed and no income protection programmes had been institutionalized for the mass of small family farmers. The fates of the latter's businesses and households were – in contrast to those of corporate agricultural producers – intimately

[68] Examples are Bates (1989) and contributions in Haggard and Kaufman (1995) and Kornai et al. (2001); on case studies, see also Nelson (1990).

linked. The traditional fallback position of family farming in hard times – production for one's own household – is no longer an option when monetary incomes are needed in order to buy not only food, but also the means of production in the marketplace.

This hole in the national social nets for highly vulnerable producers was filled by ever more intricately refined systems of tariffs, quotas, subsidies and controlled prices. These systems were designed to guarantee farmers – independently of price developments on the world market – just as high and secure an income as social policy had already secured for the industrial workforce and the majority of white-collar employees (Rieger 1995a, b).

This defensive principle has guided the agricultural policy of both the European Union and the United States, and continues to do so today. It has contributed to the continual expansion of systems of intervention and subsidy, such that in the course of several decades the rather paradoxical development emerged that ever more public resources were being spent on an ever shrinking agricultural sector. To effect this market regulation, a comprehensive protective shield had to be organized and also heavily subsidized export channels had to be artificially created, for in nearly all national economies overproduction prevailed for central commodities such as cereal, meat and milk. The world market – and in agriculture participants are primarily developing countries – became a battlefield in which countries fought with export subsidies for market shares, with fatal consequences for their domestic agricultural sector (Rieger 1999b).

Ultimately, consumers in the developed countries bear the public costs of this agricultural policy, and it is predominantly the small group of big agribusinesses that benefits from this system (Rieger 1999b). Yet, as long as governments cannot satisfy the income and security needs of the bulk of the rural economic population most seriously endangered, and as long as no functionally specialized social policy instruments exist which are compatible with an open agricultural market and, above all, with freer foreign trade, an obstinate protectionism will shape the agricultural policies of all developed countries and constitute an enduring source of international conflict.

US trade laws Compared to Western Europe, the extent and volume of social transfers in the USA are rather modest, and eligibility for and receipt of social benefits tend to be governed by much more restrictive regulations. Whereas in Germany, 5 per cent of social outlays go to means-tested benefits, in the USA this share is one-fifth (Gebhardt and Jacobs 1997). This alone reveals the already lower level of publicly provided social security – a distinguishing characteristic of the US welfare state. For our purposes, it remains critically important that, in institutional terms, the US unemployment insurance scheme – with its limited coverage, low-income replacement rate, total neglect of health care benefits, and strictly limited duration of benefit payment – is far less developed than in European countries.[69]

From this structural feature of US policy, it follows that whenever the government wanted to negotiate bilateral trade agreements or new tariff reductions within the

[69] Unemployment insurance in the USA is a state responsibility. Within a federal regulatory framework, states can set the income limits for participation in the compulsory scheme and decide on the details of benefit eligibility and financing (see Eichenhofer 1990). As a rule, eligible individuals have a right to six months of benefit receipt. Of 6.2 million unemployed persons (4.9 per cent of the labour force) in 1997, less than half were insured against unemployment (2.3 million, or 2 per cent of the labour force – US Census Bureau 1999: 430, 433).

GATT framework, it had to promise, actually introduce or expand a separate, targeted social policy for those industrial branches and segments of the labour force that would likely be negatively impacted by increased import competition.[70] In this way, the federal government attempted to dissuade such groups from mobilizing against free trade policies.

Justified by foreign economic conditions, these social benefits for special groups among the unemployed are far more generously endowed than are regular US unemployment benefits: the income replacement rates are higher and the duration of receipt is considerably longer (Decker and Corson 1995: 762). This has been fairly costly to the federal budget, but also heightened opposition to trade agreements among those groups of workers who were not privileged by the projected compensation measures. This particular domestic policy constellation, shaped by social policy programmes that are limited both sectorally and according to the level of benefits available, and which are inspired exclusively by trade policy considerations, has made it far more difficult for the USA to campaign successfully and reliably for trade agreements and GATT rounds than has been the case in European countries (Hudec 1999a; J. H. Jackson 1997b).

Thus far, we have developed the first part of the thesis, according to which social policy and import-restricting trade policy are functionally equivalent in a nation-state framework. Now we will explore the second part of the thesis, which treats the structure and governance of the world trade system.

5 The Social Regulation of International Economic Relations

The negotiations on international economic relations – their outcomes constitute the contemporary world economic order – did not occur in a vacuum, or in an international economics *nirvana*. They were and are conducted by governments solely accountable to the electorates of exclusive democratic welfare states – 'democracy' and 'welfare' both broadly understood. For this reason alone, we can assume that a systemic relationship does exist between the national socio-political agreements of the post-war period – above all the secondary consequences of their institutionalization – and the construction of a more liberal international trade system. In contrast to the regulations and practices of earlier eras, the new system of international trade relations was also to be commensurate to governments' domestic political action constraints and to put them in a position to be able to continue to fulfil their welfare state obligations. Neither GATT and the WTO nor the other organizations and agreements which govern international economic relations were or are institutions that are simply and clearly subjugated to a liberal world trade order.[71] What we can observe instead is that the national *de*regulation of foreign trade is accompanied by extensive international *re*regulation. This development has its point of departure and reference in a

70 Buttressing trade agreements with social policy measures is a peculiarity of US policy which will be discussed in more detail in chapter 3.

71 Cf. this comment by Frieder Roessler (1993: 60), Director of the Legal Affairs Division of the WTO Secretariat: 'There are exceptions in the General Agreement that permit the deviations from the basic GATT provisions necessary to achieve non-economic objectives, both of domestic and foreign policy nature. These exceptions cover such a wide range of situations that it is difficult to imagine any case in which the commitments under the GATT interfere with the efficient attainment of a legitimate non-economic policy goal.'

welfare state constitution of those countries that subordinate themselves to a world economic order. This attempt to pursue not only different but apparently contradictory goals at the same time led to an institutionalized ambivalence in the WTO system which, in our view, is perhaps the most important element in stabilizing the new world trade system as it has evolved since the Second World War.

Institutionalized ambivalence

The analysis of institutionalized ambivalence proceeds from the premise that the legal structure of WTO agreements consists of arrangements of norms and counter-norms which were deliberately created to provide governments with the flexibility of a normatively acceptable management of foreign trade required to deal with rapidly shifting states of economic affairs. It would be sociologically naïve to assume that the persistence of the more liberal trade system depends largely or wholly on the extent of national governments' satisfaction with it. The degree of contentment is only the international relation. The norms – in our case, a strongly bifurcated normative structure – of the WTO system provide the element of international *structure*.

The primary goal of establishing a freer world trade system calls for potentially contradictory norms circumscribing national trade policy. For the political definitions of the world trade system in terms of dominant legal attributes alone would not be flexible enough to provide for the incessantly varying contingencies of trade relations. Norms oriented entirely to dominant, i.e. liberalizing, rules would defeat the functional objectives of the regime. Instead, national trade policy is alternatively oriented to dominant norms and to subsidiary counter-norms also provided for in the normative make-up of the WTO system. This alternation of stances vis-à-vis foreign trade evolved as a political device for helping governments to cope with the contingencies they face as they try to fulfil their welfare state functions. This is lost from view when the trade regime of the WTO is analysed only in terms of its major attributes.

As national economic structures and world trade interact, governments activate different and abstractly contradictory norms to meet the dynamically changing needs of national governance. Only through such structures of liberalizing norms and protectionist counter-norms, we propose, can the various functions of national governments be effectively discharged.[72] Potentially conflicting norms are built into the legal definitions of WTO obligations that provide for normatively acceptable alternations of governmental actions as the state of their domestic trade scenery changes. This is an elementary platform for the alternation between differing governmental functions that

[72] An often repeated argument against this kind of analysis, that tries to make sense of something that is, in the mind of most economists, deeply nonsensical, is that it simply rationalizes a practice that has no merit at all. On the contrary, it is often claimed that the protectionist counter-norms in the WTO agreements *create* the very abuse they claim to alleviate. At heart, this is an argument based on a counterfactual, and is as such beyond empirical verification. The argument of institutionalized ambivalence tries to address an empirical reality; it is not a judgement on certain features of trade policy-making. In addition, we do not want to imply that all is well with safeguards and exceptions. It is perhaps impossible to draw a clear line between legitimate protectionist measures, i.e. those that serve a public function, and those that only attempt to create private rents. However, without the publicly acknowledged need for some social protection against the vicissitudes of foreign trade, private rent-seeking would not have much chance of success. For a more sensible view of this problem, see P. Clark (1997).

makes for institutional ambivalence. In short, the institutionalized ambivalence of GATT and other WTO agreements are *prophylactic* or *preventative* because they enable governments to join the WTO club. It is preparatory because it helps governments to anticipate special kinds of economic contingencies. And it is remedial because it helps governments to cope with troubles after they have arisen.

Safeguards and exceptions The WTO agreements, of which GATT is the most important, contain a series of regulations, mechanisms and arbitration instruments which allow governments to suspend the agreement's norms and commitments either on a permanent or on a temporary basis if certain rules are observed (Benedek 1998b). In Table 2.9 we provide an overview on the range of exceptions to WTO obligations and legitimate safeguard actions.

Under these rules, governments can take measures which contradict GATT/WTO obligations to restore their domestic economic and social stability. Those countries without elaborate, functionally differentiated welfare state structures that effectively protect workers against uninsurable risks, have, as a consequence, to rely on market-closing and anti-competition trade policy measures as the alternative means of offering non-market protection, and are thus allowed to participate in the world trade system to reap the fruits of globalization. Safeguards and exceptions provided by an international regime can serve as selective, temporal remedies, and thus substitute for more drastic and encompassing domestic protection.[73] One of GATT's historic missions – and one the WTO also now pursues – is to render the enduring tension and perpetually latent conflict between domestic, nationally conceived social goals and the desire for a liberal international economic order accessible to an agreed-upon set of regulatory procedures.

The WTO is less a substantive, or materially and legally detailed order than it is a procedural system – in effect, a permanent conference of trade diplomats.[74] At the centre of WTO agreements lie rules concerning *how* common interests of nation-states can be sounded out or determined when a trade conflict arises.[75] In terms of politics, the WTO is a continuous and by now nearly universal system of trade diplomacy, providing the governments concerned with intelligence about the moves of all the states in the system, and with a rich assortment of means to act upon them. Only to a far lesser extent does the treaty contain definite rulings on legal questions or prescriptions

73 To repeat, the central problem is, of course, the danger that domestic groups capture these escape-valve instruments for their own benefit. This very real problem is dealt with below in more detail. At this point, two remarks are in order: first, our discussion about safeguards and exceptions is not about 'good' reasons for having or for not having them, whatever the criterion, but about a hard political reality. Second, domestic groups routinely legitimate their invocation of protectionist measures with recourse basically to welfare state reasons, i.e. exposure of workers to labour market risks. But this is only possible in a context with a low degree of income protection by social policy means.

74 This characterization is not meant to depict a deficiency in the legal norms of the WTO agreements. To strengthen procedures is, rather, an indication of a mature legal order: 'It is significant that most of the provisions of the Bill of Rights are procedural, for it is procedure that marks much of the difference between rule by law and rule by fiat', so states the US Supreme Court in *Wisconsin* v. *Constantineua* (400 US 433 (1971), at p. 436).

75 Art. II:1 of the Agreement Establishing the World Trade Organization states: 'The WTO shall provide the *common institutional framework for the conduct of trade relations among its Members* in matters related to the agreements and associated legal instruments included in the Annexes to this Agreement' – emphasis added.

Table 2.9 WTO safeguards and exceptions

Temporary suspension of obligations			*Permanent exceptions to general obligations*		
Provision	*Mechanism*	*Agreement and Article*	*Provision*	*Mechanism*	*Agreement and Article*
General waivers	Allowing members to ask for permission not to be bound by an obligation. In contrast to the other mechanisms, this requires approval by the WTO Council.	WTO Art. IX	General exceptions	Measures to safeguard public morals, health, laws and natural resources, subject to the requirement that such measures are non-discriminatory and are not a disguised restriction on trade.	GATT Art. XX; GATS Art. XIV
Emergency protection	Temporary protection in cases where imports of a product cause or threaten serious injury to domestic producers of directly competitive products.	GATT Art. XIX	National security	Allowing intervention on national security grounds.	GATT Art. XXI; GATS Art. XIV *bis*; TRIPS Art. 73
Balance of payments	Restrictions on imports to safeguard a country's external financial position.	GATT Art. XII and XVII:b; GATS Art. XII	Renegotiation or modification of schedules	Allowing for the withdrawal of concessions (bound tariff reductions or specific commitments) if compensation is offered to affected members.	GATT Art. XXVIII; GATS Art. XXI
Infant industries	Governmental assistance for economic development, allowing import restrictions to protect infant industries.	GATT Arts. XVIII:a, XVIII:c			
Antidumping	Measures to offset dumping-pricing of exports below what is charged in the home market.	GATT Art. VI			
Countervailing duties	Measures to offset the effect of subsidization that materially injures a domestic industry.	GATT Art. VI			
Special safeguards	Provisions embodied in the Agreement on Agriculture and Textiles and Clothing allowing for actions to be taken to restrict trade.				

Source: Based on Hoekman and Kostecki (2001: 303f.)

of specific punishments to be exacted from contractual partners which violate these rulings (Dam 1970: 4–5; J. H. Jackson 1997a; Hudec 1999b).[76]

WTO agreements implicitly acknowledge that a fundamental, insoluble conflict exists between the welfare-democratic structures of modern societies – including the attendant sense of an almost total social governmental responsibility – on the one hand, and an interdependent world economic order without a centralized decision-making institution on the other. The WTO admits this contradiction and seeks to come to terms with it through a predominantly procedural apparatus. It is thus misleading to claim, as many in the so-called anti-globalization movement do (E. M. Graham 2000; O'Brien et al. 2000), that the WTO has a mandate simply to increase and safeguard free international trade; in effect, to give 'corporate welfare' an international re-inforcement (Nader 2000, 2002). The core function of the WTO is to protect the rights and the duties of the member states more effectively than GATT did, and that is an altogether different remit, since it is still the individual governments of the member states, the majority of which are developing countries, that decide about the governance of their own foreign trade, not the WTO.[77] For this reason, the WTO is not merely a conditioning factor for the functioning of a globalized market economy, constraining national trade policy-making; it also guarantees the autonomous existence of national welfare states by confirming the legitimacy of exclusively national obligations, *economic and non-economic obligations alike*. Conversely, this recognition of the welfare state constitution of its member states enhances the legitimacy of the international organization beyond the legitimacy flowing from its economic function.

In short, the liberal trade regime tail will not wag the national welfare state dog. The rules of the world trade system acknowledge the prior existence and precedence of certain functional prerequisites of the national welfare state – including its exacting status quo bias. As the substance of GATT norms shows, it is readily accepted in international economic relations that the social justice ideals and norms underlying a democratic polity can create special constraints and hence real and hard dilemmas for its economic governance:

76 First of all, the WTO as an international organization does not have the right to initiate proceedings against its members, however gross the violation (Blackhurst 1998). Second, the citizens of member states do not have the right to invoke GATT and other rules of WTO agreements in any domestic court, nor do they have any official access to the dispute settlement proceedings of the WTO system (Hilf and Petersmann 1993; Weiler 2000). Third, countries directly concerned or hurt do not *have* to act: GATT and WTO rules are not mandatory but permissive, thus they authorize, but do not require governments to act (J. H. Jackson 2000a: 25).

77 This function is also stressed in the new Dispute Settlement Mechanism of the WTO regime. Art. 3:2 of the *Understanding on Rules and Procedures Governing the Settlement of Disputes* (Dispute Settlement Understanding – DSU) states: 'The dispute settlement system of the WTO is a central element in providing security and predictability to the multilateral trading system. The Members recognize that it serves to preserve the rights and obligations of Members under the covered agreements . . . .' However, the DSU states as 'the first objective of the dispute settlement mechanism . . . to secure the withdrawal of the measures concerned if these are found to be inconsistent with the provisions of any of the covered agreements' (Art. 3:7). Still, as the *Annual Report* of the WTO for the year 2001 is at pains to point out with regard to recommendations or rulings of DSU panels that call for the removal or modification of the measure in dispute, 'such action is not liberalization as such – given the measure's status of incompatibility with the WTO agreements – but effective market-opening *sometimes* obtains because the measures have been in place for years or even decades' (at p. 27; emphasis added).

> The contracting parties recognize that, as a result of domestic policies directed towards the *achievement and maintenance of full and productive employment or towards the development of economic resources*, a contracting party may experience a high level of demand for imports involving a threat to its monetary reserves. . . . Accordingly, a contracting party otherwise complying with the provisions of this article shall not be required to withdraw or modify restrictions on the ground that a change in those policies would render unnecessary restrictions which it is applying under this Article. (GATT Article XII:3 (d); emphasis added)

In GATT as in other WTO agreements, detailed precautions were taken to regulate *how* countries may deal with conflicts between the national and international levels. The rules of GATT thus entail not only incomplete and strictly limited renunciations of sovereignty on the part of contracting parties, but also positive measures intended to preserve sovereignty and autonomy.[78] There are numerous indications that point to precisely this vertical synchronization, facilitated by GATT, of the transformation from industrial societies to welfare states and the creation of an international economic regime, as being responsible for the remarkable stability of the new liberal system of international trade, and for thus making GATT membership a coveted, and not dreaded status, most of all for developing countries.[79] This is all the more surprising as it is those very international norms that are well known for being rarely observed (Claude 1981).[80]

No one could have expected that the many tariff concessions and partial negations of national sovereignty which occurred during the eight negotiating rounds of GATT would turn into the most stable and most observed of all international commitments.[81] Presumably, the main reason for GATT's (relatively) conflict-free implementation is the main Western signatory states' generous and extensive socio-political systems, which, as well-established institutions independent of trade policy, help affected persons and groups to overcome the negative consequences of certain essentially foreign-driven changes for their living conditions and life chances – quite outside the trade policy sphere. Moreover, developing countries without such structures were not punished if they had to take recourse to import-blocking measures when important strata of their populations became exposed to unexpected shocks.

Thus a further factor to which the surprisingly unproblematic nature of GATT's development could be attributed is that its regulations and provisions are counterbalanced and thus relativized by articles which allow governments to deviate – under certain circumstances – from GATT rules, as long as they follow prescribed procedure. The ideal type safety valve in GATT and the WTO is the emergency escape clause. Yet, this regime also offers other mechanisms designed to make it possible for governments to virtually buy time for coming to terms with the sometimes rather disastrous consequences of international interdependency.

78 For a detailed enquiry into this double nature of GATT, see Finlayson and Zacher (1981).

79 Ruggie (1982) thus speaks of the 'embedding' of GATT in national welfare state contexts – of 'embedded liberalism'.

80 Cf. also Hudec (1999a: 163) on the quality of international jurisdiction: 'International legal arrangements have relatively more in common with the laws of primitive societies studied by anthropologists, in which litigation is still emerging as a rather tenuous alternative to dispute resolution by force.'

81 Writing in 1990, Moynihan noted that 'the General Agreement on Tariffs and Trade adjudicates international disputes by the hour. If such disputes seem marginal today, it may be remembered that for centuries European powers routinely went to war over trade issues' (1990: 156).

Safety valves for national welfare state concerns Escape clauses are intended to guarantee the fundamental validity of the norms of liberal trade policy. They reflect the fact that the concrete results of the international economic policy of comprehensive liberalization can radically restrict the ability of governments to set self-defined social or other non-economic goals and to fulfil their welfare state responsibilities. Escape clauses provide a legitimate and lawful procedure according to which governments may suspend their international commitments temporarily and in a regulated fashion (Finger 1996; J. H. Jackson 1997a: 175–211; Romero 1999). To perceive them as just 'holes and loopholes', as Hoekman and Kostecki (2001: 303–45) do, is to miss an essential point.

Because of escape and similar clauses, governments are no longer forced to make a hard choice as to whether they should give priority to national or international obligations. Under the democratic and parliamentary conditions of the quintessentially exclusive nation-state, no doubt can arise concerning the outcome of such a conflict – namely the priority of domestic preferences. Hence, the importance of the existence of such a safety valve cannot be overestimated. Escape clauses acknowledge that even though a nation as a whole may indeed profit from freer trade over the long term, specific population groups may suffer – or consider it likely that they will suffer – significant negative effects in the short term.[82] These escape clauses, then, as a matter of fact are *not* designed to deal with 'exceptional' cases of 'unfair trade' or 'social dumping'. Rather, they are conceived for the *normal* course of international trade – precisely, and quite ironically, for those shifts in the flow of goods that are supposed to occur in the wake of utilizing comparative advantages.

Basic economics tells us that in general equilibrium any action or policy of national authorities may affect international trade flows. If a member believes that another member's policy impairs its enjoyment of prior concessions, it can bring this charge before a panel. No element of national policy is immune from such an intervention, since the 'nullification and impairment' clause of the GATT (Article XXIII:1) explicitly states that no violation by another party is necessary for the complaining party to bring a case. The founders of GATT recognized that however 'obligations' may be worded, a member government could always find a way to restrict imports without violating these obligations. Thus the drafters of the GATT rules made it possible for dispute settlement to occur in *any* case in which the complaining party was being denied benefits to which the agreement entitled him. What this nullification and impairment clause in effect achieves is to ensure the status quo in the sense that only the gains from increased international trade are accepted, whereas any negative turn in the state of foreign trade affairs can legitimately be used to press for 'compensation'. If a country's industry becomes more competitive in the domestic market through, for example, more efficient public retraining programmes for older workers, and thus

[82] It should not be forgotten that the boost to national welfare expected from the international division of labour can fail to materialize due to reasons that have nothing to do with free trade. First, free trade in itself merely provides a formal framework, or an opportunity structure. If it is not taken advantage of in practice – which is by no means assured – it produces no added value and does not function as an engine of growth. Second, the 'destruction' which a transnational market economy can inflict on traditional industrial structures and economic conditions is 'creative' only under special conditions – conditions that are not provided by the free market alone. The most important framework condition, which may inhibit as well as support creative destruction, is of course the regulatory framework of the welfare state. Other major factors are culture and domestic power relations.

reduces the market share of foreign companies, that would constitute a legitimate case of 'nullification and impairment'.

Hence, to all intents and purposes, GATT rules can effectively neutralize both comparative (country-specific) and competitive (firm-specific) advantages. Carried out consistently, the WTO rules as they now stand could actually be used to effect a complete stoppage of foreign trade. Article XIX of GATT, the archetypal escape clause, stipulating general exceptions to the rule of non-discrimination, is predicated on the recognition that even a small rise in imports can create big political problems for governments and thus unleash protectionist reactions. Article XIX Paragraph 1(a) of GATT runs as follows:

> If, as a result of unforeseen developments and of the effects of the obligations incurred by a contracting party under this Agreement, including tariff concessions, any product is being imported into the territory of that contracting party in such increased quantities and under such conditions as to cause or to threaten serious injury to domestic producers in that territory of like or directly competitive products, the contracting party shall be free, in respect of such product, and to the extent and for such time as may be necessary to prevent or remedy such injury, to suspend the obligation in whole or in part or to withdraw or modify the concession.[83]

This provision must create nightmares for every lawyer. When has an 'unforeseen development' occurred? How much of an increase must take place before one legitimately can speak of 'increased quantities'? Can rising imports be determined without a doubt to be the decisive cause of slumping sales and hence employment problems of domestic firms? Or, rather, is not the increase in imports the consequence of a competitive failure, the causes of which lie in management decisions, organizational arrangements, personnel management, etc.? Or is the increase simply the result of the devaluation of a foreign against the domestic currency? How can 'like products' be distinguished from products which are less 'like' without inviting acrimonious conflict? How can one in any objective way define the time frame during which governments should be allowed to undertake offsetting interventions?

It is thus not at all surprising that there have been numerous conflicts about the application of this Article in GATT as well as ever-recurring doubts about both its actual effectiveness and the potential for abuse that it has introduced. At the same time, however, there has been a more or less constant expansion in the procedures through which conflicts of this kind can be addressed and resolved – from the notification obligations of member states impacted by defensive trade practices, to the increase in arbitration arenas, to the legitimation of counter-measures. Hence, there are good reasons to believe that it is the very fact of these conflicts, and not their absence, their vigour or their gentleness, that makes for an increase rather than a decrease in the adjustment and expansion of a more liberal international economic society. Because they are based on an essentially ambivalent legal structure, a normative system embracing opposite values without trying to force a solution, conflicts in

83 Since its ratification by the original signatory states, GATT has been amended and expanded numerous times. Its fundamentally ambivalent structure – especially with regard to the unresolved relationship between its trade policy prohibitions and mandates and the reservations and exceptions it grants to national welfare states – is preserved in the 'new' GATT as well. The latter became part of the WTO following the Uruguay Round of 1994 (cf. Odell 2000).

such an environment can fulfil a number of positive determinate functions: a balance of opposing values can be established and maintained, antagonists can be bound into a common frame of reference, and the rational elements in the management of rapid social change can be increased.[84]

Based on its wording alone, Article XIX seems to be about neutralizing the effects expected from trade liberalization – namely, changes in the flow of goods which better correspond to the comparative advantages of individual countries and thus increase the welfare of all nations. Obviously, the status quo orientation of the conservative welfare function – which underlies fundamental governmental behaviour – is opposed to the dynamic which results from the international division of labour. Yet exporting countries that increase their market share in importing countries do precisely what free trade theory and GATT's international trade policy say they should do: their firms produce better and less expensive products more efficiently. The markets reward this and increase their sales opportunities. To punish these firms and their national economies would mean to disadvantage precisely those industries whose orientation and performance correspond with the meaning and purpose of international trade policy guarantees. Nevertheless, there are good reasons to grant such escape clauses because they come with a cost. Article XIX:2 stipulates:

> Before any contracting party shall take action pursuant to the provision of paragraph 1 of this Article, it shall give notice in writing to the CONTRACTING PARTIES as far in advance as may be practicable and shall afford the CONTRACTING PARTIES and those contracting parties having a substantial interest as exporters of the product concerned an opportunity to consult with it in respect of the proposed action. . . . In critical circumstances, where delay would cause damage which it would be difficult to repair, action under paragraph 1 of this article may be taken provisionally without prior consultation, on the condition that consultation shall be effected immediately after taking such action.[85]

Escape clauses such as Article XIX thus map out for governments *how* they can and should react to problems resulting from greater economic openness and the social disruption it may bring. They acknowledge that the governments of countries exposed to increasing import competition may face extraordinary pressures – namely, those resulting from national welfare guarantees in the absence of broadly designed social insurance mechanisms. As a result, these clauses serve to demarcate a range of permissible responses and to dissuade such governments from taking recourse to internationally and – in the long run – nationally much more deleterious but politically more popular traditional instruments of trade policy aimed exclusively at serving domestic interests, such as quotas and high tariffs.

An important function of this GATT provision is to hold governments accountable for the international consequences of their making use of this exemption clause. Their action – or in some cases inaction – could be challenged in the arbitration arenas of GATT, now the WTO, and also be sanctioned by allowing the affected countries to impose countervailing duties at the end of the day. This aspect of the institutionalization of a dispute settlement instrument limits potential abuse of escape clauses. What

84 For a general discussion of the functions of conflicts, see Coser (1956).

85 Since GATT, before the WTO agreements came into force, was not an international organization, the term CONTRACTING PARTY referred to its sole decision-making body.

at first appears to be a formal legal deficit proves actually to be a procedurally secured gain for the substance of a liberal trade system. To further the overarching and long-term goal of a general liberalization of trade, the GATT system relies in many respects on often very cumbersome and complex procedural rules for resolving short-term conflicts about non-economic ends.

For the same reason, GATT abstains from strengthening the legal position of those actors who are directly involved in international trade – i.e. firms. The spectre of states besieged by private lawsuits for violations of international economic law is enough to bring about a veritable conspiracy of silence among the members of the very exclusive WTO club – namely governments – and to close tightly the door to non-governmental actors (Brand 1996/97; Davey 2000). Instead, international economic law only targets governments, attempting to subjugate their behaviour to an international order (Kessie 2000). The most important reason for this, and one that is regularly recognized by national courts, is the following: governments should retain negotiating latitude in foreign (economic) policy such that they have a free hand in domestic distributional conflicts. The central means of bringing conflicting social and economic interests into an ever newly sought equilibrium is not law, and least of all international economic law, but, rather, national social politics, which has a flexible policy of concessions at its centre.

If we look at the *political* value of dealing with increased competition and, perhaps, deflecting protectionist pressures, much the same is true of the additional mechanism that governments can use to buy time for coming to terms with the consequences of a liberal world trade order. This mechanism is the initiation of an antidumping or countervailing duty case.

Safeguards at work A theme that has accompanied international economic relations from the outset and led regularly to vehement conflicts is 'dumping'. Disputes about exactly what constitutes dumping and how it should be dealt with have repeatedly brought GATT to the brink of collapse. And antidumping is at present the most contentious issue in the WTO. The regulation that deals with this has developed into an elaborate and highly complex system of national and international surveillance, investigation and negotiation.[86]

Dumping allegations constitute probably the most common subject of conflict in international economic relations. Yet it is not precisely clear either when dumping obtains, in theory or in practice, or whether dumping truly constitutes a problem (Hudec 1999a: 143). David Hume (1788a, b) ascertained long ago that dumping practices in fact favour domestic consumers by allowing them to purchase goods at lower prices, and that they bring advantages to domestic producers either in the form of cheaper raw materials or by allowing them to devote their energies to a more profitable business. He argued further that any 'real' dumping – i.e. the selling of goods below their cost price – is ultimately self-defeating. To the extent that no one will act in a self-destructive fashion, Hume concluded, dumping is not a rational strategy that can be sustainably pursued.[87]

[86] For a short and succinct introduction, see Kerr (2001). For an exhaustive treatment, see Viner (1966).

[87] Thus the rhetorical question from Milton Friedman: 'What would you rather be, a dumper or a dumpee? A dumper is someone who sells something below cost. A dumpee is somebody who buys something below cost' (cited in Krauss 1997: 20).

Nonetheless, government measures against dumping – in response to complaints by individual firms or entire economic sectors – have been an endemic problem in both national and international economic policy. However, it may be appropriate to contend that antidumping instruments form an important mediating interface between economic systems characterized by an enormous disparity in social and environmental standards and different approaches to industrial policy. The complex and lengthy procedures for fact-finding, hearings and negotiations, one can argue, buy time for the firms concerned and thus enable them to determine their actual competitive position and to improve it in a targeted manner. Most importantly, they can do so without receiving everlasting protectionist support. Further, because measures against dumping at home and abroad are essentially – and often loudly – contested political actions, they sharpen public consciousness regarding the social and environmental framework of certain systems of production, both with regard to their positive and their negative effects.

Hence, what at first glance appears to be a dilatory mechanism actually turns out to have a deeper meaning because there is a high chance that such measures will be terminated. For this reason Hudec (1999a: 123) can conclude: 'Temporizing has a bad name that is not really deserved.' In addition, and perhaps even more important, it is by admitting and bringing them out into public discussion, and not by suppressing conflicts over dumping, that the integrity of the international economic society is maintained.

A more rigorous and internationally coordinated antidumping policy, together with more powerful institutions to combat 'dumping', would in all probability have opened up more sources for additional strife than it could have contributed to solving these systemic conflicts.[88] From the point of view of most nation-states, both the mobility of the most sought-after factors of production and trade's promise of equalizing factor prices appear as threats to the domestic status quo. In an extremely heterogeneous international economic society, intensified transnational trade harbours considerable potential for friction. Many problems that are characterized as dumping or unfair competition are essentially problems which originate in very disparate, long-established social and economic orders. Most important here are differences in the quantity and quality of the social regulation of markets and production processes, which very often appear, viewed from the outside, patently idiosyncratic. But their peculiar and perplexing nature merely reflects the fact that they embody important compromises between domestic groups and are thus essential for political stability.

At the same time, however, given the seamless web of the highly integrated national economies, there is no social regulation that does not in one way or another affect foreign trade. Of particular importance are those measures that in effect relieve companies from some of the social costs of the employment contract, e.g. a publicly subsidized maternity leave programme, or early retirement schemes that enable companies to get rid of their older workers (Langille 1996). Thus one means of achieving a more level playing field between two systems consists in accusing the less expensive system of production of dumping or of unfair trade,

[88] In fact, the Uruguay Round brought less, not more discipline to antidumping, as will be discussed in more detail below. And this means there can be too much of a good thing.

and demanding offsetting measures such as extra tariffs, or at least compensatory payments.[89]

Antidumping measures are not simply old protectionism in new clothes – if they are effectively fenced in. It makes more sense to argue that they provide a necessary safety valve for countries that practice a higher, or sometimes just a different standard of social and economic regulation and thus may suffer penalties for doing so at the hands of 'dirty competition' from less-developed countries or from countries with a different regulatory system.

Empirical investigations have revealed, for example, that 675 out of the 900 dumping complaints submitted to the European Commission during the 1980s were settled by the importer 'voluntarily' raising prices (Senti 1986: 87). In the United States, too, the mere threat of an antidumping proceeding suffices to cause importers to orient themselves to domestic prices or to accept 'voluntary' import quotas. Naturally, this method of reducing tensions is associated with considerable turbulence and expense. Yet, despite the circuitousness of international and especially national antidumping proceedings, these have made it possible to uphold the fundamental rules of GATT.

'Hypocrisy is the homage vice pays to virtue', wrote François Duc de La Rochefoucauld. Thus, despite the fact that many dumping allegations mask either homegrown problems or problems grounded in different constitutional, or quasi-constitutional (that is, welfare state) structures, their articulation always presumes that the basic norms and the ethos of free trade hold, acknowledging them in principle. Moreover, firms and governments alike must observe certain rules if they are to have a realistic chance of undercutting the competition via dumping allegations. Both antidumping and countermeasures can be challenged in WTO arenas, and a country must provide compensation to the states affected if its import restrictions are later judged to be unfounded. Just as in the case of escape clauses, here, too, the key is whether politicians *in the long term* are able to make progress towards opening their economies to trade. Again, what appears at first glance to contradict the spirit of free trade turns out, in a longer-term perspective, to be a condition of its realization.

89 The most recent example was the US move to introduce steep levies on foreign steel-makers in March 2002. The US steel industry argues that it is mostly because they employ about 140,000 workers, and are saddled in addition with the enormous burden of paying the health care and other costs of roughly 600,000 retirees. Their European counterparts do not have to bear this burden. Thanks to more generous and more tightly knit public benefit systems, European companies are free from such costs and are thus internationally more competitive. As an alternative to the introduction of tariffs and quotas, US steel companies proposed that the government assume at least $10 billion of the 'legacy costs' – the costs of retirees' pensions and health care (Pfanner 2002; Sanger and Kahn 2002; Will 2002).

As to the background of the increasing problems of US steel companies, there are, first, 'legacy costs', since steelworkers, because of their strong unionization, consistently earned over 80 per cent more than the average manufacturing wage, and hourly employment costs rose at a much higher rate than industry's output (Ignatius 2002). European steel producers argue that they modernized their industries, whereas the USA largely stood still (Fuller and Pfanner 2002). Second, on 13 March 2002, according to a report from Reuters (*International Herald Tribune*, 14 March 2002, p. 15), the US Trade Representative, Robert Zoellick, explicitly linked the strong dollar to the new tariffs. It is very unlikely, however, that a shift in stance over the dollar is on the cards just to protect manufacturers. Finally, with regard to the 'temporizing' effect of bringing the case to the WTO, it is estimated that litigation will take up to three years. The safeguard provisions of US trade law under which the tariffs were imposed allow such measures for only four years (Pfanner 2002).

The WTO and the transformation of the national welfare state

Does this reading of the origins and development of GATT also apply to the so-called new constitution of world trade? Or did the new system of world trade, centred around the WTO since 1995, free itself from its welfare state ties to such an extent that we may no longer speak of an 'embeddedness' of domestic welfare statism in the world trade order – and vice versa – as Ruggie (1994) and many other critics now claim? The opposite is true, though. The world trade order is still embedded – albeit in substantially changed welfare state contexts. And with this change, escape clauses and other safeguard mechanisms have come to play a completely new role.

There can be no doubt that the WTO has ushered in an increase in the political independence and institutional weight of a liberal world trade order vis-à-vis national governments. Legal scholars point to a much more vigorous role of international regime norms in global economic governance structures.[90] The conclusion of the Uruguay Round in 1994 not only brought progress in the opening of markets and a reform of dispute settlement procedures, it also transferred GATT into the new organizational and legal framework of the WTO (Lowenfeld 1994; Croome 1995; A. Reich 1996/97; Jackson and Sykes 1997; Preeg 1999). As a result, the world trade system became more than a mere agreement among nations – it gained a new ability to act as an organization. Whereas the administration of the old GATT had been limited to its Secretariat, which for all intents and purposes became active only in the wake of agreement on a new negotiating round, the new GATT has in the WTO acquired its own agency with dedicated personnel and significantly enhanced funding. However, compared to its sister organizations of global governance, and with regard to its declared function, its funding seems woefully inadequate, as Table 2.10 shows.

The US share of the annual budget is about $12 million out of $75 million (15.7 per cent – figures are for the year 2000). The US contribution to the WTO is much smaller than to other international organizations, including the OECD – the Organization for Economic Cooperation and Development – ($55 million), the ILO – the International Labour Organization – ($54 million), and the Organization of American States ($51 million – data in Schott 2000: 11). After all, the WTO is entrusted with the ongoing task of independently promoting international trade, supervising the observation of the rules governing this trade and adjudicating trade conflicts.[91]

90 Bederman (2001: 497) sees the WTO as 'the paradigmatic "centralizing" agency and as a solvent of traditional state sovereignty'. Shell (1995: 833) states that 'within the legal academy, the new WTO system represents a stunning victory for international trade legalists'. McGinnis and Movsesian (2000: 512) celebrate the WTO as 'the world trade constitution' and claim that 'in promoting both free trade and accountable government, the WTO reflects many of the insights that inform our own Madisonian Constitution'. On the WTO as an international organization – a status GATT did not have – see A. O. Krueger (1998).

91 As to the characterization of the WTO as an international organization, one has to note that it is the Ministerial Conference, a plenum exclusively composed of representatives of all the member states, not the Secretariat and the Director-General, which 'shall carry out the functions of the WTO and take actions necessary to this effect' (Article IV:1 of the Agreement Establishing the World Trade Organization). For the legal foundation of the supervisory functions of the WTO, see Annex 2, Trade Policy Review Mechanism, of the Agreement Establishing the World Trade Organization, and for adjudication, see the Understanding on Rules and Procedures Governing the Settlement of Disputes. The legal texts of all WTO agreements can be found at http://wto.org/english/docs_e/legal_e/final-e.

Table 2.10 Staff and annual budget of selected international economic organizations (1996)

Organization	*Number of staff*	*Annual budget $USm*
World Bank	6,781[a]	1,375
Food and Agriculture Organization of the United Nations (FAO)	5,100	600[b]
United Nations Development Programme (UNDP)	4,914[c]	1,400[c]
International Monetary Fund (IMF)	2,577[d]	475
Organization for Economic Cooperation and Development (OECD)	2,322[e]	330
International Labour Organization (ILO)	2,286	290
World Food Programme (WFP)	2,069[f]	1,200
International Civil Aviation Organization (ICAO)	759	60
World Intellectual Property Organization (WIPO)	630	121
World Trade Organization (WTO)	513	94[g]

[a] The staff figure includes an estimated 1,100 long-term consultants
[b] Sum of regular budget ($325 million) and field programme expenditure (mainly technical assistance)
[c] 1995 – the budget figure includes the core programme, support budget, extra-budgetary items
[d] Measured as effective staff years
[e] Includes 350 consultants, experts, fellows and temporary staff
[f] Plus 2,178 temporary staff employed mainly in emergency operations
[g] Includes $3.7 million for the Appellate Body of the dispute settlement mechanism. The figure of 513 for the staff includes the staff servicing the Appellate Body, but not the seven members of the Body

Source: Blackhurst (1998: 40)

Moreover, unlike GATT, the WTO features much more organizational continuity. The WTO's General Council is a primary organ, made up – just as the Ministerial Conference meeting biannually – of representatives of all member states interested in participating, and also serves as a Dispute Settlement Body. The WTO is thus not only charged with overseeing the implementation of the results of the Uruguay Round, but also with developing initiatives in various realms of international regulation, which had been handled up until then by the GATT regulatory framework and were not conclusively dealt with in the Uruguay Round. This 'inbuilt agenda' applies, above all, to the service sector,[92] the protection of intellectual property,[93] the agricultural[94] and textile sectors[95] and foreign direct investments[96] – all Agreements date to 1994. With regard to existing agreements, GATT's contracting parties must not only submit regular reports on their trade policy, but also subject themselves at regular intervals to a Policy Review.[97]

The reform of the procedures for the settlement of trade conflicts produced an institutional apparatus which 'is unique in international law in its juridical and legalistic

92 General Agreement on Trade in Services.
93 Agreement on Trade-Related Aspects of Intellectual Property Rights.
94 Agreement on Agriculture and Agreement on the Application of Sanitary and Phytosanitary Measures.
95 Agreement on Textiles and Clothing.
96 Agreement on Trade-Related Investment Measures.
97 The administration of the Trade Policy Review Mechanism is counted among the main functions of the WTO. The General Council also doubles up as the Trade Policy Review Body, as arranged for in Arts. III:4 and IV:4 of the Agreement Establishing the World Trade Organization.

system for disputes' (J. H. Jackson 2000d: 179f.). The first and most significant innovation was to make it just about impossible for a member state to block the establishment of an adjudication panel. This was meant to strengthen the multilateralism of the world trade order and to put a halt to the increasing tendency by countries to negotiate bilaterally to settle their disputes, as reflected in Section 301 of the US Trade Act of 1974 (R. A. Cass 1991). In addition to this mandate, the contracting parties introduced an Interim Review of the Dispute Settlement Panel's Interim Report and created an Appellate Body.

This juridification of arbitration instruments is the counterpart, and above all counterweight, to a further innovation: not only the setting up of a dispute settlement panel, but also the approval of a panel report, including the 'verdict', can be blocked only by consensus among all member states, thus introducing the principle of a negative consensus. A third innovation is the quasi-automatic course of such proceedings: the maximum duration of panel proceedings is limited to six months and the Dispute Settlement Body supervises the implementation of the panel's recommendation. Fourthly and finally, Article XIX itself was elaborated more precisely and its function of protecting national autonomy was strengthened; that is, its disciplining features were deliberately reduced.[98] In addition, the parties agreed to eliminate all 'grey zone measures' within four years, to set a four-year limit on import-restricting measures and to create a three-year waiting period before exporting countries can pursue countermeasures. In return, 'interim' measures were legalized and each member was allowed to make use of one exception through to the end of 1999.[99]

It has become quite clear, however, and not just because of the conflicts in Seattle, that the free trade hopes invested in the WTO have not materialized. In a certain sense, the WTO is more of an expression of the problems with which the world trade order is confronted than it is their solution.[100] Its built-in agenda consists of vexing problems that had to be left aside during the eight long years of the Uruguay Round so that this round could be concluded at all. Even though the Iron Curtain fell during this era and the nations of the socialist Second World, now saddled by complex transition problems, joined those of the First and Third Worlds, it was not merely unique, epochal historical issues that burdened the Uruguay Round. A quarter of a century earlier, the Kennedy Round had lasted four years (1963–7) and the Tokyo Round six years (1973–9). The WTO thus represents an attempt to place the governance of the world trade order itself on a new footing, because with nearly 150 member states, the old system of GATT rounds no longer promised to be effective. But as a rule-making body the WTO seems to be a failure, and in its adjudication function it appears to achieve the opposite of what was intended. In some sense the WTO has become a victim of its own success (Ruggiero 2000: xiv).

Strengthening international economic law: the trouble with success

To understand the WTO system, it is not only important to take into account *how* the rules are made – a point stressed by Finger and Dhar (1992: 8) – but also *who* is

98 Agreement on Safeguards (AS).

99 On this basis, the European Union restricted imports of Japanese autos (Benedek 1998a: 30).

100 On the ostensible masterpiece of the new WTO system, its new arbitration mechanism, consider Hudec's assessment (1999a: 126): 'It would not be the last time that governments would turn to strengthened dispute settlement as a substitute for failed substantial negotiations.'

making the rules for exactly what purpose. The main problem with the work on the new relevance of international law to world politics consists in the assumption that to have rules is per se a good thing. But this is to be doubted. It is evidently misleading to assess international economic law only in relation to the function it has of binding states together, and not also in relation to its function as an instrument of state interest and as a vehicle of transnational purposes arising out of purely domestic concerns. That was our point when we discussed the institutionalized ambivalence of the GATT/WTO system.

Rules *can* control power, but in order to fulfil this function, certain conditions need to be satisfied. Most important is the type of rules: do they impose behavioural *limits*, or do they provide *sanction* for a certain course of action? The general trend in the evolution of the international economic law first of the GATT system and then of the WTO was never solely to impose constraints on national practices in foreign trade policy-making, but also to provide *international* sanction for some of them – that is, for the less damaging ones. Thus the elaboration and ever-increasing sophistication of utilizing GATT and other WTO rules is also an exercise in applying economic and political power, not simply in its control. Rules that allow a wide range of national protective practices are also part of the solution of keeping trade freer in general, and not just part of the problem of the international control of trade matters.

The real problem, however, lies deeper. It originates in a changing domestic scene in which welfare statism in the developed countries undergoes a momentous transformation – and correspondingly it has become more difficult for developing and transition countries to install encompassing income maintenance programmes. This transformation, mostly brought about by developments internal to welfare states, is more conducive to trade-restricting than to market-opening policies.

This trend can most clearly be seen in the significant shift from safeguard provisions that impose unambiguous restrictions on governments seeking relief from their international obligations, thereby stressing that such action is exceptional, to provisions that are not associated with such autonomy costs. One result of this is the spread of antidumping measures to developing countries since the early 1990s.[101] The underlying logic guiding the creation of the original GATT rules was as follows: if the circumstances under which a particular country may impede trade are strictly specified, and obligations are imposed on those trade partners losing market shares, that country will block trade less often. However, for this logic to work out, three additional elements need to be ensured. First, the specifications of the circumstances must provide some basis for *limiting, not merely enabling* action. Second, those in charge of administering the rules have to be sympathetic to preserving the openness of the international system and are therefore hesitant to impose trade restrictions (Finger and Dhar 1992: 18). Third, trade policy-making must be free from immediate social concerns, that is, *political* apprehensions about the possible or actual repercussions of market-opening policies must be dealt with effectively by some non-trade policy means. As the dramatic rise of antidumping actions in the 1990s indicates, these conditions are no longer satisfied. From the late 1980s to 2000 the average number of countries

[101] This should not surprise anyone because governments sell trade liberalization by promising prompt and effective relief from unfairly traded and injurious imports. For this reason, the trade liberalization generated by the Uruguay Round agreements has encouraged adoption of antidumping laws in many developing and transition countries.

routinely initiating antidumping procedures has more than quadrupled, from five to more than twenty. The average annual number of cases has almost doubled, from 113 in 1987–8 to 203 in 1995–7 (Messerlin 2000: 159).

The reason that renegotiations and safeguard actions under Article XIX GATT are, in relative terms, now much less used than they were in the first three decades of GATT's existence is simple: another article provides less burdensome GATT cover. In Table 2.11 we show that the scale of use of antidumping measures is a magnitude larger than the scale of use of renegotiations and emergency actions has ever been. Simple public choice reasoning explains why antidumping became the safeguard measure of choice for governments (Finger et al. 2001: 5). First, antidumping provisions allow governments to pick out particular exporters. GATT/WTO rules do not require multilateral application. Second, governments can act unilaterally. GATT/WTO rules require neither compensation nor renegotiation. Third, domestic rules followed by governments in order to decide on the existence of an injury tend to be softer than those under Article XIX GATT. Fourth, the rhetoric of foreign unfairness provides a vehicle for building a political case for protection.[102] Fifth, the threat of formal action under the antidumping law provides leverage to force an exporter to accept a 'voluntary export restraint'.

In particular, with regard to the celebrated shift from 'power-oriented trade diplomacy' to 'rules-oriented diplomacy' (Jackson 1990), the results of the Uruguay Round have been greatly oversold. The WTO could not reverse the much stronger momentum that trade remedies – led by antidumping – have, compared to market-opening trade negotiations.[103] At fault is not, however, the new policy of legalism by itself, but domestic changes in welfare state regimes and the endemic problems of social instability in developing and transition countries. As to the former, the process has begun in the mid-1980s with the declining effectiveness of national social security systems in maintaining a firewall between the sphere of market-generated incomes and competitive labour markets on the one side, and the sphere of a societal membership backed up by public transfer and intervention schemes on the other.

In the scholarly debates there is no agreement on what exactly caused the decline of compensatory social policies and the realignment of social policy with labour markets – the rise of 'incentive compatibility' became the dominant measuring rod for the legitimacy of protective social policies – but the fact itself, the decline of social security broadly understood, is hardly disputed.[104] Replacement levels of income maintenance programmes have been lowered, the 'private' elements in pension policies have been increased, means tests have become more restrictive, 'workfare' programmes replaced 'welfare' programmes, and so on. The general tendency in all welfare states is to subordinate social policies to labour markets. Since our analysis of the move towards freer trade stressed the compensatory role of generalized welfare state regimes,

102 Frank Taussig, a professor of economics at Harvard and the first chairman of the US Tariff Commission, once noted that 'competition of any sort is unwelcome enough; competition from foreigners seems always to be regarded with particular dread' (Taussig and White 1931: 196).

103 The litigation explosion in the WTO dispute settlement system can also be seen as a decline in the general willingness of governments to subject themselves to the strictures of the new policy of legalism in the WTO framework. As Weiler (2000: 3) noted, 'measured in quantitative terms, panel and the Appellate Body activity under the new dispute settlement understanding can be described as frenetic'.

104 For a broad range of conflicting views, see Pierson (2001: 410–56).

Table 2.11 Different types of safeguard provision and their use

Instrument and agreement	*Frequency of use*
Waivers under Art. XXV GATT	113 (through March 1994) 40 in force (August 2000)
Waivers under Art. IX WTO	none
Emergency protection under Art. XIX GATT	150 actions in the years 1950–94 (3.4 per year) 49 actions in the years 1995–May 2000 (9 per year)
Measures for Balance of Payment Purposes	
• Art. VII – General Provision	3 countries had such restrictions in place at least on time during the period 1974–86
• Art. XVIII:b – Developing Countries	Used by 24 countries at least once during 1974–86 (total of 3,434 restrictions)
Releases from bindings to pursue infant industry protection, Art. XVIII	9 countries in 47 years
Antidumping duties	1,148 investigations from July 1985 to 1992 1,105 measures from 1995 to June 2000
Countervailing duties	187 actions from July 1985 to 1992 110 measures from 1995 to August 2000
Special safeguards under the Agreement on Textiles and Clothing	31 requests (1995–7)
General exceptions under Art. XX GATT	Notification not required; between 1974 and 1987, 6 developing countries notified quantitative restrictions, covering 131 products
National security exceptions under Art. XXI GATT	1 country (Thailand) notified under this article; further information not available
Periodic – three year – renegotiations at the initiative of the country desiring to raise a bound tariff rate under Art. XXVIII:1 and XXVIII:5 GATT	207 instances in the years 1955–99
'Special circumstances' renegotiations (requires GATT authorization) under Art. XXVIII:4 GATT	64 instances in the years 1948–2000

Sources: Finger (1998); Hoekman and Kostecki (2001: 307)

we must point to the declining power of the protective function of welfare states as the main reason for the return of restrictive trade policies. The invasive expansion of antidumping and thus the rise of managed, and not free, trade is a direct result of a constellation in which national governments no longer have the political cover of welfare statism with which they used to rebut the demand of domestic groups for constraining socially disruptive import competition. But since there is a wide variation across countries with respect to the scale and scope of protective social policies, we

Table 2.12 Initiations of antidumping procedures by level of economic development (January 1995–June 2000)

Reporting party	*Affected country*			*Total*
	Developed	*Developing*	*Transition*	
Developed	174	340	199	713
Developing	309	352	254	915
Transition	4	2	6	12
Totals	487	694	459	1,640

Source: WTO (http://www.wto.org)

can expect that these variations closely match those of their functional equivalents in protective trade policies.[105]

In the context of effectively functioning welfare states, i.e. of the existence of a secondary system of income maintenance underlying competitive labour markets, the establishment of rules governing international trade permitted trade issues to be discussed and resolved in their own realms, without intruding into other areas of domestic policy-making. However, the more the international trade system now involves countries that have no national systems which efficiently provide income insurance, and the more the new politics of developed welfare states weakens the protective function of social policies in order to increase their 'incentives compatibility', the more we can expect a return to foreign economic policies that are trade restricting and thus bent on reducing import competition.

The rise and near global spread of antidumping is a clear indication of this development, as Table 2.12 shows. In fact, both the weakening of the rules governing safeguard politics under Article XIX GATT and the legal structure of the Antidumping Agreement reflect a basic shift in the GATT/WTO regime. They indicate that the governments agreeing on the new rules can no longer rely on their domestic social policy systems to give them sufficient political opportunity for engaging their countries in a more liberal trade system. Instead, they deliberately weakened the discipline mandated by safeguard actions and thus lowered the costs of protectionism. The Agreement on Safeguards (AS) relaxes three existing disciplinary measures on safeguard actions under Article XIX. First, Article 2:1 AS de facto ignores the Article XIX GATT condition that import surges have to directly and unambiguously result from ongoing trade liberalization. Second, Article 8:3 AS states that exporting countries can no longer claim compensation during the first three years of a safeguard measure – in effect, a postponement of the quasi-renegotiation process demanded by Article XIX:3 GATT through the retaliation process. Third, Article 5:2 AS allows quotas as safeguard measures in a much more discriminatory manner than before. The rationale for relaxing

105 As we pointed out in more detail above, the legal norms of the WTO agreements rely on opposing values and interests. This leads us to expect that trade officials with backgrounds in different national systems of welfare provision will tend to differ in their appraisal of the same legal-economic situation. Hence one basic fact relevant to the litigation explosion in the WTO system is the vastly increased heterogeneity of the international economic society. Also, we should expect that – depending on the social environment of domestic trade policy-making – divergent criteria for the effectiveness of the WTO system would be employed by different trade officials.

the discipline of Article XIX was the competition from antidumping as a low-threshold trade remedy. But the Agreement on Antidumping (AAD)[106] does not impose any serious restraint on national antidumping practices. Instead, it gives governments virtually unrestricted permission to impose import restrictions.[107]

National antidumping proceedings are burdened with the basic problem that industries and their firms are viewed in isolation from the rest of the nation's economy. In such proceedings, consideration is given only to the impact of price competition on the firms immediately concerned, but not to the secondary and – according to free trade theory – positive impact on the manufacturing sector and consumers. No consideration is given either to the subsequent negative consequences of protectionist intervention, such as the redirection of firms' productive energies towards influence activities and rent-seeking.[108] Here, too, then, the conservative welfare function prevails in almost absolute fashion. For example, in conducting its 'fact-finding determinations', the US International Trade Commission (ITC) is prohibited from carrying out not only industry- or sector-wide assessments, but also macro-economic cost-benefit analyses. For this reason, its 'findings' are clearly predetermined (Finger et al. 1982). The notorious punitive tariffs imposed by the ITC on European and Korean steel at the request of US steel producers at the height of the Asian financial crisis in the middle of 1998 amounts to an import ban on certain types of stainless steel, thus bringing about higher prices and an improved competitive position of domestic steel-producing firms. The fact that steel-consuming firms – which would benefit from cheaper imports and the competition unleashed by them – employ thirty times as many people as the steel industry plays no role in the ITC's deliberations (Krauss 1997: 20-23). The ITC similarly fails to take into consideration the fact that tariff hikes granted to affected industries in the wake of antidumping proceedings redistribute income from domestic consumers to protected firms (Gilpin 2000: 91). Securing jobs by means of protectionist intervention is thus a very expensive undertaking.[109]

In terms of public choice, the main problem of national antidumping regulation is that it gives no effective voice to consumers or downstream producers. But also the AAD speaks only of governments, exporters and domestic producers 'of the like product' as 'interested parties',[110] and has an extremely broad range of what constitutes 'injury to domestic industry'. Article 3:4 AAD states:

106 The correct title is Agreement on the Implementation of Article VI of the General Agreement on Tariffs and Trade 1994.

107 Mark Koulen, who took part in the drafting of the new antidumping code of the WTO in the Uruguay Round, noted that the governments involved could not agree on any definite definition of dumping, but seemed to be of one mind in that they all wanted an effective means to manage their foreign trade (Koulen 1995). Peter Clark (1997: 217) noted that the 'domination of the GATT (now WTO) Antidumping Practices Committee by officials of administering authorities creates a bias in the proceedings toward effective administration. Effective does not mean enlightened or even fair. Trade liberalization is not uppermost in the minds of the constabulary.'

108 Cf. Hudec (1999a: 148): 'Economists may know that a 100 percent tariff increase on some products places other domestic producers at a comparative disadvantage, but as long as politicians and constituents do not know that, there is no incentive for compromise and restraint on foreign trade legislation.'

109 Hufbauer and Elliot have calculated that the cost of 'saving' a job through trade policy averages $170,000, and in some industrial branches runs to over $500,000 (1994: 11).

110 However, Article 6:12 AAD stipulates: 'The authorities shall provide opportunities for industrial users of the product under investigation, and for representative consumer organizations in cases where the product is commonly sold at the retail level, to provide information which is relevant to the investiga-

> The examination of the impact of the dumped imports on the domestic industry concerned shall include an evaluation of all relevant economic factors and indices having a bearing on the state of the industry, including actual and potential declines in sales, profits, output, market share, productivity, return on investment, or utilization capacity; factors affecting domestic prices; the magnitude of the margin of dumping; actual and potential negative effects on cash flow, inventories, employment, wages, growth, ability to raise capital or investments. This list is not exhaustive, nor can one or several of these factors necessarily give decisive guidance.

As the history of the US antidumping law shows, antidumping and similar measures can in fact work to keep protectionist interests at bay. From the passage of this law in 1921 through to the end of 1967, the US government had conducted a total of 706 antidumping investigations – all but 75 of them ended with a negative finding (Finger and Dhar 1992: 11f.): that is, no dumping was found. With such an antidumping instrument and the subsequent institutionalization of national systems of income protection, protectionist pressures of particular industries that would, under the old congressional regime of tariff setting, have brought Congress to enact – under the general rubric of a *social* policy – higher tariff rates, could then be diverted into antidumping or escape-clause investigations. Members of Congress could thus avoid the costly blame of not taking care of important constituent interests. Also, the few import restrictions imposed by these 'trade remedies' were more than offset by reductions agreed at the various rounds of GATT tariff negotiations.

However, in the economically more difficult 1970s and with the apparent failure of grand welfare state programmes such as Lyndon B. Johnson's War on Poverty and Richard Nixon's Family Assistance Plan, it became more important to members of Congress to win back a basic instrument to serve their industry constituents. Instead of returning to Congress the control of trade policy-making, Congress opted to continually broaden and strengthen countervailing duties and most of all antidumping measures: 'Each of the changes was made because antidumping, if expanded in a particular way, could fix a pressing political problem. The dominant question was always "How can antidumping be applied to this problem?" The question was never "Is this really a problem caused by dumping?"' (Finger and Dhar 1992: 13). Antidumping became a general mechanism for keeping import prices high enough to prevent 'injury to domestic companies', and a negative finding of the US Trade Representative (USTR) has become a rare event.

In institutional terms, the real test of dumping in a foreign market is a closed domestic market – otherwise the reimportation of domestic goods and arbitrage would eliminate the price differential. This condition is rarely satisfied. Thus it should not come as a surprise that an OECD review of antidumping cases in the United States, the European Union, Australia and Canada showed that 90 per cent of the import sales found to be 'unfair' were completely legal according to domestic competition standards – that is, they would qualify as perfectly 'fair' had a domestic competitor

tion regarding dumping, injury and causality.' This stipulation of a general interest is not thought to be effective. In fact, as the few cases of general interest clauses in domestic antidumping legislation show, they are commonly used to argue *for*, not *against*, protection (Messerlin 2000: 170–1). The core of the problem seems to lie elsewhere: normal business practices allowed for in domestic practice are not allowed for in transnational transactions, thus establishing an institutionalized bias against exporters.

made the same sale (OECD 1996; Messerlin 2000: 163).[111] With the spread of antidumping actions to developing and transition countries, this measure is not simply used as a mechanism of protection but more broadly as a tool to reshape the geography of international economic activity in patterns that do not reflect comparative advantage (Moran 2000: 234). This result is the exact opposite of what the move from power-oriented to rule-based trade policy-making should have brought about.

Trade remedies can have a powerful constituency of their own and a strong public appeal only if the particular characteristics of the welfare state in question allow for it. When one looks just at the number of antidumping cases, as may be gathered from Table 2.13, the United States and Europe have initiated by far the largest number of cases. However, per dollar of imports, ten developing countries have initiated five times more antidumping cases than did the USA, and three developed countries also come out significantly ahead of the USA. It is also quite remarkable that in particular those developed countries that made most progress in the 1990s in retrenching their welfare state and in bringing their income maintenance policies in line with more competitive labour markets – i.e. New Zealand, Australia and Canada – are among the most intensive users of antidumping measures.[112] On the other hand, conspicuously absent from the list are Japan and Norway, two countries that did not engage in retrenchment politics.[113]

All in all, there is at least some reason to believe that market-closing trade policies as much as market-opening trade policies are incidental by-products of largely independent welfare state developments. In trade policy-making, 'you get what you pay for', and only what you pay for.[114] Both under GATT and now in the WTO regime a country has to trade off concrete, short-term market access for specific goods and services in exchange for an equally concrete counter-offer. Not only as a negotiation forum for tariff reductions, but with regard to rule-making as well, the WTO proceeds only on the basis of reciprocal concessions, not mutual interests (Abbott 2001: 286).

111 In other words, in the overwhelming majority of cases the problem is not the pricing practices of foreign companies but comparative costs. As Finger et al. (1982), in a detailed study of antidumping and countervailing duty cases, showed, if a case involved a product in which US producers have comparative advantage, the case was usually determined negatively, i.e. no dumping was found. But cases involving products in which the United States does not have a comparative advantage – and where US producers are likely to be injured by import competition – usually end with a dumping or subsidy determination. As Taussig (1966 [1931]: 363) noted long ago: 'In any protective legislation the true principle of protection is best maintained by the imposition of such duties as will equal the difference between the costs of production at home and abroad, together with a reasonable profit to American industries.' For more details on the private politics of US import policy, see Finger and Murray (1990) and Finger (1991).

112 For comparative work on welfare state retrenchment, see Scharpf and Schmidt (2000), Huber and Stephens (2001) and Pierson (2001). On Australia and New Zealand, see Schwartz (2000); on Canada and the USA see Myles and Pierson (1997).

113 Of course, this analysis is very preliminary, most of all since the data on the intensity of antidumping measures do not indicate how much of national foreign trade is *in fact* restricted. For example, the distribution of WTO disputes by type of product shows that nearly half of the disputes concern agricultural products, fish and fish products, and textiles and clothes (Park 2000: 216f.). This may indicate that antidumping measures concentrate on very specific and rather small areas of international trade. On the other hand, there is a dramatic overall increase in antidumping measures, and even the rough data provided by Finger et al. (2001) reveal a clear pattern pointing to variations in welfare state make-up as an important underlying factor.

114 On this point see Abbott (2001: 286). The quote is from a USTR official.

Table 2.13 Antidumping initiations per $US of imports by economy, 1995–1999

Country/economy initiating	*Against all economies*	
	No. of antidumping initiations	*Initiations per $US (USA = 100)*
Argentina	89	2,125
South Africa	89	2,014
Peru	21	1,634
India	83	1,382
New Zealand	28	1,292
Trinidad and Tobago	5	1,257
Venezuela	22	1,174
Nicaragua	2	988
Australia	89	941
Colombia	15	659
Brazil	56	596
Panama	2	431
Israel	19	418
Chile	10	376
Indonesia	20	330
Mexico	46	290
Egypt	6	278
Turkey	14	204
Korea	37	185
Canada	50	172
Guatemala	1	168
Costa Rica	1	144
Ecuador	1	140
European Union	160	130
Philippines	6	113
United States	136	100
Malaysia	11	97
Slovenia	1	66
Poland	4	65
Czech Republic	2	45
Singapore	2	10
Thailand	1	10

Source: Finger et al. (2001: 13)

Hence, in the age of permanent austerity, now characteristic for the political economy of nearly all welfare states, this strictly mercantilist approach to international trade policy seems to guarantee that in the near future a new attempt towards freer trade will be politically unattainable. Such a stance is also conducive to the growth of 'trade remedies' of all sorts.

Under the new domestic and international conditions today's mercantilist process begins with the decline of the protective capabilities of welfare states and the consequently increasing power of national sectoral interests over national governments. The process then continues with the power which the restricting national governments may have over those national governments whose exports are curtailed. The institutionalized bias against exporting countries is one of the main results of the Uruguay Round, and it proved so powerful in practice because the domestic scene changed dramatically. Therefore, Finger and Dhar (1992: 32) are basically on the right track when they note that

> the power at the base of international differences is not the power of one country relative to another, it is the power *within* each country of import-competing interests over other interests. This power is given to them by the national trade remedies rules, the GATT rules endorse this power, and, in doing so, intensify it.

What they miss, however, is the starting point for all of this. It is not that antidumping and similar measures are 'just ordinary protection with a good public relations program' (Finger 1992: 121). Antidumping could win prominence because its institutional alternative – compensatory social policy – for reasons of its own went into decline, and antidumping has broad public support simply because it appears to perform a basic welfare state function. But antidumping is not just public policy; it is, to a certain extent, and unavoidably so, also private policy: 'It is harnessing of state power to serve a private interest' (ibid.: 141).

The new politics of trade It seems that the WTO, on its own, can achieve very little in keeping trade free. Moreover, its new structure adds further handicaps to the ones already noted. First of all, the WTO has one important drawback vis-à-vis the old GATT structure. GATT was primarily a matter of trade diplomacy, and for this reason it was constituted in a way that preserved national autonomy quasi-automatically.[115] Any agreement on new rules, or the approval of a dispute settlement panel report finding a member state guilty of breaching legal obligations, were in effect at the mercy of the veto power of a single member state – including that of the 'losing' party. This weakness from the standpoint of international economic law, however, is the main reason why governments representing unwieldy welfare states were and are prepared to accept cooperation in an international regime in the first place.[116] With a stricter policy of legalism in international economic relations becoming dominant, lawyers replace trade diplomats, and lawyers, true to their ideology and habits, express their traditional distaste for the politics of negotiation, expediency and compromise (Hudec 1987, 1996, 1999b; Weiler 2000).

Second, the organizational quantum leap in international trade regulation through the WTO provided the hitherto diffuse opposition to globalization with a clear focus

[115] GATT had only one governing body. The term coined for this body, and always capitalized in the text of GATT, is 'CONTRACTING PARTIES'. The revised text of GATT, which has become part of the WTO agreements, speaks only of member states.

[116] Weiler (2000) notes, despite the obvious lack of an enforcement mechanism, that dispute settlement under the old GATT rules achieved a surprisingly high compliance rate. But appearance may be deceptive, as can be seen from an observation by Robert Hudec (1999a: 203–4) on US practice under the old GATT, noting a strong base of coercive diplomacy and a thin superstructure of legalism: 'Today, it is the United States more than any other GATT country that imposes conditions on others *before* agreeing to panels, that blocks panels' adoption of adverse reports, that blocks requests for authorities to retaliate, and, for good measure, that takes its time about complying with adopted panel rulings' (emphasis added).

for effective resistance. Scepticism vis-à-vis the promises of free trade grew and found lasting expression in Seattle and elsewhere. The WTO and its members were unable to respond to the criticism (House of Commons 1999). The failure of the WTO conference in Seattle in late 1999 cannot be attributed exclusively to the mobilization of NGOs, however.

This quasi-democratic resistance is part of a more general trend of domestic closure. For example, during the Uruguay Round in 1994 it was resolved to open a new negotiating round on the Agreement on Agriculture at the end of 1999 so as to subject the various national systems of both lavish as well as idiosyncratic subsidies and encompassing market 'organization' to stricter regulation. Yet despite this agreement, the European Union's Agenda 2000 reforms ratified in Berlin in March 1998 affirmed the status quo in European – and in consequence as well in US – agricultural policy all the way through to 2005 (Rieger 2000). The conspicuous failure of the Multilateral Agreement on Investment means that, for the foreseeable future, foreign direct investment will be negotiated exclusively in the context of bilateral trade policy and cannot be protected in the framework of a multilateral treaty.

Third, these developments demonstrate that it was hitherto more GATT's institutional and organizational weaknesses than its strengths that ensured its success (Bello 1996). The new organizational independence of the WTO, above all the procedures for dispute settlement, have thus far sparked opposition among governments, most of all from developing countries, to embrace social and environmental standards in the regulatory substance of the WTO, for they fear that negative consensus[117] does not sufficiently guarantee more sensitive national interests. Rather, it is designed to strengthen the supranational character of the world trade order at the expense of its international or intergovernmental elements.[118] Moreover, the world trade order was strengthened at the expense of its balkanization. First, the WTO is anything but an integrated normative structure; rather, it consists of highly diverse legal regimes. Second, at present none of the various plurilateral trade agreements,[119] supposed to break new ground in international regime-building in very contested areas, binds more than twenty-nine members, if one counts the European Union as a single member.[120]

The WTO's institutional stagnation is just the flip side of the new trade policy activism and interventionism on the part of the governments of the leading economies. In other words, the new features of the world trade order brought about an upsurge

117 Article 6:1 of the Understanding on Rules and Procedures Governing the Settlement of Disputes (Dispute Settlement Understanding – DSU) states: 'If the complaining party so requests, a panel shall be established at the latest at the Dispute Settlement Board (DSB) meeting following that at which the request first appears as an item on the DSB's agenda, *unless at that meeting the DSB decides by consensus not to establish a panel.*' For the adoption of panel findings, Art. 16:4 DSU states as a general rule: 'Within 60 days after the date of circulation of a panel report to the Members, the report shall be adopted at a DSB meeting . . . [unless] the DSB decides by consensus not to adopt the report.' On the new dispute settlement mechanism, see Hudec (1993, 1999a), Croley and Jackson (1996), Petersmann (1997), Davey (2000).

118 On the supranational, or constitutional character of the WTO, see D. Z. Cass (2001). A good example of this problem is provided by the United States. Congress tied the ratification of the outcome of the Uruguay Round to the Dole Amendment: the United States retained the right to withdraw from the WTO if the latter were to violate its sovereignty (Gilpin 2000: 111).

119 These agreements include the Agreement on Trade in Civil Aircrafts, the Agreement on Government Procurement, the International Dairy Agreement, and the International Bovine Agreement.

120 In the voting procedures of WTO organs, each member state of the European Union has its own vote.

in unregulated economic nationalism and thus a much more particularistic welfare state landscape by trade policy means. During its first term (1992–6), the Clinton administration pursued an aggressive, results-oriented trade policy vis-à-vis Japan and other countries, which allegedly did not import enough US goods and were thus declared to be responsible for the enormous US trade deficit. David Sanger of the *New York Times* (29 October 2000) characterized the *raison d'être* of the more than 300 bilateral trade agreements concluded during Clinton's two terms as 'making the world safe for Motorola in Japan and General Motors in China'. Both NAFTA and the Single Market Programme of the European Union (and the single Market Programme's continuation in the Economic and Monetary Union (EMU)) are attempts to replace world markets with more exclusive free trade zones and customs unions in order to subject global capitalism once again to a stronger degree of political control.

But NAFTA and the EMU are just the tip of the iceberg. It is estimated that at the end of the twentieth century more than a hundred customs unions existed, and that nearly every member of the WTO was also a member of one of these quintessentially tariff-protecting organizations (Gilpin 2000: 109). These efforts to form defensive economic blocs are part of a general pattern. Already in the wake of the Kennedy Round, and even more so following the Tokyo Round, it became quite clear that non-tariff barriers were increasingly taking the place of tariff barriers. The more the most intensively regulated branches of national economies were affected by globalization – e.g. pharmaceuticals, financial services, communication technologies and basic utility industries – the more the trend towards non-tariff barriers shaped world trade. It seems as if the attempt to strengthen the legal aspects of the WTO order – that is, to force conflicts arising out of regulatory encounters to a liberal conclusion instead of institutionalizing them – has weakened and not strengthened trade liberalism. The institutionalized ambivalence of the WTO legal system seems unable to withstand the pressure created by welfare state reforms.

The new policy of legalism in the WTO system introduced a rigidity which apparently overstretched the consensual basis of governance of international economic relations by means of an international organization. As of 1 October 2000, from the 205 cases brought under the revised dispute settlement process, 106 (51.7 per cent) were still in progress, 53 cases (25.9 per cent) had been resolved by an adopted panel or by an Appellate Body report, and 46 cases (22.4 per cent) had been determined by other means, mostly by bilateral settlement (15.1 per cent of all cases) (Park 2000).[121] In all adopted legal rulings, the losing party declared that it would comply with the ruling.

But apparently governments have a major problem with compliance. In one third of the allegedly resolved 53 cases, the required action did not transpire. This compliance problem is mostly due to the fact that governments often face grave difficulties in reversing measures that, by definition – otherwise they would not have been taken – enjoy significant political support at home (Hudec 2000: 221). In addition, de jure and in point of fact, dispute settlement panels and the Appellate Body do constitute a

[121] It is not clear if the cases 'resolved by other means' are in fact resolved. In its report for the year 2001 the WTO states that although Article 3:6 of the Dispute Settlement Understanding states that 'mutually agreed solutions to matters formally raised under the consultation and dispute settlement provisions of the covered agreements shall be notified', notifications of outcomes have not been registered for some portion of complaints that have not proceeded to the panel stage, *indicating an apparently dormant status* (WTO 2001: 27).

public authority with the right and responsibility to make decisions which determine the organization and structure of *domestic* political and legal power, and the distribution of goods and opportunities in *domestic* society. For that reason questions of *democratic* legitimacy and governance figure massively in the conflicts over the 'constitutionalization' of trade law (D. Z. Cass 2001).

Finally, the compliance problem is exacerbated by a fundamental imbalance in the institutional structure of the WTO: the consensus requirement de facto makes it impossible for the 140-plus member governments of the WTO to override legal rulings. No WTO legislature in the traditional sense exists.[122] In judicial systems with strong courts of last resort, such as those of the United States or Germany, the legislature can overrule courts when they reach decisions that are politically unacceptable to the community at large. Every court action takes place in the shadow of legislative corrigibility and thus maintains a basic rapport between the law and the political community. As Hudec (2000: 223) noted, 'to the extent that the WTO is unable to legislate correction to unwise or unwanted legal rulings, it will place even greater strain on the political viability of its dispute settlement machinery.' What Renato Ruggiero (2000: xiv), Director-General of the WTO from 1995 to 1999, noted with regard to the whole of the WTO – namely, institutional overstretch and thus the danger of becoming a victim of its own success – is even more true for the dispute settlement system.

The important point, however, lies in the fact that the juridification of the world trade system also extends to that part which provides a legal cover to antiliberal trade practices and thus, in effect, at least to some extent serves to stabilize the overall system. Of course, the national protective trade policy measures now in vogue betray a basically mercantilist orientation and reveal an unyielding status quo thinking, in which changes in employment and incomes are perceived solely in terms of absolute risks and losses. Such conservative, economically purely nationalist trade policy is easy prey for domestic political exploitation of its procedures by firms and – in the case of the USA – by unions and other 'private' parties.

In some sense, however, this is the price to be paid to maintain the liberal thrust of the international trade system. By tolerating such conflicts, however nonsensical they may appear from the point of view of rational economics, this system avails itself of a central stabilizing means. Moreover, it is in particular due to the fact that antidumping policies and procedures form an extremely complex and, in institutional terms, highly differentiated structure, that the regulatory encounters which provide the starting point for all international trade conflicts do not trigger more fundamental conflicts. The organizational messiness of antidumping prevents trade conflicts from accumulating. As a rule, antidumping procedures are not synergistic. On the contrary, they *allow* a wide range of conflicts to be dealt with simultaneously *and* in a segmented fashion, each of them concentrating solely on very esoteric 'facts' of the case at hand.

Thus one can say that the multiplicity of dumping-related trade conflicts stands in inverse relationship to their intensity. Viewed in this way, antidumping procedures are not a trade liberals' pandora's box, but a safety-valve institution that leads to a

122 The only body in the WTO system that even faintly resembles a legislature, the Ministerial Council, meets only every two years. It is, given the direct impact of international trade law on shaping *societal* opportunity structures, not representative in the sense of being elected by an international trade constituency to fulfil the function of representing that constituency on trade matters.

functionally extremely important constellation in which governments no longer need to reach a final solution of unsatisfactory states of affairs, but merely to release the tensions which arise from them.[123] That this in fact is a *positive* contribution to the maintenance of a liberal trade order can be gathered first of all from the observation that up to now no trade conflict – or even the repeated trade wars – has provoked a country into exiting from the international regime, and, second, that countries did not give up on regulating their economies, but, sometimes, changed the form of regulations only.

Despite appearance to the contrary, there are no strong indications that because of the move to constitutionalize a world trade law, interdependence is now less regulated than it was under the old GATT regime (D. Kennedy 1995; Goldstein and Martin 2000; Litan 2000; Nye and Donahue 2000). Nonetheless, the new domestic conditions framing and most of all constraining compensatory social policy in the national arena are a significant cause of the revival of protectionism and of regionalization in world trade.

The same caveat applies to this relationship between the new politics of the welfare states and the turn towards a more undisciplined protectionism as it did to the equally reciprocal relationship between compensatory social policy and a deregulated national foreign trade policy as it existed at the outset of the globalization movement: the *fact*, not merely the *possibility*, of a relationship is decisive. In this regard, one has to note that the WTO regime is still on a trial run.

The actual situation consists of criss-crossing trends and counter-trends and precludes any categorical statement. The same notion of a basic ambiguity is also true of a correlation that has attracted far more attention than the positive complementarity of trade and social policy which marked the onset of the globalization process, namely the claim that globalization is laissez-faire writ large, induces rampant locational competition and thus necessarily implies the end or at least the radical curtailment of the welfare state. Instead, it makes much more sense to argue that it is, in particular, welfare states that are still the most important providers of order in the international economic society.

6 Welfare Democracy and Trade Policy

For many observers globalization manifestly means the end of national social policy. At the same time – and in most cases they do not notice this inconsistency – it is claimed that globalization brings about the constraints incidental to fiscal federalism and thus contains a clear political message for social policy. But any political message is meaningless if something will occur anyhow, fully independent of what the actors want to happen. On closer view, the theoretically arrived conclusions of fiscal federalism do not fit the actual forces shaping welfare state developments. Moreover, this model underestimates the extent to which the mature welfare states support the global economic order independent of global governance structures.

Applied to the globalization–welfare state conundrum, fiscal federalism entails the notion that in an open national economy, domestic institutions of social policy are not only ultimately shaped by conditions abroad but bring about the opposite of the

[123] On the sociological foundation of this insight, cf. Coser (1956: 156).

beneficial effects that social legislation is thought to achieve.[124] A country that raises the level of living standards of its poorest citizens above their market wage by means of redistributive social policy and then calls on its more wealthy citizens to finance such a policy drives the latter abroad and attracts instead the foreign poor. Abroad, the profits attained by owners of scarce factors of production fall, while those of immobile suppliers of productive factors, who usually lack capital, rise. For the foreign tax state, the influx of net payers and the emigration of net recipients of state benefits produce a budget surplus that may be used for social ends. The effectiveness of foreign social policy increases without any effort added. At home, the effectiveness of equalizing social policy decreases, because the emigration of the owners of scarce factors of production and the immigration of financially weak persons enlarge the gap in gross wage rates between these two groups. Factor emigration thus undermines the effectiveness of equalizing social policy at home, while strengthening it abroad:

> In the theoretical extreme case of complete mobility, the effect of national social policy would end up in smoke abroad. The distribution of net incomes domestically would be determined by conditions abroad, independently of national redistributive measures. There would thus be no reason to attempt national social policy. (H.-W. Sinn 2000a: 13; 2000b)

There is, however, no evidence of the existence of that kind of national locational competition or social dumping – i.e. a zero-sum locational competition – that somehow 'necessarily' leads to a dismantling of the welfare state or to a fully (market) incentive compatible social policy (Drezner 2000). This is true of conditions both globally and in Europe, even though it is precisely in Europe that the expectation had been that the near complete realization of a single market would force social policy change in the direction of massive welfare state curtailment (S. Sinn 1992; Mussler 1998).[125] In the European Union, the exact opposite seems to take place, i.e. a move towards *social* centralization (Schuster 2000; Rieger 2001). We do not dispute the theoretical plausibility of the effects of locational competition, nor do we seek to pass judgement on whether an antagonistic locational competition with the said effects *should* exist or not. Social science, which understands itself as a science of reality, is interested more in *why* these effects have not come about – and why they should not be expected in the future.

The following section attempts to provide an answer to these questions. Not only can and did the welfare state further globalization through its social policies by making freer trade possible, it also provided a direct, positive contribution through its tax policy. *Of their own volition*, governments of welfare states *privilege* mobile capital.

124 The *locus classicus* for the model of fiscal federalism is Thibout (1956). On the theory and some evidence of the social effects of fiscal federalism in the US context, see Rose-Ackerman (1981), Winer (1983), C. C. Brown and Oates (1987), Peterson and Rom (1989) and Cheikbossian (2000).

125 On the face of it, fiscal federalism is ambivalent about its true political message: it can be used to argue the futility of redistributive social policy. But it can also be used to argue for a centralization, or nationalization of social benefit systems. The first to take this latter line of argument was the British economist Edwin Cannan. Writing in 1896, he said: 'Measures adopted to produce greater equality are, however, exceedingly unsuitable for local authorities. The smaller the locality the more capricious and ineffectual are likely to be any efforts it may make to carry out such a policy. It seems clearly desirable that all such measures should be applied to the largest possible area, and that subordinate authorities should be left to act, like the individual, from motives of self-interest' (C. C. Brown and Oates 1987: 307).

This expedient alliance between governments and the pillars of capitalism is as old as politics itself, because state power has always been based on *territorial* control. As long as an international society of effectively segmented political systems exists, mobile capital and governments will come to terms in one way or another. To be politically effective, i.e. to revalue the domestic voice of its owners, mobility, or transferability, of capital of all sorts presupposes territorial sovereignty, and hence its effectiveness is necessarily limited as well. Governments have always attempted to compensate for this weakness by organizing policies transterritorially. It is precisely this compensation that stands again today at the forefront of the international economic order – and canalizes the impact of globalization in a very particular way.

Welfare mercantilism and the tax state

The facts presented in this chapter can be read as follows: both in national and international trade policy, the rules governing competition are followed when and only as long as they serve welfare state ends. As the analysis of GATT has shown, in the international economic order the principle of an open market economy with free competition is not only compromised in many respects, but is also dependent on its near complete concurrence with *positive* benefits for *individual* governments. In a dynamic system with an international division of labour, however, such a coincidence is – for systemic reasons – an open question.

It is beyond the computation and the political regulatory potential of any single country to determine whether – and at what price – a global economy offers its population the 'secure sustenance' that welfare statism, in the final analysis, demands. Countries can – as, for example, Ireland has done with great success in the deregulation of one sector after another – provide new service sector firms with a productive and above all affordable climate. But they have no means of hindering large US technology firms from pulling out as a result of falling stock prices on Wall Street.[126] Yet in democratic welfare states, governments must find a way of providing secure sustenance to the mass of the population, and – by means of the political predominance of the propertyless in numerical mass democracies – this moment sets a clear standard for politics. In democratic welfare states, the dominant concerns guiding all policy decisions are jobs, the incomes hereby attained and the tax yield of the national economy.

The legitimacy of political leadership ultimately depends on its measuring up to the expectation of providing welfare – by whatever means. The national division of labour and numerous other – ethnic, religious, regional – divides generate inequalities among persons and groups. These inequalities tend to correspond, sooner or later, to differentials in political power as well. *Whose* welfare increases the legitimacy of a government also depends on *how* political power is organized and who bears it. The concrete means of welfare-democratic politics can vary greatly, but its general thrust is unwavering, marking a crucial difference to other political regimes. Such politics is defined in national terms and thus is, by necessity, fundamentally egalitarian.[127] Governments

[126] 'Irish officials seem well aware of the perils. "We live or die by internationally traded goods and services"' (*New York Times*, 31 October 2000, Section C, p. 8).

[127] For a magisterial overview on the forms and history of government, see Finer (1999). This study also indicates what kind of revolution the rise of democratic welfare statism represents in world history.

of welfare states have always attempted to use foreign policy to compel the international economic division of labour to serve immediately tangible domestic ends (Viner 1949; Katzenstein 1978).

It is not blind coincidence that the experiment of democracy in ancient Greece was accompanied by a strictly mercantilist urban-territorial economic policy and that the flourishing of the Roman Republic went hand-in-hand with its becoming an economically inspired and militarily driven great power (Tandy 1997; Weber 1896).[128] In the seventeenth century, mercantilist policy offered nascent nation-states just as viable a means of manipulating foreign trade for purely domestically conceived ends as did military geo-politics in the twentieth century to the competing great powers of England, Germany, Russia, Japan and the United States (Heckscher 1994 [1935]; Magnusson 1994).

At the end of the twentieth century, the most important tool for manipulating free trade is national and particularly international trade policy. The governments of developed welfare states have attempted to create the requisite levers by establishing international economic organizations. The purpose of these organizations is to enhance the foreign power of the state leadership for domestic purposes. It is thus not surprising that the integration and contraction movements of the global economy are accompanied by an increase and decrease respectively in the growth of inter-state organizations. Between 1875 and 1919, international organizations grew in number at a rate of 25.6 per cent annually, in the interwar period of 1920–44 by only 11.1 per cent, and after the Second World War (1945–64) again by 24.3 per cent (Wallace and Singer 1970: 281).

Since the importance of international law does not flow from the willingness of governments to abide by its principles to the detriment of their interest, but from the fact that they so often judge it in their interest to conform to it, this interest deserves closer attention. It is neither fixed for once and for all, nor does international economic law create a strong and at least potentially countervailing supranational body to the international community of states. However, under conditions of economic interdependence the ability to politically control essentially transnational market forces is a common concern of states in the shaping of international economic relations. Put differently, in the eyes of governments – as in the view of the bulk of the electorate – free trade is merely *one* instrument among many for achieving essentially welfare state goals. In cases in which this instrument does not achieve the desired effects, it is replaced by others. If not unconditional free trade, what then is the guiding principle of foreign trade policy?

If welfare state principles are transposed to national and international trade policy, we can speak of welfare mercantilism. It is typical of welfare democracies that governments – and even more so, the opposition parties seeking to take their place – treat the population as if it consisted solely of clients of their social policy. An attempt is made to somehow draw all citizens into the state's sphere of influence and to tie

128 The welfare statism of these early experiments in democracy was in particular pointed out by Weber (1896): 'At some time or another, to be sure, cities like Athens or Rome become dependent on imports for their grain supply. But such conditions are highly abnormal; and in all these cases the *community* takes over the responsibility of supplying these goods. The citizens are not inclined to leave this task to uncontrolled private trade nor can they afford to do so.'

their interests to it. All are supposed to benefit from it and to show their gratitude at the next election. In this way, social standards are introduced into the shaping of foreign trade. A principle of every mercantilist policy is thus also to improve, reinforce or salvage as many domestic income sources as possible. Foreign economic policy, then, follows the principle of creating as many foreign sales as possible, 'and indeed to the greatest extent possible . . . for such products in which a maximum amount of domestic labour is invested' (Weber 1978: 820). This is a core element of modern welfare state mercantilism. For this purpose, all countries have developed a broad range of instruments to actively promote exports, ranging from public credit facilities[129] to countertrade as an instrument of industrial policy[130] to export subsidies.[131]

A second core element of welfare state mercantilism is the empathetic treatment of domestic capital which is mobile and thus capable of emigration. Locational competition and mobile capital constitute the mechanism which gives this form of mercantilism its dynamic and structures domestic burden-sharing. Who pays which taxes and finances which programmes? Essentially, welfare-democratic motives provoke a mercantilist reaction to globalization by actively promoting it. Welfare mercantilism and economic openness may well go together, as Max Weber noted with regard to the very similar constellation which obtained at the end of the nineteenth century:

> Today communities in which the propertyless have seized power are often very cautious towards the propertied. Municipalities under socialist control, such as the city of Catania, have attracted factories with substantial tax benefits, because the socialist rank and file were more interested in better job opportunities and in directly ameliorating their class situation, than in 'just' property distribution and 'equitable' taxation. Likewise, in spite of conflicting interests in a given case, landlords, speculators in building land, retailers and craftsmen tend to think first of their immediate class-determined interests; therefore, all kinds of mercantilism have been a frequent, though highly varied, phenomenon in all types of communities. This is all the more so since those concerned with the relative power position of a community also have an interest in preserving the tax base and great fortunes capable of granting them loans; hence, they are forced to treat personal property cautiously. Thus, even where the have-nots are in control, personal property may either

129 The Federal Republic of Germany, for example, provides an export safeguard in the form of *HERMES* guarantees and credits.

130 The foreign buyer can make countertrade a condition for the conclusion of the deal in order to 'earn' the means necessary to purchase imports. Countertrade used to shape trade with Eastern Bloc countries. Today, it is most common in the case of exports of capital goods from industrial countries to developing nations. One of the main reasons for countertrade is the lack of international competitiveness of the goods offered in exchange, so that exports would not otherwise come about. Exporters who are in a position to accept such countertrade thus enjoy a competitive advantage. Countertrade, however, is not limited to trade with developing countries: 'Industrial countries commit themselves to countertrades when the value of the business is very high and when political entities are involved or in the role of a buyer (as in the case of infrastructural installations or the procurement of military equipment). As a rule, they are guided in such matters by employment policy considerations, i.e. furthering the maintenance or creation of jobs' (Grafers 1999: 212).

131 In the agricultural sector, industrial countries everywhere grant export subsidies. The prices that are guaranteed to producers are typically much higher than world market prices. In order to create a safety valve for sales in conditions of overproduction, exports are subsidized. In the framework of the WTO, an Agreement on Subsidies and Countervailing Measures was passed in 1994, but it explicitly excluded agriculture (Article 3:1).

> expect mercantilist privileges or at least exemption from liturgies and taxes, *provided* a plurality of communities competes with one another among which the property owners can chose their domicile. (Weber 1978: 352)

This privileging mercantilism is anything but a recent development. Democracy with a universal and equal franchise has always run into 'peculiar difficulties' when trying to tax mobile property – and behaved accordingly.[132] Welfare state mercantilism – not the dismantling of the welfare state – represents the standard reaction to antagonistic locational competition. Moreover, the difficulties of raising taxes 'have greatly affected the rise of modern capitalism':

> Even where the propertyless strata are dominant, the taxation of personal property meets certain limits as long as the propertied can freely leave the community. The degree of mobility depends not only on the relative importance of membership in this particular community for the propertied, but also on the nature of the property. Within compulsory associations, particularly political communities, all property utilization that is largely dependent on real estate is stationary, in contrast to personal property which is either monetary or easily exchangeable. If propertied families leave a community dependent on a market economy, and particularly a labor market, the have-nots may find their economic opportunities so much reduced that they will abandon any reckless attempt at taxing the haves or will even deliberately favor them. (Ibid.: 352)

Thus the more developed a community's welfare state, the more attention we can expect it to pay to mobile capital. The enormous budgetary demands of welfare democracy indirectly reinforce globalization by leading governments to consciously privilege and woo capital. They thus have exactly the opposite effect of what is normally assumed to be caused by welfare states' heavy fiscal burden, namely to slow down or retard globalization.[133] A by no means covert alliance of expediency thus exists between the political agents of the welfare state and the pillars of global capitalism. This alliance stems primarily from the fact that political rule is territorial rule, whereas market

132 Schumpeter (1918: 51) even claimed that the tax state is the natural complement to a free market economy. The critical element is, of course, the forms and the incidence of taxes.

133 The Law Introducing an Ecological Tax Reform (*Gesetz zum Einstieg in die ökologische Steuerreform*), passed by the German *Bundestag* on 3 March 1999, illustrates with the necessary clarity how the fiscal burden is shifted around, giving contemporary substance to Weber's historical lesson: 'If personal ("mobile") property is dominant, the propertied everywhere unburden themselves . . . and shift the tax burden to the masses' (Weber 1978: 353). In its effort to make energy more expensive – and thus to provide incentives for a more rational use – the first stage of this 'ecological tax reform' (which went into effect in April 1999) raised the mineral oil excise tax by 6 pfennigs per litre for petrol and diesel fuel, by 4 pfennigs per litre for heating oil and by 0.22 pfennigs per kwh for natural gas, and introduced a new electricity tax of 2 pfennigs per kwh. The additional revenues expected from this are used to finance transfers by the federal government to the statutory pension insurance scheme, allowing the latter to lower its contribution rate by 0.8 per cent to 19.5 per cent. Taxes are thus being raised on two mass consumption goods – petrol and electricity – which are among those most territorially bound. And the tax burden is being lowered on the factor labour, which, in light of sharply increased locational competition, has been catapulted to the forefront of new distributional struggles. Swedish fiscal policy in the 1990s moved in the same direction: it sharply increased the tax burden of its workers, and it cut the corporate income tax by half. The aim was, of course, to make the Swedish welfare state safe for globalization (Henrekson and Jakobsson 2001). For a more detailed comparative perspective, see Scharpf (2000b).

relations can to a large extent be separated from geography.[134] The invention of exclusive welfare states thus brought about the birth of modern capitalism:

> At the beginning of modern history, the various countries engaged in the struggle for power needed ever more capital for political reasons and because of the expanding money economy. This resulted in that memorable alliance between the rising states and the sought-after and privileged capitalist powers that was a major factor in creating modern capitalism and fully justifies the designation 'mercantilist' for the policies of that epoch. (Ibid.: 353)

An internationally segmented system of welfare states is thus not only the precondition of a market capitalism capable of functioning as an engine of growth. It also created a situation in which governments *invented capitalist* protectionism of their own accord, something that continues today in various forms.

Keeping companies at bay

Capitalist protectionism, however, does not mean that governments are now at the mercy of the transnationally mobile owners of much sought-after capital. The competition among territorial units described by Weber strongly suggests a second, complementary form of welfare mercantilism, to some degree offsetting the growing voice of mobile capital in domestic politics. The privileged position of mobile capital can be attributed to a situation in which nations carry out their policies independently. Some coordination of their foreign trade relations offers at least a possible means of a political control of antagonistic, or anarchic, locational competition, and thus of also easing the mounting burden of the majority who are nowadays generally immobile. Locational competition generates a common interest among states to construct a counterweight to it through international organization. Though not much noted, with this project welfare states are quite successful.

Modern mercantilism as a system of *external* power formation is welfare state oriented. It is not, unlike classical mercantilism, oriented towards fiscal monopoly; that is, it no longer aims primarily at controlling and exploiting industry by giving firms concessions, granting them monopoly status and allowing them to form cartels. Yet in one respect, old and new mercantilism are alike.

With regard to a free market economy and autonomous capitalism, both are deeply irrational. There is a critical difference between capitalism that is oriented towards the politically fashioned and controlled consumption of mass populations, and capitalism

[134] It is thus also true that, for example, in the United States the role of the corporate income tax in total tax revenues has rapidly declined in recent decades and that in recent years a whole series of firms not only paid no taxes, but even received tax refunds, despite high profits (Anelauskas 1999: 282–6; 'Study Finds That Many Large Companies Pay No Taxes', *New York Times*, 20 October 2000, Section C, p. 2). There is, however, a welfare state or, more precisely, a tax state flip-side to this coin: US government revenues from *personal* income taxation increased over the course of the 1990s from under 8 per cent of GNP to over 10 per cent ('Washington Bets that a Bear Will Never Come', *New York Times*, 13 October 2000, Section C, p. 1). We should further note with regard to *corporate* income tax that it is ultimately never organizations, but *individuals* who pay taxes, and that, from a micro-economic perspective, these taxes are generally passed on to consumers. To tax propertied individuals more efficiently is thus offsetting the more lenient tax treatment of firms.

that is oriented towards market opportunities which are created autodynamically and independently by means of private entrepreneurial efforts and performance. The optimum conditions for the *formal* rationality of voluntaristic economic action are the exact opposite of the *substantive* demands welfare states make on the economic system.[135] What the welfare state does, and what constitutes its *raison d'être*, is to try to correct the *systemic* defect that *no* economic system can directly translate the socially constructed *subjective* feelings of need into *effective* demand; that is, into demand that is – to a sufficient degree and for a longer time period – taken into account and satisfied through the *market-based* production of goods and services. It is profitability alone that provides capitalists and entrepreneurs with incentives to take care of the needs of consumers. Besides, it is not just demand ('wants') as such, but *effective* demand for goods and services which regulates their production in free markets dominated by profit-making firms. Thus welfare states, in essence, take measures to effect *directly* the distribution of employment, incomes, goods and services (Weber 1978: 93, 105, 108, 111). This general principle will become the stronger the more the national economy becomes part of international economic society, which no individual country can effectively control.

Both historically and presently, the basic point is the same: that the 'development of a *modern* system of economy is accompanied by the phenomenon that the masses increasingly satisfy their demand through interlocal and finally international exchange of goods' (Weber 1896: 141; emphasis in original), is preconditioned *either* on a parallel system of public transfers effectively compensating for the risks of interlocally or internationally provisioning populations with their basic needs, *or* on strictly regulating foreign trade, that is, by means of a discretionary trade regime, by coercive trade diplomacy, by international power politics – or, today, by international organization.

Contemporary welfare state mercantilism conveys governments' attempts to take advantage of the benefits of global economic integration. At the same time, however, governments seek to strictly limit the imported economic change that accompanies the deepening and broadening of the international division of labour, which consists, in their eyes, in more 'destructive' than 'productive' effects. One of the results of this typical welfare state dilemma is the protection of declining industries, which can be observed in all welfare democracies and which runs diametrically counter to the logic of an international division of labour (Bhagwati 1988).

A second result is that welfare mercantilism expresses itself in governments' assumption that international trade is a zero-sum game. The advantages of one country are seen as the disadvantages of another and vice versa. This attitude provides the key to understanding why progress in international trade policy has taken the form of so-called concessions which countries reciprocally grant each other. In terms of the mechanisms and dynamics of the international division of labour, this fundamental

135 With regard to England, its 'rational' capitalism (Max Weber) was not the product of a national economic policy. Rather, it developed parallel to the monopolistic fiscal policy of mercantilism because it found an ally in Parliament which put a strong check on the evolution of a bureaucracy, making it incapable of independently promoting welfare statism, quite in contrast to the development in Continental European countries (Weber 1978, 1981 [1923]). This Parliament represented, however, the propertied bourgeoisie. A parliament constituted by an equal franchise would, most likely, have pursued a different economic policy and particularly a different foreign trade policy, by imposing most of all substantive demands on the performance of markets in the interest of 'social justice'.

reciprocity indeed makes no sense, but it does ease the process of domestic legitimation – and ratification – of commercial treaties (Krugman 1997).

The political control of international economic relations can thus be succinctly characterized as follows: at their core, these regimes are government of governments, by governments, for governments.[136] It was a mercantilist policy that led to more free trade in the post-war period. Both the WTO and the IMF and World Bank are institutions that are controlled by governments. As organizations they are strictly limited to closely supervised executive functions. They have neither a formally independent basis nor any informal capabilities that would permit them to oppose governments. Their political latitude emerges first from governments' common interests and second from differences in their interests, which create some space in which, at times, an ingenious leader of an organization can push forward his own position. These regimes are always – at least – one arm's length away from the real pillars of the global economy: the corporations. The latter have no direct access to international organizations, nor are they themselves the addressees of international economic policy. Not only are the autonomy-enhancing norms, safeguards, escape clauses and the like directed exclusively at governments, so too are the *liberal* market norms of international economic relations. They constitute basically 'voluntary' commitments by states, to which private persons cannot – or may only in exceptional cases – successfully appeal (Kessie 2000). These norms cannot be translated into private actors' claims to state regulatory abstention, which are judicially enforceable on an individual basis as subjective rights. This makes transnational economic transactions a discretionary privilege, not an entitlement protected by the courts.

The main difference between international politics and domestic politics is the fact that the institutional pattern governing business–government relations in the former is *informal*, and not formal, as in the latter. At least there are no *formally* determined methods for producing the domestic or private interest input to both rule-making and adjudication in international economic regimes. And in most cases there are no hard constitutional or juridical means by which private actors can control their government for its behaviour in international forums, thus giving rise to a 'double edge diplomacy', which significantly increases the autonomy of national governments vis-à-vis domestic political actors – including companies (Putnam and Bayne 1987; Putnam 1988; Moravcsik 1993b, 1998b).

At the same time it is obvious that in effectively *globalized* markets regulated by *national* policies *individual* economic interests of companies can be decisively advanced by a government policy – or nullified. In the politics of international economic regimes the decisional input of the official bearers of international 'public' relations may be made as a consequence of informal bargaining or of some type of implicit coordination between private actors and their governments. But the normative and the decisional output produced by the international organizations will most certainly have consequences for private actors, even though for them the very peculiar decision-making process in the international forum is a black box – i.e. non-transparent – confronting them with results that may differ enormously from what they have asked

[136] That we phrase this point as an echo of Lincoln's description of American democracy in his Gettysburg address, a 'government of the people, by the people, for the people', is not meant to imply a fundamental non-democratic nature of international governance structures – the exact opposite is the case – but to denote its basic modus operandi.

for. One has to assume that international attempts to balance the private interests involved in trade conflicts will result, at best, in a pale reflection of the true weight and complexity of the competing private interests involved.[137]

This shortcoming marks the decisive difference between international economic regimes, including GATT and the European Union. Only in the European Union do the legal acts of the Community also give individual market citizens judicially enforceable rights – even vis-à-vis individual member states (Cowles et al. 2001). More important, however, is the fact that it is exactly this relentlessly defended limitation which provides governments with real power vis-à-vis the transnationally active firms in international economic affairs. The much fêted policy of legalism in international economic governance is usually silent on the peculiar quality of this move towards juridification: that *states* successfully monopolize the dispute settlement mechanism of the WTO.

True enough, as a code of general governmental conduct, the GATT in principle promotes *non-intervention* by governments in international trade. The overriding goal of GATT is an open world trading system unimpeded by government restrictions. GATT as well as other WTO agreements are based on the desideratum of a free international market between independent private buyers and sellers.[138] However, and contrary to what one can expect to flow from this characterization of the international trade regime, GATT entails no 'Bill of Rights' for individuals.[139] In addition, and making this picture even more problematic from the point of view of free markets, the WTO as an organization is unable to help when it comes to the needs of corporations confronted with governments acting arbitrarily.

Formally, the GATT, and now the WTO, are, to all intents and purposes, member-driven diplomatic international entities, with a very limited organizational role with regard to autonomous leadership and independent advocacy capability, not to mention access to resources.[140] In both an institutional and a legal sense, firms simply do not exist in the WTO system and have no obliging ally within it. Moreover, and even more important for the private interests involved, even if the domestic industry of a member state is directly hurt, that country has no obligation to act: GATT and WTO rules are not mandatory but permissive; i.e. they authorize, but do not require, governments to

137 As Dean Rusk, then US Secretary of State, said in 1962: 'I don't believe that the U.S. can afford to stake its interests in other countries on a particular investment in a particular situation' (Barnet and Müller 1974: 84).

138 For this reason, J. H. Jackson (2000a: 47) sees the European Union as the model for an approach in international politics that aims at limiting government officials vis-à-vis the economy.

139 One has to acknowledge the possibility that companies might not be interested in an international economic law with teeth, i.e. one that is autonomous vis-à-vis national governments as a result of granting rights, that is, giving 'direct effect' to international norms, because such a structure may have more negative than positive effects. Spiro (2000: 571) notes that 'non-state actors themselves may prefer the unaccountability of informal power. Corporations and NGOs able to work through agent-states are able to avoid the institutional constraints that would come with direct representation in public decision-making fora, as well as the prospect of being held directly responsible to formal legal regimes.'

140 See Henderson's (1998: 112) summary on this point: 'The dominant actors throughout the story [of the Uruguay Round] were the member governments: it was their attitudes and decisions that decided at each stage the agenda for the officials working in the GATT in Geneva – secretarial and delegates alike – and largely determined what it was possible for them to achieve or even attempt.' For a more extensive treatment on the limited role of GATT's organization vis-à-vis governments in the transition from the GATT to the WTO regime see Croome (1995) and Preeg (1995).

act (J. H. Jackson 2000a: 25).[141] What is the policy of legalism in international trade relations trying to achieve if it ignores private interests? If, as Weiler (2000: 14) pronounced, the panels of the Dispute Settlement Mechanism are a court in all but name and should more appropriately be called 'The International Court of Economic Justice', then the question is 'justice for whom'?

That neither the GATT nor any other WTO agreement – including the new Dispute Settlement Mechanism – have 'direct effect', i.e. do not provide private interests with any legal remedy against countries violating treaty obligations, is the most important *legal* fact of this international regime (Bogdandy 2001: 265).[142] There is a strong call in favour of correcting this systemic defect of the WTO's legal order. Otherwise, so the argument goes, the WTO does not only lack legitimacy; it will also be unable to provide companies with a basis on which the material benefits of a global market economy may be realized for all countries involved:

> Since most people spend most of their time on the production of goods and services (such as education) as a means to acquire other goods and services inside and outside their home country, the frequent double standard cultivated by many lawyers and courts (that is, their preference for, and higher level of scrutiny accorded to, civil and political rights rather than to economic and social rights, and their disregard of the increasingly transnational exercise of individual rights in the modern global economy) *reflects a strange legal anachronism and disregard of the actual individual preferences of the modern homo economicus.* (Petersmann 1997: 400; emphasis added)

In short, if the efforts spent on creating a stable regime of international trade responded to the genuine needs of companies, the means employed seem to be fundamentally in conflict with the requirements of the situation.[143] But, for better or for worse, there is a reason for this state of affairs. Since international law is formulated by the exclusive club of states, we can expect that *systemic* demands respecting 'sovereignty' – or at least to reduce the 'autonomy costs' of international economic governance – will tend to impose themselves on any demands by private interests.[144] Given the essentially welfare-*democratic* nature of most states, we can assume that governments will agree

141 Given the immense discrepancies in real economic might, smaller countries in particular may refrain from taking action against an economic superpower. As a result of a complaint against the USA for its use – contrary to GATT norms – of import restraints on imported dairy products, The Netherlands was authorized to utilize restraints against importations of US grain, but never acted on that authorization. However, this moderation had no effect on US behaviour vis-à-vis The Netherlands (J. H. Jackson 1997a: 116).

142 For Weiler (2000: 17), echoing a lawyer's ethos, 'the notion of excluding voices affected by one's decision and not hearing arguments by them runs counter not only to the ethic of open and public process but to the very principles of natural justice'. On the standing of third or private parties in international law regimes, see J. H. Jackson (1992), Croley and Jackson (1996), Brand (1996/97), Carmody (1997), Hilf (1997), O'Connell (1999) and G. E. Evans (2000).

143 Despite the fact that 'direct effect' is essential for European integration, the European Court of Justice rejects a direct application of WTO rules in order to guarantee as much international freedom of action as possible to the Community organs and to the national legislatures and executive branches (Berkey 1998; Prechal 2000: 1065, with references to the relevant judicial rulings).

144 To repeat, neither the WTO agreements in themselves nor the newly designed Dispute Settlement Mechanism is about freer trade per se. A case in point is the banana dispute, which involved two countries that hardly even *grow* bananas and which was finally resolved outside the WTO arena in a way that cemented the bureaucratic state of affairs in the European banana market (Lavery 2001).

in keeping companies away from the legislative, executive and juridical forums of international governance and thus avoid putting themselves in a position where a powerful lever is created against them.

Stated in more general terms, the rise of global business fundamentally altered the relationship between public and private government, creating points of converging and diverging interests. For governments, global corporations are a source of national welfare and a potential frustrator of national policy. The power of global corporations comes from control of the means to create wealth on a worldwide scale. However, and of more significance, for global corporations governments are both a nuisance and a basic necessity. They cannot create the institutional basis for becoming truly transnational firms, and they are not able, just by themselves, to defend the market positions and the profits they gained abroad. To create and to regulate markets is still a right of sovereignty. It is thus basically a *national* capitalism, with companies grounded in domestic politics, that uses the machinery of government to fight for the markets upon which their success depends. International economic law, like any other law, is a device for political purposes of all kinds, and the furthering of a liberal world trade order is only one of them. Also, the strength of international law, again like that of any other law, domestic or international, lies not in those who formally make it, but in the support brought to it by those over whom it rules, i.e. states. Because of this it does not make much sense to see international economic regimes in opposition to welfare states.

Welfare states and international economic order

If one accepts these propositions concerning the foreign trade policy of democratic welfare states and the characteristics of the 'liberal' international economic regimes, how does one then explain the rise of globalization and the increased free play of an international division of labour? Three causal factors play a role here: first, governments' common interests; second, the welfare-democratic quality of globalization; and, third, governments' interest in protecting welfare democracy from itself.

Let us begin with the third factor, for it describes the particular point of departure of the foreign trade policy of developed welfare states. The second factor provides the substantive content of this policy, and the first describes the formal preconditions of successful international political coordination.

This third factor renders clear why international economic policy until now has taken a decidedly liberal direction. As the apparently unstoppable expansion of the welfare state demonstrates, the democratic revolution was extremely successful in its attempt to create a counterweight to the capitalist market economy. This development points, however, to an old problem of every mass democracy: how is a market economy possible at all in a mass democracy on an enduring basis? How can welfare democracy be protected from the danger of undermining its own foundation, namely the revenue-generating power of the national economy? The political order of democracy and its authorized pillars – parties, parliaments and governments – are by their very nature ill-suited to provide such protection. Indeed, it is precisely this order that is the point of departure of welfare democracy.

Two institutional answers to the above question are the separation of powers and the protection of basic rights, especially property rights. Neither of these, however, corresponds to the logic of democracy. In a democracy, the *demos* strives for the greatest possible control over the fate of its members' lives. The separation of powers and the guaranteeing of inviolable basic rights restrict the freedom of action of a democratic government. Another answer is international policy as an attempt by governments to achieve increased credible governmental commitments by means of a vertical separation of powers. The point of departure here is the insight that although it is in the interest of both the government and the governed to have a well-functioning and thus productive market economy, this functionality is very difficult to maintain because of the ongoing temptation to correct both market outcomes and market processes by means of intervention and regulation (Weingast 1995; Quian and Weingast 1997).

Sooner or later, governments in all welfare democracies find that after a certain point in time they are no longer in a position to control social policy or to reinstil life into the market economy. Democratic institutions are hardly in a position to effectively strike and maintain a balance between a market economy and socio-political systems of (re)distribution (Marshall 1972: 123–36). This universal experience can become the groundwork of a shared interest among the governments, in particular of the more advanced welfare states, to voluntarily tie their hands through international economic policy, in order thereby to give the market economy greater and politically more secure freedom from government intervention. This shared interest is the point of departure for a truly supranational order of economic relations. We have shown above that – and why – this order is subject to numerous provisos. Most importantly, however, we should not lose sight of the point of departure of international free trade regimes: common government interest. For this shared interest defines the scope as well as the limits of potential action by this regime of a government of governments for governments in a community of states (M. Huber 1910).

A global economic government?

No one, not even the sharpest critic of globalization, goes so far as to claim that parliamentary democratic governments have finally given way to a government of unaccountable business leaders. Indeed, critics of globalization appeal to public opinion and to governments to put global capitalism on a political regulatory leash. They would certainly not do so if they assumed that neither of these organs of democratic society was in a position to fulfil this demand. At the same time, critiques of globalization cannot disguise the fact that, in the years since 1985 in which globalization unfolded, public opinion and democratically elected governments have been anything but neutralized, silenced or condemned to impotence. Citizens only accept the norms of a liberal trade system when these do not deny some end that they are determined to obtain, and the same is true with regard to welfare statism. Having both the constitutional and the institutional means at hand to change the basic course of economic policy, any long period of failure will induce the electorate to try the alternative to welfare statism, or, if markets and companies do not deliver on their promise of improved welfare, to turn back to the state.

The crisis of the welfare state, which is allegedly produced by globalization, is largely ideological, not political. More precisely, the concept of the welfare *state* overlooks the decisive point: what we are really dealing with here is welfare *democracy*. And there is no turning back from this, any more than there can be a return to an economy without machines and computers. The welfare state and the global market economy do get along very well, as is proven anew each day. In fact, the welfare-democratic reaction to big business is more democracy – if big business does not want to appear incompatible with welfare democracy, and this is something it cannot afford. It is less a matter of dependency on or subordination to the relationship of democracy to the market economy, than of a balance which is lost and which is then regained. It is not government but companies which create jobs, but in order to behave in a way that brings about this result, companies in turn need governments. The deregulation of markets and firms represents an attempt by governments to endow the liberal economic foundations of welfare democracy with a new dynamism. Conversely, corporations, too, are continually reminded by governments that they must earn anew their privileged status as artificial persons with limited liability. Property rights are essentially political artefacts, and their enforcement is dependent on a legal infrastructure which firms themselves cannot create (Coleman 1982; Braithwaite and Drahos 2000: 143–74; Soto 2000). Such shifts and re-orderings in the power relations of the state and the economy are perennial – striking a balance was and is the task of politics in a welfare democracy.

Politics in a welfare democracy is, in the final analysis, governed by public opinion. The operation of a market economy, too, is ultimately anchored in public opinion – not merely in high-priced lobbying. Public opinion is the definite arbiter in the fight between welfare state protagonists and those attracted to the market mechanism. The national deregulation initiatives of the early 1980s, which formed the point of departure for globalization, were an entirely *democratic* response to excessive welfare state intervention. The paradigmatic case of this pattern is Sweden. When the 'cradle-to-grave' welfare state in Sweden, with public expenditures fluctuating between 60 and 70 per cent of GNP, proved to be too heavy a burden on the economy, public opinion shifted to freer markets as the more promising source of welfare, and provided the parties with the political space necessary for economic reforms.[145] Table 2.14 shows the long-term decline of the Swedish economy and the inversion of public opinion on the relative merit of entrepreneurship and company formation. In the mind of the Swedish public the social policy apparatus of the most highly developed welfare state on the globe had endangered what the large, territorially bound majority expects of every capitalist market economy: attractive employment positions and a higher standard of living. The calculation of Henrekson (2001) shows that from 1970 to 1998 GDP growth in Sweden was normally one percentage point below the OECD average: 1.7 compared to 2.7 per cent per year. If we take OECD's purchasing-power-adjusted GDP per capita as a yardstick, Sweden developed very unfavourably relative to other OECD countries. Whereas in 1970 Sweden ranked fourth among the 23 richest OECD countries, it slipped to ninth place in 1990 and fell to eighteenth place in 1998. In the words of the OECD and its *Economic Survey* of March 2001, however, the performance of the Swedish economy has 'continued to be impressive', averaging around 4 per cent (OECD 2001: 10). The Swedish economy, the report noted, 'is probably stronger and better balanced than at any other point during the past three decades' (ibid.: 23).

145 'Turning Sweden around' was by no means a smooth process, but involved bitter fights – the social sciences being one of the main arenas of struggle (Korpi 1996, 2000; Henrekson 2001). Moreover, the political success of this turn-around is the more remarkable because the size of the grantee classes – persons depending for their livelihood primarily on the public purse – is remarkably high in Sweden. As OECD data show, the share of transfer recipients aged 16–64 – nearly all of them eligible to vote – rose from 26.5 per cent of the total workforce in 1965 to 67.0 per cent in 1995, and has been slowly decreasing since then, to 64.2 per cent in 1999 (2001: 103).

Table 2.14 Economic decline and shifting public opinion in Sweden, 1963–1997

Growth of real GDP per capita (1973–1991)		*Share of respondents believing that it is important to encourage entrepreneurship and company-formation*	
Year	*%*	*Year*	*%*
		1963	50
		1967	41
1973–89	1.7	1978	30
1990	0.6	1981	72
1991	–2.4	1985	74
		1997	88

Sources: Henrekson and Jakobsson (2001: 22); Korpi (1996: 1737)

Since the late 1980s a number of policy measures have been implemented, which, taken together, have replaced the traditional Swedish model with something very different.[146] After the Social Democrats' return to power in 1994, the public expenditure share of GDP shrank continually from 67 per cent to 54 per cent in 2001. In 1991 the corporate tax rate was cut in half and by 2001 stood at 28 per cent. The wealth tax on unlisted stock has been abolished, and a uniform 30 per cent capital income tax replaced a steeply progressive schedule. The highest marginal tax rate has been lowered from close to 90 per cent (1980) to roughly 55 per cent (2001). Labour markets have been deregulated, and the wage bargaining system, the pride of the Swedish model, has been vigorously decentralized. The extensive deregulation of previously regulated markets – such as domestic airlines (1992), the financial sector (1993), postal services (1993), telecommunications (1993) and electricity (1996) – has opened new arenas for entrepreneurial expansion. In the social services – most of all in health care, care for the elderly, and pre-school child care – there is now a significant share of private-sector production (OECD 2001: 118). In all income maintenance and transfer systems, replacement rates have been lowered and elegibility rules tightened. In 1998, Parliament adopted the requirement that municipalities and counties had to balance their budgets by 2000.

At the same time, public resources were shifted to more productive use, i.e. to the educational system and active labour market policy, helping to bring the unemployment rate down from over 10 per cent (1992) to 3.7 per cent (2002). Table 2.15 illustrates, by comparison, the great emphasis that Sweden puts on adult education. There should be little doubt, however, that the sweeping return to market mechanisms in Sweden, as well as in other mature welfare states, will encounter a negative political response and a return to the state when it is no longer accepted as materially benefi-

146 The following synopsis is based on Lindbeck (1997), Henrekson and Jakobsson (2001), Henrekson (2001) and OECD 2001.

Table 2.15 Share of population in selected age groups undertaking full-time education

	15–19 years	*20–9 years*	*30–9 years*	*Above 40 years*
Sweden	86.1	30.4	13.3	2.7
Germany	88.3	21.7	3.0	0.2
United States	74.2	21.4	5.6	1.6
OECD	76.3	20.4	4.4	1.2

Source: OECD (2000b)

cial by significant proportions of the population, as nation-state democracies provide a sounding board for such a response and also the institutional means to engineer it. The latest progression in antidumping practices is a telling example of such a turn of events.

Historically, capitalist market economies and democratic governance had to reach a fresh equilibrium on a regular basis:

> There is something about the government that makes it grow when it is attacked. The public likes competitive power systems. It wants both democracy and a high standard of living and thinks it can have both provided it can maintain a dynamic equilibrium between the democratic and the capitalist elements in the regime. The public is willing to try to get along with the capitalist system provided it can maintain alongside it a democratic political system powerful enough to police it.
>
> What has the equilibrium done to American government? It has meant that big business has had to be matched at all points by what Paul Appleby calls big democracy. Every change in the organization, technology, and scope of the economy has had to be matched by parallel changes in the organization of political power. The point is that governmental change becomes possible when it is necessary to preserve the equilibrium. Once we understand this proposition a host of other data fall into place because the necessities of the equilibrium determine what can and what cannot be done. (Schattschneider 1975 [1960]: 120f.)

Globalization is not the end of democratic governance. Rather, the new spatial and global economic environment has relegated governance to one of its conditioning factors. Moreover, in order to understand what is happening with organized, that is, *welfare* democracy, it has always been necessary to pay attention to what its main competitor for public influence does, and not only to the governmental-bureaucratic expressions of welfare democracy. The global economy, too, has to find legitimacy in the public arena. And in this arena, not only are the rules of the game of a very peculiar nature, but social standards are used to gauge the results of both welfare statism and markets. In private conflicts, the strong can dominate the weak, but in the public arena of welfare democracy, the many weak have united in self-defence and forged the weapons they need: social policy and the tax state, anti-trust legislation and competition authorities. More recent additions to this arsenal are international economic regimes. Transnationally active companies as the main bearers of the global economy have no such means of collective action. The surprising and, because of its welfare state underpinnings, quite precarious growth in the effectiveness of global governance structures is simply the flip side of economic globalization. Through international organizations – institutions of governments for governments – state officials have expanded a role that has always ranked among the tasks of the bearers of legitimate public power: mediating on the basis of social standards between the 'inside' (their populations) and the 'outside' (external power centres).

This counter-movement occurs almost automatically, is hardly visible and is made up of a myriad of discrete measures. It is almost never perceived to be what it is, because it is only seldom perceived as a response to globalization. Similarly, previous movements seeking to counter or to compensate for the concentration of private economic power have developed silently and quasi-automatically:

> The sense of urgency behind the drive to preserve the equilibrium is so strong and the compensatory changes in the government are made so easily that we are hardly aware of them. The reaction is almost automatic. That is how it happens that most of us do not know that we have created a new government. We thought that we were merely rallying to preserve the status quo. (Schattschneider 1975 [1960]: 123)

The perpetual process that Schattschneider is trying to address is constitutional political control, or managing large-scale social change. What he observes on the domestic scene can also be seen in the international setting: the creation of a new governance structure. But despite its far-reaching nature, this new mode of government is hardly noticed, because it is based on governments in welfare states, not on international organization.

States, and states alone, are themselves the principal institutions of the international *economic* society of states. It is first and foremost welfare state governments that 'protect' the rules of international economic law through the domestic political actions that it takes to set the national *social* scene so that the international rules will have a *sustained* chance to be effective. All the measures taken by governments of operational welfare states to control social conflict, to appease political dissatisfaction, to remove social and economic grievances small and big, to counter a disintegration that threatens to bring about the breakdown of society, presuppose an effectual national autonomy. Viewed in an international perspective, what these fundamentally *domestic* political acts have in common is that they are all directed towards the preservation of a liberal international economic order, not by directly upholding its rules, but by producing, fashioning and managing the social environment in which the rules operate *nationally* in such a way that they may continue to do so *internationally*. This kind of domestic social politics belongs to a sphere of action which the norms of international economic regimes themselves do not and cannot regulate, and may even obstruct, but which their successful operation nevertheless presupposes. The rules that sustain order in a basically non-interventionist international economic society can operate only if conditions obtain in the *domestic* political system that enable them to do so (Bull 1995 [1977]: 59).

In addition, as a second basic condition for order in the international economic society, the rules that sustain this order can only operate effectively if and to the degree that a sense of *common* interests among governments continues to exist, which they try to translate into a precise guide of conduct (Huber 1910; Bull 1995 [1977]: 73). It is thus quite misleading to see social policy, or welfare statism, in opposition to economic globalization and international interdependence. In some basic sense domestic social politics is a process whose central and distinguishing feature is the attempt to shape national decisions in foreign economic trade matters in relation to an agreed body of international legal rules. In consequence, both the existing forms and the prospects of economic globalization are bound up with the prospects of the welfare state culture that at present underlies its workings. This is not to deny that there is a basic conflict between the norms of international governance structures and the domestically determined notions of social justice. However, this conflict serves not only important *integrative* functions in the management of international economic relations; it is also asymmetric in the sense that its unwavering point of departure is a series of faits accomplis brought about by the forces of welfare democracy.

7 Outlook

This chapter cannot but end on a sceptical note. The material facts of welfare democracy forbid us simply to conclude from the complementary relationship between the expansion of welfare state benefit systems and the stabilization of a liberal foreign trade order, as seems a posteriori suggested, that this relationship is politically defensible, much less that this is somehow automatically guaranteed. Every international division of labour is grounded in national conditions which it itself can neither create nor safeguard. Liberal foreign trade policy is economically desirable, yet socially and thus politically improbable due to the particular nature of the economically most advanced nation-states, whose entire mode of governance is oriented towards the primacy of domestic welfare.

The unlikely emergence of a system of open and increasingly integrated national economies, the 'accidental success' (A. O. Krueger 1998: 4) of international trade after the Second World War, was made possible by an autonomous social policy. The latter pursues goals which are, strictly speaking, inevitably at variance with those of a liberal trade policy – the social politics of welfare democracies is not driven by export interests, not to mention import interests. The tangible *results* of comprehensive welfare statism could bring a turn towards a more socially unconcerned trade policy. The claims for social protection and for the compensatory equalization of distributional market outcomes for the politically and electorally significant groups in society had to be effectively fulfilled before foreign trade barriers could be lowered.[147]

It is precisely this circumstance that renders the world trade order quite fragile. It is dependent on conditions which it itself has neither created nor can, by itself, sufficiently sustain. Similarly, social policy is not, or at least not primarily, judged on which foreign trade conditions it permits, complicates or even precludes. Both sides of the relationship that produced a liberal world trade order and thus globalization – national

147 The basic consensus which, according to Streeck, shaped the post-war order in the Federal Republic of Germany, had its foreign trade and trade policy elements as well. With regard to the conditions that had to be fulfilled to allow the establishment of a market economy in the Federal Republic, he comes to the same conclusion concerning Germany's domestic situation as our investigation of the foundations of the new foreign trade order: 'Under the conditions of the West German post-war compromise, those who wanted to transform Germany into a liberal market economy had to accept the reincarnation of numerous traditionalist institutions of status-assurance – for farmers, civil servants, the middle classes etc. – as well as a comprehensive welfare state and well-established unions' (Streeck 1999: 17).

systems of social protection and a GATT framework compromised by national welfare state demands – have been in a state of continual flux since the 1970s.

Yet increasingly, these changes occurred more for autonomous reasons inherent to each side of the relationship than because of closely coordinated reactions between the two sides. In part, this can be attributed to the fact that organizations and institutions inevitably tend to follow a logic of their own the more they become entrenched. So social policy in developed welfare states, like trade policy in an institutionalized international regime, is increasingly confronted with problems which it itself has generated. In other words, the personnel and the immediate beneficiaries of these institutions developed an ever greater interest in these institutions' survival and expansion, and paid ever less attention to the secondary consequences of this for other realms of economy and society.

There is nothing in the complementary – but essentially unintended and thus accidental – relationship between social and trade policy which could provide anything like a foundation for guaranteeing a Leibnizian 'pre-stabilized harmony' of that relationship.

Trade policy arguments and foreign economic relations as a determinant of national welfare play virtually no role in contemporary reform debates on the restructuring of social insurance schemes – even though the impending decisions on social policy are highly relevant to trade policy and foreign economic relations. Almost all contemporary reform agendas and projects – whether workfare programmes, the privatization of parts of the health insurance system or the individualization and marketization of pension insurance accounts – would lead ultimately to a greater dependence of living conditions on the market. Admittedly – and usually rightly – such measures are justified with reference to a much greater incentive compatibility to labour markets. Such a turn may streamline public expenditure, but it may eventually bring down a free trade regime.

Under the twin conditions of a rapidly progressing technological revolution and a deeply antagonistic locational competition among governments, can those social protection needs, which are essential to the preservation of an open national economy, be met? It is even more true of the 'old' than of the 'New Economy' that its technical basis is revolutionary. Thus Marx's description still applies today:

> Modern industry never views or treats the existing form of a production process as the definitive one. Its technical basis is therefore revolutionary, whereas all earlier modes of production were essentially conservative. By means of machinery, chemical processes and other methods, it is continually transforming not only the technical basis of production but also the functions of the worker and the social combinations of the labour process. At the same time, it thereby also revolutionizes the division of labour within society, and incessantly throws masses of capital and of workers from one branch of production to another. Thus large-scale industry, by its very nature, necessitates variation of labour, fluidity of functions, and mobility of workers in all directions. (Marx 1977 [1867]: 617)

The establishment of a capitalist market economy swept away, 'with all repose, all fixity and all security as far as the worker's life-situation is concerned' (ibid.: 618). The security provided by social insurance schemes took its place. The latter not only made the new economic conditions – a 'ceaseless human sacrifice' (ibid.) – and the attendant employment, income and status losses acceptable to those individuals directly and (at first) negatively affected; non-market insurance also made it possible for national governments to pursue trade policies that opened up national economies, and still keep them open today.

However, neither free trade nor an international division of labour by themselves create jobs. Rather, they free incomes that can then be invested more productively. Whether and to what extent this occurs in actual fact depends on politically fashioned and thus not very reliable conditions. Social and particularly educational policies are only two of the factors that determine how creative and productive the ongoing destruction of the relations of production in the final analysis will prove to be. Open capital markets and liberal trade regulations not only can but, much more important, *have to* compensate the effects both of institutionally rigid individual and collective labour law and of higher taxation of labour for financing social protection schemes. To bemoan 'institutional rigidities' in labour markets and a high social burden on firms and consumers misses the crucial fact that social protection, to be effective, has to be unyielding.

This, however, is not an argument for etching worker protection *as we know it* in stone or for continuing the traditional forms of social insurance. One can think of forms of social rights which do not compromise its substance and are nevertheless more incentive compatible than the present ones. It is not only the complementarity of social and trade policy which scholars until now have considered insufficiently, but also the exact nature of social policy institutions and their consequences for companies and labour markets, i.e. their incentives compatibility.

Ultimately, it is not ideas and values but the concrete *outcomes* of trade and social policy, and thus the reactions of the citizenry, which are decisive for the future course of both trade policy and social policy. Under the democratic conditions of modern politics, there can be no doubt that a restrictive trade policy and economic nationalism constitute an ever-available means for responding politically – with intervention and regulation – to the 'devastating effects of social anarchy' (Marx 1977 [1867]: 618) unleashed by an open market economy. The core of the problem from a national political perspective is knowing whether domestic producers and consumers understand the trade-off involved and are prepared to shoulder the costs of a social policy – by way of higher taxes and thus consumption abstinence – that is capable of effectively and sufficiently providing compensatory non-market incomes. Those who profit from free trade are not by necessity willing to pay for this social infrastructure. It is also true, however, that not every advancement in social policy is compatible with free trade policy.

3

Defensive Globalization in the Welfare State: Foreign Trade Policy and Social Policy in the USA

The chaos of structure and function is matched by a chaos of political process. . . . The system of American government flaunts virtually all tenets of legislative responsibility and administrative effectiveness. It appears always to be wasteful of manpower and money. At times it threatens the very democracy it is established to maintain. But it works, it works – and sometimes with beauty.

Morton Grodzins 1966: 7

1 The Problem

Life courses in Germany, just as in other Western European societies, have long been embedded and anchored in welfare state systems of social protection (Mayer and Müller 1986, 1989; Mayer 2001b; Leisering and Leibfried 1999). This not only collectivizes most economic risks faced by the employed population, but also – the flip side of the coin – cultivates a negative disposition on their part towards changes in their personal situation in life. Workers tend to perceive their jobs and working conditions, as well as the corporatist management of the labour market by so-called social partners,[1] as a property right.[2] This makes the process of adapting to economic and technical change a major problem. For this reason alone, public discussions of 'globalization' in Continental Europe since the beginning of the 1990s have been largely conducted in negative terms. For broad strata of the population globalization is a worrying phenomenon, as a result of which politicians are discouraged from adopting it as a means of engaging in more radical socio-political reform.

One side emphasizes changes in demand for social policy goods as a consequence of the individualization of life courses, the dissolution of traditional forms of the familial division of labour, increased life expectancies and nursing care needs, new educational wants, and challenges of immigrant integration. Coming to terms with these new realities, they argue, requires expanding existing social policy offerings and creating new ones that are better suited to and more closely related to the workings of labour markets (Lampert 1995, 1999; F.-X. Kaufmann 1997a; Lindbeck 2001). The

1 Employer and employee associations have a shared, constitutionally guaranteed, and very broad authority over workplace matters, which is intricately linked not only to wage determination but also to a company's policy.

2 A consequence of this attitude may be illustrated by an agreement between Italian trade unions and the managers of the two airports of Milan, allowing early retirees to fill their posts with members of their own family (*FAZ*, 27 April 2002, p. 7).

other side of this policy debate underscores the necessity of deregulation, of reducing transfer expenditures and of turning unproductive transfer expenditures into productive educational ones. They argue for a restriction of the supply of social policy goods in order to give domestic companies in the new, seemingly boundless global economy opportunities for growth and innovation, which would, in turn, foster new occupational and biographical prospects for employees (Siebert 1996a, b; Hüther 1997; OECD 1997).

In this chapter, we suggest that both sides of this discussion fail to take into account the functional and thus reciprocal relationships that exist between open world markets and socio-politically organized, intrasocietal capacities to react, adapt and shape up. Compensatory social policies, we propose, are, in both theory and practice, an instrument to defend the public interest in trade policy-making. It helped to discipline those protectionist trade policy practices that could compromise society's overall interest – namely, freer trade. Whereas the interface between 'inside' and 'outside' is alternately praised and vilified, its precise form and significance are seldom examined. In this chapter, these interrelationships will be described and analysed in terms of their societal causes and consequences – above all for foreign trade policy-making – using the surprisingly unfamiliar case of the strongest economic power in the current global market, the United States of America.

At first glance it might appear as if regulatory burdens in the realm of social protection play a minor role in the United States' overall system of state, market and personal welfare production as compared to (Western) European welfare states. This might be used to explain the tremendous competitiveness of US firms and the attractiveness of the USA as a market and production site. We will show in the following, however, that this is misleading. With regard to the *political* responsibility assumed for the welfare of its citizens, the United States is not an exception. Focusing on the USA's lower levels of social and public expenditures as a proportion of GDP and lower tax burdens on both individuals and corporations – cited again and again as a locational advantage – underestimates the importance of, for example, the extent of the expansive social regulation of the workplace, of extensive consumer protection and of a vast scope of rigidly enforced employee benefit schemes.[3] Employee protection rights in the workplace, consumer protection and government regulation – not only via the tax code – of the market supply of social policy goods are functionally equivalent to the transfer-oriented European-style welfare state (Stevens 1988; Howard 1993, 1997; Jacoby 1997a; Nivola 1997).

The welfare-*democratic* commitment of the US government is not weaker than that of other states. It does not consciously abstain from regulation and political intervention in the interest of the greater good of market efficiency. Rather, this engagement merely assumes different *forms* because political actors are confronted with a federally divided polity and an extremely heterogeneous population. Further consequences follow from this as well, not only for social policy but also for other realms of public

[3] Nearly three-quarters of all employees in the USA in 1999 received health insurance from their employer (Green Book 2000: 796). The employer expenditures associated with this can be seen in the amount of revenue lost to the federal government as a result of employer tax deductions of their health insurance contributions. The estimated cost for 2001 amounted to $359 billion. Occupational pensions, meanwhile, cost the government $373 billion in lost revenue. This *fiscal* social policy will soon amount to almost two-thirds of federal social expenditures (ibid.: 780; US Census Bureau 1999: 386).

policy. The public sector's welfare-democratic engagement in the USA is evident in its socio-politically driven and highly intensive regulation of foreign trade. The US government attempts much more than its European counterparts to influence employment and wage levels through micro-management of foreign trade. US trade policy thus constitutes, to a very great extent, a system of welfare state intervention. For this reason, the relationship between trade policy and social policy in the USA differs greatly from that in Western Europe. Globalization in the USA thus rests on very different trade policy foundations, assumes different forms and leads to different consequences for social policy. The politics of socialized trade of the USA is guided by an exclusive foreign economic nationalism, which impels it to use its position of global economic dominance for purely domestic purposes.

The US situation is surprising in that it combines several cumulative factors: an economic boom, which extended throughout the entire decade of the 1990s, international attractiveness measured in an extraordinary influx of capital and a commanding international position of many US companies in their economic sectors. All of this contrasts in peculiar ways with the country's foreign economic and trade *policies*, which would lead one to expect dire economic conditions.

The US case shows, first, that economic conditions – and, above all, the daily decision-making behaviour not only of managers but also of investors and large segments of the employed workforce – can achieve a surprising degree of independence vis-à-vis the politically determined framework and government attempts at shaping and influencing economic behaviour. The US economy has achieved its success not *as a result of*, but *despite* US trade policy. In other words, the domestic market is still much more important than world markets for the performance of American companies. Nevertheless, it is to be expected, second, that (trade) policy realities will catch up sooner or later with economic conditions. For this reason, too, the US case is of particular interest. That which occurs in the USA has direct consequences for the rest of the world economy. Furthermore, governmental micro-management of trade policy tends to have long-term consequences, since it invites corporate rent-seeking.

2 The Political Nature of Economic Internationalization

Globalization, understood as the integration of national economies and the approximation of national systems of social, economic and fiscal policy, is chiefly caused, so the argument commonly goes, by two factors: the first is the revolution in transport and communication, the second the rebirth of the liberal market economy in the wake of the democratic revolutions which, since 1989, have put an end to the socialist 'second' world.

However, there are several problems with this understanding. First of all, technological progress is a cumulative and continuous historical process (M. Brown 1966). Over the last 150 years, though, phases of international integration have always alternated with phases of disintegration. Second, productivity levels among developed economies have not developed – even remotely – evenly, much less convergently. Around 1870, those fifteen countries that, together with the USA, formed the core of the international economy of the time, averaged only 77 per cent of US productivity. This ratio fell to 57 per cent by 1929, finally reaching its lowest point of 46 per cent in 1950. By 1979, however, it had climbed back to 75 per cent (Abramovitz 1986:

391). If one compares the global economic situation around 1900 with that of today, it becomes clear that the contemporary realities of trade and economic policy in a fragmented world of states are the product of a fundamental *de*-globalization. Third, contrary to an often-voiced sentiment, the progress towards global market integration has little to do with greater cognizance on the part of economic policy-makers. The argument that the international division of labour leads to greater market efficiency was supplied by Adam Smith and David Ricardo long ago, and this theory has become the largely unquestioned dogma ever since (Sykes 1998). Yet most real world markets have been shaped by extremely protectionist national trade policies. Only Great Britain constituted an exception in this until the First World War – confirming the obtaining protectionist rule elsewhere.

For these reasons, Paul Krugman does not see technical progress, and the economic policy imperatives that are said directly to result from such progress, as the foundation of the new global market economy. Instead, he points to the essentially political causes of growing world trade and increasing economic integration:

> International economists . . . tend to view much, though not all, of the growth of trade as having essentially political causes, seeing its great expansion after World War II largely as a result of the removal of the protectionist measures that had constricted world markets since 1913. At least implicitly, therefore, they also tend to see the trend towards growing integration as potentially reversible. (1995: 328)

Krugman does not elaborate this argument on the politics of globalization any further. Yet his understanding of the essentially political nature of economic globalization goes to the heart of the matter. He underscores how precarious the steps towards global market integration are, and thus considers them to be reversible.[4] Prerequisite to a national economy's sustained integration in the world market under conditions of mature welfare *democracy*, therefore, is the supporting role of domestic and, above all, social policy.[5] In this perspective, globalization is the product of a development created by *individual* states. Its course is determined by *how* these states operate in the globalized world. *No* government simply executes the allegedly imperative duties necessary actually to sustain a globalized economy – *every* government is exclusively concerned with its *own* economy. The electorate makes sure this is so. For this reason, the institutional foundation of global market integration is anything but stable. The quite

[4] Alan Greenspan, Chairman of the Federal Reserve Board, in the First Annual Stavros S. Niarchos Lecture at the Institute for International Economics, shares this essentially *political* view of globalization and recognizes the political power of the 'dissidents' favouring 'politically imposed systems, employing the power of the state to override the outcomes arrived at through voluntary exchange': 'Technological advance and globalization distress those who once thrived in industries that were at the forefront of technology but which have since become increasingly noncompetitive. In each step of incremental advance, the distance between gainers and losers is necessarily narrow. So it is understandable that our exceptionally complex system for the international distribution of goods, services, and finance is not universally recognized as successful at enhancing standards of living and promoting civil values worldwide. Indeed, those who perceived the need to protect economies from open trade have endeavored since its inception to slow or even reverse the forces supporting global expansion' (Greenspan 2001: 2).

[5] The analytically and politically most vexing question concerns, of course, the exact particulars of social policies, i.e. the adequacy, or the functional relations between provisions for social security on the one hand and the prerequisites of markets, particularly labour markets, on the other hand. On this point see below chapter 4, pp. 187 ff.

unexpected fact of the persistent *reality* of global market integration is thus what calls for an *explanation*.

That a world economy with globally active corporations emerged at all is ultimately the product of, and dependent upon, the fact that governments dismantled their protective barriers to foreign trade for endogenous, domestic reasons. They did not do so in the interest of a global market economy. Globalization is thus by no means an independent entity external to governments, which confronts them with an ineluctable fate, thereby eroding the economic foundations of the traditional nation-state.[6] Rather, it is a product of *simultaneous* and *parallel* national economic and especially trade policy decisions. The equi-directional process in which the advanced economies have opened themselves up to world markets has its foundation in *shared* problems of domestic economic and social policy. At their core is the phenomenon that in a democratic political framework governments are themselves faced with the challenge of striking a balance between the ever-present demand by electorally dominant majorities for social policy goods and the essentially minority problem of taking care of the functional demands of a market economy. The move by electorally dependent governments to international institutions provides a quasi-constitutional device to credibly commit governments to abstain from troublesome economic micro-management and expansionist social policy. The common problem of governmental overload due to an excessive amount of discretionary interventions into economy and society provides the decisive foundation for every impulse to coordinate and organize truly international institutions of freer trade, and, by implication, rule-bound domestic economic and social politics: *shared* or at least *complementary* national interests. In the final analysis, then, it was the domestic predicament of governments having to manage mature welfare democracies which paved the way for that which we call the globalized economy: private actors making use of the new liberal international economic framework. In other words, the globalized economy is, to a very large degree, the unintended consequence of a solution for some other problem.

For this reason, there is admittedly no guarantee that this formation will not turn against its political creators. Demands for a 'civilizing' or 'taming' global capitalism, even if they are draped in the seemingly harmless form of a call for a 'global financial architecture', appear to be precisely such a counter-reaction, while confirming in their own way the fundamentally political nature of this type of capitalism.

Yet how does globalization's dependency on national policy play out in practice? What role does social policy play in this context, and what is the relationship between foreign economic and trade policy and social policy? And, conversely, what are the implications of the new national and international economic environment for the fate of national social policy?

New challenges for social policy

Even if one seeks not to raise globalization to the status of a hegemonic behemoth, there can be no doubt that a series of economic changes is occurring which has a formative impact on society and politics. The following changes are particularly significant:[7]

[6] See also the carefully chosen words with which Alan Greenspan describes globalization: 'Globalization as generally understood involves the increasing interaction of the world's peoples *through the national economic systems*' (Greenspan 2001: 1; emphasis added).

[7] Cf. Ringlstetter and Skrobarczyk (1994), Osterloh and Weibel (1996), Proff and Proff (1996), Baron (1997), and Proff (1997).

1. The expansion of markets and the emergence of global patterns of consumption are creating new opportunities to make use of economies of scale and scope. Spending on research and development have to bear fruit more quickly, for in the information economy competitive advantages are usually only temporary in nature.
2. The economic integration of regions with unequal levels of development opens up new possibilities for linking firm-specific (competitive) with national (comparative) advantages. With globalization, geographic differences in input costs translate into improved chances of sourcing out individual elements of the value chain to countries with comparative advantages.
3. Improved investment conditions yield new opportunities to invest capital abroad (portfolio investments), to circumvent national barriers to market entry by developing production sites abroad, to transfer marketing, distribution and customer service abroad and thus to aim these activities at specific markets, bring them closer to the customer and develop lobbying power through local firm presence. Such a lobbying presence has become more important, particularly in the granting of government contracts and in the influencing of national trade and economic policy.

What consequences for the welfare state arrangements of advanced Western industrial societies do these changes in their economic environment have? And what implications do they have for the action horizon of national social policy?

The ornate institutions of the welfare state, liberal economists claim, make it more difficult for managers to adapt to competitive conditions and to adopt organizational innovations quickly and to the extent required. Social regulation of employment, they argue, increases the potential for resistance among employees who are seemingly negatively affected by restructuring measures; social rights function as disincentives; and the forms of financing social policy together with the collective bargaining policy of the 'labour market cartels' of unions and employer associations create their own brand of market-entry barriers to protect current job-holders (Shlaes 1994; Rüthers 1996, 2000). Moreover, generous welfare state support of a growing mass of unemployed persons reinforces the labour market cartel: despite new labour market and competitive conditions, as liberal economists observe, real wages of employed persons have remained stable.[8] Further, the scale and structures of national social policies still largely reflect nation-state conditions of times long gone by. There is a serious misalignment between welfare state structures and contemporary social and workplace conditions (Lindbeck 2001). In the meantime, however, the foundations of a nation-state economy and thus also of strictly inward-looking, exclusionary trade and social policies have given way: controls of capital flows, import restrictions in the form of tariffs and autonomous currency policy have now been definitely relegated to the past. In addition, the rationale for clinging to traditional forms of social policy has diminished, so the liberal argument goes (Berthold 1997; Tanzi 2000).

A sociological perspective on the development of social policy

What are the scientific merits of these arguments? Initial grounds for caution are due to the fact that the conditioning factors of the individual elements of this ostensibly unambiguous constellation can easily change. The current cost-benefit calculation with

[8] This seems to be a German peculiarity in the context of globalization (Prasad 2000).

regard to national social policy and global economic conditions, regularly considered to speak unquestionably against the traditional system of social policy, could easily reverse. As the examples of Japan and then of the Southeast Asian countries after 1996–7 have shown, institutional arrangements between the market and social policy, which initially were seen as advantages, can very quickly turn into disadvantages. Precisely because the new global market conditions may trigger very rapid, equidirectional and thus powerful reactions by large groups of independent economic actors, national competitive advantages can undergo a *Gestalt*switch virtually overnight. It is then that the value of welfare state institutions could become manifest, for these can serve as buffers, giving the affected economies and firms the time and flexibility they need to rebuild their institutional infrastructure. Karl Polanyi called attention to the fact that the swiftness of processes of economic change constitutes the critical variable for successful adaptation strategies.[9] In periods of accelerated and kaleidoscopic economic change in which the final direction of change is not yet discernible, but decisions about adaptation have to be made, nevertheless, on a continuous basis, time is a scarce resource, for it determines the rationality of these measures: 'The incredible rate at which the economy and society is changing causes people to lose their bearings' (Fogel 2000: 82).[10]

Second, particularly in Western Europe, national systems of social protection arose in the context of open national economies. In the German case, for example, export dependency and import competition are by no means new phenomena, and thus in all probability are already reflected in and accounted for in the institutional structures of German welfare statism. Therefore, one must look more closely to see which forms of social policy could – or, according to some experts, will inevitably – be jeopardized by globalization. The demographic transition to a top-heavy age profile, for example, looming in all advanced economies, sets the reform agenda for both old-age pension and health care systems. Globalization, meanwhile, especially with regard to capital markets, facilitates a solution to these problems more than it feeds into their causation (Pierson 1998, 2001: 80–104).[11]

Third, and even more crucial to an understanding of the current fate of welfare states and their socio-political horizon of action, the relationship between social policy and economic development is structurally indeterminate. Neither the macro- nor the micro-economic consequences of socio-political intervention and welfare state institutionalization follow a monodirectional logic. Both periods of high growth and deep recessions are typically conducive to increased social spending, the first because of a 'growth dividend', the latter because of pressing social need. In addition, the institutional and organizational particularities of the institutionalization of social policy measures is decisive for their *secondary* consequences for companies and for the

[9] 'The rate of change is often of no less importance than the direction of the change itself; but while the latter frequently does not depend upon our volition, it is the rate at which we allow change to take place which well may depend upon us' (K. Polanyi 1957 [1944]: 36–7).

[10] Bhagwati and Dehejia (1994: 36) see the 'increased randomization of comparative advantage in different manufactures' as the main source of more rapid turnover among workers and thus heightened anxiety about job loss.

[11] Moreover, openness vis-à-vis immigration can slow the demographic transition and hereby considerably lower its economic costs (Borjas 1994, 1995). The internationalization of capital markets eases the transition to funded forms of old-age insurance, for it reduces dependence on the national stock of capital and on the national savings rate.

national economy, since it may either assist in or block adaptation to changing circumstances. To complicate the picture even further, economic success is also possible *in opposition to* and *despite* limiting framework conditions. Hence, to transform disadvantages in the external environment – and this includes as a rule the political-institutional framework which cannot, or at least not without great difficulty, be changed – into *conditions* of strategic action, has always been a prominent task of effective management.[12] Finally, in terms of its rationale and legitimating values, social policy is an independent entity. Neither the political forces behind it nor its fiscal scope are driven solely, or even principally, by prospects of corporate profits or increases in macro-economic productivity. On the contrary, there are powerful groups which 'view societal organization based on the profit motive and corporate culture as fundamentally immoral' (Greenspan 2001: 2).

In general, social policy is oriented towards *social* needs that have their origins in the *subjective experience* of specific social wants, which in democracies will sooner or later be acted upon by political entrepreneurs and thereby find their institutional expression. The distributional outcome of the market economy is a *cause* of the demand for social policy goods, but not the gauge of that which is politically possible (Marshall 1949, 1972; Rieger 1998a). Finally, the process of social policy must always reckon with what Max Weber called the 'substantive features of so-called "democracy"' (1978: 215). The most important of these features is that in a democracy it is far more pivotal *how* political conflicts are resolved and especially *who* makes these decisions than what their material content is or their end–means rationality measured in terms of objective functional relationships (Lewis 1952).

Thus, apart from the fact, discussed above, that advantage–disadvantage constellations can be reversed, there are also ongoing conditioning and adaptation processes that run in *both* directions. On the one hand, socio-political interventions and institutions set the framework conditions – not easily influenced by firms – for business activity. On the other hand, markets judge in their own way which social policy and how much of it is acceptable, as is evident in the development of capital in- and outflows, unemployment, and productivity and profitability.

In both respects, reformers act in an open setting. In this setting, only the often unintended consequences or the long-term effects of the shifts in the relationship between social policy and a market economy, between social regulation and deregulation (often ignored for reasons of political short-term payoffs) play out: such as impoverishment, rising social and regional inequalities and mass unemployment, capital flight, the rise of an informal economy and excessive overtime. But even then it is only rarely possible, in terms of rational political action, to attribute *specific* outcomes to *unambiguously identifiable* causes, much less to convincingly derive political policy recommendations and secure their passage in the legislative process. Such elements of uncertainty, or even ruptures, are inherent in a matter shaped by dynamic reciprocal states, not by unilateral dependencies. Moreover, on both sides in industrial relations, institutional conditions and the organizational details of collective action have considerably influenced the potential to confront economic challenges successfully. In any

12 This statement is meant as an observation of an *empirical* state of affairs. This implies neither that the present-day, largely politically fashioned framework conditions are acceptable by standards either of egalitarian justice or economic efficiency, nor does it deny that concerted efforts are being made to change them.

case, determining the 'appropriate' amount and the functionally most adequate form of social policy *ex ante* – even if *all* politicians, and their opponents, claim this of their policies – lies beyond the capacity of political control in a democratic welfare state.

In many respects, the example of the United States is instructive with regard to the interrelations between social policy and market development:

1 First of all, the development of US trade policy since the end of the Civil War shows how tariff policy was burdened first and foremost with social functions, and how the introduction of national institutions of social protection during the Great Depression created a freedom of action, which had been lacking up until then, and which allowed for the liberalization of trade policy. Ultimately, this development demonstrates how certain peculiarities of US trade policy – mainly its use as a discretionary tool, its concentration on specific sectors of the US economy, its broad range of activating mechanisms and its multitude of interventions and transfers – can be attributed to specific deficits in the scope and efficiency of the US welfare state itself.
2 Second, recent developments of US trade policy show how welfare state institutions can function as a precondition for the further lowering of trade barriers and for the toleration of increased import competition – and where the *social* and thus also *political* limits of a further opening of US markets lie.
3 Third and finally, a hardly noticed development in the realm of US fiscal welfare reveals which new structural forms of social policy are more compatible with – and thus have better chances of realization in – the new market, company and international competitive context than the traditional intervention and transfer programmes of social insurance and social assistance. It also suggests how, despite or precisely because of these welfare state reform projects, US trade policy became more protectionist.

3 The Protectionism of the United States

After the UK, which it would soon overtake, the USA was, in the second half of the nineteenth century, the capitalist country par excellence. Here, capitalism and the market economy – unhindered by traditions of rigid social strata and absolutist state intervention – could frame societal conditions which then provided them with optimal prospects for development (Sombart 1976 [1906]). Yet in one respect the USA did not follow the UK example: the USA comprehensively and enduringly closed itself off from the rest of the world through the middle of the twentieth century. In its economic development, it was strictly inward-looking (Irwin 1996b). Table 3.1 shows the relatively limited degree of global economic integration of the US in various periods.

Viewed from an historical-comparative perspective, the USA is a latecomer in the development of a welfare state. Whereas Bismarck and Lloyd George had founded the modern social-insurance state well before the end of the 'long nineteenth century', the USA needed the political challenge of the economic catastrophe of the Great Depression to neutralize resistance to comprehensive federal competencies in the organization of publicly run income security programmes (Amenta 1998; Pierson 1995). This was also due to the fact that tariff barriers were long understood by politicians and the electorate to be the functional equivalent of social policy (Eaton and

Table 3.1 The world market integration[a] of the USA, the United Kingdom and Germany, 1913–1998

	1913	*1950*	*1970*	*1987*	*1998*
US	3.9	2.9	4.4	7.4	11.9
UK	27.7	13.1	16.6	21.1	27.4
Germany	19.9	9.8	17.4	23.3	28.3

[a] Average of exports and imports as % of GDP

Source: Krugman (1995: 331) and own calculation based on IMF (1999a)

Table 3.2 A comparison of tariff barriers, 1913

Country	*Tariffs as % of total imports*	*Average tariff rate (manufacturing)*
US	21.4	44
UK	5.7	0
Germany	7.9	13
France	8.7	20

Source: Bairoch (1989: 77, 139)

Grossman 1985). This trade policy condition first delayed and then distorted the formation of a welfare state, and ultimately produced a unique brand of welfare statism.[13] After the Civil War, the policy of high tariffs was legitimated and justified with the argument that they allowed the USA to protect its internationally comparatively high income levels and to stabilize employment.[14] Employers valued import tariffs because they provided compensation for higher wage costs, thus compensating for this competitive disadvantage vis-à-vis foreign competitors, and because they had the additional benefit of creating a *private* rent. As we can show in Table 3.2, the USA in 1913 constituted a more strongly protected fortress than any of the countries of Western Europe. President Benjamin Harrison characterized the 'tariff protection system' of the USA in 1892 as:

> [a] mighty instrument for the development of our national wealth and a most powerful agency in protecting the homes of our workingmen from the invasion of want. . . . A general process of wage reduction can not be contemplated by any patriotic citizen without the gravest apprehension. It may be . . . possible for the American manufacturer to compete successfully with his foreign rival in many branches of production without the defence of protective duties if the pay rolls are equalized, but . . . the distress of our working people when it is attained . . . [is] not pleasant to contemplate. (Cited in Eckes 1995: 279)

13 On the latecomer status and the different type of welfare state in the USA, see the discussion in Glazer (1988: 168–92, 204–5; 1998), Hacker (2002), and Amenta and Skocpol (1989).

14 In his classical explanation of the conspicuous absence not only of socialism, but also of a social welfare state, Sombart (1906: 81–126 [English 1936]) statistically supports his contention that in most sectors US wages were twice as high as in Europe.

Foreign trade and social policy in the New Deal

The integration of US markets into the international economy is thus a relatively recent phenomenon. Its institutional foundations, which still determine trade policy today, were not created until Franklin D. Roosevelt's New Deal of 1933. The New Deal not only nationalized and institutionalized social policies; it also effected a divide in US trade policy. Only four years after the infamous Smoot-Hawley Tariff Act of 1930 – which raised protective tariffs to record levels and thus increased the economic difficulties of the Great Depression – came the Reciprocal Trade Agreement Act (RTAA) of 1934, which put an end to the 'American system' of protective tariffs (Lusztig 1996; Irwin and Kroszner 1999). With this law, the US Congress empowered the President to engage other countries in binding negotiations on bilaterally lowering tariffs and, more importantly in political terms, to implement the resulting agreements without seeking Congressional approval. Step-by-step, the US market for imports was opened. By 1945, thirty-two bilateral trade agreements had been concluded with twenty-seven countries on the basis of strict reciprocity, and the average tariff rates sank by 44 per cent (Destler 1986: 10). The RTAA of 1934 brought about a sharp rupture with the previous regime of extreme protectionism, and this law then laid the foundation for US efforts after the Second World War to secure a new liberal order in world markets. In the end, and despite its tortuous ways, this led in 1947 to the General Agreement on Tariffs and Trade (GATT), through which, subsequently, particularly since the 1970s, the opening of world markets was organized and stabilized.

As in earlier periods of extreme protectionism, in the New Deal as well, social ruptures found their political-institutional answers. In the minds of protagonists and their followers, the protective tariff policy served to stabilize employment, to forestall changes in primary income distribution and to rebalance patterns of distribution and consumption, all of this step-by-step and at a self-determined, i.e. *politically* controlled pace. The institutionalization of national social policy programmes during the Great Depression – in particular the introduction of an unemployment insurance scheme, active employment programmes and elements of federal social assistance – provided the Roosevelt administration with the means to directly address US social problems in a domestic political context, and at the same time to shape its international trade more freely.[15] This new latitude in trade policy formulation as a result of the enhancement of welfare-statist income protection was not the product of reflected, rational planning in which the relative advantages and disadvantages of trade and welfare-statist income protection were weighed. Roosevelt himself was elected on an economic-nationalist platform. In his inaugural address he declared: 'Our international trade relations, though vastly important, are in point of time and necessity secondary to the establishment of a sound national economy' (cited in D. M. Kennedy 1999: 388).

In any case, a glance at the literature of the time shows that the social legitimation of tariff policy was discursively and functionally separated from the issue of its factual consequences for the economic well-being of the population. The main beneficiaries of high tariffs were certain groups of producers whom tariff policy provided with two sets of opportunities: first, to cream off profits due to the exclusion of competition, at

[15] An overview of this socio-political development is provided by Heclo (1995). The theoretical connection between protectionist trade policy and social policy discussed here can be found first in Corden (1997 [1974]: 4). It is further elaborated above in ch. 2, pp. 63–5 ff.

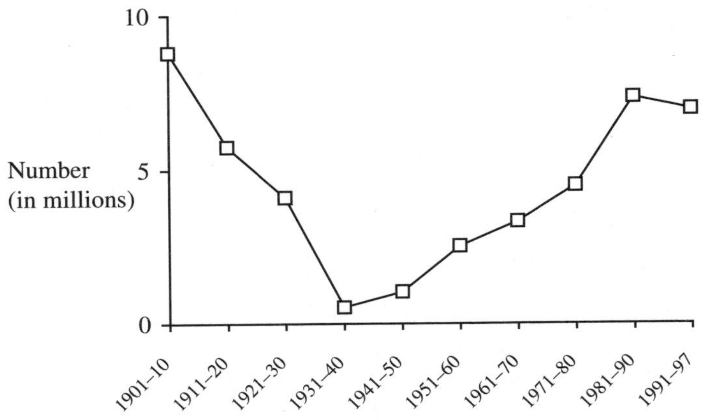

Figure 3.1 Immigration into the USA, 1900–1997 (in millions)
Source: US Census Bureau (1999: 872)

the expense of consumers, and secondly to organize cartels – which, in the context of the industrial labour relations of the time, occurred to the detriment of workers (H. Levy 1905; Hobson 1907). Their cartel organization enabled these employers very successfully to counter both the wage demands of workers and their attempts to unionize (Montgomery 1987).[16] Compared to Continental Europe, the USA was a high-wage country and thus a correspondingly attractive immigration magnet (Sombart 1976 [1906]; J. Williamson 1998a: 154–8). Transatlantic mass migration then greatly contributed to undermining the privileged position of labour (J. Williamson 1995, 1996; Goldin 1994; Goldin and Katz 2000). Declining real wages in the final decade before the outbreak of the First World War mobilized a union movement against a liberal immigration policy. The restrictive immigration laws which were then passed after the First World War put the finishing touches on US protectionism (M. Jones 1992 [1960]). Figure 3.1 shows how US immigration developed in absolute terms after 1900. The massive restriction of immigration after the First World War led to a demographic situation in which the share of the US population born in the USA increased steadily from 71.3 per cent in 1900 to 94.4 per cent in 1970. Due to increasing immigration since then, this share has fallen back to just under 90 per cent in 1997 (based on data from US Census Bureau 1999: 872). The factor that is probably most responsible for the formation and development of this protectionist foreign trade policy is the country's early democratization – the introduction of the universal male franchise[17] – and the formation of a two-party system in which the social needs of wage labourers represented a central issue in competition for votes. It was the Republicans who equated tariff protection with public welfare. The US economist and former chairman of the US International Trade Commission, Alfred E. Eckes, Jr., details in his history of US

16 Prior to the First World War, US anti-trust laws were enforced far less often against firms than against unions, and were thereby the most significant means of obstructing the labour movement (A. T. Mason 1969 [1925]).

17 In 1830 the last state repealed its provision stipulating minimum property ownership as a precondition for the franchise. To this day, the USA lacks a uniform national electoral law (Keyssar 2000).

trade policy how the Republican Party was able, by means of an ostensibly employment-oriented high tariff policy, to win 14 out of 18 presidential elections between 1860 and 1928 (1995: 281).

This expressly social motivation for tariff policy is thus part of the reason why the US did not introduce federal social policy programmes on the model of those of Bismarck or Lloyd George until FDR's New Deal.[18] The social policy of the New Deal, in particular the new national social assistance programme and the similarly national – albeit run by the states – unemployment insurance programme, gave the federal government leeway to increasingly back off from protectionism and to implement and maintain a liberal foreign trade policy (Lusztig 1996: 49–70).

With this radical reversion in foreign economic policy brought about by the New Deal, a principle became dominant in the USA which Max Corden (1997 [1974]: 74) terms the conservative welfare function. In ideal-typical exactitude, it expresses the following maxim of government action: 'Any significant absolute reductions in the real income of any significant section of the community should be avoided.' According to Corden, this is 'conservative' because, in practice, albeit not being exactly the same, it largely presumes the existing distribution of income to be the best and thus worthy of preservation. In such a welfare function, and expressed in terms of welfare weights, income *losses* are weighted far more than their equivalent in income *increases*.

The 'conservative welfare function' helps us understand why tariff policy is intricately linked with the social policy objectives of providing income and employment security. Further, it renders clear the liberating effect that the introduction of social policy can have on the regulation of trade policy. To the extent that *social* objectives can be achieved through *social policy* itself, governments need not take recourse to tariffs or other foreign economic policy tools with which they would otherwise attempt to reduce or eliminate the pressure of import competition on the domestic economy. The social efficiency of the welfare state thus increases. Tariffs can then be lowered, which can result in lower prices for domestic consumers and cheaper primary products for industry. This promises not only economic but also political dividends.

Let us put this differently: until a country is equipped with such an institutionally autonomous social policy infrastructure, it is not, in an effectively democratic framework, in a position to allow extensive integration of its economy in world markets and thus to take advantage of the international division of labour. In the US case, it

[18] A further important reason is the revenue basis of the federal government. Until the First World War, tariffs were the single biggest source of revenue. The very first law passed by the US Congress under its new Constitution was a measure to raise tariffs. The delegate James Madison introduced the measure, with the justification of providing the federal government with revenues and protecting industry (Duty Act of 4 July 1789, see O'Halloran 1994: 2). The US Constitution gives Congress, and not the President, sole power to conclude commercial treaties, and, at first, it prohibited the introduction of a nationally levied direct income tax. The 16th Amendment (1913) then gave the federal government the power to exact an income tax. The income tax was raised in part to remove the fiscal need for high tariffs and thus to give the country greater room for manoeuvre in trade policy, i.e. to lower tariffs (Hody 1996: 58 and 68). Already in 1894, in the context of the repeal of the rather high McKinley Tariff and the enactment of the Wilson-Gorman Tariff, Wilson's Free Trade Act tried to pre-empt the effect on the federal budget that tariff reductions would have by introducing an income tax (Terrill 1969). The income tax law, however, was rejected by the Supreme Court in 1896 as unconstitutional. The income tax law which went into effect in 1913, like its predecessor, was introduced as part of the tariff-reducing Underwood Tariff. On the relationship between US trade policy and the fiscal basis of the federal government, see Baack and Ray (1985) and J. M. Hansen (1990).

is evident that Roosevelt's initiatives in social and foreign trade policy stabilized each other.[19] First, these initiatives provided the foundations for an opening of US markets in exchange for corresponding export opportunities for US industry. Over the course of time, these new growth prospects for the economy translated into greater latitude in social policy. One cannot argue, however, that Roosevelt and the architect of the new trade policy, Cordell Hull, carried out this volte-face in foreign economic policy in order to generate the fiscal basis necessary for a more expansive social policy.[20] Yet it was indeed Cordell Hull who, as a member of Congress in 1907, introduced a federal income tax law which, after passage of a constitutional amendment, came into operation in 1913 (Hull 1948: I.48–61).

Trade policy compensation for welfare state deficits

After the Second World War, US free trade policy was by no means absolute – it was always compromised by a myriad of limitations and provisos (Magee and Young 1987; Goldstein 1988; Irwin 1994; Rodrik 1995; M. A. Cameron and Tomlin 2000). First of all, from the start, agriculture was excluded from the RTAA. In the subsequent GATT negotiations, the USA requested and was granted a waiver for its protectionist agricultural policy, which continued, albeit in different forms, until the end of the Uruguay Round (Dam 1970: 260). With this removal of agriculture from the new liberalized framework of world trade, the fate of this sector – also in the developing European Union – was sealed. It enjoys an exceptional status through to the present day. Family farming has been the reason why the USA, and later most other countries, have clung to agricultural protectionism – at least that is the public relations side of this public intervention. But there is more to it, otherwise the rhetoric would not have worked over such a long time. In contrast to other economic sectors, in agriculture the social unit of the household and the economic undertaking are *not* distinct. For this reason, such family enterprises are considered to be socially and economically particularly vulnerable. Moreover, for those working in these traditional economic units there existed no – or at least no sufficient – functionally differentiated income protection schemes such as those prevalent in the industrial sector. Thus duties, import

19 This opposing logic in the reciprocal stabilization of trade and social policy, which assumed institutional forms in the legislation of the New Deal, is to this day hardly understood: 'Policy logic might have inclined them toward protectionism in the 1930s, since in the New Deal they [the Democrats] were the party that became committed to aggressive intervention in the US economy. Instead, throughout the 1940s and 1950s they maintained their low-tariff tradition' (Destler 1986: 29). Unlike the period between the Civil War and the First World War, after the New Deal the Democrats' 'low tariff tradition' for the first time became a politically feasible alternative, because now first-best public policy instruments could provide some measure of social security.

20 In the sections of his two-volume autobiography that deal with trade policy, Hull does not make any mention at all of the New Deal social policy as a potential consideration in the passage of the Trade Agreement Act. Hull does recount, however, the bitter resistance of the Roosevelt administration's social policy faction to the liberal turn in trade policy (Hull 1948: I.353). Yet trade agreement policy after 1934 was not dogmatically, but, rather, pragmatically free trade orientated. It was formulated by a newly created coordinating committee within the administration which carefully explored the probable impact of every contemplated tariff reduction: 'It studied our trade with that nation, to see which imports from it could receive lower duties *without competing unfairly or injuriously with our domestic industry or agriculture*, and which of our exports should receive lower duties from it by way of compensation' (ibid.: 366; emphasis added).

quotas, guaranteed prices and export subsidies remain the principal means by which governments attempt to achieve goals which, in the employment relations of other sectors, are realized not only more effectively through social insurance and social assistance programmes, but also with a less trade-distorting foreign economic impact (Rieger 1995a, b; 2000).

With the exception of the agricultural sector, US trade policy in the post-war era – despite its fundamentally free trade orientation – has been distinguished by the fact that all significant changes in foreign trade policy, from the various GATT rounds to NAFTA, were accompanied by special compensatory measures. This has assumed various forms. First, far-reaching Trade Assistance Acts programmes that are targeted on the income protection and retraining of workers who have been 'dislocated' – i.e. become unemployed – as a result of increased import competition have been periodically enacted since 1962 (J. H. Jackson 1997a: 201–3; Schoepfle 2000). Further, the lowering of tariff barriers in those sectors that are particularly labour-intensive has been typically less extensive than in those in which fewer jobs were at stake (Hillman 1982; McKeown 1984; M. Wallerstein 1987; Bhagwati 1988: 77). Finally, the negotiation of so-called voluntary export restrictions, which temporarily reduce import competition, was an important means of granting firms time to adapt, that is to restructure, their operations or retrain their employees (Tonelson 1994).

Even after the institutionalization of direct, welfare-statist solutions in the New Deal and thereafter, the US Congress has regularly been loath to grant the executive branch comprehensive authority to negotiate international trade agreements. For constitutional reasons, every such trade policy empowerment of the President is temporary and occurs with the proviso, repeatedly underscored by the Supreme Court, that Congress is responsible for trade policy. In the multilateral GATT rounds, just as in bilateral negotiations, the executive branch follows a point-by-point procedure in close coordination with the Senate. Congress has thus sought to ensure that in every single case the maxim 'no injury to domestic industry' is upheld. Thus, it has reserved the right to intervene in order to protect firms or workers in specific sectors. In order to be able to reduce tariff barriers more rapidly, the Kennedy administration then developed a negotiation package which bundled together a range of issues. In order to receive the authority to negotiate such a package, it fashioned a new compensatory instrument designed to cushion the social consequences of growing import competition in the early 1960s:

> Appreciating that future tariff cuts would affect some U.S. industries and workers adversely as reciprocal concessions created new export opportunities, administration strategists chose to eviscerate the escape clause. Instead, the president would obtain authority to provide adjustment assistance to import-impacted workers and firms. . . . In his own public statements President Kennedy lauded the adjustment assistance option. He told the December 1961 AFL-CIO [the umbrella organization of US unions] convention that this new program of safeguards would 'provide a recognition of the national responsibility in the period of transition for those industries and people who may be adversely affected'. (Eckes 1995: 186)

According to Aho and Bayard (1980), the Trade Adjustment Act (TAA) of 1962 brought the decisive breakthrough for the internationalization of the US economy. It paved the way for the passage of the Trade Acts of the 1970s and 1980s and for the success of the three ensuing GATT rounds. The US Trade Representatives could move from point-by-point negotiations to a broad, though temporarily limited authority to effectively conclude trade treaties on its own. This led to a massive acceleration of tariff reductions and to a quantum leap in the scope of goods which were encompassed by them.[21]

The size of the US economy and its international significance made US trade policy a decisive element in the international economic order. The TAA of 1962, and especially the expansion of this instrument over the following two decades, put the US government in a position to instrumentalize foreign economic relations to serve geopolitical and security objectives. Until the TAA, the escape clause was the primary means by which the President could, in the case of a recommendation by the International Trade Commission, reimpose higher levels of duties or introduce import quotas in order to protect domestic firms from 'harmful' competition.[22] This form of trade policy, however, entailed a twofold problem. First, it called into question GATT, which, in Article XIX, provides for a regular multilateral procedure to deal with increased import competition in the wake of tariff reductions. Second, it provoked protectionist countermeasures by the governments of the export countries affected. Conversely, in US domestic politics the critique is often voiced that priority given to foreign and above all security policy considerations habitually are detrimental to the country's own national economic interests. Congress and the White House were thus regularly at odds over how trade policy should be managed. For Congress, domestic policy considerations took priority, whereas for the White House, foreign policy considerations were usually paramount. The stance of the Senate and the House of Representatives in their dealings with the executive branch was unambiguous: 'No U.S. industry which has suffered serious injury should be cut off from relief for foreign policy reasons' (Eckes 1995: 216).

The exclusively economic-nationalist escape clause policy, fuelled by domestic politics via Congress, thus severely restricted programmatic cultivation of democracy abroad, geopolitical and above all security policy latitude, and traditional concerns of the executive branch of government. At the same time, foreign policy goals and constraints of the USA as a global power repeatedly prevailed over the escape clause, thus limiting its social effectiveness. The TAA provided an alternative which was neutral in both foreign policy and trade policy terms. Table 3.3 shows how, in the wake of the institutionalization and then successive expansion of the TAA provisions, recourse to the purely tariff policy-oriented escape clause became increasingly unnecessary. The TAA of 1962 reflects the United States' relatively underdeveloped unemployment insurance and social assistance programmes (Aho 1985).[23] First of all, the unemployment insurance scheme can hardly be compared to its Continental European cousins. One

21 For a more detailed discussion, see ch. 2, p. 85 f.

22 Since 1935, an escape clause was a standard component of bilateral trade agreements negotiated by the USA. Although their respective form and concrete procedures could vary based on circumstances, their substance was always the same: protection of domestic industry from import competition from low-wage countries deemed to thus have a competitive advantage (Eckes 1995: 220). The escape clause balanced traditional tariff *protection* policy with the liberal policy of tariff *reduction*, which had succeeded it.

23 On the historical origins of the USA's restrictive anti-poverty policies including the influence of the Puritan heritage, see Katz (1983) and Patterson (1994). For a systematic and broad first assessment of the reforms in means-tested US social policy in the 1990s, see Schelkle (1999), Blank (1997), Weaver (2000), Blank and Haskins (2001), and Heclo (2001).

Table 3.3 Escape clause proceedings and their success rates, 1975–1993 (USA)

President	*Number of cases filed*	*ITC recommends relief*	*President provides some remedy*	*% of cases serving remedy*
Ford (1975–7)	15	9	6	40
Carter (1977–81)	29	18	9	31
Reagan (1981–5)	10	5	3	30
Reagan (1985–9)	7	2	1	14
Bush (1989–93)	2	1	0	0

Source: Eckes (1995: 245)

third of US workers are not covered at all, the income replacement rates are low and the duration of benefit receipt is limited to a maximum of twenty-six weeks. Upon expiration of benefit there is no subsequent equivalent to Germany's unemployment assistance benefit (*Arbeitslosenhilfe*), which does not know any time limits, nor is there any kind of regular transition into the social assistance scheme (O'Leary and Wandner 1997). Moreover, unlike European systems of unemployment insurance, the US unemployment programme does not ensure any health care benefits. The average weekly benefits in 1999 ranged from a high of $288 in Massachusetts to a low of $156 in Mississippi (Green Book 2000: 293f.).[24]

The stinginess of this system was compounded in 1986 when unemployment compensation was made taxable. Those who received less than $10,000 in unemployment compensation during a tax year became subject to a tax rate of 5.6 per cent, a rate that rose progressively as the income increased. In 1998, the average rate at which unemployment benefits were taxed was 18.3 per cent.[25] A person working forty hours per week at the federal minimum hourly wage of $5.15 was earning a weekly wage of $206. Assuming no vacation, this yields gross earnings of $10,712, less about $600 in income taxes. This shows that unemployment compensation barely sufficed to keep an individual worker above the (then) poverty level of $8,667, let alone to secure a reasonable living standard.[26] This weakness of passive labour market policy with regard to income maintenance in the USA is matched by the virtual absence of active labour

24 The income replacement rates range from 50 to 70 per cent (cf. Green Book 1998: 340–1).

25 Cf. table 4.4 in the Green Book (1998: 339). According to the data in Goodin et al. (1999: 169–71), the taxation of social benefits in the USA neutralizes any positive effect which anti-poverty policies might have on the income situation of beneficiaries. The phenomenon that government takes from the poor with one hand that which it had given them with the other can be observed in other welfare states as well, albeit not in the same magnitude as in the USA. In Germany, the Federal Constitutional Court attempted to prevent this by declaring incomes up to the Social Assistance programme's minimum subsistence figure to be tax-free (BVerfGE (Decisions of the German Constitutional Court. Official Collection), vol. 87: 153–81, and other decisions). Goodin et al. base their investigations on panel data from the period 1985–1994. One can assume with regard to the US case that the expansion of the Earned Income Tax Credit in 1996 significantly increased the efficiency of the country's anti-poverty policy. This reform and its effects on poverty (and trade) are discussed and analysed in more detail below.

26 For a four-person household with two adults and two children, the US poverty level in 2001 was $17,960 (US Census Bureau, Poverty 2001 – Poverty Thresholds 2001; http://www.census.gov/hhes./poverty/threshld/thresh01.htm – 9 Nov 2002).

market policies.[27] Moreover, the horizontally (according to problem types or problem groups) and vertically (the distribution of responsibilities in a federal system) fragmented social assistance programme is hardly geared to the risks and needs of larger segments of the labour force. It concentrates on peripheral groups such as ethnic minorities and single-parent families – and these two groups often overlap (Sandefur and Tienda 1988; Marmor et al. 1990; Quadagno 1994).

Contrary to the case in Western Europe, in the USA, *government* social policy institutions are not seen as benefit programmes whose function should be and is *solely* to guarantee an appropriate degree of income security for the average worker (Ellwood 1988). Free-market forms of private provision for future contingencies, and employee benefit programmes incorporated into employment contracts, play a role at least as significant as that of public social protection programmes (Stevens 1988). This means, however, that a market participant's social security is largely tied to his or her employment status and trajectory. Health care for three-quarters of American workers depends on company-provided insurance, and corporate pensions account for about 30 per cent of US retirement assets outside social security (Martin 2002). It is for this reason that large segments of the population are so worried about foreign trade relations – above all, competitive imports and dependency on exports – and that concern over 'unfair' trade and 'dumping' is almost a national obsession.[28] In the peculiar welfare state constellation of the USA, foreign trade is a *directly* relevant factor in their personal social security, and *not* one whose effects can be adequately compensated by income from social benefit programmes.

As *voters*, US workers have something like a veto power over import-easing legislation, except when this restriction is bought off by government promises of targeted compensation by federal social programmes. When trade policy threatens to harm their welfare, they can force the government to undertake countervailing and compensatory social policy measures. This is precisely the function of a *supplemental, trade-related* social policy instrument, which uses federal revenues to offset job losses of workers harmed by heightened import competition – including income losses stemming from loss of seniority in a given firm (Finger 1982; Mussa 1993). Table 3.4 shows how, in two samples, the recipients of Trade Adjustment Assistance differed from 'normal' unemployed workers as well as from those whose unemployment insurance claim was exhausted. It is striking here, first, how trade-related social assistance comes to the aid primarily of those workers who have been employed the longest, and thus received better employer benefits, and that union membership is probably the decisive lever for having access to trade-related social policy goods in the first place. The ambivalence and the contradictions of US trade policy are thus determined, among other things, by a welfare state system which, in the eyes of workers, offers insufficient social protection. This has made it necessary to regularly attach political chains to foreign trade

27 Heclo has pointed out repeatedly (1994, 1995) that the demise of a national, legally anchored active labour market policy at the end of the 1940s, which had been implicit in the New Deal legislation, paved the way for the retrogression of the US welfare state after the 1970s. The question of why the USA has never enduringly pursued an active labour market policy is examined in Schmid et al. (1992) and Weir (1992).

28 For an elaborate defence that 'dumping' and 'unfair trade' is in point of fact, and not just allegedly, a major problem for the US economy, see Ragosta and Magnus (1997), two Washington-based trade lawyers. This is a minority view, since most social scientists do not find either the political or economic case advanced by them to be credible (Horlick and Clarke 1997).

Table 3.4 Features of previous employment positions of Trade Adjustment Assistance (TAA) and unemployment compensation recipients respectively, and of the unemployed generally, before and after 1988 (USA)

	TAA recipients		*UI exhaustees in manufacturing*		*Displaced workers*	
	Sample					
	before 1988	*after 1988*	*before 1988*	*after 1988*	*before 1988*	*after 1988*
Mean weekly wage ($)	*448*	*458*	*394*	*379*	*408*	*435*
	Fringe benefits (%)					
Paid vacation	95.4	93.5	78.0	70.7		
Paid holiday	96.3	94.8	83.6	77.9		
Paid sick leave	53.6	57.1	45.6	40.6		
Health insurance	93.4	93.4	74.9	70.6	75.1	72.5
Pension plan	85.5	78.8	53.7	47.8		
	Tenure					
Mean tenure (years)	14.6	12.2	9.0	7.0		
10 years and more (%)	59.3	54.2	36.0	24.7	34.3	35.3
Union member (%)	72.7	65.5	37.2	29.9	16.2	15.9

UI = Unemployment insurance

Source: Decker and Corson (1995: 762)

legislation. The deeper reason why this peculiar US path could be pursued at all is rooted in the US Constitution. Article I, Section 8 declares: 'The Congress shall have the power . . . to regulate commerce with foreign nations.' The sole responsibility for foreign trade of federal *representative* institutions gives US trade policy its distinctive social-democratic character and makes it particularly susceptible to protectionist instrumentalization.[29]

Despite the great expectations associated with Trade Adjustment Assistance as an alternative to protectionist control of US foreign economic relations, this instrument could not fulfil its promise. A complicated, lengthy application procedure and broad discretionary powers of an independent federal agency, which at the same time is subject to Congress's power of the purse, made this form of protection against imported economic turbulence politically unreliable and socially ineffective (Aho 1985: 235–9). The demise of trade-related social assistance was further accelerated by the transition from an industrial to a service and ultimately to an information society, as well as by the weakening of the political influence of US unions. Figure 3.2 shows the development of expenditures on Trade Assistance programmes. A first problem of Trade Assistance – compared to the social rights which, for example, social insurance schemes

[29] Thus Hudec (1999a: 127): 'For fans of direct democracy Smoot Hawley [the zenith of US protectionism at the beginning of the 1930s] has to be one of their all-time favourite statutes. Seldom has so much of the US electorate had so much direct impact on so many details of a major statute.'

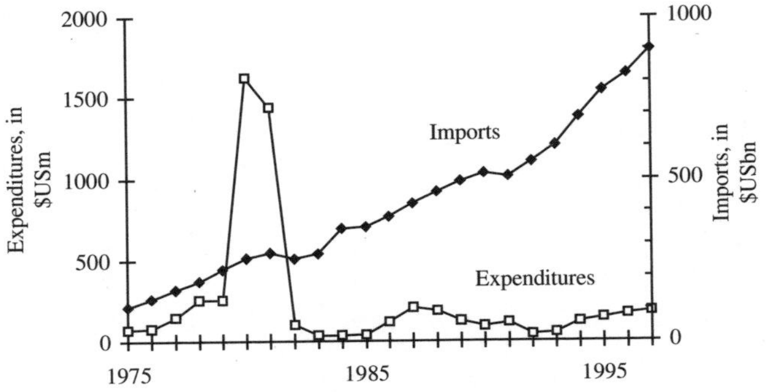

Figure 3.2 Expenditure on Trade Adjustment Assistance (TAA) and imports in the USA, 1975–1997

Sources: Green Book (1998: 388) on TAA; IMF (1999a: 132 f.) on imports

can guarantee – is its intrinsic uncertainty: can a *specific* case of unemployment or a *specific* factory closure really be concretely and indubitably attributed to a sudden, unforeseen increase in imports? The less this is the case, the more such a programme will become the object of political manipulation. And further, can one rule out that technological progress, sinking productivity, management errors or changed consumer behaviour were the decisive factors for the turn to the worse? Given these systemic elements of uncertainty in the fate of businesses, how can a government agency justify paying different rates of income replacement to different affected groups, or granting them differential access to subsidized retraining programmes? Thus instead of treating social risk situations in such a way that they remain intrinsic to the economic arena – and functioning there as performance incentives, setting free productive energies to whatever extent possible – it is precisely the ostensibly 'targeted' programmes of social trade assistance, with their highly discretionary elements, that become the source of new, now *politically* directed distributional conflicts, and independent objects of opportunistic behaviour.[30] Trade-related social policy is thus also an institutional ersatz social policy to the extent that it cannot be fashioned as a social right of citizenship governed by general rules. The excerpt from the description of Trade Assistance by the Committee on Ways and Means of the US House of Representatives in Box 3.1 gives an impression of how and under what conditions benefits can be applied for under the Trade Assistance Act.

A second problem inherent in this form of protecting the labour force against the risks of market openings is its social ineffectiveness. The instrument of trade-related social policy is designed to win the political support necessary for the approval of commercial treaties. It aims neither at a structural effect in the sense of providing an easily accessible and effective economic security, nor at assistance for occupational mobility. Its decision-making process is highly contingent on circumstances and power relations. Figure 3.3 shows that despite the markedly increased globalization of the

30 To this extent, trade-related *social* policy continued the peculiar US practice which dated from the post-Civil War era, namely that of congressionally brokered distributive, discretionary benefits with patronage character. Civil War pensions for union soldiers were financed by customs duties which Congress controlled. These gave Representatives and Senators the means to pursue a special kind of nurturing of their electoral districts (Bensel 1984; Amenta and Skocpol 1989; Skocpol 1995).

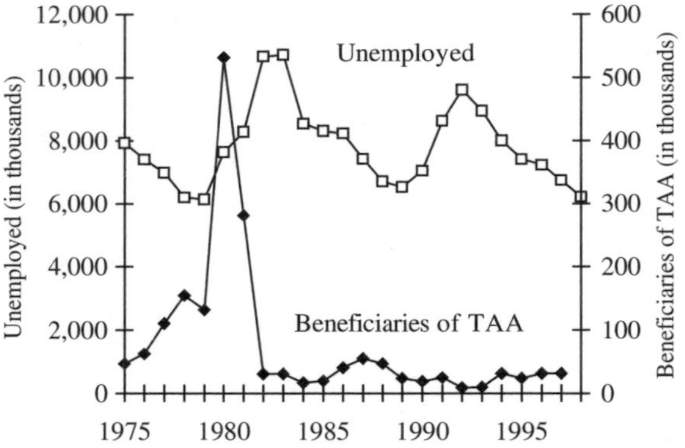

Figure 3.3 The unemployed and recipients of Trade Adjustment Assistance (TAA), 1975–1997

Source: Green Book (1998: 388) on TAA beneficiaries; US Census Bureau (1999: 879) on unemployment

Box 3.1 Prerequisites of entitlements to Trade Adjustment Assistance

A two-step process is involved in the determination of whether an individual worker will receive trade adjustment assistance: (1) certification by the Secretary of Labor of a petitioning group of workers in a particular firm as eligible to apply; and (2) approval by the State agency administering the program of the application for benefits of an individual worker covered by a certification.

The process begins by a group of three or more workers, their union, or authorized representative filing a petition with the ETA [Employment and Training Administration of the Department of Labor] for certification of group eligibility. To certify a petitioning group of workers as eligible to apply for adjustment assistance, the Secretary must determine that three conditions are met:

1. a significant number or proportion of the workers in the firm or subdivision of the firm have been or are threatened to be potentially or partially laid off
2. sales and/or production of the firm or subdivision have decreased absolutely; and
3. increased imports of articles like or directly competitive with articles produced by the firm or subdivision of the firm have 'contributed importantly' to both the layoffs and the decline in sales or production.

. . .

The *Secretary* is required to make the eligibility determination within 60 days after a petition is filed. A certification of eligibility to apply for TAA covers workers who meet the requirements and whose last total or partial separation from the firm or subdivision before applying for benefits occured within 1 year prior to the filing of the petition.

Source: Green Book (1998: 384)

US economy, trade-related social policy lies beyond the reach of the vast majority of the unemployed, with the exception of the circumstances of the early 1980s. It remains largely untouched by trends in unemployment levels. The substance of trade-related social policy – exactly which benefits are paid to exactly which groups, for how long, at what level and on the basis of which criteria – depends on political power relations, both within Congress and between Congress and the White House. Of central signifi-

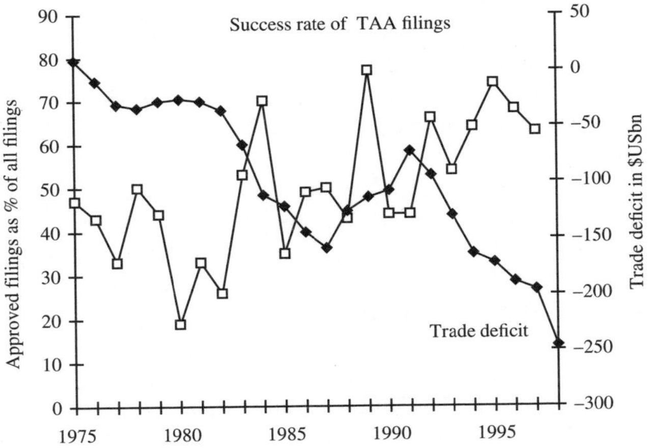

Figure 3.4 Success rates of TAA filings and the US trade deficit, 1975–1998

Source: Green Book (1998: 385) on TAA filings; IMF (1999b: 928f.) on trade deficit

cance in this regard is the influence of unions. To what extent is a given president indebted to unions or do his prospects for re-election depend on the votes of union members? The same is true for members of the House of Representatives and Senators. The political supply of social trade policy as a reward to labour groups for tolerating trade liberalization never exceeds that which is absolutely necessary at a given moment to get a commercial agreement – or a mandate to negotiate such agreements – past the various hurdles of the legislative process.

A third problem is the way in which trade-related social policy is implemented. Given the ambiguous criteria of what exactly constitutes 'foreign' injury to 'our' industry, the discretionary powers of government agencies are necessarily vast. At least the highly varying rates of certification and approval, depicted in Figure 3.4, lead one to believe that it is not merely the social problem of heightened import competition which determines the way in which this instrument is employed. In any case, the success chances of TAA petitions rose with the rising probability of a trade deficit.

The trade policy backlash of 1997

The subsequent waves of market openings in the 1940s, the 1960s and particularly since the 1980s were relatively far-reaching by US standards and thus led to striking increases in import competition. They would not have been politically possible without the social buffer of the unemployment compensation and social assistance programmes.[31] The mechanisms described in the last section are mere *supplementary* institutions, which in and of themselves would not have permitted a liberal trade policy.

[31] To stress the political dimension of a welfare-democratic cost-benefit analysis of opening American markets should by no means downplay the subsequent welfare-enhancing results of the politically anonymous social policy of the market: cheaper and most of all a broader range of products for consumers and more jobs because of the new opportunities to export. Without these tangible benefits to large strata of the population, market openings would not be sustainable.

A completely different question, however, is whether the level of social protection currently attainable by the average worker is sufficient to safeguard US trade policy from the temptations of protectionism. A more recent episode of US trade policy, which observers consider to be more indicative of the future course of the American welfare state than the failure of the health insurance reform initiative of Clinton's first term, suggests the contrary.[32]

In November 1997, Congress denied President Clinton the so-called fast-track authority for his project to deepen NAFTA and expand it to include Latin America. Despite repeated attempts, Congress continued this oppositional stance throughout the remainder of Clinton's second term – and beyond to President Bush – and extended it to the issue of Chinese integration into the WTO under US leadership. Fast-track authority means that Congress must decide to adopt or reject commercial treaties as a whole. The House of Representatives and the Senate cannot attach strings to these treaties, which the White House must then accept as the price of passage. Rather, Congress can merely accept or reject the overall package as the executive branch has fashioned it.

In US foreign economic policy since the RTAA, fast-track authority – or some functional equivalent – has always provided the political foundation for the administration to conclude commercial treaties with other countries or to engage effectively in GATT rounds. As long as every agreement between countries can be watered down or fundamentally called into question by subsequent domestic political and interest-group demands in Congress, no country has been or will be willing to engage in negotiations over commercial treaties with the US government. The failure to grant fast-track authority then led directly to the breakdown of the negotiations with Central and South American states on the expansion of NAFTA and the stronger integration of Latin America into the North American trade sphere (Baldwin and Magee 2000).

The opponents of fast-track empowerment were primarily concerned with the social consequences that might follow a further lowering of protectionist trade barriers vis-à-vis countries with lower wage and social benefit standards than the US: a further decline in wage levels, greater economic insecurity and rising unemployment. This could have enduring political consequences not least because, in the aftermath of the radical welfare reform of 1996, US anti-poverty programmes in their present shape – above all, Temporary Assistance to Needy Families (TANF) and Food Stamps – clearly send no signals to workers that there will be a protective safety net *beyond* the labour market which will mitigate the risks of the USA's intensely competitive-capitalist style of labour utilization. The social assistance reform passed in 1996 as the Personal Responsibility and Work Opportunity Reconciliation Act (PRWORA) indeed fulfilled Clinton's promise 'to end welfare as we know it' (Teles 1996). The transformation of Aid to Families With Dependent Children (AFDC, originally ADC) and various welfare-to-work programmes into TANF amounted to a nullification of the social assistance policies of Franklin D. Roosevelt's New Deal and Lyndon B. Johnson's Great Society. With its restriction of lifetime benefit eligibility to a maximum of sixty months regardless of need, the toughening of work requirements for TANF recipients, and the new empowerment of the states to design their own additional work-requirements, TANF constitutes a radical curtailment of US social assis-

[32] Cf. 'Clinton rebuked', *International Herald Tribune*, 12 November 1997, p. 8, as well as T. L. Friedman (1997), J. K. Glassman (1997), Pfaff (1997), and Scott (1997).

tance programmes.[33] Between January 1994 and June 1999, the number of persons claiming social assistance halved, from 5 to 2.5 million. The number of Food Stamps recipients has fallen sharply as well, so that now fewer people receive AFDC/TANF than in 1971 (Blank 2000: 4).[34]

Against the background of an already weak and fragmented social net, these reforms represented a decisive loss of social rights and a signal turn against any social policy aiming at suspending, curtailing or correcting market forces. In cases of loss of employment, they further reduced the chances of social compensation and thus increased the risk of not only income but also status loss.[35] In our perspective, this loss of publicly guaranteed and functioning social security in 1996 had to have a much stronger effect on the general climate in which decisions on the scale and scope of the American welfare state were taken than the unachieved gain in social security entailed in the failure of Clinton's 1994 universal health insurance initiative (Hacker 1997, 2002; Skocpol 1997). In a direct response to this new socio-political environment, President Clinton promised to include again special social programmes – federal funds for regional and sectoral, passive and active labour market policies – in his trade initiative. Such declarations of intent did not suffice, however, to convince either the Democrats or the Republicans in Congress to grant him fast-track authority. After at first encountering the same sort of resistance as his predecessor, President Bush, having significantly improved assistance and benefits to dislocated workers, received fast-track authority from the Senate in the form of 'trade authority' on 1 August 2002 (Baucus 2002; http://www.sice.oas.org/Trade/tradeact/act1.asp).

The reticence to further liberalize US demand markets is thus unsurprising. US trade policy decisions are made in a socio-political context characterized by a high poverty risk and increasing income inequality. Table 3.5 depicts the latter in international perspective.These data show that in the USA income inequality is not only far more extensive than in Germany or Sweden, but also that this inequality has increased considerably since 1979. In Sweden, by contrast, it has remained essentially stable and in

33 Cf. e.g. Gebhardt and Jacobs (1997), Kamerman and Kahn (1997), Weaver (1997, 2000), Wiseman (1997), Gebhardt (1999, 1998, 1997), Blank (2000), Blank and Haskins (2001) and Heclo (2001). A broader discussion of these programmes' pursuit of labour market integration can be found in Freeman and Gottschalk (1998) and Card and Blank (2000). On the implementation and effects of TANF, see the overviews in Blank (2000) and Schoeni and Blank (2000); for a preliminary stock-taking of state implementation of TANF see Nathan and Gais (1999) and Blank and Haskins (2001), and on the entire reform complex, see the publications from the Urban Institute's project 'Assessing the New Federalism' (www.urban.org). Brauner and Loprest (1999) provide a summary analysis of studies examining the fate of social assistance 'leavers', i.e. of persons who have exited AFDC or, since 1997, TANF.

34 Blank (2000: 19) points out that Clinton's welfare reform only partially explains this development: 'This is the result of a conflux of events that all came together at the same time: a strongly expanding economy, substantial revisions in public assistance that emphasized work and reduced benefit eligibility, and major policy changes that increased the return to work and the subsidies to support work, particularly among single mothers.' Further, a clear, enduring trend towards an increase in willingness to work and assumption of work among certain demographic groups worked as a 'push factor'.

35 TANF was implemented on the golden eve of a period of employment growth – unforeseeable at the time – which would turn out to be the most favourable labour market environment of the past thirty years. For this reason, the full significance of this loss of social rights will only be fully perceived when less favourable labour market conditions return. Moreover, Congress froze programme funding at the 1994 level, a year with relatively high claimance rates. The decline in claimance rates has thus created unprecedentedly favourable conditions for the states to finance training programmes and child care ('reform niches'). These initiatives could disappear with the next recession. In any case, the entire TANF legislation is scheduled to be revised in 2002 (cf. Weaver 2000).

Table 3.5 Income inequality in the USA, Germany and Sweden from the mid-1970s to the mid-1990s

		Median	*Ø*	*Gini-coefficient*	*% <0.5 of the median*	*% >1.5 of the median*	*90:10 ratio*
USA	1974	15,906	17,593	0.317	15.9	21.2	10.17
	1979	17,092	18,640	0.303	15.9	21.4	8.96
	1986	18,077	20,251	0.336	17.9	24.7	11.03
	1991	17,715	20,172	0.340	17.9	24.7	11.14
	1994	17,511	20,736	0.364	18.5	26.5	13.50
Germany	1981	13,159	14,497	0.245	5.6	16.6	4.97
	1984	12,948	14,234	0.250	6.5	16.3	5.16
	1989	14,417	15,849	0.248	5.6	16.3	5.29
	1994	14,150	15,722	0.272	8.5	17.7	6.59
	1994*	13,659	15,143	0.264	7.5	17.2	6.09
Sweden	1975	11,359	11,719	0.214	6.4	11.3	4.26
	1981	11,440	11,872	0.196	5.2	10.4	3.88
	1987	11,623	11,977	0.217	7.3	10.5	4.76
	1992	13,508	14,295	0.228	6.5	13.1	4.99
	1995	12,476	13,127	0.220	6.5	11.8	5.21

Note: The absolute amounts of median and average income refer to standardized equivalent income. The median income is the point of income in the overall income distribution scale above and below which 50 per cent of all income is located, i.e.'the middle person'. Median income is a measure better protected against a few outliers, i.e. a few millionaires, than average income is. Using equivalent income produces comparable data as economies of scale are taken into account. The Gini-coefficient is a classical measure of inequality, which may vary between 1 and 0: with a Gini-coefficient of 0, each household has the same income, while at 1, one household appropriates all incomes; 50 per cent of median income is a standard measure for the size of the poverty population, while the percentage of people with more than 1.5 the median income describes the size of higher income groups. The 90:10 ratio measures the concentration of income distribution: it reports how many times bigger the income of the top 10 per cent is relative to the bottom 10 per cent. The numbers for Germany 1994* include the New Eastern States.

Source: Osberg (2000: 13)

Germany it has increased only slightly. Inequality as such, however, is not necessarily a problem of social or poverty policy, because all contemporary societies are cast in such a way that they are bound to aim at the reduction of poverty while preserving an inegalitarian income structure.[36] What, then, is the reality behind these figures and what are its political consequences? This question is of particular importance because during the same period in which the number of poor persons in the USA increased and income inequality grew, its global market integration vigorously advanced as well. Between 1960 and 1994, the traditionally rather small share of the sum of imports and exports in Gross National Product more than doubled, from 8.9 to 22.3 per cent (Cline 1997: 32). As figure 3.5 shows, the trade deficit increased significantly during

[36] For this reason T. H. Marshall recommended that 'when the subject being studied is inequality, the use of the term "poverty" should be avoided altogether' (Marshall 1981: 52).

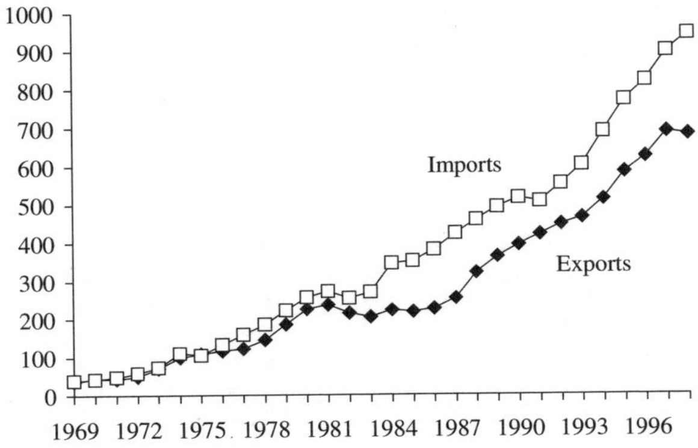

Figure 3.5 US exports and imports, 1970–1999 (in $US bn)

Source: IMF (1999a: 128f., 132f.)

the 1990s. In light of the more or less simultaneous increase both in income inequality and employment insecurity, this rising trade deficit put increasing pressure on trade policy. We are not interested here, however, in whether an objective causal relationship between global market liberalization and the development of income distributional patterns can be found to explain this correlation, as public opinion holds it to be true, and thus constitutes an important political reality.[37] Our concern, instead, in light of this particular context, is which trade and social policies were pursued, and what was the *functional* connection between them?

Changes in the labour market

Together with increased income inequality, two labour market developments became focal points of US public policy confrontations. The first is declining real wages among large segments of the population, and the second is the growing difficulties of families to make ends meet. Table 3.6, based on three-year averages in order to neutralize cyclical effects, shows that in the 1980s market incomes declined for the lower strata of the gainfully employed, that significant income losses spread well into the middle classes and that income inequality increased markedly.[38] That family incomes declined less rapidly is largely a result of the fact that partners, primarily women, shifted to paid work in ever greater numbers. Even though the double-income household increasingly became the norm, wages were less and less able to meet conventional family

37 On the social and political power of pseudo-facts see Merton (1987: 4), who noted that 'strongly held theoretical expectations or ideologically induced expectations can lead to perceptions of historical and social "facts" even when these are readily refutable by strong evidence close at hand'. The globalization discourse is particularly exposed to the tendency of pseudo-facts to induce pseudo-problems. 'Social dumping', 'unfair trade', and the 'race to the bottom' in regulatory politics are prime examples. The reason for this is, as Merton also notes, that there is a competition among groups or collectivities about the public interpretation of reality.

38 Whereas between 1968 and 1970 the wealthiest disposed of 11.44 times as much total family income as did the poorest, between 1988 and 1990 it was 17.45 times as much.

Table 3.6 The development of average US family incomes ($US), 1968–1970, 1978–1980, 1988–1990 (family head aged 18–64)

Year	*All*	*(Bottom)* *1*	*2*	*3*	*4*	*Decile* *5*	*6*	*7*	*8*	*9*	*(Top)* *10*
						Total family income ($US)					
1968–70	30,182	6,275	13,502	18,078	21,813	25,252	28,763	32,818	37,966	46,536	71,778
1978–80	32,535	5,372	12,855	18,087	22,871	27,263	31,691	36,615	42,624	51,736	76,230
1988–90	34,522	4,966	12,237	17,900	22,979	27,775	32,756	38,422	45,457	56,185	86,837
						Annual earnings for employed family heads ($US)					
1968–70	23,034	4,106	10,139	14,236	17,583	20,051	22,377	24,495	27,328	31,375	50,427
1978–80	23,376	3,448	9,454	13,240	16,559	20,006	22,800	25,794	28,821	33,504	48,389
1988–90	22,889	3,567	8,283	12,146	15,500	18,219	21,193	24,369	28,155	33,320	51,251
						Employment rate for family heads (%)					
1968–70	92.9	69.7	85.9	91.8	94.6	95.9	96.8	97.2	97.6	98.3	98.4
1978–80	98.6	59.8	80.0	87.1	92.2	93.2	95.2	96.0	97.6	97.3	97.8
1988–90	88.8	55.2	80.6	87.1	90.8	93.2	94.5	95.6	96.2	97.2	97.5
						Annual hours worked for employed family heads					
1968–70	2,187	1,685	2,001	2,119	2,159	2,229	2,241	2,245	2,287	2,315	2,418
1978–80	2,117	1,518	1,875	2,013	2,094	2,142	2,179	2,217	2,230	2,260	2,418
1988–90	2,121	1,426	1,877	2,022	2,109	2,149	2,179	2,212	2,238	2,266	2,382
						Annual earnings for employed spouses ($US)					
1968–70	8,319	1,831	3,393	4,303	5,282	5,934	7,198	8,576	10,101	12,261	15,653
1978–80	9,956	2,204	4,050	5,213	6,493	7,526	8,800	10,127	11,812	13,938	17,871
1988–90	12,624	1,523	4,582	6,120	7,794	9,316	10,787	12,763	14,814	18,121	24,844
						Employment rate for spouses (%)					
1968–70	54.2	41.3	45.1	46.3	46.4	51.7	55.5	60.1	63.2	65.9	58.9
1978–80	64.4	40.5	47.4	56.3	62.6	63.6	67.0	70.0	74.0	76.0	69.1
1988–90	73.7	47.1	56.3	66.5	71.3	74.8	77.4	80.0	83.5	84.4	80.8
						Annual hours worked for employed spouses					
1968–70	1,411	1,095	1,099	1,167	1,221	1,279	1,409	1,500	1,597	1,672	1,729
1978–80	1,454	1,054	1,091	1,186	1,325	1,369	1,454	1,408	1,599	1,666	1,675
1988–90	1,644	1,194	1,291	1,410	1,545	1,606	1,659	1,718	1,760	1,827	1,842
						Proportion of husband-wife families (%)					
1968–70	88.4	58.8	78.3	86.1	91.0	93.0	93.8	94.7	95.2	95.8	96.7
1978–80	85.2	47.7	71.4	80.3	87.3	90.3	92.5	94.4	95.4	95.9	97.0
1988–90	86.8	48.1	77.4	85.1	89.0	92.0	93.1	94.6	95.4	96.0	96.8

Source: Fogel (2000: 277f.)

Table 3.7 The share of US households running a deficit, 1973–1974, 1994 (in income deciles)

	All	*1*	*2*	*3*	*4*	*5*	*6*	*7*	*8*	*9*	*10*
1973–4	20.4	52.9	50.4	33.0	23.7	16.3	10.7	7.0	4.8	3.0	2.0
1994	37.3	80.5	65.8	56.6	44.9	34.6	30.0	22.6	16.0	13.8	8.8

Source: Fogel (2000: 279)

Table 3.8 Income and expenditure of US households by income deciles, 1973–1974, 1994

Decile	*1973/74*			*1994*		
	Income	*Expenditure*	*Savings*	*Income*	*Expenditure*	*Savings*
1	2,146	2,948	–802	5,302	11,281	–5,978
2	3,545	3,949	–404	10,189	14,297	–4,109
3	5,449	5,085	364	14,797	18,575	–3,778
4	7,484	6,177	1,307	19,997	22,470	–2,473
5	9,546	7,210	2,336	26,050	25,649	402
6	11,637	8,149	3,488	32,676	29,369	3,309
7	13,891	9,163	4,728	40,853	34,584	6,269
8	16,552	10,473	6,079	51,154	39,492	11,662
9	20,214	11,766	8,448	65,082	47,547	17,535
10	29,336	15,775	13,561	103,638	66,626	37,012
All	11,981	8,070	3,911	36,981	30,993	5,987

Source: Fogel (2000: 280f.)

needs. This is even more true of the lower income groups, for there employment rates and annual work hours declined most dramatically, and compensatory mechanisms, such as double-earning, were least prevalent.

Table 3.7 gives a sense of the greater social vulnerability of US family households. The share of households whose expenses exceeded their income has nearly doubled and has greatly increased the risk of impoverishment above all among lower income groups. One must speak of a vastly increased *risk* pool of families threatened by economic hardship because one cannot assume that these are the *same* households as those that are in continuous economic difficulty. The increasing share of households running deficits, manifest in all income groups, indicates a considerably greater likelihood among far larger segments of the population that a loss of or decline in income might lead to a grave household financial crisis. Table 3.8 clearly shows further that relative household deficits have also increased significantly. With regard to average living standards, not only the lowest 20 per cent, as is to be expected, but now the lowest 40 per cent of households are confronted with an imposing deficit.

The growth of a population at risk and the consequences for trade policy

The US Census Bureau identified 13.9 million persons (5.1 per cent of the total population) in 1998 whose household incomes did not exceed 50 per cent of the official poverty line, and a total of 34.5 million (12.7 per cent) whose incomes remained below the poverty line. The number of poor rises to 46 million (17.9 per cent) when one includes the 'almost poor', i.e. those whose incomes exceed the poverty line by 25 per cent or less (data based on Dalaker 1999). A different survey instrument yields a more precise picture of poverty in the USA. According to data from the Survey of Income and Program Participation (SIPP), in 1994 about 40 million people could be considered poor, an average monthly poverty rate of 15.4 per cent. The composition of this poor population changes markedly over time, even from month to month, indicating that a rather large proportion of the overall population is at risk of becoming destitute. However, only about one-third of those identified as poor based on average monthly income in 1993 and 1994 were poor throughout the entire respective year. Of the 21.4 per cent who were recorded as poor one month during the year 1994, roughly a quarter (5.3 per cent) were poor throughout the entire year.[39] This highly dynamic picture of impoverishment and the combination of a relatively small hardcore population of poor people with fuzzy though quite broad margins may help to explain the low priority that anti-poverty politics has on the public agenda.

In the USA, poverty entails more than simply low income. It can also exclude those affected from gaining access to essential services. The same data source shows that during the entire year of 1993, roughly 19.4 million Americans lacked health insurance.[40] Over a 28-month period, 73 per cent of all Americans were continually health-insured, meaning that 27 per cent, or 66.6 million people, had no claim to physician or hospital services for at least one month during this time span. Among those Americans who were employed during the entire period, 86.5 per cent had access to health services. This figure drops to 73.5 per cent among those who had at least a part-time job during the entire period, and to 58.1 per cent for those whose employment relationship was interrupted at least once. These data make clear the extent to which a long-term full-time employment position is prerequisite to gaining access to welfare state and/or occupational benefits systems in the USA.

The distribution of access to health insurance across the labour force continues to be of critical importance for the appearance and the social effectiveness of the American welfare state. First, the willingness or capacity of firms to offer their employees health insurance varies significantly across sectors. In agriculture and commerce, 35.5 and 26.7 per cent of employees respectively are without health insurance. Second, it is above all those with high incomes who enjoy occupational health insurance benefits. Thus, 49.2 per cent of employed persons with a household income below the poverty line have no insurance. Of those in the income class twice and three times the amount of the poverty line, 35.6 and 20.3 per cent respectively have no occupational health insurance. Third, age also plays a decisive role. Among the 31.1 million employed persons under 30 years of age, 27.5 per cent have no insurance, and among the 37.7 million workers aged 30–39, 17.7 per cent are

39 See Naifeh (1998). The SIPP data give insight not only into poverty rates, but also into the numbers of entries into and exits out of the poverty population, as well as into the average duration of poverty episodes. On the fundamental aspects of this poverty dynamic see Leisering and Leibfried (1999: 55 ff.).

40 See Bennefield (1998). Health insurance refers to the following benefit programmes: public health insurance for retirees (Medicare), means-tested health care for the poor (Medicaid), health insurance for members of the army and their dependants, employer and union health insurance benefits, and private health insurance (see also Currie and Yelowitz 2000).

uninsured, despite the critical role of this life phase in terms of family formation and child-rearing.[41]

A fourth factor conditioning unequal access to health insurance protection is race and ethnic identity. Among non-Hispanic Caucasian employed persons, 11 per cent have no insurance; among Asians this figure is 20.8 per cent, among African-Americans 21.2 per cent and among Hispanics 33.4 per cent. Finally, a fifth factor correlating with health insurance coverage is geography, for there is indeed enormous regional variation. According to Census Bureau data, from 1997 to 1999 an average of 16 per cent of the population was without health insurance. Of these, Texas fared the worst with 24.1 per cent and Minnesota the best with 8.8 per cent uninsured.[42]

The data of the SIPP show further that in 1995 nearly 49 million Americans – about one in five – lived in a household that had difficulties providing the essentials of life.[43] This refers to households that were unable to pay either the gas, heating oil or electricity bill or the rent or mortgage payment, or that could not afford to go to the doctor or dentist. Of the 11 per cent of Americans living in a household that was confronted with more than one of these difficulties, roughly a quarter were unemployed. In 1995 more than 11 million Americans reported that they could not afford to buy enough groceries. It is very instructive to see who actually helped these families meet their basic needs: 17.2 per cent of all Americans reported having received assistance in a situation in which they could no longer sufficiently provide for themselves; 4.9 per cent were helped by government institutions, 6.1 per cent by their family, 2.4 per cent by friends and 1.6 per cent by communal agencies. These data suggest that the capacity of the US welfare state to prevent poverty and deprivation is very limited.

In figure 3.6 we sketch how the efficiency of welfare state reduction of poverty can be measured. On the horizontal axis, persons or households are depicted as cumulative percentages of the total population, on the vertical axis are income levels. The solid diagonal line represents market income, the dashed line market plus transfer income. If one takes the poverty line as a measure, then A + D is the income poverty gap, excluding public transfer income. The total volume of transfers is A + B + C. Of these transfers, A and B go to the poor, while C supports the non-poor. Although the amount B goes to people who are poor, it goes beyond the poverty line and thus constitutes, just like C, 'wasteful spending'. Only the amount A reduces the income poverty gap. The measure of the efficiency of poverty reduction is thus A/(A + B + C). D is the poverty gap which remains even after welfare state intervention. The overall efficiency of poverty policy is thus A/(A + D).

In an international context, the US scenario is striking for two reasons. A detailed comparative analysis using matching sets of micro-economic data seems to suggest that, first, its market incomes lift the workforce more efficiently over the poverty line than do those of other countries.[44] The income poverty gap resulting from the primary income distribution generated by labour markets was 6.1 per cent in the USA (1995),

41 The data refer to 1996 and can be found in the 1998 Green Book (855). Since 1997 the Urban Institute in Washington has been carrying out a periodic national family survey which is concerned above all with the development of health insurance access (http://www.urban.org).

42 On ethnic and regional variation see Pear (2000).

43 On this and what follows see Bauman (1999).

44 One cannot infer statements about the entire poverty population from these microdata. This standardized data source can shed light, however, on the relative roles of the market and social policy in the production of national welfare in comparative perspective.

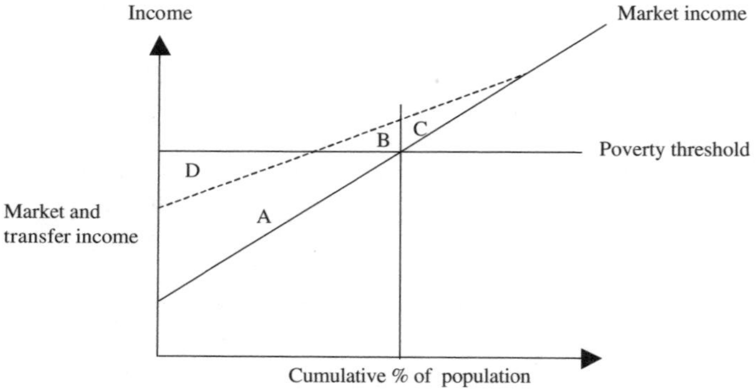

Figure 3.6 The efficiency of welfare state poverty reduction

Source: Beckerman (1979), in H. Kim (2000: 5)

8.7 per cent in Germany (1994) and 10.4 per cent in Sweden (1995).[45] Second, welfare state transfers in the USA reduce the poverty gap far more modestly than elsewhere. These transfers effect a 61 per cent reduction in the poverty gap, whereas in Germany the reduction is 89 per cent and in Sweden 88 per cent (our calculations are based on data in Kim 2000: 13). Thus, in international comparison, the income poverty gap 'after social transfers' is substantially larger in the USA than in European countries. In the USA this D of figure 3.6 thus amounts to 2.4 per cent, in Germany to 0.9 per cent and in Sweden to 1.3 per cent. The comparatively high overall efficiency rate of the US transfer system – 51.3 per cent, as opposed to 46.4 per cent in Germany and 41.1 per cent in Sweden – can be attributed above all to the country's less extensive market income poverty. For this reason, the very low transfer rate of the US welfare state does not affect the efficiency of anti-poverty policy to the extent often assumed. In the USA (1997), the overall (net) sum of welfare state transfers constituted 7.4 per cent of total household incomes. In Germany (1994) this (re)distributional rate was 16.8 per cent and in Sweden (1995) 22.5 per cent (Kim 2000: 13).[46]

These figures all refer to the period before the 1996 welfare reform. This reform indeed made US social assistance practice even more restrictive than it had already been. Yet it also introduced a far-reaching modification in an already well-established, though low-ranking, programme of the American welfare state, which, based on everything we know this far, has led to more effective anti-poverty policy: the Earned Income Tax Credit (EITC). How this programme works and what its trade policy implications

[45] See Kim (2000). His calculations are based on the microdata collection of the Luxembourg Income Study (LIS).

[46] A differently designed study of the LIS's income microdata similarly shows the limited significance of welfare state transfers for the living standard of US workers. De Nardi et al. (2000: 26f.) find that the average gross income of the labour force (aged 25–64) in the USA (1994) consisted of 84.4 per cent employment income but only 2.4 per cent social insurance and 1.3 per cent social assistance income. In Germany (1994), the share of employment income was 82.2 per cent, of social insurance 4.8 per cent and of social assistance 1.6 per cent. In Sweden (1995) the share of labour market income was 74.9 per cent, of social insurance transfers 16.2 per cent and of social assistance benefits 2.3 per cent.

are will be discussed in the next section. We should first take a closer look, however, at the socio-political side of US protectionism in foreign trade.

Because US employees do not have the benefit of universal social protection – the mark of Western European welfare states – and since the apparatus of social trade policy has remained limited, it should not come as a surprise that an expansion of unilateral and 'results-oriented' trade policy since the early 1990s was provoked by increasing import competition in the wake of the globalization of the US economy. In an environment in which the personal situation already depends more intensely on the labour market, the growth of new forms of trade protectionism was politically inescapable. The growing foreign trade deficit, i.e. the far greater volume of imports relative to exports, seems to have sent clear signals to trade policy. Its political significance stems from the welfare state conditions of the USA. The compulsion to participate in the labour market is much stronger in the USA than in European countries. Due to the prominent role of employment-based social benefits there, the financial and thus social protection attainable by an individual and by families are dependent upon the direct yield of this labour market participation and on a person's private assets.[47] For the US workforce, the probability of procuring the basic means of existence, of gaining a position in life and of finding inner satisfaction are swayed to a very large extent by markets – and the perpetual scramble even to keep one's station in life is a basic constant of the American social structure.

If import competition is perceived as a threat, and this is precisely what is suggested by the trade balance figures, and at the same time the already limited public social protection instruments are further restricted, this potential foreign commercial threat to jobs and incomes will, under the special conditions of the US political system, very easily and directly lead to demands for a stronger ostensibly 'social' regulation of import competition and a more discretionary, or managed export policy with immediate, tangible results for the most vocal parts of the population. Indeed, this has been a growing tendency during the 1990s. Since the ratification of WTO entry and the NAFTA treaty, trade policy itself has lacked drive and direction (Lovett 1999). The never fully silenced resistance to further liberalization of foreign trade has not only grown, but burgeoned. This has led to politically powerful coalitions consisting of environmental advocates, industrial workers and ideologically motivated economic nationalists (Matthews 1997; Cohen 2000: 239–59).

The foundation for the enormous increase in employment levels in the US economy during the 1990s was tremendous productivity growth. However, this harbours considerable potential for social conflict. If, as in the first half of 2000, employment growth of 1.8 per cent translates into real economic growth of 6 per cent, then an economic growth rate of 2.5 per cent entails a *drop* in employment of nearly 1 per cent. An enduringly low unemployment rate is only possible with very high and steady

47 Despite the 'great bull market of the century', beginning in 1982 and sending the Dow Jones industrial average up about 1,400 per cent, two-thirds of US households have not become wealthier in retirement after adjusting for inflation, or have experienced a drop in the value of their pensions, compared with households led by people of comparable ages in that year. The gains of the 'great bull market' went disproportionally to the rich. Households that had less than half of pension wealth – those in the 50th percentile – experienced a drop in income of 13 per cent from 1983 to 1998, while those in the 65th percentile kept their position and those in the 80th percentile increased their retirement wealth by 19 per cent. But the really big gains went to the rich: those in the 95th percentile enjoyed a rise in pension wealth of 176 per cent over 15 years (Madrick 2002).

economic growth, for growth in productivity has proven to have ever-decreasing employment effects. In the first half of the 1990s, an economic growth rate of 1 per cent effected a growth in employment of 0.78 per cent. In the second half of the 1990s, an economic growth rate of 1 per cent translated into only a 0.1 per cent increase in employment. Commenting on this trend, an editorial in the *New York Times* observed:

> If consumers were in sounder financial shape, the job losses that a slowdown might bring would not be so worrisome. But instalment debt and stock market margin debt carried by consumers are now an astounding 245 per cent of disposable personal income. It is off the charts thanks to margin debt, which now accounts for more than 3.5 per cent of disposable income, up from an average of 0.78 percent for the 30 years ended in 1995. This debt load also means that consumer spending could contract significantly, exacerbating the downturn. (Morgenson 2000)

In the USA, contrary to Western Europe, social policy for inactive members of the labour force is not designed to preserve the living standard enjoyed during employment. For the US economy, the low rate of social transfer implies that welfare state benefit systems do not function well as automatic stabilizers during periods of decreasing economic growth, which guarantee firms a stable demand climate. This does not mean, however, that there is less demand for social and economic security in the USA than in Europe. It merely assumes different forms – and this makes all the difference for trade policy.

In Table 3.9 we describe the most important instruments with which US trade policy can achieve results and thus compromises the principle of liberal foreign trade. It exposes the tremendous extent to which US foreign economic relations can be shaped by particularist interventions providing protective assistance to specific interest groups. It reveals as well the myriad of political actors involved in the trade policy-making process, and shows how the essentially political competition for protection privileges works.[48] These instruments form the institutional foundation for the USA's 'contingent' protectionism. The differentiated legal and constitutional underpinnings of this interventionist order, especially with regard to the political clout of workers and firms to independently occasion proceedings aimed at import protection, if necessary with judicial support, make clear the extraordinary employment consequences of trade policy. The contingent character of US protectionism can be seen above all in its far-reaching dependency on transitory labour market and income developments.[49] It is a 'stand-by mechanism' used only when needed. Nevertheless, the question arises, who actually profits from this social trade policy? Without a doubt, only a truly social protection and income securing rationale can justify such a discretionary foreign trade regime. The procedures entailed in this trade policy-based system of social protection are extraordinarily complex, always influenced by politics and necessarily restricted to specific sectors or even firms. Due to this complexity and politically induced fragmentation with regard to actual access, the secondary consequences of such a policy go

[48] A description of this diversity of 'constitutive interests' in US trade policy is offered by Deardorff and Stern (1998), and an overview of attempts at explaining the special path of US trade policy can be found in Rodrik (1995).

[49] The term 'contingent protection' was coined by Rodney Grey, the Canadian trade representative for the Tokyo Round of GATT negotiations (Rugman and Anderson 1987: 9).

largely unnoticed – precisely by the weaker, unorganized groups affected by imports and trade policy, not to mention by the vast majority of consumers. This means that many of those entitled to benefits do not actually receive them.[50]

The limited transparency and openness of these proceedings makes them highly susceptible to manipulation and corruption. The US trade policy system is known for the systemic rent-seeking which it triggers and encourages. For the national economy, this means wasted resources.[51] Taking into account only those cases of 'damaging' or 'unfair' import competition actually pursued by the International Trade Commission (ITC) leads to an underestimation of the *secondary* consequences of this interventionism. On average, ITC initiates four proceedings per year. For each case in which an official proceeding is actually launched, there are at least a hundred cases in which the petitioner withdraws the complaint – usually because importers 'voluntarily' raise their prices in response to Commerce Department inquiries into whether a case of dumping exists or an import product is reducing market shares of domestic producers. The ambivalence, or uncertainty, of such a discretionary policy means that domestic clients do not have any guarantee of achieving the desired result, since the government can signal to lobbyists that an official proceeding is inopportune at the present time – but it is also true that it can use informal channels to foreign governments to achieve the desired effect (Noland 1997: 3). Figure 3.7 depicts the development of the two most important trade policy instruments with which the USA attempts – outside of GATT or the WTO system – to protect itself from unfair trade and dumping. These have almost completely superseded import protection via escape clauses.

The commercial treaty concluded with China in the summer of 2000 is a prime example of results-oriented and watertight trade policy aimed at forestalling negative trade consequences for employment and wages. The White House portrayed this agreement to the most virulent critics of a 'permanent normalization' of trade relations with China – unions and agricultural interest-groups – as a no-risk, one-sided deal in their favour.[52] China promised to significantly lower its agricultural and industrial duties and in addition guaranteed minimum import quotas and market shares. In return, the

50 V. C. Jackson (2000) argues that the extensive juridification of US proceedings, particularly the right to contest their outcome in court, enables the administration to ward off the claims of special interests. She underestimates, however, the extent to which this system not only breeds special interests, but is also predicated on them. Interest group politics, not the functional prerequisites of free markets, steers US trade policy. In an article in *The Economist*, Jagdish Bhagwati identified the cause of this: 'It's the process, stupid' (*The Economist*, 27 March 1993, p. 69; also in Bhagwati 1998: 145–8). The incentives of this system are for more, not less, protectionism. A political logic lies at the root of this. In October 2000 the *New York Times* reported on a proposed amendment drafted in the Senate which stipulated that the additional revenue generated by a 'successful' antidumping proceeding should no longer flow into the Treasury, but be returned to the industrial branch that had launched the proceeding ('Protection on the Sly', 23 October 2000, A23).

51 For a classic account of rent-seeking, see A. O. Krueger (1974), as well as Magee et al. (1989), for whom the regulation of US foreign trade amounts to a 'black hole'. For Bhagwati (1982), trade policy is a prime example of '*d*irectly *u*nproductive, *p*rofit-seeking DUP activities'. In an article in the *American Economic Review* (1994), Grossman and Helpman characterized US trade policy as 'protection for sale'.

52 The US Trade Representative at the time, Charlene Barshefsky, in a speech at the John F. Kennedy School of Government at Harvard University on 13 April 2000, described the trade agreement as a 'one-way concession' (China's WTO Accession in American Pacific Strategy, The White House and China Trade Relations Working Group; http://chinapntr.gov/speeches/barshevsky0413.htm – 7 November 2000).

Table 3.9 Major US instruments for the regulation of imports

	Statutory reference (as amended)	*Agencies involved*	*Is there a statutory time limit?*	*Can citizens initiate complaints?*	*Is there a public hearing?*	*Reasoned determination to be published?*	*Judical review provided by statute?*
Escape Clause[1]	Trade Act of 1974, §201	ITC/President	yes	yes	yes	yes	no
Antidumping[2]	Trade Agreements Act of 1979, §101	ITA(DOC)/ITC	yes	yes	yes	yes	yes
Countervailing Duties[3]	Trade Agreements Act of 1979, §101	ITA(DOC)/ITC	yes	yes	yes	yes	yes
Complaints against foreign government actions[4]	Trade Act of 1974, §301	US Trade Representative /President	yes	yes	yes	yes	no
Unfair trade practices[5]	Trade Act of 1974, §341 (Tariff Act of 1930, §377)	ITC/President	yes	yes	yes	yes	yes
Nonmarket economy safeguards[5]	Trade Act of 1974, §406	ITC/President	yes	yes	yes	yes	no
Textiles[6]	Agricultural Act of 1956, §22	President	no	no	yes	yes	no
National security[7]	Trade Expansion Act of 1962, §232	DOC/President	yes	yes	yes ('if it is appropriate')	yes	no
Dairy products[8]	Agricultural Adjustment Act of 1933, §22	USDA/ITC/ President	no	no	yes	yes	no
Meat[9]	Meat Import Act of 1979, §1	President	no	no	yes (public consultation)	yes	no
Tax measures (Houdaille)[10]	Internal Revenue Code, §103(a)(7)(D)	President	no	no	no	no	no
Generalized system of preferences[11]	Trade Act of 1974, Title V	President	no	no	no	yes	no
Voluntary restraint[12]	Trade Expansion Act of 1962, §252	President	no	no	no	no	no
	Agricultural Act of 1956, §204	President	no	no	no	no	no
Tariffs[13]	Tariff Act of 1930, §516	Treasury	yes	yes	yes	yes	yes

Notes: ITA = International Trade Administration; ITC = International Trade Commission; DOC = Department of Commerce; USDA = Department of Agriculture

[1] When imports are increasing and are harming national industry substantially, this programme empowers the President to limit imports via tariffs or fixed quotas. These measures may last up to five years.

[2] When the prices of imported goods are lower in the market of the exporting country, the price difference may be made up by a tariff.

[3] Punitive tariffs may be used in addition to normal tariffs when imports are subsidized by the government of the country of origin.

[4] US companies and citizens may use this procedure to raise complaints about foreign economic policies of other countries which affect them disadvantageously. The US government is required to follow up such complaints. If such a complaint is deemed justified, the government may take up negotiations with the government complained against so as to remove the cause of complaint. The President may take all appropriate measures to make that foreign government remove the source of complaint.

[5] The US government is empowered in a plenary fashion to take steps against 'unfair trade practices'. This refers not only to imported goods but also to infringements on patent and copyright legislation and other legal monopolies. Based on this law the International Trade Commission may ban such imports. The President may veto such a decision.

[6] In the context of the GATT International Multifiber Agreement a US national law empowers the President to negotiate bilateral treaties with textile exporting countries such as to limit such US imports.

[7] This measure relates to dangers for US national security which may result from imports which harm US industry. Until now, only complaints against imports of products in the oil refinery business have been successful.

[8] This law provides the basis for quotas relating to a series of milk products.

[9] This law allows the US government to tie the import of meat products to the development of corresponding US demand and supply.

[10] This measure relates to stipulations in US tax law privileging US competitors who rely on imported goods in their chain of production that are taxed at relaxed rates as compared with US companies relying on national products only.

[11] According to this programme, goods from developing countries may be imported without any tariffs. The President may review and change this list at regular intervals.

[12] Except for the agricultural and textile sector there is no legal basis for the President negotiating with foreign governments about limiting their exports to the US. 'Voluntary export limitations' fill this vacuum and have acquired quasi-legal standing.

[13] Tariff laws in the US require declarations for each and every good imported. The tariffs vary strongly but have been lowered in many sectors in recent years.

Source: Jackson (2000a: 293–4)

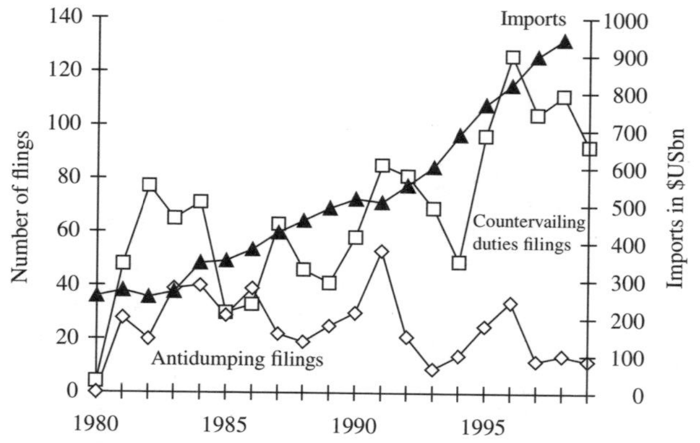

Figure 3.7 Punitive duties and antidumping proceedings in the USA, 1980–1999
Source: See ⟨*http://ia.ita.gov/stats./cvdrevl.htm*⟩ on countervailing duties and antidumping filings; ⟨*http://ia.ita.gov/stats./adrev1.htm*⟩ on imports; IMF (1999a: 132f.)

USA made no concessions whatsoever, and was even able to expand its traditional enforcement mechanisms against unfair import competition.[53]

The import-restricting and export-enhancing effects of this interventionist foreign trade system are impossible to quantify. On the contrary, to all appearances there seems to be no effect at all, but instead we seem to witness the presence of a strong free trade regime. The global market integration of the USA, if one takes only the gross sum of imports and exports as a measure, has considerably accelerated since the 1980s. As figure 3.8 shows, goods that could be imported into the US duty-free were, by the late

[53] The legal basis for this normalization is the extension of the Most Favoured Nation (MFN) trading status to China. MFN is the basis for the entire US system of trade agreements and applies to 160 countries. Besides China, only Afghanistan, Cuba, Laos, North Korea, Serbia/Montenegro and Vietnam are denied MFN status. The text of the law approved by the Senate comprises 69 pages. For the (re)establishment of 'normal' trade relations, half a page suffices. The rest specifies enforcement and protective regulations and begins with the classic protection clause: 'If a product of the People's Republic of China is being imported into the United States in such increased quantities or under such conditions as to cause or threaten to cause market disruptions to the domestic producers of a like or directly competitive product, the President shall, in accordance with the provisions of this section, proclaim increased duties or other import restrictions with respect to such product, to the extent and for such period as the President considers necessary to prevent or remedy the market disruption' (Calendar No. 575, 106th Congress, 2nd Session, H.R. 4444, p. 6). The law contains tougher enforcement mechanisms, prescribes lower thresholds for antidumping proceedings and stipulates additional protective mechanisms which go beyond those regulatory and defensive measures hitherto at the disposal of national trade policy as well as those provided by the WTO. Finally, it provides additional resources for the supervision of trade with China: it enlarges the divisions of the Commerce Department and the ITC that are responsible for the implementation and supervision of both the treaty and China's WTO membership by 100 and 75 per cent respectively, and increases their budgets as well. In his 2001 Budget, the President proposed expanding the loan programme for trade with China and introducing a special programme to provide assistance via the internet to small businesses in accessing the Chinese market: 'an export advisor on every desktop' ('Labor Aspects of PNTR: Benefits for American Workers and Farmers', The White House – China Trade Relations Working Group, June 6, 2000; http://www.chinapntr.gov/factsheets/Labor%20Aspects.htm – 7 November 2000).

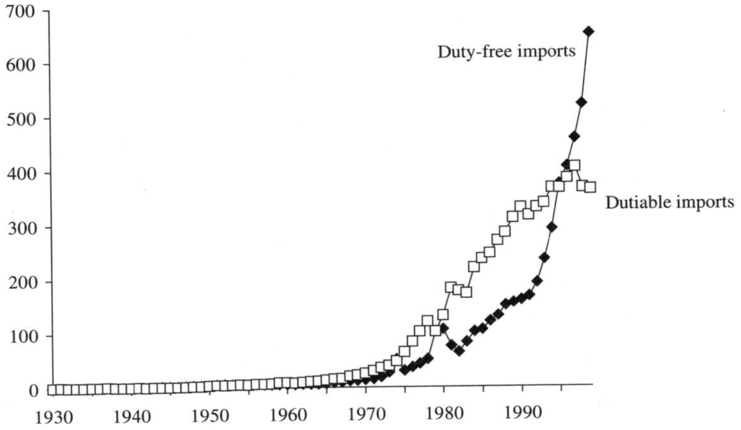

Figure 3.8 Duty-free and dutiable imports into the USA, 1930–1998 (in $US bn)
Source: US International Trade Commission (2000: 4)

1990s, outnumbering those that carry a tariff. A few observations on this diagram are necessary. First, every import occurs in the shadow of the threat of very powerful trade policy intervention. Every import is subject to the proviso that it inflict no injury – i.e. that it neither affects the sales of domestic producers nor has any other negative effects on employment and wages. Yet *whether* and above all *how* this proviso is fulfilled is another question. The well-known fact that, until now, political slogans notwithstanding, positive economics has not succeeded in bringing the dramatic increases in imports into an empirically observable connection with economic difficulties among low-wage employees seems to attest to the efficiency of US trade policy.[54]

Second, the NAFTA and similar preferential treaties[55] are means of *redirecting* trade from a free foreign economy supervised only by the multilateral GATT and the WTO into a territorially limited free trade region characterized by a far higher, bilaterally

[54] Empirical evidence of this *failure* to establish a causal relationship can be found in Krugman and Lawrence (1994), Krugman (1995), Davis et al. (1996), and Pryor and Schaffer (1999). This negative finding could, however, be due to the fact that the nature of this relationship is not properly understood. Thus in their previously cited, highly influential articles, Krugman and Lawrence have attempted to show that the actual share of imports from low-wage countries ('2.8 per cent') stands in no credible relation to the massive downward trend in wages during the same period. Leamer (2000: 37) notes the following in this regard: 'Do you remember the case of Krugman Air, which uses a secret input – Mexican power – to fly its airplanes at low cost? When Krugman Air started to compete in the U.S. market, it offered to fly U.S. routes at half the going price. The response of U.S. carriers was to match the price and find various ways to cut cost including lowering hourly wages by 30% and expanding hours per week by 10%. "Not us," explained the economists who worked for Krugman Air, "We couldn't have been responsible for all that reduction in wages. We are too small. We only have a 2.8% market share."'

[55] Trade agreements besides NAFTA include the Generalized System of Preferences, in effect since 1976, governing trade with developing countries (in 1999, 1.3 per cent of total imports); trade privileges on the basis of the Caribbean Basin Economic Recovery Act, in effect since 1984; the US–Israel Free Trade Agreement (1985); and the Andean Trade Preference Act (1992). These special trade agreements are negligible in terms of their volume. In 1999 they constituted less than 1 per cent of total imports.

negotiated level of protection.[56] Imports from Mexico and Canada constituted 18.4 per cent of total US imports in 1999. If trade with Mexico continues to grow at the same pace as it has in recent years, it will exceed trade with Europe by 2004 (Weiner and Gori 2000: 12). Contrary to the case in the multilateral negotiating arena of the WTO, in bilateral trade agreement policy it is much easier for the USA to accommodate domestic interest groups such as unions or environmental protection organizations. 'Free trade agreements' are not really about free trade. As Andreas Lowenfeld noted with regard to NAFTA, it should have taken only two or three pages to mandate 'free trade'. Instead, the text of NAFTA is 1,500 pages long – 1,500 pages of exceptions to free trade (referred to in Ragosta and Magnus 1997: 89).

The free trade agreement between the United States and Jordan signed on 24 October 2000 ties the abolition of all duties and import restrictions to Jordan's compliance with *sanctionable* labour and environmental standards.[57] Article 6, Paragraph 1 of the draft treaty defines the regulatory framework of the ILO as the standard for Jordanese worker rights. Article 6, Paragraph 2 refers explicitly to the problem of social dumping in trade relations:

> The Parties recognize that it is inappropriate to encourage trade by relaxing domestic labour laws. Accordingly, each Party shall strive to ensure that it does not waive or otherwise derogate from, or offer to waive or otherwise derogate from, such laws as an encouragement for trade with the other party.

Paragraphs 3–5 initially emphasize national autonomy in social policy, but then concede the contractual partners supervisory rights regarding compliance with social standards. They even render contractual violations sanctionable and establish a mechanism to coordinate enforcement.[58] The free trade agreement with Jordan is the first

[56] See some of the essays, entitled 'Free Trade Areas Are Not Free Trade!', republished by Bhagwati in his 1998 collection (pp. 269–312). According to Bhagwati, this trade policy reversal expresses the interests of a 'selfish hegemon'. NAFTA and similar commercial treaties, he argues, are used by the USA to increase the social and environmental production costs of its 'low-wage' competitors. Contrary to the case in the multilateral arena of the WTO, in its bilateral trade policy the USA can bring its economic superiority directly to bear.

[57] The ratification of this agreement by Congress occurred on 28 September 2002 and was certain because the volume of trade with Jordan had been less than $300 million and because – far more importantly – Jordan is considered to be an ally in the context of US foreign policy in the Middle East (Office of the United States Trade Representative, 'The US–Jordan Free Trade Agreement Fact Sheet', 27 October 2000; 'Labor Praises Social Agenda Of Trade With Jordan', *New York Times*, 25 October 2000, C1 and C12; http://www.jordanembassyus.org). Contrary to President Clinton's original plan, the trade agreement with China obligates it to obey neither the UN Human Rights Convention nor the ILO conventions. Corresponding amendments, which were introduced first in the House of Representatives and later in the Senate, could not win a majority ('Senate Votes to Lift Curbs on US Trade with Beijing: Strong Bipartisan Support', *New York Times*, 20 September 2000, A1 and A12).

[58] Of the eight major conventions of the ILO, the US has ratified only two – the abolition of child labour and of forced labour. Neither the conventions defining workers' unionization rights (Conventions 87 and 98), nor the anti-discrimination conventions (Conventions 100 and 101) were accepted by the USA. Accordingly, US workers have no legal recourse to these conventions. Jordan has ratified seven of these eight conventions. The exception is Convention 87 concerning freedom of association and collective bargaining. Thus Jordan actually has more grounds than the USA to insist on compliance with social standards. The non-ratification of the ILO conventions has not hindered the USA, however, from being an active member of the ILO. This is especially true of employer representatives, who, because of the ILO's corporatist structure, dispose of an independent influence in the organization (Power 1968). The non-ratification is generally explained with reference to the country's federal structure. It lacks a uniform labour law, and in some states laws exist which make union organization by workers extremely difficult (Sørenson 1952; Rogers 1990).

such accord ever in which issues of compliance with social standards play a central role.[59]

Third, a substantial share of international trade is a transaction between national divisions of one and the same firm. As a result of the growing significance of US multinational corporations, an ever greater segment of US international trade is now in fact intra-firm trade (Coldwell and Reid 1998). One-third of all US goods exports and more than two-fifths of its goods imports in 1994 occurred within one multinational company (Zeile 1997). Contrary to genuine transnational market transactions, intra-firm trade occurs largely independently of competitive conditions, price and currency fluctuations, and changes in the overall economic climate in the target and host countries. The market does not, therefore, at least not directly, shape this segment of international trade; rather, internal company decisions do.

Intra-firm trade involves an internalization and thus an exclusion of transnational market risks. Far from representing a relationship between independent market participants, such transactions are largely a bureaucratic family affair. Intra-firm trade is also a means by which firms can protect themselves against the risks of interventionist, situational and opportunistically exploitable trade policy.[60] It is thus no coincidence that US intra-firm trade plays a particularly prominent role in the country's commercial relations with nations with which it is regularly engaged in trade conflicts. On average, during the period 1983–94, US merchandise trade with Japan was 72 per cent intra-firm trade, with Germany only 55 per cent. In both cases, the level increased during this period: from 68 to 77 per cent with Japan, and from 52 to 63 per cent with Germany (Doremus et al. 1998: 123). For the firms involved, intra-firm trade has the advantage that a large share of their *in-house* international commerce cannot and need not be influenced by the classic instruments of national trade policy – i.e. customs duties, protective and special rules and antidumping proceedings. On the contrary, it is safe to assume that companies utilize intra-firm trade precisely to avoid conflict with trade policy institutions (Bonturi and Fukasaku 1993).[61]

For the countries concerned, intra-firm trade has the considerable advantage that its effect is largely neutral vis-à-vis the existing distribution of income. Contrary to more traditional 'trade at arm's length', two potentially very different welfare state

59 This statement is not entirely accurate in that Public Law 106–200 of 18 May 2000 makes the President's trade policy vis-à-vis forty-eight African and twenty-four Caribbean states conditional on these states' compliance with ILO Convention 182, the abolition of child labour. This law that empowers the President to conclude commercial treaties is, by itself, not a treaty. In this respect we should note that in various cases the ITC has treated the existence of an unemployment insurance scheme in an exporting country as an unacceptable subsidy of an import good, potentially justifying imposition of higher duties. In the 1980s the ITC imposed counter-tariffs, for example, on the import of tyres from the Michelin Tyre Company of Canada and on the import of Canadian fish, citing the Canadian unemployment insurance scheme as the reason. The procedural rules of the ITC on antidumping and punitive counter-tariff proceedings stipulate that the benefits of the US unemployment compensation system should *not* be taken into account in the assessment of the 'fact' of an 'unfair' subsidy of foreign producers (Rugman and Anderson 1987: 43, 46). Clearly, there is a double standard here.

60 Destler and Odell (1987) discuss the rather ineffective but nonetheless prevalent resistance of some US corporations to the erratic, contingent protectionism of US trade policy – chiefly due to Congressional intervention.

61 For example, pricing in intra-firm trade involves not market but transfer prices set internally by company units. They can be fixed in such a way as to avoid taxes and customs duties to whatever extent possible. They thus pose a considerable problem for tax authorities. Moreover, it is the USA, precisely because of the vast scope of its intra-firm trade, that has major problems targeting punitive tariffs on only those products that are genuine imports, thus affecting only the export country.

worlds cannot collide here. The danger that absolute differences in wage costs might exert pressure on domestic wage levels is, accordingly, more remote.

In sum, we see that US trade policy differs from that of the European Union or Japan, both in terms of its institutional structures and its governance. Every step towards liberalization, like the openness of demand and supply markets in general, is conditional on the organization *de nouveau* of compensatory social policy and interventionist protectionist trade policy measures. This is true whenever larger segments of the population are exposed to risks of loss of employment and income. What then, in this context, is the significance of the 1996 welfare reform, which transformed welfare into workfare? This can be assessed only if we turn our attention away from social assistance narrowly understood and examine broader changes in US anti-poverty policy, particularly the growing tax-based social assistance for the working poor. This programme, the Earned Income Tax Credit (EITC), has given the entire US approach to social assistance a new focus.

A new social policy: the EITC's negative income tax

The two main forms of welfare state income maintenance are social insurance and social assistance. Social insurance schemes are typically financed by contributions, tied to an employment contract and designed to maintain standards of living in case of temporary or permanent incapacity to work. Social assistance benefits are subject to a means test and aim at guaranteeing the needy a politically defined subsistence level.

Both forms of security provision have lost much of their original legitimacy and rationality. Under the combined influence of demographic shifts in the age profile of populations in developed welfare states and of changes in the labour market – e.g. high rates of long-term unemployment and the proliferation of flexible and so-called irregular employment contracts – social insurance schemes have become at once expensive and cumbersome institutions: expensive, because they can translate into high non-wage labour costs; cumbersome, because they constitute something like property rights of large segments of the population and as such stand in the way of more radical reform. As a result, social insurance schemes are largely resistant to attempts to reconstruct the welfare state as a whole from a system predominantly public to one based mostly on the private production of social policy goods.[62] Traditional social assistance programmes can be counter-productive in two ways: first, in that they function as poverty traps, locking their clients into their existing dependency instead of integrating them into the labour market; second, because they serve as disincentives and thus undermine the efficiency of labour markets. Arguments like these were used to justify and win passage of the fundamental reform of several US social assistance programmes discussed above.

As figure 3.9 shows, AFDC, hitherto the core US social assistance programme, has been overlaid with a programme that has pioneered a new path in social policy: the EITC is a nationally uniform negative income tax exclusively funded by the federal government (Howard 1993, 1997; Green Book 2000; Haveman and Wolfe 1998).[63] Yet, as

[62] On these two problems of social policy in advanced welfare states and their interrelationship, see Pierson (1994, 1998), Rüthers (1996) and Rieger (1998a). On the limits of this line of argumentation, see Leisering and Walker (1998) and Leisering and Leibfried (1999).

[63] All other cash-based anti-poverty programmes with potential labour market overlap are funded cooperatively by the federal and state governments.

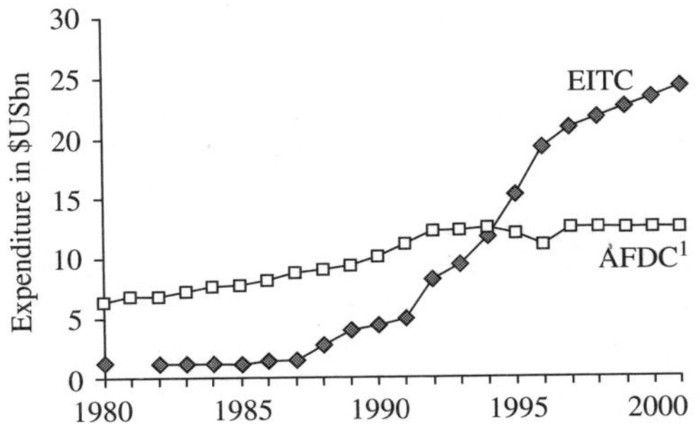

Figure 3.9 US federal expenditure on EITC and AFDC (TANF), 1980–2001[2] (in $USbn)

[1] Since 1997 federal payments for Temporary Assistance for Needy Families (TANF), introduced in 1996, have been block grants to the states and have replaced expenditure on Aid to Families with Dependent Children (AFDC), Emergency Assistance for Needy Families (EA) and Job Opportunities and Basic Skills Development (JOBS). The size of the block grant is determined by one of the following factors, whichever is higher: average expenditure in 1992–4, in 1994 or in 1995. In toto, block grants for AFDC, EA and JOBS in 1997–2002 amount to $US16.6 billion. The expenditure on AFDC alone is unknown; thus, after 1997 – for the sake of contrast – we simply continued the level of expenditure as it obtained in 1994. Expenditure on AFDC does not include state expenditure or administrative costs.

[2] Data for 1997–2001 are based on budget requests only.

Source: Green Book (1998: 1357, table 1–5; 1359, table 1–6 for EITC; 411, table 7–4; 503 ff. for AFDC (TANF))

the name suggests, its benefits are limited to wage earners. Until 1994, eligibility was further limited to working families with children. Although this is no longer the case, the programme is still designed to give the bulk of benefits to families. The EITC is aimed at overcoming the poverty gap and is now seen as the primary instrument of a 'work first' and 'making work pay' strategy (Lerman 1999: 11–14). If employment-generated income falls below a certain level, the Internal Revenue Service (IRS) reimburses paid taxes or, in case this proves to be insufficient, provides monetary transfers. At present, and as one feature of the organization of EITC, the employer is directly subsidized in that the government or social insurance fund allows him to forgo paying the social insurance contribution on behalf of the employee and instead to pay out its cash value directly as a wage supplement to the employee, if the latter is eligible for EITC.[64] Box 3.2 shows how the IRS calls on employers to give their employees access to the EITC.

In the USA, then, wages are systematically subsidized, as first occurred on a large scale in England in the village of Speenhamland in Berkshire at the turn of the

64 Since 1998, the payroll tax (social insurance contribution) payable to the IRS totals 15.3 per cent, and is shared equally by employer and employee. For an annual average income of $27,583 the employee share is $2,110. For an income half this, i.e. the poverty level, the contribution burden is $1,055. It is this contribution that the IRS targets with the additional $100 in wages mentioned above, depicted in Box 3.2 (1997 data from the *Congressional Research Service, The Library of Congress*: CRS Report for Congress (94–27 EPW), Social Security: Brief Facts and Statistics, Updated 1 May 1998; http://concordcoalition.org/entitlement/crs050198.html – 7 August 2000).

Box 3.2 EITC notification for employers

Are you interested in providing your employees with the benefit for increased take home pay at virtually no cost to your enterprise? The Internal Revenue Service (IRS) has a program called the Advance Earned Income Tax Credit (Advance EITC) that does just that. Employees can get extra money in their paychecks rather than having to wait until they file their tax return.

This is how it works. You make the advance payments to your employees from the employment taxes you would normally deposit or send to the IRS. The amount is paid to the employees – with no income tax withheld. You then claim the amount as a timely payment on your quarterly employment tax form (Form 941).

Signing up for the Advance EITC payment is easy. All your employees need to do is give you a Form W-5, Earned Income Credit Advance Payment Certificate. You do not need to send Form W-5 to IRS. Just keep the form on file.

Over 15 million workers may qualify for this paycheck 'boost'. To qualify for Advance EITC, working parents or grandparents must have at least one qualifying child and their annual income for 2000 must be less than approximately $27,000, or less than approximately $31,000 with two or more qualifying children. For many workers receiving the Advance EITC each paycheck can make a difference in buying groceries, paying rent, and meeting other daily needs. For example, an employee who earns minimum wage would see their take home pay increased by over $100 each month.

Source: Tax Information for Business, EITC Information for Employers IRS (http://www.irsustreas.gov/prod/bus_info/eit-emp.html (14.06.00))

eighteenth century, with the social protection instruments of the time (K. Polanyi 1957 [1944]: 77–86). Speenhamland, however, was judged to be a catastrophic mistake, for this social policy led to a situation in which the already steady downward trend in wage levels went into free fall. Employers knew that the gap between wage levels and a subsistence income would be filled with public money and they thus lowered wages all the more (Blaug 1963; Stadermann 1995). In the USA, policy-makers have attempted to forestall this effect of wage subsidies through minimum wage legislation. Hence, since President Clinton's inauguration in 1993, the legally mandated minimum wage has always been raised at the same rate as EITC increases. Still, it is reasonable to assume that the considerable decline in real wages suffered by large segments of the US workforce since the 1980s has also been supported by this wage subsidization. As a rule, the minimum wage is so low that the income it yields does not suffice to lift even a one-person household over the poverty or social assistance threshold.[65]

The EITC was first enacted under President Nixon in 1974. At first, it was a small, fairly insignificant programme. Its socio-politically revolutionary component, family assistance, had been rejected by Congress (Moynihan 1973; Burke and Burke 1974;

[65] As of 1 Oct 2002, the federal minimum wage was $5.15. The federal minimum wage law applies to all firms with sales of more than $500,000. Smaller firms fall under this law when they engage in interstate commerce and their employees thus use federal transportation and communications infrastructure. Moreover, the working conditions of all government employees in federal, state and local institutions, including hospitals and schools, fall under this law. The majority of states has a minimum wage statute. If the state-prescribed minimum wage is higher, it takes precedence over the federal standard; if it is lower, it applies only to employment relations, which are exempt from the federal law. As of 9 Nov 2002, in California and Massachusetts, the minimum wage was $6.75; in New Mexico $4.25; in Kansas $2.65. See http://www.dol.gov./esa/minwage/america.htm.

Patterson 1996: 720). Since the mid-1980s the programme has expanded greatly, due chiefly to three major amendments since 1986 (Green Book 1998: Appendix K). In terms of numbers of claimants, the EITC some time ago became the country's largest social assistance programme, although programme benefits per claimant – as wage supplements – are much lower, for example, than in AFDC/TANF. During 1994, the average monthly number of claimants was 54 million, as opposed to 34 million in the means-tested medical assistance programme Medicaid, 14 million in AFDC and nearly 29 million in the food assistance programme Food Stamps (all data based on US Census Bureau 1996: 371). As figure 3.9 showed, federal expenditures for EITC since 1993 have exceeded those for AFDC and later TANF. This gap has widened steadily.

In the US South, a traditional low-wage region, 16.6 per cent of all taxpayers received EITC benefits in 1992, claiming average annual benefits of $954. In the North-east, 8 per cent of taxpayers received benefits ($865), in the Midwest 10 per cent ($890) and in the West 11 per cent ($895) (Myles and Pierson 1997: 463). Between 1989 and 1998, EITC benefits for families with one child were raised by 90 per cent and for families with two or more children by 214 per cent. This effect was augmented by four successive increases in the minimum wage during this period (1990: $3.35; 1997: $5.15). Overall, due to these measures alone, the total income of lone parents with one child increased by 26 per cent, and that of those with two children by 40 per cent (Blank 2000: table 2).[66]

Even though the general (not only the political) mood was not disposed towards social policy, and particularly not towards welfare (Gilens 1999), it was not only the EITC that was spared drastic (welfare) or even minor (social insurance) reforms.[67] The EITC was even gradually expanded, most recently with a major increase in 1993, so that one can now speak of a development from a welfare state towards a 'workfare state'.[68] The corresponding legislative initiatives were proposed and enacted by Republican and Democratic Congresspersons alike. It has not been possible to discern divisions vis-à-vis the programme along the lines of political party affiliation or economic interest – in part because the programme expansions were always components of broad package deals. The political function of EITC expansion is evident in the fact that such expansions have always occurred simultaneously with tax cuts favouring the propertied and middle classes (Myles and Pierson 1997). The classic Southern objection to the expansion of the social programmes does not apply in the case of the EITC: in stark contrast to minimum wage legislation, which is controversial (Schelkle 1999), the EITC does not impact regional differences in wage levels, but, rather, indirectly reinforces them.

66 Meyer and Rosenbaum (1999) attributed roughly half of the marked rise in labour market participation by lone mothers during the period 1984–96 to the expansion of the EITC. While such 'pull effects' are largely uncontested, this is not true of the very slow increase in the number of work hours or of improvements in the quality of employment positions held (Schelkle 1999: 51 f.).

67 Yet in connection with this programme, which up to this point had seemed foolproof, there have been public debates about fraudulent claims, making the programme controversial and thus politically vulnerable (Blank 1997: 113 f. More detailed evidence can be found in Schelkle 1999: 54). 'The [crucial] question being whether assessing the eligibility via tax declarations is inherently more fraud prone than the old-fashioned way of assessment by caseworkers' (Schelkle, op. cit.).

68 Since its introduction in 1974, the EITC has been marked by an enduring and *uninterrupted* expansion in the range of incomes eligible for supplementation, the kinds of household eligible and the level of benefits provided (Green Book 1998: Table 13–12). This runs completely counter to the trend in other areas of US social policy during this period.

Five circumstances have given the EITC particularly favourable chances of passage and survival in the contemporary competitive business and economic climate:

- First, its social effectiveness. By definition, the programme avoids work disincentives, i.e. incentives to obtain an income outside of the labour market from the welfare state: the precondition for receipt of this benefit is the existence of an employment contract.[69] The US version of the negative income tax conspicuously *lacks* any elements of a 'guaranteed minimum income' for *all* citizens independent of current or previous employment status.[70]
- Second, the neutrality of its benefits vis-à-vis regionally divergent wage costs. This is guaranteed by the fact that this instrument – in contrast to the minimum wage – imposes no direct burden on employers.
- Third, the programme's social efficiency. The EITC is administratively rather easy to organize, for it is a part of the US Treasury administration.[71] In contrast to other social assistance programmes, it requires no (labour-)intensive supervision of applicants' living situations. The comparatively limited budgetary costs of the programme because of its predominantly fiscal nature – in 1994 Food Stamps alone cost over $27 billion – neither endangers the goal of a balanced budget, nor conflicts with the objective of a 'lean' government.
- Fourth, the EITC's compatibility with productive and competitively oriented business organizations. In the new global competitive climate, a business organization's effectiveness is negatively associated with the degree to which social policy gives employees 'exit' and 'voice' options vis-à-vis management decisions, and positively

69 Minimum wage legislation is also tied to the existence of an employment relationship. This instrument has occupied such a prominent position in the Anglo-American legal tradition because of the historical and to a large extent contemporary lack of generally binding collective bargaining agreements fulfilling equivalent functions. In the case of the minimum wage, like the EITC, substantial increases in benefit levels have occurred since the early 1990s after years of stagnation during which inflation ate ever further into the poverty-fighting significance of minimum wage legislation (cf. Blank 1997: xvii and 114 ff.; 2000: 16 ff.). The last increase occurred, not coincidentally, in 1996 – to a certain extent a 'waving with the carrot' just prior to welfare reform. The minimum wage was raised in two steps from $4.25 to $5.15. In inflation-adjusted terms, even after these increases, in 1999 its value still lay 19 per cent below that of 1979 (J. Bernstein 1999: 1; J. Bernstein et al. 2000). Since in the case of the minimum wage, as opposed to the wage-subsidizing EITC, the employer bears all of the costs, its employment effects are always the subject of controversy (ibid.: 115). Moreover, regional differences are considerable, not least because of the Southern states' traditional reservations regarding a raise of the wage floor.

70 Its linkage to employment makes this model interesting also for German policy-makers (Scharpf 1995; Zukunftskommission 1998: 223–68; Paqué 1999a), as the 1999 discussion of the low-wage sector in the Partnership for Work (*Bündnis für Arbeit*), a consortium of the social partners and the national government, showed. Associated with this policy, however, at least in the US case, is the *abdication* of any kind of government guarantee of a minimum standard of living for those *outside* the labour market. In Germany such a policy would surely encounter far stiffer political and even constitutional resistance. Since in Germany a far more effective and constitutionally secure basic level of provision exists in the form of Social Assistance, a supplemental social assistance programme tied to employment has the potential to be far more effective there (Leibfried et al. 1998; Schmähl 1999a, b, 2000).

71 Roughly ten states, especially since the mid-1990s, supplement federal EITC benefits with their own EITC programmes administered autonomously at the state level (Johnson and Lazere 1998: 9–10; Blank 2000: 10). By providing such negative income tax benefits in relation to their own state income taxes, these states hope to reinforce the federal programme's goal of 'making work pay'.

associated with the degree to which the incentive effects of management decisions are allowed free rein (Ramaswamy 1994).

- Finally, the EITC's limited visibility and thus limited political vulnerability. Only a portion of its benefit is actually paid out; the bulk of it consists of forgone income taxes and social insurance contributions. The EITC is thus less conspicuous on the expenditure and anchored on the revenue side of the budget (Blank 1997: 114). The EITC is fiscally thus largely hidden, including in terms of the overall tax burden on employers and employees.

But what are the effects of EITC as the new social policy instrument of choice for the foreign economy policy-making of the USA? For trade policy, or more precisely, for the trade policy latitude of the US government, the result of the EITC is not to reduce, but rather to augment domestic political pressure for protectionism. This form of social policy does not politically unburden trade policy, but, rather, makes its likely employment effects an even more prominent focus of domestic politics. Every labour market downturn which can be remotely attributed to foreign commercial relations directly translates into very powerful and effective demands for trade policy intervention. This is because the EITC is *not* primarily an income *replacement* benefit.[72] As import and export figures show, the volume of US foreign trade has grown to such an extent that in nearly all companies, international factors play a decisive role. Under these new conditions, the country's enormous trade deficit, which has always been adduced as 'proof' of an overly generous import policy, has become an even greater handicap to US foreign commercial relations. That this trade deficit is more than equalled by net inflows of foreign capital hardly resonates in domestic politics. This is most probably due to the fact that the positive employment effects of foreign direct investment are rather limited. Between 1977 and 1991, the share of workers in foreign-owned firms rose from 1.7 to 5.3 per cent. By 1997, this share had fallen to 4.9 per cent, while the output of these firms increased from 5.5 to 6.3 per cent of total production between 1992 and 1997 (Zeile 2000: 141, 146). Moreover, as early as the 1970s it had been noted that new jobs were not emerging in those economic sectors that were subject to increased import competition. They arose instead either in those sectors that, due to technological progress, did not (yet) face foreign competition, or in those that were less vulnerable to such competition, such as the service sector (Eckes 1995: 217).

Since EITC does not relieve worker anxiety, it should not come as a surprise that in a poll conducted by the Pew Research Center for People and the Press in 2000, 78 per cent of respondents answered that 'protecting the jobs of American workers' should have top priority in deciding US policies about trading with other countries (Kletzer and Litan 2001: 1). The Trade Act of 2002, cleared by Congress on 2 August 2002,[73] is reflecting this negative disposition towards trade liberalization as it binds trade authority for the White House to three conditions: first, much improved trade adjustment assistance, both with regard to coverage and benefits; second, introduction

72 The EITC provides income replacement only for those incomes that are so *low* that they fall under the provisions of the programme. For households with no earnings whatsoever, the EITC can of course provide no income replacement.

73 On 6 December 2001, the House of Representatives voted to extend fast-track authority by a 215-to-214 vote and the Senate agreed by a 64-to-34 vote on 1 August 2002.

of 'wage insurance';[74] and third, compelling US trade negotiators to pursue labour rights and environmental provisions: the so-called Jordan standard (Baucus 2002).

4 Outlook

A look at the United States can enrich the comparative analysis of social policy and welfare state structures. A first finding is that it is impossible to calculate clearly the effects of welfare state institutions on the sustainability and dynamism of an internationally open market economy. This would be true for structural reasons alone: social policy reform, even or perhaps precisely when, as in the US case of expanding EITC, it leads to more effective poverty prevention, can lead to discretionary trade policy – and not social policy – being perceived as the most effective means of social protection. The USA has increased its protectionism over the last decade, and has expanded its unilateral instruments at the expense of integration in a multilateral system of international trade policy.[75] As early as the 1980s it had already become clear that the administration of contingent protectionism was costing several times as much as the US contribution to the operation of the WTO – not to mention the money that foreign firms were having to spend on lobbyists and lawyers when their imports landed on the Congressional agenda or were challenged before the ITC (Rugman and Anderson 1987: 45).

US trade policy has become much less predictable for its trading partners. Its central rationality criteria are not the rules and procedures of an international economic order, but, rather, positive, tangible results in terms of US employment and wages and simultaneous avoidance of any threats to these by import competition. 'Building prosperity at home' is the underlying principle guiding US foreign trade policy.[76] For this reason, whenever ostensibly threatening import competition looms, the USA makes use of its national trade policy instruments instead of following the procedures provided for in Article XIX of GATT (Finger et al. 1982). Given this state of affairs, there can be no talk of an 'unconditional free trade' orientation in the USA. Precisely the opposite is the case. For example, one Senate version of a trade bill giving President Bush fast-track authority identified a number of WTO decisions against US trade laws and directs the Administration to develop a strategy for remedying these decisions or lose fast-

74 'Wage insurance' works as follows: eligible workers would receive some fraction of their wage loss – which would vary by age and tenure of the worker – for up to two years following the initial date of job loss, but would begin to be paid only when they found a new job. The basic idea of this programme is to address the real needs of workers and at the same time to contain incentives for workers to accept new jobs more quickly, and in a broader scope, than they do now (Kletzer and Litan 2001; Baucus 2002).

75 As Anne O. Krueger wrote in the mid-1990s: 'US administered trade laws have become increasingly restrictive in a number of ways and thus have acquired increasingly protectionist overtones. . . . Threats of administered protection have induced trading partners to accept other bilateral measures, such as voluntary export restraints, in preference to the trade remedy alternative. By the mid-1980s, the United States was the largest single user of administrative trade law remedies' (1995: 35). For background on the more general ambivalence of US politics vis-à-vis international institutions, cf. Luck (1999).

76 'Building prosperity at home' was a key phrase used in a speech given by President Clinton's Trade Representative Charlene Barschefsky to the World Affairs Council in Los Angeles on 25 September 2000, in which she took stock of US trade policy during the Clinton years ('Trade Policy 1992–2000: The Clinton Record and the Road Ahead', 4).

track authority: 'These decisions are unfair and overreaching; in effect, they add new WTO rules on trade laws that have not been negotiated and could not have been negotiated' (Baucus 2002: 4). Trade policy consists of a set of instruments used in an organized way to facilitate or obstruct the cross-border traffic of a nation's economy based on *domestic* political and thus, in the final analysis, social criteria. This says nothing about the economic rationality or irrationality of these plans. Trade and social policymakers alike are career politicians on a short-term contract, and are accountable solely to a *national* public. Their material destiny is determined by this constituency alone. Thus, foreign trade can and will always be guided by social policy concerns. This is particularly true in the United States.

Further, the structure and political constitution of a welfare state can give hints as to what *kind* of trade policy is at all possible within it, as well as to what social policy strings can be tied to the opening of domestic markets in order to reach this goal. The hard facts of a welfare state are critical variables in the probability of counterproductive behavioural changes on the part of its actual and potential beneficiaries when the latter are confronted with demands for fundamental adaptation in their firms. However, negative incentives exist in trade policy as well:

> The U.S. Farm and Steel Support Bill recently signed by the president included a unique steel provision that gives U.S. steel companies compensation from tariffs levied on foreign steel imports as a result of successful antidumping suits. This is a drastic departure from the typical protocol, where tariff revenues go to government coffers. At a time when the steel industry is reeling from poor pricing, this new legislation will add fuel to the rising tide of antidumping suits filed by steel companies against their foreign competitors. (Moreno 2000: 1)

The more accessible the instruments of protectionist trade policy, the greater the probability that those who feel threatened by import competition will react in ways that are 'directly unproductive'[77] and that are short-term rather than economically productive and long-term-oriented. When faced with what they perceive to be impending challenges 'from abroad' in the interest of 'foreigners', employees and their representatives, as well as management, ask themselves whether they should try to politically eliminate these threats, thus helping to establish a discretionary trade regime with its accompanying regulations of domestic markets which can easily turn out as fetters, or have faith that they will be able to compete under a basically intervention-free regime. The institutions of the welfare state can, literally, insure them against the political risks and economic costs of protectionism (H.-W. Sinn 1995, 1996). As it stands in the USA, unions and firms alike expend substantial resources on trade policy lobbying, first to protect their domestic market from foreign competition, and second to gain secure access to foreign markets. The latter is the goal of a 'results-oriented' trade policy and managed trade, the hallmarks of the Clinton era. The high influx of foreign direct investments into the USA is largely a product of the fact that goods cannot easily be exported into the country; if one wants to sell to the US market, one has to produce there. Also the high pressure of migration movements on the borders of the USA can be explained by the fact that *not enough* trade is permitted. When goods are not

[77] Bhagwati (1982) coined the term DUP (*D*irectly *U*nproductive *P*rofit-seeking) activities to demarcate more clearly the essence of rent-seeking.

allowed to pass borders, then people come instead. Free trade in goods and effective international freedom of movement and settlement are functionally equivalent (Dowty 1987; Wellisch and Walz 1998).

The functional co-equality of trade and social policy also means that the structures of political governance of the welfare state determine to a large extent whether and how its institutions can or will change in response to new economic and especially business conditions with its promise of more welfare, i.e. jobs, higher wages and more consumer goods. Here again the question arises, does government attempt to preserve these welfare state institutions in the face of pressure to reform, *or* does it reform them in conformity with market forces? The pivotal factors in this decision are, first, the identity of the median-voter, second, the institutions of the separation of power, including federal constitutional elements, and, third, the weight of corporatist channels of influence vis-à-vis those of parliamentary democracy.

With regard to the first, it is largely a matter of whether the majority of the electoral population is more interested in consumption or in gainful employment, or, put differently, what role markets and thus competition play in determining their current and future situation in life. The greater the consumption orientation to be satisfied by public means, i.e. the greater the share of pensioners and other grantee classes, including public employees, in relation to those whose situation in life and employment fate are determined by market prospects, the greater the probability that it is not future but present interests that will shape their choice of political party. The USA has clearly always been a work-oriented society in which employment, and thus profit, interests stand at the centre not only of economic but also of party competition. Nearly 70 per cent of the US population is gainfully employed, and the trend is rising. Indicative of this culturally dominant employment orientation is the passage of the Senior Citizens' Freedom to Work Act of 2000. This law allows workers to retain their jobs beyond the age of 65 *without* suffering reductions in social security benefits.[78] In social policy reform projects, a central role is played by social policy institutions' market conformity – i.e. low non-wage labour costs, the absence of negative work incentives and the greatest possible flexibility for governments and firms in shaping social policy. In this opinion climate, social policy that runs *counter* to the market logic is taboo. Instead, efforts are made to find ways and means to use private interests and market instruments to achieve social policy goals.

With regard to the second point – the possibilities for an ongoing regime of 'politics against markets' allowed by the constitution – it is a matter of whether the system of political opinion formation and decision-making is designed to facilitate timely and effective decisions, or designed to slow down the legislative process so as to allow contradictory voices (via counter-majoritarian elements) the greatest possible influence. These opposite poles are represented by the English and the US constitutions respectively. The 'efficient secret of the (English) constitution' is the fusion of the executive and legislative branches (Bagehot 1928 [1867]: 9). The government and the administration – that is, the state – are to get the laws they need. The opposite is intended by the US Constitution: it gives each of the three branches of power the means to block

[78] Heretofore, old-age pensioners aged 65–69 lost $1 in social security benefits for every $3 they earned. This rule was repealed (*Social Security Earnings Test Elimination Bill Unanimously Passed by Senate*, ElderWeb.com Newsletter, 22 March 2000; http://www.elderweb.com/news/nws000322a.htm – 7 September 2000).

the legislative process. The guiding principle here is that it is better to allow some good legislative proposals to fail than to have to deal with the consequences of the mass production of 'bad' ones (Hamilton et al. 1999 [1787–8]: 411 f.).

As the social policy reforms of the last decade show, these veto powers have little relevance for the effectiveness of a legislative process aimed at achieving *negative* goals – e.g. deregulation or the repeal and restriction of benefit laws. It is much easier to find a negative than a positive consensus. Fundamentally opposed positions can agree on rejecting something, for to do so these positions need not be articulated and no persuasion must take place. Implementing positive political action and institution-building, however, is a far more ambitious project. In the US political process, a veto of a positive policy has much greater chances of success than does loyalty to a specific programme. Further, the existing degree of societal and cultural heterogeneity attained in the USA implies enormous political costs of the kind of majority orchestration required for institution-building and thus rules out the introduction of the kind of welfare state income protection that would replace discretionary and social protection-oriented trade policy and ease the transition to a genuine free trade regime.

In terms of the relative influence of corporatist vis-à-vis democratic parliamentary channels of influence, the key is who has the last word in which policy areas. The Norwegian social scientist Stein Rokkan captured the relative importance of both of these channels of influence as follows: 'Numbers count, but resources decide.' The USA has neither a centralized economic order based on constitutionally guaranteed tariff independence nor autonomous social insurance administrations borne by nationally organized social partners. This places narrow limits on the potential effectiveness of efforts at labour market cartelization.[79] This is reinforced by the liberal economic principles inscribed in the Constitution, which led to state 'right to work' laws and narrowly limits the potential scope of action of unions (Feinman 1976; C. Fried 1984). In the USA, the influence of workers as well as of employers can only be manifested through and in Congress. Due to these ultimately constitutional constraints, socio-economic demands are steered chiefly into trade policy channels where their function is primarily negative as a force of disruption and obstruction.

As the US example shows, trade policy-making consists of decision-making processes, which are in the final analysis determined by social structures that lie beyond a government's disposal and which lead to a specific – yet, in terms of its outcome, unpredictable – relationship between foreign trade and social policy. Globalization itself dictates neither an optimal quantity nor an optimal quality of social policy. Social policy has its own standards, and its decisions are taken in arenas that are autonomous both in terms of their constituent actors and the rationale of the substantive content of their choices. It thus independently establishes a framework for the various market citizens, workers and managers in relation to which they then orient their behaviour.

[79] In the USA it has been, and remains, far more difficult to exempt the labour market from general anti-trust laws. For this reason, the argument that free market competition has a positive impact on labour relations and also benefits the individual worker plays a far greater role there than in the European context. The classic justification is provided by Armen A. Alchian and Harold Demsetz (1972), who stress that the relationship between business owner and customer differs in no way from that between business owner and employee. Both the customer and the employee should have the freedom to leave the business when they are not content with the way in which they are being treated.

Conversely, certain forms of social policy are fundamental to an open foreign trade policy. Without this openness, under the (ultimately always social) democratic conditions of the universal franchise, no globalization can occur. Yet from this we cannot derive any compelling justification of the socio-political status quo. On the whole, we call for a broader perspective in social policy analysis and comparative welfare state research. Our work clearly points to the need to take seriously a society's foreign trade dimension as a determining factor of its welfare state and above all welfare-societal development. In the course of globalization in general, and especially that occurring in the economies of Europe, the nation-state shells that until now have shaped the relationship between institutions and individuals – and have thus institutionalized life courses – have not only become thinner and more porous, but are being formed anew. The products of this transformation regularly turn out differently from what is expected or desired. The need for compelling explanation and comprehensive orientation has grown enormously. This is a challenge not only for social policy research, but also for the social sciences as a whole.

The USA is perceived to be the chief advocate and chief propagandist of the internationalization of markets. It is thus particularly important to examine the domestic political preconditions of free trade policy there. Social policy and trade policy are closely interrelated. Both aim at correcting the primary distribution of income in the market and thereby form a system of communicating pipes tending towards equilibrium. In order to understand the further development of social policy in the age of a global economy, special attention must be given to the interactions between trade and social policy. Economic models of equilibrium are very helpful here: 'It is essential to take into account general equilibrium, in which everything affects everything else in at least two ways' (Krugman 1995: 328). Trade and social policy are so closely intertwined because the demand for economic and social security is inflexible; when it is not satisfied by socio-political means, it will be content with the instruments of a protectionist trade policy.

4

Two Worlds of Welfare Democracy: Global Capitalism and Social Policy Reform in Germany and the USA

The trial by market everything must come to.

Robert Frost 1916: 106

1 The Problem

At the very beginning of the new century, Germany and the USA appeared to belong to two different worlds. Harvard political scientist Peter Hall, a veteran, knowledgeable observer of Germany, saw it facing its biggest crisis since the Second World War (1997: 313). Unemployment figures continued to hover at levels comparable to those that plagued the end of the Weimar Republic, and no improvement is yet in sight. The labour market's inflexibility and limited absorption capacity call into question the productivity of the 'German model', i.e. of a 'co-ordinated economy' (Soskice 1990, 1999) coupled with a transfer-intensive welfare state (Hall and Soskice 2001; Schmidt 2002). In the free-market economy of the United States, by contrast, the prevalent view was that the Promised Land had been reached, in which continual economic growth, low unemployment and low inflation go hand-in-hand (S. Weber 1997). Within a decade, the fronts had thus been completely reversed. At the beginning of the 1990s, the same institutional conditions were evaluated conversely: US economists considered social regulation of the US labour and commodities markets to be a decided disadvantage in global competition (Nivola 1997). Although the causes of this drifting apart of the two national economies – including the more general question of the causal significance of political-institutional context in economic growth – remains a matter of controversy, nowadays one version or another of an 'American model' is regularly offered in Europe as a model for economic policy. Yet social progress and economic growth are generally achieved more *at the expense* of the prevailing natural and social conditions than *in concert* with them. Extensive social regulation need not have a paralysing effect on economic action, but can instead provoke an increase in individual and collective effort.

If one looks beyond model metaphysics, mechanistic conceptions and fashion- and media-driven attention cycles, both countries – despite their radically opposite economic fate in the last decade of the twentieth century – have one thing in common: the protagonists of their welfare state institutions have gone on the defensive and have been being criticized for a long time for similar, if not identical, reasons. Not least because of the new global economic environment, this criticism appears to be having an effect or at least seems to be gaining greater resonance (Seeleib-Kaiser 2002). Above all, the effectiveness of traditional means-tested social programmes without a closely controlled recourse to labour markets has been called into question. Rather than serving as a social net of last resort, it is argued, these programmes have provided incentives to the poor to withdraw themselves from the labour market, resulting in the creation of 'poverty traps'. These programmes themselves are said to constitute, rather than solve, the problem of poverty and exclusion (Murray 1994, 1999). In both Germany and the USA, criticism of welfare state benefits provided to the average citizen has been on the rise. The working man, it is said, has 'maturated', has grown beyond the confines of the traditional welfare state. Money is distributed to groups of people who are more than capable of supporting themselves. With this in mind, Meinhard Miegel (1983) called attention relatively early to the 'silent revolution' in the income and property relations of the Federal Republic of Germany.

In the new international environment of globally competitive markets and of stock exchanges as a major source of wealth, the general evaluative standard has shifted by which the costs and benefits of state-provided social protection and services can be judged. In both countries members of compulsory social insurance schemes, in particular pension schemes, ask themselves whether their investment in the form of high social insurance contributions brings a sufficient yield. At present, and despite the collapse of the new e-markets, these yields are rather meagre relative to average asset growth in investments in stocks (Börsch-Supan 2000a, b). The 'great bull market of the century', which began in 1982, sent the Dow Jones industrial average of the New York Stock Exchange up about 1,400 per cent, and stock markets of other developed countries and some transition countries saw similar developments (Madrick 2002).

These debates are, upon closer examination, as old as the welfare state itself. The transformation of 'solutions' into 'problems' (Flora 1981) seems to be inherent to the nature of social policy. However, the rationality and the legitimacy of this critique will not be further examined here. In this chapter we are concerned with a different problem: what is the social policy status quo in both countries, above all with regard to welfare state reform policy? How vigorous and how enduring has criticism of their welfare state arrangements been? What role has globalization played in social policy debates in each country? And what has been the relationship between the new national and global economic environment and the political environment in these well-developed, democratic welfare states? In the final analysis, the essentially social democratic combination of interest-driven party competition and a mature welfare state has always yielded considerable risks of obstructing the functionality and developmental potential of market structures (Olson 1982, 2000; Higgs 1987). Has this problem disappeared with globalization, which allegedly, with regard to control over the course of societal development, inevitably and necessarily enhances the role of the market relative to the state?

When one compares the social policy institutions of Germany and the United States, one sees that their fundamentally different structures have led to distinct challenges and thus to completely different results in the endeavour to adapt, in the wake of globalization, welfare state institutions to changed macro-economic conditions. If one accepts what some consider to be a manifest economic imperative and others to be the 'terror of economics', then Germany, with its full-income guarantee through the welfare state, will soon have to reform its labour law and social policy to bring it into strict conformity with free-market principles. Conversely, there is some reason to

Table 4.1 Economic growth and social expenditure in Germany, 1991–2001

	1991	*1993*	*1995*	*1997*	*1999*	*2001*
Social expenditure	100	119	132	138	147	155
GDP	100	110	120	126	131	138

Source: *FAZ* (7 March 2002: 14); these data are reported from BMA 2002: 367ff. (*Sozialbudget*)

believe that in the USA, extraordinary economic growth coupled with a considerable increase in income and asset inequalities will provoke a counter-movement, which will manifest itself in more heavily redistributive social policy. Tocqueville claimed long ago that democracy not only breeds material envy, but also gives citizens the political means to redress material inequalities (Tocqueville 1994 [1835–45]: I. 200–2). To what extent can such decisions and developments be observed in each country?

Four sharply contrasting and unexpected states of affairs are of relevance here. First, Germany is pursuing a reform policy that contradicts the trend set by globalization. The Schröder government did not only repeal the (few) socio-political measures that had been passed under the Kohl regime in the latter's attempt to relieve companies of social and labour regulatory constraints; it also intensified social regulation of part-time work, making it more expensive. The provisions of the three most important pieces of legislation are summarized in Box 4.1. In the USA in 1996, the federal structure and benefit provisions of the welfare programme were placed on a new footing. Opportunities to claim benefits outside the labour market were radically curtailed, and central competencies in welfare policy were relegated to the states. At the same time, federal legislation raised the minimum wage considerably and further enhanced the negative income tax for low-income working families (EITC).

Second, despite lower economic growth rates and much greater fiscal stress, during the 1990s German social expenditure grew faster than GDP, whereas in the USA federal social expenditure as a percentage of GDP decreased from 22.0 to 20.8 per cent. In Germany, social expenditure consumes 31 per cent of GDP (*FAZ*, 7 March 2002, p. 14; Green Book 2000: 1334). As Table 4.1 shows, public expenditure on social programmes continually outpaced growth of GDP. Only in 1997, the year before it was voted out of office and a Social Democratic and Green Party coalition government took over, social expenditure grew a paltry 0.6 per cent. In the USA social expenditure as a percentage of the GDP peaked in 1985, reaching 23 per cent, and then continually decreased down to 20.8 per cent. Perhaps more remarkable is the fact that non-discretionary social spending – outlays for social security and Medicare – shrank in the second half of the 1990s from 4.6 to 4.2 per cent in the case of social security and from 2.5 to 2.3 per cent in the case of Medicare (all figures percentages of GDP – Green Book 2000: 1334f.).

Third, fundamental data on labour market development in Germany and the US point in opposite directions. In (West) Germany, the population grew from 55 to 63 million between 1960 and 1990, a gain of 15 per cent. The number of employed persons increased in the same period by 8 per cent, only slightly more than half the

Box 4.1 The first social policy measures ('counter-reforms') of the Schröder government

Law to Correct Social Insurance and Guarantee Employees' Rights (25 November 1998)
Suspended for 1999 and 2000 the pension- 'dampening' 'demographic factor' in the statutory 'pension formula' as it had been just introduced through the Pension Insurance Reform Act of 1999 by the conservative Kohl government. Repealed all cuts in invalidity pensions.

Extended the insurance obligation to all those self-employed considered to be de facto employees ('pseudo-self-employed'). Spread out protection against dismissal further downwards again: from companies with 10 to those with only 5 employees. Restored as of 1 January 1999 continued payment of full remuneration in case of sickness or spa visits. Dropped the sunset clause (August 1999) in the protective regulation for seconded workers from other EC member states – making this legislation permanent.

Law to Strengthen Solidarity in Social Health Insurance (10 December 1998)
The following measures were taken to decrease the financial burdens on the insured and patients: copayments for prescription drugs were reduced from 9 to 8, 11 to 9 and 13 to 10DM for small, medium and large prescription units respectively. The chronically ill were relieved of copayments for transportation, drug and other treatment-related costs, if in the previous year they had incurred out-of-pocket costs in treating their specific chronic illness amounting to more than 1 – previously 2 – per cent of their income. The automatic increase of copayments concomitant with rising increases in contribution rates was revoked. The 'hospital surcharge' (*Krankenhausnotopfer*) of 20DM per insurance member was suspended for 1998 and 1999.

To undo new 'elements of private health insurance' the following steps were taken:[1] sickness funds were prohibited from introducing non-obligatory copayments (which would have allowed the lowering of contribution rates) and from offering contribution refunds or additional services (for extra contributions) in their by-laws. The insured person's right to chose between in-kind provision (*Sachleistungsprinzip*) and reimbursement for expenses was restricted to the few voluntarily insured. The recently introduced mandate was rescinded that a reimbursement system replace in-kind provision for dental prostheses and orthodontal treatment. The standardized and only partial payment for dental prostheses was also given up and the pre-1997 system of in-kind provision restored. Dental prostheses for young persons born after 1978 were again fully insured. Dentists were de novo prohibited from charging privately for their services.

Law to Regulate Marginal Employment Relationships (4 March 1999)
It set the lower earnings threshold for mandatory insurance contributions at earnings of 630DM per month. It allowed the current standardized (*Pauschalbetrag*) income tax of 20 per cent plus Church Tax and Solidarity Surcharge to be replaced with a social insurance contribution (12 per cent pension plus 10 per cent health insurance). Now there are three modes of income taxation for marginal employees: normal income tax according to *Lohnsteuerkarte* (wage tax card), standardized income taxation and the new option of paying a social insurance contribution of 12 + 10 = 22 per cent in lieu of taxes.

[1] The Law Reforming Public Health Insurance after the Year 2000 of 4 November 1999 purported to correct competitive imbalances between Social and Private Health Insurance by discouraging the movement of older patients from Private to Public Health Insurance, thus hindering further differentiation of the risk pool. Premiums for older patients in the Private Health Insurance sector are to be standardized, and increases in these premiums are to be contained by lowering the rate schedule which private (sick fund) doctors can charge older patients.

Source: German Council of Economic Experts (1999: 112–17)

rate of the population increase. After Reunification, the number of employed persons fell continually from 37.8 (1991) to 35.9 million (1998). The US population grew between 1960 and 1998 from 181 to 270 million, an increase of 50 per cent. The employed population rose in the same period by twice this rate, or 100 per cent.[1]

Fourth, in the 1990s, elements of a social-interventionist trade policy became a focus of domestic political conflict in the USA. Defensive foreign trade regulation aimed at obstructing import competition is a traditional feature of US trade policy. Market openings always entail the proviso that domestic producers may not be harmed. During the 1990s, bureaucratic control of national economic borders and official discretion in implementing restrictive measures rose far more in the USA than in other countries (A. O. Krueger 1995; Russell 1999). Antidumping proceedings and countervailing duties – punitive and retributive customs duties conceived as a response to allegedly unfair trade practices (subsidies, etc.) of exporting countries – emerged as one of the most important instruments of US trade policy. At the end of 1995, 294 antidumping measures were in effect in the USA, compared to only 133 in the European Union. Between 1991 and 1995, the USA launched an average of 49.4 antidumping proceedings annually, while Europe launched only 32.4.[2] In 1988 the Exon-Florio Amendment to the Omnibus Trade and Competitiveness Act expanded US regulation of foreign trade to also encompass foreign direct investment into the USA (Kang 1997). This enhanced protection against imports has been supplemented by attempts to increase exports through a series of bilateral trade agreements. In both of President Clinton's terms of office, it was tangible domestic, employment-related concerns, not the multilateral regulations of an international economic order, which determined the ends and means of US trade policy. For Germany, on the other hand, the guiding principle remains that trade policy is far less subject to state regulation. This fact can be attributed less to the Europeanization of trade policy and to the European internal market than to Germany's Foreign Trade Law (*Außenwirtschaftsgesetz*) of 1962, which declared that in the realm of imports and exports, everything is allowed that is not explicitly prohibited.

Below, we will show how these opposing developments and contrasting structures are linked, and how they can be explained through this linkage. We are interested here not only in historical and contemporary differences in the development of social policy, labour markets and trade policy, whose causes, forms and consequences will be described and interpreted. Our paramount concern is to demonstrate that both in the USA and Germany, the welfare state as an economic reality is underestimated, and globalization as a political reality is overestimated. The respective institutional contexts – the political conventions in each country, together with the power relations among their main societal groups – determine to a large extent how economic change since the middle of the 1980s has transpired, as well as why each country has reacted as it has, and not otherwise, to such change. The spatial revolution of globalization

1 Own calculations based on data prepared by the German Council of Economic Experts (1999: 214f.).

2 The data are from the Congressional Budget Office (1998: Appendix B: Statistical Tables). According to the statistics of the Congressional Budget Office, at the end of 1995, 25.1 per cent of all antidumping measures in effect worldwide stemmed from the USA, and only 15.9 per cent from the European Union. Other countries that have made considerable and increasing use of antidumping procedures are Canada and Australia. In protectionist trade policy, antidumping measures are the policy of choice in advanced industrial countries.

takes place not in a politically unclaimed space, but first and foremost in the confined capillary system of a national economy bound to the nation-state. And the concept of the welfare state veils the most important element of its emergence, the foundation of its continued existence and the ever renewed point of departure of its dynamic: its systematic linkage to representative democracy. A concept more fitting than welfare state is welfare *democracy* (Marshall 1972: 105). It is the structure and above all the unique domestic concentration of power of welfare democracy which determine the management of globalization in individual countries. Welfare democracy is solving the purely domestically conceived social problems of globalization by internalizing the attendant conflicts in parliaments devoted to compromise and concessionary politics.

2 Social Regulation and the Market Economy

Before analysing the German and US social policy environments more closely, let us first elaborate on the analytical perspective of this enquiry. The question is, first of all, which developments in these countries merit a social science interest and attempts at explanation, and why?

In examinations of social policy in the context of globalization, not only are the problem-solving and cost effectiveness of state measures of relevance, but so too are their secondary consequences. Questions of effectiveness and efficiency can be directly and fairly clearly answered, at least on a theoretical level, as long as there is agreement on the goals of social policy and thus also on the social policy yardstick. The globalized market economy and, in particular, globalized production processes have, however, rendered certain aspects of social policy visible in other realms of the economy and society – realms that had hitherto commanded less attention, even though they considerably complicate welfare state relations and their political guidance or control. These non-state repercussions of social policy are much more ambiguous, and their political relevance is thus far more difficult to gauge. A social scientific investigation can at the very least clarify precisely where the problems confronting the responsible actors lie.

A first such problem is the role of welfare state regulation for job creation and destruction. Employment conditions mould economic environments, and nowadays these employment conditions are to a large extent the product of social policy intervention and regulation. Such measures not only impact on the cost of an employment position to an employer, they also substantively and organizationally constrain an employer's economic action, set goals for such action and provide the means to pursue these goals (Lindbeck and Snower 1996). Nowadays, a profoundly socialized labour law, and not merely the freedom to conclude employment contracts, guides the investment of productive means into 'labour' as a factor of production (Zöllner and Loritz 1998: 6).[3]

[3] The more formally regulated the use of labour is, the more incentives exist to evade the rigours of labour law – at least there are strong empirical indicators suggesting that the more developed welfare statism is, the greater becomes the share of the underground economy. In 2000, the following estimates of the share of the underground economy as percentage of GDP were calculated: Sweden 20 per cent, Germany 14.7 per cent and the United States 8.9 per cent. In those countries in which workplace security traditionally compensated for a lower transfer intensity of social policy, the underground economy is even larger: Italy 27.8 per cent, and Spain 23.4 per cent (F. Schneider 2000).

A second question is the significance of the welfare state for trade policy. Here we see that social policy institutions are also at work in realms in which their traditional concerns – income maintenance, occupational safety and the provision of health care and other services – are not primarily or directly at issue. In contrast to the attempt to assess the effectiveness or efficiency of social policy, we are faced here, first, with a fundamental ambivalence, not least because we are always confronted with two – or even more – conflicting evaluative standards: market-based meritocracy and the egalitarian justice of the democratic welfare state (Esping-Andersen 1990; Marshall 1949, 1965). This points to a first, central difficulty for a social science perspective: in such empirical studies, value conflicts lie at the centre of attention, which, by their very nature, are extremely hard to address in a direct way. A social science investigation, then, must first render these value conflicts explicit, and then reveal their causal significance in the context of explanations which attempt to satisfy objectivity criteria. A second, not only scientific, but also political difficulty lies in the fact that in these secondary, but no less important, consequences of social policy, unintended results can have the effect of reshaping existing structures and creating new ones.

In the context of a more general welfare state perspective that takes into account not only the currently employed population but all persons willing to work, the outcome of the labour market, which forms the departure point for social policy in a market economy, is in the final analysis the aggregate of a very large number of decisions made continuously and ever anew in a vast number of individual companies. This clearly constrains the potential efficacy of social policy, which seeks by means of legal coercion to put its stamp on the distributional outcomes of a market economy sustained by private actors operating on their own accord. Indeed, for those who make first and last decisions in the labour market – employers and employees – welfare state framework conditions and the socio-political intentions of policy- and lawmakers are essentially only one factor among many. In companies, decisions are made on the basis of alternatives. Precisely how workers, managers, entrepreneurs and investors act is ultimately beyond the control of lawmakers, for the final decision is made by independent individuals. The most decisive factor for every order in a sociological sense, i.e. for its de facto capacity to influence the decisions of a large number of private entities via direct commands, is the distribution of political power in the given community, and this distribution of power is ultimately determined by spatial relations (Weber 1978: 330). Mobility – the ability to escape the spatial sphere of organized political control – has always been the most basic means of resisting state power, which consists essentially in territorial sovereignty and thus is always spatially limited and bound (Ratzel 1923: 63). One of the first tasks in an investigation of the forms and consequences of a globalization process, therefore, is to decipher, by analysing political developments, its spatial conditions and its dependency on spatial relations, and then to explore its role in shaping key substantive realms of politics and policy-making. Space is an independent political force, not merely a neutral conduit of political power. Every development which brings about changes in spatial conditions or standards is of critical importance, for such developments exert a lingering effect on societal conditions on all levels (Ratzel 1940).

A second factor limiting the potential efficacy of social regulation stems from the fact that labour market outcomes are determined not only by companies' personnel decisions concerning hiring, promotion, dismissal, wage levels and employee benefits, but also by decisions made in further links in the production chain – above all, by decisions on site location. In its attempt to impose certain rules on the investment of the productive factor 'labour', or to achieve certain outcomes by means of intervention, social policy, in particular individual and collective labour law, is limited in the scope of its potential influence to only one sphere of the company.

Indeed, there are further spheres of the company that similarly condition the scope of its autonomy in personnel management. These are distinct, reciprocally independent and in terms of their potential internal and external impact to a certain degree interchangeable realms, which also produce primary socio-political effects, without however being accessible to social or even economic policy. Even when lawmakers attempt to strictly influence the structuring of employment contracts, however, the outcomes cannot only lag far behind policy-makers' expectations, but can even turn out to be the opposite of what was intended. Thus in advanced economies, the direct result of excessive labour law regulation has typically been an increasing informalization of economic activity – above all, in the form of undocumented employment. In developing countries the formal employment sector is much smaller than the informal sector, and state bureaucracies have little or no ability to control this.

A third factor limiting the potential efficacy of statutory regulation designed to achieve specific, corrective effects on a market economy, in contradiction to its inherently open-ended nature, is the plurality of institutional contexts in which individual companies find themselves. These contexts can vary greatly. One effect of globalization is that the intra-national market conditions to which companies are exposed no longer have a common macro-economic denominator. One and the same social policy measure can trigger completely different reactions among companies. These reactions can vary not only according to the company's economic sector but also according to company size and market conditions. With the globalization of markets and production processes, the probability increases that welfare state regulations and interventions produce effects that directly contradict policy-makers' intentions.[4] Under the new global economic conditions, knowledge of actual market conditions is naturally much more limited among the makers and implementing organs of social policy than among those who are continually exposed to these markets and whose fate is immediately dependent upon them. The more intricate and far-reaching market conditions are, the less predictable are the potential effects and side-effects of social policy for those who fashion it.

Fourthly and finally, with the establishment of global markets, companies and their investors are confronted with a vastly expanded range of choices in many realms. In this new environment, any government's social policy initiative faces limits due to locational competition among states. This fragmented world of welfare states suffices on its own to limit the action horizon of social policy, for in planning any social policy expansion or new regulation, policy-makers must take into account the probable reaction of those who may be burdened by it.

The extent to which these limits become manifest in practice differs from case to case. When confronted with tax and regulatory pressures, managers and investors are, for example, not as cosmopolitan as Adam Smith had assumed,[5] and managers,

4 To describe this phenomenon, organizational theory has coined the term 'post-decision surprise' (Harrison and March 1984).

5 'The proprietor of stock [in contrast to the land owner, who is tied to his land] is properly a citizen of the world. He would be apt to abandon his country in which he was exposed to a vexatious inquisition, in order to be assessed to a burdensome tax, and would remove his stock to some other country where he could either carry on his business, or enjoy his fortune more at his ease' (Smith 1937 [1776]: 800).

investors and fund administrators operate with a much stronger home bias than would be expected from an economic or globalization perspective (Obstfeld and Rogoff 2000). The issue of social policy in advanced welfare states is thus not a single, general problem, but, rather, always a series of individual problems in specific countries, which must be discussed separately. On a more general level one can say only that even in a 'coordinated' national economy, it is ultimately the wage level set by competitive markets that determines employment prospects. Levels of welfare state benefits, including entitlements as well as workplace safety and co-determination rights, influence wage rates, just as do individual training, knowledge and motivational level. Shifts in the relative value of work stemming from technological change, which are not allowed to effect changes in wage patterns, result in unemployment. If wages for whatever reason do not do justice to these developments, this has a negative effect not only on employment generally, but also on the individual market participants who are interested in getting a higher return on their investment in human capital.

One can further observe that despite all 'hard' components of globalization, above all with regard to the new communications and transportation technology infrastructure, companies continue to have to operate in a fundamentally politically created and managed environment – and this will not change appreciably in the future. Globalization has not been able to somehow free companies from the influence of the state. No matter where companies and investors turn, they will always be confronted with state actors. The latter not only have their own interests, but also marshall their own instruments of power. The most important of these is always the protection of private property rights (Anderson and Young 2000; Jay 2000: 284–310; Soto 2000: 153–205). How these inescapable welfare state environments affect micro-economic decision-making cannot be deduced a priori, but rather must be determined empirically. It is, however, beyond doubt that they can make a decisive difference, for example to the extent that they further or impede company evolution and social change (Wolff 1996, 1999).

The reference to globalization is normally associated with the universal argument that governments can no longer influence globalization by means of public policy, because the new technologies ignore state borders. Yet technology as such creates only opportunities; it does not produce any realities. It needs human beings who use it – entrepreneurs who explore new opportunities, and employees who are willing to collaborate creatively in pursuing them. For these, state action is deemed necessary, above all with regard to the safeguards or fire walls of a global economy which is constituted by a multitude of individual national economies. Despite a comparatively efficient infrastructure – the gold standard is an example of this, for it not only eliminated any currency risk, but also put 'golden reins' on governments (Schumpeter 1927) – earlier globalization tendencies were already subsequently strongly limited by changes in their political and social framework conditions (J. G. Williamson 1998a, b).

The increasing interdependence brought about by global markets, evident in the fact that since 1985 world trade has grown at least twice as fast as Gross World Product,

---

That things are more complicated than this is demonstrated, for example, by the history of the income and property tax in Switzerland. Today, there is still largely uncoordinated tax competition among the cantons, even though Article 129 of the Swiss Constitution presciently tried to preclude this: 'The federal government establishes principles governing the harmonization of direct taxes from the federal, canton and local governments' (Cohn 1889).

is not a one-way street; rather, countries could choose to apply brakes to or to opt out of at least some of the alleged 'imperatives' of globalization (Krugman 1995: 328; Jay 2000: 286–88; Greenspan 2001; Keohane and Nye 2001). This could happen for a variety of reasons. One of these is inherent to the economic realm: business can turn its attention to domestic markets, because it sees greater and above all more secure opportunities to make a profit there. The US Department of Commerce's *Survey of Current Business* finds, for example, that foreign direct investment is often considerably less profitable than directly comparable domestic investment.[6] Another reason is the mutually reinforcing and increasingly politically successful resistance by social groups which see their income and status wholly or partially threatened by the dynamic of global capitalism and import competition. Whether imagined or real, these fears guide human behaviour, and there are plenty of politicians who, with protectionist slogans, are able to transform such fears into electoral votes (Kletzer and Litan 2001). This trend can be seen in many countries again and again. Thus in foreign trade practice during the twentieth century, free trade was the exception and protectionism the rule. The majority of human beings are risk-averse and consider it 'unfair' when someone's income is significantly reduced due to external forces which the government – at least theoretically – could control.[7] This issue is regularly thematized, in particular in mass democracies with party competition.

First of all, then, one must ask precisely which forms of social policy are related to which foreign trade practices and policies and how, and exactly which, labour market conditions result from this. Neither the establishment nor the maintenance of externally free markets, whether for labour, goods or services, are unaffected by social policy. Indeed, social policy impacts the ability of both governmental and private actors to adapt to the conditions of a global market economy and to come to terms with the ongoing pressure to either adapt or resort to the protectionist trade measures. In answering the first question one is confronted with a second one: are the various efficiency dimensions of social policy – income maintenance, job creation, the upholding of free trade, societal integration and cost efficiency – simply additive, or are there *trade-offs* among them? In other words, does success in one of these dimensions necessarily or inevitably occur at the expense of the development in one of the others?

In what follows we will concentrate on these questions and sketch several answers. First, we describe how globalization represents a technological and spatial revolution for industrial and company organization, as well as what consequences for the social policy environment emerge from this systemic transformation. We then give a short overview of the social policy structures and most recent social policy reforms in each country. Further, we attempt to explain the unexpected path of German social policy

[6] During the period 1988–97, the average *return on assets* (ROA) for foreign-owned US companies was 5.1 per cent, compared to the corresponding industrial average of 5.7 per cent. In 22 of 30 non-finance sectors, the average ROA for foreign direct investments in the USA lay below that of US domestic investments. The two main causes for the lower ROA are first the market share and second the 'age' of the investments. The higher the market share, the lower the differential relative to the ROA of comparable US domestic investments. The same is true of the age of the investments: the longer ago the investment was made, the greater the probability that it yields a return similar to those achieved by its domestic US competitors (Mataloni 2000).

[7] This accords with the 'conservative welfare function' of Max Corden (1997 [1974]: 74–6; Deardorff 1987). Corden's concept is particularly helpful in understanding the functioning of foreign trade policy relative to social policy.

reform under the conditions of a globalizing economy. Finally, we elucidate why social policy reform in the USA had paradoxical consequences, even though at first glance it appears better suited to the imperatives of globalization.

3 Pathways of a Global Market Economy and Challenges to the Welfare State

For companies, globalization means two things. First, it means a considerable expansion in opportunities to obtain competitive advantages beyond the borders of the home market. The reverse of this is true as well. Thus companies, which heretofore were protected from foreign competition by the comparatively higher costs of doing business internationally, must now reckon with increased foreign competition in their home markets. The technological leaps that have occurred since the 1980s have dramatically reduced transportation and communication costs and have thus clearly limited the independent significance of geographic location for the determination of industrial and company structure (Schaefer 1998; Benvenisti 1999). Partly driven by these developments, but also for other reasons, governments have continued – by means of multilateral agreements or unilateral measures – to eliminate or reduce trade barriers. Finally, to some extent on their own, and to some extent in international coordination in the context of first GATT and then the WTO, governments have laid the legal foundations for an internationalization of production (Hudec 1999a; J. H. Jackson 1997a, 2000a–d).

The internationalization of the relations of production

It is above all the internationalization of production which gives globalization its critical significance.[8] The ways in which companies invest resources – above all capital and management resources – have hitherto assumed new forms. These involve an expanded horizon of alternatives for corporate action, but also new types of risk. Whereas in 'classic' export activity, resources were invested almost exclusively within the home country, in the case of independent subsidiaries, the utilization of company-specific competitive advantages occurs almost exclusively abroad. Figure 4.1 depicts the various levels of intensity of corporate internationalization. Export transactions are made between legally and economically independent contractual partners, whereby the company either utilizes independent marketing organizations or delivers directly to a foreign customer. International licensing contracts involve the marketing of *know-how*. It is not only immaterial goods that can be licensed, enjoying as a result, like patents and labels, commercial protection, so too can such products that can be made use of only through contracts, i.e. company-specific production technologies or marketing concepts. Their great significance stems above all from the fact that, despite the new infrastructure, transport costs can still be prohibitively high. In one study, half of the companies surveyed listed transport costs as the reason why they sold a licence abroad, and a quarter listed the high costs of developing their own distribution channels (Welch 1993, cited in Schanz 1995: 35). In addition to the costs of physical transport, the

8 The following overview is based above all on Schanz (1995), Osterloh and Weibel (1996), Coldwell and Reid (1998), Grafers (1999), and Tilly and Welfens (1999).

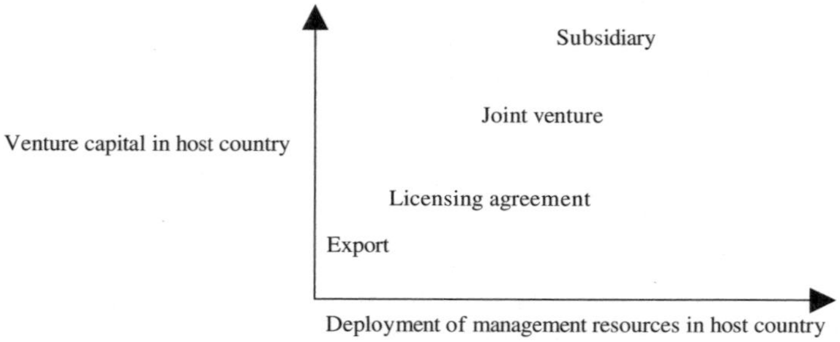

Figure 4.1 Degrees in the internationalization of business
Source: Schanz (1995: 16)

costs of developing international commercial ventures and of monitoring contracts contribute to markets' continued strong home bias and the corresponding macro-economic segmentation (Obstfeld and Rogoff 2000). In the case of direct investment, companies purchase a company abroad in order to have decisive influence on, or complete control of, the decisions of the acquired company. Under the influence of globalization, the significance, above all, of joint ventures has dramatically increased. In the environment of high tariff barriers and restrictive investment laws of the 1960s and 1970s, they were most often *second-best* strategies for the exploitation of markets, while today they are increasingly the *preferred* strategy. Both joint ventures and the other forms of direct investment are almost never inspired by trade and economic policy concerns, but, rather, nearly exclusively by micro-economic concerns. Equal treatment of foreign and domestic investors in economic and, above all, a coordinated tax policy, which has now become (nearly) the rule in advanced economies,[9] however, contrasts with the fact that production via newly established foreign subsidiaries, which carry out all or at least the most important manufacturing stages, is of at most marginal significance in the world's most important economy, the United States. Of the $282 billion in foreign direct investments that flowed into the USA in 1999, $276 billion was used to purchase US companies, while only $6 billion was used to found new companies (Howenstine and Troia 2000: 63).

Globalization offers companies not only a new technical infrastructure, but above all a vastly reduced risk associated with committing resources abroad. For this reason, companies are driven ever more in their decision-making by the prospects of exploiting their own competitive advantages internationally, by the need to respond to the foreign commercial activities of their competitors and by differential site conditions in the home and guest country, i.e. the return on capital investment, market size, factor costs and exchange rate developments.

The consequences of this are well known. Since 1983, world trade has developed at twice the pace of production. The cumulative increase in the export of goods in 1993 amounted to 70.5 per cent, while the corresponding growth in production was 34.6 per cent (Preeg 1995: 12f.). Not only politically, but also for the world economy

[9] The 'exceptions', which, as with the USA and Germany, can still be of great significance, are described and discussed below.

Table 4.2 Selected indicators of the world economy in the 1990s

	Value of current prices ($USbn)			*Annual growth rate (%)*				
	1996	*1997*	*1998*	*1986–90*	*1991–5*	*1996*	*1997*	*1998*
GDP at factor cost	29,024	29,360	n.d.[b]	12.0	6.4	2.5	1.2	n.d.[b]
Exports of goods and non-factor services	6,523	6,710	6,576	15.0	9.3	5.7	2.9	–2.0
FDI inflows	359	464	644	24.3	19.6	9.1	29.4	38.7
FDI outflows	380	475	649	27.3	15.9	5.9	25.1	36.6
FDI inward stock	3,086	3,437	4,088	17.9	9.6	10.6	11.4	19.0
FDI outward stock	3,145	3,423	4,117	21.3	10.5	10.7	8.9	20.3
Cross-border mergers and acquisitions[a]	163	236	411	21.3	10.5	10.7	8.9	20.3

[a] Majority-held investment only   [b] n.d. = no data

Source: UNCTAD (2000: 2, table 1.1)

1989 was a turning-point, for since then in the developed economies more than half of national production has been performed by companies that are foreign-owned (Dunning 1997a: 9). Today, the world economy is no longer driven by trade alone, but also by foreign direct investment. Already between 1980 and 1992, the amount of global direct investment grew four times as fast as international trade in goods (Nunnenkamp et al. 1994: 6f.). Table 4.2 depicts the globalization of trade, production and investment in the 1990s. Despite declining global economic growth, the growth rates of trade, direct investment and international mergers and acquisitions are up to several times that of the Gross World Product production. According to the figures of the United Nations Conference on Trade and Development (UNCTAD), the number of countries that liberalized investment rose steadily during the 1990s. Of the 145 statutory changes that were recorded by the UNCTAD in 1998 (2000: 9), 136 eased foreign direct investment, while 9 made it more difficult. Table 4.2 gives an idea of how, under conditions of globalization, the 'complex interdependence' of national economies works. The so-called 'Asian crisis', which originated in a comparatively insignificant newly industrialized country, not only spread at breathtaking speed and destroyed within 24 hours holdings that had been built up over decades, but left hardly any national economy untouched.[10] Compared to this, the debt crises of the 1980s unfolded in slow motion (Keohane and Nye 2000: 109).

[10] Under the title *Global Contagion – a Narrative: Networked Economies, Stunted Lives*, the *New York Times* published in February 1999 a series of articles which explored the origins and the consequences of the 'Asian crisis'. The authors have since published their material in book form (Kristof and WuDunn 2000). On the experiences of the individual countries in East and Southeast Asia and 'lessons' from the financial crisis, see W. T. Woo et al. 2000.

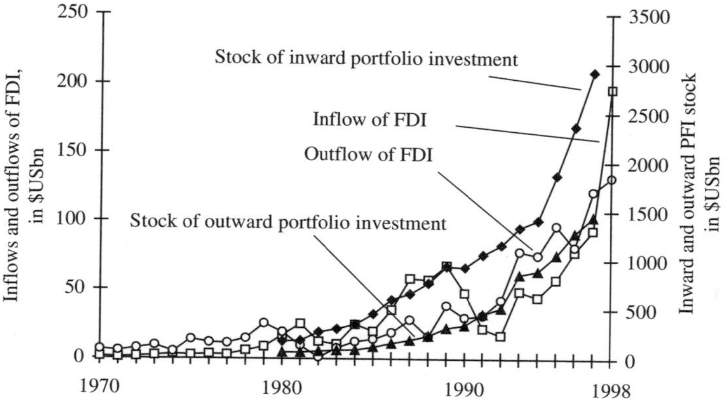

Figure 4.2 The USA in the global economy: influx and outflow of foreign direct investment (FDI) and the change in stock of domestic and foreign portfolio investment (PFI), 1970–1998
Source: IMF (1999a: 928f.)

Due to its size, liberal structure and dynamic growth, the US market is of unique importance for the new global economy. Its attractiveness is reflected above all in the influx of foreign direct investment. As figure 4.2 shows, after the decline from 1987 and the slow recovery from 1992 on, the influx of foreign direct investment exploded during 1998, a trend that continued in 1999. The same is true of the influx of portfolio investments. The stock of these foreign direct investments in 1997 amounted to 36 per cent of the US Gross National Product. The enhanced opportunity to penetrate national markets from abroad is a consequence of the globalization of the economy and is of enormous importance for national social policy and its reform.[11] The cost of market entry for foreign companies has fallen dramatically. The epochal transformation from an industrial to a service and then to an information economy has, similarly, lowered the minimum costs necessary for market entry or exit. Historically, however, customs duties and a wide range of non-tariff trade barriers have produced and stabilized unique national economic structures in which social policy plays a formative role in company and labour market organization as well as in the shaping of the market and the political sphere. The principal challenge to the existing relationship between the market and the state, and to the institutional structure of social policy, is posed by this externally rooted increased contestability of hitherto nationally fragmented markets, which had been subject to uniform political control. These two factors – the dramatic decline in the costs of transport and communication, and the expansion of the service economy – determine the nature and severity of the problems encountered by individual states in adapting their welfare state institutions to the new global economic environment.

The rise of the welfare state and the disintegration of the world economy

It is certainly mistaken to believe that a reciprocal isolation of national economies in the past made it easier for countries to develop and implement independent models of

[11] The standard work on this subject is Baumol et al. (1982), albeit without reference to globalization.

labour policy and the welfare state – usually in the form of social insurance schemes. Precisely the opposite occurred. National labour and welfare state regimes are the flip side of that de-globalization of national economies which, from the end of the nineteenth century through to the 1950s, created the internationally fragmented world of welfare states that only now is growing back together.

The introduction of welfare state transfer systems and the intensification of social policy regulation of companies were among several political answers to the internal problems of developing industrial societies in the final decades of the nineteenth century (S. Neumann 1949; Olson 1963; Rimlinger 1977; Przeworski and Sprague 1986). Trade policy was often – and in some cases always – the substitute for a social policy which, in the course of democratization and parliamentarization, had become unavoidable, and through which the representatives of the propertyless, wage-dependent segments of the population entered the centres of political power. This was true above all in the USA, where income maintenance was pursued not by means of social policy but through tariff policy (Huston 1983). Federal or state social policy per se, however, does not make protectionist trade policy necessary (Knorr 1951a, b). Of critical significance are the institutional forms chosen for social policy, and in these decision-making processes foreign trade concerns played almost no role whatsoever – which is not to say that the structures of trade policy and foreign trade as framework conditions outside the focus of the actors had no influence. Yet 'social' objectives can be pursued in many different ways, from price controls to socialization of companies and sectors to social insurance policy, and from individual or collective labour law to holding companies directly accountable for the financial well-being of their employees. Each of these policy options has different consequences for foreign trade. Yet social policy – in particular discretionary social policy that endeavours to protect specific sectors, regions or population groups – can achieve its goals only if it can effectively control the national borders, via the instruments of foreign trade policy. For agricultural policy, which essentially is a form of social policy against the market, this has historically been the rule, and remains so today (G. Wright 1964; Rieger 2000). The decisive point for the world economy at the end of the nineteenth century, though, is that, increasingly, and as a rule also without considerable resistance, foreign trade policy was determined by an exclusively national social policy. Motivated by welfare state concerns and favoured by the universal franchise and new democratic elements in national constitutions, this protectionist trade policy caused nations to grow ever farther apart after they had moved closer together from the middle of the nineteenth century through to the outbreak of the First World War.[12]

It is also erroneous, however, to believe that the welfare-democratic revolution was the cause of de-globalization, or – put differently – that every comprehensive social policy regime necessarily involves protectionist trade policy, as is repeatedly asserted (Voigt 1992: 26–8; Krauss 1997: 35–59). History tells a different story.

Germany's organized capitalism and the transition to protectionism In Germany, the driving force behind protectionism lay in the formation of cartels. This reorganization

12 The English socialist Richard Crossman termed this system, which in Western Europe and North America after the Second World War was able to hold its own against both the socialist and liberal market challenges, 'welfare capitalism'. The welfare state, he argued, was the culmination of a long process in the course of which capitalism was 'civilized' and to a large extent reconciled with democracy (Marshall 1972: 104).

of the economy from below hindered the development of a liberal order. State social policy had, at most, an indirect influence on trade policy. Freedom of trade, which was introduced in the North German Confederation in 1869 and then throughout the German Empire in 1871, combated, according to the prevailing opinion of the time, only state, not private competition constraints. In the *Kaiserreich*, cartels spread ubiquitiously. Among the larger industrial nations, the German Empire was the only one to protect cartel pacts under civil law. Not least for this reason, Germany's supra-corporate constructions proved to be structurally more enduring and effective than their foreign counterparts (H. Schröter 1996: 132f.). The High Court of the German Empire ruled in 1897 that cartels were fundamentally permissible. It found that freedom of trade was not violated 'when industrial partners join forces to pursue in good faith the goal of preserving the viability of a branch of industry by forestalling the devaluation of its products and other disadvantages which stem from individual companies' attempts to undercut prices' (cited in Mussler 1998: 24). Every domestic regulation of prices had, however, if it was to be effective, also to protect domestic producers from lower-priced foreign goods. Cartels increase profit-margins and signalize profit opportunities, even to foreign companies. Cartels thus achieve their objective only when, by means of tariffs or non-tariff trade barriers such as licences or quotas, they generate protection against foreign commercial competition.

In this way, the protectionist trade policy of the German Empire was also a direct consequence of the cartelization of the economy. Despite cartelization's elective affinity with the mercantilist-authoritarian state tradition, contemporary observers emphasized its private-sector origins. Gustav Schmoller, the *Kaiserreich*'s most influential economist, described cartels as 'a system of justice and of fairness', its directors were 'educators who sought to secure victory for the overall interests of a branch of industry against selfish group and individual interests' (cited in Mussler 1998: 24). He emphasized their guild-like cooperative character. The majority of legal scholars in the *Kaiserreich*, as in the Weimar Republic, considered it to be clear that on the issue of cartels, the law had to adapt to the economy and not vice versa. One of their leading representatives, Hans Carl Nipperdey, observed at the National Lawyers' Annual Convention (*Juristentag*) of 1928 that the purpose of the civil legal order was neither to stem economic development, nor to apply pure ethics to the economic sphere (ibid.: 25).

Classical liberal economy theory, together with its real-world pendant, free trade, was also dismissed as 'pure ethics':

> The liberal economic system offered us the opposite theory of a cosmopolitan economic order uncoupled from the individual state. This order seeks to create out of the microcosm of individual economic activity the macrocosm of a world economic order, but foundered on the natural resistance of national economic policy. The latter developed strongly during the second half of the 19th century and reduced the cosmopolitan back to a national economic order. This development should not be attributed to state initiative, however. Rather, it is a product of economic and social conflicts that gained form and content on the foundation of newly won freedom and with the help of a powerfully growing economic system. The outcomes of these conflicts constituted nearly fully formed building blocks which the government could then utilize in course of the ever more comprehensive and complicated expansion of the national economic order. (Tschierschky 1924: 25)

The politicization of the economy and the socialization of the state had a socio-political dimension as well. The cartelization of the economy was predicated on a nation-state framework that provided it with the necessary protection against foreign commercial competition. This economic interest coincided with an independent interest on the part of the political pillars of the Empire – and later of the Weimar Republic – in a welfare state. In Bismarck's view, protective tariffs had to achieve two objectives. First, they had to generate income for the Imperial government. This would render it less financially dependent on the transfers of the individual states and, as a result, less politically dependent on the Upper House of the German Federal Parliament (*Bundesrat*), freeing it from the 'free-loader' role. This new source of income was supposed to provide the state with the means 'to counteract the needs for socialism in a reformist way'.[13] Secondly, an activist tariff policy was designed to secure greater economic security: 'to grant protection . . . to domestic national labour and production – in the country as well as in the city, in industry as well as in agriculture' (Bismarck in his address to the *Reichstag* on 8 May 1879, cited in Gerloff 1913: 158). For Bismarck, tariff policy was a means of securing autocratic rule: it won the allegiance both of Prussia's East Elbian ruling class and of the new industrial magnates in the Western half of the Empire. For industrial interests, it was essential that the financial burden of new socio-political obligations be mitigated by additional tariff protection (Gerschenkron 1943).

In Germany as in the USA, protectionism emerged for political reasons. In both countries, too, it favoured the formation of supra-corporate interest group representation aimed at political influence, thus giving rise to cartelization.[14] Cartelization, moreover, promised a more effective defence against the challenge of socialist unions, for both individual companies and the state. Indeed, socio-political motives were expressly invoked in favour of cartelization. In his Freiburg dissertation under Max Weber, Robert Liefmann noted that the state can impose socio-political financial and regulatory burdens much more easily on an economy that is coordinated via cartels and similar contractual arrangements than on a free economy (1897: 198). As the development in the early years of the Weimar Republic and then the economic policy of the National Socialists would show, this conception of a *leiturgic* satisfaction of socio-political needs had a thoroughly prophetic quality (F. L. Neumann 1963 [1942]: 38).

The social politics of US protectionism In the long-term development of the relationship between US social and trade policy, three turning points were decisive in laying the groundwork for an independent path of welfare-democratic development. Hereafter they were also responsible for the enduringly exceptional status of the US welfare state and US trade policy.

13 Bismarck in his address to the *Reichstag* on 12 June 1882, cited in Gerloff (1913: 141). This hope was, of course, never realized. The famous '*clausula* Frankenstein' cemented the financial particularism of the Empire: 'All revenues from tariffs and tobacco levies which exceed the sum of 130 million marks in one year shall be transferred to the individual federal states according to the population which formed the calculation basis for their contribution to the expenses of the Empire' (ibid.: 162).

14 Schumpeter maintained that in the USA, contrary to the German case, protective tariffs did not exploit consumers, for the large US domestic market forestalled genuine monopoly formation. It did, however, increase the rate of profit, and thereby furnished the country's rapidly developing industry with additional capital (Schumpeter 1940: 173).

The first such turning point was the Interstate Commerce Act of 1887 and the Sherman Antitrust Act of 1890. Both were instruments of a mass anti-cartel and anti-trust movement which was increasingly able to exert political influence. Although under the influence of protective tariffs, trusts and cartels both in the USA and in the German Empire became an increasingly dominant feature of the economic structure, in the USA this course of development was viewed with increasing criticism, and then expressly fought. By 1914, the competitive, anti-monopolistic orientation of US economic regulation – although somewhat limited in its effectiveness – constituted the principle of corporate organization.[15]

The second critical turn which would shape the course of future development was the gearing of politics towards consumers. The enormously heterogeneous demographic development of US society in the course of mass immigration from 1870 on made the consumer the common denominator of competition among political parties (Hofstadter 1972 [1955]: 171–3). Between 1870 and 1914 the population increased from about 40 million to 100 million inhabitants, of whom 75 million were new immigrants. More than four-fifths of these immigrants came neither from Great Britain nor from Ireland, countries which in earlier decades had provided the bulk of immigrants and which shared a similar culture and language (figures calculated based on US Census Bureau 1976: 8, 105–6). Issues such as consumer protection against monopolistic price-fixing, food industry inspection, regulation of utilities' fees and bank regulation became foci of national party politics. Existing administrative institutions were reformed or new ones were created to address these problems, because consumer interests promised to be a common denominator for a population that had almost nothing in common except for their identity as consumers and their interest in democratic political participation.[16]

A third turning point was the ever stronger retreat from protectionism. Here, too, the politicization of consumer interests played an ever greater role. The Republicans' argument that, on the whole, protective tariffs increase public welfare in the form of higher wages and greater employment security was too striking a contradiction of actual conditions and was perceived to be economic nonsense (Edwards 1970). A first attempt to lower tariffs under President Taft failed. This led, however, to an amendment to the Constitution, the sixteenth Amendment, which in the course of tariff law

15 Until the 1920s, the Interstate Commerce Act and the Sherman Antitrust Act were of more than mere symbolic significance. Protected by a Supreme Court ruling, they were employed as a means of limiting to whatever extent possible the ability of the working classes to organize and to engage in industrial conflicts. They were also invoked to declare the introduction of an income tax by Congress in 1894 unconstitutional (Wiebe 1967: 92). But there existed a marked difference between the federal and the state level. The Supreme Court did grant the state supreme courts considerable scope for interpretation, in terms of both public interest trust regulation and social policy and tax legislation (ibid.: 81). The Sherman Act did not begin to bite big business until Theodore Roosevelt's presidency and his successful foundation of a Bureau of Corporations in the equally new Department of Commerce and Labor (ibid.: 191). The Hepburn Act of 1906 – according to Wiebe (ibid.: 192) the most important piece of legislation of Roosevelt's entire presidency – gave the Interstate Commerce Commission the regulatory power which Progressive reformers had long demanded. In any case the Webb-Pomerance Act, passed under Woodrow Wilson, suspended anti-trust legislation vis-à-vis the activity of American industry abroad. The Edge Act from the same period institutionalized the support of private sector banking by the US Federal Reserve (J. G. Williamson 1974: 94).

16 Under pressure from consumer organizations, the Pure Food and Drug Act was passed in 1906. It set a new precedent for federal regulatory jurisdiction (cf. Wiebe 1967: 191).

reform made possible the introduction of a federal income tax and thereby largely eliminated the fiscal justification for protectionism (Hody 1996: 58, 68). The two decisive arguments against a policy of high tariffs were as follows. First, the increased competition in domestic markets brought about by foreign competition would lower costs and be beneficial to consumers, weakening the trusts and monopolies. Second, a willingness to sink customs duties would help exports by providing US products with targeted access to foreign markets.[17]

This development found its first political expression in Woodrow Wilson's New Freedom programme. This movement peaked in 1934, the year in which the Trade Agreement Act was passed. The latter brought about a final departure from protectionism and institutionalized free trade as a fundamental principle of foreign trade policy.[18] Technically, the Trade Agreement Act was an amended version of the Trade Act of 1930. Its importance was twofold. First, it created instruments with which customs duties could be reduced (Feiler 1937; Larkin 1937). Second, it entailed a surrender by Congress to the executive branch of all of its prerogatives in the realm of foreign trade. This secured a new course against 'capture', i.e. the co-optation of Congressional trade policy by the business interests which since the administration of Andrew Jackson (1829–37) had put their stamp on the country's trade policy (Taussig 1888; Kreider 1940, 1943; Q. Wright 1944; Destler 1986: 9–36; 1998).

In contrast to the case in Germany, in the USA social policy has never been sufficiently developed to render protectionist trade policy superfluous. The principle of free foreign trade has been and remains juxtaposed with the institutional realities of a politicized and highly discretionary and arbitrary regulation of imports and exports. Elmer E. Schattschneider's observations in 1935 on the relationship between economic reason and political calculation remain true today:

> The history of the American tariff is the story of a dubious economic policy turned into a great political success. . . . The very tendencies that have made the legislation bad have, however, made it politically invincible. (1935: 283)

As will be shown below, important reasons for this lie in the organization of federal social assistance.

The determinants of societal burden-sharing

Globalization is neither Behemoth threating civilization nor an iron cage. Precisely because globalization seems to elude a comprehensive political definition, and apparently attacks and dissolves existing social and economic conditions without shaping or ordering them anew, it is important to recall the fundamental principle of 'methodological individualism': that also this spatial revolution, which leaves no social order untouched, can ultimately and systematically be described and explained in terms of concepts of action and behaviour of one or more individuals (Weber 1978: 7; Arrow 1994).[19] Globalization is on the one hand the result and, more importantly, simulta-

17 Even opponents of protectionism maintained that tariffs were a necessary compensatory measure for the higher US labour costs compared to other countries (Hody 1996: 62).

18 Wilson had enunciated this principle in his inaugural address: 'For trade is reciprocal; we cannot sell unless we also buy' (cited in Hody 1996: 63).

19 Individualism as a scientific principle can, but need not entail a political agenda (Lukes 1971, 1973; Buchanan 1989).

neously and inevitably also the point of departure for collective social action. To understand it, it is of critical importance to enquire into actions as they are *subjectively intended* and not merely into objective-functional social forces. The key is how people react to their experiences with globalization. Since globalization is constantly being 'made' anew, we must remain conscious of the always contingent, artificial, and self-made character of all the pertinent 'facts'. They could have turned out differently. Contrary to the givens of inanimate nature, social facts are neither characterized by an inherent, immutable law which explains them, nor do they determine what will or even should happen (Arendt 1967: 564).[20] This point characterizes not only the core problem of every social science, but it also allows for the possibility of human freedom.[21]

Observed regularities in the historical relationship between processes of globalization and the welfare state can be used for orientation and comparison, but no objective, generalizable truth independent of space and time exists which might enable us to ascertain with any degree of certainty what effects welfare state regulatory measures or programmes will have on economic behaviour. The eminently political character of the situation and the open-endedness of the situations in which globalization puts people are for many an uncomfortable but inescapable reality. The particular circumstances in the context of which actors face questions and seek answers must be taken seriously as conditions of their action, for they can be decisive. Reflections on a 'pure' theory, which proceeds from a priori postulates and identifies potential general or typical effects of economic globalization processes on national socio-political conditions, for example, through the experimental designs of game theory, constitute a further means of developing a more precise understanding of the actual difficulties confronting political actors today. Yet neither historical experiences of globalization nor the 'geometric truths' of a 'pure' economics deduced from a priori reasoning can provide a basis for predicting the future nature of the relationships between the welfare state and globalization, or how actors will respond to this. Both describe in their own way objective possibilities, yet neither is capable of predicting with any kind of certainty what will happen. The same is true of the question of what should happen.

Seeking to infer generalizations intended to predict future events is not a promising approach. Historical experience suggests, moreover, that it would be mistaken to conceive as opposing categories *the* economy – whether global or national – versus *the* government or the political sphere, and vice versa. The actual relationships are far more complex. An often underestimated point is critical here: the economic order is a product of political processes. It is largely the result of compromise between opposing interests. This is especially true of foreign trade. Whoever controls decision-making in the realm of foreign trade, above all with regard to its forms and degree of openness, also determines to a very large extent the form and effectiveness of the national political economy. It is a question of whether a government attempts to control its foreign trade or not. In the late nineteenth century, a new climate of free trade and globalization emerged, accompanied by far-reaching domestic and, above all, democratic control, i.e. the rule of mass public opinion over foreign trade (Verdier 1994). In the last fifteen years of the twentieth century, this development was seemingly reversed.

[20] For this reason, Stuart Kauffman, a natural scientist and winner of the McArthur Genius Award, writes in his *Investigations*: 'The concept of an agent is, inherently, a non-equilibrium concept' (2000: 8).

[21] 'That we can change the circumstances under which we live at all is because we are relatively free from them' (Arendt 1967: 563).

The political sphere in general and trade and social policy in particular appear to have become dependent variables, products of global economic conditions, and thus to have lost their autonomous capacity for action as the prerogative of democratic sovereignty. Cuts in social programmes and the crisis of the welfare state are regularly cited as 'proof' of this. For most observers, it is considered beyond doubt that the contemporary structure of markets and industries not only limits any further redistributional attempts of national social policy, but also creates grave social and political problems for the existing socio-political order, for the new global market conditions are no longer compatible with the old welfare state arrangements.

This perspective is, however, oversimplified. It does not sufficiently take into account either the changes that have actually taken place in welfare state institutions, or that which has not changed contrary to widespread expectations. The same is true of the rhetoric on this issue. Which arguments have in fact been used to justify or to block reforms? And, finally, it has now become clear that social policy frameworks can be reformed in reaction to the same new market conditions in thoroughly different ways. How can we come to a better understanding of a reality that has become problematic? Precisely which changes have, in the context of globalization, challenged the welfare state status quo, and how does the status quo place limits on reform policy?[22]

Since people are typically more struck by those things that harm or threaten to harm their immediate personal interests, than by those things that benefit them, it is of particular interest how globalization affects the existing distribution of the tax burden among different societal groups (Avi-Yonah 2000).

The relationship which exists at any given time between the fiscal burdens a welfare state occasions and the socio-political benefits it provides – a relationship that shapes the interactions between various social groups – can often be explained only with reference to history. There is *always* a misalignment between welfare state structures and social structures, depending on the scale and scope of social change. Fundamentally, this relationship is driven by domestic power relations. When the framework conditions, within which a stable balance between burdens and benefits has emerged, undergo decisive changes as a result of exogenous influences, citizens tend to perceive this as 'unfair' or 'irrational'. The previous consensus on the standards of measurement of these burdens and benefits becomes more fragile and ultimately breaks down altogether.[23] In this situation, representative democracy, whose role had been to balance the relationship between the free market and social solidarity, and between distribution and redistribution, can no longer readily fulfil this function. The 'voice' of resistance is expressed in electoral behaviour, in the mobilization of protest and in other forms of political action on the part of those who are dissatisfied with the status quo. This resistance exists in an alternative or complementary relationship with the 'exit' of those who are dissatisfied (Hirschman 1970). However, exit can take the place of voice, and exit weakens the voice of those who remain behind. The elimination of capital controls and the now virtually equal treatment of nationals and foreign citizens in advanced economies means that the political exit entailed in capital transfers no longer needs to be coterminous with physical departure from the state. The new exit chances imply that the expanded international comparative horizon of opportunities for capital investment no longer, or at least no longer to the same extent,

22 On the role of the status quo in reform policy, see Fernandez and Rodrik (1991).

23 For a more detailed elaboration of this perspective, see Simmel (1992 [1908]: 687–790).

need to express themselves in the national political arena as voice (Benvenisti 1999).

There is, however, a countervailing second factor which limits the effectiveness of voice. Since the 1950s a series of international and, above all, supranational institutions have been formed, ranging from the European Union to the International Monetary Fund to the Group of Seven negotiations, by means of which governments have won new freedom of action at the expense of their national legislatures (Sykes 1999; Gruber 2000). The former decentralized mechanisms of forcing political responsibility for the free play of exit, voice and loyalty have lost their effectiveness due to the rise of these international organizations peopled exclusively by state actors. This is true precisely because, in the latter, policy is made by and for governments.[24]

If one observes at first only private actors, and above all those who can be characterized as globalization winners, it is clear that in societal burden-sharing the financial and tax contributions which can be demanded of these internationally mobile groups is sinking sharply. This downward movement translates into a challenge to the welfare state status quo. In Germany, for example, it can be seen in the fact that the myriad of historically evolved, and thus now often hardly intelligible cross-subsidies between social insurance institutions are viewed by the schemes' contributors as an unfair burden, for they receive no direct return in exchange. For this reason, there are calls, for example, for tax financing of 'non-insurance' types of social policy expenditure, i.e. for the use of contributions from one scheme to pay benefits to persons who did not contribute to the scheme, or for purposes foreign to the scheme. During the US presidential election campaign of 2000, the Republican Party's unofficial – and as a result all the more effective – battle cry ran: 'We want our money back.' The foreseeable budget surplus of the coming years was supposed to benefit those persons who had filled the state's coffers in the first place, and not those who had proven to be unable to take advantage of the new economic opportunities.[25]

The changed framework conditions of the market economy lead to welfare state institutions suddenly being seen in a different light and to their programmes' benefits being measured by different standards. This special circumstance can help us to understand why the 'crisis' of social policy is so hard to grasp and why, with the exception of the USA, rhetoric has far exceeded actual reforms, and why we should not expect greater changes in the future.[26] In addition to the new global economic facts, the nor-

[24] This is also true of the European Union, as Moravcsik (1993a, 1998a), Moravcsik and Nicolaïdis (1998, 1999), Pollack (2000), Rieger (2001) and McKay (1999) have shown. The influence of the European Commission on public opinion and decision-making has steadily declined, a development that has at times been overshadowed by the exceptional presidency of Jacques Delors. An article in the *Frankfurter Allgemeinen Zeitung* from 7 August 2000 sheds light on this: 'Prodi's (the current President of the Commission) presentation to the Council of Ministers of the report of his three "wise men" at the summit of October (1999) was met by the cool arrogance of the national leaders. "We are the wise men who matter", admonished the Spanish Prime Minister Aznar' (Peter Hort, 'Prodis harte Prüfungen', p. 1).

[25] See, for example, an editorial in the *Plain Dealer* from 11 October 2000: 'We work hard for our money, and we would like to keep it and spend it as we wish – not as Gore wishes. We want our money back and a cut in taxes. We want less government' (8B).

[26] This is also true when the reform agenda is predicated on indubitable rationality criteria. As Henry Aaron (1989: 1) observed in his Richard T. Ely-Lecture to the American Economic Association, 'Despite our professional pride in determining our priorities, history strongly suggests that the President's priorities will shape the research agenda of economists . . . more than ours will shape his.' Cf. also Aaron (1994a) and Sawhill (1995). On the US case one must further note that the reform project that – to a far greater extent than welfare reform – was put on the agenda for substantive rather than 'ideological' reasons, i.e. health-care reform, failed.

mative arguments invoked for and against reforms are of interest as well. They can point to separate elements of reform endeavours which are essentially welfare state democratic in nature. These elements are not only opposed to new economic interests induced by globalization, but derive from thoroughly different value spheres, which are inaccessible to economic efficiency criteria. More than one-and-a-half centuries ago, Alexis de Tocqueville enquired why in democracies the passion for equality is greater than the passion for freedom:

> The advantages that freedom brings are shown only by the lapse of time, and it is always easy to mistake the cause in which they originate. The charms of equality are every instant felt and are within the reach of all. . . . The passion for equality penetrates on every side into men's hearts, expands there, and fills them entirely. Tell them not that by this blind surrender of themselves to an exclusive passion they risk their dearest interests; they are deaf. (Tocqueville 1994 [1835–45], II: 96, 97)

Different social groups are by no means uniformly affected by these changes in societal framework conditions brought about by globalization. The legitimacy of the reform agenda can therefore be easily challenged, for the changes are caused by foreign, exogenous forces. For this reason, in the eyes of those who believe themselves to have been negatively impacted by globalization, the material gains of globalization winners cannot be claimed as a contribution to the commonweal, rightly meriting an entitlement to tax, social insurance contribution or regulatory relief.

Under hitherto existing conditions, a balance between the welfare state and the market economy had taken shape which had an air of normalcy, not least because spatial conditions changed little through the mid-1980s. Resistance to change is especially strong because social policy itself, as a system of subjective social rights, hardly changed. In Germany, the magnitude of social benefit systems measured in terms of national income has remained roughly constant since the beginning of the 1980s. Its intermediate position relative to other countries in terms of its social benefits and expenditures remains unchanged since the 1970s (Alber 1998, 2001a).[27] However, the same welfare state facts that had previously been considered hard-won political achievements are now considered to be locational disadvantages, and occupational safety and health measures earlier perceived as contributing to the 'humanization of work' are now seen as regulatory impediments to job-creation and tools of unionist obstructionism blocking efficient corporate organization. The social and labour policies themselves have not changed, yet they now reveal, independently of their original justifications, thoroughly different effects. Yet why should these well-earned rights to benefits and protection suddenly be illegitimate?

Every beneficiary of welfare state institutions attempts to maintain his claim – which, if not earned, is perceived subjectively as justified – to a given benefit. And he fights, if he can, the cutting of benefits and the shifting of economic risks onto his own shoulders. Under the political conditions of numerical democracy and party competition, this resistance can be very effective. It is further enhanced by the impression that this new wealth is largely 'unearned', e.g. 'only' due to lucky speculation. Because

[27] According to data from EUROSTAT (1999), German social expenditure since 1980 has ranged from 28 to 30 per cent of Gross National Product.

acquired without personal effort, this wealth is not socially esteemed.[28] The new mobility of capital, its expanded opportunities to compare production sites according to the return they promise, and to employ this comparison as a weapon in domestic distributional conflicts, are rooted in an infrastructure that these owners of capital did not themselves create and the use of which costs them nothing or close to nothing.[29] It is this perception of essentially 'unearned' advantages that gives resistance to reforms aimed at making social policy more suited or compatible to the free market its characteristic moral weight. It is not merely the 'technical', or veto power-facilitating impediments to decision-making in a majoritarian democracy, augmented in the Federal Republic by 'cooperative' federalism, that can be blamed for the non-reform of social and labour policy. What is decisive, first, is whether reform efforts are considered to be legitimate, and then, which social forces can be mobilized by the various interest groups in the political arena.

The logic of the reform agenda

No matter what the causes and the legitimacy they enjoy as reasons for welfare state reform, the situation is as it is. The environment for social policy, as for business activ-

28 An announcement in the *New York Times* (6 September 2000, A14) summarized resistance to the repeal of the estate tax with the slogan: 'Can you be wealthy and have a conscience at the same time?' The core of the debate on the estate tax is the social responsibility of the new, stock market-created wealth in the USA (Stevenson 2000). The advertising campaign against the repeal of the estate tax was carried out by a group ('Responsible Wealth') of some of the most wealthy Americans (Buffett 2000). In the 2000 presidential campaign, the fact that Dick Cheney, the Republican vice-presidential candidate, had donated less than 1 per cent of his income to charity organizations – even though he had become a multimillionaire after leaving public office in his capacity as a member of the board of directors of an international oil company, almost turned out to be a major handicap (Campbell 2000; Kinsley 2000; Lichtblau 2000; Clymer 2000).

29 The American Lori Wallach, who runs *Global Trade Watch* and organized the protests against the Ministerial Conference of the World Trade Organization in Seattle, blames low infrastructural costs for the economically profitable, but ecologically absurd international goods trade:

Moisés Naím: Give us an example of how the current trading system isn't working.

Lori Wallach: One of my personal favorites is that under the current trade rules, it is profitable – or these companies wouldn't be doing this – for U.S. companies to harvest wood in the Pacific Northwest, make it into disposable chopsticks, wrap them in paper, with a note written on the exterior in Japanese, 'For a single use, please dispose', put them on a boat, and send them off across the Pacific to Japan. Meanwhile, a Japanese company – this was two years ago – harvests timber in Sarawak, Malaysia, processes it into toothpicks, wraps them in plastic, and ships them to the United States. Somehow, it makes economic sense for those two boats to pass in the dark and go off to their respective destinations. Somehow, with all that transportation, all of that extra processing and labeling and translating, that trade is more worthwhile than trees in the United States going into our toothpicks, and the trees in Asia going into the Japanese market.

Moisés Naím: What sort of regulation would you establish to avert this kind of trade? Some people will tell you that your example represents entrepreneurial freedom and free markets in action.

Lori Wallach: Well, yeah, in that particular instance, the number one freedom there is corporate welfare, and subsidies of public funds being used for private gain. And that is particularly the case with transportation systems. I mean, what makes that doable is, basically, the system of petroleum pricing. But also, all the ports and roads that make it reasonable to schlep all that stuff around, to cut it down here and ship it there, and put it on a truck there, and take it here. (Foreign Policy 2000: 44f.)

ity, has radically changed, and this has consequences. As a result of globalization, the costs of 'over-regulated' labour markets and 'ossified' wage structures have risen relative to the *status quo ante*. They have translated into high and enduring unemployment, widespread tax evasion, the development of a black market economy and limited attractiveness for foreign direct investment. They have, however, in the main not triggered augmented reform efforts.

Under the new conditions of 'deep' transnational integration, and expressed in the theoretically derived terms of a more 'rational' social policy, the transfers for those in need are to be financed without burdening the economy, i.e. by the government through general tax revenues (Siebert 1996a, b, 1999a: 241–55). If one observes the new competitive global market on its own, the micro-economic logic of this argument is indisputable. This global market imperative for national social policy reform is additionally buttressed by a new macro-political environment: balanced state budgets, low interest and inflation rates and lean government are rewarded by high levels of investment and a greater influx of foreign direct investment (Tanzi 2000). Extensive bureaucratic social protection systems and state social services, whose benefits constitute social entitlements tied to employee status and increase non-wage labour costs through the burden of contributions, do not seem to fit into the new economic landscape. Expanding public employment is no longer an option for ameliorating poor labour market conditions. Private insurance, entrepreneurially provided social services and transfer systems employing strong income incentives are considered far more suitable to the new *Zeitgeist* of frugal state budgets and deregulation. Marketizing the production of social policy goods and stressing labour market-oriented income incentives are said to have become the new and dominant principles of welfare states. The introduction of real or quasi-markets for the delivery of social welfare services is thought to have positive competitive effects on the public sector and to reduce the probability that service providers can win over for their own interests those politicians and agencies who are supposed to supervise them. The barely controllable opportunity structures for opportunistic behaviour which the mature welfare state provides are expected to disappear with the introduction of the new competitive mechanisms. The autonomous and – for reasons of path dependency alone – self-perpetuating character of this transformation is also thought to reduce the probability that specific political orientations will be punished for this in the voting booth (Snower 1997).

Direct interventions in primary income distribution – whether through minimum wage legislation or a negative income tax – apparently constitute a lesser threat of market distortion, for they always presuppose employment. Measures of this kind do *not* primarily set in after income has been earned in order to redistribute resources via taxes and transfers, i.e. through a *secondary* income distribution (Phelps 1994; Snower 1997; Jerger and Spermann 1998; Kletzer and Litan 2001). *Primary* income earnings and distribution are supposed already to satisfy social needs. Minimum wage legislation as well as wage subsidies do not undermine the market laws of supply, demand and largely free price-setting, but only modify the constraints and opportunities to which all market participants are subject (Barr 1993: 743). Similarly, the introduction of 'quasi-markets' (Bartlett et al. 1998), e.g. in the health care sector, constitutes an attempt to link up with the self-interests of the political leaders, managers and employees of these systems' various funding agencies in such a way that the latter can be harnessed to the common good. To suppress and to attempt to drown out self-interest and opportunism by idealistic appeals to professional or societal responsibility is ultimately futile. Rather, private utility should be marshalled in the service of the public good via the 'visible hand' of the legislature or regulatory agencies (Baier 1999).

The changing structure of work and corporate organization

Technologically driven change has dissolved companies' traditional organizational boundaries and has confirmed anew what M. Jensen and Meckling (1976: 310) observed a quarter of a century ago: 'Most organizations are simply legal fictions which serve as a nexus for a set of contracting relationships among individuals.' In shaping their internal organization, companies increasingly turn to market mechanisms, and, in structuring their relationships among one another, employ hierarchical elements (Picot et al. 1996). Inter-company cooperation today is supported by a wide range of instruments; strategic alliances without reciprocal equity participation and functionally specific inter-company networks have become normal structures of economic organization (Markusen 1995). Hierarchical capitalism is, according to John Dunning, being replaced by 'alliance capitalism' (1997a; see also Wilkins and Schroeter 1998). That management is today rewarded above all for its organizational abilities points to a major shift in what is needed to attain competitive advantage: entrepreneurial abilities and the art of optimally combining heterogeneous resources are at least as important today as possessing one's own resources, which had been paramount heretofore (Dunning 1997a: 15).

Under the new global market conditions of intensified 'creative destruction', corporate reorganization is never final, and organizational strategies and structures which are universally valid and optimal for all economic branches and societies do not exist (Milgrom and Roberts 1990). The ordering of production domestically and abroad is subject to a continual process of adaptation. It is driven by the new micromanagement entailed in 'flexible production', by incessant and fundamental efforts to improve product quality and by competing hierarchies within companies themselves (Best 1990). Corporate organization itself is becoming a strategic variable (Osterloh and Weibel 1996: 125). To an ever greater extent, the efficiency of the organization of work processes depends on whether employees are able to react constructively to unexpected developments.[30] Such ability can be captured in advance by labour contracts only to a limited extent; if it is to be achieved, it must be fostered and upheld by means of the unceasing management of incentives.

Above all, with regard to the investment of the productive factor 'labour', corporate organizational strategies thus no longer emphasize coordination alone, but also motivation (Wolff 1999). Labour has been revalued as a source of knowledge and ideas; its purely physical and psychic qualities are fading, at least in developed countries, into the background. The instruments of personnel management are thus being revolutionized in the direction of a stronger socialization of individual resources. The need to encourage and utilize interactive learning amongst a wide range of groups of independently acting employees at all levels of the production chain nowadays stands at the centre of organizational work policy. A systematic, theoretically well-founded management of incentives has become a focus of corporate reorganizations.

30 See MacLeod (1995: 12), who describes the current state of Japanese personnel management.

This shows not only the extent to which companies today are dependent upon *voluntarily* enacted, highly individual components of employee performance, but also the degree to which, precisely for this reason, the framework conditions of the work process are set by social policy. It also suggests which opportunities social policy opens or precludes for companies in the shaping of their internal organization. Social policy provides employees with exit options from the labour market – or with incentives not to work, depending on the perspective of the observer. These exit opportunities are also, however, the foundation of an orientation towards so-called post-material values. These, in turn, pave the way for essentially individual freedom, on the basis of which new work contents and forms can develop. It is nearly impossible to generalize about the effects of social policy, which are omnipresent and leave virtually no sphere of work organization untouched. It can only be said that its institutions, regulations and benefits play a central role in the development and guaranteeing of the moral economy of markets and in the policing of non-contractual aspects of labour relations. For this reason, companies and their lobbies have a far greater interest in influencing their welfare state environment in a targeted way.[31] Framework conditions, corporate work organization and corporate strategy have not only become more interrelated, they now also interact, in that their relationships to one another are being deliberately changed by employers in order to generate competitive and locational advantages (Aoki 1996).

The blueprints of reform and of adaptation processes, even when their inner logic is convincing and the external circumstances appear compelling, do not translate automatically into a new, more adequate social policy. The reform agenda must not only be formulated, but also implemented. Whether, and above all how, the alternatives to the status quo enter the political decision-making realm is an independent variable which shapes the relationship between 'globalization' and the 'welfare state' (Pierson 1998). The main difficulty lies in the fact that those who are, in institutional terms, responsible for enacting reforms have at one and the same time a vested interest in the old order. Their power basis derives from this order and hence they have a clear interest in defending the status quo. In the new global framework, however, the nation-state arrangement has lost its monopoly position. Every government is now only a particular actor, which, moreover, competes with the legal orders of other states (Franck 1999, 2000). Hence, state actors have lost their firm anchorage in an historically evolved relationship between state, economy and society, together with the attendant ability to influence the course of events, just as have the employer and employee organizations.

[31] To the extent that virtually all companies have become at least potentially multinational, the relationship between institutional context, organization and strategy has changed not only in the realm of welfare state conditions: 'While older management theory paradigms proceed from the assumption that companies must adapt to their environment, newer approaches maintain that companies achieve a strategic competitive advantage precisely by proactively influencing their environment and changing the rules of competition' (Osterloh and Weibel 1996: 124). The pendant to this paradigm shift in corporate strategy is a new view of free trade. The foundations of the 'new' foreign trade theory are the company-based and thus manipulable competitive advantages rooted in economies of scale and scope (Krugman 1987), and no longer the geographically fixed comparative advantages in the international division of labour presumed by David Hume, Adam Smith and David Ricardo.

Globalization means that labour relations have received a new foundation, without this translating immediately and directly into a new order for conflict resolution. The new constellation is marked no longer by conflict-oriented strategies bound to the logic of the zero-sum game, but by cooperative and collaborative strategies. This simple fact makes reform even more difficult to achieve, since it multiplies veto positions. Most classical forms of industrial action aimed at improving wages and workplace conditions, from the open strike to the silent resistance of inner obstruction, are no longer habitually resorted to, for under the new economic conditions they would have self-destructive effects. This is also true of employers: in the age of *just-in-time* production and markets, they can be rapidly overtaken by foreign competition, and hence can simply no longer sustain traditional industrial conflict (Gentz 1999).[32] The same is true of state nationalization and more intensive regulatory strategies vis-à-vis multinational corporations. The low costs of capital mobility and the high degree of import penetration in most markets has rendered these classical strategies too blunt to be used in normal conflict situations; they are now only suitable as a last resort. Correlatively, voluntary cooperation defines not only companies' internal relations, but also their relations with one another and with actors from the state, the union and the philanthropic (whether traditional or NGO) spheres.

Incentive systems have thus attained pivotal importance, both on a macro-organizational (state) and on a micro-organizational (company) level. State actors today participate in locational competition for free capital, and companies compete for highly qualified employees. The environment of social policy has thus changed fundamentally. The old environmental conditions – which were conducive to the comprehensive social protection programmes of the post-war period, whether these took the form of social insurance schemes or means-tested income transfers – have disappeared.

As a result of the Fordist transformation of both private and public workplaces, large and uniform classes of employees faced the same or similar employment conditions, but these are now being replaced by far more fragmented and individualized groupings. Families, too, no longer function as a type of reinsurance for a labour market in which, predominantly, men are active. Women have also become active in the labour market in large numbers; to the extent that the labour market allows it, this condition will continue (Esping-Andersen 1999, 2002; Lindbeck 2001). As with employment conditions, so too do personal relationships fragment ever more, becoming more discontinuous and heterogeneous. With increasingly diverse educational opportunities and skill levels, income disparities are rising – contrary to the long-standing assumption that income inequality would be neutralized societally and hence politically by social regulation (Aghion 1998; F. Levy 1998; Fogel 2000). In Germany, this latter objective took on a quasi-institutional form in the wake of the Supreme Court's interpretation of a constitutional guarantee of 'uniform living conditions' for all in Article 106 (par. 3 no. 2), and Article 72 (par. 2) of the Basic Law, seen as disallowing regional disparities. It was further strengthened in social and economic policy terms by both the interdependent structures of the federal system and by the strong centralization and juridification of the collective bargaining system (Abromeit 1992; Renzsch 1997).

32 This does not imply that we believe that logic or economic rationality *in fact* governs industrial relations. It simply means that the new conditions make some strategies more costly; they do not rule them out.

4 The Real Worlds of Social Policy Reform: A Collapse of the Welfare State Paradigm?

The global market economy is not the only force that drives social policy reforms. If one takes stock and comparatively examines welfare state arrangements from the perspective of their greater or lesser compatibility with the new economic conditions alone, one runs the danger of overlooking conditioning factors other than domestic and foreign trade structures, as well as functions other than those inscribed in employment contracts. Such a perspective can overestimate the resistance capacity of institutions and arrangements which for completely different reasons are afflicted by problems and thus being put to the test. Even without the challenges of the global market economy, there are reasons to take a more careful look at the institutions of the welfare state (Siebert 1996b; Kaufmann 1997a; Pierson 1998).

Since the 1970s, there has been a growing impression in the public sphere and among social scientists that the welfare state is increasingly losing its *raison d'être*. The criticism that the welfare state's redistribution from the rich to the poor constitutes little more than 'robbing Peter to pay Paul', that it sets poverty traps and creates a 'culture of dependency', found popular support – first in public opinion and then in the voting booth. The general impression was that 'something must have gone wrong' if a veritable 'economic miracle' or economic growth in general creates greater rather than lesser demand for social policy. At the same time, 'new' poverty risks were discovered, making it even more difficult to identify the 'truly' poor who were more deserving of support than much of the traditional social policy clientele (Leisering and Leibfried 1999: 188ff.). Beside the costs of social policies and difficulties in financing them, the problem of dependency – i.e. behavioural effects attributed to dependency on public income transfers – commanded ever more public attention. Up to now, a clear causal relationship between social expenditures and negative work incentives could not be proven, despite intensive research (Moffit 1992; Atkinson 1999). For precisely this reason, though, public discourse could be dominated by rumours, isolated cases and exaggerated depictions of benefit abuse.[33] No matter how convincing one finds this critique, it has, up to now, produced no institutional consequences – with the exception of the United States and its notorious 'ending welfare as we know it' of 1996. This is attributable not least to the fact that the expansion of social rights has always been connected to the introduction of control mechanisms.

The causes of the independent dynamic of social programmes, which amounted to a seemingly unstoppable growth of the welfare state, are therefore in all likelihood not to be found in any kind of personal character deficits of welfare state clients, but, rather, in a systematic peculiarity of the welfare state itself. A major part of this is the inherent difficulty, in the context of democratic social policy shaped by party competition, in determining the 'true' preferences of voting citizens and making these guide

[33] Barr (1993: 745) has pointed out that in the absence of an empirical income distribution without welfare state interventions, one can just as easily argue that social policy does not mitigate, but aggravate or cause poverty – as Murray (1994) has done so effectively in the case of the USA. In other words, the thesis of an unconditional relationship between socio-political benefit expansion and negative work incentives is, in the form in which it is regularly and effectively presented, impossible to falsify. This is the reason why it has been so successful.

Table 4.3 Federal means-tested benefits in the USA as a % of the federal budget, selected fiscal years, 1968–1996

	Medical aid	*Cash aid*	*Food aid*	*Housing aid*	*Education aid*	*Jobs training*	*Energy*	*Services*
1968	1.54	2.83	0.50	0.44	0.48	0.40	0.00	0.22
1973	2.71	3.49	1.57	1.37	0.74	0.38	0.00	0.69
1978	3.18	3.50	1.85	1.60	0.89	2.11	0.06	0.75
1983	2.92	2.77	2.24	1.54	0.92	0.56	0.25	0.41
1988	3.63	2.85	1.90	1.38	1.05	0.35	0.17	0.42
1990	4.00	2.91	1.90	1.40	1.10	0.32	0.13	0.33
1991	4.71	3.19	2.12	1.43	1.12	0.33	0.14	0.39
1992	5.69	3.53	2.37	1.59	0.98	0.36	0.12	0.42
1993	6.03	3.79	2.47	1.70	1.02	0.34	0.11	0.41
1994	6.40	4.34	2.47	1.65	1.00	0.33	0.13	0.52
1995	6.69	4.48	2.43	1.65	1.00	0.31	0.11	0.40
1996	6.64	4.46	2.38	1.61	0.98	0.25	0.07	0.35

Source: Green Book (1998: 1420)

decisions about which socio-political goods are to be publicly produced and in what quantity. In any case there can be no doubt that the current structures and benefit catalogues of welfare state institutions do not adequately come to terms with the actual risks of unemployment, persistent low income and sudden income loss – risks that can only be covered by the public sector. But it is not at all clear whether covering these risks is at all possible. Social policy at once does too much and too little, and the one is the cause of the other (Barr 1993: 742). The original causes and dynamic of this gap have nothing to do with globalization, but the latter's new realities have enlarged it.

The thesis that the institutions of the state have lost their power to shape developments and/or that their impact is countered by far stronger market forces is politically more current in the USA than in Germany, even though at first glance the US experience provides far less evidence for this view. The volume of means-tested programmes relative to social insurance schemes is far greater in the US than in Germany. Social insurance schemes' share of total public social expenditures amounted to 62 per cent, while that of means-tested benefits was 27 per cent, i.e. barely 5 per cent, of GNP. In Germany, social insurance schemes' share of the 'social budget' was 68 per cent, while that of social assistance was only 4 per cent. Even when one adjusts for inflation, government social assistance expenditures increased fourfold between 1968 and 1996, whereas the population grew by only 32 per cent during this period (Green Book 1998: 1414). Federal expenditures on social assistance benefits rose from 6.5 per cent of the federal budget in 1968 to 17.1 per cent in 1996.[34] As Table 4.3 shows, an ever greater share of federal income and means-tested programme expenditures has been consumed by health assistance for the poor, largely due to rising costs of the Medicaid pro-

[34] Our calculations, based on data from the US Census Bureau (1999) and the Statistische Bundesamt (1999). Educational expenditures were excluded.

gramme.[35] This development reflects, one the one hand, the lack of an encompassing public health insurance scheme in the USA (though not in the UK or Canada – see Hacker 1998) and, on the other, the technical advances in medicine which have translated into a cost explosion. In the USA, the institutional differentiation of welfare state programmes reflects ethnic and other divisions that undermine general social solidarities *ab initio*. Nationally defined solidarities are the precondition for successful redistributional policies (Quadagno 1994; Skocpol 1995; Rieger 1997, 2001). Ultimately, the fragmentation of income transfer and other social programmes for low-income groups contributes to the impression of the loss of political – or institutional – control. Despite discretionary means-testing and the possibility of far-reaching bureaucratic control, the growth rates of means-tested programmes have always been higher than those of the seemingly more attractive social insurance schemes. Whereas in 1962 federal expenditures on social insurance schemes amounted to seven times those on means-tested programmes, this ratio was cut in half by 1999.[36]

Table 4.4 summarizes the most important quantitative indicators of differences in emphasis and magnitude of welfare state programmes in both countries. If one analyses social expenditure in relation to national income, one is struck by the fact that Germany spends roughly 10 percentage points more than the USA. The difference between the two countries' total public expenditure is of a similar order. Health care spending is a different story, however. Despite Germany's comprehensive and generous statutory health insurance, its public expenditure on health care constitutes only 1.6 percentage points more of GNP than in the USA. This reverse situation becomes even more clear if one takes into account private health expenditure. Total spending on health care expressed as a share of national income is 3.4 percentage points higher in the US than in Germany. In this sector of the welfare state, the greater responsibility assumed by the public sector in Germany translates into stronger control of spending. In the US system, meanwhile, untamed growth in spending is juxtaposed with limited or no access to health care for large groups within the population (Alber 1988; Newhouse 1996; Pauly 1997; Reagan 1999; Gottschalk 2000; Hacker 2002).[37] The enormous difference in the scope of the welfare state is also reflected in social policy's ability to provide income to citizens beyond the market. In Germany, 17 per cent of incomes are welfare state transfer payments, whereas the corresponding share in the US is 7 per cent. Thus German social policy's capacity to reduce the 'poverty gap' is more than twice as high.

The coverage rates of welfare state benefit schemes in both countries evince several additional disparities:

1 The first pillar of public *pension* insurance in the US (social security) covers 70.7 per cent of the population aged 15–65, more than Germany's 56.3 per cent. This

[35] In inflation-adjusted terms, state and local welfare expenditures rose between 1968 and 1998 at nearly the same rate (+392 per cent) as federal welfare expenditures (+401 per cent). This parallel development was the product of a matched funding mechanism which was repealed in the welfare reform of 1996 (to be discussed further below).

[36] Our calculations, based on data from the Congressional Budget Office (2000).

[37] In her comparative analysis of German and US health care reform policy, Weide (1998: 110) summarized the difference between the two countries as follows: 'In the United States, regulation must protect the public by limiting the market forces in health care. In Germany, it must give the patients more collective power to protect themselves.'

Table 4.4 Selected indicators on the German and US welfare states, 1995–1998

		Germany	*USA*
1	Social expenditure (% of GDP, 1995)	28.1	16.1
2	Social expenditure (% of public expenditure, 1995)	54.8	44.8
3	Total expenditure on health (% of GDP, 1998)	10.6	14.0
4	Public expenditure on health (% of GDP, 1998)	8.1	6.5
5	Scope of welfare state public transfers (% of total income,[1] 1994–7)	16.8	7.4
6	Poverty gap, reduction and net poverty		
6a	Gap before transfers (% of total income before taxes)	8.7	6.1
6b	Reduction by transfers (% of total income after taxes,[2] 1994 (USA) 1997 (Germany))	7.8	3.8
6c	Poverty after transfers (% of total income after taxes,[2] 1994 (USA) 1997 (Germany))	0.9	2.4
7	Coverage of old age insurance[3] (%, 1996)	56.3	70.7
8	Coverage of unemployment insurance[3] (%, 1995)	55.3	89.0
9	The scope of the welfare state: coverage of public health insurance[4] (%, 1997)	92.2	45.0
9a	Health gap: coverage of total health insurance[4] (= 9a + private health insurance) (%, 1995)	99.9	84.2
10	Coverage of accident insurance[5] (%, 1995)	95.1	85.4

[1] 'Extent of welfare state' is defined as share of net transfers in the sum total of post-tax income. Figures for Germany are for 1994, for the USA, 1997

[2] Unless otherwise indicated figures for Germany are always for 1994, for the USA, 1997. 'Poverty gap' (line 6a) denotes societal poverty – measured as 50% of net mean household income – before any government tax take or government transfer. 'Reduction by transfers' (line 6b) denotes by how many percentage points this gap is closed by government action – relative to all post-transfer incomes. Line 6c shows the amount of post-transfer poverty remaining

[3] Insured as % of population between 15 and 65 years old

[4] Insured as % of total population

[5] Insured as % of employed population

Sources: OECD, Health Data, 1999b (lines 1, 2, 9a); US Census Bureau 1999 (lines 3, 4); Kim 2000: 13 (lines 5, 6); VDR 2000 (line 7); Statistisches Bundesamt 1999: 58, table 39; 62, table 3.14; 452, table 19.3.2. (lines 7, 8, 9b, 10); Green Book 1998: 8, table 1–2; 328 (lines 7, 8); US Census Bureau 1999: 15, table 14; 397, table 629; 411, table 649 (lines 7, 8, 9b, 10); BMA 2000: tables 2.6A and 8.14; 2.3 (line 8); US Department of Health and Human Services 2000: 339f., table 128, 129 (line 9b)

is due not only to higher labour participation rates in the USA, particularly among women, but also to the inclusion of the self-employed in the scheme and to the fact that in families, those who do not work (mostly women) and who hence lack direct access to social security protection become independently vested in the scheme after 10 years and do not, as in Germany, have only indirect access to benefits through family relations. Moreover, the USA has a lower *de minimis* limit – the floor at which contributions start – than Germany. The US system is mainly oriented towards eliminating the risk of poverty in old age among the greatest possible share of the population. German pension policy is oriented far more strongly towards preserving the standard of living which individuals have attained during their occupational lives – a mission that is left to second (occupational) and third (personal) pillar pension plans in the USA. In both countries, the historical motivation for the state pension scheme still determines its mission. In the USA, the New Deal sought to provide rapid and above all effective income security for the future elderly population which had been most gravely afflicted by the mass unemployment and asset depletion caused by the Great Depression. Germany's point of departure in the 1880s was the political motive of winning the loyalty of the 'labour aristocracy' over to the Reich. A funded scheme was adopted, meaning that benefit entitlements accumulated only slowly. Over the ensuing decades the scheme was expanded step-by-step, yet without striving for greater equality among pension levels than reigned among market incomes. As a result, an increasingly large share of pensioners was in need of a separate old-age social assistance programme.

2 In the realm of *unemployment* insurance, too, the US coverage rate of 89 per cent – versus 55.3 per cent in Germany – reflects the New Deal tradition of broad-based protection. In the USA, the already much larger share of the population employed has also been more broadly insured. The financing is incumbent upon employers alone. This unemployment insurance is, however, much more limited in the benefits it provides than its German counterpart. First, the eligibility criteria are more restrictive. Second, its benefit levels are much lower. Third, they are paid for a much shorter period of time. This benefit set-up is geared towards overcoming brief periods of income loss. In cases of mass or long-term unemployment, it thus leaves a growing share of the insured without further benefits, not even means-tested ones. An additional peculiarity of the US system is the 'experience rating': the more employees that an employer fires, the higher his contributions to the scheme become.

3 If one takes into account Germany's private *health* insurance sector as well as its version of Medicaid (health care assistance provided through Germany's social assistance programme – *Krankenhilfe der Sozialhilfe*), 99.9 per cent of the population has health insurance (Statistisches Bundesamt 2000: 62). The German health insurance 'gap' of 0.1 per cent is extremely small, whereas the US one of 14.6 per cent, or 41 million Americans, is considerable – although in recent years progress has been made in closing this gap for children (Herz et al. 2000; Riley and Herz 2000). Here we still see the old pattern of exclusion of the working poor by the US welfare state, which in recent decades has been clearly broken, however, by the financial transfers of the EITC. For the middle classes in the USA, health insurance is accessed through the employer and constitutes a part of the social wage (Hacker 2002). Only pensioners aged 65 and older are subject to compulsory health insurance providing basic coverage (Medicare). Beyond this, the Medicaid programme provides minimum, means- (income- and assets-) tested health protection to limited, categorically defined groups of poor persons.

4 In Germany, statutory *accident* insurance covers over 90 per cent of the population and thus more than twice the share covered by the US workers' compensation system (Statistisches Bundesamt 1999: 45; US Census Bureau 1999: 8, 397). The difference is due above all to the fact that in Germany school attendance is treated, in insurance terms, like employment. Yet even when one compares the employed populations in the two countries only, the German accident insurance system still covers 10 per cent more than does the US system.

In interpreting Table 4.4, two points must be kept in mind with regard to the US case. First, not only can employee benefits go a long way in substituting for direct state production of social protection and provision, but companies can supplement this private sector supply of social policy goods on their own initiative. Second, as has been mentioned several times above, there are alternative systems of non-market protection of jobs and income. One is union organization, another is protectionist trade policy.

From 1998 to 2001, Congress and the White House were in the happy position of quarrelling over the distribution of a budget surplus. At the same time, in the course of the New Federalism institutionalized in the welfare reform of August 1996, the core elements of social assistance policy have been devolved to the states. These two developments have contributed to a dramatic lessening of the conflict potential of US social policy. It has not only won new distributional latitude, but also now disposes of an institutional and thus automatic control mechanism in the form of decentralization, which in the US federalist context independently thwarts the expansive autodynamic growth of social programmes (Kramer 2000).[38] Together with the traditional restrictive elements of US social policy – mainly minimum benefits, an individualized equivalency principle and a strong orientation towards the company – this development has made the structures of US social policies better suited than those of the Federal Republic to harmonize with the forces of the global market economy.[39]

President Clinton's welfare reform of 1996 ushered in a shift in responsibility for one's own livelihood from the public sector to the individual. The 1996 reform increased the pressure on individuals to earn their livelihood through wage labour, whether it be directly through compulsory workfare or through various forms of forcing indirect or direct exiting from social assistance programmes (Gebhardt and Jacobs 1997; Gebhardt 1998; Weaver 2000). The new rule that social assistance may be claimed for a maximum of five years over the course of one's entire life makes the paradigm change unmistakably clear. Yet just as important for the new hegemony of the labour market over income distribution is the rapid ascendance made in the hierarchy of US social policy by the Earned Income Tax Credit (EITC) – a kind of negative income tax for low-wage workers. If one declares market conformity to be a paramount criterion for the rationality of social policy measures – i.e. creating as few incentives as possible to leave the labour market – then a programme of this type is an optimal instrument for allowing workers to achieve socially sufficient income through gainful employment. Taken together, the United States' traditionally limited unemployment insurance system, its minimalist social assistance programme restricted to those actively engaged in labour markets and the strict temporal limit on benefit receipt all compel a far more efficient functioning of the labour market than in Germany. More importantly, the US minimal wage legislation has cushioned the fall

[38] Graebner (1977) and Wallis (1984) show how Franklin D. Roosevelt's New Deal shifted the vertical distribution of power in favour of the Federal government. On the effects of a federal governmental structure on social policy, see Rose-Ackermann (1981), Peterson and Rom (1989) and Pierson (1995). On locational competition as a means of constraining social policy, see Thibout (1956), C. C. Brown and Oates (1987) and Weingast (1995).

[39] For critical commentary on the most recent federal and state legislation, above all on state competition's negative consequences for the poor, and in particular the high disparity in levels of provision among states, supported by key Supreme Court decisions, see V. C. Jackson (1998, 2000), Cashin (1999) and Little (1999).

Table 4.5 Composition of poverty population for selected demographic groups in the USA, selected years 1959–1998 (% of poverty population)

	1959	*1966*	*1975*	*1985*	*1994*	*1998*
Aged	13.9	17.9	12.8	10.5	9.6	9.8
Children	43.6	42.6	42.1	38.8	39.6	38.3
Non-aged adults	42.5	39.5	45.1	50.7	50.8	51.9
Individuals in female-headed families	26.3	36.0	47.4	49.5	52.8	53.5
Individuals in all other families	73.7	64.0	52.6	50.5	47.2	46.5

Source: Green Book (2000: 1288)

in real wages which could be observed in nearly all markets as a result of shifts in skills demand, a technological revolution in the production sphere and globalization.

Labour market participation is of great significance with respect to social security in old age or illness, for membership in first- and second-pillar schemes – social and occupational insurance respectively – is tied to employment. Social insurance schemes, like occupational plans, are oriented towards the labour market and are not designed to serve as a corrective to it. US social policy shows itself to be more market-oriented than its German counterpart in that it largely lacks redistributive components. As Table 4.5 demonstrates, American social policy is more effective in helping groups outside the labour market to stay above the poverty line than those inside. In sharp contrast, the two main redistributive elements of the German system are the family orientation of the compulsory health insurance system – spouses and children are co-insured at no additional cost – and the various forms of crediting 'socially useful' activity in the calculation of old-age pensions – primarily child-care periods and other care work, but also periods of apprenticeship training, continuing education or compulsory military service. US public and occupational insurance schemes' more market-conforming design has a drawback, however. When more or less all types of transfers, allowances and services of secondary distribution can be accessed only through employment, these become part of primary distribution. Thus, when the state provides no income independent of employment and the earning trajectory, economic and ultimately social pressure become concentrated on gaining political control of the access to – and exit from – the employment sphere.[40] One means of achieving this goal is unionization and a policy of regulating the labour supply, wages and labour demand (closed shops).[41]

40 The more that access to health care is solely dependent upon continued employment, the more labour market dislocations – unemployment and above all disparities in the risk of unemployment among different population groups – have a direct impact on employees (Bowman 1999: 2). In 1997, 13 per cent of those insured at the time reported that for some period during the past two years they had no health insurance whatsoever (ibid.). Among African-Americans and Hispanics, this figure is much higher.

41 Cf. Freeman and Medoff (1984). In England in the nineteenth century, the unions invented their own form of domestic protectionism in order to keep out competition: 'Some unions divide the country round them into districts, and will not permit the products of the trades controlled by them to be used, except within the district in which they have been fabricated. . . . At Manchester this combination is particularly effective, preventing any bricks made beyond a radius of four miles from entering the city. To enforce the exclusion, paid agents are employed; every cart of bricks coming towards Manchester is watched, and if the contents be found to have come from without the prescribed boundary the bricklayers at once refuse to work' (Cairnes 1874: 307).

This path was foreclosed – for political reasons, but also due to the transformation of the economic structure and corporate organization caused by technological progress (Rogers 1990; Freeman and Rogers 1999; Teixeira and Rogers 2000).

Protectionism promises a further means of getting labour markets under political control. Defending wages and employment were and are the dominant motives in the US for protectionism (M. Wallerstein 1987; Eckes 1995; Frank 1999). Due to this essentially social view of foreign trade, US – in contrast to European – regimes have at no time had both hands free to put their country on the path of free trade and thus to integrate the US economy into the global economy in a lasting way. One hand was always preoccupied with finding ad hoc means of granting additional social protection – but not only, and sometimes not even predominantly, to workers. Democratic, i.e. Congressional, control of policy on trade accords is, for constitutional reasons, far more extensive in the USA than in Europe. 'To regulate commerce with foreign nations' is a prerogative of Congress, i.e. the legislative branch, but not of the President, i.e. the executive branch, as laid out in Article I, Section 8 of the US Constitution. The US Congress sets foreign trade policy and as a result severely limits the President's room for manoeuvre (Franck and Weisband 1979). The enormous increase in power which US presidents have gained since the Second World War by employing Executive Orders and Executive Agreements, allowing their foreign policy to become not only independent of Congress but also nearly immune to Congressional supervision, never extended to the 'low politics' of foreign trade relations (L. Pauly 1997). The populist democratic slogan 'no injury to domestic industry' has always forced US governments either to make the dismantling of trade barriers dependent on the probability of negative employment effects, or to mitigate resistance by means of compensatory measures in the various Trade Adjustment Acts or by providing workers with some other form of compensation for the risk of job loss from increased import competition (Bhagwati 1988; Tonelson 1994; Deardorff and Stern 1998, 2000). The former has had the consequence of securing much more effective protection against foreign trade for those industries that are labour intensive and organized in large corporations. The latter has had the consequence that the White House and Congress have had literally to buy off the resistance potential of groups which felt threatened by trade liberalization.

Beside labour market and employment concerns, a further, independent source of resistance to foreign trade liberalization is the principle of democratic sovereignty. With regard to trade policy, the average US citizen is worried not only about foreign trade liberalization, but also about surrendering economic policy-making authority to international organizations in which the USA is only one member among many and in which democratic control of governments cannot be forced directly.[42] Moreover, and

42 At a hearing of the Senate Committee on Foreign Relations on the issue of US entry into the WTO, Ralph Nader, founder and chairman of the country's largest consumer protection organization, commented: 'When historians look back on this period . . . either they will focus on it as a moment in which Congress resisted the anti-democratic WTO or they will view it as the moment in which Congress ceded authority to safeguard the interests of this country and its inhabitants to this new autocratic body' (cited in Aaronson 1996: 176). In March 1995, two of the most influential senators, the Republican Bob Packwood and the Democrat Daniel Patrick Moynihan, published a joint letter to the President of the United States: 'We are writing to propose that the WTO establish its headquarters not in Geneva (where it will be viewed as simply a continuation of the GATT) but . . . here in Washington, D.C. Locating the WTO's headquarters in Washington would do much to . . . help build the support of the American public for its work' (cited in Aaronson 1996: 168). On the 'Great 1994 Sovereignty Debate' on the conclusion of the Uruguay Round of GATT and the founding of the WTO, see J. H. Jackson (1997b).

this is of great importance in the USA, with its strong democratic tradition, the limitation of the country's own sovereignty in matters of trade policy entailed in joining the WTO was criticized, thus weakening the position of the WTO vis-à-vis the USA (J. H. Jackson 1997a).[43]

Even for the USA, the ability to export is predicated on allowing imports. The latter can generate social costs. People orient their current behaviour towards the events that they think will probably occur in the future, especially as they feel a pressure to minimize risks and avoid losses. Resistance to changes in employment and income relations has existed at all times and in all places; it has political consequences, however, above all when a foreign source of disruption can be identified (Krugman 1997).

In global capitalism the pace of change has increased greatly. The demands for government relief and compensation on the part of those negatively impacted have developed accordingly. In the USA in particular, the danger of a reversion to protectionism has grown, and it has become a daily task of the White House and the ITC to try to prevent this. Protectionist initiatives emanate from Congress on a regular basis, and every step taken towards the easing of trade is conditional on the offer and enactment of parallel social protection measures.

Whether such compensatory measures are economically rational and efficient is another matter (Baldwin 1985b). In any case, they assuage any opposition from the most active elements of the wage-earning classes – such as unionized workers and the elderly – who generally have more to lose and are less able to cope with adjustment and dislocation. In the electoral strategy of politicians, who now as always are elected within the framework of a nation-state, these groups are critical (Decker and Corson 1995).[44] In terms of their magnitude and scope, these programmes – relative to the entire US social budget – might appear insignificant. Yet politically, they are indispensable, as President Clinton learned to his cost when in 1998 he sought to obtain Congressional approval for proxy authority to negotiate foreign trade agreements – the so-called fast-track authority – without such appeasing measures. This proxy, which previous presidents had always received in exchange for compensatory social and labour-market policy measures, was denied Clinton through to the end of his presidency (Destler 1997; Gilpin 2000: 249) and an equivalent 'trade authority' was recovered by President Bush on 1 August 2002.

This highly situative social policy has foundations outside of welfare state benefit schemes, in that it is intertwined with trade policy, and is strongly limited in terms of its scope. Such a 'social trade policy' can be found neither in Germany nor elsewhere in Europe. In Continental Europe there indeed exist traditional protectionist niches, above all in agriculture and the declining heavy industries (steel, coal and shipbuilding), but this protectionism does not constitute a daily nuisance for those who

[43] Every member of an international organization reserves the right to sovereignty in the sense of being able to withdraw from the organization. Nonetheless, the US Congress's ratification of the outcome of the Uruguay Round of GATT and the therein inscribed transition to the WTO was contingent upon a proviso, contained in the Dole Amendment, that any limitation of US sovereign rights would be countered with US withdrawal from the organization (Gilpin 2000: 111).

[44] On the origins of Trade Adjustment Assistance, see Aho and Bayard (1980). On social trade policy, which was a topic of hot political controversy in the NAFTA debate, see Conybeare and Zinkula (1996).

manage import and export policy.[45] In Western Europe, as opposed to the USA, comprehensive protectionism has existed mainly only in theory (Kahler 1985), even though in EU trade policy rudiments of a 'strategic' industrial policy do exist (Fröhlich 1994; Freytag 1995).

Despite this caveat, the crucial difference in the foreign trade policy of the two countries can be summed up in the formula that, with regard to imports and exports, 'In Germany everything is permitted that is not explicitly prohibited, whereas in the USA everything is prohibited that is not explicitly allowed.'[46] Because of the open language of the Commerce Clause, US courts have tended to regard the powers of Congress over foreign commerce as the most sweeping of all its powers over commerce, including the authority to absolutely prohibit foreign importations (Morrison and Hudec 1993: 93). In consequence, as a much-quoted Supreme Court decision put it, 'no individual has a vested right to trade with foreign nations' (*Buttfield* v. *Stranahan* (192 US 470 – 1904).[47] The US government, US courts and prevailing constitutional doctrine view individual freedom to import and export unequivocally as a privilege, and not as an individual right that could be invoked as a cause of action against discriminatory or disproportionate governmental foreign trade restrictions. In 1989 the Court of Appeal for the Federal Circuit stated that over the past 200 years there has apparently not been one single US court decision that has upheld a right of importers to overturn a congressional exclusion of any product from importation: 'When the people granted Congress the power "to regulate Commerce with Foreign Nations" . . . they thereupon relinquished at least whatever right they, as individuals, may have had to insist upon the importation of any product.'[48] Even though this theoretical 'ban with exemption proviso' is diluted by the existence of numerous general clauses providing exemption from normal duties, a US exporter must always be prepared to declare and prove which of these exceptional authorizations sanctions his export. In Germany, by contrast, this

45 Foreign trade authority has not been fully delegated to the European Union, despite this general impression. Notwithstanding the case law of the EU Court of Justice, arguing for an exclusive Community competence for a 'common commercial policy', the EU also in this field does not enjoy 'sovereign powers' but possesses merely derived, limited and enumerated powers 'as provided in this treaty' (Article 3 of the EEC Treaty). As a result, there is a fundamental ambiguity in the external economic relations of the European Union. On the one hand, the WTO sees the Union as a single economic area, and the Union as a whole is also a WTO member. On the other hand, in decision-making processes, it is the votes of the individual states that count (Benedek 1998a: 16). Far more important than this, however, is the fact that the ongoing control of imports and the support of exports continue to be a purely national matter (Epping 1998). With regard to foreign trade beyond the borders of the EU, member countries continue to have considerable autonomy (Woolcock 2000).

46 See Long (1989) and Grafers (1999: 89f.). Article 1, Paragraph 1 of Germany's Foreign Trade Law (*Außenwirtschaftsgesetz*) stipulates: 'In principle trade and commerce with foreign economic areas is free as goods, services, capital, payments or other economic transactions between residents in foreign assets and gold'. In addition, the general constitutional guarantee of liberty (including economic liberty) in Article 2 of the German Basic Law is recognized by courts to confer 'standing to sue' against all governmental restraints of individual liberty including foreign trade restrictions. The Foreign Trade Law was enacted on 28 April 1961. Before it went into effect, the Allies' exchange regulations governed essential sectors of West German foreign trade. The occupying powers applied the US foreign trade principle that 'everything that is not explicitly authorized is prohibited'.

47 The European Court of Justice, too, does not recognize a *right* of individuals to engage in extra-Community trade. Moreover, and in sharp contrast to American practice, there exist no standard procedures for the Commission to arrive at decisions in those fields of commercial policy in which it can act autonomously (Völker 1993: 142).

48 *Arjay Associated Inc.* v. *Bush*, 891 F.2d 891, 898 (1989).

burden of proof rests with government officials, who in each case must determine which ban has been violated. To be able to leave the country, every piece of merchandise – and especially 'intelligent' products – must either be covered by an already existing licence (authorization), or receive one ad hoc. The latter occurs in roughly half of all cases. For exports to developed countries whose relationship to the USA is, in American eyes, a competitive one, and where the USA is concerned to protect its competitive advantages, export licences are required in 90 per cent of all cases (Long 1989: 2).[49] The same competition-driven reservation applies to foreign direct investment. Since 1988, the USA has had its own supervisory and regulatory authority, the Committee on Foreign Investments in the United States (CFIUS), which must be notified of every sizeable foreign investment in the US economy.[50] How can this fundamental difference in trade policy approach be explained?

One possible explanation is that which in recent years has been most criticized with regard to Germany's foreign trade and welfare state status – what Josef Joffe in the *International Herald Tribune* once called the German 'full-income society'. The transfer-intensive welfare state in Germany produces – in contrast to the US case – a trans-sectoral climate of economic security for almost the entire population. Thus in Germany, trade and social policy are institutionally distinct from each other and politically decoupled, whereas in the comparatively underdeveloped US welfare state this is not the case. In Germany, trade policy themes rarely appear on party platforms and play virtually no role in electoral campaigns. They emerge usually only in connection with one of the above-mentioned industries, while in the USA they are omnipresent and a decisive element in candidates' prospects for electoral success. Depending on how the labour market is doing, trade policy either climbs up or down the rungs of the agenda of the White House and Congress. The lower the levels of unemployment, and the better the prospects for earnings, the less attention trade policy receives. Every increase in unemployment, however, is immediately associated with foreign trade and leads to a search for trade policy responses.[51] It is above all the 'third' parties which regularly tap the isolationist mood of large segments of the population and thereby force the two main parties to address the concerns of these voters. In the presidential election of 1992 it was the independent candidate Ross Perot, and in the 1996 campaign the Republican candidate Pat Buchanan, who forced both the Democrats and

49 According to an article in the *New York Times Magazine* (22 October 2000, p. 42), the list of products whose export is banned includes a disposable underwater camera made by Kodak, the Cadillac Deville, inflatable boats and airbags.

50 Originally, the creation of this office was justified in military and national security terms: 'Prudent mergers and acquisitions advisers recommend that investors report acquisitions of any domestic company that has cutting-edge technology or products, even if it does no defense-related business. They also advise reporting investment that the public might construe as being related, even indirectly, to national security' (Kang 1997: 303). The CFIUS thus concerned itself with the sale of a company that grew tulip bulbs. The CFIUS does not, as a rule, block any sale involving foreign direct investment, but it can cause severe delay in such sales, make them more expensive via regulatory fees, or simply serve as a deterrent (cf. *Frankfurter Allgemeine Zeitung* from 25 August 2000, 19: 'Deutsche Telekom muß mit FBI rechnen').

51 Here lies the reason why in the USA, economists' calls for free trade have never been heard. In light of this reality, Krugman considers the obsessive engagement with the theory of free trade to be a 'sociological phenomenon' (1993: 362). His colleague McCulloch characterizes the theory of the absolute preferability of free trade as a 'religion' (1993: 367). Mussa responds to the question concerning the causes of difficulties in the theory's application with the refrain 'jobs, jobs, jobs' (1993: 373).

the Republicans to adopt protectionist trade policy guarantees (Aaronson 1996: 9; 2001). In the 2000 campaign it was the Green Party candidate Ralph Nader who ran on a platform of stronger political control of foreign trade.

Rapidly increasing import penetration of US markets and, with it, much greater dependence on foreign trade, is a comparatively new phenomenon. The sheer magnitude of the US domestic market has always not only provided domestic industry with unique growth opportunities, but also served as a magnet for foreign entrepreneurs. In contrast to US industry, German companies have been strongly export-oriented ever since German unification in 1870. On this ground, there is reason to expect Germany to display greater willingness to accept or at least allow imports in exchange. Yet this was not originally the case. Despite its export orientation, Germany was already raising its customs barriers steadily higher in the early years after the foundation of the Empire. Ultimately, in the wake of the Great Depression, this led to the autarchic economic policy of the National Socialist regime (Hirschman 1980 [1945]). Shielding one's own economy from the welfare-threatening competition of the world market appeared to be part of the logic of the developmental path towards a welfare state, and is reflected most strongly in the fact that hardly any national constitution explicitly protects the transnational exercise of the economic freedoms and property rights of its citizens. In the contemporary view, progress in the area of domestic social integration and political democratization led simultaneously and inevitably to international economic disintegration (Moffat 1928; Carr 1945; Röpke 1942). Even during the first two decades after the Second World War, leading international social scientists ruled out the prospect of a development towards, or a return to, freer trade (Myrdal 1957; Deutsch and Eckstein 1961). In order not to endanger the newly restored democracies of Western Europe in their collective front against the Soviet Union and the Eastern Bloc, priority was given to providing comprehensive social security to citizens (Knorr 1951a). Politicians from across the political spectrum proceeded from the assumption that this priority would preclude any further opening of the economy. Ironically, it was precisely this move towards a 'social market economy' that later allowed governments increasingly to dispense of price controls, quotas and customs duties.[52]

At present, Germans have access to a range of welfare state benefits, which are relatively easy to receive, do not stigmatize and, though means-tested, reach a consider-

[52] One reason why Germany's and Western Europe's agricultural sectors, in which independent family farms predominate, have been granted continued protection is that they had already been subject to state protection to an increasing extent ever since the late nineteenth century. The essentially employee-oriented social insurance schemes, which were vastly expanded from the 1950s, were not a suitable starting point for the social protection of an agricultural sector in which the household and the enterprise are inseparable. Protective agricultural tariffs could thus be justified with socio-political arguments. The organization of economic security through tariffs is, however, usually only *second best*. The incomes of independent family companies can also be protected against loss of income through other instruments – e.g. a type of negative income tax, or private insurance subsidized by the public sector at levels differing by the economic condition of the individual enterprise. Nevertheless, agricultural protectionism was not only transferred to the European level, but also expanded there. The lack of a democratically controlled policy on the European level has made it possible for protectionism to endure not only in the agricultural sector, but also in the coal and steel industries (Rieger 1999b). The share of the electorate that still works in these sectors is so small, and the relative cost of protectionism so absurdly high, that there can be little doubt that in a democratic parliamentary European regime, such protectionism would have virtually no chance of survival.

able share of the middle classes.[53] These programmes provide a measure of economic security outside the labour market. They also help beneficiaries to deal with new challenges, e.g. by allowing them to invest in education and training. Despite several attempts in recent years to sharpen the workfare regulations in German social policy, nearly all wage earners are, for example, covered by unemployment insurance and, subsequently, by unemployment assistance on a temporally unlimited basis. In addition, if they become unemployed, they have access to a broad palette of passive labour market measures, which are equivalent to an activating policy.[54] Even more important is the fact that the labour and social administrations operate independently of each other, both institutionally and financially, and are furthermore federally fragmented. The labour administration belongs neither to the national nor to the communal administration. It is parafiscally organized, and thus located outside government budgets. From a political perspective, it is part of the apparatus of the social partners' autonomous labour market regulation. As a result, for institutional reasons alone, the guidelines and measures aimed at bringing social assistance clients into the labour market are bound to be ineffective. Social assistance case-workers cannot assign jobs to clients and thus have little power to penalize negative behaviour. The engagement of labour market policy and social policy with Germany's economically active population is thus shaped by different actors respectively, whereas in the USA coordinated efforts are under way to subordinate social policy to the labour market.

This rough picture may help explain why German workers, both in principle and in practice, are in favour of free trade. In stark contrast to their US counterparts, German unions do not reject the principle of an open economy; exports mean jobs and imports mean cheaper primary products and consumer goods. Yet this acceptance has its price. Social assistance and the benefits and services provided by the labour administration are, first, components of a very expensive welfare state. In 1996, Germany spent 30.5 per cent of its GNP on social protection (EUROSTAT 1999). Nearly half of this comprised pensions expenditure.

The conclusion that only such an extensive welfare state equipped with these particular emphases is in a position to make tolerable the economic and social risks of global market integration, and thus politically not to obstruct such integration, is not compelling. One should keep in mind that decisions about the forms of German social policy were not made with an eye to foreign trade relations. On the contrary, the fundamental decisions for parafiscal organization, contribution-based financing and a largely decentralized structure express strong reservations vis-à-vis the autocratic order of the *Kaiserreich*. The German states in particular, then, were anxious to avoid grant-

53 Examples are housing allowances (*Wohngeld*), care insurance (*Pflegeversicherung*) and a wide range of government services such as day nurseries (Lampert 1994).

54 The German Council of Economic Experts (1998: 35), which counsels the government in economic policy and produces an Annual Report on the state of the nation's economy, estimates the rate of disguised unemployment – those employed in the secondary labour market, i.e. in positions wholly or partially financed by public funds – compared to that of official unemployment as follows:

	Unemployment	
	official	disguised
Old federal states	9.8	3.6
New federal states	20.1	16.7

ing the federal government its own tax authority, even though it was precisely for his social policy that Bismarck sought to raise income by taxes. It was domestic and, above all, power politics alone that led to the forms of social policy in Germany that still exist today. The same is true of German labour law, which developed well beyond its origins as liberal labour contract law into a comprehensive system of worker protection rights. Over time, both socio-political institutions and labour law have become institutionally independent. One can expect, for the reason above, just as in earlier periods, that changes in the framework conditions of these institutions will have consequences that were originally quite unexpected. Even though in the past these changes have caused massive problems of adaptation, not only for companies but also for social policy, they have not led to decisive changes.

Second, German social policy – and this is decisive for its further consequences in the course of a globalized national economy – influences German companies. With the expensive growth of welfare state benefit systems and the intensification of social-legal regulation of employment contract conditions, social policy became an independent motor for the perpetual creation and destruction of employment positions which is inherent to a dynamic market economy.

In Germany, social policy's function can still be described as guaranteeing a full-income society. Yet not only is the share of the population that profits from this desired goal steadily shrinking; in addition, more and more people are enquiring whether this mission for social policy, in terms of its economic logic, can be sustained. The stability of real wages, despite mass unemployment, shows that the labour market is split between insiders and outsiders. Germany's socio-political arrangements not only exacerbate this division, they are also its prerequisite. The social partners' autonomous regulation of labour markets has increasingly given the impression that their collective bargaining agreements are forged to the detriment of third parties, at whose expense job holders have protected their income levels. In Germany in 1995, 28.9 per cent of workers were organized in unions, yet the contracts concluded by union representatives applied to 90 per cent of the workforce. In the USA, the level of organization is 14 per cent, and collective bargaining coverage is 11 per cent (ILO 1997: tables 1.2, 3.2). The much higher share of long-term unemployed in Germany, which since the early 1980s has always constituted at least one-third of all unemployed persons, shows this ability of the German unions to shape the labour market for the benefit of their members (Paqué 1998: 21; German Council of Economic Experts 1999: 88).[55] Without the parafiscally organized Federal Labour Office's continued generous transfers and the social assistance programme, which is financed mostly by the municipalities, resistance against the current 'autonomous' system of fixing wages would be considerably greater.[56]

The same is true of employment regulation and employees' workplace rights. Rulings by labour courts in particular have strengthened the rights of workers and

[55] In the USA between 1983 and 1993, despite rising unemployment, the share of long-term unemployed among the total unemployed population sank from 20 to 12 per cent (Paqué 1998: 21). For a comparative perspective on union organization, see Western (1997). On the structure of industrial relations in Eastern Germany and their implications for job creation and job destruction, see Schroeder (2000).

[56] Despite claims to the contrary, up to now the majority of company-level tariff agreements, aiming at a better match of labour conditions and labour contracts to the individual and specific needs of companies in economic distress via the introduction of opening and hardship clauses, did not result in more jobs but in more job security for those already in employment.

provided unions with powerful tools with which they can discipline companies for their behaviour in collective bargaining negotiations and in the implementation of collective bargaining agreements (Rüthers 1996).[57] Besides the comparatively high wage levels, this relative overregulation of the German labour market blocks the creation of new jobs. Moreover, wages constitute a major portion of small companies' fixed costs, which are of major significance for the dynamic and highly competitive markets of the service, information and communications industries.

Opportunities for German companies to experiment with new forms and structures of compensation – including tying wages to the performance of the company – are highly constrained by German labour law, labour court decisions and the presence of unions in companies (Badura 1999; Stege 1999). Strategies such as those of the American Nucor Corporation, a very successful new company in the steel industry in the USA, are blocked in Germany by a centralized tariff system. Nominally, Nucor pays its employees only 60 per cent of average wages in the industry, but it effectively doubles this through a performance-based bonus system. Not only the wage structure, but all forms of performance-based or profit-sharing compensation systems must meet with the approval of the two main actors: the employer and employee organizations. The contemporary structure of industrial democracy hinders wage experiments small and large, especially those proposing a mix of market and public-sector sources of income. The latter could be a necessary precondition for the creation of jobs for the hard-to-place unemployed. (On Germany and the broader European context, see Wood 2001a, b; Ebbinghaus and Visser 2000; Esping-Andersen et al. 2000.)

This is not only a result of the current constellation of political forces. Different political-philosophical traditions shape policies and legislation towards markets in both countries. In Germany, the material status of the individual in the context of the collective lies at the centre of social thinking. The individual's consumer needs – or that which is thought to be a legitimate standard of living – shape the direction of politics. The idea of a 'just wage' is still the standard by which the effectiveness of the economy's satisfaction of basic needs is measured. The Schröder government's policy of driving the '630 DM' jobs out of the market by regulating them and making them more expensive, or of at least generating new revenues with which the pension insurance funds could be stabilized, is guided – as is the struggle against 'irregular', i.e. short-term and flexible employment – by conceptions of an economy that is to some extent moulded or organized from above. Herein we see a way of thinking that is oriented towards the status quo. 'Order' is seen as a means of constraining fundamental change and of keeping changes under control. Markets and competition are seen as secondary, for they are open-ended and potentially disruptive. This is not simply because of distrust vis-à-vis markets' ability to generate and distribute income. Rather, there is a deep-seated mistrust of the ethos and manner of how a market economy functions. To base societal organization on the profit motive and shareholder culture is viewed by the majority of Germans as fundamentally immoral. It is not only in present times that it has been a major problem for German social policy that the majority of the population is oriented towards the conception that 'the ultimate and only value by which the conduct of their affairs is to be decided is good administration and

57 According to Bernd Rüthers (1998), a labour lawyer, the case law directing court decisions in conflicts about the labour contract is still guided by the notion of a 'life-long relationship' first developed in the Third Reich.

Table 4.6 A measure of income inequality[a] (Gini-coefficients) in Germany, 1984–1996

	Market income[b]			*Net income*[c]		
	Old Länder	*New Länder*	*Total*	*Old Länder*	*New Länder*	*Total*
1984	0.4371			0.2794		
1988	0.4190			0.2665		
1991	0.4234	0.3928	0.4385	0.2775	0.2183	0.2947
1996[c]	0.4443	0.4754	0.4537	0.2936	0.2441	0.2896

[a] Incomes are equivalence weighted, i.e. the income of the whole household is not simply divided by the number of household members, but weighted by some mostly age-graded factor smaller than one. This procedure responds to economies of scale which increase with household size. Equivalence weighting thus reflects the fact that, for example, a 2-person household does not need 2 but only 1.4 times as much as a 1-person household to attain the same level of need satisfaction
[b] Including employer contributions to social insurance but pre-tax and pre-transfer (i.e. pensions etc.)
[c] Including Migration Sample D

Source: German Council of Economic Experts (1999: 192)

provision for their needs by officials (that is 'good' in the purely technical sense of rational administration)' (Weber 1918a: 158).

This value orientation gives social policy its standards and direction. In terms of its own measure, it has been successful to date. Despite the spatial revolution of the micro- and macro-economy entailed in globalization, social inequalities in Germany have remained fairly stable since the mid-1980s. Table 4.6 depicts the development of the most important measure of inequality, the Gini coefficient.[58] It shows, first of all, the strong influence which the German transfer and tax state has if one observes the difference between market and net incomes. It shows, further, that the increase in inequality is concentrated mainly in eastern Germany and thus reflects a special situation. The most important finding of this table, however, is that inequalities have increased only marginally.

A further measure of inequality is the calculation of proportional values out of different decile boundaries. It can give more precise information concerning whether and in what order of magnitude social inequalities in Germany have changed. The 90:10 ratio, for example, expresses the relation of the income threshold of the ninth decile

[58] The Gini-coefficient is a summary statistic of inequality derived from the Lorenz curve. The Lorenz curve plots cumulative percentages of total income received against cumulative percentages of income recipients, starting with the smallest income recipient. A point on the curve gives the percentage of the population that accounts for a given percentage of total income. The Gini-coefficient gives the area between the observed Lorenz curve and line of absolute equality as a proportion of the total area under the line of absolute equality. The Gini-coefficient has a maximum value of one (absolute inequality) and a minimum of zero (absolute equality).

Table 4.7 Income inequality in Germany: decile shares and decile ratios, 1984–1996 (equivalence-weighted net incomes[a])

	Old Länder				*New Länder*		*Total*	
	1984	*1988*	*1991*	*1996[b]*	*1991*	*1996[b]*	*1991*	*1996[b]*
				Share of deciles[c]				
1.	3.4	3.5	3.1	2.7	4.1	3.4	3.1	2.8
2.	5.3	5.3	5.3	5.1	6.3	5.9	5.0	5.2
3.	6.5	6.6	6.5	6.4	7.4	7.0	6.1	6.5
4.	7.5	7.6	7.4	7.4	8.2	8.1	7.2	7.5
5.	8.4	8.6	8.5	8.4	9.0	8.9	8.2	8.4
6.	9.6	9.6	9.6	9.5	9.8	9.8	9.4	9.4
7.	10.7	10.8	10.8	10.8	10.9	10.9	10.8	10.7
8.	12.1	12.3	12.4	12.6	12.1	12.2	12.6	12.4
9.	14.2	14.5	14.9	15.2	13.7	13.9	15.2	14.9
10.	22.4	21.1	21.4	22.1	18.5	19.8	22.3	22.2
				Decile ratios				
90:10	3.37	3.36	3.54	4.15	2.69	3.00	4.01	3.99
90:50	1.74	1.79	1.83	1.92	1.57	1.62	1.97	1.91
50:10	1.94	1.88	1.94	2.16	1071	1.86	2.04	2.09

[a] On the concept of equivalent income see note a of Table 4.6
[b] Including Migration Sample D
[c] Share of the total equivalent net income held by each decile

Source: German Council of Economic Experts (1999: 193)

to that of the lowest decile.[59] Table 4.7 describes changes during the period 1984–96. These data show that in Germany, if we leave the new federal states aside for a moment, a remarkable stability characterizes the middle range of income recipients. One also observes, however, a considerable decline of equality at the bottom, while relative improvement over time is concentrated in the ninth and tenth deciles. The data for the new federal states reveal a massive shift to the detriment of the lower income classes. If one takes into account that the basis of these changes is the transition from a socialist command to a market economy, the relative stability for the majority of Germans over time is astounding. It is primarily due to the intra-national compensatory transfers and above all to the welfare state maintenance of the greater part of Eastern German income recipients that this revolutionary social transition could proceed stably. Even far more than in the West, in the new federal states wages and income are strongly subject to political manipulation. In the United States, by contrast, the price for labour power, which is determined by market competition, is viewed also normatively as the 'correct' price and as a 'just wage'. For this reason, both individual and collective distributional labour market outcomes are considered in the USA, compared to Germany,

59 The threshold of the first (ninth) decile is defined as the smallest part of income not exceeded by 10 per cent (90 per cent) of the population.

to be far less the responsibility of the political sphere. For US social policy, therefore, only a minimum standard of living – in the form of a minimum wage and a poverty line – is of political relevance. The individual is viewed abstractly, as acting independently on the basis of her own fundamental rights, and as solely responsible for all consequences of her actions.

As Table 4.8 shows, this thoroughly different orientation is reflected also in the far greater scope of inequalities and, above all, in a greater tolerance for increases in inequality in the population. The different methods of data collection and processing make a direct comparison between the two countries difficult. Table 4.8 allows us at least to perceive, however, what, in contrast to the German case, has changed over the course of time. Despite this limited comparability, one can still ascertain that in Germany there are fewer poor and fewer rich. In Table 4.8 two further US peculiarities are striking. First, the progress made by lower income groups between 1949 and 1969 was more than merely reversed in the period that ensued: the lowest 20 per cent of families had in 1996 a smaller share of total income than in 1949. This loss of the terrain that had been won throughout the early 1970s is also reflected in the Gini coefficient. It sinks until 1969 and then rises sharply thereafter. Second, this reverse movement applies to all income groups – with the exception of the wealthiest 20 per cent. The members of these groups have been able to increase their share of national income considerably. Compared to them, the middle-income groups have shown relative stability. Signs of 'American conditions' can be seen, however, in the new federal states, as well as in terms of the risk of social decline for the middle range of incomes. This assessment must be supplemented by three points, though.

First, one must recall the altogether different magnitude of labour market transformation in Germany and the USA. In the USA, the workforce has doubled since the Second World War, while in the Federal Republic it has grown by less than 10 per cent.

Second, in the USA, socio-political progress takes different forms and employs very different mechanisms from those in Germany. On the one hand, states compete fiercely with one another in their regulation of the private market for health insurance benefits. State mandates on which type of preventive medicine companies must offer their female employees, for example, constitute an effective means of attracting scarce human capital in the context of the new interstate competition (Lewin 2000). On the other hand, for the same reason, corporate personnel departments have become very

Table 4.8 Shares of aggregate family incomes in the USA, in quintiles, 1947–1996

Year	*(Bottom)* *1.*	*2.*	*Quintile* *3.*	*4.*	*(Top)* *5.*	*Top 5%*	*Gini-coefficient*
1947	5.0	11.9	17.0	23.1	43.0	17.5	0.376
1949	4.5	11.9	17.3	23.5	42.7	16.9	0.378
1959	4.9	12.3	17.9	23.8	41.1	15.9	0.361
1969	5.6	12.4	17.7	23.7	40.6	15.6	0.349
1979	5.4	11.6	17.5	24.1	41.4	15.3	0.365
1989	4.6	10.6	16.5	23.7	44.6	17.9	0.401
1996	4.2	10.0	15.8	23.1	46.8	20.3	0.425

Source: Levy (1998: 199)

creative at using insurance benefits to bind workers to the company. The health insurance benefits of the three major auto manufacturers, for example, now extend coverage to their employees' same-sex life partners (Swoboda 2000). Ford Motor Company estimates that the additional costs of this coverage amount to $5 million annually. Compared to the $2.4 billion that Ford spends on health insurance and health care benefits, this does not seem like a lot of money. It looks like a very large sum, however, when one considers the conservative climate of opinion in the USA and the constraints this imposes on federal social policy. A national health insurance bill containing such provisions would have no chance of passage. Furthermore, there is another mechanism that drives corporate employee benefit plans, so that their effect is widespread, allowing them to grow regularly and rapidly beyond their initial personnel policy motives and specific labour market causes (Halaby 1986; Dobbin et al. 1993; Sutton et al. 1994). This essentially market-mediated progress in social policy has a disproportionally strong and enduring effect because the companies must offer their social benefit packages to all employees in order not to run the risk of being sued for employee discrimination. The decisive levers are the Civil Rights Act of 1964 and the related Equal Employment Opportunity legislation. The latter permits individual employees to use the courts to force changes in working conditions, including employee benefits.[60] The explosion in the costs of corporate health benefits in recent years can be attributed to a considerable extent to these social rights, which are largely beyond political control and have been forcibly expanded by an independent judiciary (Freudenheim 2000; Verhovek 2000).

Third, there is a flip side to these new forms of progress in labour and social insurance law. Besides the civil law possibilities for winning economic rights for workers, in the last two decades state legislation, and to some extent court decisions, have weakened the traditional foundation of the freedom of the employment contract – the 'employment at will' doctrine – and mitigated it with rights of appeal in the case of 'unfair dismissal' (Lazear 1990; A. B. Krueger 1991; Miles 2000). This legal development brings with it an increased risk to employers of being sued when they terminate an employee's contract. Companies have responded to this by hiring temporary workers and making use of short-term employment contracts – i.e. seeking workers who are not covered by this new labour and social insurance law. Since 1979, this segment of the US labour market has grown five times as fast as the labour market on the whole (Autor 2000). Thus, in the low-wage sectors, temporary and short-term labour contracts predominate, because companies want to avoid the additional costs of the new social insurance law mandates imposed upon them primarily by the courts. This corporate reaction is arguably the main reason why employee benefits have remained limited to the higher income groups. Thus, in the USA as well as in Germany, legislation and court rulings aimed at enhancing the social rights of the economically most vulnerable workers end up producing precisely the opposite effect.

60 In addition to the two already mentioned laws, other laws useful to employees for pressing the courts regarding their social and economic rights are the Equal Pay Act (1963), the Age Discrimination in Employment Act (1967), the Rehabilitation Act (1973) and the Americans with Disability Act (1990). The effectiveness of these laws owes a good deal to the amendment of the Civil Rights Act in 1991, which allows for punitive damages and thus sends strong signals to employers about permissible personnel policy, forcing them to adopt a more progressive stance in human resource management. For a view on the populist leaning of the American judiciary, see Sherwin (2000); for a broad and critical overview, see Nivola (1997).

5 The Social Arithmetic of Welfare Democracies

The differences between Germany and the USA, in terms of both their labour markets and the dynamics and forms of their social policy reforms, could, perhaps, be explained by the different states of their economic development. On the path to a service and information economy, Germany is a latecomer. In the USA, between 1973 and 1993 the share of the economically active population employed in industry sank from 33 to 24 per cent; in Germany during the same period, it sank from 47 to 37 per cent (Paqué 1998: 26). One could argue that as a result of these sectoral emphases in the German economy, the nature of companies' organization and employment positions are not (yet) advanced enough to give new forms of social policy – market-based, incentive-oriented, rule-oriented and selective – sufficiently fertile ground and impetus for growth. In this view, the transition would be only a matter of time and not a problem in itself. Sooner or later, all developed welfare states would follow the path towards a market-oriented – or at least a market-adequate – production of social policy goods and, in the process, design their remaining welfare state benefits in a more selective and decentralized fashion.

Germany's social structure differs, however, in several fundamental ways from that of the USA, buttressing its traditional forms of social policy organization and impeding reform. Demographic conditions favour the current structure of the social pension and health insurance schemes. The combined effect of the epochal demographic transition to a top-heavy, i.e. rapidly greying, population and quasi-universalist social insurance schemes leads to a strong equi-directionality of interests and political orientations – which imbues reflection on new socio-political paths with a conservative hue.[61] Old-age pensioners in Germany make up 24.8 per cent of the total population and are thereby the largest single-issue constituency. In electoral terms, they are matched by a labour force that constitutes 40.7 per cent of the population.[62] However, among economically active individuals there are fundamental differences in the types of employment relations that obtain. In absolute numbers, as well as 20 million old-age pensioners, there are also 21 million individuals employed in the private sector in the production of goods. Of these, 12 million are active in service industries or in commerce. Only this private sector group is dependent, using a phrase coined by Hans

[61] In a more theoretical perspective, it could be argued that the much greater spread of incomes in the USA should help politicians to win over some parts of the publicly insured employees for a decrease in the coverage of social security, i.e. old-age insurance and Medicare, and thus to participate in a system providing retirement security via competitive markets, promising a higher return on their 'investment'. The two probably most important reasons why this shift has not happened to date is, first, the dramatically increased income insecurity in the past two decades, limiting the potential for private, or market-based strategies to provide for long-term retirement security, and, second, the sharply amplified volatility of the stock market since the beginning of 2001. In addition, for several years now the American saving rate has been negative. This fact indicates, first, that social security as forced saving is still the most reliable way for American society to provide for old age, and, second, that the distribution of wealth is much more unequal than income distribution. Data from 1992 show that a quarter of American households reach retirement with little or no wealth at all, and that half of all households do not hold any of the assets that have delivered relatively high returns, i.e. neither bonds and stocks, nor real estate or businesses (Lusardi 2001).

[62] These and the following figures are from the *Statistical Yearbook of the Federal Republic* and cover the year 1998 (see Statistisches Bundesamt 2000).

Rosenberg, on the 'anonymous social policy of the market' (1976 [1967]: 217). In light of the relative homogeneity of societal interests, it is no coincidence that the two major German parties differ only marginally in their positions on pension reform, and that only the smaller and far more programmatic parties – the Liberals and the Greens – attempt to change the status quo by proposing market solutions or a basic pension.

A second factor that constrains a more radical departure from social policy reform is the vast number of people who work in the administration of the various components of the German welfare state. If one adds together those employed in the public sector, the health sector and the administrations of the social insurance schemes, it amounts to nearly 8 million employees. In order to achieve passage of a reform in the direction of more market-oriented and selective welfare state programmes, these groups would have to be convinced that it would not be at their expense. At present, there is not even a discussion about how one might win over these politically decisive groups for such a reform initiative. They need not even explicitly exercise their political power as an interest and electoral group, for party competition by itself and in its own way manages to protect their employment enclaves. In 1999, for example, the Bavarian governor Edmund Stoiber, faced with a proposed health and pension insurance reform – initiated by his party ally Horst Seehofer during his tenure as Federal Health Minister – which would restrict access to spa treatment and thus cost some jobs in his state, decided to veto the measure. Moreover, Germany's mass unemployment, which extends into the middle classes, is not particularly conducive to large-scale experiments in labour market policies.

The social-structural scope of social insurance schemes thus helps determine the magnitude of the transition costs, and these – in an environment of party competition – can be not only considerable, but also prohibitive. Moreover, the degree of homogeneity of those social groups that owe their jobs to the state determines the choice of social policy innovations. The more universal and the more centralized welfare state benefit schemes are, the greater will be the political costs of a transition to a new order. If, as in the case of highly unified institutional structures, there is only a small number of welfare state programmes, there are limited opportunities for institutional experimentation and learning. If systems are more fragmented and their administrative structures more decentralized, as in the case of the USA, then a more rapid adjustment to changes in the economic environment can be expected. Social policy innovations can then cross the boundary more rapidly not only between the public and private production of socio-political goods, but also those of political geography (Inman and Rubinfeld 1997a, b; Oates 1999). Federal structures can be conducive to not only democratic, but also social policy experimentation, and thus can lower the risks of undesirable developments on the national level (Osborne 1988).[63] For this reason, one

[63] A counter-position is argued by Donna Shalala, Secretary of Health and Human Services in both of President Clinton's terms of office. She defends 'big government' as a necessary corrective, in terms of the national polity, to the irresponsible results of American federalism: '"To me, it's a fundamental debate about federalism", she said. "It depends on what you believe you should have a national government for. I believe that justice and opportunity ought not to be determined by geography – or by country of origin or by your parent's income." The federal role, she argued, "is to reduce variation." To conservatives, of course, that sounds like redistribution of resources."That's exactly what we're talking about," Dr. Shalala said, with nary a flinch. "*Redistribution defines us as a country*. That's what the national government does. But it ought to be in a limited way, just for the fundamentals. And in debating what those fundamentals are, we define what the country is about, what our character is about, what we care about"' (Toner 2001; emphasis added).

can also expect that in the USA the above-sketched 'perverse' effects of enhancing worker rights via state legislation and court decisions will unleash a counter-movement. There are two further reasons why this is likely: first, unions are now too weak to push through a national response, and, second, achieving a federal harmonization of labour law is politically impossible.

In the face of the ostensibly compelling demands of globalization, German politics attempts, to whatever extent possible, to preserve the institutions of the welfare state (Alber 2001c). Even minor deregulatory initiatives, such as those enacted by the Kohl government just prior to the change of government, which were part of a programmatic adaptation to the new global market conditions – chiefly the easing of protections against dismissal and the introduction of a demographic factor into the pension formula – were denounced by Social Democrats in the election campaign of 1998. The promise to return to the *status quo ante* by way of 'counter-reforms' was one of the pillars of the Social Democratic success, and the cautious reformatory measures of the Kohl government were subsequently overturned upon victory.

This is not simply a matter of a small transfer of electoral votes between the two major parties. The language of class conflict and class struggle is being revived, together with its welfare state slogans. Whereas in 1980 only 25 per cent of Germans surveyed believed that a 'class-struggle' and 'irresolvable conflicts' existed between employers and employees, this figure had climbed by 1997 to 44 per cent (Noelle-Neumann 1998). This could give a misleading impression of actual attitudes, however. Jan Ross's assessment in *DIE ZEIT* (1999) is probably more accurate: the overall situation, of which the electoral victory of the Social Democrats is only a part, is shaped by the fact that in the struggle between the market and the welfare state, the latter has maintained the upper hand – equality has prevailed. If one follows Tocqueville's expositions of the 'democratic passion for equality', this outcome appears less surprising. On the contrary, his reflections lead one to expect that an increase in inequalities in the economic sphere would lead to a far greater equalizing counter-movement in the political sphere – if the political preconditions for this are in place. Globalization, then, following this sociological expectation, should lead to more, not less, social policy, for it occasions an enhanced, material interest in state authority. The truly interesting question, therefore, is why in the United States this equalizing reaction of the welfare state has not materialized.[64] The key to answering this question is what John E. Cairnes termed 'non-competing groups' (1874: 71–4). Their income is largely immune to the vicissitudes of the market.

The pivotal struggles occur between those who have a strong interest in the continuation of social policy or for other reasons have no reason to fear wage competition, and those who want to – or are compelled to – seek their opportunities in the marketplace. In Germany, the former group is numerically much stronger, and because of the equi-directionality of their interests it is an easy target for mobilization in favour of the status quo. It includes not only pensioners and beneficiaries of long-term trans-

[64] This perspective was first put forward by Felix Somary (1929). He discussed the welfare state realities of the Weimar Republic in terms of 'democratic socialism'. Future-directed against present-day-directed interests don't carry much weight for low-income groups and those in old age. To reduce consumption in order to save presupposes a sufficiently high income and strong intergenerational family bonds. He also pointed out, however, that a high degree of wealth inequality facilitates investments and is thus conducive to higher growth rates of the economy.

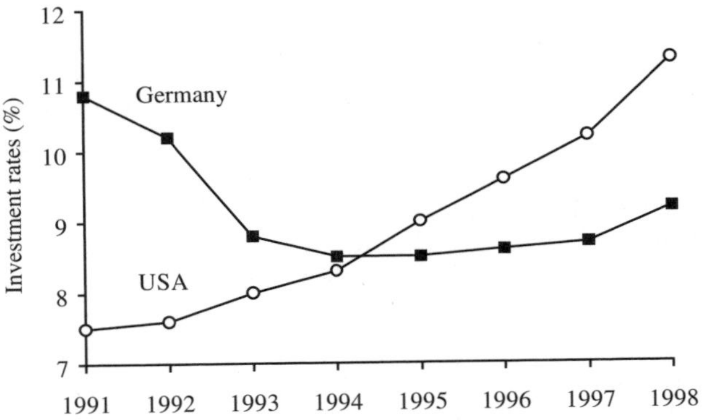

Figure 4.3 Investment rates in Germany and the USA[1]

[1] Real production investment as % of real GDP

Source: German Council of Economic Experts (1998: 69)

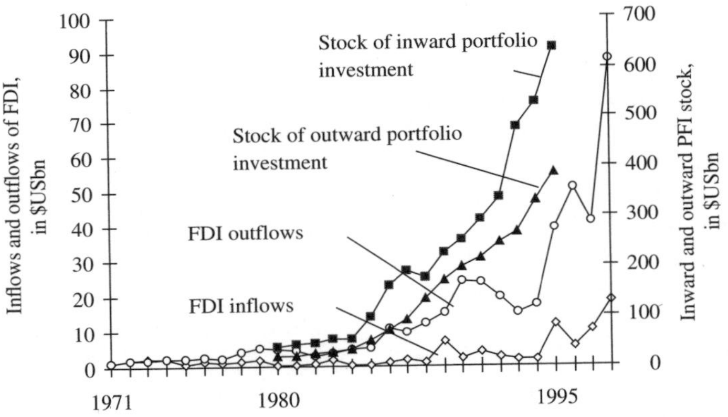

Figure 4.4 Germany in the global economy: influx and outflow of foreign direct investment (FDI) and the change in stock of domestic and foreign portfolio investment (PFI), 1971–1998

Source: IMF (1999a: 458f.)

fers, but also all those who can reckon with fairly secure incomes through fixed fee schedules or, in the case of farmers, a nearly total economic regulation.

For a democratically organized society, the numerical preponderance of these groups means that, very probably, future welfare will be sacrificed for that of the present. Public expenditure which is essential to productivity but which has only long-term effects, e.g. for infrastructure, education and research, tends, due to the logic of a parliamentary democracy, to be displaced by spending on consumption whenever the size of the non-competing groups becomes so large that their interests become determinant. This problem of strongly discounting the future is exacerbated by the fact that public investments also strongly influence private investment behaviour, for private capital becomes productive only with the help of non-private infrastructure. In figure 4.3 we depict the reverse trends in the development of investment rates in Germany and the US. As this and figure 4.4 show, long-term-oriented venture capital is increasingly migrating out of Germany. Socio-political and labour-law conditions constitute only one factor among many influencing rates of investment (depicted in figure 4.3) and international movements of investment capital (depicted in figure 4.4). Such highly aggregated indicators can easily hide conflicting tendencies, for many decisions made independently from one another flow into them. Social policy and labour law do at the very least have effects that are relevant to investment decisions, and capital movements express a judgement about welfare state conditions, i.e. about how the institutions of social and labour market policy are used to respond to new framework conditions of economic action.

Compared to the US case, the far greater emigration of venture capital out of Germany is striking. Total foreign direct investment in Germany in 1995 amounted to just under 4 per cent of GNP. Contrary to venture capital, however, portfolio capital seems to see Germany as an attractive investment location. The total stock of portfolio capital in 1995 equalled roughly 26 per cent of GNP. This difference reflects the greater orientation towards the present in the German national economic culture.

Despite the global market economy, then, domestic societal relations still determine the political answers to the new challenges and thus legislation as well. The rules of the democratic game dictate that it is elections that, with their strictly numerical calculus, decide the direction of societal development. Parties orient themselves to the composition of the electorate and to the identity of the median – or even pivotal[65] – citizen, who is decisive in election campaigns. For example, Paul Pierson's calculations of the size of major welfare state clientele as a proportion of the electorare showed that it is quite low in the United States (32.9 per cent), around 50 per cent in Germany and reaches 57.3 per cent in Sweden (Pierson 2001: 413).[66] In all European countries the fraction of the adult population, and approximately also of the electorate, whose income is almost completely determined by political expenditure decisions, is higher than 50 per cent. One should not forget that politicians still have only a domestic power basis, whereas companies have no choice but to look outward. Contrary to economic markets, political markets are exclusively reserved for citizens of the nation-state.

6 Outlook

'The trial by market everything must come to', wrote the poet Robert Frost (1916: 106). Yet this does not mean that the market can compel a specific decision. Robert Frost did not sell his Christmas trees, which are the subject of his poem, at the price offered by the visitor from the city. That was his decision. And he knew the opportunity costs of his choice.

The interdependent markets on which global capitalism is based disclose the economic and social costs of national social policies. By itself, however, this abstract truth is devoid of empirical content. If we restrict our analysis to the costs of doing business in mature welfare states that have risen relatively due to the technological revo-

[65] In his theory of the 'pivotal actor', Pierson (2001: 417–19) sees much less viable space for policy reform than the median-voter and 'minimum-winning-coalition' argument grants.

[66] Pierson's calculations are quite conservative. The much more detailed statistical analysis of Lindbeck for Sweden shows a ratio of tax-financed to market-financed individuals of 1.83 for the year 1995. In 1960, this ratio was 0.382, and in 1990 it was 1.51 (1997: 1279).

lutions, it is indeed true that political leaders in these countries can no longer make decisions on national economic and social policy without taking into account the reactions of world markets. Yet this is just as meaningless – in a literal sense – as it is true. Governments can, but are not obliged to, obey the price signals of the global economy for their labour and social policy. Two further difficulties characterize welfare state politics in the age of globalization. First, the very same signals of global capitalism and the world market mean different things to different people. And this is pivotal. One and the same situation does not look the same to people situated differently in the social structure. For some, it proves the need for more, for others, for less social policy. This fundamental ambiguity of the challenge of global capitalism means – and this is the second problem – that the contents and the pace of socio-political reforms in all probability are not determined by an economic rationality calculus alone. In a democracy, it is not the 'geometric truth' of arguments – no matter how convincing they may be on theoretical terms – that is decisive, but the number of votes that competing political positions can muster. Citizens act and vote based on their own personal truths and interests, and these can be the complete opposite of that which globalization and socio-political reform suggest as necessary for securing society's future.

In the process, 'welfare' can thus easily fall by the wayside. Even welfare democracy is no guarantee for the persistence of welfare statism. Societal decisions on public welfare are not the same as the aggregation of individual interests via the market mechanism, and they are also somewhat different from the political decisions of a majoritarian democracy. In contrast to the market, the point of departure and reference for the welfare state is that the value of the individual is not reducible to his market value. An essential element of the welfare state is taking goods and services – including 'incomes' – out of the market, or at least controlling or modifying the market's effects on the distribution of goods, services and incomes. At the heart of social policy lies the concern to achieve outcomes that the market itself, left to its own devices, would not have produced (Marshall 1985 [1965]: 15). Welfare states today are welfare democracies. Every social policy is preceded and followed by elections. There is no reason to assume, however, that this political, democratic mechanism enables the body politic to ascertain with sufficient certainty, and to implement, that which is indeed necessary in the field of social policy. Democratic vote-casting is just as oriented towards self-interest as is the ostensibly egotistical behaviour of the market citizen.

There is no denying that globalization forces its own agenda. The outcomes of reform policy, however, might very well be quite different from what many wish for – or fear. Democratic politics has always been characterized by unpredictability, for the rules of the game do not determine the substance, but merely the form of political action. And these forms can maximize a highly heterogeneous input. Thus the probability of democratic reform policy leading, for example, to precisely those outcomes that some consider under conditions of globalization to be clearly compelled by economic reason is very low. There is no cause, however, for premature pessimism – or optimism. This is true, first, because an additional feature of democratic politics is that it can always correct its negative outcomes, and, second, because the realm of that which is politically disposable and fashionable is always limited. For this reason, there is always a possibility that economy and society are successful precisely in nullifying political designs and interventions. In any case, and this point is not to be underestimated, this general demand for more, not less, politics is – despite conflicting goals depending on the political faction – a double-edged sword. Guests can show up at this party who were not on anybody's list. In a democracy, the guests are not only fundamentally equal in status, they are also the final arbitrator and, ultimately, determine the direction of politics.

The signals of the global market economy mean something different – and inspire different political responses – for each affected group, depending on its social-structural status. It is a grave error to believe that the ostensibly obvious realities of the new economy set indisputable parameters for reform to which politicians must now orient their decisions. The expansion of the welfare state has led to a condition in developed economies in which social policy and the market constitute alternative determinants of individuals' life situations (Janowitz 1976). For this reason the realities of global market integration are simultaneously welcomed and bemoaned. The conception that these new realities are unarguable normative standards, to which politicians should orient themselves in the interest of the public welfare, is an illusion. Expanding the global market economy and improving the prospects of sustaining it constitute merely one among many other equally conceivable objectives. This competes with a plethora of other goals. From a social science perspective, there are no grounds for considering one or the other to be meaningless per se. As Max Weber noted:

> The distinctive characteristic of a problem of social *policy* is indeed the fact that it cannot be resolved merely on the basis of purely technical considerations which assume already settled ends. Normative standards of value can and must be objects of *dispute* in a discussion of a problem of social policy because the problem lies in the domain of general *cultural* values. (1904: 56)

By its very nature, social policy reform involves culture wars. It entails decisions about core societal values. The reform proposals of every side 'really', and not just 'fictitiously', seek to increase welfare. All parties involved claim this for themselves. Social science can merely, first, attempt to make clear to all parties in the course of a social policy reform that all action and non-action in pursuit of a desired goal brings with it more or less high costs in the sense of predictable losses vis-à-vis other goals. Which goal political actors should focus upon is a question that cannot be resolved by science. Once a goal *is* decided upon, social science can help, second, to bring about more political realism about welfare state reform in the sense that it can develop a conception as to how this goal can be achieved. Of crucial importance here is a rational calculus not only with regard to the objective condition of the market economy and the strength of the interests of those who profit from it, but also concerning the potential resistance of those who will be negatively affected by a reform and are in a position to obstruct it.

5

The Welfare State and Social Policy in East Asia: Religion and Globalization

No one can understand what makes the present age what it is. They are mystified by certain insistencies.
William Carlos Williams 1986 [1927]: 272

1 East Asia as a Challenge for Comparative Welfare State Research

Because of the 'Asian miracle', the surprising fact of overcoming the barriers to development, there has been strong academic and political interest in the role of the state in the economic rise first of Japan and then of the East Asian rim countries, i.e. South Korea and Taiwan as well as the city-states Singapore and Hong Kong. One aspect of this development remains insufficiently addressed, however – social policy. For many, the astounding economic success of these countries serves as proof not only of the superiority of Western market institutions, but also of the feasibility, if not inevitability, of transferring them to non-Western cultures and social environments. But, in this West–East context, the development of social policy and the welfare state has for a long time been neglected by social science research. Moreover, since it was the active authoritarian state, the near-absolute rule by officials, that was seen – and more often than not expressly praised – as the central agent in bringing about the economic miracle in Japan and the 'four tigers', globalization, with its claim on the unavoidable 'end of the nation-state', should have had a much deeper impact in East Asia than in the developed Western countries with their more clearly marked-off and thus more autonomous economic sphere. Furthermore, since they stress familism, group obligation and communitarian concepts of social order, and since they rely much more on occupational, i.e. company-provided, welfare, East Asian welfare states should be particularly pressed to rebuild their social policies according to Western lines, because, as is often alleged, they run counter to those values that are functional for a globalized market economy. As Max Weber implied, group-oriented loyalty and the market are antithetical, and so he pointed out that 'the great achievement of . . . the ethical and ascetic sects of Protestantism was to shatter the fetters of the sib' (Weber 1951 [1915]: 237).

A short glance at OECD or IMF statistics already shows that the course of welfare state development in East Asia did not follow the path of Western modernization. In addition, judging from international newspapers and journals such as *The Financial Times*, the *Wall Street Journal*, the *New York Times*, *The Economist* or even the *Far Eastern Economic Review*, social policy in East Asia is not exactly headline-grabbing. It is, rather, a part of low not of high politics. This is surprising, even more so because exponents of modernization theory claim that here we have the confirmation of our postulate of a systemic relationship between the development of a free-market economy and a liberal, representative democracy – that is, between two out of the three core elements of modern or, rather, Western societies.[1] For this reason, the question of social policy in these countries is of signal sociological interest because the answer may shed new light on the power of and the limits to economic globalization.

Modernization theory assumes that a country's political constitution directly influences its welfare state development. The core mechanism of representative democracy – party competition for electoral votes – was already considered by Schumpeter to be an *independent*, not merely a derivative, motor of social policy (1950 [1942]: 208). South Korea in particular and, to a lesser extent, Taiwan are treated as dream cases of political modernization theory (Przeworski and Limongi 1997: 162). But the welfare state itself, independent of the respective form of political constitution, is also considered in modernization theory to be a *systemic* element of a comprehensive, functionally differentiated and interdependent structure of developed societies. Variants of this theory may differ in how they locate the origins of the welfare state, in their positioning of it in the stages of societal modernization and in the mechanisms to which they attribute its rise and expansion (Flora and Heidenheimer 1981; Alber 1987; Swaan 1988; P. Baldwin 1990; Esping-Andersen 1990). Yet the exponents of theories of modernization agree on one point: the welfare state as an autonomous sphere, like parliamentary democracy and a liberal market economy, is a necessary and inevitable product of modernization (Flora et al. 1977; Ashford 1986: 300–18; Rose and Shiratori 1986).

The development of the Western European and North American welfare states appears to prove them right. The welfare state as a systematic, state-organized institution – which intervenes in society to minimize the material consequences of social and biological risks and to correct deficits in the exterior circumstances of life, performs social services and financially helps meet existential needs – has become an essential component of the Western model of democracy and the market economy. It is, of course, debatable whether welfare state regulations and systems of intervention and transfer are – in their contemporary scale and scope – indispensable, existential and functional features of a society characterized by democracy and a market economy. Unquestionable, however, is the fact that their institutionalization and continued expansion constitute a general phenomenon, at least in Western industrial countries. Despite national differences in the organization and scope of intervention, *all* these countries have aggrandized social policy as an institutionally and politically independent field of activity in response to purportedly general problems of societal development. Because of this sweeping transformation, three groups of question concerning social policy and the welfare state in East Asia arise:

1 What institutional social policy structures can be found there? And which material and political resources were available for the implementation of social policies?
2 How effective have the dynamics of social politics been in enforcing social rights? Or how do East Asian social policies differ from those in the West?

[1] For an argument to distinguish between modernization and Westernization, see Huntington (1996: 101). Modernization includes industrialization, urbanization, the spread of literacy and education and an increase in social mobility. The basic cultural features of the West are the separation of spiritual and 'worldly' authority, individualism, the stress on rationality, the rule of law and representative politics.

3 How can these differences be explained? And, closely related, what impact does economic globalization have on them?

The answers offered here are, in abridged form: first, East Asian socio-political institutions are more restricted, group-bound and particularistic than their Western counterparts. Second, these institutions lack key psychological, sociological and political motors that drive welfare state development in the West. Third, Confucian culture can be identified as the fundamental cause of an independent path of welfare state evolution in East Asia. We suggest, therefore, that economic globalization sharpens rather than mitigates the distinctiveness of social policy structures in East Asia, in particular their low political profile. Globalization, we will argue, involves mobilizing cross-country differences as much as it dissolves them, adjudicates rather than overrides contrasts, or forces them into some pallid ecumenical whole. In short, *this exploration comes to the conclusion that the distinctive course of welfare state development in the West should be traced to particularities in religious formation and development*, just as it should in East Asia. The prominent role and particular dynamic of social policy in Western industrial societies has specifically Judaeo-Christian roots. Western values have decisively shaped the social politics of *Western* countries and continue to do so, but they have been unable to leave a decisive mark on social politics in East Asia. In East Asia, the Confucian elements of social organization and culture have (until now) impeded a more far-reaching institutionalization of social policy as an *independent* formative power vis-à-vis economy and society.

Section 2 depicts modernization theory's account of the driving forces of and formative influences on welfare state development. In section 3 we will describe the main institutional features of social policy in East Asia and highlight the chief differences between the paths of welfare state development and regulation as posited by modernization theory, on the one hand, and the actual patterns of socio-political intervention in East Asia, on the other. We argue that these are not merely developmental, transitory differences, but they are due to a systematically rooted discrepancy in the basic organization of social policy. Confucian norms and values are adduced as the reason for this special path of development (section 4). Certain features of Confucian ethics strongly limit, as remains to be shown, the development of an autonomous state social policy along Western lines. These same norms and values, however, made possible a highly successful economic policy and corporate organization. Thus it is not culture per se that explains patterns in welfare state building, but their social, political and economic advantage. At the same time, though, there are indications that the impact of Confucian ethics on the development of a market economy in East Asia and on companies' ability to adapt to change has not been exclusively positive. Conversely, an examination of East Asian culture in terms of its significance for social policy yields an insight into the way in which, in the West, the norms and value determinations of Judaeo-Christian ethics have shaped the development of the welfare state and have independently affected the course of economic development. We will also attempt to show how, and to what extent, the Western model of development – and the modernization theory predicated upon it – is, despite marked changes and permutations, *dependent* upon, and shaped by, *Judaeo-Christian* traditions. Finally, we pose a series of questions that emerge from the above analysis: what are the chances of the East Asian variants of social policy and the welfare state of endurance and survival, i.e. what potential for adaptation do they possess, in the face of the new, partially endogenous, partially exogenous challenges to East Asian economic policy and corporate organizational structures posed by globalization (section 5)?

Three additional explanatory remarks concerning the design of this chapter appear to be in order. The first concerns the selection of countries. The second addresses the actual and assumed problems with cultural explanations, i.e. the *causal* treatment of ethics and religion in the context of *empirical* investigations. And the third remark underscores the preliminary and speculative character of the reflections presented here.

In this book, Hong Kong, Singapore, South Korea, Taiwan and Japan are collectively referred to as 'East Asia', even though, geographically, this is not entirely accurate. Further, we include Japan, a country whose social policy is characterized by a rather long developmental history – not only by East Asian standards – and whose economy is comparatively well advanced. This grouping of countries is permissible insofar as we are concerned only with the general features of their socio-political development. We limit our analysis to the key institutional foundations of social policy in these countries, as well as to the dynamics and autonomy of their development. We are not investigating the quantitative aspects or attempting to explain the concrete institutional arrangements of their welfare states, nor are we detailing the history of particular social policies. The impetus for our line of enquiry was the remarkable economic success story of this group of countries, which gave rise to the question: 'How did Japan and the four little dragons achieve such a rapid industrial transformation? Why did a few peninsulas and islands, dots on the East Asian periphery, gain such Promethean energy and accomplish so much at this particular time?' (E. Vogel 1991: 1). A priori there is no reason to believe that a plausible explanation of the peculiar economic path of development of this group of countries might not also yield an explanation of their socio-political peculiarities – and vice versa.

Cultural explanations have a bad reputation, often for good reason. First, cultural factors, be they 'values' and 'norms' in general or 'ethics' and 'religion' in particular, are typically invoked in attempts to explain economic development and structural formation in an ad hoc fashion, as a *deus ex machina* (Boudon and Bourricaud 1992: 659). 'Culture' is thereby often placed in opposition to 'economy'. Analytically, however, it is hardly fruitful to perceive of these as separate, free-standing entities.[2] More promising are approaches that comprehend these two moments as distinct and independent expressions of *one* reality, to be addressed in *one* framework.[3] In other words, it is not very sensible to situate 'economic' in opposition

[2] Such an ontological point of view has been suggested, for example, by Peter Koslowski: 'Ethics are the corrective and the compensation for market failures, religion the corrective and the compensation for ethical failures' (1988: 40). Micro-analytically, this requires the postulation of an independent 'ethical will' as the carrier of ethical action and as a normative instance of appeal for ethical behaviour.

[3] Religion and ethics as particular types of social action and organization thus become topics of an 'empirical science of concrete reality: Our aim is the understanding of the characteristic uniqueness of the reality in which we move. We wish to understand on the one hand the relationships and the cultural significance of individual events in their contemporary manifestations and on the other the causes of their being historically so and not otherwise' (Weber 1904: 72). On the fundamental difference between the (subjective) validity of normative postulates and the (objective) soundness of determinations of fact, which forms the point of departure for empirical research, Weber observes: 'The fact that one investigates the influence of certain ethical or religious convictions on economic life and estimates it to be large under

to 'non-economic' values and then try to measure their relative strength. In point of fact, there are *only* non-economic values. Economics is not a value in and of itself. As a technique, it is a way of weighing one value against another, to help in decisions on the distribution of limited resources between different uses, and as a positive science it tries to establish the causal significance of values (Hayek 1935: 121; Sowell 2000: 305).

Second, in cultural explanations the relationship between ideas and interests often remains obscure, as do the mechanisms of their mediation. Immediate plausibility and anecdotal evidence often play a larger role than do the systematic generation of hypotheses and their empirical testing. Values, as other phenomena, do not impact behaviour in an unmediated way; no 'organizationless self-enforcement' of their norms occurs (Troeltsch 1994 [1912]: 981). The misleading opposition of 'ideas' and 'interests' divides science into (hermeneutic) *Verstehen* (understanding) and (objectivistic) *Erklären* (explanation), which is methodologically rather fruitless.[4]

Third, *culturalist* explanations are commonly based on ideal-typical stylizations. They proceed – especially in discussions of religion – from ideological systems, which are logically closed, essentially static and cut off from the profane world (Boudon and Bourricaud 1992: 283–90). For this reason, attempts to (re)construct cultural factors often become highly ahistorical and tautological. Authors tend not to be interested in the empirically observable consequences of culture and religion, but in their theoretically derived ethics, without any notion about how and when they shape reasoning and motivation. This is misleading for several reasons. First of all, systems of practical ethics, no matter how other-worldly and abstract their orientation, are also and always concerned with this world.[5] For this reason, we are interested here in culture as a complex of *actual* determinants of human conduct. Likewise, 'religion' for us denotes the conditions and effects of a particular type of social action. Second, cultures are often contradictory and thus open to opposing interpretations (W. James 1987

---

certain circumstances does not, for instance, imply the necessity of sharing or even esteeming those casually very significant convictions' (Weber 1917a: 12). Of importance here is thus not what is 'true' or 'false' with a view to the success of economic development and the stability of a political order, nor the 'better' or 'worse' of ethical norms and social principles. These normative facts are just empirical material and as such are accessible to value-neutral observation.

4 A description and critique of the current renaissance of these old conflicts in the field of cultural history can be found in Nitschke (1996). Max Weber's well-known formula points to one way of overcoming this opposition: 'Not ideas, but ideal and material interests, directly govern men's conduct. Yet very frequently the "world images" that have been created by "ideas" have, like switchmen, determined the tracks along which action has been pushed by the dynamic of interests' (Weber 1920: 280). For Weber, there is also in economic action a place for 'ideal' interests: 'All economic activity in a market economy is undertaken and carried through by individuals acting to provide for their own ideal and material interests' (Weber 1978: 202). However, he also stressed that 'religious or magical behavior or thinking must not be set apart from the range of everyday purposive conduct, particularly since even the ends of the religious and magical actions are predominantly economic' (ibid.: 400). For a more elaborate discussion of Weber's approach to ideas and culture, see Lepsius (1986). For a critique of Western reifications and projections in the treatment of 'other' religions, see Benz (1959) and Matthes (1993).

5 William James made the same point when he noted the *empirical* evolution of religion: 'Religions have *approved* themselves; they have ministered to sundry vital needs which they found reigning' (1987 [1901–2]: 303).

[1901–2]: 478; Simmel 1984: 100).[6] Moreover, the meaning of their component parts can change over the course of time, and is contingent not least upon the outcome of political disputes. Finally, these systems' effects depend upon the broader constellations in which they are embedded (Wildawsky 1987: 11–12). It is therefore necessary to be clear about exactly which cultural or religious values and norms are identified as being causally relevant to which developments and structures, and in light of which positive explanatory problems. The objective cannot be to describe a certain ethical system as such – closed, temporally invariant and independent of its context – and then use it as an *explanans* in explicating socio-economic developments.[7] Instead, we attempt to describe the psychological and sociological ideas of Confucianism as it applies to the organization of social policy and to the relationship of social policy with the economic and political spheres. We do not attempt to elaborate a cultural explanation as an alternative to economic or political interpretations. Here, ideas and values are viewed first as conditioning and then as conditioned factors of societal development – except that here only one, namely the first side of this two-way relationship, is emphasized. 'Culture' does not suspend economic and political laws. These laws obtain within cultural frameworks.

On a formal level, we do not seek to develop a model in opposition to the *homo oeconomicus* and her rational choice as the analytical point of reference for positive theory. Modern economics is distinguished precisely by the fact that it is, first, neutral relative to the preferences of the individuals it studies, i.e. it accepts these as given. It does not say anything about the utility itself which is being maximized (Rothschild 1992: 14–16).[8] Second, it conceives the traditional economic theme, coping with scarcity, as restriction-guided behaviour. Rules of whatever kind, including religious ones, according to this line of thinking, canalize behaviour by limiting the horizon of permissible actions. Institutional reform, social change or culture shifts alter the relative advantageousness of alternative courses of action and thus trigger corresponding adaptive reactions (Pies 1993: 41). Thus, thirdly, economics expands to the extent that its subject matter ultimately encompasses no longer merely the central fact of life of having to cope with scarcity, but also the regulation and institutionalization of scarcity-induced conflicts (Brennan and Buchanan 1985). Economics then gains its own access to the world of institutions and culture as conditions of social action; it becomes part of a '"realistic" science of the ethical' (Weber 1904: 97).

In terms of the methodological nature of this chapter, we should emphasize its speculative and preliminary character. Marion Levy is certainly correct when he warns that without knowledge of the language and of the original philosophical and socio-

6 See Weber's general warning (1920: 291) against cultural determinism: 'Neither religions nor men are open books. They have been historical rather than logical or even psychological constructions without contradiction. Often they have borne within themselves a series of motives, each of which, if separately and consistently followed through, would have stood in the way of the others or run against them head-on. In religious matters "consistency" has been the exception and not the rule.'

7 On systematic misunderstandings in particular in the sociology of religion, which ultimately can only be understood in cultural-historical terms, see Matthes (1993: 26ff.).

8 Cf. Schumpeter for this clarification: 'The economic interpretation of history does not mean that men are, consciously or unconsciously, wholly or primarily, actuated by economic motives. On the contrary, the explanation of the role and mechanism of non-economic motives and the analysis of the way in which social reality mirrors itself in the individual psyches is an essential element of the theory and one of its most significant contributions' (1950 [1942]: 10f.).

political literature, it is inappropriate to engage the subject of Confucian culture and the development of the welfare state (1995: 206). This chapter is (perhaps) primarily justified by the fact that it contributes to the more precise formulation of research questions – above all, those concerning the points of departure, the fundamental forms and the dynamics of *Western* political and social development.

Furthermore, this chapter is based on Max Weber's study of Confucianism and Taoism (1989 [1915]). Weber's work certainly no longer corresponds on all points with the state of research on Chinese culture and ethics; and it has attracted a comprehensive, and to some extent extremely critical, literature.[9] Much of the criticism overlooks, however, the fact that Weber consciously approached Confucian culture from the perspective of a *positive* question. He was not concerned with describing and evaluating Chinese culture and ethics as such. Weber's limited focus makes his work useful for this study. Even if the questions explored here were not explicitly treated by him, he was interested not merely in a narrowly conceived economic ethic and its significance for the rise and development of modern capitalism, but also in the related problem of demonstrating the significance of religious-cultural motives 'for the substance of the socio-political ethic, i.e. for the nature of the organization and functions of social communities from the convent to the state' (ibid.: 189). It is precisely this hypothesis, of important, that is, *consequential* linkages between religion and social policy, that makes his reflections relevant, both then and now, for a better understanding of welfare state developments.

2 The Trouble with Modernization Theory

Like democracy, the welfare state can be seen as an increasingly probable consequence of market and industrial development. This is one of the central ideas of traditional modernization theory. Or, alternatively, it can be attributed to independent, non-economic causes. In light of the observable variance in market and democratic developmental paths, it seems reasonable to suggest that one cannot simply proceed from the assumption that there is a necessary and somehow inevitable connection between the market and industrial transformation of societies, on the one hand, and their democratization and parliamentarization, on the other. Civil rights are the lever for freeing individuals from traditional bonds and helping to bring about a meritocratic distribution of individuals among the new status positions of industrial society, which is then, perhaps, supplemented by the social rights of welfare states.

In this vein, in a study of the chances of a civil society emerging in Russia in the first decade of the twentieth century, Max Weber argued:

> [I]t is quite ridiculous to attribute to today's high capitalism, as it exists in America and is being imported into Russia, to this 'inevitability' of our economic development, any 'elective affinity' with 'democracy' or indeed 'freedom' (in *any* sense of the word), when the only question one can ask is how all these things can 'possibly' survive at all in the long run under the rule of capitalism. (1906: 69)

9 A compilation can be found in Schluchter (1983).

Weber opposed any deterministic understanding of societal development and emphasized instead the significance of political mobilization for a liberal order *against* the material conditions and constellations of interest which are created or modified by them:

> The outlook for the chances of 'democracy' and 'individualism' would be very poor indeed if we had to rely for their development on the effects produced by the 'laws' of *material* interests. These interests point as clearly as can be in the opposite direction. The *housing of the new serfdom* is ready everywhere: in America's 'benevolent feudalism', in Germany's so-called 'welfare provisions', in the factory system in Russia, and it is just waiting for certain conditions to make the masses 'compliant' enough to enter it once and for all – a slow-down in the tempo of technical and economic 'progress', the victory of 'dividends' [*Rente*] over profits [*Gewinn*], together with the exhaustion of the remaining 'free' land and markets. (ibid.: 68)

Weber's allusion to the form and direction of contemporary socio-political development, i.e. to its decidedly company-based orientation and its instrumentalization as a means of keeping the workforce in line, also implies that some general features of forms and levels of industrial development – despite there being considerable differences in these countries' political framework – give particular kinds of social policy a greater and others a lesser chance of success and survival. Which model of the welfare state is in fact fashioned in a country is decided in the political realm in concrete historical situations depending on cultural resources, and the path that is thereby charted is in turn influenced by these conceptions of political and social order and guiding ideas which exist in a given place at a given time (Castles 1989; P. Baldwin 1990; Rieger 1992a: 70–150).

In the strain of comparative historical welfare state research that took the notion of an autonomous path of social policy development seriously, the focus has usually been on the timing of social policy initiatives relative to socio-economic developments, not on their being shaped through culture and religious ethics.[10] The main example given for welfare state development attributable to independent, non-economic forces is the social policy of Bismarck. It largely served purposes of political integration and manipulation. These purely politically derived objectives played a greater role in the causal nexus that drove the *Kaiserreich*'s welfare state development than did its state of economic development or some socio-economic inequalities the system could not tolerate (G. A. Ritter 1983: 28–41; Hennock 1987; Rieger 1992a,b). Further non-economic factors that, according to this literature, could spark far-reaching socio-political intervention include state legitimation interests, mass wartime mobilization and nascent processes of state- and nation-building (Mann 1988). The UK experience during the Second World War of Germany's socially indiscriminate air raids – bombs struck rich and poor, elites and masses alike – was an essential impetus for the institutional reconstitution of the British welfare state. Beveridge, who led the reform, distinguished himself from his predecessors with his National Health Service, in particular by virtue of its pronounced universal-egalitarian features (Klein 1983: 1–30).[11] These

[10] But see Heidenheimer (1983) and Kersbergen (1995).

[11] The empirical core of the analysis of Goodin and Dryzek (1987), for example, is formed by the massively increasing social insecurity reaching across social classes in the wake of the war. They thus proceed from the assumption that the disappearance of this socially indiscriminate insecurity will lead to the

unique circumstances point to a social policy that can be an independent dimension of societal order and development. The genesis and political significance of the need for economic security and for societal mitigation of social inequalities can have autonomous political roots and thus is subject to a logic of its own. Notwithstanding empirical observations to the contrary, economic-determinist conceptions of welfare state development, though, dominate modernization theory.

Modernization theorists assume that social policy is an essential component of modernization processes, in that it systematically interacts and varies with economic and political development. They point to the fact that with increasing national income not only does the transition from autocracy or dictatorship to democracy become ever more probable, but that representative democracy is also marked by a greater likelihood of stability and survival (Huntington 1968; Eisenstadt 1973; Flora 1975: 9–33; Berger 1986). Seymour Martin Lipset (1959) speculated that growing prosperity enables democratic regimes to palliate distributional conflicts, and described social policy as a generalized system of alleviating economic inequalities. Welfare statism is thus an insurance against revolt by the economically disinherited. An interpretation of a somewhat different camp sees the welfare state as a direct consequence of economic growth. Thus Walter Rostow, for example, maintains that 'significant expansion in social welfare has . . . been largely a function of the rate of growth itself' (1971: 182; cited in Flora 1974: 82).[12] In this view, the welfare state is a mere dividend of economic growth, and it remains unclear which actors with which interests and under what conditions drive this development. It remains unclear also what consequences economic stagnation or depression may have for social policy: is social policy in such situations still simply a function of economic development, or does a policy of welfare state retrenchment have a different logic from one of welfare state expansion? (Pierson 1994, 1996).

There are also schools of thought claiming that the absence of democracy is a precondition for successful economic development.[13] In this view, democracy is a mechanism that furthers consumption at the expense of production and investment, and social policy is equated with democracy. Thus, only autocracy or dictatorship, or a strong *republican* regime of checks and balances coupled with property rights effectively out of reach of electoral majorities, are capable of creating and maintaining the

weakening of the universal-egalitarian moments in British social policy. However, as Janowitz (1976: 37f.) has pointed out, the events of World War II strengthened the ideal of equality, which was able to continue to grow with profound vigour and impact because of one of the main achievements of total wartime mobilization: the creation of administrative structures and of an administrative elite that was adapted to large-scale societal innovation. For the first time, the state had the capacity to alter the social structure.

12 The classic articulation of the thesis that the welfare state is the product of the 'logic of industrialization' stems from Harold Wilensky: 'Economic growth is the ultimate cause of welfare state development' (1975: 24). In this interpretation, however, the decisive variable is not the growth dividends yielded by economic development which can then be redistributed by the public sector, but rather the social problems associated with such development.

13 For Hayek (1947: 107–8) this notion has taken on the quality of an iron law: 'In a democratic society, at any rate, once the principle is admitted that the government undertakes responsibility for the status and position of particular groups, it is inevitable that this control will be extended to satisfy the aspirations and prejudices of the great masses. There is no hope of a return to a freer system. . . . The hopelessness of the prospect for the near future indeed is due mainly to the fact that no organized political group anywhere is in favour of a truly free system.'

conditions necessary for successful economic development.[14] Walter Galenson argues, for example, that as the degree of democratization increases, so does the rate of allocation of resources from investment into consumption (1959: 3). Karl de Schweinitz also considers successful institutionalization of a market economy to be dependent on the limitation of democratic freedom and popular participation in the political process (1958/9). The same argument is formulated by Samuel P. Huntington and Jorge I. Dominguez (1975) as a condition for successful catch-up development in Latin America and East Asia.[15] These conceptions are supported by certain versions of public choice theory, in which political variables are treated as endogenous to models of economic policy decision-making. They blame mechanisms of representative democracy for systematically privileging merely redistributive and unproductive policies and for the resultant thwarting of the market (Olson 1982; Magee et al. 1989).

One problem with this interpretation is that both autocratic and republican regimes, too, are subject to a high degree of integrative and legitimatory pressure, which they regularly attempt to ease by means of social policy and welfare state intervention, especially when they seek to thwart or weaken broad-based political participation. In addition to the Bismarckian case mentioned above, the National Socialist regime's extensive use of social policy can be adduced here as well (T. Mason 1978; Tennstedt 1988). Also, as Roosevelt's New Deal politics demonstrate, social democratic mass politics can override counter-majoritarian constitutional constraints.[16] Moreover, the social policy forms observed in these cases are tailored to precisely those groups with the loudest potential voice. For this reason, interventions aim to bring about a perceptible change in the social conditions of these vocal groups, in order to attain the desired objective – political acquiescence. These vocal groups, however, are seldom identical to those who, in terms of their socio-economic condition, are most in need of social policy transfers and services. This concessionary social policy often results in benefit schemes which are inequitable by any standard of distributive justice, yet, in terms of the sheer quantity of transfers, positively comparable to those of Western democracies. The development of social policy in both the Soviet Union and Latin America furnish empirical examples for this (Rimlinger 1974; F.-X. Kaufmann 2001c: 828–43; Mesa-Lago 1978, 1990, 1991), as does the 'benevolent feudalism' of US American welfare capitalism (Jacoby 1997a). There are thus strong indications that the phenomenon of welfare state expansion is largely independent both of the respective political system and of the system of interest representation and mediation.

14 In welfare state research the identification of representative democracy with social policy is relatively new. With regard to the origins of the modern welfare state, one finds the opposite claim, namely that from very early on autocratic rule is the central condition for socio-political progress. In the controversial German exhibit at the world's fair in St Louis in 1904, the Wilhelmine Ministry of the Interior attributed Germany's pioneer role in social policy vis-à-vis Switzerland, France and England to the contention that liberal parliamentarism in those countries impeded socio-political progress. Parliamentarism, it claimed, made concessions to the enfranchised working classes necessary, and the latter were not interested in social policy but in organizational empowerment and collective bargaining autonomy.

15 For a more sophisticated view, see Boulding (1976: 96). For a comprehensive assessment of the empirical and theoretical relationships between a liberal market economy and democratic development see Rueschemeyer et al. (1992) and the essays in Midlarsky (1997).

16 For a view of the New Deal as an authoritarian turn toward large-scale social planning and thus reconstructing social structures see Lippmann (1937). In a letter at that time Lippmann complained: 'The people are selling their liberties' (quoted in Steel 1981: 322).

A brief stock-taking of various theorems stemming from modernization research reveals not only a diverse complex of postulates and claims, but also a series of contradictions among them. First, the various versions of modernization theory each find a different point of departure for the institutionalization of social policy; it seems to be by no means unambiguously determined by economic development. Second, modernization theory arrives at differing assessments both of the role of parliamentary politics as an independent cause of welfare state expansion, and of the dependency of social policy either on the material yield of economic growth or on the social consequences of industrialization, which, as 'social problems', inevitably compel state intervention and compensation. This analytically indeterminate state of modernization theory and the contradictions of its central claims appear to demonstrate that it bears no – or only a modest – heuristic value for the analysis and interpretation of social policy in East Asia under conditions of economic globalization.

Apart from these differences in analytical demarcation and substantive weighting vis-à-vis specific features of welfare state development, exponents of modernization theory agree on four points. Yet this unity is not acknowledged as such and, precisely because of its apparent taken-for-grantedness, is not perceived as something that calls for closer examination and explicit explanation. Moreover, this consensus is predicated, *pace* Weber, upon the existence of systemic relationships and dependencies among a liberal market economy, representative democracy and the welfare state, and hence of common *cultural* roots of the myriad manifestations of the welfare state in *Western* societies.

The first such commonality of welfare state development assumed in modernization theory is that the timing of social policy initiatives, as well as their concrete forms and substance, cannot be merely deduced from industrialization and the institutionalization of a market economy. Of central importance remains the fact that – no matter where the respectively distinct goals and emphases of social policy may lie – to an often surprisingly large degree its institutionalization occurs independently of the concrete state of affairs of the market economy. There is no inevitable, systemically conditioned harmony of economic and welfare state development, but, instead, potential for massive disintegration. This follows from Esping-Andersen's empirically derived assumption that social policy is regularly pursued 'against the market' (1985), and from T. H. Marshall's view that the characteristic feature of the democratic welfare state is that 'civil rights and the capitalist class system are at war with each another' (1949: 84).[17] Welfare state measures and institutions are very rarely viewed just as pieces of a machinery specially designed to cope with deficiencies of the moment, not merely means to an end, but in a certain sense ends in themselves, 'progressive' features of society and the very embodiment of civilization. Even when they do not explicitly reject the capitalist market economy, proponents of welfare statism typically hold 'that there are some elements in a civilized life which rank above it and must be achieved by curbing or superseding the market' (Marshall 1961b: 272).[18]

17 Marshall noted early on 'that the standards by which that progress [of social policy] was assessed were constantly rising, and that ever deeper probing into the social situation kept revealing new horrors which had previously been concealed from view' (1961b: 258).

18 This hostility to the capitalist market economy, or free enterprise system, is reflected in the near total absence of markets as positive sources of welfare in social policy research. Instead, the organization of the economy itself shows up only negatively, in that the welfare state 'will slay the dragon of "*capitalism*", the father of everything evil and source of all unrest', as Weber (1917b: 89) has put it.

The second commonality refers to the way in which social policy becomes established and is sustained. Social policy is developed in a highly autonomous institutional complex governed by a separate sphere of values and norms. This sphere's development proceeds, at least potentially, separately or autodynamically in the sense that it can also run expressly counter to the capitalist economic order.[19] The two most important reasons for this are, first, the interest of every organized activity to defend itself even as its original *raison d'être* ceases to exist, and, second, the influence of purely philosophical speculation on the moral perfectability of men and the 'good society' (Parsons 1938; Stinchcombe 1968: 8; Weber 1978: 82–6). In this way, and viewed from the standpoint of economic rationality, the social politics of welfare states can become successively 'irrationalized'. One decisive mark of welfare statism is the specialization of a particular, often university-trained group of persons in the continuous operation of social policies, who are permanently associated with particular norms and values and who are closely linked to specific social groups. Moreover, the characteristic nature of welfare state expenditure has become more and more a system of self-sustaining expansion in response to *politically* created definitions of welfare requirements. In other words, once institutionalized, social policy has become a political world in its own right, where some balance of power, not the distribution of needs, will determine the allocation of resources.

The third point of unexpressed unity is modernization theory's strong interest – guiding its hypotheses and research – in the peculiar dynamics of welfare state development, and in the search for the reasons why the latter can confront business and government with formidable challenges of adaptation and control. The culture of the welfare state is intensively individualistic, and 'the claim of individuals to welfare is sacred and irrefutable and partakes of the character of a natural right' (Marshall 1953: 236). Until the 1980s welfare state research was fascinated by the seemingly unstoppable expansion of social policies, and since then by the equally surprising fact that welfare statism, despite programmatic political efforts to the contrary, has proved to be extremely difficult to roll back (Kangas 1991; Green-Pedersen and Haverland 2002).

A fourth point, related to social policy's independent foundation and dynamic, is the tendency towards universalization and egalitarian levelling in the course of welfare state development. Marshall's description of this development indeed leaves open the question of what exactly drives it, yet indicates its direction:

> Citizenship is a status bestowed on those who are full members of a community. All who possess the status are equal with respect to the rights and duties with which the status is endowed. There is no universal principle that determines what those rights and duties shall be, but societies in which citizenship is a developing institution create an image of an ideal citizenship against which achievement can be measured and towards which aspiration can be directed. The urge forward along the path thus plotted is an urge towards a fuller measure of equality, an enrichment of the stuff of which the status is made and an increase in the number of those on whom the status is bestowed. (1949: 84)

19 See also T. H. Marshall, who contends that the key aspect of the development of civil status is that its three components – civil, political and social rights – took separate paths, 'travelling at its own speed under the direction of its own peculiar principles' (1949: 73).

Not only the market-induced, methodically depersonalized and rationalized 'masterless slavery' (Adolf Wagner) of the modern working classes, but also feudal-corporative, familial and company-based dependency relations are viewed as contradictory to the ideal of personal autonomy to be achieved through social policy. For example, in the last century of the *Kaiserreich*, liberal academics such as Max Weber and Lujo Brentano joined socialist unions in rejecting company-based welfare state institutions. They viewed their legal prohibition as comparable in significance to the eradication of feudal agricultural relations in the first half of the nineteenth century (Mommsen 1974: 107–32, esp. 126f.). If in comparative social policy research the universalism and egalitarianism of the ideal-typical social democratic welfare state serve as seemingly neutral yardsticks of societal development, this is due to a fundamentally hostile orientation towards both particularist social-structural relations of all kinds and 'amoral' rationalized economic institutions.[20] But this type of thinking and the resultant social structure are unique to the West.

Thus it is quite unfortunate that in nearly all publications on East Asian social policy there is the assumption that, in this macro-region, social policy will develop into welfare states of the European-Atlantic model. European social policy – income maintenance through universal social security based on social rights, which aims at personal autonomy – became, implicitly or explicitly, the paradigm of a developed or a modern welfare state. This entire line of research seems to be off the mark. It has tacitly assumed that social policy originated in Europe alone. In fact, the development of social policy in Europe and North America is – in a world-historical perspective – highly idiosyncratic. European social policy presented itself as a project to remodel state, economy and society. The strikingly original characteristic of the Western welfare state is that it concentrates on subjective social rights.

As will be shown below, social policy in East Asian countries differs from that of its Western predecessors in four respects. It is less heterogeneous to economic realities and far more strongly integrated in and coordinated with these. Moreover, its potential to be employed as an independently conceived ordering model counter to existing economic, social and political relations is far more limited. Further, its path of development is tied far more closely to general economic and corporate development, occurs in a more gradual tempo and is primarily *stataric*.[21] This contrasts with the Western social policy dynamic, which, because of its dominant focus on social rights, threatens again and again to overwhelm politics and the social order. Finally, universalism and egalitarianism do not appear to be formative principles of social policy in East Asia.

20 The main exponent of this view is Esping-Andersen (1990). For a critique see Rieger (1998a). The central problem of nearly all welfare state research is the near total silence on the market economy. It is only seen as the grim cause of social policy, not as a way of satisfying the needs and wants of the population. Once 'welfare' had been elevated to the top rank of political objectives, the politically controlled, bureaucratic provision of means to meet needs gained a significant advantage against the impersonal working of markets.

21 *Stataric* is old Greek and means leisurely, here in the sense of slow and measured. Hegel used the term to describe Chinese society and politics in his *Philosophy of History* (1961 [1840]).

Table 5.1 Basic East Asian economic data, 1990s

	Year	*Hong Kong*	*Singapore*	*South Korea*	*Taiwan*	*Japan*
Population (millions)	1996	6.3	3.0	45.5	21.4	125.8
Activity rate (%)	1996	50.0	56.9[a]	46.4[a]	43.5	53.5
Unemployment rate (%)	1996	2.8	2.7[a]	2.0	1.1	3.4
	1998	5.0	4.5	8.4	4.0[b]	
Degree of urbanization[c]	1970	88.0	100.0	41.0	—	71.0
(%)	1996	95.0	100.0	82.0	—	78.0
GNP[d]						
• $USbn	1996	153.3	93.0	483.1	272.0	5,149.2
• per capita ($US)	1996	24,290	30,550	10,610	12,710	40,940
Foreign trade quota[e] (%)	1996	142.1	186.6[a]	34.4	50.5	8.3

[a] Data for 1995
[b] Data for the end of 1997
[c] Degree of urbanization = urban population as % of total population
[d] GNP = Gross National Product
[e] Foreign trade quota = export/import as % of GNP

Sources: IMF (1997), C. Jones (1990b: 447); Jacobs (1998); World Bank (1998); Republic of China (1997); *Frankfurter Allgemeine Zeitung* (2 December 1998: 21) and our calculations

3 The Welfare State and Social Policy in East Asia

Tables 5.1 and 5.2 give an overview of the most important quantitative indicators of economic and welfare state development in East Asia.[22] The first and, for our argument, decisive point is the comparatively low levels of social expenditure. The impressive catch-up and most of all the societal intensity of industrial economic transformation in these countries would lead one to expect much higher social expenditures. They remain low despite the fact that in the field of health care policy East Asian countries made decisive steps during the 1990s towards de facto universal coverage (Ramesh and Holliday 2001). If one looks at historical patterns of welfare state expansion in Western Europe, one sees that there, at considerably earlier stages of industrialization and urbanization, higher social benefit levels had been attained than presently obtain in East Asia. In the German Empire in 1910, for example, the share of social and educational expenditures relative to GNP was 5.3 per cent, rising to 16.8 per cent in the later Weimar Republic (1929) and to 23.3 per cent in the Federal Republic (1958).[23] Quantitative indicators on public spending, however, can be misleading

22 The historical-comparative literature on social policy and the labour market in East Asia is sparse, in particular with regard to the role of cultural factors. An exception is the comparative literature on income distribution: Fields (1984, 1985, 1994), P. W. Kuznets (1988), Galenson (1992), Ranis (1993), and Krongkaew (1994).

23 Our calculations based on the data in Flora (1983) and Flora et al. (1987).

Table 5.2 Social expenditure in East Asia in international comparison, 1990s (% of GNP)[a]

	Japan 1992	*South Korea 1995*	*Taiwan 1996*	*Singapore 1995*	*Hong Kong 1995*	*Germany 1993*	*USA 1993*
Total social expenditure	16.14	8.70	11.00	5.08/10.29[b]	5.52	32.97	20.84
Income transfer[c]	7.25	3.12	5.71	0.79/6.00[b]	1.22	21.00	9.28
Health	5.27	0.24	—	1.21	1.67	6.43	5.85
Education	3.70	3.73	5.00	1.78	2.63	5.60	5.20
Housing	—	1.56	0.38	1.29	1.40	0.24	—

[a] The figures are based on the OECD categories
[b] Includes expenditures of the *Central Provident Fund*
[c] Income transfers = social insurance and public assistance

Source: D. Jacobs (1998: 46f.) and our calculations

because of the functional equivalence of social regulation of labour markets and corporate behaviour. Therefore, the ensuing description and discussion of social policy realities in East Asia deal less with their statistical properties than their qualitative aspects. Moreover, the focus is on the institutional side of income maintenance via social policy, and not on the effectiveness and efficiency of income policies, redistribution and anti-poverty programmes. With the exception of the educational sector, we are also leaving aside most welfare state infrastructural measures and services, i.e. public hygiene and health, child care, etc.

Patterns and foci of welfare state development in East Asia

Leaving national peculiarities aside, East Asian countries share four institutional features of welfare state development:

- a conception of social protection as a last resort dominates the state's social policy orientation;
- social insurance is restrictive and fragmented and thereby particularizes risks; but the organization of education, housing and health care is more group-transcending;
- old-age insurance schemes either do not exist or are designed to provide minimum benefits; they are funded schemes and thus have hardly any redistributive effects;
- a special role – both relative to other areas of social policy and compared to European countries – is played by an expansive educational system.

At first glance, the institutional structure of social policy in East Asia seems to follow Western models. Indeed, in many cases, these are institutions that are the legacy of a colonial or occupying power, not the result of endogenous developments predicated on national or regional traditions.[24] Even after independence, welfare state development in East Asian countries has often been decisively influenced by foreign social policy concepts – a phenomenon that is further strengthened by the historically conditioned, highly competitive relationship of these countries with each other. One reason for this social policy dynamic is that in these countries, external competition among states is far more important than internal competition among parties. Yet in sharp contrast to party competition having a decisive influence in Western welfare states (Castles 1978; M. G. Schmidt 1982, 1996; Korpi and Palme 1998; Huber and Stephens 2001; Kitschelt 2001), state competition there was not a systemic feature of expansive welfare state development. State competition remains dependent on rather coincidental foreign

[24] As the example of Hong Kong shows, this form of initiating social policy does not necessarily involve the social policy of the mother country being used as a model. Hong Kong's social policy was, due to the city-state's colonial status, determined to a very large extent by the British administration. Yet while in Great Britain the universal welfare state ascended in the post-war period to become the prevailing international model for the achievement of social integration, the same ruling parties which, in the mother country, had all supported this policy into the early 1980s, in the crown-colony pursued a completely opposite, yet also highly systematic, residualist social policy (McLaughlin 1993: 106). Not until just prior to surrendering the crown-colony did the British break out of this mould with a radical proposal for pension reform (Kwon 1998a: 43) that interestingly now stood in opposition to the more residualist domestic reform project of Margaret Thatcher. Singapore's Central Provident Fund, which bundles together the city-state's most important social policy functions in a kind of functionally centralized insurance fund, is similarly a British creation. Yet here, too, no British model was followed. By contrast, the institutional core of the Japanese public welfare system is to a very large extent the product of the US Supreme Commander for the Allied Powers and directly inspired by Roosevelt's New Deal (Thränhardt 1995: 429; Kwon 1998a). South Korea's and Taiwan's social policies, on the other hand, are clearly marked by the influence of their former colonial ruler, Japan. To this extent, both were and remain indirectly Western – and directly Japanese – influenced. An example of this can be seen in the South Korean health insurance reform of 1977, which in 1988 and 1989 was expanded to include agricultural workers and the self-employed respectively to achieve universal coverage: 'In developing this system, the post-war Japanese health insurance plan served as a model. The combination of such principles as the division of the population into the employees and the remaining others (together with a number of privileged occupational groups), the operation of autonomous enterprise-unit or community based medical insurance societies, and the point system for medical fee payment is a Japanese innovation' (H. K. Lee 1992: 160). A further form of external influence on social policy, e.g. on the South Korean health insurance reform, is often overlooked: 'Following recommendations from the USA attached to the aid loan in 1975, National Health Insurance became a compulsory programme in 1977' (Kwon 1998a: 51). On Japanese influence on Korean development in general, see Kobayashi (1996). A Japanese connection can be found as well in the colonial period itself, in that Taiwan's social policy institutions served as a model for Japan: 'In fact, from pre-protectorate days, the Japanese in Korea looked to Taiwan for educational models for Korea' (Tsurumi 1996: 293). Moreover, again at the end of the 1980s and during the 1990s, a reverse reform competition can be observed between the two countries: 'But Taiwan was influenced by Asian nations as well as Western ones. When the South Korean government announced in 1991 that almost 95 percent of its population would be included in its National Health Insurance program, some Taiwanese officials publicly asked "why South Korea could and Taiwan couldn't". The leaders of Taiwan reasoned that if South Korea, a close neighbour of Taiwan which shares similar social and economic features, could initiate universal National Health Insurance, there was no reason why Taiwan could not' (Tang 1997: 75). This was expressed also in party competition: 'In the Legislative Yuan the DDP [Democratic Progressive Party, the opposition to the Kuomintang] successfully argued not only for democratization but also for social welfare including the early implementation of the National Health Insurance scheme. A speech by the DPP's legislator Yu Chen-shien illustrated one aspect of the nature of the NHI debate, when he asked: "Why can Korea afford to have National Insurance but not Taiwan?" He added, "Does it mean that Taiwanese lives are less valuable?"' (Kwon 1998a: 49).

policy constellations and thus did not allow social policy to become independent by means of its own dynamic.

The Western origins and inherited organizational form of many social policy institutions in East Asia do not mean, however, that they are also comparable with their Western forebears in terms of their political function or effects, and even less in terms of their developmental potential. The differences between East Asian and Western models lie not so much in the formal structures of the social policy institutions themselves as in the sentiments that guided their founding, find expression in them and influence their further development. The often observed social policy 'system deficits' (Thränhardt 1996: 51) in East Asia are, thus, in fact structurally determined. They are not perceived by these countries' social policy actors themselves and for this reason do not influence policy-making; they are visible only from the external perspective of the developed Western welfare state.

A first, general difference relative to the Western model of development can be found in the fact that in East Asia welfare state institutions play a different role in the overall system of societal welfare production. The institutions of state social policy are fundamentally subsidiary to families and companies and are organized in such a way so as not to contradict the latters' peculiarities or functional principles. Rather, they appear as an organic complement to them, without any distinct institutional significance. A further general difference is that social policy plays a different role in East Asian countries than in the Western system of political governance. Contrary to social policy's mediating role between state, economy and society in Western welfare states, in East Asia it has not become an independent agent – located beyond economy and civil society – of autonomous social and system integration, i.e. a comprehensive and self-driven system of social equalization and political compensation. Because of this structural disparity, East Asian social policy institutions are endowed with different societal functions and cultural significance. They produce different incentives for, and effects on, processes of political mobilization (and demobilization), economic policy-making and companies' latitude in personnel and organizational decisions.

In contrast, in Western societies the most basic mechanism of bringing about the universalistic, rights-based social policies typical of Western welfare states was the development of economically derived social classes acting as political entities and more or less exclusively dominating the political arena (Marshall 1938; Dahrendorf 1959). In East Asia this kind of social and political transformation of social structures never reached the scale and scope necessary to turn the state into a vehicle of economic redistribution, and thus never functioned as the deliberated (re)construction of a particular social order. This also means that in East Asian societies the tendency of groups or factions to use the law as a means of exercising political rights for collective privilege is much less pronounced than in the West.

The institutions of public assistance The public assistance, i.e. means-tested, policies of these countries can be best understood in terms of Western models of development. This is largely due to the disruptive consequences of socio-economic modernization, i.e. the institutionalization of a competition-oriented liberal market economy. The influence of Western models can be seen most clearly in the fact that in Japan and other East Asian countries no indigenous poor law tradition existed at either the state or communal level (Leibfried 1994; Goodman 1998: 140–4). In Japan it was Buddhists and, after the Meiji Restoration, Christians who sustained a basically philanthropic welfare sector (Foreign Press Center 1995: 55, 57).[25]

The comparatively prominent importance of public welfare institutions in several East Asian countries is rooted, first, in these countries' social problems, which stem from rapid industrialization and urbanization. The earlier, traditional forms of emergency care by familial and kinship networks were embedded in local neighbourhood relations and the structures of the extended domestic economy, which in turn strongly limited their adaptability to modern social realities. As will be discussed below, however, key elements of this general understanding of the transition to a mobile industrial society are in need of revision. The overwhelming traditional, i.e. familial and household-bound, forms of social security[26] do not automatically or necessarily lead to the creation of public welfare provision and the expansion of social insurance systems.

A second origin of the strong role of the state in welfare provision lies in the massive destruction and uprooting of large population groups in the wake of the Second World War and the Korean War. Under circumstances in which external sovereignty and domestic autonomy had been substantially surrendered, in the first case by Japan and later by South Korea, social assistance policy was set by the USA. During and after the Korean War, the USA bore both the financial and the administrative burden of welfare provision in South Korea – a product of the fact that no indigenous Korean welfare system existed (Chang 1985).

Influenced by Western organizational models of public and philanthropic care, Japan and the city-states Hong Kong and Singapore introduced welfare systems. In the case of Hong Kong, this was the system of Comprehensive Social Security Assistance (CSSA). Japan, pressured by the US occupying forces, introduced a comprehensive welfare system in 1946, which endowed the needy with far-reaching legal rights to benefits.[27] Hong Kong's social assistance and welfare system was, because of the city-state's colonial status, designed by Great Britain (Hodge 1973; Chow 1998). This notwithstanding, it was expressly guided by familial values, in sharp contrast to the

[25] In Japan, which, compared to other East Asian countries, has a very extensive social assistance programme, only 586,106 households, or 883,112 individuals (0.7 per cent of the population), received social assistance in 1993 (Foreign Press Center 1995). In the USA, 7.7 per cent of the population claimed means-tested benefits (Aid to Families with Dependent Children and Federal Supplemental Security Income – US Department of Commerce 1996: tab. 599) in 1994. In Germany, 2.45 million persons (3 per cent of the population) were on non-institutional social assistance in 1993 (*Laufende Hilfe zum Lebensunterhalt außerhalb von Einrichtungen*; BMA 1998: tab. 8.16, 2.1).

[26] One need only consider the Korean situation in 1988, which suggests completely different familial constellations: 'Three out of four Koreans aged 60 and over lived with their married or unmarried children, while one in four lived only with his or her spouse or alone, away from his or her children' (Choi 1992: 150). In Japan this is no longer quite as often the case, yet it is still much more so than in Germany: the share of three-generation households among all households in Japan was 17 per cent in 1975. This share sank by 1991 to 13.7 per cent. In the Federal Republic, the corresponding share was 2.2 per cent in 1976 and 1.2 per cent in 1991 (Seeleib-Kaiser 1996: 162).

[27] In an amendment introduced at the end of 1946, the Japanese were able to introduce two important changes to the strictly individualistic and unconditional conception of the occupying power. First, families were made responsible for their members, extending – in contrast to Western practice – to cousins. Second, refusal to work was made grounds on which benefits could be denied (Thränhardt 1995: 429).

development in the mother country.[28] The same was true of Singapore's Central Provident Fund (CPF) introduced in 1953. It, too, was a British creation just prior to Singapore's independence,[29] and constitutes the best-known form of the East Asian 'provident fund approach' (Tyabji 1993: 54). The latter model strongly influenced social policy in the entire region, and in Singapore is associated with a rather minimalist welfare policy beyond the CPF.[30]

In general, it can be said that the eligibility criteria of these schemes are comparatively restrictive and stigmatizing, and their benefits relatively minimal. In the post-war period, they were for a long time predicated on the provision of benefits in kind.[31] These features reflect the schemes' lack of any basis in the separate economic classes of an industrialized society. They have no 'natural' counterpart in those social products of societal differentiation through which socio-political interest mobilization or status competition between distinct social classes or strata as expansionist engines could have evolved.[32] Moreover, welfare policy is not only strictly subsidiary, but also more strongly locally bound and more 'community' oriented: it addresses individuals not as individuals, but, rather, as members of some primordial or equivalently esteemed group.[33]

On the whole, state welfare policy is custodial, not emancipatory (Deyo 1992: 304). It is conceived as a social technology to augment the family order's social functions –

28 Lau speaks of a political orientation of 'utilitaristic familism' (in Kwon 1998a: 41). Kwon also calls attention to the fact that Hong Kong, in its condition as a 'temporary society' resting 'on borrowed land', was unable, unlike other East Asian countries, to develop any stable policy direction of its own with regard to the socio-political tasks of society and politics (ibid.: 42). This might also explain why a minimalist social policy orientation was developed furthest there, and why not even a provident fund approach or social health insurance programme could be introduced. For a recent description, see Chow (1998).

29 For an overview of the CPF and of the social policy of Singapore, see Asher (1995), Deyo (1991) and Tremewan (1998). The CPF is composed of several clearly distinct sub-funds or accounts: Ordinary, Medisave and Special Account as well as life insurance in the Dependants' Protection Scheme and voluntary supplemental health insurance in Medishield and Medishield Plus.

30 Cf. Kwon: 'In Singapore: there is almost no social security for those who have no CPF account. Only about 2,000 people receive public assistance benefits after passing a strict means test. According to Asher's calculation, the level of public assistance is at least 25 per cent below the minimum household expenditure for more than one-person households. . . . In short, Singaporeans do not have social rights to a safety-net other than their CPF' (1998a: 34f.).

31 The prevalence of benefits-in-kind in Taiwan's social assistance programme is described by Gordon Chan (1985: 344). Closely related to this is the common practice in other benefit programmes of providing one-time and lump-sum payments.

32 A semi-official description of the origins and characteristics of the Japanese social assistance system runs as follows: 'The system of welfare services that grew up after World War II was a complete departure from the wartime structures. During the Allied occupation Japan instituted a series of welfare laws, which were general in that they emphasized public responsibility for the welfare of everyone in the nation and made no distinction among different groups of recipients, but specific at the same time in that they called for a specialized professional welfare service tailored to the characteristics of each client group' (Foreign Press Center 1995: 58). This shows clearly what was different about this public assistance policy from the Japanese perspective.

33 Kwon (1998a: 53f.) reports on South Korea: 'The reason for the failure of the Public Assistance Programme is also partly because the selection procedure is not solely based on an income test. The local officials who are responsible for the selection of beneficiaries often use their local knowledge and the records of previous years to identify those in need.'

also, and particularly, where these do not yet or no longer exist. Familial orientation and its normative significance for the organization of social security in East Asian countries by no means constitute an unbroken tradition of social structure, but are a product of deliberate public choice, and thus provide a good illustration of the invention of tradition according to strictly contemporary needs.[34]

However, this fundamental familial orientation means that the institutions of public welfare provision are relatively isolated within these countries' overall institutional structures. Further, it indicates that they lack developmental potential both for individualization and for the juridification of social rights, and thus also for a differentiation of social insurance branches.[35] Although after the Second World War Japan could boast of unemployment, health, accident and old-age insurance schemes, in 1951 it still spent 44.3 per cent of its total social expenditure on public welfare, and only 8.5 per cent on social insurance schemes (Thränhardt 1995: 427). In South Korea, social expenditure after the Korean War was even more lopsided because of the embryonic condition of the country's social insurance system – even fifteen years into the post-war period.[36] As of 1965, public welfare, which was claimed by nearly 14 per cent of the population, still consumed 73 per cent of social spending (Kwon 1998a: 53); only 27 per cent was spent on social insurance schemes and social services (H. K. Lee 1994: 12).[37]

Taiwan was involved in the Second World War to a lesser extent than Japan and far less so than Korea in the Korean War. Thus in the immediate post-war period, Taiwan was not afflicted nearly as extensively by a need for public assistance. The then extant state welfare had to a large extent been put aside and, during the 1950s and early 1960s, affected less than 1 per cent of the population. Subsequently, Taiwan imported the 'War on Poverty' approach of the USA, so that, by 1965, 9.3 per cent of the population was claiming social assistance. The proportion of public assistance in social spending rose from a mere 2 per cent in 1951 to 14 per cent in 1980 (G. Chan 1985: 333). Furthermore, compared to Korea, social insurance schemes emerged very early in Taiwan. Labour Insurance, a health insurance scheme, was introduced as early as 1950, well before the first wave of industrialization. This was a result of the migra-

34 Cf. this summary of the Japanese situation: 'The features of postwar Japanese society so often labelled as vestiges of a familial, neo-Confucianist, or feudal past tend upon closer examination to have been adaptions of social controls, legitimated perhaps by traditional symbols and ideological claims, designed to satisfy a basic need for security against risks the state is unwilling or unable to provide' (Haley 1991: 181).

35 This is also reflected in the pronounced status uncertainty among the staff of the state welfare institutions concerning their public function (C. Jones 1990b).

36 At that time Korea operated an experimental, in its coverage very limited, 'general' health insurance scheme introduced in 1963, as well as pension allowances for civil servants (1960) and the military (1963). In contrast to the 1990s, no social protection beyond the social assistance programme existed in those days for the average worker.

37 In Korea the situation had been reversed by 1987: social assistance now made up only 20 per cent of social expenditure, while social insurance and social services consumed 80 per cent (H. K. Lee 1994: 12). The social assistance rate must have been between 5 and 6 per cent of the population (Kwon 1998a: 53 – with further data on welfare dependency between 1965 and 1995). This did not change in any way, however, the fundamental characteristic of welfare without a legal entitlement to benefits (Kwon 1998a: 54): 'The fundamental cause for the inadequacy of the Public Assistance Programme is that it is similar to the English Poor Law in the seventeenth century. It does not embody a guaranteed social right to a decent life. Its aim is to provide a minimum level of relief, so that no work disincentive is introduced. This brings up the question of why the concept of social rights has not been brought into the area of public assistance.'

tion of the Kuomintang government from mainland China to Taiwan in 1949. In the context of the Chinese civil war, the Nationalists under General Chiang Kai-Shek had agreed as early as 1945, i.e. before moving to Taiwan, on a national health service based on the British model, and had inscribed this in Article 157 of the Chinese Constitution (Tang 1997: 74; Ku 1998; Kwon 1998a: 47).

Social insurance schemes Social insurance schemes in East Asia are focused predominantly on health and accident insurance.[38] These institutions are less oriented towards income replacement and status maintenance, and more towards the securing of a basic level of health care and thus of fitness for work. Even in hospitals, family members often assume the lion's share of the burden in the treatment and care of the sick. The pattern of welfare state initiatives and expansions here is more top down, and reveals a variegated landscape of occupationally related privileges bestowed by piecemeal social policy. This has led over time to the evolution of rather complicated structures, most elaborate in Japan (Jacobs 1998: 12–15, 105–14). First, civil servants and military personnel[39] were provided for, followed – a peculiarity of East Asia – by school teachers. In Taiwan, teachers and school administrators (1980), as well as their spouses (1985) and children (1990), have their own health insurance scheme (Kwon 1998a: 45). In Japan, too, a separate old-age pension scheme is granted to teachers (ibid.: 59).

South Korea's National Health Insurance Scheme consists of a series of group-specific social health insurance funds. In 1984, separate funds were created for civil servants and teachers (Choi 1992: 157; H. K. Lee 1992: 159f., 165). The origins of the universalizing system date to 1963, but this was only a limited social experiment. In 1977, the first institutionally grounded, far-reaching health insurance scheme was launched, with two branches. Type I, health insurance for industrial workers, was based on social partnership and was designed for employees in larger firms. Type II was self-insurance for small firms and several categories of the self-employed, i.e. regional health insurance. Further, there is a public welfare programme providing some cash payments for the sick (Medical Aid System, i.e. Medicaid). The health insurance system covered 42 per cent of the population in 1983, was extended in 1988 to the rural population and in 1989 to the urban self-employed (H. K. Lee 1992: 169). Together with the public welfare programme for the sick, by 1989 it covered the entire population (Jacobs 1998: 115). For Type II-insurance, the government paid half of the self-insurance contribution. At the same time, as the initially merely experimental health insurance scheme was launched in 1963, a universal accident insurance scheme was introduced for the industrial workforce. By 1996 it covered about 40 per cent of the working population.

In the two city-states a more comprehensive, uniform model prevailed: in Hong Kong that of public assistance (Hospital Authority) and in Singapore that of compulsory insurance for the less serious conditions (Medisave Account). In Singapore there

38 You (1995: 147, fn. 7) emphasizes the following detail in the South Korean case, which eased the path of such schemes: 'Note that, unlike measures which reduce the costs of job loss, the Industrial Accident Insurance encourages hard work.'

39 Taiwan had the first 'secret' social health insurance scheme : 'The Insurance for the Military Program was the first social insurance program to be enacted in Taiwan after 1949. Both the financial budget and the number of insured are regarded as national defence secrets and therefore are not made public. As a result, the social insurance system for the military remained independent from other social insurance systems even after the implementation of the NHI in 1995' (Tang 1997: 63, fn. 7).

were two optional supplementary schemes for more expensive illnesses (Medishield, Medishield Plus) and, since 1993, a complementary public welfare programme for the sick poor (Medifund).

The share of social expenditure taken up by occupationally specialized welfare arrangements can be considerable. In Taiwan at the beginning of the 1990s three-quarters of all social expenditure was thus earmarked.[40] Only after such select state-related groups are publicly insured do we see socio-political coverage being extended to the entire population. Generally, health insurance seems to be the type of scheme most susceptible to universalization, as well as, in the eyes of political entrepreneurs, the one most capable of generating mass loyalty.

The potential for universalization is limited, however, by the nearly complete break-up of East Asian populations into separate risk groups, resulting in a pluralized system of occupationally specific schemes, as well as by the attendant fragmentation in the system of financing.[41] This is true above all in Korea: the health insurance scheme is composed of more than 500 funds organized according to occupation, without any kind of financial equalization mechanism (Kwon 1998a: 52f.). This not only rules out the compensation of differential risks and horizontal redistribution, but also drives up the costs of the system as a whole.[42] In Japan, too, the structure is mostly fragmented,

[40] For Taiwan, the following applies: 'Still in 1991, 74.9 per cent of the total welfare expenditure by the central government was spent on military servicemen, government employees, teachers, veterans and retired MPs. Considering that there were no social policy programmes for ordinary citizens except the Labour Insurance programme, the state must have been seen as protecting the interests of the privileged, although, until the lifting of martial law in 1987, there was little explicit criticism' (Kwon 1998a: 47f.).

[41] Cf. Kwon: 'This method of financing social welfare [with the state functioning only as "regulator"] has resulted in a fragmented welfare system in which the pooling of risk is narrower than in an integrated system. In the South Korean health care system, for instance, the public employees, the industrial workers, the self-employed and the farmers have their own health insurance schemes between which there is no financial transfer. In varying degrees, this is the case in Japan and Taiwan. Even in Singapore where the welfare system is integrated in the Central Provident Fund, there is no transfer mechanism between members' accounts within the Central Provident Fund. It should be noted, however, that the role of the state in the financing of social welfare in these countries is expanding' (1998a: 66). If one considers the far greater equality in primary income distribution in the East Asian territorial states compared to Western welfare states, one can speak of a 'redistribution from bottom to top' as a notable feature of the latters' social policy profile: 'The redistributive outcomes of social policy differ in East Asia from countries in the West such as Britain, due to their different methods of financing welfare. Elsewhere, I have compared the redistributive effects of state intervention in Japan and South Korea with those in Britain (Kwon 1997). That study showed that the distributions of market income and disposable income in Japan and South Korea are more equal than in Britain. Social policy intervention in Britain, however, is more redistributive than in Japan and South Korea where the better off get the lion's share of social policy benefits. This is, *inter alia*, largely due to the regulatory type of welfare financing' (Kwon 1998a: 66; see also 1997: 475; 2001).

[42] Cf. Kwon (1998a: 56): 'The pooling of risk was so narrow that the National Health Insurance could not flatten the rate of contingencies across the different risk categories. For instance, public employees, who tend to have good health, have their own National Health Insurance fund, while farmers, who are less healthy on average, had their own separate funds. The expected medical cost will be higher in the farmers' insurance fund than in the public employees'. If these two groups were integrated into one health insurance fund, the expected cost of health care would be the mean of the expected costs of the two funds, but this did not happen in the National Health Insurance system. Indeed, the fragmentation of National Health Insurance also raises the issue of social solidarity. Social insurance programmes can bring about social solidarity by pooling different risk groups, so that people in need can get help from the better-off. Under the prevalent system of National Health Insurance, such redistribution could not take place. As well as these shortcomings, the absence of any transfer mechanism between health insurance funds led to a high level of financial inequality between them.'

although demographic developments have strongly shaped the health insurance reform process and have marginalized particularistic elements of the system's organization (ibid.: 60ff.). In Taiwan, administrative integration across all risk groups seems to have taken place in 1995 (ibid.: 44f.).

Unemployment insurance does not exist in the region except in Japan (1947) and South Korea (1995). In Hong Kong, since 1978 unemployment is supposed to have been covered by a non-means-tested allowance for the unemployed (Tyabji 1993: 59). This is an employer benefit provided in case of dismissal; in other cases individuals are entitled only to welfare payments from the CSSA. In Taiwan there has been talk only of a 'virtual' unemployment insurance since 1979: 'The unemployed in Taiwan receive no statutory welfare support. While the revised Labour Insurance Act of 1979 stipulates that unemployment is a contingency covered by labour insurance, the provision of unemployment benefits is indefinitely suspended because unemployment has been so insignificant in the past two decades that such benefits are considered unnecessary' (G. Chan 1985: 348f.). Tang (1997: 59 n.1) writes, however, as if this unemployment insurance is now in force, yet 'strictly limited to very poor citizens', and thus resembling discretionary welfare rather than insurance.

Japanese unemployment insurance is comparatively weak. It targets primarily persons with standard, full-time jobs. Only about one-third of the part-time employed are insured. According to the Japanese Labour Force Survey, the share of benefit claimants among the unemployed is around 33 per cent. Unemployment assistance does not exist in Japan, but there is a 're-employment bonus'. Beyond unemployment insurance in a broader sense, one should also mention the well-developed system of corporate 'labour market adaptation subsidies', which supports the system of lifelong employment. This has obviated the need to institutionalize a more individualistic employment promotion policy with statutory entitlements (Seeleib-Kaiser 1996: 135–41). In the meantime, the traditional buffer sectors for continued employment beyond the age of 55 (retail, agriculture, construction and subcontracting) are themselves endangered or – with the exception of subcontracting – have been deprived of state protection against primarily foreign competition. The unemployment insurance scheme organizes transition assistance to pensioner status via a so-called wage subsidy for employed persons over the age of 60 (Seeleib-Kaiser 1999, 2002). In effect, the unemployment insurance scheme is used to a large extent to fulfil functions achieved in the West by social assistance programmes. A de facto full-employment policy which functioned in and for an essentially paternalistic corporate world through the 1990s, was, on the other hand, the functional equivalent of a public insurance scheme.

In South Korea there were efforts from the beginning of the 1990s to introduce contribution-based unemployment insurance in the context of the Seventh Economic Five-Year Plan, 1992–6 (H. K. Lee 1992: 171f.). Such a scheme was enacted in 1995.[43] In light of the developments of 1997–8, the IMF and the World Bank have without success urged the expansion of the unemployment insurance scheme as an essential component of the country's adjustment programme, in order to give employers the opportunity to undertake large-scale restructuring measures ranging from the reduction of excess personnel to the closing of entire factories (Holla 2001).

Since assets such as real estate can serve as a social insurance for prolonged spells of unemployment or old age, one has to note that in both mercantile city-states one

43 The contribution rate is 1.35 per cent: 0.3 per cent is paid by the employee and 1.05 per cent by the employer (Kwon 1998a: 53).

finds a distinctly socially oriented housing policy, the strongest and most comprehensive being in Singapore.[44] In Korea and Taiwan, but also in Japan, one observes equally marked, albeit weaker engagement in this area.[45]

Pension insurance schemes For the most part public pension insurance schemes are funded according to strict actuarial criteria rather than financed by a pay-as-you-go method – which has a much greater potential for group-transcending redistribution – and the introduction of non-actuarial benefits. Hence, risk-pooling does not predominate (Tyabji 1993: 54).[46] Hong Kong's parting British Governor Patten's proposal in July 1994 to set up a pay-as-you-go, strongly redistributional pension scheme failed. It would have represented the first complete departure from East Asia's restrictive social policy tradition.[47]

In terms of benefit levels, these pension schemes are minimalist, i.e. they are neither strongly related to the living standard achieved during occupational life ('full income maintenance') nor do they take the form of payments on a regular basis for the rest of one's life. Rather, they tend to be structured around a one-time lump-sum payment[48] and are more strictly based on the equivalence principle, and in this sense have less elaborate 'social' ('non-insurance') redistributive elements.

In analysing public pension systems, it is important to take into consideration as well, however, certain elements of corporate social policy – i.e. employee benefits such as severance and length-of-service bonuses. In Japan and Korea, these are fixed features of the *primary* income distribution, in most cases in the form of lump-sum payments, and had to be coordinated or fused with the subsequently introduced pension

44 In Singapore the CPF assists primarily in saving not for retirement, but for the purchase of a home. About 90 per cent of the population now live in their own home – certainly an international high point. Kwon attributes this much higher home ownership rate in Singapore than in Hong Kong to Singapore's state- and nation-building concerns, which shaped housing policy. In the wake of national independence in 1968, housing savings were made possible in the context of the Ordinary Account of the CPF, an account which could also be used for other purposes. The housing component consumes three-quarters of the social contribution, which is 40 per cent (Kwon 1998a: 37, 34; Tremewan 1998). On Hong Kong, cf. Jacobs (1998: 134).

45 Cf. for all three states the data in Jacobs (1998: 114, 122f., 130). On housing policy for seniors in Korea, see Choi (1992: 159f.).

46 Yet Kwon reports (1998a: 31): 'In Japan and South Korea, public pension programmes are arranged under the social insurance principle. These pension programmes combine elements of flat-rate and earnings-related principles so that higher-income earners who contribute higher premiums will have higher pensions in money terms, but low-income earners will receive a better return for their money. Because of this mechanism, intra-generational redistribution can take place.'

47 Cf. Kwon: 'As we have seen in Singapore, it is not unusual for the British to introduce a pension programme before they leave a colony. However, the Hong Kong proposal cannot be treated simply as a measure for an honourable retreat since the proposed OPS [Old Age Pension Scheme] was quite different from the provident fund normally introduced in former British colonies. Patten's OPS proposed a pay-as-you-go system in which the present elderly could receive immediate benefits from the contributions of the current working population. This would also have had a redistribution effect between income groups as well as generations since the contribution was to be 5–10 per cent of taxable income, with benefits at a flat rate. Such a pension proposal had never been conceived before in Hong Kong and was as radical as Patten's political reform' (1998a: 43). Patten's suggestions collided with an existing old-age insurance system which consisted above all in a Social Security Allowance (SSA) and a Higher Social Security Allowance. As in the case of the CSSA, the SSA provides welfare benefits, while the Higher SSA consists of programmes which provide non-means-tested, limited benefits financed exclusively by taxes.

48 As in the case of the (small) pension element in Taiwan's Labour Insurance scheme, see G. Chan (1985: 338).

schemes.[49] Since Hong Kong has no pension scheme whatsoever, something called Long Service Pay exists here on its own beside the city-state's minimalist systems of public assistance and welfare. In most cases, pension insurance schemes in East Asia are structured according to the same privilege-based design already found in health-insurance schemes; their pattern of institutional development is similarly top-down with a rather weak trickle-down effect.[50]

The Japanese pension insurance system is much further developed than South Korea's or Taiwan's. It covers the entire population and is long established, i.e. it has long been capable of paying claims. And also – with its 'basic pension' element paid by the state – it deviates from the provident fund approach (Kwon 1998a: 59). Japan's pension system thus receives a more elaborate state subsidy; the public sector goes beyond a mere regulatory role and assumes a provider role. Japan is an exception also in the sense that the longer institutional history of its pension policy has increasingly created an independent dynamic, which, in interaction with the demographic transition towards a top-heavy population pyramid, led to those typical policy problems with which Western welfare states are confronted as well.

With the exception of Japan, long-term care insurance schemes do not yet exist in East Asia.[51] South Korea, for example, has the maxim: 'Family care first, social secu-

49 In Korea a telling conflict emerged on this issue: 'The fourth issue [in implementing the National Pension program in 1988] was the relationship between the national pension and the severance allowance system that has been in operation since the Labour Standards Law of 1953. The 1973 National Welfare Pension Law did not specify this relationship. . . . [The capitalists] insisted on an "either/or" choice. In other words, if to introduce the national pension insurance with capitalists' contributions together with the workers, the employer's burden of the severance allowance which comes up to 8.9 per cent of monthly remuneration should be reduced or eliminated. On the part of the workers, elimination of the severance allowance system, which is the responsibility of the employer and already an established right for workers by law, and its replacement by the National Pension Insurance for which workers share the contribution with employers, was not acceptable. The compromise was the gradual merging of the severance allowance into the national pension, as well as the creation of Unemployment Insurance' (H. K. Lee 1992: 171). The implementation of the unemployment insurance scheme did not occur, however, until 1995. On the Korean pension system, see also Kwon (1998b, 1999b).

50 The effect of the highly fragmented social policies can be discerned from the following data: 'Currently, 65,000 or 3.3 per cent of older Koreans aged 65 and over are receiving these special pensions. This is also the total number of pensioners in Korea in 1990' (Choi 1992: 155). The reason for the latter is that the General Pension Insurance Scheme is still under construction. One can compare this to the social assistance figures: 'The number of elderly recipients of the LP [Livelihood Protection Act of 1961] has been around 200,000–270,000, or 12–16 per cent of the total elderly population aged 65 and over, or 9–14 per cent of the total LP recipients. It is notable that the proportion of elderly recipients has shown an increase in recent years' (ibid.: 156). This social policy landscape is further complicated by the fact that since 1991 a special (social-assistance-style) basic pension (Old Age Allowance) exists, which is designed to bridge the period until the General Pension Insurance Scheme becomes operative (ibid.). Against this background, the Retirement Benefit paid by companies as a gratuity according to the Labour Standards Act of 1953 unfolds its particular importance: 'The RB [Retirement Benefit] is paid as a lump sum when the worker leaves the work-place because of having reached retirement age or for other reasons. Currently, this programme is the principal income maintenance programme for most retirees in Korea, covering some 4.8 million, or 29.5 per cent, of Korean workers' (ibid.: 157). On the RB, Choi adds: 'However, its benefit level is not sufficient to maintain a minimum living standard' (ibid.: 151).

51 Japan introduced a mandatory Long Term Care Insurance scheme on 1 April 2000. It is administered by the municipalities and financed by multiple sources: 12.5 per cent by the municipalities and prefects, 25 per cent by the central government and 50 per cent by the insured, among which those over age 65 would pay 17 per cent and those aged 40–65 would pay 33 per cent (*PKV Publik* 7/98: 79; cf. also Eto 2001).

rity second' (Choi 1992: 161). This indeed reflects societal conditions there: 'As regards living arrangements, 99.7 per cent of Koreans aged 65 and over are living with their families or alone in the community, whereas only 0.3 per cent are living in institutions' (ibid.: 150).

This third element of welfare state development in East Asian countries, the pension system, consists once more – in terms of both its institutional structure and political governance – of comparatively free-standing institutions. They are not the organic, politically engineered extensions of social structures that are typical of Western countries, or systemic outgrowths from private or self-organized institutions such as welfare funds, savings banks, or mutual sickness and invalidity insurance funds, which in Europe at the end of the nineteenth century constituted the main agents of social welfare provision (Swaan 1988).

The emergence of pension schemes in East Asia is not only closely connected with the functional conditions and problems of the corporate-industrial economic order, but also rigidly limited by the perceived demands of international industrial competitiveness. Through the 1980s, social policy reform has always been initiated by state bureaucracies without significant social pressure or political mobilization from below (Garon 1987; Wilkinson 1994). Already for this reason, social policy never tested the limits of public households or overtaxed employers. Moreover, in all East Asian countries after the Second World War defence of the state and social order against labour movements came to be equated with defence of the capitalist economic system that supported that order.

These conditions of emergence explain as well why social policy schemes encounter considerable resistance not only among employers but even among the sharply separated employee groups, which were almost never able to speak with one voice. In addition, in South Korea and Taiwan there have been considerable difficulties implementing welfare state regulation effectively (Deyo 1992: 299).[52] In South Korea, for example, there is almost always an enormous time gap – sometimes decades – between enactment of legislation and the actual budgeting of funds and organizational implementation (H. K. Lee 1992).

The extremely functional orientation of social policy is expressed further in the fact that in some countries it is used routinely to provide long-term, inexpensive financing for state infrastructure or to subsidize industry. Japan's pension insurance scheme and Singapore's CPF[53] constitute the two most important examples of this. South Korea first crossed the universalization threshold in the pension insurance sphere with the National Pension Act of December 1973. It incorporated broader segments of the population into the pension scheme for the first time. Yet this expansion in coverage was motivated exclusively by the need to generate additional

52 In Taiwan, the unions were invited, but chose not to participate in, the drafting of comprehensive occupational health and safety legislation which was to unify the previous provisions in the fields of labour contract law, working hours, the consequences of accidents at work, maternal leave and retirement. Thus the Ministry of Labour represented workers vis-à-vis employers (Deyo 1992: 303; Weggel 1991: 283).

53 Kwon reports on the CPF: 'In 1994, the CPF fund stood at . . . 73.19 per cent of GDP in that year. Of this . . . 55.37 per cent of GDP was invested in government bonds and the rest was held as advanced deposits with the Monetary Authority of Singapore. The function of advanced deposits is as a reserve fund for withdrawal by members of the CPF. The government in turn has invested these funds at home and abroad, though the details of its portfolio are not made publicly available' (1998a: 35).

savings for the next capital-intensive wave of industrialization (H. K. Lee 1992: 158f.).[54] The prominent role of private wealth formation in social protection and public assistance, reflected in a traditionally high rate of savings, together with the wide range of corporate employee benefit schemes, prevent the state from ascribing a comprehensive responsibility for the social status of individuals or from developing political support for the idea of citizens' social rights and their attendant welfare state politicization.[55]

The educational system The fourth common feature of East Asian welfare state development consists in the comprehensive and intensely achievement-oriented educational system (Ashton and Green 1996). In Korea and Taiwan, the Japanese colonial administrations in many ways laid the foundations for the entire educational system.[56] In these countries there was a strong convergence of interest in education on the part of both the population, including the old agrarian-aristocratic classes,[57] and the state, which exhibited a strong orientation towards strategic human capital formation. Taiwan appears to have been even more active than Korea in this regard (M. L. Lee et al. 1994: 276). The high demand for educational goods and the central importance of examinations for access to both higher educational institutions and employment in the public and private sector led to a broad supply of non-state schools, educational institutions and tutoring programmes in all East Asian countries.[58] Public expenditure on education remains very high even today, and the pressure to achieve on pupils and students is enormous. The educational system is thus structured far more universally than the system of social policy. Education – and not compensation for status loss – serves as an engine for social policy. Finally, it is only in educational policy, but not in other realms of social policy, that the two territorial states (i.e. non-city-states) Korea and Taiwan evinced an unbroken, historically cumulative, advanced level of development in the twentieth century:

54 'As a means to raise the rate of private savings by popular masses, workers were forced to join the National Welfare Pension Fund, which required a 20-year contribution. The Korea Development Institute [an official and influential entity] estimated that the national pension scheme would mobilize about 100 billion won in less than two years' (H. K. Lee 1992: 159).

55 On Japan, see Thränhardt (1995: 432).

56 On Korea, see J. H. Woo (1991); on Taiwan, see A. Kohli (1994, 1997) and Yu (1989: 215f.). Tsurumi (1996) observes Korea (294–308) and Taiwan (279–94) together: 'In both Taiwan and Korea, education was made a central pillar of colonial development' (279), although he is referring here primarily to popular, not elite education, and Korea had a far less bumpy path of development. As shown by the example of Taiwan, however, where in 1928 the first university – Taihoku Imperial University (now National Taiwan University) – was opened, slowly but surely the entire Japanese educational system was implanted.

57 Hye Kyung Lee (1992: 148 n.1) calls attention to an interesting interaction between educational expansion and land reform in Korea, which makes clear the new strategic significance of educational qualification for social mobility and societal differentiation: 'The fundamental bent for education, which lay in the traditional culture itself, was accelerated by the decline of the landlord class due to the land reform. In order to maintain their former social status, many of the former landlords were obliged to invest their residual resources in the education of their children. The educational drive and the agrarian reform were mutually reinforcing.'

58 In Korea, the corporate world and the school system merged in certain cases: 'Tapping the well known educational zeal, many companies established secondary schools on the company premises to attract young workers from poor villages and reduce worker turnover' (You 1995: 122).

> Perhaps the most immediate legacy of the Japanese colonial era was the existence of the hundreds of thousands of educated South Koreans and Taiwanese who became the core of the post-war political and economic elites. Most were the products of the public-school systems that the Japanese had developed in Korea and Taiwan to train literate manpower and inculcate the local population with Japanese cultural and social values. By 1940, about 38 per cent of school-age children attended elementary school in Korea, and about 58 per cent of school-age Taiwanese children did so. During the 1930s some children of elite families in both societies began to take the road of higher education. (Kobayashi 1996: 325)[59]

Summary Tables 5.3 and 5.4 summarize the essential institutional features of social policy in these East Asian countries. The focus is upon the specific characteristics of their welfare state organization and the scope of their social policy schemes. When these institutional features are seen in relation to the data on social benefits in these countries, the nature of the peculiarity of welfare state development in East Asia becomes clear.

The missing welfare state: interpretations and explanations

Both the institutional peculiarities of welfare state developments in East Asian countries and their low levels of public spending relative to GDP suggest that they inhabit an entirely different welfare state universe. Figure 5.1 depicts this enormous institutional break between East Asian and Western welfare states and identifies the main factors that could be relevant for an explanation of the differences. Hardly any systematic comparative studies of social policy in East Asia and Western welfare states are available; the majority of the literature is empirical and descriptive. Nevertheless, among the – usually implicit – explanatory attempts for the generally observed lack of the development of a comprehensive welfare state in East Asia, we can distinguish three principal approaches.

A first approach, which shapes most of the discussion on socio-political developments in East Asia, lies within the confines of traditional modernization theory. Essentially, it sees only a *time lag* in socio-political relative to industrial development, yet no systematic difference from the Western pattern of development. Exponents of this school point chiefly to the institutional, or formal, development of state socio-political interventions and their close resemblance to counterparts in the West.[60] To the extent that such interpretations are always predicated on presumptions of future development, yet at the same time can supply no time frames or critical thresholds the fulfilment of which would constitute confirmation of the 'theory', these explanations are empirically impossible to test.[61] Steve Chan's study (1997) is an exception, since it

[59] More recent revisionist historiography emphasizes the exceptional colonial status of Taiwan and Korea compared to Western colonies. This leads directly to the development surge in both countries after the Second World War: 'As Professors Myers and Eckert point out, the encouragement of industrial development in colonial areas was unique to Japanese imperialism. No other modern imperialist power, with the possible exception of the British in India, embarked on such an extensive program of colonial industrialization' (Duus 1996: xxxiii). The export of the Japanese educational system through a programme of colonial enculturation was a component of Japan's imperialistic policy (Tsurumi 1996).

[60] Cf. Patten (1988), who, as the last governor of Hong Kong, sought to introduce a general, pay-as-you-go pension scheme and to thereby actively support this interpretation and development.

[61] But see Marsh's carefully designed case study of the 'great transformation' of Taipei, Taiwan, to test 'neomodernization' theory (1996).

Table 5.3 Features of state welfare provision in East Asia

Japan	*South Korea*	*Taiwan*	*Singapore*	*Hong Kong*
		Social security		
Statutory, discretionary, closely confined public assistance. + Old-age assistance: since WWII 2-level: mandatory nat. basic pension ins. for residents aged 20–59 (1985); income-related suppl. mandatory ins. for employees (1944ff.) & other groups; contributions by employers and employees of 8.675% each; 1/3 of benefit level paid by state as lump sum in cases of disability; social security contribution ceiling. + Accident ins. (1911) + Unempl. ins. since 1947 (amended 1975/94); employee contrib. 0.4%, employer 0.75%, with risk surcharges of up to 10.5%.	Statutory, discretionary public assistance. + Contribution-financed national pension ins. since 1973, expanded in 1986 (1998 employee contrib. 3% of gross wages, employer contrib. 6% of total wage bill of the company); no social security contribution ceiling; state assumes portion of admin costs & subsidizes costs for farmers and fishermen; separate systems for public employees, the military and private school teachers; disability pensions. + Accident ins. since 1953; since 1963 employer contrib. ranges from 0.6% to 29.9% of wages acc. to risk group (avg. 1.7%). + Unempl. ins. since 1995 in dev't.	Statutory, discretionary public assistance. + Mandatory worker pension ins. since 1950s with 6.5% contrib.: employee 1.3% (self-employed 3.9%), employer 4.55%, state 0.65% (2.6% for self-employed) plus adm. costs; social security contribution ceiling; lump sum payment as a rule at retirement age; disability pension. + Accident ins. (since 1929, reformed in 1958/94); employer contrib. only: ranges from 0.09% to 3% of wages acc. to risk group (avg. 0.39%). + No unempl. ins.	Statutory, discretionary minimum public assistance. + Indep. pension policy since 1953: mandatory ins. in Central Provident Fund (mandatory saving with employer and employee contrib. of 20% each; no social security contribution ceiling; lower contrib. for employees over 55; favourable tax treatment of CPF); benefits above all for home purchase (Ordinary Account 30 Points), for old-age bonus (Special – 4 contrib. points – & Ordinary Account) & for disability; separate systems for public employees & some categ. of priv. empl. + Accident ins. since 1929 (last expansion 1985); employer liability + No separate unempl. ins.	Since 1970s 2-level system of public assistance: (1) statutorily regulated general (Comprehensive Social Security Assistance, CSSA) & old-age related (Old Age Assistance, OAA within Social Security Assistance, SSA) public assistance, (2) old-age (from age 70, higher OAA within SSA) & disability assistance (within SSA); both are tax-financed. + 2-level accident ins.: public assistance (1971) & Employer Liability Ins. (1953). + Unempl. assistance within CSSA (1978) can be provided in addition to an employer provided severance bonus.
		Public welfare		
Mainly voluntary & communal organizations; networks of voluntary organizations.	Mainly voluntary organizations.	Public welfare institutions & subsidized voluntary organizations.	State funds (financed in part by employee contributions); networks of voluntary organizations.	State subsidies & funds; networks of voluntary organizations.

Table 5.3 (continued)

Japan	*South Korea*	*Taiwan*	*Singapore*	*Hong Kong*
		Health		
Priv. sector dominates benefit provision; 2-levels: since 1938 National Health Ins. (NHI), usually communally admin.'d (or by Mutual Aid Associations (MAAs) above all for the self-employed), since 1961 for all residents outside of state Employee Health Ins. scheme (EHI since 1927), above all for self-employed, pensioners etc.; NHI replaces lost earnings; EHI consists of *c.*1,900 orgs. in 4 groups: Social Insurance Agency (small & mid-sized firms), occup. health ins. (large firms), sailors' ins. & ins. assocs for public employees & teachers (MAAs); in NHI state pays 50% of total expenses & adm. costs; rest financed by contribs of varying rates & communal subsidies; EHI-financing: employer	Since 1963 slow (1988 still only 2/3 of pop. covered), since 1989 (via suppl. Regional Health Ins.) sweeping progress towards universal coverage; covers farmers, self-employed, pensioners & employees in small firms; 1995 health ins. scheme newly reformed; separate systems for public employees & private school teachers (contrib. of ins. & employer 2.3% each, military (free) as well as ind. employees (contrib.'s of employers & employees each 1–4% of wages before bonuses (avg. 1.52%) – fund adm.'d jointly by employers and employees [1992: 420 funds]); state pays adm. costs & a % of other costs (in Regional Health Ins. 50%). Only rudimentary financial equalization mechanism; subst.	1950 intro. of limited state health ins.; special schemes for public employees, for teachers & for children & pupils (1989 an additional 38% of pop.); means-tested, free medical care; mainly private beside some state and philanthropic medical aid for the poor (1994 for *c.*50% of pop.). 1995 introduced a soon-to-be universal (except for unemployed) National Health Ins. scheme; contrib. depends on ins. plan, i.e. for employees in indust. & trade: employee contrib. 1.275% for employee & for each add. fam. member up to 5; employer 2.55% & 2.4225% for each addit. fam. member; state contrib. 0.425% for each fam. member & assumption of any deficits. Large co-payments. Limited	State and state-subsidized private health care system with patient co-payments; Medisave Accounts in the CPF cover primarily hospital care, financed by 6 out of 40 contribution percentage points; beyond this, voluntary suppl ins. Medishield & Medishield Plus for expensive services (catastrophic care ins.) utilized by 85% of those eligible; further, continued wage payment by employer for 14 days per year, for a max. of 60 days in cases of hospital stay. Medifund, a state foundation independent of the CPF which is financed by the interest on state-provided capital, subsidizes the hospital costs of the poor.	State (Hospital Authority (54%)) & state-subsidized medical assistance for the poor (28%), as well as purely private medical assistance for the poor (18% of patients in 1988); no state health ins. scheme (14% private ins., mostly via employer); overburdened state health service for out-patient care, *c.*65% of patients visit private doctors; in cases of illness (after a 3-day waiting period) continued wage payment by employer for up to 120 days at 80% of wages, otherwise social assistance (CSSA).

and employee each pay 4.3% of basic wage, state pays 13% of benefits; co-payments; since 1961 comprehensive coverage of pop. with broad range of benefits. EHI has rudimentary financial equalization mechanism. Since 1972 free med. care for seniors.	co-payments and min. benefits. State-subsidized services for selected groups; no provision for loss of earnings. Virtually no private health ins., but partially (1/5) private service providers. Supplement for poor via Medicaid (free med. care only for seniors & disabled).	continued wage payment: after 3-day waiting period 50% of wages for up to 6 months (in some plans 1 year).		
		Education		
9-yr. compulsory school attendance (6 elementary & 3 middle school), admission to 3-yr. secondary school (rate of attendance 94.8%) via highly competitive examinations, especially in private schools; highly competitive, 2-level admissions test for (mainly public) university admission: 1st level – standard, state, 2nd level – designed by each university separately. Rates of attendance: 2-yr. college 12.4%, university 26.4%.	Mixed system of public and private schools; 9-yr. compulsory school attendance for elementary & middle school, 7 years of which are free; highly competitive. Extremely selective access (via examinations and lottery) to high schools – rate of attendance 84% (1992); state-controlled.	Exclusively state system, 9-yr. compulsory, free school attendance; free school materials for the needy; rate of attendance: 98%. Elementary school usually state, as are 1/3 of middle schools; predominantly standardized curriculum set by Min. of Ed.; attendance rates of high school, vocational school and junior college (1/3 state-run): 90% each; attendance rate of university (private, subsidized): 29% of 18–21 yr. olds.	10-yr. compulsory school attendance; predominantly state or state-subsidized school system (only elem. school free); attendance rate of middle school (75% of which are private): 87.4%; highly competitive examination system; state-controlled curriculum in state-run or subsidized schools; some independent schools with curricular discretion.	9-yr. compulsory school attendance (elem. & middle school; attendance rate: 99%); mixed system of state and state-subsidized schools (84%) & private schools (16%); (state) high school attendance rate: 83.8%; standardized, state-controlled curriculum; highly competitive examination system. University attendance rate (mostly private, yet subsidized): 19.6%.

Table 5.3 (continued)

Japan	*South Korea*	*Taiwan*	*Singapore*	*Hong Kong*
		Housing		
Low share of publicly constructed housing (9% of new construction 1945–90); somewhat subsidized (31%); high share of rental housing in large-scale housing construction (60% purely privately financed); low housing allowance for state employees.	Low share of publicly constructed housing; selected subsidies above all for middle classes; comprehensive, price-damping housing-market control by Korea Housing Bank.	Selected subsidies; 80% of the population live in their own home; 5% of housing stock is state property; subsidized mortgages for purchasing own home.	87% of pop. live in state-constructed housing (Housing and Development Board, 1997); 81% of pop. owns apt. or house (CPF, via Ordinary Account).	High share of publicly constructed housing (1989: 47%). 1996 35% of households in Housing Authority (HA) apts., 11% of pop. finances home purchase with HA-mortgages. Targeted housing policy for low-income population.

Sources: Social Security Administration (1997) and Jacobs (1998); as well as G. Chan (1985), Chang (1985), Jones (1990b; 1993), Leibfried (1994) and Chiang (1997)

Table 5.4 Types and coverage by welfare state institutions in East Asia in the mid-1990s (%)

Programme	*Instrument*	*Type*	*Coverage*
	Japan (1995)		
Health Care	Employee Health Insurance (EHI, government managed)	insurance	30
	EHI (society managed)	insurance	26
	National Health Insurance (self-employed, etc.)	insurance	34
	Public Employees Mutual Aid Associations (MAAs, part of EHI)	insurance	9
	Medicaid	assistance	0.54
Invalidity, maternity, occupational injury	EHI (government managed)	insurance	30
	EHI (society managed)	insurance	23
	National Health Insurance (self-employed, etc.)	insurance	—
	Public Employee Mutual Aid Associations (MAAs, part of EHI)	insurance	8
	Government Employee Accident Insurance (1993)	insurance	7
	Workmen Accident Compensation Insurance (1993)	insurance	70
Old age, survivor & disability	National Pension Insurance	insurance	47
	Employees Pension Insurance	insurance	49
	MAAs – public sector	insurance	8
	MAAs – private sector	insurance	1
	Public Assistance	assistance	4.5[a]
Family	Child Allowance	allowance/employer liability	63[b]
	Child Support Allowance	allowance	106[c]
	Public Assistance	assistance	9.2[c]
Unemployment	Unemployment Insurance (1993)	insurance	50
	Public Assistance	assistance	0.06[d]
	South Korea (1996)		
Health Care[e]	Civil Servants and Private School Teachers Health Insurance	insurance	11
	Industrial Employees Health Insurance	insurance	37
	Regional Health Insurance	insurance	50
	Medicaid	assistance	4
	Free medical care for the military	state provision	1.4

Table 5.4 (continued)

Programme	*Instrument*	*Type*	*Coverage*
Invalidity, maternity, occupational injury, old age, survivor & disability	Industrial Accident Compensation Insurance	insurance	40
	Labour Standards Law	employers' liability	20
	National Pension Programme	insurance	35
	Government Officials' Pension Programme (1994)	insurance	5
	Private School Teachers Pension Programme (1994)	insurance	1
	Labour Standards Law	employer	—
	Livelihood Protection Act	public assistance	4[f]
Family	Livelihood Protection Act	public assistance	—[g]
Unemployment	Employment Insurance Programme	insurance	20
	Taiwan (1996)		
Health Care	National Health Insurance	insurance	93
	Free medical care for the military	state provision	1.7
Invalidity, maternity, occupational injury	Labour Insurance	insurance	80
	Farmers' Insurance (only maternity protection)	insurance	19[h]
Old age, survivors	Labour Insurance	insurance	80
	Government Employees Insurance	insurance	7
	Farmers Insurance (only for survivors)	insurance	19[h]
	Old Age Allowance	allowance	20[j]
	Farmers Old Age Allowance	allowance	22[j]
	Public Assistance	assistance	0.54[f]
Disability	Labour Insurance	insurance	80
	Government Employees Insurance[i]	insurance	7
	Farmers Insurance (only for survivors)	insurance	19[h]

Hong Kong (1995)			
Health Care, invalidity, maternity, occupational injury	Hospital Authority (1998)	State provision	82[k]
	Invalidity Pay	employer liability	84.3[l]
	Maternity Benefit	employer liability	84.3[l]
	Occupational Injury Pay	employer liability	84.3[l]
	Medicaid (part of the Comprehensive Social Security Assistance, CSSA)	public assistance	0.48[m]
Old age, survivors	Old Age Allowance – OAA (part of Social Security Assistance, SSA)	allowance	54[n]
	Higher OAA (also part of SSA)	allowance	82[o]
	Long Service Pay	employer liability	—
	CSSA benefits	assistance	14[j]
Disability, family, unemployment	Disability Allowance (SSA)	assistance	1.11[p]
	CSSA	assistance	0.16[p]
	CSSA (for single parents)	assistance	0.15[p]
	Unemployment Severance Pay	employer liability	84.3[l]
	CSSA (for the unemployed)	assistance	0.62[p]
Singapore (1996)			
Health Care	Ministry of Health	state provision	—
	Medisave Account of the Central Provident Fund (CPF) (1995)	provident fund	80[q]
	MediShield (CPF) (1995)	provident fund & insurance	50
	MediFund (independent state foundation)	assistance	3[r]
Invalidity, maternity, occupational injury	Invalidity Pay	employer liability	83[l]
	Maternity Pay	employer liability	83[l]
	Occupational Injury Pay	employer liability	83[l]
Old age, survivor	Special and Ordinary[s] Account (CPF)	provident fund	70[t]
	Civil servants' pension	employer liability	—
	Dependants' Protection Scheme	provident fund & insurance	70[t]
	Public Assistance	assistance	0.8
Disability	CPF	provident fund	70[t]
	Dependants Protection Scheme (CPF)	provident fund & insurance	70
	Public Assistance	assistance	—

Table 5.4 (continued)

Notes: As a rule (following Jacobs, 1998: 11), we have listed only those programmes for which coverage figures exist. The reference year for the degree of coverage is listed next to each country's name (deviations are listed next to programme titles). For health insurance (and 'Provident') programmes, coverage is presented as the share of potentially eligible individuals (not of those actually receiving benefits) relative to the general population (and for income-replacement benefits relative to the economically active population). For allowances or other government assistance, the data refers to the share of recipients relative to the total population or to the relevant population group (e.g. those 65 or older in the case of the Old-Age Allowance). The concepts 'insurance', 'allowance' and 'assistance' are used in the conventional (ILO) sense, with public assistance being largely means-tested, whereas higher-level government assistance ('allowance') allows for generous exemptions of assets and income and thus approaches statutory entitlements

[a] As % of elderly households

[b] As % of children under the age of 3 years old

[c] As % of all lone-parent households

[d] Recipient households other than elderly, disabled and lone parents as % of labour force

[e] Excluding cash benefits (maternity grant, funeral grant, etc.)

[f] All recipients (including non-elderly) as % of total population (more precise figures not available)

[g] Cannot be precisely determined

[h] 30% of those covered by Farmers' Insurance are older than 65 and hence probably not included in the statistics on the economically active population, so that the 19% figure here is overestimated

[i] Includes Retired Government Employee Insurance and Insurance for Teaching and Administrative Staffs of Private Schools

[j] As % of the population aged 65 and older

[k] The entire population is entitled to benefits but a minority chooses to opt out of the public sector, paying high user fees in the private sector

[l] Available to all civil servants as well as private sector employees

[m] As % of the economically active population

[n] As % of the population aged 65–70

[o] As % of the population aged 70 and older

[p] As % of the general population (share of the disabled population unknown)

[q] Co-insured dependants must be added (data not available)

[r] Based on number of claims filed, not on number of benefits recipients

[s] Minimum sum and final withdrawal

[t] Proportion of active members of CPF in the labour force

Source: South Korea (Jacobs 1998: 17, Table 3), Taiwan (Jacobs 1998: 19, Table 4), Hong Kong (Jacobs 1998: 22, Table 6), Singapore (Jacobs 1998: 24, Table 8), Japan (Jacobs 1998: 14, Table 2).

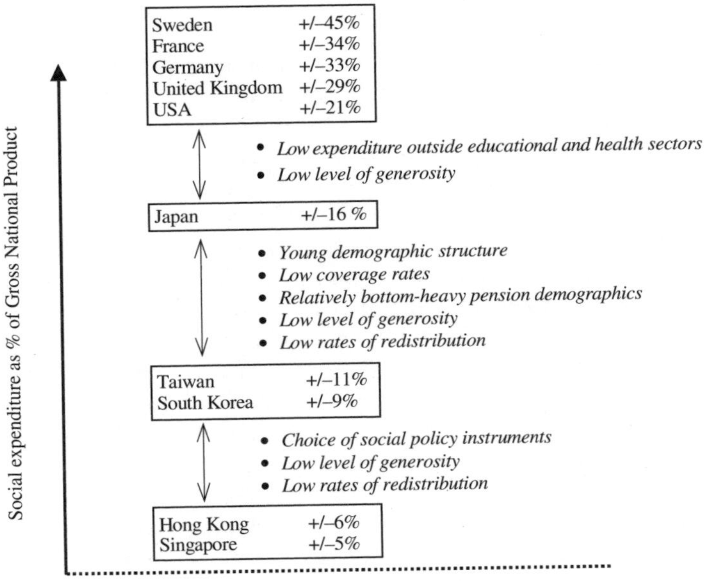

Figure 5.1 The main causes of differences in social benefit levels

Note: The figures cited are based on the OECD definition. For the Western countries and Japan they are based on the year 1993; for the Newly Industrializing Countries they are based on 1995

Source: Jacobs (1998 : 90) and the authors

focuses on the data available. He examines the influence of the democratization of Taiwan and South Korea on these countries' social expenditure, using Singapore as a contrasting case. For both territorial states his findings indeed show significant increases in per capita expenditure on education and social security, yet no shifts in the percentage share of these spending categories within the public household. This development seems to speak for an influence of democratization. However, changes in spending levels in specific policy sectors – education, health care, social security and housing – do not follow any uniform pattern, and they do not differ fundamentally from developments in Singapore.

A second line of interpretation focuses on the political conditions of welfare state development, especially anti-communist repression of unions and labour parties. The latter policy was shaped by the front lines of the Cold War and was long supported by the USA, and undoubtedly owed much of its endurance and impact in this region to their support (Berger and Borer 1997: 3–9; Berger 1997). Both the rapid development of a modern social structure in the context of urbanization and industrialization, and the successful demands by unions and labour parties for socio-political gains in income security and income equalization across groups and strata, suggest, according to this view, the existence of welfare state development along Western lines. This development was blocked, however, by the fact that in the interest of an employer-controlled market economy and of the hegemony of traditional elites, the representatives of the new social groups were oppressed. If it were not for the war-related repression and weakening of labour parties, the argument goes, social policy would have attained a level of magnitude accordant with these countries' level of industrial development (Wilkinson 1994: 204–7; Pei 1998: 46f.).

A third interpretation – compared to the other two it is more implicitly argued – views economic prosperity itself as the main cause of socio-political moderation. The premeditated choice to pursue consistently a fiscally conservative public policy instead of building up an interventionist tax state along European lines is the factor that has precluded a policy of welfare state expansion (World Bank 1993). In one variant of this interpretation, public intervention and the institutionalization of extensive government transfer programmes became superfluous to the extent that welfare is produced for the population by the market economy itself in the form of rising incomes, or by companies in the form of American-style 'welfare capitalism'.[62] In another variant, the low level of socio-political intervention is seen as the direct result of a conscious decision in favour of the effectiveness of the market mechanism as opposed to state public action, explicitly attributed in part to the 'puritan' economic ethic of Confucianism.[63] Authoritarian rule in East Asian countries is thus viewed as the decisive factor explaining why they were able to establish the most adequate economic policy. The foundation for the economic success of these countries is thus not laissez-faire capitalism, according to this interpretation, but, rather, strict state control of the political-economic framework and the pursuit of strategic industrial policy (Amsden 1989; Wade 1990b; Root and Weingast 1996).[64]

62 Drèze and Sen (1991: 22) call this a strategy of 'growth-driven security' and contrast it with 'state-provided security'. While in the first strategy, economic growth is given priority, the second concentrates on making available socio-political goods and services *before* the economy generates higher levels of employment and income. With regard to the effectiveness of these strategies, they ascertain that in a ranking of the countries with the highest success rates in the reduction of child mortality (under the age of 5) during the period 1960–5, Hong Kong ranked first (83 per cent), followed by Chile. The average GNP per-capita growth rates were 6.1 per cent in Hong Kong and –0.2 per cent in Chile. Also the subsequent rank order is inconclusive: the United Arab Republic, Costa Rica, Kuwait, Cuba, Singapore, China, Jamaica and South Korea (ibid.: 23).

63 One could argue that it is precisely because Confucian culture, while not bringing forth its own brand of capitalism, was essential to capitalism's successful implementation, that social policy was prevented – as an opposite pole to the market and its supporting values – from becoming dominant. For Max Weber, the disciplining, rational qualities of modern capitalism were the feature that distinguished it from other, historically precedent economic forms. For this reason, he was interested in connections between the particular economic rationalism of capitalism and the 'economic ethic' of the world religions. His thesis and argumentation on the role of the 'Protestant ethic' need not be further elaborated here. In his examination of Confucianism, Weber emphasized its eminent compatibility with economic rationalism: 'In the sense of the absence of all metaphysics and almost all residues of religious anchorage, Confucianism is rationalist to such a far-going extent that it stands at the extreme boundary of what one might possibly call a "religious" ethic. At the same time, Confucianism is more rationalist and sober, in the sense of the absence and the rejection of all non-utilitarian yardsticks, than any other ethical system, with the possible exception of J. Bentham's' (Weber 1920: 293). Beside this fundamental worldly-sober disposition, Weber highlights the willingness to save, diligence and discipline which characterize members of Confucian-influenced societies, i.e. social qualities which in Europe could only laboriously be cultivated in non-Puritans. Above all, the lacking or lax work discipline in factories was one of the major impediments to the *take-off* of industrialization in Europe. In any case, following in Weber's footsteps, Robert Bellah interprets the Japanese form of Confucianism as a functional equivalent to the 'Protestant ethic', to which he attributes Japan's economic ascendance (1985 [1957]).

64 In particular it is argued that the distinctiveness of economic development in East Asia lies in the credible commitments of governmental elites. Property rights are for the most part politically secure, and the framework conditions are designed such that the macro-economic fruits of prosperity are distributed widely throughout the population, not monopolized by select groups (Campos and Root 1996: 174–7).

Table 5.5 Agrarian protectionism in East Asia, 1955–1982

	1955–9	*1960–4*	*1965–9*	*1970–4*	*1975–9*	*1980–2*
Japan						
Rice	50	72	99	160	263	249
Wheat	37	62	97	127	276	278
Beef	113	142	165	146	284	181
weighted Ø	44	68	87	110	147	151
Korea						
Rice	−14	−9	6	55	138	154
Wheat	−22	−8	18	16	47	128
Beef	3	5	55	88	281	354
weighted Ø	−15	−5	9	55	129	166
Taiwan						
Rice	−31	−8	−13	4	58	144
Wheat	48	25	39	32	57	92
Beef	−4	8	20	37	162	153
weighted Ø	−21	2	2	17	36	55

Note: The figures represent the degree to which domestic prices were higher or lower than world market prices (%)

Source: Anderson et al. (1986: 22)

One objection to the above interpretations is that East Asian development does indeed follow the Western pattern in one sphere, namely agriculture. Just as in the historical development of Western industrial societies, in East Asian countries agrarian protectionism has increased much more than just proportionately with levels of modernization and prosperity. Within a period of only a few years, these countries built up elaborate systems of protective tariffs and subsidies, thoroughly insulating their national agricultural sectors from the rest of the world (see Table 5.5). The main policy goal of this protectionism was to guarantee income security for the agriculturally employed population (K. Anderson et al. 1986).

This development not only demonstrates the receptiveness of East Asian political systems to socio-political pressure, it also makes clear that under specific conditions free-market policies can be put on the back burner if issues of income security and income distribution are considered to be of greater political relevance. This is no small matter. Agrarian protectionism considerably raised the cost of living for the urban industrial workforce and thereby massively helped to erode the main comparative advantage – a low-wage economy – to which not only the four 'tiger' states but also Japan owed their international economic success. Not surprisingly, then, the East Asian countries tried to cushion the effects of their welfare-state agricultural policy by subsidizing food prices. East Asian countries' protectionism in the agricultural sector is not exceptional; their general export orientation has been matched by a relatively restrictive import policy. This moment, too, has socially conservative, or welfare state roots: it is based on the American tolerance over many years of protectionism in light of these countries' foreign and defence policies (L. B. Krause 1989; Shin 1994). These countries pursued restrictive import practices in an effort to block potential negative effects on their social structures and income distributions (Haggard and Moon 1983; Baldwin et al. 1995; El-Agraa 1995; Huff 1995; Lindlar 1995; Sato 1995). Moreover, in South Korea and Japan, a concern for national political autonomy played a central role in the limitation of direct foreign investment.[65]

The example of agriculture points to a further objection to the idea of an authoritarian repression of socio-political mobilization. For in Taiwan and South Korea in particular, and to a considerable extent also in Japan, broad-based social movements existed in favour of land reform. In dealing with this issue, governments, despite their undoubtedly conservative leanings, did not help the agrarian aristocracy to uphold the old order. Rather, the state's strength and ability to act independently was demonstrated precisely in its succumbing to populist pressure to implement far-reaching land reform, against the resistance of traditional rural elites (Haggard 1990; Dorner and Thiesenhusen 1990; Jenkins 1991: 206ff.). Similar successes of independent, populist mobilization can be found in the area of housing policy. In Hong Kong, such mobilization efforts promoted public housing to the central element of state social policy (Castells et al. 1990; Castells 1992). These examples show that neither authoritarian state repression nor its policy pendant, social quietism, can alone explain these countries' limited and – despite rapid industrial development – stataric social policy.

In refuting the argument of political obstruction of socio-political progress, we should recall that, historically, Western welfare states as a rule were introduced over the objections of unions and working-class parties, or at the very least were confronted by the latters' considerable reservations. This was the case even more so in countries in which the labour movement was more autonomous and decentralized and thus able, independently and without state intervention, to pursue its company-level interests, which were oriented more towards shaping wage levels and workplace conditions than towards securing state-provided social security.[66] South Korean development is particularly instructive in this regard. The unions there were concerned primarily with fighting for collective freedoms – for a greater 'equality of weapons'. Here, just as in earlier Western development, the feeling of not being acknowledged as a partner of equal status in the distribution of the fruits of prosperity by state authorities, managers and firms played a major role (Lindauer et al. 1997; Marshall 1949).[67]

A final characteristic of East Asian socio-political development is that those features of their institutional framework that derived from European history, i.e. either from the Protestant-Calvinist poor law tradition (minimal, stigmatized welfare benefits and the principle of providing benefits-in-kind) or from Catholic social philosophy (status-based differentiation and localism/subsidiarity), had in the East Asian context

65 For the period 1971–2, Lindlar (1995: 314) arrives at the following average annual values for the amount of foreign direct investment as a percentage of gross domestic fixed investment: Singapore 21.6, Hong Kong 7.3, Taiwan 2.0 and South Korea 1.0.

66 Cf. Skocpol (1992: 24ff.) and the literature listed there.

67 Above all, with regard to South Korea, the relatively less inegalitarian primary income distribution, which has been largely stable over time, is overestimated. Roughly 40 per cent of all households are not included in income statistics. Further, the increase in asset inequality is underestimated. The concentration of landed property has grown enormously. It is estimated that in 1988, 44 per cent of South Korea's landed property was in the hands of 1 per cent of the population, and about 77 per cent in the hands of 10 per cent. The value of landed property rose between 1974 and 1989 roughly three times faster than national income (Leipziger et al. 1992). The frustration of the working classes is directed above all at this kind of inequality.

a different effect on the course of welfare state development. Whereas in Western countries in the nineteenth and twentieth centuries these features, under pressure first from the labour and then from the civil rights movement, supported the formation of legally grounded claims to social benefits, in East Asia they did not unleash political reactions of the same nature or effect (K. V. Friedman 1981; Marshall 1964b, 1965).[68]

The interpretation that the ruling elites deliberately abstained from extensive public intervention in order to increase the efficiency of markets is contradicted by the fact that economic development in these countries is largely state-initiated and -coordinated. This is particularly true of the large-scale provision of capital, the development of infrastructure, the education and training of the workforce and, finally, the protection of industry from foreign competition and the flip side of this, capital export restrictions.[69] This concerted, massive public engagement makes it improbable that powerful state bureaucracies would demonstrate tactical reserve in another sphere – namely social policy – and that this would also find popular acceptance. All East Asian governments played a far greater and much more active role in the industrial 'revolutionizing' of their societies than did the governments of Western Europe and North America in the nineteenth century (Garon 1987; E. Vogel 1991: 4–5; Hikino and Amsden 1994).[70] An explicit – not merely culturally mediated and thus implicit – socio-political minimalism would thus produce grave credibility problems for these governments among their electorates (Weingast 1993).

The question of East Asian welfare statism

The limits of previous attempts at explanation Until now, authors seeking to explain this development have focused on certain factors that quite plausibly help explain East Asia's special socio-political path of development. Objections can be made, however, to each of these interpretations, based either on these countries' pattern of historical development or on contradictions between this pattern and that of Western welfare states, from which standard modernization theory derives.

In East Asia, one can identify neither strictly endogenous nor exogenous paths of development towards a welfare state along Western lines. Social policy appears neither

68 Already in 1913 Richard H. Tawney in a lecture delivered at the London School of Economics noted that in the second half of the nineteenth century the 'problem of poverty' turned into 'the problem of riches'. In the years between the two Poor Law Reports of 1834 and 1909, he went on, 'the centre of interest in social studies shifted from pauperism to poverty, from poverty to the distribution of wealth, from the distribution of wealth to the control of industry' (quoted in Marshall 1964b: 39).

69 The special, active role of the state in economic development is explored in detail in area studies by Amsden (see all works cited in the References), Deyo (see all works cited in the References) and Wade (1989, 1990a, b).

70 Hikino and Amsden (1994: 296) point to a logical relationship between such state activism and East Asia's striking income equality – in contrast to Europe – during industrialization: 'Assume, that unequal income distribution implies access to a disproportional share of resources by small groups in agriculture or industry, the more concentrated economic power is, the more these groups can both bypass state sources of investment finance and buy government favours.' As a result of successful land reform and an initially very weak industrialization, after the Second World War the three East Asian territorial states found themselves in precisely the opposite situation from that cited here. For a critical discussion of the statistical validity of the claim that, despite economic growth, primary income distribution continued to develop in a comparatively equal, and above all stable, fashion, see the references in Leipziger and Dollar (1992).

to be part of an inevitable logic of industrialization, nor of a concessionary integration ideology and strategy of autocratic-patriarchal regimes. With regard to the former, the aforementioned general indicators show that these countries' industrial expansions (measured as persons engaged in the industrial and service sectors relative to the total workforce) have been far more dynamic than the development of their social (transfer) expenditures (measured here as a share of national income). In light of the political history of South Korea, Taiwan and Singapore, and even of Japan, the hypothesis of an 'autocratic' course of social policy expansion appears to be quite plausible at first sight. Despite the US-induced democratization of Japan after the Second World War and the political liberalization of South Korea in the mid-1980s and of Taiwan in the 1990s, these countries' institutions were shaped by bureaucratic-authoritarian forms of rule. Singapore still adheres to this form of political organization and emphatically defends it. Below, we will address in greater detail certain cultural factors to which this political traditionalism can be attributed, at least to some extent.

Here we point out that in historical perspective, it was precisely those (exclusively Western) countries whose political constitutions had a bureaucratic-paternalistic cast, which, in marked contrast to liberal democracies, were the first to introduce social insurance systems (Flora and Alber 1981: 47, 72). In the wake of devastating wars (Korea and Japan), nascent state- and nation-building (Taiwan and Singapore) or an enormous influx of refugees (Hong Kong), all East Asian countries faced an extensive integration challenge. It was met, however, not as in the West with a massive expansion of welfare state provision and public income security; rather, they executed a socio-political restraint which continues to the present day, despite recent political changes. Although there are indications that democratization in South Korea and Taiwan could lead to an augmented socio-political dynamic borne by new competition among political parties for electoral favour, the institutional fruits of this phenomenon remain meagre.[71]

[71] In Taiwan, the opposition's proposals for the introduction of a general pension insurance scheme during the communal elections of 1993 led to a competition among political parties, familiar in the West, to see who could offer more: 'In a short period – less than a month – pensions became a big issue all over the island and the size of the allowances grew and grew. . . . After the election, some local authorities held by the DPP [Democratic Progressive Party, the opposition party] tried to implement its promises but schemes soon terminated because of shortage of money. And on the KMT side [Kuomintang, the governing party] the policy draft on a national pension system is still only a draft. Nearly everything is still in the original situation. No significant welfare development has been achieved' (Ku 1997: 248). In the first free presidential election, in 1996, it was generally expected that socio-political themes would play a bigger role than heretofore under the autocratic rule of the Kuomintang. Yet the Chinese military manoeuvre and the resulting threat to the national integrity of Taiwan pushed socio-political issues into the background. The security threat reinforced the existing primacy of economic efficiency and global competitiveness (ibid.: 249). A counter-example is the simultaneous, sweeping Taiwanese health care reform of 1 March 1995. Its introduction five years earlier than planned occurred thanks to the increasing dynamic of political competition (Chiang 1997: 229; Tang 1997: 87–100). It was enacted by the Kuomintang with an eye to the parliamentary elections of late 1995 and the presidential elections of 1996, and constituted a significant step on the way towards a national health service. It extended the mandatory membership pool from about 50 per cent of the population in 1994 to 93 per cent in 1996. The contours of the reform were given top-down (Tang 1997: 61), but the sense of its urgency and necessity was a product of democratization. In South Korea, since the transition to free presidential elections in 1987, one can observe a similar dynamic of change, as is evident in the comprehensive expansion of the social health insurance scheme in 1988 and 1989 and of the general pension reform in 1988 (Kwon 1998a: 55f.).

A reformulation of the problem The puzzle we try to address is the surprisingly limited standing of social policy in East Asian economic and societal development. The gradations in public and social expenditure levels in East Asia versus the West do not point to minor differences in the relative economic significance of the welfare state, which become smaller over the course of time. Rather, they lead us to assume that in East Asia the orientation towards social policy and its potential role in the state, economy and society is fundamentally different from what obtains in the West. This diagnosis of a fundamental difference is supported by the already highlighted condition of industrial transformation and urbanization *not* leading to socio-political mobilization, and by these countries' rejection of the Western model in essential realms of social policy. This is true above all for the general rejection of redistribution and the orientation towards minimal state provision of socio-political goods.[72] We focus on these moments in the remainder of this chapter.

The study of welfare state development in East Asia inevitably leads to the problem of the more general structure and configuration of the model of economic growth in these countries. The thesis of a – up to now only vaguely defined – crucial influence of culture on societal developments neither excludes the possibility that values or more or less ordered worldviews and ethical motives are themselves subject to change, nor that their effect lies alone in a stabilization of the social order. The typically conservative, or defensive, thrust, not only in Singapore but also in other East and Southeast Asian countries, of certain politicians' championing of 'Asian' values – as opposed to Western liberal values and universal and statutory civil rights – presents a misleading picture of values and ideas.[73] Nowhere do values create some particular economic conditions unless certain possibilities of transformation – which seem to originate purely from 'ideas' – are also present in the existing social relations and opportunity structures. In fact, in most cases the direction of influence runs the opposite course, in that the needs of economic life and political compromise manifest themselves regularly either through a reinterpretation of cultural 'dogmas' or through being bypassed casuistically.

If, as claimed here, Confucian culture and ethics play an essential role in the shaping of East Asian socio-political institutions, then it must also be explained, or at least made explicable in principle, *how* this peculiar complex of factors could have determined the direction of development or the structure of institutions. If one proceeds, as a culturalist approach usually does, from the assumption that cultural traits are particularly enduring, or unalterable, one is confronted with the problem of explaining their change. The influence of fundamental shifts in economy and society are obvious causal factors here. Another is the competition between worldviews and religions. It was Weber himself who noted at the beginning of the twentieth century with regard

72 The influential Japanese social scientist and philosopher Yasusuke Murakami noted as the most conspicuous failure of Western representative democracy its inability to achieve an equality of opportunity for individuals without being transformed into a tool for bringing about equality of outcome, forced by a 'mechanical system' of majority votes (1996: xxiv). For a collection of essays on Murakami, see Yamamura (1997).

73 Cf. this admonition by the champion of cultural explanations himself, Max Weber: 'For public political activity leads to a far greater surrender of rigorous ethical requirements than is produced by private business activity, since political activity is oriented to average human qualities, to compromise, to craft, to the employment of other ethically suspect devices and people, and thereby oriented to the relativization of all goals' (1978: 593).

to the Asian people that 'at the present time' all these people import the 'commodity' of 'technical economic rationalism' as 'the most important Occidental product' (1978: 630). One can conclude from this, then, that Confucian culture and ethics alone cannot be decisive for welfare state development, including its repeated ruptures. Also, culture cannot be invoked as an explanatory factor the way a light switch can be turned on or off.[74] To complicate the picture even more, a further explanatory factor to consider in East Asian development is the dynamic relationship between a country's domestic situation and the international environment, as a combination of imperatives and opportunities.

To come back to the problem of cultural explanations, we have to note that in earlier periods of East Asian and Chinese development there were already examples where Confucian ethics was a catalysing rather than a retardant factor. In such cases, its democratic egalitarianism and meritocratic educational ideal were turned against ossified social hierarchies. Indeed, Confucianism itself historically originates in an explicit attempt to come to terms with a secular crisis of the social order; the core of historical Confucianism is the reflective search for a comprehensive, explicitly political framework of meaning and order (Jaspers 1957: 157–85; Bary 1991). From this, it derived, in terms of its content, an integrative character and, in terms of its form, the character of a practical ethics or ethical philosophy (Roetz 1995: 8, 16; Bary 1998). Conversely, there are also examples of how, under the influence of Confucianism, societal development stagnated. Confucianism's development into a state religion, its aristocratic justification of elite rule and its rigidification in ritual are undoubtedly closely related. Both cases clearly demonstrate that Confucianism can be turned against itself.

Confucianism, therefore, can be interpreted and politically harnessed both against the status quo, leading society out of a crisis of order and meaning, and in favour of the status quo as an essential moment in the stereotypification of social and political rule. Confucianism harbours the potential to be both a mere cultural reflex of the 'hegemonic' power relations, as well as an ethical contrast image which ruptures these hegemonic relations (Moritz 1998: 173f.). This moment of fundamental ambivalence has in a way guaranteed its integrity and, therefore, also its capacity to shape the state, economy and society over a period of 2,000 years. This is not to say, however, that Confucianism can be used to justify anything, revolt or restoration, progress or stagnation. However, both these poles of social action have foundations in Confucian psychology and sociology. Their implications for a radical socio-political reorientation form the subject of the concluding sections of this chapter.

[74] A related problem is the often claimed causal significance of Confucian (or 'Asian') values for the economic ascendance of the East Asian countries. The same values to which Weber attributed the economic *stasis* of China and East Asia – discipline, sense of duty, familial solidarity and social solidarity – have been adduced since the 1970s to explain the economic success of the East Asian periphery (e.g. Fei 1995). Until this time, Japan was not at all considered to be a Confucian society (Eisenstadt 1990: 444). With regard to the Weberian interpretation, a closer examination of the history of Confucian ideas and their consequences reveals not only considerable differences between the development in China and that in the East Asian periphery, but also the pivotal importance of strategic manipulation or reinterpretation of Confucian conceptions on the part of political elites, in the interest of either state- and nation-building (e.g. in Japan, see Ikegami 1995; in Korea, see Deuchler 1992) or economic modernization (e.g. in Singapore, see Wong and Wong 1995 and Schein 1996). Moreover, the internal adaptability of Confucian cultures, resulting from their lack of a 'church' or any other kind of organized institutional manifestation, has been, and continues to be, repeatedly underestimated (Bary 1988: 109; 1991).

These examples call attention to the fact that the influence of cultural factors as such – here, a religious ethic – cannot be clearly predicted. Explanations, therefore, have to acknowledge the pivotal significance of more or less coincidental constellations. What happens in social politics is irregular, and it is rare for a social policy to last.[75] This implies considerable limitations on the potential to extract policy lessons from East Asian development models, as from the earlier success stories of Protestant-Puritanical societies. Depending on the constellation of structural forces, the influence and role of cultural moments can vary.[76] It is fair to assume, however, that the interaction of these forces follows certain patterns.[77] The Weberian category of 'elective affinity' points not only to the contingent nature of structural variations, but also to the historical uniqueness and thus the chance of sudden discontinuities in institutional developments.[78] Successful economic modernization can be planned only to a limited extent. The same is true of the 'optimal' relationship between social policy and markets. The measure of economic – as for private and societal – 'success' is culturally determined.

Here we propose that three basic details of welfare state development are shaped by cultural factors. The first consists of general dispositions. A culture's interpretations of meaning and visions of social order determine its evaluations of socio-political alternatives, and sometimes even prevent alternatives from being perceived. In this way, culture channels *basic* welfare state *trajectories*. Here, we are, above all, interested in the particularistic nature of socio-political development in East Asia and in the heavy burden of socio-political responsibilities on families and companies that result from it. A second important detail is the *pace* of socio-political developments, or the temper of social politics. Here, we are interested in the question of why welfare state development in East Asia unfolds more statarically, i.e. more slowly and restrained, than in the West. Culture can confer on societal actions a particular emotional intensity and a more or less significant potential for instability and disruption. The third extremely consequential detail is the *autonomy or heteronomy* of social policy. Here, we are interested in the question why, in East Asia, social policy appears *not* to constitute an idiosyncratic, independent dimension of societal development or political mobilization, but, rather, remains closely tied to social-structural or company-based relations; whereas in the West, social policy forms an autonomous sphere that can be and is turned *against* the economy and *against* society in the name of establishing an order of things *de novo*. Culture, therefore, conditions a society's institutional arrangement in the sense of a more or less explicit linking or interweaving of its individual elements in a consistent pattern.

This kind of interpretation suggests that the analysis of welfare systems requires at its base an understanding of the categories of meaning by which the participants

75 See also Burckhardt's relativistic reference to civilization history: 'As soon as one admits that the emergence of something occurred in a specific historical moment, it becomes clear that it cannot eternally exist on earth' (1982 [1905]: 139).

76 On the related problem of generalizing explanations, see the apt phrase of Geertz (2000: 219): 'The motive to general reflection about politics in general is radically ungeneral.'

77 These 'patterns' are, following Weber, 'relations of adequacy' (1978: 341). They refer to 'elective affinities' between the structural forms of social, economic, political and cultural life, i.e. 'whether they further or impede or exclude one another – whether they are "adequate" or "inadequate" in relation to one another' (ibid.).

78 See Weber's original formulation of this concept (1978: 341), and for a more detailed reformulation in the context of welfare state development, see Rieger (1992b).

themselves comprehend their experience and orient themselves towards one another in their everyday lives. The institutions of class and family, household and market, power and privilege, far from being submerged by such an analysis, are seen to depend for their very impact on the broader system by which knowledge itself is produced. The significance of both the substance and the procedure of social rights – who gets what and on what terms from the welfare state – is seen to reside in their capacity to operate as systems whose significant features are far more extensive and interrelated than our now commonly accepted disciplinary divisions may embrace. Seen in this way, social policy and social science are not just inextricably linked to one another; they actually constitute two sides of the same configuration.[79]

For the sociologist, then, social politics constitutes a realm within which it is possible to see people acting in accordance with their deepest assumptions and beliefs, in which assumptions on human nature and social order are put to the test of scope and implication. Accordingly, and looking at actual social policies, it is precisely in the concepts and relationships encountered in the social order that many of the presumptions and procedures of organized public welfare find their predominant genesis and ultimate acceptability. Thus we are interested in the concepts by which communities categorize and order their experience of an otherwise chaotic universe into sets of meaning, symbolically grasped and manipulated in social politics, because these concepts provide a key to the understanding of social policies. In describing the conceptual ordering and institutional enactment of social politics, we can arrive at a fuller understanding of what exactly *drives* social policy and what gives welfare states their particular institutional stamp. Therefore, the regularities that we will point out are not the work of some cultural versus economic, political or psychological factors, but the *fit* between the institutional format of social policies and the cultural concepts and social relations to which they are inextricably fixed. In fact, we believe it impossible to arrive at a clear understanding of the differences between the real worlds of welfare states without an investigation of the religious concepts through which decisions on the institutional format of social policies make sense.

4 Religious Roots as Driving Forces of Welfare State Development

The main body of the remaining part of this chapter confronts the religious origins of the institutional designs of social policy. The procedure is a combination of the analytical and the empirical. But because our main way of proceeding involves mapping connections between religiously derived ideas and visions of social policy, between structures of social policy and ethics, we concentrate on a description and discussion of these links. This seems all the more necessary in that welfare state research dominant today tends to ignore these connections. In order to see them, we have to appreciate the place of religion in the evolution of social policy structures. In more than one way, religion provides an inescapable framework for social politics. This chapter, however, is but a prelude to our being able to come to grips with the *theology* of social policy. Social politics and social policies are much richer in religious sources than we

[79] Weber went so far as to argue that 'social science . . . [is] the historical and theoretical treatment of the same problem the practical solution of which constitutes "social policy"' (1904: 67).

commonly believe, but this richness does not – until now – feature on the map of most welfare state research.

What do we mean when we talk about culture or religion in the context of globalization and the fate of national social policy? In light of the extraordinary progress which revolutionized science and technology in the nineteenth and twentieth centuries, and which conferred on them an unprecedented, supposedly levelling influence on societal development and governance, culture seems, above all in its religious forms, to be a dusty collection of exhibition pieces in a museum of the history of ideas. 'Ethics', too, appears in 'modern' society to be limited to lamenting in a helpless and futile fashion the hard social facts of an interdependent world in which markets coordinate economic and social life. Its typical means of expression, as a protest and appeal, suffices in popular estimation to demonstrate its irrelevance. Moreover, in the acid bath of modern social theory, seemingly 'ethical' behaviour is regularly reinterpreted to be nothing more than nicely clothed egotistic rational choice. Very often, however, it is precisely behind this façade of irrelevance and hypocrisy that one finds a presence and force that are all the greater, and behind claims of the universality of apparently completely demystified values and both undoubted and superior rationality criteria, one discovers their contingency and hence dependency on cultural and institutional context.[80]

Western political – and social science – preoccupation with culture and ethics can be quite misleading with regard to the true significance of these spheres. The misunderstanding stems, according to accepted wisdom, from the fact that these dimensions of action and their reflection seem to comprise a distinct, 'other-worldly' reality which is sharply divided from *this world*, i.e. from that which seems to be accessible only via a positive social science. Already here we can see, ironically, the influence of the Christian worldview. It hinders not only an adequate examination of *other* socio-political cultures, but also the fundamental observation of the specifically Western origins, forms and consequences of one's *own* socio-political culture. The division into the 'other-worldly' and 'this-worldly' is itself culture-specific. It confers on ethical behaviour and values a supernatural character. But this conception does not put them out of reach of an empirical investigation, nor does it make them irrelevant. On the contrary, they can develop for precisely their transcendental qualities a peculiar dynamic and idiosyncratic autonomy which puts them in a position to explode the framework of existing conditions or to explicitly and independently shape them in an image not found in the world as it is.

In our approach, 'culture' is seen as a system of values, opinions and attitudes that transports 'envisioned order', and 'ethics' as an essential means of its attainment.[81] Ethics imbues the psychological and sociological dimensions of constructions of reality with the normative, and hence supra-individual, quality, which renders these constructions social facts. Through ethics, cognitive structures of perception and

80 For spirited defences of the continuing role of culture in the world's variety, see Sahlins (1999) and Geertz (2000). For an intellectual history of the concept of culture, see Kuper (1999).

81 Although we are of a more 'positivistic' bent in our approach, we share Kroeber's and Kluckhohn's answer to a standard objection to cultural analysis: 'If we are asked, "How can a logical construct like culture explain anything?" we could reply that other logical concepts and abstractions like "electromagnetic field" or "gene" – which no one has ever seen – have been found serviceable in scientific understanding. Analytic abstractions summarize an order of relationship between natural phenomena, and relations are as real as things' (1952: 190).

interpretation become reality. In the context of 'culture', then, they are articulated by distinct social carriers – be they non-conforming intellectuals, state bureaucrats, political entrepreneurs or crusading social reformers. 'Culture' thus encompasses an area whose poles represent on one side the forms of everyday knowledge and on the other 'those categorical forms of thinking which as a sort of "historical a priori" are inaccessible even to thought itself' (Raulff, quoted in Gilcher-Holtey 1998: 488). 'Culture' is thus a potency that must be activated, and which in this process is subject, depending on the situation, to shaping and reshaping. This prohibits us from claiming a unilinear dependency between 'culture' and societal institutions.

Culture as such cannot fully explain socio-political development. The connection between established cultural convictions and socio-political decision-making is always *mediated*, and *causal relationships can run both ways, in particular when new economic situations arise or when new forms of political rule develop*. In such cases, religious norms are often ambivalent or silent with respect to new problems and practices. Moreover, neither culture nor religion creates social policies unless – in the existing socio-political structures and constellations – there are also interests providing specific possibilities of, or even powerful drives towards, a socio-political transformation of hierarchies and distributions. In addition, the functional needs of *directly* provisioning the disprivileged and those outside of the labour market can make themselves manifest either through a reinterpretation of religious imperatives or through simply bypassing them. Thus religious ethics can penetrate into social institutions in very different ways. The case that interests us most, because it had revolutionary consequences, is an ethic that is able theoretically to organize the world from a religious perspective into a systematic, rational cosmos. In this case, 'its ethical tensions with the social institutions of the world are likely to become sharper and more principled: this is the more true the more the secular institutions are systematized autonomously. A religious ethic evolves that is oriented to the rejection of the world . . . . Indeed, the very tension which this religious ethic introduces into the human relationships towards the world becomes a strongly dynamic factor in social evolution' (Weber 1978: 579).[82]

82 This point seems to suggest that the more the modern, formally rational market economy threatens to turn into an 'iron cage' (Weber) or 'prison' (Lindblom), the higher the potential to challenge it from a substantive, strictly value-oriented ethic, because its result is, from the point of view of the individual, irrational. The sole *criterion* according to which a competitive market economy can claim to be rational is a strictly procedural one: it is an impersonal process in which anyone's productive contribution is interpreted, tested and corrected *by others*, a process that *may* create things that are greater than any individual mind can ever fully comprehend (Hayek 1945: 15, 7). As Hayek himself noted, 'our personal sense of justice . . . frequently revolts against the impersonal decisions of the market' (ibid.: 21). Starting from the same notion, Weber (1920: 275) went on to argue that the *need* for an ethical interpretation of the 'meaning' of the distribution of fortunes among men '*increased* with the growing rationality of conceptions of the world' (emphasis added). Perhaps it is not too far-fetched to claim that the economic gospel à la Milton Friedman and similar prophets present a secular version of a theodicy of good fortune for those who are fortunate, giving substance to Weber's argument that the economically privileged are seldom satisfied with the fact of being privileged. Beyond his fortunate position he needs to know that he has a *right* to his good fortune: 'He wants to be convinced that he "deserves" it, and above all, that he deserves it in comparison with others. He wishes to be allowed the belief that the less fortunate also merely experience his due' (Weber 1920: 271). According to Weber, such a theodicy of good fortune is anchored in highly robust ('pharisaical') needs of man and thus a powerful motor of affirmative ideologies. Hayek argues for a more heroical attitude. He acknowledges that in a competitive market order the concrete results of the individual's effort in making the most of his abilities and resources are judged by its utility to others and is thus 'objectively' just, but not subjectively, since the

Therefore we are primarily concerned with constellations in which a religious culture develops not only autonomously, but also in studied contrast to socio-political institutions and established social structures. Depending on the political programmes it engenders, it can produce revolutionary consequences, in particular when its ethic is based on some steadfast inner faith. But also in this case we are, *empirically*, very often confronted with an extraordinary capriciousness and thus utter unpredictability of the exact weight religious postulates will carry in any particular application. If we take these reservations seriously, we then have to admit that the values and ideas that are supposed to explain socio-political institutional forms and decisions cannot be reconstructed on the basis of them alone. Claiming linear or exclusive dependencies oversimplifies complex interactions, which must in fact be analytically differentiated in each individual case. Culture structures the universe of socio-political alternatives, yet does not *determine* socio-political decisions.

The reality of religion

The aspect of religion that interests us most is its theoretical attitude towards the world. The more worldviews and religious ethics are marked by an 'inner' truth and absolute obligations, the more they penetrate into social institutions not in some silent, discrete way, but in pronounced battles that sometimes resemble civil war. The more this is the case, the more the very tension which a religious ethic of this type introduces into the social relations towards the world as it is, the more it becomes a strongly dynamic factor in social evolution. However, as Weber noted, it is exactly such a constellation that makes the successful moulding of social institutions in the image of a radicalized religion contingent on the strength of its rivals: 'To the extent that a religious ethic organizes the world from a religious perspective into a systematic, rational cosmos, its ethical tension with the social institutions of the world are likely to become sharper and more principled; this is true the more the secular institutions are systematized autonomously' (Weber 1978: 578f.). At present, at least in the West, both politics and economic life form spheres of their own, and thus exhibit a great potential for conflict, or culture wars, because these spheres are also expressions of distinct cultures.

The moments of welfare state development on which we focus, the long-term dynamics of social policy structures, their autonomy in the system of societal institutions and political governance, their normative independence relative to the values guiding the other spheres of social life and the universalism, i.e. group-transcending quality, of the associative or communal relationships induced by social policy are always the direct result of individuals' decisions. But in the remainder of this chapter we will not reconstruct the historical nitty-gritty of exactly how religious ethics made itself felt in social politics and thus was able to mark welfare state institutions. Rather, we must be content here with identifying those cultural factors with which the

---

result frequently does not correspond to its subjective merit. Yet, he says, 'if the individual is free to choose, it is inevitable that he should bear the risk attaching to that choice and that in consequence he be rewarded, not according to the goodness or badness of his intentions, but solely on the basis of the value of the results to others. We must face the fact that the preservation of individual freedom is incompatible with a full satisfaction of our views of distributive justice' (Hayek 1945: 21–2). It is exactly this fact that 'welfare democracy' tries to correct.

general orientation, the pace and the autonomy or heteronomy of welfare state development in East Asia can, at least as a first approximation, be rendered more comprehensible.

Religion or, better, religiosity can be equated neither with (seeming or supposed) naïveté nor with moral idealism. Religion is the *form* of a coherent answer to the fundamental questions of human existence, and is thus an inevitable feature of social life.[83] As such, it always includes faith, or make-belief, for the simple reason that naked reality is never able to give an answer to the question of what one *should* do.[84] There is no worldview without intellectual construction. Religion is oriented towards, and provides, 'final' causes and answers. From this flows its capacity to be an independent standard of evaluation and action, to establish values and organize them in an overarching context of meaning. In examining religion, there is, further, no reason to 'treat [its values] as Platonic ideas which, from their empyreum, guide the sub-lunar world of institutions. . . . Values are nothing but collective preferences which appear in an institutional context and which, by the means of how they arise, govern this context' (Boudon and Bourricaud 1992: 659).

In our concept of religion we follow William James (1987 [1901–2]) and Max Weber (1978).[85] Three points mark our perspective. First, religion is to be seen as a *peculiar kind of reality*, which cannot be reduced to 'real' realities and is not rationally or logically deducible from it, and which is thus fully capable of existing and surviving in a secularized world (James 1987 [1901–2]: 50). It is, as Max Weber pointed out, the idiosyncratic autonomy of the religious domain that enables political entrepreneurs to directly harness religion to extra-religious purposes (1978: 433). Secondly, religious convictions relate to first and final causes, and the truth that is imputed to them is the first and last word. Because it can surround both intellectual and political protest with an incontestable religious aura, religion can be a powerful vehicle of social change. In the words of Max Weber, 'the conflict between empirical reality and this conception of the world as a meaningful totality, which is based on religious postulate, produces the strongest tensions in man's inner life as well as in his external relationship to the world' (ibid.: 451). This points to the utopian qualities of religiously influenced worldviews: 'The ultimate question of all metaphysics has always been something like this: if the world as a whole and life in particular were to have meaning, what might it be, *and how would the world have to look like in order to correspond to it?*' (ibid.: 451; emphasis added). Thirdly, religion ultimately signifies a distinctive and additional dimension, one that provides the subject with a sphere of power which charges her with energy. The experience of religious feelings and the associated condition of faith and trust enlarges 'spiritual strength', 'are exerted on the personal centres of energy' (James 1987 [1901–2]: 455, 461). Thus, depending on the cultural logic of social politics, it has more or less capacity to generate and drive social change.

83 Hence it is possible, and, as we propose, theoretically and analytically fruitful, to speak of the culture of capitalism or of democracy. However, as we also try to point out, this is in fact the case because both capitalism and democracy as practised in the West have religious foundations.

84 For a similar perspective on religion, see T. S. Eliot, who, in his *Notes Towards the Definition of Culture*, observed: 'Any religion, while it lasts, and on its own level, gives an apparent meaning to life, provides the framework for a culture, and protects the mass of humanity from boredom and despair' (quoted in Kuper 1999: 38).

85 Simmel developed very similar ideas (1984: 100–19).

Relations of culture and religion

Starting from James's social psychology of religious experience and Weber's sociology of religion, we will assume that social politics involves 'strong evaluations' in the sense that it discriminates between right and wrong, acceptable and not acceptable, necessary and possible, unavoidable and needless, which are not rendered valid by some unambiguously 'rational' or technical reaction to social problems, but, rather, because of their essentially idiosyncratic nature, stand independent of these and are thus able to offer standards by which they can be judged to be legitimate, to command respect – and to exact taxes and contributions.[86] It is the quest for legitimacy and thus the acceptance of legal obligations and fiscal burdens that provide the link between the complex of religious doctrines and the operative principles of social policies. Religion, or culture in general, involves robust claims about the status of persons and the nature of social order. Hence, a social policy is an assent to, an affirmation of, a given ontology of the human and the social. For this reason, it is also to be expected that *every* social policy response is essentially contested, and religion gives this contest a particular flavour – a flavour that can matter decisively.

Social policy is a universal phenomenon, but, like everything else in society and history, this type of organized reaction to social problems receives a variable shape in culture. And this shape is inseparable from religiously derived 'strong evaluations'. Religion is an inescapable framework of social politics and of social policies. But 'inescapable' does not mean the working of any 'iron law'. The contrary is the case.

Religiously grounded 'strong evaluations' are not a conditioned response to the challenges posed by modernization and globalization, engineered by some blind forces of history, as Huntington's analysis (1996) seems to suggest, but a *creative* response *contingent* upon providing *useful* formulas for, in our case, social policy. Precisely because it is, to some degree, malleable, open to deliberate ideological redesign, the religious dimension can be so important in politics. It is because of their immediate 'cash-value' that religious beliefs and convictions can have a substantive, and often politically aggravating, effect on domestic social politics. They shape the context of interaction among principal actors by structuring the terms of debates among actors, who use religiously legitimated ideas and ideals to gain advantages over their adversaries or to change outcomes more in their favour. Having to make arguments within the framework of substantive religious principles lends this self-interested behaviour an aura of legitimacy that masks bitter conflicts between the primary players. Socio-political battles are turned into ideological zero-sum games. Effective claims on religiously derived principles of social organization can drastically reshuffle the balance of power among principal actors, moving it towards those actors most capable of legitimating their claims and staking out their positions on the underlying religious rationale. In social politics, religious beliefs are made to matter for results and outcomes, and, in the process, benefit some actors over others. To introduce religious elements into the social politics of welfare states leads to a set of winners and losers that is distinct from the set resulting in a religiously neutral context.

The general point of departure in cultural-sociological as in culturally comparative analyses is thus the claim of the (relative) independence of religious worlds of thought

[86] We owe the felicitous term 'strong evaluations' to Taylor (1989: 4).

and conviction. Their ideas and values have a distinct structure and internal logic. They can be neither directly nor fully attributed to economic and social conditions or developments; the latter can, however, condition them or afford them a greater or lesser chance of success. Of importance here, though, is the assumption that these religious conceptions exert an independent influence on the social order.

The psychology and sociology of Confucianism

First, religious convictions always have psychological and sociological substance. They characterize or describe conceptions of human nature and, predicated upon these, of social order (Troeltsch 1994 [1912]: 34). In their extreme form, adherents organize their church and religious community in strict opposition to the rest of society and the state in autonomous, isolated circles – or, at the opposite end of the spectrum, seem to subject themselves to society as it is (ibid.: 69). Confucianism is an example of the latter.

In contrast to Western religion(s), Confucianism is more a religious concept regarding the ordering of general social life than a form of organization of religious life. It has no 'believers' who declare their faith in it, no church or clergy, and no other organizational substratum whatsoever. Its key propagandists were and are literary figures, philosophers and bureaucrats. Its ethics speaks primarily to familial, household and workplace behaviour, and is practised above all in the context of action and organization (Wei-Ming 1988; Bary 1988).

Second, the religious idea influences existing social and economic conditions. Here, we are interested in

> [the] ideal, religiously derived concept of a sociological structure . . . . This idea has a tremendous historical mission, regardless of the more socially conservative or revolutionary consequences resulting from it. Once in power, it will transform the sociological arrangement in which men relate to each other. Social and political consequences are inevitable and will colour the existing order in distinct ways. There is no doubt that the grappling with and the accommodation to the political-social is anything but an easy and smooth process. (Troeltsch 1994 [1912]: 51f.)

Ethical-religious convictions can, at the same time, have psychological and sociological consequences that are thoroughly ambivalent in the sense that they can differ in interaction with similar states of affairs. This does not mean, however, that they are purely accidental.[87] The foundation both of the external adaptability of religious ideas as well as of their survivability is their potential to give rise to different social ideals. Their social autonomy can also be seen in the fact that they are never fully congruent with the socially dominant relations, but, rather, can be used to pass judgement on them.

In the following paragraphs we will examine two paths of influence, or mechanisms of transmission, of ethical-religious factors on economic and welfare state developments. We encounter them, first of all, in the 'practical motives to act derived from

[87] Troeltsch shows, for example, how the individualism and universalism of the Christian faith can yield two fundamentally different social consequences: idealist anarchism and communal love-communism on the one hand, or social conservatism on the other (1994 [1912]: 72).

psychological and pragmatic relations' (Weber 1989 [1915]: 85). In this analysis, religion and ethics are treated as systems of social regulation which, depending on their foundation in specific beliefs, possess in varying degrees a potential for dynamism or statarism, for heterogeneity or homogeneity, for autonomy or heteronomy, and for a universalistic or particularistic social policy orientation. Our attention is therefore called to behavioural imperatives which transport an ethic as a principled teaching of typical motivations and courses of action. We are also interested in how such behavioural imperatives shape general attitudes towards social differentiation and poverty, above all regarding the toleration of inequality and interpretations of its causes, forms and effects. We are further concerned with conceptions of order that they express. A second path of influence, which we will examine more closely, is a society's culturally mediated perception and localization of social responsibilities as well as the identification of the latters' institutional carriers and set of tasks. We assume that these ascriptions, together with social-structural and political moments, set the course of economic and social policy to the extent that they make certain welfare state paths of development more, and others less, likely.

The religious origins of socio-political dynamics

A central feature of Confucian societies to which observers repeatedly call attention is the 'tremendous stress on familial piety' (Weber 1978: 579). This refers to a complex of convictions which goes far beyond the social-structural conditions and which, at least to some extent, is independent of these.[88] This complex appears to exert an immediate influence on the dynamic and evolutionary potential of social policy, in two ways. First, it sets sharp limits on social policy's potential for universalism and redistribution, and, consequently, Confucianism has thus decidedly particularistic effects. A second consequence is that individual self-understanding is derived from the perspective of the community. Here, too, this sponsors a more stataric than dynamic social policy.

With regard to the first point, Confucianism seems to place strict limits on – if not completely preclude – certain forms of social policy. This means that conceptions of 'brotherhood' which go beyond the sphere of kin, blood relations and household members, as well as attendant conceptions of a group-transcending sense of responsibility incumbent upon each individual, are not only lacking in Confucianism, but explicitly scorned. The 'injunction of brotherly love' is especially characteristic of congregational religion and can contribute very effectively to the emancipation from political organization. The second type of connotation is the strictly communal, or family- and household-based, way of perceiving and evaluating other people. In Confucian thinking, it is the familial, or relational context that constitutes someone's identity, not the other way round. This narrowly limits social policy's potential to function as an independent formative power counterpoised to existing social relations.

[88] The actually observable familial and household structures in East Asia do not, as such, make possible a judgement on the empirical validity of Confucian conceptions. The more typical use of Confucianism in family and social policy is to use it as an ethically charged yardstick for social and political realities. In consequence, ideas can become more important and politically decisive the more social reality and religious postulate are at odds. As Weber (1978: 579) notes, 'the very tension which this religious ethic introduces into the human relationships towards the world becomes a strongly dynamic factor in social evolution'.

Confucian social policies form a system which, by its goals, its sources of legitimacy and its particular relationship with the larger societal environment, evinces very little autonomous impact on social and political structures, because so much of its authority and impact depends on its systematic incorporation into other realms of social life. Confucian social politics remains resolutely pragmatic, tries to minimize independent effects on social and economic structures. Social politics is not seen as an endeavour in generating new social obligations and relationships, and thus a new social order. Nor do Confucian politics conceive social policies as the preferred vehicle for the reconstruction of society according to some vision of social justice. This does not mean that Confucian social policies are poorly developed, but, rather, that they are consistent and logical in their own way. Their legitimizing principles and concepts are measured against different cultural standards.

With regard to the capacity to generate social change and to give social policy a direction of its own, two peculiarities of Christian thought should be given special attention here, for they inform underlying conceptions of the nature and tasks of social policy and express basic welfare state orientations in the West. They characterize an understanding of social policy that differs sharply from that which prevails in East Asian countries.

The first peculiarity is rooted in the fact that, 'as economic differentiation proceeded, customs of mutual neighbourly assistance in work and in meeting immediate needs were transformed into customs of mutual aid among various social strata' (Weber 1978: 581). However, as will become more clear in a moment, for this to happen depends on specific religious facts.

The second peculiarity is the tendency to abstract social welfare activities from concrete persons, to rationalize them as independent subjects and to transform them into objects of premeditated public regulation, to systematize this public activity and institutionalize it, and ultimately to dress the originally quite malleable claims on benefits in the form of subjective legal claims.

Both moments intersect in the uncoupling of the notion of 'helping the poor' from the concrete person and her social lineage, a process that is enormously advanced by the fact that membership in a religiously defined community is predicated on faith in salvation alone. Salvation religions are congregational religions – that is, the individual actively participates in the worship of the single supreme deity qua individual with her own inalienable tie to that deity. The individual is part of an organized collectivity of equal fellow-believers; they aspire after personal inward perfection.[89] An essential feature of congregational religion is that simply by virtue of the fact that members proclaim their devotion to shared abstract ideas (*pneuma*), a strong sense of belonging develops, which not only competes with family and kinship bonds, but can also expressly negate these. In the religiously derived and constituted congregation, no ruler has a superior status.[90]

Since the status of the religious believer is distinct from that of the political subject, it can have tremendous consequences for remoulding the latter in the image of the first.

[89] On the distinction between the hierarchical organization of the church and the congregational organization of the sect, see Troeltsch (1931).

[90] As Troeltsch (1931: 457) pointed out, 'the sects . . . are connected with the lower classes, or at least with those elements in Society which are opposed to the State and to Society; they work upwards from below, and not downward from above.' On the 'churches of the disinherited', see also Niebuhr (1954, 1964 [1951]).

Confronted with the sometimes extraordinary emotional dynamics of salvation religion, class and status barriers can give way to fraternization, or, in social politics, to universalistic social policies.[91] Therefore, the principled absolutist ethics of religious sects have to be viewed as truly revolutionary forces in social politics because they give rise to new social relationships, new social identity and new forms of collective action. In fact, the very concept of citizenship, which lies at the centre of welfare statism, has its origins in the communally founded city of the Occident, a form of social, political and economic organization unique to the West (Weber 1958 [1921]). The city, as Weber noted, has been 'the major theatre for Christianity', and provided an institutional home for the 'pneumatic piety of the ancient religious community, for the mendicant monk orders of the high Middle Ages, and for the [Protestant] sects of the reformation up to pietism and methodism' (Weber 1920: 269).[92]

The origin of this principle of organized welfare, which most radically transcends the traditionally closed circle of personal relations and memberships in status groups or social strata, is 'loving your enemy'. In Confucianism, this form of affective neutrality is not only rejected, but considered to be in violation of *raison d'état* (Weber 1978: 350).[93] Social duties extend alone to organically given personal relationships:

> A universal 'love of mankind' was turned around by Mencius with the argument, that this would eliminate piety and justice: Not to have father and mother exemplify animals. The content of the duties of a Confucian Chinese was always and everywhere piety against concrete, alive or dead men, associated to him by the extant social order, but never vis-à-vis an other-worldly good and hence never vis-à-vis a holy 'calling' or 'idea'. (Weber 1989 [1915]: 62)

As a consequence of this way of thinking, trust remains limited to kin, quasi-kin, household or quasi-household type groups.[94]

The flip side is a general mistrust of persons and social forms outside of these personal spheres – a disposition that also hinders the development of both free markets and formal organization, since both depend ultimately on strictly voluntaristic notions

91 On generalized commitments as a typical feature of public policy, see Janowitz (1976: 37), who, discussing British and American social policy, simply takes it for granted that 'the welfare state is a political arrangement that emphasizes universalism'.

92 As we will elaborate in more detail below, it is important to note that salvation religion can have world-shattering consequences for social and political order because individuals' deliverance demands a collective revolutionary transformation of the world in the direction of a more ethical status (Weber 1978: 506). Since it seems impossible to conduct a meaningful life as required by a religious ethic in the world-as-it-is, there is a strong urge to reshape the world – or to regress into an apolitical, romantic intellectualism à la Rousseau. As to the latter, an 'anti-rational inner attitude characteristic of religion of unlimited trust in god may occasionally produce an acosmistic indifference to obvious practical and rational considerations. It frequently produces an unconditional reliance on god's providence, attributing to him alone the consequences of one's own action, which are interpreted as pleasing to god' (ibid.: 567). Both in fundamentalist Christianity and Islam, this anti-rationalist attitude is sharply opposed to 'empirical' knowledge.

93 Karl Jaspers (1957: 171) also points out this contrast to Christian value conceptions: 'When Lao-Tse teaches to counter enmity with good deeds, Confucius answers: "And how then to repay good deeds? Enmity counter with justice, and good deeds repay with good deeds."'

94 For Confucius, to truly behave as a human being means to fulfil five cardinal relationships: parent and child, ruler and minister, husband and wife, elder and younger, and friend and friend. On the rights and rites of being human, see Kwok (1998).

of the individual. Similarly, it indicates group-bound orientation in the choice of social policy tools. Also, as one of the typical results of Confucian thinking in social politics, the formation of *grantee classes*[95] – as a systemic by-product of the rise of welfare statism – and the typical socio-political socialization of competitive electoral groups, this development is firmly inhibited; this is due to this basic communalism. In the West, however, the evolution of grantee classes has been a major factor in the transformation of social structure. The basis for this is the primacy of abstract criteria in the evaluation and the institutional design of social order. The overall effect of this type of welfare statism on the process of political socialization is to separate and in fact isolate its clients from the larger social structure (Janowitz 1976: 105). For that reason it is a means *par excellence* for nation-state-building and for creating political bonds in a new polity (Adams 1990; Bendix 1977 [1964]; Lunch 1987; Shklar 1991).

The radical theology of social rights To view the individual as an isolated unit, an object of public interest politics, is also a precondition for large-scale social engineering and thus for a creative social policy as the midwife to a new social order. Georg Simmel called attention to a paradoxical moment of Christian alms-giving. Even though the act is occasioned by the recipient, i.e. by her social plight, it is the motivation of the donor, and not the plight of the recipient that is decisive. The objective of the deed is to improve the fate of the donor, not that of the recipient:

> When Jesus told the rich young man: give your property to the poor, what mattered was not the poor, but the soul of the young man; for the salvation of the soul this renunciation is merely a means or symbol. The future Christian alms-giving is of the same nature: it is nothing but a form of asceticism, or a 'good deed', improving the other-worldly fate of the alms-giver. The spread of beggary in the Middle Ages, the futility in the distribution of alms, the demoralization of the proletariat through indiscriminate giving, counteracting all rational reform – this was virtually the revenge of alms for the purely subjectivistic motivation of its giving, concerned only with the giver, not the receiver. (Simmel 1992 [1908]: 516)

Much like Tocqueville (1835) before him, Simmel describes the developmental trajectory within industrial society from Christian caritas to state welfare policy as a shift of the reference point from the salvation of the individual donor to the welfare of the social whole. In neither case, however, does the poor person as such, or the concrete nature of her needs, any longer play a decisive role in welfare policy. Simmel deduces from this a certain rationalization capacity of caritas, since, in the interest of an abstract conception of 'society' yet to be created, it guides welfare provision:

[95] Following Weber, 'class' means all persons in the same class situation, and 'class situation' means 'the typical probability of (1) procuring goods, (2) gaining a position in life, and (3) finding inner satisfaction' (Weber 1978: 302). The two main types of classes are, for Weber, (a) a 'property class', which is primarily determined by the disparity of property, and (b) a 'commercial class', which is determined by the marketability of labour, goods and services. In an analogous way one can talk of a 'grantee class' if their income position, public status and their self-image is primarily determined by public transfers or public employment.

> It takes place, voluntarily or enforced by laws, in order for the pauper not to become an active, harmful enemy to society, to restore his diminished powers, to prevent the degeneration of his offspring. The pauper as a person, the impression of his situation on his feelings, is of no concern, as it is of no importance for the one who for the sake of his soul is giving alms; true enough, the subjective egoism of the latter is revoked, however, not for the sake of the pauper, but for the sake of society: that the pauper receives alms is not the final goal, but merely a means, just like in the first case. The domination of the social motive over alms-giving becomes apparent in the fact that just because of it it can be denied – particularly so when individual pity or the embarrassing situation of refusal will move us to give. (ibid.: 516f.)

However, as it turned out in the course of rising representative democracy, a rational public interest in controlling claims and entitlements was no match for the driving and sustaining fact that these can have a *moral* underpinning that makes them virtually unmanageable. Conceptions of *subjective public rights* – not their existence as such, but the magnitude of their authority – have religious roots in Christian and in particular in Protestant thought. Their justification and wording evince their origins in a source that cannot be infringed upon, either by the state or by the power of the status quo.[96] The social effectiveness of subjective public rights is, in consequence, not just a matter of the specific content of these rights. Notions of 'natural' rights or 'natural' law were familiar not only to Greek and Roman antiquity, but also to Chinese culture (Roetz 1992: 129, 231; Bary 1998; Bary and Weiming 1998). Decisive here is the religious grounding of rights as 'inalienable', as a quality of the individual that is inviolable by any worldly power and that cannot be outweighed or compromised away by any worldly advantage.[97]

A strictly societal legitimation and rationalization of social policy as opposed to organic, personal aid is predicated upon a specific conception of poverty's causes. Just like the instrumentalization of caritas for societal ends, the thinking of the potentially entitled individual also reflects a high level of social policy abstraction and can lead to amoral individualism: 'A social perspective in which the individual is just the product of his societal milieu gives him the right to claim a compensation for every calamity and loss' (Simmel 1992 [1908]: 514f.).[98] In the Christian tradition of aid as a categorical end-in-itself and in its rationalization into comprehensive social policy, Simmel identifies considerable potential for the development of a formal – and theoretically unlimitable – 'right'. She whose means do not suffice to meet her ends is already poor

96 Herein also lies the cause of the uncoupling of subjective rights from tradition, i.e. the fact that the social politics of the welfare state has become reflexive, or self-referential (Luhmann 1981: 97; 1990: 39–45).

97 Marshall stated one important aspect of this problem of institutional control of social politics in the following way: 'If you concede to a poor person an absolute, unconditional right to relief, the question then arises how to deny him the right to become poor if he so wishes' (1965: 90).

98 For this reason Luhmann (1990: 21) notes that the contemporary welfare state cannot be understood adequately as a simple response to the negative effects of industrialization: 'In one way or another, everything an individual experiences appears as socially conditioned and, consequently, as an undeserved fate requiring compensation, including his own action.' However, as our comparative analysis should make clear, Luhmann's general theory of the welfare state, putting a universalizing tendency to compensate at its core, reflects a culturally predisposed course of social politics. For 'welfare' to become an *indeterminate* principle, a project with unlimited scope and no end (Robson 1976: 174), is a cultural artefact.

(ibid.: 548). There is no point zero of conclusively satisfactory conditions. Rather, the experience of poverty is subjective, giving rise to endemic socio-political relativism: 'The pauper, feeling his situation as an injustice of the worldly order and virtually claiming relief from life itself, will easily make every accidental individual in a better situation than himself solidarily liable for this claim' (ibid.: 515).[99]

The demand for social rights can be historically traced and understood as the natural supplement to civil and political liberties, and accordingly is buttressed in part by the other-worldly justification of those rights, i.e. their appeal to the inviolable, intrinsic value of the autonomous individual as paramount to all other interests. Hence it can lead above all in social policy to amoral individualism. But here we also see the ultimately religious roots of the understanding of modern social policy as an eschatologically grounded 'decommodification' of labour power, as the defence of the dignity and intrinsic value of the individual against the power of the market's invisible hand.[100] This further development, or, rather, transportation of 'civil rights' into the social sphere of an ethically mandated equality of economic results renders comprehensible both the tension between its elements – economic, political and social-status rights – and the intensity of the conflict among them. Here as well, we see an individualistic unconditionality projected onto visions of political order. These, in turn, are indebted to a culture in which the value of the individual is not reducible to her social role, but in which, conversely, societal relations have to be justified in light of the value of the individual.[101] This idea is clear even in its most extreme perversion, namely the conception that the individual is a product of society. For even in the West, this idea is always employed only as a secularized version of a negative, never of a positive theodicy. According to the latter, society owes the individual 'reconstitution' when – and, indeed, precisely when – she proves herself to be incapable of supporting herself and, building on this, of integrating herself socially. Empowerment and not compensation is the issue.

In sum, precisely because, under the influence of Christian and in particular Protestant Calvinist ideas, personal and direct caritas became the point of departure for systematic programmatic social policy, social policy debates are very often indefatigable battles of conviction or virtual holy wars. This appears to be much less the case in East Asia.[102] In Western countries, however, social policy is about much more than

[99] As a character in Philip Roth's *The Human Stain* (2000: 331) muses, every kind of incapacity became asserted as a privilege.

[100] Marshall (1949; 1965) elaborates the internal logic of the civil rights movement and the irresoluble tension between civil rights – the foundation of a market economy and its 'spontaneous' order – and the hierarchically established social rights of the welfare state. In his investigation of Western paths of welfare state development, Esping-Andersen (1990) declared 'decommodification' to be the focal point of social policy altogether. For a critique of this seemingly impartial characterization, see Rieger (1998a).

[101] See Boudon and Bourricaud's description of participants in the US civil rights movement: 'One can hardly describe them as religious in the strict sense of the word. They seem, however, to be marked by an at once charismatic and prophetic dimension. The most active of their members are inspired by an absolute subjective conviction .... They view a rejection of their message, or even indifference, as sacrilege' (1992: 426).

[102] Of particular significance here are the beginnings of socialism in Japan at the end of the nineteenth century. Of the forty founding members of the Socialist Society, out of which Japan's Social Democratic Party later emerged, all but one were Christians (Duus and Schreiner 1998: 152). The elective affinity between Christian and socialist thought is by all appearances stronger than that between Confucianism and socialist thought.

merely repairing the damage that the free market economy – purportedly or actually – leaves behind. It is also, for all intents and purposes, about saving the world.[103]

The monotheistic backbone of social rights The Western social policy conception of an individual 'right' to social protection emanates not only from the paradoxical organic-institutional rationalization of caritas, but also from a different, deeper source: the notion of an other-worldly, personal God.[104] The latter augments the revolutionary significance of social rights in such a way that they can be employed effectively and expressly *against* the distributive results and the 'spontaneous order' produced by the free market.[105] Thus there is a heightened chance that social politics will centre on a commitment to fundamentalist reform and a blanket rejection of the powers that be. As Weber (1978: 542) stressed, 'religious virtuosity, in addition to subjecting the natural drives to a systematic patterning of life, always leads to a radical ethico-religious critique of the relationship to society, the conventional virtues of which are inevitably unheroic and utilitarian.' In the view of monotheistic religions, God, the universe, man and society are part of a single, meaningful whole. The world is presented to the believer as his responsibility. He will have the obligation to transform the world in accordance with his ideals, in which case he will become a rational reformer or a revolutionary on the basis of a theory of 'natural' rights (ibid.). It is thus the translation of monotheistic religious values into the operating principles of social policy, the institutionalization of social rights and the formation of new types of social relations that results in the West in social politics against markets, in an autonomous sphere of justice separate from the economic.

In the monotheistic view, the human being is a moral, purposive creature whose ultimate objective is personal redemption. Moreover, the notion of an other-worldly, personal God enhances the value of the self enormously and accentuates the fundamental and final pre-eminence of the individual over the primordial community.[106] 'Community' thereby becomes in essence a consensual community, and 'society' a union based on rationally calculated expediency. At the centre of both are voluntariness and the idea of contractual, terminable relations as the basis of all social relationships. Because the politically achieved social rights of citizenship brought into play a unique resource, social relations here are seen as not only subject to call, but also dependent on conditions that are shaped by equal, contractual partners acting on their

103 Boudon and Bourricaud too call attention to this inter-sphere transportation of the motivational dynamic of salvation religiosity: 'The opposition between the profane and the holy has lost nothing of its relevance, even if its content has changed so much that the enthusiasm of zeal of the believers nowadays becomes inflamed by issues and problems which earlier were judged to be worldly' (1992: 427).

104 On the importance of an exclusive personal religious relationship to god, see Weber (1978: 569).

105 That this feature of Western societal evolution owes less to some social-scientific, rational engineering than to 'rash do-good-ism', perpetually disturbing the status quo by the invasion of ever new enthusiasts, was also pointed out by Boulding (1950: 190): 'It was not the economists who liberated the slaves or who passed the Factory Acts, but the rash and ignorant Christians!'

106 Salvation religiosity can promote a fierce individualism in so far as an 'ever-watchful' preoccupation with one's own fidelity to a divinely revealed law forces upon the believer 'a desperate struggle, no longer for the respect of others, but for self-respect and a sense of personal worth' (Weber 1978: 497). Judging from the social and political results, Weber also notes that 'the struggle for a sense of personal worth must have become precarious again and again, threatening to wreck the whole meaning of the individual's pattern of life, since ultimately the fulfilment of God's promise was the only criterion of one's value before God at any given time' (ibid.).

own will. Societal power and traditional forms of authority, most importantly those resulting from material inequalities and the rights of property, are thereby effectively neutralized.[107] Congregational religiosity and the enhancement of the value of the individual, which in the West became essential motive forces and determining factors of systematic – as opposed to caritative, i.e intermittent – socio-political measures, are both completely lacking in Confucianism.[108]

Confucianism, like Western culture, has a conception of the self that goes beyond the social. As in the West, it recognizes the individual's interest in not becoming a device of external forces, and in maintaining her moral integrity relative to the 'world'. The oft-cited willingness of individuals loyally to adapt to their social environment and their interest in social harmony are thus both subject to a moral reservation (Roetz 1995: 91). Yet, in contrast to Western culture, this individualizing aspect of the Confucian ethic is not buttressed by conceptions of a hereafter and of a relationship to a personal God which stands above all else. The reference point in Confucian culture is the self-cultivation of the individual. This culture is thus always ultimately and intimately related to social qualities. Confucianism therefore lacks, despite its positive relation to the self, any kind of heroic-unconditional stance against the world (ibid.: 80f.). In general, 'world-rejecting' behaviour is only understandable against the backdrop of an 'other-worldly' orientation. If this other-worldly orientation is lacking, as is the case in Confucianism, then ethics remain an accommodating ethics of responsibility, without the possibility of constituting an absolutist ethics of conviction that explicitly abstains from enquiring into the consequences of behaviour in this world (Weber 1978: 348).[109]

107 Consider the assessment by Professor Xu Xin (Nanking, China) of the relationship between a 'brotherhood ethic', monotheism and contractual thinking: 'China has never had a conception of God. There is not even a definitive Chinese expression for God. We believe that the monotheistic idea gives human beings a new world perspective: it makes it possible to share things with one another. With the idea of a God it is much easier to accept all human beings as brothers and sisters. The idea of a compact between the people of Israel and God, the idea of a personal relationship between the individual and God, contrasts with the Chinese concept of a ruler (Emperor) and his people. China, too, had a concept of a compact between the Emperors and "heaven", in order to legitimise domination, but with a very important difference: the ruler–people relationship was predicated on authority. In the Jewish man–God relationship, authority is obtained through a contract. Both sides have rights and duties, while in China one side – the people – had all the duties and the Emperor all the rights. The Chinese rulers always demanded total obedience. I believe that over the centuries, the Jewish concept of a two-way-relationship (dialogue) brought forth democracy' (cited in a letter to the editor by Emanuel B. Krauskopf to the *Frankfurter Allgemeine Zeitung*, 24 August 1998, 8).

108 Alexis de Tocqueville also called attention to this consequential difference and its religious roots, although he associates both orientations with forms of Christian thought. He leaves no doubt, however, as to which of the two worldviews will survive and what consequences this will have, in his opinion, for the fate of the individual and society. In his *Memoire sur le paupérisme* he writes that there is a basic form of welfare, which consists in each individual's inclination, according to his means, to redress the want that he observes in his immediate surroundings. This has always existed, and it begins with the experience of human misfortune. Christianity made a virtue of it, known as caritas. The other form of welfare is less instinctive, more rational, less emotional and often stronger. It leads society itself to deal with the misfortune of its members and makes it willing systematically to redress their suffering. This type of welfare has its roots in Protestantism and develops only in modern societies. The first form of welfare is a private virtue which is remote from societal regulation. The second, on the other hand, is cultivated and steered by society (Tocqueville 1835: 11). The society Tocqueville denotes is, of course, the democratic mass society of individuals governed by representative bodies.

109 Roetz (1995: 93) clearly notes at one point: 'The primary concern to keep one's state of mind pure, to keep – like the typical Taoist – one's own hands unsullied by the "dirt of the world", is rejected in the *Lunyu* of Confucianism.'

The social politics of salvation religion The transport of the ideational framework of a salvation religion into perspectives on social structures accentuates a radical transformation of the terms of social politics. Salvation religiosity's interest in transcendent justice and material equalization is predicated on reference to a fundamentally different, truer and better world and thus makes social policy arguments basically irrefutable. Since a salvation religion is about *the* truth, it is dogmatic in its thought and in its practice. Dogmatic means that salvation religions hold that theirs is the only true way to salvation. Such dogmatism is absent in the case of Confucianism, and this is the reason why it trails salvation religion in socio-political consequences.

Social politics in the context of salvation religion are typically oriented towards conviction-ethics, which does not much care for the actual results of social reform and thus has a high toleration rate for perverse effects.[110] What counts is the confirmation of principle, i.e. to pass a law. The absolutism of salvation religiosity is complemented by a tendency to programmatic, symbolic politics, which in the final analysis, as Weber put it, is accessible only via empirical psychology (Weber 1989 [1915]: 98). Even after its religious roots have died out, a this-worldly uncompromising ethical habitus retains, after its socio-political institutionalization, considerable chances of survival and influence due to its selective advantages.[111] Even in the absence of declared religiosity, men seek certainty, and it lends their actions effectiveness and vigour: 'In America we are all Methodists now!' (Boulding 1950: 183).[112]

In addition to the unconditionally and intrinsically valuable self, the second conviction-ethical root of the independent dynamic of Western welfare state development is the categorical equality of all human beings before God. This creates a fundamental and insurmountable tension vis-à-vis existing inequalities. Here, too, we see differences in the evaluation, and ultimate origins, of this tension. Its religious origin in the West gives it deeper roots and entails more far-reaching consequences for fundamental decisions in social and economic policy. In the evaluation of social relations, horizontal moments of equality are emphasized far more strongly than vertical moments of pre-eminence and subordination (Roetz 1995: 76).

In short, our claim is that in the West welfare democracy could bring about a revival of the idea of salvation *in this world* precisely because it provided the political and

110 The definitive description of this type of behaviour stems from Weber (1919: 360): 'The person who subscribes to the ethic of conviction feels "responsible" only for ensuring that the flame of pure conviction (for example, the flame of protest against the injustice of the social order) is never extinguished. To kindle that flame again and again is the purpose of his actions, actions which, judged from the point of view of their possible success, are utterly irrational, and which can and are only intended to have exemplary value.' A more poetical expression can be found in T. S. Eliot's *East Coker*, the second of the *Four Quartets*:

> For us, there is only the trying.
> The rest is not our business.

On policy paradoxes as the normal result of the clash between lofty but nonetheless zealously pursued ideals in public policy-making, see Stone (1997). On endemic unintended consequences in twentieth-century America, see Gillon (2000).

111 For this reason Boulding (1957: 223) can note that 'ethical behavior . . . is not essentially different from economic behavior, for ethical behavior too involves choice among selections according to some value ordering'.

112 Despite a differing denomination, Luttwak (1999: 17–20), stressing the enduring authority of Calvinism, makes the same point.

institutional means – the political and social rights of citizenship – to make the *ethical* transformation of social order a going concern of politics. It is for this reason that the originally *other-worldly salvation* could be so powerfully transformed into an interest in the 'liberation from the senseless treadmill' of modern economic life, into a potent critique of the impersonal order of the market economy and the 'commodification' of labour. As Weber noted, 'the hope of salvation has the most far-reaching consequences for the conduct of life when salvation takes the form of a process that casts its shadow before it in this life already' (1978: 528).[113] The most important mechanism to transport religion into social politics is for the individual to anticipate his own personal salvation through a revolution of the existing social structure, whereas Confucian thinking provides a cultural frame in which the individual seeks to fit his future status into the existing, strictly hierarchically ordered social structure (ibid.: 494). In the latter there is, accordingly, also much less room to develop 'compensatory hopes', as Weber calls the 'divine promises relating to this world' (ibid.: 496), and thus much less tension between actual social position and, because of the very limited potential to reform the real world, 'perpetually fruitless expectation and hope' (ibid.: 497).

The sublimation of the salvation idea is essentially responsible for the development of Western social policy as a distinct worldview. And a religiously inspired countervailing, absolutist conception of truth has helped it to become an independent pillar of the material world.[114] In this context, certainty can inspire in believers the additional audacity necessary for them to fight, and attempt to reshape, the status quo. Herein lies the selective, competitive advantage of Christian religiosity. Depending on the religious *status quo ante*, then, secularization can mean many different things and produce different outcomes. In the context of salvation religiosity, it involves a transfer of equalizing interests and equalizing hopes from the other-world to this world.[115] It retains, however, and this point is decisive, its abstract-universalistic moments, which can give socio-political development an extremely rationalist, politically centralizing and often utopian stamp. The theoretical and practical ideas of Jeremy Bentham and Robert Owen, despite opposite philosophical points of departure, provide good examples of social policy design radically removed from the entire empirical world (K. Polanyi 1957 [1944]: 103–10).[116]

The heritage of salvation religion: social politics against markets Alan Greenspan is on Weberian terrain when he observes that the political problem of globalization is the morally rooted clash between those 'who believe that relatively unfettered capitalism is the only economic organization consistent with individual and political freedom' and those who view 'societal organization based on the profit motive and

113 Because of the dismal real-world background of the capitalist expansion of his day, Weber could state that 'it is my opinion that there is no way to eliminate socialist convictions and socialist hopes. Every working class will always return to socialism in some sense or other' (Weber 1918b: 302).

114 On these features of Judaeo-Christian religion, see Assmann (1998: 73–102).

115 In particular, it is monotheism, which is stressing the fundamental equality not only of economically separated men, thus furthering the economic interests of disprivileged classes, but also of the sexes. This tendency to allot equality to women is a characteristic of monotheistic religions, providing them with an unusual degree of emancipation from conventions (Weber 1978: 488–90).

116 Another example is the socio-political 'salutism' of the Salvation Army, which Clasen (1913) investigated from a cultural-sociological perspective. Such developments have no equivalents in the Chinese cultural sphere.

corporate culture as fundamentally immoral' (2001: 2). The modern cultural conflict we see at work in the globalization battles is the principled struggle between ethical rationalization and the process of rationalization in the domain of economics. As Greenspan notes, the strife we witness over economic globalization is 'the twenty-first century's version of debates over societal organization that go back at least to the dawn of the industrial revolution, and many of the intellectual roots of those debates go back far longer' (ibid.: 1).

Now and then the real reason for religious or quasi-religious hostility towards the expansion of 'free' markets is connected with the attitude of religious ethics towards the imperatives of rational profit-making. As Weber pointed out:

> [It is] above all the impersonal and economically rationalized (but for this reason ethically irrational) character of purely commercial relationships that evokes the suspicion, never clearly expressed but all the more strongly felt, of ethical religions. For every purely personal relationship of man to man, of whatever sort and even including complete enslavement, may be subject to ethical requirements and ethically regulated. This is true because the structures of these relationships depend upon the individual wills of the participants, leaving room in such relationships for manifestations of the virtue of charity. But this is not the situation in the realm of economically rationalized relationships, where personal control is exercised in inverse ratio to the degree of rational differentiation of the economic structure. There is no possibility, in practice or even in principle, of any caritative regulation of relationships arising between the holders of a savings and loan bank mortgage and the mortgagee who has obtained a loan from the bank, or between a holder of a federal bond and a citizen taxpayer. Nor can any caritative regulation arise in the relationships between stockholders and factory workers, between tobacco importers and foreign plantation workers, or between industrialists and the miners who have dug from the earth the raw materials used in the plants owned by the industrialists. The growing impersonality of the economy on the basis of association in the market place follows its own rules, disobedience to which entails economic failure and, in the long run, economic ruin. (1978: 585)[117]

The Confucian ethic rests on the general presupposition that

> power-relationships in both the economic and the political spheres have a purely personal character. In these spheres of the execution of justice and particularly in political administration, a whole organized structure of personal relations of subordination exists which is dominated by caprice and grace, indignation and love, and most of all by the mutual piety and devotion of masters and subalterns, after the fashion of the family. Thus, these relationships of domination have a character to which one may apply ethical requirements in the same way that one applies them to every other purely personal relationship. (ibid.: 600)

117 On the 'market community as such . . . as the most impersonal relationship of practical life into which humans can enter with one another', see Weber (1978: 635–40). It was, of course, Adam Smith who celebrated exactly this impersonality as a positively valued, liberating quality of market transactions: 'It is not from the benevolence of the butcher, the brewer, or the baker, that we expect our dinner, but from their regard to their own interest. We address ourselves, not to their humanity but to their self-love, and never talk to them of our won necessities but of their advantages. Nobody but a beggar chooses to depend chiefly upon the benevolence of his fellow-citizens' (Smith 1981 [1778]: 27). In neo-classical economics, 'impersonality' is a basic precondition for a competitive order. G. J. Stigler states in *The Theory of Price* (1946) that 'economic relationships are never perfectly competitive if they involve any personal relationships between economic units' (cited in Hayek 1946: 97).

This ethically grounded order of political and economic life sharply contrasts with the *homo politicus* and the *homo oeconomicus* of Western modernity. Both perform their duties best when they act without regard to the person in question: '*sine ira et studio*, without hate and without love, without personal predilection and therefore without grace, but sheerly in accordance with the impersonal duty imposed by (their) calling, and not as a result of any concrete personal relationship' (ibid.). Because of its formalism, the rational economic association of modern capitalism and the rational personnel management of modern business organization brings about a fundamental *depersonalization* which is beyond the control of a material ethic that is always and directly concerned with *particular* individuals and *particular* groups.

It is the 'extreme artificiality of the market economy' which enables this type of social coordination to travel across cultural divides. It is most of all the 'commodity fiction . . . which supplies a vital organizing principle in regard to the whole of society' (K. Polanyi 1957 [1944]: 73).[118] In general, institutions of culture provide a protective covering which limits the 'commodification' of labour. However, different cultures are differently predisposed to provide a principled defence. For example, at the beginning of the nineteenth century the 'commodification' of labour was seen as a device and principle of individual economic freedom because of its strongly Puritan underpinning.[119] In their *History of Trade Unionism*, Sidney and Beatrice Webb quote from the report of the Select Committee of 1811:

> No interference of the legislature with the freedom of trade, or with the perfect liberty of every individual to dispose of his time and of his labour in the way and on the terms which he may judge most conducive to his own interest, can take place without violating general principles of the first importance to the prosperity and happiness of the community. (cited in Marshall 1949: 76)

Powerfully assisted by the heroic ethics of Puritanism, in England both the early Factory Acts and the 'new' reformed Poor Law offered protection and relief only to those who, 'through age or sickness, were incapable of continuing the battle, and to those other weaklings who gave up the struggle, admitted defeat, and cried for mercy' (ibid.: 80). The Factory Acts provided a protection confined to women and children, 'and champions of women's rights were quick to detect the implied insult. Women were protected because they were not citizens. If they wished to enjoy full and responsible citizenship, they must forgo protection' (ibid.: 81).[120] However, the ascendancy of democracy put an end to this negative concept of social rights.

118 Following Marx's depiction of the satanic mill of modern business organization, Karl Polanyi (1957 [1944]: 73) argued that the 'alleged commodity "labor power" cannot be shoved about, used indiscriminately, or even left unused, without affecting also the human individual who happens to be the bearer of this peculiar commodity'.

119 A heroic, individualistic ethic is a natural correlate to the concept of a discontinuous social order. For example, Hayek (1945: 25) speaks in terms of an almost Camusian existentialism of 'the necessity, in any complex society in which the effects of anyone's action reach far beyond his possible range of vision, of the individual submitting to the anonymous and seemingly irrational forces of society . . . to adjust himself to changes which may profoundly affect his fortunes and opportunities and the causes of which may be altogether unintelligible to him. It is against these that modern man tends to revolt unless their necessity can be shown to rest upon "reason made clear and demonstrable to every individual."'

120 In the United States the argument of the courts – that enforced protective measures curtailed the civil right to conclude a free contract of employment – imparted a powerful brake on social reform until Roosevelt's New Deal (Arkes 2000), and is still a constraint on trade unionism and on expansionist, rights-based social policy (Epstein 1985).

The political rights of citizenship are a unique resource in distributive struggles because they entail the use of the coercive machinery of the state to change the outcomes arrived at through apparently *voluntary* exchange of competitive labour markets, where 'nobody bothers about any but his own economic problem' (Hayek 1935: 121). The level of incomes and the distribution of goods and services are subject to political, rather than the spontaneous determination of impersonal economic forces. Under conditions of fully institutionalized welfare democracy, a return to a truly competitive order solely based on private property is ruled out.[121]

Thus free market policies, or deregulation, are less a principled attempt to restore laissez-faire but a political project to realize the *socialist* potential within corporate capitalism. It aims at the sovereign consumers empowered by democratic politics, not at producers (Livingston 1997). In a welfare democracy, free-market policies have to accept the rules of the game set by welfare statism, i.e. the supremacy of *political* rights derived from *needs* over *economic* rights derived from *productive* efforts.[122] Only a powerful political organization – not the 'spontaneous order' of free markets – can *directly* translate the subjective, *politically* empowered feelings of need into *effective* demand. 'Need', however, tends to become a purely rhetorical device. The new, essentially democratic politics of an unceasing procession of social questions revolves not merely on how to divide the jointly produced wealth of the nation, but, at the same time, on how to adjust rights and obligations. The effect is a fusion of economics and politics: 'In the most fundamental sense, the rights and benefits of social welfare are not to be argued in terms of the needs of particular individuals or specific classes of social groups. To the contrary, the moral criteria are those of distributive justice' (Janowitz 1976: 112).

It seems unlikely that without traditions of radical, monotheistic salvation religions in the West, socialism could ever evolve as a quasi-religious eschatology. For Arnold Toynbee, communism was a Christian heresy (Boulding 1952: 206), and for Max Weber it was beyond doubt that socialist movements were based on specifically religious needs: 'The plebeian and pariah intellectuals of Germany, like that of the Latin countries, increasingly took a radically anti-religious turn, which became particularly marked after the rise of the *economically eschatological faith of socialism*' (1978: 515; emphasis added).[123] Conflicts around globalization resemble wars of religion because they involve a clash of two messianic eschatological faiths – free market economics and welfare statism – with the promise of commodification standing against the one of decommodification. *Both* faiths aim at a rationalized *ethical* transformation of the world, and they have a *common* origin in the absolute transcendental quality of

121 On the social transformation of 'true' democracy, see this summary by Lord Acton, as cited by Hayek (1945: 30): 'The true democratic principle, that none shall have power over the people, is taken to mean that none shall be able to restrain or elude its power. The true democratic principle, that the people shall not be made to do what it does not like, is taken to mean that it shall never be required to tolerate what it does not like. The true democratic principle, that every man's will shall be as unfettered as possible, is taken to mean that the free will of the collective people shall be fettered in nothing.'

122 On this point, see also Lenski (1966: 84): 'In many ways this centuries-old conflict to enhance the value of common citizenship can be viewed as an attempt to reestablish the ascendancy of *need* over *power* as the dominant principle of distribution.' Part of this transformation of the political economy is the change in the meaning of 'productive work', which now entails, as grounds for effective claims on the public purse and public services, family care and even the time spent in educational institutions.

123 For a more detailed discussion, see Weber, who views syndicalism in Western Europe as a variant of socialism 'equivalent to a religious faith' (1978: 515).

Judaeo-Christian beliefs and their very powerful 'eschatological emotional dynamic' (ibid.: 524).

Reading the social philosophy literature from the English Fabians to John Rawls, it becomes obvious that what had happened was the transfer of salvation religion into the politics of this world.[124] The *social* achievement of welfare statism as a *systematic* regulation of markets is also a project of salvation.[125] The more strong this salvation ethic is, for example in the Puritan underpinnings of US welfare-to-work policies as well as in the ethically rigorous universalism of the Swedish welfare state, the more social politics is stripped of its character as an unmethodical and miscellaneous succession of discrete actions dealing with the social problem of the day. In both cases, social policy is marked by a peculiar dynamic because it is seen as a methodology of salvation. Of course, there is a limit to this – in the final analysis – religiously motivated influence upon economic behaviour and its order. But there are no fixed or absolute bounds to this influence, because at heart it is a conflict between strictly opposing value orientations, or, rather, a conflict over what is the best *means* to achieve a fundamentally religious end.

The eschatology of free-market politics Both basic economic thinking and bureaucratic welfare statism – or its civil society equivalents – in their typical *Western* forms carry the hope of salvation and are thus able to have the most far-reaching consequences not only in the West but in other parts of the globe as well. In both cases, a certainty of salvation motivates rational reformist activity and furnishes attempts at a transformation of the world in a rationalized *ethical* direction. Both classical economics and the social philosophy of welfare statism are, at heart, a radical ethico-religious critique of society-as-it-is, and thus it has to be changed. For both, the world is not simply given for all eternity, but for 'work'. Both require from their followers work within the institutions of the world, but also in opposition to them. Their protagonists believe it to be their task to transform the world in accordance with radical ideals, and are typically more or less 'rational' reformers breaking off from tradition on the basis of a theory of 'natural' rights. In short, both market liberalism and welfare statism *in their Western forms* are able to produce revolutionary consequences, and thus result, despite being clothed as a 'solution', in more, not less, conflict.[126]

It is therefore not accidental that the revival of a more doctrinaire and radical free-market liberalism, denouncing government *in toto* as the problem, not the solution, to

124 The same happened in economics, where departments and faculties became temples of social engineering: 'As religious faith retreated among the intelligentsia in the nineteenth century, modernist faith flowed in' (McCloskey 1985: 6).

125 The curiously systematic character of modern welfare statism as an attempt to create a social order of its own was noted by Karl Marx in its first incarnation as factory legislation: 'that first conscious and methodological reaction of society against the spontaneously developed form of its production process' (Marx 1977 [1867]: 610).

126 Since both market liberalism and social democratic welfare statism are a religiously rooted ethic of convictions, they acquire their ability to revolutionize 'at the price of acquiring a whole complex of problems which becomes greatly intensified and internalized. The inherent conflict between the religious postulate and the reality of the world does not diminish, but rather increase. With the increasing systematization and rationalization of social relationships and their substantive contents, the external compensations provided by the teachings of theodicy are replaced by the struggles of particular autonomous spheres of life against the requirements of religion. The more intense the religious need is, the more the world presents a problem' (Weber 1978: 578).

the modern social question (Ronald Reagan), started in the Anglo-Saxon world. For in Protestant-Puritan thinking it was always beyond doubt that public political activity leads to a far greater surrender of rigorous ethical requirements, produced by private business activity, since, as Weber put it, 'political activity is oriented to average human qualities, to compromises, to craft, and to the employment of other ethically suspect devices and people, and thereby oriented to the relativization of all goals' (1978: 593). The basic motive at work here is 'the theoretical insight that the political apparatus of force could not possibly provide a place for purely religious virtues, whether uncompromising rational ethics or acosmistic fraternalism' (ibid.). And Weber went on to point out that it was exactly this motive that provided one important source 'of the affinity between inner-worldly asceticism and the advocacy of the minimization of state control such as was represented by the laissez-faire doctrine of the "Manchester school" ' (ibid.).

What was then the Manchester school is now the 'Washington consensus' underlying the politics of the IMF and the World Bank. And, of course, then and now free-market economics as the 'proven method for demonstrating salvation' compromised with the facts of political power struggles.[127]

Behavioural imperatives: toleration or rupture of existing relations

In examining East Asia's prominence of egalitarian educational policies – just as in the case of its overall more amicable socio-political orientations and certain 'harmonious' features of corporate organization – the question arises whether such choices of emphasis stem from the rational calculation inherent in successful late or 'catch-up' modernization, or whether it can be described better as a by-product of Confucian culture in the sense that it could provide organizational formulas and thus help to legitimize particular socio-political strategies. An analysis of Confucian traditions speaks for the latter interpretation.

The element of the Confucian ethic that is probably most instrumental to East Asian countries' economic success is its high esteem of education. It is, above all, the link between education and the ideal of lifelong learning, on the one hand, and democratic-egalitarian and meritocratic elements, on the other, that gives this realm of welfare state policy its enhanced significance. From an historio-genetic perspective, the Confucian patrimonial bureaucracy's successful self-assertion against the aristocratic feudal order resulted in an 'official theory' according to which not birth but – in principle universally accessible – education decides whether one belongs to the 'plain folk' or to the 'literati':

127 On mainstream free-market economics as a moral science, or an absolute ethics, whose protagonists are concerned first and foremost that the flame of pure conviction never be extinguished, see this quote from a memorandum circulated in May 1983 among the staff at the Council of Economic Advisors: ' "Mankiw's Maxim: No issue in economics has ever been decided on the basis of the facts." "Nihilistic Corollary I: No issue has ever been decided on the basis of theory, either." "Frisch's Restatement: Never let the facts stand between you and the right answer." "McCaleb's Policy Prescription Principle: All policy implications drawn from economics are matters of faith" ' (McCloskey 1985: 31). The reader should note that our view on the poverty of economic modernism is not meant to give comfort to the enemies of the Washington Consensus or the 'Chicago boys'. First of all, economists themselves noted their dogmatic impulse. Second, dogmatic impulses can be found in the other social sciences as well, and are perhaps less controlled than in economics. On the distinction between an 'ethic of principled conviction' and an 'ethic of responsibility', see Weber (1919: 359).

> Of course, 'equality' . . . did not mean an unconditioned equality of all natural qualities. Men differ in what comes easy to them because of some natural aptitude and what requires work. But at least with regard to what Confucian bureaucratic reasons of state and social ethics demanded everybody could achieve, since it never reached for the sky. And thus everybody had, given good public administration, to look for the reasons of worldly and inner success or failure within himself. Man as such is good, bad things enter him from the outside, through the senses, and differences in the quality of men were differences in the harmonious development of the individual person. . . . Basically it is the material situation in life which set men apart. Equal economic situation in life and equal education make for identical characters. And indeed . . . was material wealth . . . from the ethical point of view, not primarily a source of temptations (although positively recognized as such), but rather: the most important means to advance morals. (Weber 1989 [1915]: 338f.)

The fate of society – its 'goodness' – one's family and oneself depend exclusively on the effort of the individual, on her true nature and the extent to which her innate good can be brought to the surface and thus rendered effective. 'Thus everything turned into a problem of education with the objective of self-directed advancement out from one's own disposition' (ibid.: 347). This personal disposition is not affected by any transcendental notions. Rather, it is a complex which, according to Weber, is thoroughly focused on this-worldly, primarily socially conditioned objectives.[128]

Restorative social policies Corresponding to this is the dominant Confucian notion of the 'world-organizing bureaucrat' (Weber 1978: 512), whereas in the West the success of the societal order emanates from an 'invisible hand', and societal prosperity results unintentionally from the essentially independent – and, according to Mandeville (1988 [1724]), 'amoral' – pursuit of interests (L. Schneider 1987). Moreover, the notion of 'original sin', radical evil and negative conceptions of societal determinism are foreign to Confucianism. Adverse socio-economic conditions such as individual misfortune are attributed to 'mistakes', and these mistakes are seen as the product of a deficient education and insufficient individual effort (Weber 1989 [1915]: 347; 1978: 438). For this reason, the learning process and contact with new subject matter are not restricted to a specific life stage, but instead have always constituted a lifelong, ever renewed process (Weber 1989 [1915]: 359).[129]

At the same time, and as a natural correlate in the realm of social organization, one of the dominant interests of Confucianism has always been state-led social reform.[130]

128 'In the catalog of goods in the *Shih ching*, the highest rewards promised to the Chinese subjects for their correct performances of the official cult and their fulfillment of personal religious obligations are wealth and long life, while there is a complete absence of expectations in regard to another world and any compensation there' (Weber 1978: 527).

129 These utilitarian moments in Confucianism, together with a strong collectivist orientation, can be seen as a 'public good'. They endow East Asian societies with advantages in competitive contexts in which the capacity of the members of a company or organization to learn and adapt constitute a pivotal factor in survival and success. The characterization of a value system as a public good implies that it cannot be easily generated or rationally disposed of: 'Successful self-interested, utilitarian behaviour in market environments requires the presence of collective resources, common values and shared expectations that rationally acting individuals cannot normally generate, protect or restore even if they fully recognize their vital importance' (Streeck 1989). On the utilitarianism of Confucianism, see Tillman (1982) and Roetz (1992).

130 See Weber (1978: 445), who notes that 'Confucius was centrally concerned with influencing princes in the direction of particular social reforms'.

Since Confucian ethics were always devised by political actors and imposed by political force, they could never become something sacred and thus unalterable. Without such qualities, there is little chance for them to become a source of iconoclastic heresies.[131] Social protest cannot acquire a religious aura and thus win extra strength and capability to overturn the existing order. It is most of all the sacredness of a divinely revealed faith that can successfully oppose tradition because the sacred is the ultimately unalterable. Hence, an explanation for the deep concern for *radical* social reform, for *freshly* unifying people, for *founding* communities and societies is to be sought on the religious grounds of a salvation ethic, chiefly because this type of activity constitutes the theatre of God's will.[132] In general, any direct harnessing of religion to extra-religious purposes, something that is a recurrent typical feature in the history of Western societies, presupposes an idiosyncratic autonomy of the religious domain. One way in which the idiosyncratic autonomy of religion becomes apparent is the phenomenon of 'Reformation', i.e. innovations in religion. A reformation liberates society from its previously achieved social equilibrium and is thus a principal historical agency in bringing about critical social change.[133]

Confucian social politics has far less evolutionary potential in terms of the emergence, expansion and establishment of group-transcending welfare state benefit systems – i.e. systems that bind individuals who do not and will never know one another and nevertheless are willing to entrust large portions of their incomes, through taxes and contributions, to impersonal agencies that then dispose of the money according to their own prescriptive, abstract criteria. The moral basis of this behaviour is congregational religiosity:

> Congregational religion added the fellow worshipper and the comrade in faith to the roster of those to whom the religiously founded obligation of assistance applied, which already included the blood-brother and the fellow member of clan or tribe. Stated more correctly, congregational religion set the co-religionist in the place of the fellow clansman. (Weber 1978: 580)

131 See, for example, Hayek (1947: 109), who wants to tap this resource and consequently admonishes his fellow economists to 'pay deliberate attention to the moral temper of contemporary man . . . to set a definite task to the reformatory zeal of men . . . to point out reforms which can be fought out by unselfish men'.

132 It is by no means Judaeo-Christianity per se which, in the final analysis, provides the driving force for such a direction of social politics. As Weber pointed out, it was difficult for such an emotionalist faith as Lutheranism to generate anti-traditionalist, rational patterns of conduct, and thus it lacked any drive towards the rational control and transformation of the world. It lacks any motivation 'towards revolutionary attitudes in social or political attitudes and any inclination towards rational reformist activity' (1978: 570). It is the belief in predestination that can produce in its most consistent followers the strongest possible motives for acting in accordance with God's pattern. Hence it is no surprise that the Puritan belief in predestination was regarded by the powers that be everywhere as dangerous to the state and as hostile to authority, 'because it made Puritans sceptical of the legitimacy of all secular power' (ibid.: 574).

133 Boulding (1952: 202) pointed out the general pattern that innovations in religion preceded and paved the way for innovations in economic life: 'Indeed, the most important innovation in any society is the *idea* of innovation itself, for this represents the Rubicon between the traditional stationary type of society, in which each generation repeats the patterns of its elders, and the "economic", dynamic society, in which innovation becomes an accepted and profitable role. . . . Once iconoclasm has succeeded in the most traditional and "sacred" area of life, once "free enterprise" has been successful in religion, the spirit of innovation seizes upon all other areas of life.'

One feature of 'ethical' religions like Confucianism is their basic distrust of impersonal relationships and therefore also of the 'market' as well as of 'societal' – as opposed to 'community-oriented' – social policy (ibid.: 584f.).[134] One basic result of this makes for much more amicable social politics. In contrast, in the West the fundamentally religiously derived capability of social policy to revolutionize social and political structures comes at the price of acquiring a whole complex of problems which are, because of their religious sources, greatly intensified and internalized.

Contrary to the taxing ethical requirements of salvation religiosity, Confucianism is predicated on realistic behavioural assumptions, i.e. that material and sexual interests constitute the principal driving forces of human action. These behavioural assumptions, paired with a highly personalized ethic of responsibility, lead to a high level of acceptance of coercive political power and social subordination, and mitigate these at the same time with rationalized and meritocratic elements. The need to fit into hierarchic social relations follows already from the simple fact of the scarcity of means relative to needs. Constraints are easily accommodated and are not a cause for revolt: 'The coercive order as such, the differentiation of wealth and factional economic conflicts posed therefore no principled problem' (Weber 1989 [1915]: 348). It is not a matter of subordination per se. A democratic element can be seen in conceptions of reciprocity that are fundamental, and inflected in a personalized, egalitarian way. They have their roots in rural neighbourhood associations' social ethic of exchange (ibid.: 358). A consensus orientation follows from this, pursued through discussion of common problems, which transcends hierarchy. Moreover, the political order is not seen as something external to the individual; rather, the individual is an integral part of the order in that her behaviour directly influences its quality. These conceptions are diametrically opposed to Christian ideas and have drastic socio-political consequences.

The radicalization of conceptions of a socially independent self, responsible ultimately only and exclusively to God, provides the individual with an immense potential for resistance to the 'unreasonable demands' of this world. Further, the wish or, more precisely, the religiously inspired need for an enhancement of this independence has typical socio-political consequences. It leads to a strong interest in 'hard' social rights, i.e. in means to overcome or mitigate individual dependencies vis-à-vis the market and the state bureaucracy.[135]

134 East Asia's strong emphasis on personal relationships both in business and in the relationship of business to politics, as opposed to the West's apparently successful, culturally mediated, detached relationship to the market, in which the market is seen as an impersonal mechanism that coordinates interests, is explained by Cho and Lee (1995) with the argument that Confucian values lower the costs of implementation of firm and economic policy decisions, for the Confucian ethic expressly and effectively rewards cooperative and loyal behaviour. Kahn (1979: 121–2) sees in this factor the most significant competitive advantage of Confucian-shaped cultures. In the wake of the economic crisis that befell all of East Asia in July 1997, Western commentators, in view of the highly personal nature of economic relations here, asked whether the entire system might not be plagued by *crony capitalism*. This view is probably exaggerated, although it accurately identifies the potential danger of this form of capitalism. As Weber pointed out, in the sphere of economically rationalized relationships, *personal* control is exercised in inverse ratio to the degree of rational differentiation of economic structure.

135 On individualism in Western thought, see Taylor (1989), Boudon and Bourricaud (1992: 219–27) and Luhmann (1989). On the precarious individualist foundations of socio-political modernization in Japan, see Koschman (1996).

In the Confucian context, on the other hand, the development of the individual is not an end in itself, but remains limited to her function in the immediate community of the family, the clan and the neighbourhood association, or the company. Confucianism does not imply any 'natural law' that sanctions a personal sphere of freedom. Other than private property, in Confucian societies there are no legally guaranteed freedoms, and even the 'right of property' is, according to Weber, 'secured only in a factual-situation and thus relative way', without that aura of inviolability that determined the structure of development of *constrained* political rule in the West. This limited significance of personal freedoms, ultimately rooted in the nature of patrimonialism, gives interventionism a specific paternalistic welfare state colour. It expresses itself in a subsistence policy with a clear

> preference for the utmost equality in the distribution of wealth in the interest of social order [which is paired] with an Egyptian public storehouse policy to control prices. Material justice, not formal law, was also in this realm the ideal of patrimonial rule. Thus property and acquisition continued to be problems of practical utility on the one hand, of social-ethical aid in sustaining the masses on the other, but not of a natural law, individualistic social ethics, as it sprung in modern times from the tension between formal law and postulates of material justice. (ibid.: 340)

Because of their predominantly company-level locus and orientation, East Asian socio-political institutions are more compatible with the functional requirements of highly regulated markets and companies, for in companies, too, the community and not the autonomous individual constitutes the core of order. Therefore, one could argue that in fact Confucianism has a theory of the social – albeit only an implicit one – which is in its own way adequate to an *organized* market economy. In Western culture the social is understood far more, by contrast, as being opposite and adversarial to the logic of an *impersonal* market-oriented social development. This results in greater scope for alternative visions, and thus in Western social politics, public policy schemes can rise to the status of an autonomous power, shaping social and societal relations according to some plan. As a form of large-scale social engineering, it is not tied to the immanence of the empirically given. Instead, it can orient itself to utopian conceptions of a good society, one that transcends prevailing conditions and has yet to be created. This type of order is, in essence, derived from voluntary agreement, purposefully thought out, based on impersonal bonds and enacted through general, positive laws (Weber 1920: 299; 1978: 37). Conversely, Confucianist social policy is left only with the recourse to tradition to justify corrections to social conditions. This results in a widespread disdain for purely legal rule, i.e. rule by virtue of positive statute (Weber 1978: 36).[136]

The problem of order in the welfare state Herein might lie the actual core of Confucianism's ethics of adaptation, which Weber depicts as its constitutive feature, a characterization that Roetz rejects. Weber was no doubt bearing in mind this fundamental, psychologically and socially highly consequential difference between an ulti-

136 On the significance and historical fate of legalism in Chinese ethics, see Roetz (1992) and Granet (1985). Reference to the notion that positive legal rule is illegitimate is also made by Granet: 'For the Chinese, the concept of a law is foreign' (1985: 288).

mately other-worldly and an ultimately this-worldly orientation in the understanding of the self and the soul. This contrast will not become fully clear, however, until one considers not only Weber's, but also Ernst Troeltsch's work on the basic features of Christian thought and their ethical and socio-political implications. It is this moment that imparts upon Western individualism its enormous, fateful significance and renders it the exclusive reference point of a liberal political order and a free competitive economy. Looking at this ultimately religious origin of Western individualism demonstrates clearly that the institutional core of Western welfare states – their understanding of social rights as property rights or subjective (public) rights – derives from the same roots as these states' political and economic liberalism (Homann 1988; Marshall 1949; Boulding 1952). The institutionalization of social rights which occurred in the course of welfare state expansion, as well as the status quo orientation that is regularly bemoaned in times of crisis, do not, in this understanding, constitute a universal socio-political phenomenon, i.e. are not the product of a certain level of economic development, but, rather, have roots and driving forces that lie more deeply in Western culture. Moreover, this institutionalization of social rights, and thus welfare statism as well, is to some degree inherently unstable, since its essentially religious root is a virtually unlimited potential of self-criticism and social discontent that always turns against any societal achievement. If social positions become negotiable, ideals and expectations will always outgrow actual achievements and thus set the problem of institutional control of relentlessly expansionist as well as divisive social politics in a particular, never-ending way (Knight 1947: 83). In East Asia, however, we can observe a fundamentally different situation, in particular when we look at the problems that companies typically have to face in a rapidly changing world economy.

The economic cosmos brought about by the central mechanism of economic globalization, the 'Washington consensus', is a cosmos that should allegedly not be judged in terms of 'social justice'. In so far as it results in order, it is an order emerging from disorder. This paradoxical social organization, however, is based on images of the self, attitudes and values that cannot be understood without systematic reference to a very particular theological tradition. Moreover, the transformation of the very private and very energetical pursuit of self-interest in some public good without any premeditated design smacks of alchemy. Not only is this thinking, when it is turned into a public policy, regularly contested; in addition, it still presents us, *pace* Hayek, with the puzzle of precisely *how* an order forms itself without design. Confucian thinking clearly favours mercantilism and welfare statism. If there is order in economy and society, it is the work of the legislator, who has to smooth out human interactions to the end of achievement of general prosperity.

Simmel's analysis of the peculiar psycho-social transformation of a theologically grounded tradition of social policy suggests that Western welfare states are not characterized by an excess of solidarity, or 'collectivism', but that the problem is rather one of excessive individualism. In the West, great stress is placed on the individual: the capacity of each person to fashion his or her own inner self and then to take that self and grant it – and this is one of the central ideas of the welfare state – a full range of socio-political support. Originally, this support was provided by religious faith. Replacing family, kin and neighbourhood, the institutions of the welfare state form an outer structure that provides the material that will cohere in the person, but will not force any particular course upon her or him. Since the institutional framework of the welfare state organizes rather than governs, social control of the welfare state is a perennial problem of welfare state governance.[137]

In the social politics of Western welfare states, individualism is expressed in the juridification of social claims and their interpretation by supreme courts and other instances as a constitutionally protected property right (Reich 1964; Marshall 1965; Heinze 1984). The 'new equity' created by the welfare state links nearly every person in one way or another to the state's administration and thus creates a fundamental interest in its continued existence. It thus introduces an institutional rigidity, which forms the background for the diagnoses of 'overload' and 'sclerosis' in the political governance of welfare states (Janowitz 1976; Olson 1982; Higgs 1987; Bok 2001). Administrative categories that singled out persons and groups and allowed them to make needs-based claims created 'automatic', politically sacrosanct entitlements and, in the process, 'disabled the state' (Stone 1984: 13; Tynes 1996).

This is the new social and political situation which, since the 1970s, in all developed welfare states of the West turned 'welfare state crisis' into a permanent feature of the 'new' politics of the welfare state (Pierson 2001). To regain institutional control of the social politics of welfare states became a holy grail. For Simmel, writing at the turn of the nineteenth century, public welfare was still exclusively a matter of discretionary precautions of the state's administration, and the receipt of assistance was strictly conditioned on entering the poorhouse and abdicating the rights to vote and to serve on a jury. These measures prevented a recurrence of the medieval 'revenge of the alms'. As the development of social policy after the First World War shows, the restrictive conditions of the provision of public welfare could not be maintained in the context of the universal franchise, party competition and the mass politics of representative bodies.[138] Herein lies one of the main sources of the welfare state dynamic of Western industrial societies. It is precisely this particular psycho-cultural foundation that is lacking in East Asian societies.[139] This is the reason why a universalistic-abstracting approach to socio-political relations exists there only at a rudimentary level: 'belonging' is more important than individual autonomy.[140] Membership in a com-

137 The problem of social control in the welfare state formed the centre of the sociological work of Morris Janowitz. For an overview, see Suttles (1985).

138 The problem gained a particular significance because of a basic shift in both the rationale and the practice of means-tested programmes. In the 1960s all advanced welfare states' bureaucratic discretion ceased to be seen as a brake on generosity and a safeguard for incentives to work and were instead conceived as a positive, not a negative, instrument of social policy, to be exercised in broadening the services rendered to those whose need for them was apparently most pressing. The means-test became a needs-test (Marshall 1965: 88). Courts came to be seen as a 'quality control mechanism' over bureaucrats and politicians (Birkinshaw 1985: 3). Law was converted into a tool to achieve specific ends, to be used instrumentally, i.e. for the partial purposes of directly implementing positive social objectives (Cranston 1985; Galligan 1986; Handler 1986).

139 Thus also the institutional foundation for a *social* rule of law is lacking. 'In East Asia predictability necessary for economic prosperity lies less in a system of laws and more in the leadership's commitment to its professed policies and principles. The rule of law is secondary to the sincerity of officials and the steadfastness of individual leaders in carrying out their programs. The adversarial, indeed game-playing, spirit of Western legal practices, is seen as whimsical when contrasted with the reassuring consistency in judgement of stolid officials with long terms of office' (Pye 1988: 85).

140 Discussing the Anglo-American scene, Janowitz (1976: xii) characterizes the welfare state in the following way: 'The ideological, political, and moral justification of welfare expenditures is that the state can intervene in the management of the economic system in order to assist each household and each person *to pursue goals of their own choosing*' (emphasis added).

munity understood as primordial, i.e. not open to influence by state laws, is the characteristic social attribute. At the same time, communities are organized hierarchically according to the model of a patriarchally understood family or a patrimonially organized household. As a result of a person's existence being far more strongly determined by social ties, and because of the emphasis on an individual's social functions, sociopolitical benefit claims are far more dependent on situation and context. They are the product of an 'objective' situation which can change, and not an expression of a 'subjective', unchangeable personal status or position.[141] East Asian social politics is much more pragmatic, because it lacks a distinctive theological foundation.

The religious dimension of personnel management One important consequence of the Confucian ethic is that companies in East Asia are confronted primarily with 'coordination problems', and less with 'motivational problems'. The distinction between coordinative and motivational problems is based on the fact that a problem's technical resolution does not automatically entail that it is also susceptible to implementation (Hurwicz 1973; Wolff 1995; Ledyard 1989). Beside coordination or feasibility issues related to production and communication, a second hurdle to the implementation of decisions is constituted by motivational problems, i.e. problems related to the 'natural incentives' of the participants. Pointing to the same insight is the distinction between 'resource constraints' and 'incentive constraints' (Myerson 1989: 191). According to this view, these 'natural incentives' are regularly evident as opportunistic behaviour – 'self-interest seeking with guile' (Williamson 1993: 224). In the West, occupational positions and levels of income are seen as entitlements, and since these entitlements have strong normative qualities, they cannot be taken away without cost. Approval of a company's restructuring as well as 'trust' become things that have to be calculatingly negotiated for.

Judging from the history of organization theory and the exploding literature on 'change management' there is reason to believe that this status quo orientation of individual behaviour in organizations has cultural roots inasmuch as its ultimate origin is the conception of the absolute sovereignty of the individual, which shows up, in the words of James Madison in Federalist Paper No. 55, as a certain 'degree of depravity in mankind which requires a certain degree of circumspection and distrust' (Hamilton et al. 1999 [1787–8]: 314).[142] In Japan, by contrast, job descriptions – in the sense of proprietary claims of employees to the types of work they must perform – are unknown (Kieser 1998: 48f.). This feature is a central and critical variable of organizational and institutional change, especially in advanced Western industrial societies. It has received far too little attention in the theory and practice of political and business change management (Wolff 1999).

141 This perception is of course never fully absent in the West. Thus Heinze points to this German Constitutional Court ruling: 'The authority of the legislature to determine the content and limits [of property rights in public entitlements] is more extensive, the more this property is part of a social relation and social function' (1984: 54). Our interpretation hinges, however, not on the existence or lack of a certain point of view as such, but on the differing psycho-cultural motivations and groundings of welfare state benefit claims, their ability to be marshalled against existing conditions, and the differing independent dynamics that can result.

142 On the development of an 'individual theodicy of personal destiny' in Judaeo-Christian religiosity, see Weber (1978: 495).

The distinction between coordination and motivation problems has its origins, if one follows our interpretation, in the West's individualistic culture, in which stubbornness and self-interest are not only legitimate, but also highly esteemed categories of perception of self and others. These traits are much weaker in Confucianism. This is related to the fact that the value of a person is measured above all in terms of his or her social relationships and functions (Nakane 1970).[143] The nature of the sinicized legal systems of East Asia, giving rise to regimes of public law that almost exclusively stressed duties, thus precluded the development of the concept of 'legal rights' (Haley 1991: 21).[144]

Integration in the group and a high level of flexibility in intra-group behaviour is matched, however, by conservatism in the behaviour of the group as a whole.[145] The status quo orientation, which in Western societies is focused on the individual and enhanced by the legal anchoring of social benefit rights and by welfare state labour regulation (Streeck 1992), finds its roots in East Asian societies in the group. Only in extraordinary circumstances is change considered to be a problem: 'Radical organizational innovation and strategic orientation that forces some constituent groups to make a sacrifice would in general occur as a matter of organizational survival in response to drastic environmental shocks' (Aoki 1988: 298).

On the other hand, Stiglitz (1996) emphasizes the fact that the practice of guaranteed lifelong employment in East Asia renders employees far more willing than in Western companies to propose productivity-enhancing innovations to management. If employees in Western companies do so, they run the risk of furthering rationalization processes, which end up costing them their jobs. The, perhaps decisive, difference between the two cultures lies not in favouring reaction rather than change, but in the possibility of resisting (unreasonable) behavioural demands that are to lead to change. In East Asia, there is no recourse to the welfare state and its social or labour law in this regard. The effectiveness of familial or group-based rudiments in the company-based fiduciary community is enhanced by the this-worldly orientation of Confucian practice. Organizational adaptation is a simple case of discretionary bureaucratic politics, given that the goal of personal effort is not independence, but, rather, adaptation to the world: the 'hallmark [of Confucianism] is an absolute lack of feeling for a need

143 Bray (1986: 170) notes the strong influence of distinctive models of the management conflict, cooperation and control developed in the context of East Asian wet-rice technology on organizational behaviour in companies. Both in modern, large-scale companies and in rice cultivation systems the *systemic* nature of change exerts heavy pressure to conform: 'In order to ensure access to water and labour, even the most privileged members of rice-growing societies have traditionally been obliged to cooperate closely with their fellow-farmers. On the other hand where essential resources are in short supply – labour and land for instance – conflicts inevitably arise. To some extent such organizations as irrigation societies and labour exchange groups have the effect of reducing social inequalities and promoting communal harmony; nevertheless social and economic hierarchies are to be found in all village societies where there is pressure on resources.'

144 This also implies that both in the company and vis-à-vis the state, law, or rules, are an instrument of top-down control, not an instrument of bottom-up control (Haley 1991: 22).

145 The central place of communal relationships in East Asia can also be glimpsed from the fact that infraction of rules is punishable by expulsion from the community (Bray 1986: 172). For a comparative perspective, see Fenwick (1982), who notes as a basic difference in the organization of social control between Japan and the US that 'conformity (in Japan) is more a function of the threat of exclusion from social groupings rather than formalized punishment that might be meted out by the criminal justice system' (at p. 64f.).

of salvation or for any transcendental anchorage for ethics. In its place resides what is substantively an opportunistic and utilitarian (though aesthetically refined) doctrine of convention appropriate to a bureaucratic status group' (Weber 1978: 476).[146]

Continuous versus discontinuous conceptions of social order

An explicit peculiarity of Confucianism is the idea of expressly designing the social order as the foundation and form for achieving individual religious-ethical goals. Ethical values are seen as being in a continuous relationship with, and dependent upon, life's material basis and social and political organization. Confucianism proceeds from the assumption of an immediate relationship between ethical-spiritual values and social (and economic) organization. The ethically guided behaviour of the individual is an indispensable prerequisite to social order. Individuals directly and functionally serve the supra-personal social order and draw their value from this alone (Moritz 1998: 209). In this worldview, the cosmic order does not differ from the cultural order (Granet 1985: 293).[147] In symmetric-continual fashion, Confucianism organizes loyalties and bands together not only the state, economy and society, but also men and nature: correct behaviour becomes obligatory in order to secure or restore the regularity of natural events (Roetz 1995: 40; Moritz 1998: 210). 'Sin' and 'piety' are viewed as integral powers, and integrative behaviour becomes a categorical imperative (Weber 1978: 438; Roetz 1995: 8; Moritz 1998: 212).[148]

This contrasts with the position of traditional Christianity, according to which the state and the social order cannot claim any specifically religious dignity and are hence ethically neutral. They only 'become relevant for Christianity in terms of their external and superficial functions' (Troeltsch 1994 [1912]: 73). In the West, social order and individual behaviour are seen as conceptually – and morally – distinct, and power, law and social justice are seen to reside in and to result from essential impersonal and thus amoral structures. This fundamentally discontinuous relationship between the individual and society, which characterizes Western culture, is a remarkable feature with decisive consequences. Only in the West did the notion of 'spontaneous' order evolve, or of a 'public good' as the result of an 'invisible hand' determining the results

146 Also Wolferen (1989: 9f.), noting the relatively weak sense of transcendent norms as moral imperatives as one of the reasons for the relatively easy acceptance of top-down patterns of governance, stressed the religious origins of this behavioural trait: 'Concepts of independent universal truths or immutable religious beliefs, transcending the worldly reality of social dictates and the decrees of powerholders have of course found their way into Japan, but they have never taken root in any surviving world-view. . . . The fact that Japanese have situational instead of general moral rules and hold particular values rather than universalistic ones provides crucial clues to Japanese behavior.'

147 For this reason, the Chinese philosophers have, according to Granet, 'persistently expressed contempt for jesters. For when they stand on their head, it could be that they turn the world upside down as well' (1985: 272). Here we clearly see the intensity of the pressure to socially conform, which is also reflected in notoriously low crime and imprisonment rates.

148 Morality is reduced to the utility resulting from reciprocally benevolent behaviour: 'He who loves others will most certainly be loved by others as well. He who uses others will most certainly be used by others. He who hates others will most certainly be hated by others. He who inflicts harm on others will most certainly be harmed by others' (Mo Di in Roetz 1995: 40). In this line of thinking, the strategic behaviour of individuals is also equated with moral behaviour; they cannot be in opposition to each other. The societal order 'flows' from individual behaviour, and, conversely, a 'good' order is predicated on the correct behaviour of each individual: 'The foundation of the world is the state, the foundation of the state is the family, and the foundation of the family is the self' (Menzi in Roetz 1995: 80).

of individual action.[149] State social policy in East Asian countries instead has greater affinities to familial and kinship structures and is limited by these in its sphere of action and potential for legitimization.[150] In East Asia, therefore, public policy and individual morality are seen as entirely consonant, and the institutionalization of social policies includes the local practice of communities.

This Confucian notion of a consonant social order also contrasts sharply with an understanding of social order in which the latter is not built directly from the individual behaviour of society's members, but, rather, emerges spontaneously and independently – behind their backs, as it were.[151] Such a conception of an order achieved by means of the invisible hand has its foundation in an absolute individualism according to which each individual is responsible only to herself and to her personal God, and pursues, according to her best knowledge and conscience, solely her own interests. This Western notion of individuality depicts a self-directed and self-fashioning person whose psychic structure generates someone who, whatever her overt manifestations, is deeply and truly private. In Western thought, the individual possesses an inner driving force that directs actions. Intent is seen to lie within, and to be sufficiently distinguishable from overt acts that one can ask God and man to judge one by one's intentions and not one's deeds. Only the ethical individual who acts out of autonomously derived, inner choices can comprehend the transcendence and unity of God. This individualism precludes any conception of order which claims an immediate continuity or unmediated correlation between individual behaviour and social order or, what amounts to the same thing, societal welfare.[152]

The theology of methodological individualism: the church of Weber To clarify the difference between concepts of a continuous versus a discontinuous social order, we can use Weber's sociology as our empirical material. A specific, positively valued social determinism is the result of a particular institutional order, as are voluntaristic notions of social order. Weber's concept of an 'interpretative sociology', envisioning the individual person and her action as the basic unit, is clearly indebted to the Judaeo-Christian culture.[153] To take the individual person as 'the sole carrier of meaningful conduct' is a typical Puritan concept. Weber's sociology is based on the philosophy of discontinuous history. He draws a strict line between his interpretative sociology and the totalizing *physique sociale* of Comte and Durkheim. His scrupulous nominalism allows him to pursue lines of structural analysis, but he never goes so far as to equate 'structure' with social reality.

149 On the history of the concept of 'spontaneous order', see Hayek (1969) and, for a short description, Garrison and Kirzner (1989). On the 'invisible hand', see Vaugh (1989) and Zamagni (1989).

150 The guiding conceptions of Confucian familialism are in fact matched by a still vibrant practice of the provision of familial assistance. In the course of industrialization and urbanization this tradition has proven to be astoundingly capable of survival and adaptation (Kwon 1997; Kono 2000).

151 See also the 'Great Teaching', which is attributed to Confucius: 'Before the elders told the whole world the essence of pure virtue (or the politically correct attitude), they put their own state in order. Before they put their state in order, they took care of their family. Before they put their family in order, they disciplined themselves. Before they started with their education, they straightened their character. Before they formed their character, they examined themselves' (cited in Geldsetzer and Han-ding 1998: 35).

152 This lack of normative individualism is echoed by the lack of an assumption of freedom of the will in Chinese ethical philosophy (Granet 1985: 293).

153 In discussing Weber's image of man, Gerth and Mills also note that his 'decision-making, morally responsible individual is, of course, a specifically modern and Occidental type of personality' (Gerth and Mills 1946: 70).

Structural explanations attempt to account for the motivation of systems of action by their function as going concerns rather than by the subjective intentions of the individuals who act them out. For Weber, despite his fears of the unstoppable growth of a totalitarian bureaucracy in all spheres of life, is always aware that something profound is going on in the social universe that is not fully calculable in advance. Life and social structures are persistently open to radical innovations that cannot be deduced from previous categories and concepts of thinking. For Weber, societies are communities of agents evolving along an 'edge of chaos' between over-rigid and over-fluid behaviour.[154] The social universe is, for him, a vastly non-repeating one, and hence his interest in charisma, profit-seeking capitalists, entrepreneurial politicians and salvation religion's prophets. The social structure is a space of possibilities. For him, emergence and persistent creativity in the social universe and in institution-building are real. As a sociologist he is interested in the causal analysis of regularities, but this is not denying the fact of autonomous agents. Institution-building and structures are about *constraints*, or, more to the point, the *constrained* release of social energy. Social action is often directed to construct routines and institutions as constraints on social action, which then constitutes further social action. Thus, for Weber, 'structure' and 'organization' are not static, but dynamic concepts, because for him they do not deny the emergence of novel functionalities. Despite actors themselves aspiring to it, particularly in the form of large-scale social engineering, social life is, in the final analysis, something incalculable, and for that reason 'laws' are, for Weber, merely tools of analysis, or heuristic devices, but not congruent to reality, or an 'expression' or 'reflection' of reality, and no concrete reality can be deduced from 'laws' (Weber 1904: 75). For Weber, the social universe is a pluralistic one, and this rules out totalizing notions of theory.

Despite his sometimes overly fatalistic tendencies, it is worth noting that Weber, in the conception of his 'interpretative sociology', starts from the notion that the *individual* is *ordinarily* in tension with the social roles and routines of everyday institutions. Moreover, in the context of the rise of a global capitalism he stressed that 'the need for an ethical interpretation of the "meaning" of the distribution of fortunes among men *increased* with the growing rationality of conceptions of the world' (1920: 275; emphasis added). And finally, because of the basically antinomical structure of his thinking, he noted early on that welfare statism evolved as a major counterpole to modern capitalism (see Mommsen 1989: 34–43). To note the hegemony of capitalism does not mean that there are no contending forces. Since it fits the empirical realities typically found in Western societies, one of his more fruitful analytical tools is the notion that societies are made up of conflicting 'life orders' (Weber 1920: 323), consist of a plurality of 'contradictory systems of order' (1978: 32).

The political philosophy of a correlative social order In Confucian thought, society and individual are both merged into one natural, divine cosmos. The social and po-

154 We owe the phrase an 'edge of chaos', indicating the line between autonomous agents constantly pushing their way into new territory, and the interest in establishing regularity and order, to Stuart Kauffman, for whom this notion is part of a General Biology (2000: 22). The starting point of Kauffman's *Investigations* is 'the stunning fact that autonomous agents do, every day, reach out and manipulate the universe on their own behalf. Yet that truth is nowhere in contemporary physics, chemistry, or even biology' (ibid.: x).

litical implication is that the societal order is held to be grounded in this divine cosmic order. Social conformity is thus reinforced with religious sanction. The cosmological monism of Confucianism contrasts with salvation religion, marked by a sharp dualism between this world and the supernatural world, which is also the world of the hereafter. Thus, salvation religion involves the rejection of this world in favour of the more real one, beyond and above it. Since salvation religion centres on the idea of the one, supreme Creator, salvation is open to everybody and, at the same time, requires religious action. Religious life becomes separate from everyday life, piety is modelled on the behaviour of the religious, and, since this behaviour can have dramatic unintended but positively valued real-world consequences, may feed back into the society at large, transforming it in the process.[155] Since no political authority can monopolize religious leadership, the problem of legitimating power presents itself in a totally new way. The subjects cannot be ruled anymore qua their role as believers. Moreover, and exacerbating the problem of political authority and social order, salvation religion provides a new, independent ideology and the social cohesion for rebellion and reform movement, and it can serve to legitimate and reinforce created social orders.

The correlative philosophy of social order in Confucianism gives a completely different trajectory to political organization (narrowly conceived) and to prospects for initiation and expansion of state social policy than exists in the West. This occurs in two ways.

First, it precludes the idea of the autonomous individual as the bearer of subjective rights and thus also hinders those rationalizations of the relationship between citizen and state which in the West led to elaborate systems of impersonal accountability and checks and balances to control officeholders. Officeholders in the West are seen by the population as representatives, whose actions must be controlled and sanctioned, whereas in East Asian cultures they are seen as role models.[156]

Second, the Confucian conception of the state excludes notions of equal-ranking and hence competing powers within one body politic. This radically limits the potential for the development of a pluralistic political system, and it also rules out the existence of guaranteed non-state spheres, such as collective bargaining autonomy for the social partners. The free formation of communities and individual pursuits of salvation are seen in the Confucian worldview as illegitimate competition. They appear as sources of 'emancipation from domestication at the hands of the institutions of the state' (Weber 1920: 283).[157]

155 This is, in a nutshell, Max Weber's story of the rise of the Protestant ethic.

156 See the description in Granet, which implies a fundamentally different understanding of politics. 'The human being is nobler than other beings only to the extent that he occupies a certain position in society and in this way is able to participate in the maintenance of the social order, which in turn constitutes the model for the cosmic order. Out of the great mass of beings, only the prince, the sage and the nobleman rise above. These conceptions are in harmony with a world-view which is not anthropocentric, but instead characterized by the overarching significance of the concept of influence on society. The cosmic order is an emanation of the virtue of the prince' (1985: 258). Weber points to the 'purely religious factor' that in China the conception of a rationally regulated world had its point of origin in the ceremonial order of sacrifices, that 'everything', especially the indispensable regularity of metereological processes for rice economies, depended on the unalterable sequence of correct behaviour: 'According to both classical and heterodox Chinese views, these processes were held together by the ethically proper conduct of government that followed the correct path of virtue' (1978: 448).

157 'Confucianism, the ethic of a powerful officialdom, rejected all doctrines of salvation' (Weber 1978: 504).

The strictly personalizing features of Confucian politics in combination with the authoritarian character of political rule can help to understand why autonomous industry-wide unionization in East Asia has been an uphill battle. Instead, the labour movement there is not oriented towards conceptions of conflicts of interest, which are viewed as basically insurmountable because they are anchored in the individualistic structure of society, but is shaped into more particularistic and instrumental forms. An 'institutionalization of conflicts', which has become typical for Western industrial relation politics, becomes necessary only in a context in which conflicting values are seen as irreducibly diverse.[158]

Accordingly, in East Asia in general, opposing interests have no independent legitimacy and hence there seems to exist no need to independently institutionalize fundamental social conflicts. This also explains why the development of collective bargaining, to the extent that such development actually occurs, involves a high propensity for violence on the part of both 'free' unions and state authorities. Here it is not merely a matter of securing the economic interests of employers by employing state power, i.e. the police and the army. The norms of the political community, which are called into question by union formation along Western lines, are also violated. The political Confucianism of the 'world-organizing bureaucrat' has its essentially democratic qualities, yet ironically these preclude – in the interest of social levelling and fighting against those status privileges *not* resulting from the politics of bureaucratic rule – the autonomy of independent social formations, whether they be unions or sects and churches.[159] In addition, the more strongly a political association is shaped and controlled by the bureaucracy, the more it seems to fight such formations as competitors of its rule.[160]

Confucian conceptions of order colligate the state, economy and society as well as the individual, family, group and political association, and they directly link these realms of action to one another. Confucianism thereby constitutes the foundation for an isomorphism that gives East Asia's modernization path its own direction and characteristic shape. These countries lack the perpetual, in the final instance, irresolvable tension between democracy, the market economy and the welfare state as realms of action which are differentiated, independent and (in theory) reciprocally correcting. This characteristic tension in Western society was captured by T. H. Marshall in the term 'the hyphenated-society' (1981: 123–36), and, since Karl Marx's *The German*

158 To argue, as Bernard Williams (1973: 183) does, that it is within the moral sphere 'surely falsifying of moral thought to represent its logic as demanding in a conflict situation one of the conflicting oughts must be totally rejected', presupposes a moral and political universe in which such a behaviour vis-à-vis the clash of values is a regular feature. On the independence of values and the limits of trade-offs between values, see Lukes (1992).

159 Max Weber describes this tendency of political bureaucracy in its struggle with the nobility and the estates (1989 [1915]: 111). With regard to Confucianism, he refers to the struggle of 'Confucian official cultural campaigns against the Buddhist, Taoist and sectarian search for salvation of all kinds' and the various compromises which emerged from this, amounting to a kind of coexistence (ibid.: 112).

160 For an example of this anti-pluralist stance in Japanese educational politics, see Aspinall and Cave (2001). On the problem of finding, or rather founding, a civil society independent of the political construction of the state, see Gayle (2001). On the 'subversive, combative character' of 'civil society' vis-à-vis the state in post-war Korea, see Koo (1993, quoted from p. 232), who nonetheless states that the history of civil society in South Korea is 'short in history and relatively underdeveloped in institutional features' (ibid.).

Ideology, has been typically analysed in social theory under the rubric of 'contradictions' (Walzer 1983; Przeworski 1985; Bowles and Gintis 1986; Dahrendorf 1988).

The familial orientation of Confucianism sets decisive emphasis on the organization of political power and rule in East Asia. Subjugation to familial authority dominates the societal and political order and results in strong elements of patriarchalism and patrimonialism. To characterize this element, Weber cited the Confucian adage that 'insubordination [is] more reprehensible than brutality', indicating that obedience to family authorities is the distinctive mark of all social and political qualities (Weber 1978: 579).[161]

> Just as patrimonialism has its genesis in the piety of the children to the house toward the patriarch's authority, so Confucianism bases the subordination of the officials to the ruler, of the lower to the higher-ranking officials, and particularly of the subjects to the officials and the ruler, on the cardinal virtue of filial piety. (Ibid.: 1050)

According to Weber, this link between culture and the organization of power in Confucianism is more systematic and fundamental than in the West.

The Confucian ethic leads, therefore, 'far more systematically' to a 'theory of the welfare state' in the domestic affairs of East Asian societies and to a mercantilist approach to trade policy (ibid.). Yet with the 'theory of the welfare state' Weber still refers to the patrimonialism and cameralism of absolutist politics, not to the welfare state as an independent functional entity. Patrimonial welfare state practice in the West, he argued, was shaped far more by kin particularism, and interventions in the economy occurred rather sporadically and were guided by predominantly fiscal interests: 'In normal times this seems to have led to far-reaching restraint on the political authorities toward the economy, restraint which very early on found support in theoretical laissez-faire principles' (ibid.: 1051).[162]

The religiously enhanced quality of an individualized, formal law tradition was secularized in Western development to the extent that it soon left its original sphere – rights to freedom of conscience, assembly and association – and effected a corresponding revaluation of rights of civic participation – e.g. property rights and the right of settlement and occupation – and political participation.[163] This happened predomi-

161 An often cited Confucian passage describes how a son is punished by state civil servants for having denounced his father for having committed a crime (Roetz 1992: 410). Weber (1978: 579) contrasts this with the 'directly opposite accentuation of general virtues of life [which] is found in those more radical types of congregational religion which advocate the dissolution of all family ties. "Whosoever cannot hate his father cannot become a disciple of Jesus".'

162 Following Wittfogel's seminal work (1931, 1957), Bray (1986: xv) points out that the development of social institutions depends on the staple crop that feeds the population and fills the coffers of landowners and the state and is thus inseparable from the development of the agricultural systems that produce the crop: 'Rice and wheat have quite different characteristics and requirements: farming systems based on these crops are presented with a different range of technical choices, and they experience different patterns of social and political development in consequence.'

163 This is, in summary form, Georg Jellinek's thesis on the origins of the 'rights of man and citizens' (1927 [1895]). He shows that natural law theory alone would not have yielded a legal claim to civil rights. Rather, he traces the origins of human and civil rights to the struggles over religious freedom. For a discussion of this thesis, see Schnur (1964). From the perspective of the history of ideas, John Locke's interpretations have been decisive (1996 [1689]). On their social consequences, see Andrew (1988). The *locus classicus* on the subject of 'bourgeois' possessive individualism is Macpherson (1964).

nantly under the pressure of historically specific circumstances, i.e. the consolidation of absolutist-bureaucratic rule and these rulers' interest in having subjects with equal status. Accentuating, and ultimately rendering absolute, subjective rights, i.e. those that emanate only from the individual, is a reaction against the rationalization of absolutist state power. This reaction occurred against the background of certain religious convictions, which gave it direction and dramatically enhanced its effect. From this flows the declaration of the sovereignty of the people as a natural equivalent to the sovereign individual. The birth of the state from a contract among autonomous individuals is not a fiction, but, rather, became reality in the founding of the North American colonies. The conception of the state as no more than a means of achieving personal well-being or individual welfare is now here to stay. This ushered in pure individualism as a possible motor for an incessant overturning of social relations via application of an unconditional ethical standard (Wahl 1909: 84).

A constitutional conception predicated upon separation of state and society, pluralistic political and social institutions and party competition are factors that favour the development of a welfare state integration ideology as well as an expansive social policy following its own criteria of rationality and legitimacy. The success of the Western pattern of modernization is based perhaps more on its inner contradictions and tensions, which give the market economy and the welfare state, as sharply divided realms, a greater dynamic and a strong impetus to self-directed development. By contrast, the East Asian pattern is characterized more strongly by a continuity of social and system integration, the common basis of which is the Confucian ethic.

An essential factor in the development of social policy as an independent realm in Western welfare states is, first, party competition in parliamentary democracy. Party competition in the West originates, however, not only in the parallel development of political and economic markets, but also in the state's role as an arbitrator vis-à-vis competing interests. In the welfare state this balancing act entails privileging different social groups on a continually rotating basis. This second moment plays a far lesser role in East Asian countries. Socio-political privileging there is much more static. There is no express status competition which might translate into an independent socio-political dynamic.

Thus, Heinz Lampert sees the 'central significance of social policy . . . in its contribution to the transformation of the legal norms of the liberal and social constitutional state out of the world of the written constitution and into the form of guaranteed formal rights – substantive rights and opportunities actually usable in real life' (1994: 415). This moment undoubtedly exists as well in East Asian countries. Yet there, the political goal of providing compensation to actually or presumedly underprivileged groups is not characterized by such an unconditionalism. Accordingly, this moment has not developed into the pivotal element of the political process. Bureaucratic patrimonialism, which continues to be the prevailing model of political order, has set limits to such a development in East Asia.[164]

The patriarchal familialism of primary groups and companies is paralleled and reinforced by the bureaucratic-patrimonialist organization of the state. Faith in the 'omnipotence of discipline' (Weber 1951 [1915]) pervades state, economy and society. Bureaucratic patrimonialism is particularly significant in East Asian societies: national

[164] On the Confucian understanding of politics and constitutionalism, for a historical perspective see Wang (1913), and for present-day developments, see Pye (1985, 1988).

economies there are dominated by large firms, and cartel, or alliance, capitalism, under strong political influence, structures the interaction of the economy and the state. This bureaucratic patrimonialism expresses itself not only in a comparatively repressive style of politics, but also in far-reaching surveillance of public life and the press. This has been true not only in Singapore, but also – into the 1980s – very markedly in South Korea, where the media were used by the government to control the public sphere and to represent state interests, rather than functioning as the 'fourth estate' along Western lines (Beng-Huat 1994; Woodiwiss 1998).

The oikonomistic welfare state The continuous or correlative philosophy of political and social order in Confucianism corresponds to its *oikonomistic* understanding of the family, household, company and state.[165] We describe as oikonomistic those conceptions that are not oriented towards a model of functional societal differentiation. Such conceptions can find expression in various institutions, amongst which, typically, structural isomorphs can be observed. Bureaucratic patrimonialism, however, as a form of organization of political-territorial entities, exhibits features of an *oikos*, as does familial community in biological reproduction. In the economic sphere, companies, too, can be *oikonomistic* to the extent that they are oriented less towards market production than towards meeting the needs of those who belong to the company (Weber 1978: 381). Common features of all three realms are centralist-hierarchic organization, the fusion of functions and a segmented-mechanical relation of units to one another.[166]

Viewed ideal-typically, an *oikos* system is at the other end of the spectrum from the modern enterprise. It seeks to meet the consumption needs of its constituent parts comprehensively and is functionally undifferentiated. The *raison d'être* of economic production is not market exchange for profit maximization. The latter can also play a role in an *oikos* system but remains, however, ultimately subordinate to the meeting of consumption needs. This characterization of business organization and management can help us determine the type and scope of functions that can, in a mediated fashion, be associated with the company's interest in the narrower sense – i.e. the selling of goods and services on the market for the maximization of profit. Here it is essentially a matter of determining the extent to which companies, besides producing and selling goods and services, genuinely – and not only strategically – fulfil socio-political functions, and the extent to which their market rationality is thereby compromised.[167]

165 Catherine Jones speaks of an 'oikonomistic welfare state' (1990b, 1993).

166 For our comparative perspective it is important to note that the institutional format of *oikos*-structures do not rule out capitalist acquisition or strict market-orientation. The essence of an *oikos*-orientation is that it utilizes capitalist enterprises and markets for non-economic goals in the sense that it is the main task of political governance to expressly prevent the emergence of a 'spontaneous' order, i.e. an order that is allegedly not only more complex and intricate than any 'planned' order and thus more efficient and more capable to adjust to change, but also cannot be explained in terms of deliberate efforts to achieve coordination (Weber 1978: 381–3).

167 In Western economic thinking, contract law and contractual constructs are essential tools in the rational (and instrumental) shaping of the market (and company) organization (Wolff 1995). See the telling observation by Nakane (1970) on Japan, that the relationship between employer and employee cannot be explained by exclusively contractual concepts. This is to say that the 'contractual partners' believe that their relationship is not fully reducible to a contract. This should be distinguished from contract theory as an interpretative approach in economics. In the latter, *every* organizational problem can be described and explained as a contractual problem (Buchanan 1988; O. E. Williamson 1985: 22).

This question is important above all in constellations in which external circumstances – such as, at the present time, economic globalization – force companies to adopt greater market rationality, and in which the assumption of functions by the state, family or other market-type institutions becomes critical to companies' continued existence and survival.[168] Of particular interest here is whether the principles of lifelong employment and seniority-based compensation, which structure labour markets above all in Japan and South Korea, and fulfil essential socio-political functions by substituting for the expansion of differentiated systems of income maintenance in unemployment and old age, can be maintained under conditions of heightened import and export competition. This will depend less on these institutions as such than on the question of whether their potential for flexibility suffices to master the challenge to adapt. It may well be that in the process, lifelong employment and seniority themselves prove to have been elements of a previous era's rational adaptation to the social and economic conditions of its time – e.g. the labour shortage in Japan in the immediate post-war period and in South Korea during the phase of heavy industrialization – and thus later fall away under the pressure of changed circumstances and make way for greater labour market mobility and performance-based wages. Or it could turn out that these institutions have a resilience which is nourished by their own – cultural-religious – roots, and which itself limits and shapes companies' scope for action and adaptation.

A further feature of an *oikos* orientation is the methodical avoidance of market risks. Thus Max Weber contends that the Confucian ethic is fundamentally consumer-oriented. Yet the ethical problem for Confucianism consists less in the pursuit of profit as such than in the peculiar effects of this pursuit on social relations, as well as in the transient nature of success in economic activities pursued solely for their own sake. Greed as such is considered to be a source of social unrest, for it inevitably polarizes interests and generates conflict: it pits producers against consumers, creditors against borrowers, and employers against employees. In such a framework, occupational risks, too, argue against allowing capitalist enterprises to pursue exclusively their own ends, for this would disturb the balance and harmony of the soul (Weber 1951 [1915]).[169] Apart from these two reservations, Confucian ethics esteem the value of economic

168 Roetz makes reference to this to the extent that he notes that the enduring emphasis on morality in Confucianism is 'at odds with the modern understanding of economic rationality, which has proclaimed itself independent of ethics, and for which the only constraint on strategic economic calculation is law' (1995: 65f.). This assessment is predicated, however, on the Western conception of 'free' markets which are not bound by substantive ethical norms. Instead, the partners in an exchange relation assume that each will be interested in the future continuation of the relationship. Thus, insofar as an 'ethical' attitude exists, 'honesty is the best policy' (Weber 1978: 637). Of course, the rights-based defence of laissez-faire claims that the market is a *moral* institution par excellence, because, according to marginal productivity theory, in a competitive market each factor of production – labour, credit and other forms of capital – will be paid an amount exactly equal to the value of its marginal product (Henry 1983). The American economist John Bates Clark was one of the first to clearly – and carefully – formulate this idea in an article published in 1886: 'As (competition) came gradually into existence it demonstrated its capacity for dividing products with a certain approach to justice. It commended itself to men's sense of right, and was established . . . on a moral basis' (cited in B. H. Fried 1998: 219).

169 These elements of a culturally mediated disciplining of individual ambition and the attendant interest in social equalization as a going concern of public policy perhaps explain as well the markedly egalitarian character of income distributions in East Asian societies. This feature distinguishes them both from Latin American countries and from historical conditions in European countries during the period of industrialization.

activity very highly, as expressed in the comparatively early development of economic theory (ibid.: 154). Ultimately, the reservations vis-à-vis the capitalist pursuit of profit appear to have been limited essentially to the behavioural ideal of the civil service, whose 'gentleman ethic' was incompatible with the pursuit of profit (ibid.: 354).

Beside the *oikos* orientation, a further expression of continuous-integrative conceptions of social and political order in East Asia is familialism. Familialism affects economic and company structure in a twofold fashion: a large proportion of companies are family businesses; and familialism functions as an integration ideology and control instrument for personnel management. East Asian businesses vary in their structure between the two poles of family business and large company. In both cases, familialism functions as a barrier to the initiation and development of state social policy. In both cases, too, even the company itself becomes an essentially socio-political institution.

A typical example is the practice by many South Korean *chaebols* (large industrial conglomerates) of continuing to pay striking workers their wages for as long as several months. The familial identification of workers with the company is matched by management's assumption of social responsibility. The latter is not negated or relativized by sharp conflicts of interest and resulting strategic behaviour.[170] In the Hong Kong and Taiwanese economies, small family businesses predominate, whereas in South Korea and Singapore large and very large firms do.

In both instances one can observe an oikonomistic structure of business organization. Yet patriarchalism has a different meaning in each case. In smaller family companies, patriarchalism is the point of reference for a real, existing community, whereas in large and very large firms it is a tool of integration, one that is often used excessively. Employees, including those in middle management, see a contradiction between patriarchalism and a clearly structured, top-down organizational hierarchy. In the Korean *chaebols* in particular, the metaphors and images of the Confucian family serve as a central means of closing rank and of social control. Organizational hierarchies are interpreted and understood in analogy to the order of the Confucian family.

Through its well-developed familialism, Confucianism imparts a patriarchal character on the social structure and a patrimonial tone on business organization. It thereby lays the basis for a vertically oriented and segmented social structure in which social responsibilities are concentrated in distinct, independent segments. Durkheim (1964 [1902]) termed this feature of social organization 'mechanical solidarity', as opposed to the 'organic solidarity' of societies differentiated by a division of labour. In the framework of such a segmented order, however, social protection and basic security guarantees are by no means provided in a one-sided relationship. Rather, they are an expression of an immediate reciprocity that not only binds and regulates the behaviour of rulers through their cultural roots, but also evinces rational foundations in so far as the ruler has his own interest in preserving the subjects' economic capacity (Weber 1978: 1023).[171] In business organizations, this moment of explicit and immediate

170 The social and cultural-anthropological study by Janelli with Yim (1993), based on several years of participatory observation, offers a range of similar examples.

171 Woodiwiss (1998) discusses the extent to which the patriarchal *enforceable benevolence* which is predicated on this reciprocity constitutes a functional equivalent to Western constitutional rights, and whether hereby the ostensible contradiction between 'Asian values' and 'universalist' human rights disappears.

reciprocity becomes particularly significant when, in the wake of the transition to an information economy, traditional means of objective, process-oriented performance control must give way to result-oriented control. In the process, employees' motivation and flexibility become decisive variables in the success of the company. This factor negatively influences companies' ability to carry out large-scale organizational restructurings, as do the aforementioned rather restrictive effects of other typical elements of East Asian labour organization – e.g. employment and seniority.

Summary

In light of the peculiar religious-historical roots of social policy in the West, we must reassess the transferability of Western institutions to countries with a different cultural foundation as well as our standards of measurement of progress in the development of a welfare state. What appears to Western eyes as inexplicable hesitancy in the social policy realm may seem to actors in East Asian countries to be an equally incomprehensible presumption for social policy models which do not at all suit their cultural, social and/or institutional context. Thus it is not East Asian, but Western social policy that appears exotic, quite deservedly so, and thus in need of explanation.[172] Moreover, there is not much reason to believe that under intensified pressure of a rapidly globalizing capitalism the 'strong evaluations' underlying social policy choices – including those of a low political profile – will give way to more uniformity in the institutional design of social policy. Each system has its own potential to adapt without losing its identity in the process.

The schematic depiction in Table 5.6 below summarizes the focal points of the previous section. The main emphasis is not on the institutional features of social policy institutions per se, but, rather, on individual characteristics, which, as a result of specific, ultimately religiously rooted convictions and imaginative horizons, play a central role in social policy practice. Here we are dealing of course with ideal-typical abstractions. Such an analysis thus serves less to provide a sufficient, detailed description of the conditions of the welfare state than to facilitate an understanding of its fundamental moments providing direction to its main driving forces. Research that concentrates exclusively on the quantitative aspects of welfare state expansion misses the specifically cultural factors that shape social policy. The same is true of research that

[172] From this it follows as well that there is no universally valid social policy concept and thus no uniform measure of social policy progress, i.e. of the necessity or desirability of specific welfare state conditions. For example, the International Labour Organization (ILO) is a bearer and propagandist of specifically Western norms and ideals of social policy design. This can be observed in its difficulties in understanding the social policy behaviour of East and Southeast Asian countries in their economic crisis of the late 1990s. This is especially true of the realm of social protection against unemployment and disability, where the ILO expressly calls upon governments to increase their engagement and raise state expenditures: 'Of Southeast Asia's four most severely affected countries (Indonesia, South Korea, Thailand and Malaysia), only South Korea pays a minimal and short-term unemployment benefit. *For the ILO it is a mystery why not even Singapore or Hong Kong introduce an unemployment insurance scheme, given that their per-capita incomes are higher than those in some industrial countries.* The traditional social networks which were counted upon have proven in the contemporary crisis to be thoroughly insufficient, it says. Moreover, in periods of economic growth, a social insurance scheme would have cost East Asian countries only minimal additional costs' (*Frankfurter Allgemeine Zeitung*, 'Mit Sozialpolitik Not in Asien dämpfen', 2 December 1998, 21; emphasis not in original). See also Segal (1998) and Domenach (1998).

Table 5.6 Social policy features and their religious roots

Social policy features		*Christianity*	*Confucianism*
autonomy		truth of divinely revealed religion	
	heteronomy		ontologically fixed immanence
heterogeneity		transcendence of salvation religion	
	homogeneity		inviolability of tradition; social ritualization
dynamism		unconditional ethic of conviction	
	statarism		ethic of responsibility; stressing the logic of consequences
universalism		pneumatic community-building	
	particularism		community of descent

deals only with formal, institutional features of welfare state institutions. Much more important and, as we would like to claim, decisive for the general outlook of a 'world' of welfare statism, is the fundamental drive, or temper, of social politics as an action system. The principal finding of this exploration is that it is less the case that the Confucian welfare states fail to fit the general developmental mould than that social policy in Western society is shaped by special conditions. In the West, social policy became a complex of more and more consciously grasped independent values, which now exist in their own right. Here, social policy took over the function of this-worldly salvation, no matter how this may be interpreted. It promises a salvation from the routines of everyday life, and especially from the increasing pressures of theoretical and practical rationalism of economic life. With its claim and promise of 'decommodification' social policy achieved a redemptory function, and social policy could begin to compete directly with salvation religion. Thus in the West, neither free-market capitalism, nor democracy, nor welfare statism are carriages, which one may arrest at will. They are based on values conceived as historical ultimatives, not something easily compromised upon, and therefore there is an inevitable tension between them, sometimes erupting into culture wars. Because they are bound to specific cultural roots, salvation religion, they do not travel well across cultures.

The one exception is free-market capitalism, because of the apparent social and political neutrality of its most basic institutional architecture. The money economy is based on an essentially impersonal relationship. Because it is shallow vis-à-vis existing social structure, and because it is unable to build social structures and communities of its own, the market can be compatible with a wide range of different cultures and social systems. This is not true for representative democracy and universalistic social policies. Moreover, when we look at the current trend of globalization, free-market capitalism looks like an pervasive and unifying affair, absorbing other cultures into its own image, and enabling numerous institutional interweavings to give way, without much ado, to a set of parallel forces heading in the same direction. But appearances may be deceiving. The personal networks underlying the 'crony capitalism' of much of Asia reflect a strong resistance to hand over the material fate of groups and societies to some 'invisible hand' (Lipset and Lenz 2000). Of course, economic globalization presents a hard reality. But, and this is often forgotten in the typically 'principled' Western perspective, what counts in the end and thus decides the fate of societies and communities is not values per se but the behaviour and the institutional structures selected and formed on their basis – that is, actual results, and these results are critically dependent on their social context.

In East Asia, successful modernization and the new societal wealth are taken as proof of moral and cultural equivalence, and thus bolster the claims to cultural distinctiveness and, at times, greatly help to assert the superiority of their values and ways of social organization. It assists governments in rebuffing Western standards in and designs of economic, political and social governance. Obviously, 'culture' can be directly at the service of economic interests to a very large extent. But even in the absence of successful modernization, it is quite remarkable that the 'Washington consensus' embodied in IMF politics, Madisonian concepts of limited government, and human rights as the ultimate yardstick of socio-political progress always needs considerable backing of coercive diplomacy to gain at least a nominal acceptance.

When we broaden our perspective, then we see that what really drives globalization, understood as a peculiar *culture*, is the quasi-religiously derived obligation to crusade. The protagonists of welfare statism, in whatever political cloth, are also, in their own realm, crusaders driven by principled convictions and very often unassailable faiths, but what distinguishes them from global capitalists and their backers in neo-classical economics is the fact that welfare statism is still a nation-state project, or an undertaking of territorial politics, whereas for global capitalism national borders are a pointless nuisance. But this does not mean that the welfare state will simply disappear.

5 Culture Under Conditions of Globalization

In this chapter we may have focused too strongly on contrasting the courses of social policy development in East Asia versus the West, and too little on eliciting their commonalities. We also may have devoted too much attention to ahistorical cultural patterns and not enough to the present and to expected imminent ruptures with the past. In globalized economic society, it is widely assumed, the same forces are at work everywhere. Thus all societies, whichever civilization they belong to, are seen to face the same challenges of transnational competition, and the institutional conditions of this competition are becoming increasingly uniform.

With inescapable necessity, then, a universal economic order appears to be taking shape – one that moulds not only individuals and companies, but also cultures, according to its needs. The regulatory framework of WTO agreements no longer stops at the borders of nation-states, and this is particularly true for the intervention regimes of the IMF and the World Bank. These structures of international governance no longer merely regulate interstate trade, but extend deep into the domestic affairs of national societies. Nearly all aspects of welfare state regulation of company-based production – from product safety regulations to mandates for (national language) labelling, to rules of origin and local content regulations stemming from domestic political forces – are subject to review in light of their effects on transnational competitiveness, i.e. whether they hinder the import of goods and services or of foreign investment (Kahler 1995; D. Vogel 1997).

The fate of social policy, which until now was an exclusive national matter in that it expressed a country's choice of a social order, seems to be directly affected by this development. Most observers proceed from the assumption that the enormously enhanced independent dynamic of the capitalist market economy – borne by new forms of corporate organization and driven by new corporate strategies of a transnational *alliance capitalism* (Dunning 1997a) – in concert with a truly international and effective framework of relevant *policy regimes*, creates the socio-political institutions that are optimal for its functioning. For the East Asian welfare states this poses the quite dramatic question: are kin structures, above all the family, as separate and independent sources of welfare, an evolutionary dead end in social policy development? At the same time, this independent dynamic is thought to set effective limits to the expansion and independent development of the welfare state, for the market immediately punishes every 'wrong' social policy initiative – which is then measured in labour-market statistics, the balance of payments and the health of state budgets (e.g. Berthold 1997; Krauss 1997).

This understanding does not accurately reflect reality, however. The conditions of globalization will neither directly nor unambiguously determine decision-making in the realm of social policy. The pursuit of complex goals such as welfare or social security cannot be reduced to a merely socio-technical public choice problem. In these matters, empirical statements – which at least in principle can be tested by confrontation with reality – can hardly be distinguished from normative beliefs, which are not only impossible to prove, but also often – at least for outsiders – difficult to define in an unambiguous way. Even the declaration, 'social policy A is unconditionally preferable to social policy B, because B would bring about the result b, and because b is disadvantageous', deduces a normative conclusion from two statements of which one is empirical ('result') and the other normative ('disadvantageous') (Boudon and Bourricaud 1992: 610, 612). Therefore, in the social policy decisions of the present and the future, the question of the role of convictions or values does not disappear, and, accordingly, neither does that of the influence of the different cultures which underlie the inescapable frameworks of 'strong evaluations'. On the contrary, precisely for this reason they gain considerable significance, for values guide the search for suitable means to realize societal objectives: 'From the very moment individual and collective preferences become more complex, their attainment necessitates the assent to commonly shared values' (Boudon and Bourricaud 1992: 613). Another expression for assent to convictions, collective preferences and commonly shared values is 'culture'.

Much more interesting than the question of the distributive latitude which globalization supposedly denies or allows social policy is thus the question of the culturally predefined *action horizon* of social policy alternatives. Culture, or religion, is not outside social policy but integral to it. Three points are important here, and for all of them the observations on East Asian welfare state development are instructive: the persistence of a differentiated world of welfare states amidst a globalizing economy; social politics as the dominant motor for the creation of new forms of divergence; and the renewal of social policy rather than a decline of social policy as the most probable outcome of increased global capitalist competition.

In our *first* point we suggest the continuity of welfare state divergence. Uniform global pressures to modernize and adapt need not give rise to uniform institutional social policy responses. This proposition is by no means new. Rather, it has been the point of departure for historical-comparative welfare state research since the 1970s. A glance at East Asia shows, further, that the horizon of alternatives for the political organization of social security is far more expansive than the developmental history of the welfare state in the West would lead one to expect. It shows, too, that the commonalities of Western developmental paths are far greater than suggested, for example, by Esping-Andersen's 'three-world' theory.[173] Viewed against a Confucian background, the ostensibly considerable Western differences are revealed as stemming from the same roots and as determined by the same driving forces.

Despite differentiated national forms, the Western welfare state – especially its character as an independent sphere and an essential, albeit intensely *contested* idea – is the product of the singular Western development, above all of parliamentary democracy and of the reaction to the rise of a capitalist market economy. These three core elements of the Western societal order all have the same cultural-religious roots in the ultimately deeply Judaeo-Christian conception of the inalienable, intrinsic value of the individual, and in the attendant possibilities, problems and limits with regard to the production of public goods, because such an order is inherently hostile to any notion of society as the foundation of organized *communal or communitarian welfare.*

Whatever the collective outcome, though, these three elements are systematically interrelated. Whether a market economy, representative democracy and a welfare state coincide at any particular place in time is a historical question. That they can do so is evident in the common, Christian-influenced history of the West. To stress the conflict-ridden social politics of the West is important, since it is by no means obvious that, as Samuel Huntington (1996: 65) has put it, in Africa and Asia neither Adam Smith nor Thomas Jefferson – and we will have to add Bismarck to this list – will meet the psychological, emotional, moral and social needs of urban migrants and of the rising mass of young and volatile people. But if they do, it will happen on their own terms. Looking at East Asia, the point is not whether welfare statism along Western lines could not be grounded in Confucian values and concepts. Of course it can, given the richness of this tradition. Social rights and welfare statism were never justified monolithically by one particular socio-moral theology. However, even while one might grant that the Confucian values are compatible with the distinctive traits of welfare state-building in the West, there remains the question why Confucianism in fact did not assist a development along Western lines. The actual result is different, and it will be different in the future. In other words, they have their own Adam Smith, Thomas Jefferson and Otto von Bismarck.

[173] Attempting to gauge the dimensions of this East Asian horizon of alternatives, which differ fundamentally from those of Western imaginative horizons and interpretative models, seems to us to be a more promising methodological strategy than undertaking further additions to the typology of Esping-Andersen, e.g. *Confucian welfare states* (C. Jones 1993: 214; but also Kwon 1997). Jones's earlier approach to *oikonomic welfare states* (1990b) engaged the subject more clearly from a cultural angle, from which we proceed as well. 'The influence of Confucian tradition in both countries is a rather negative one in the sense that it provides a strong basis of political rhetoric opposed to introducing certain social programmes' (Kwon 1997: 477). This reference already strongly suggests that there is a fundamentally different horizon of alternatives for welfare state development in East Asia. At this point it is also important to stress that to 'find' a proper name for the peculiarities of Western and East Asian welfare state developments is just the beginning, not the end of research. Names do not solve research problems: 'That word names the universe's principle, and to possess it is after a fashion to possess the universe itself. "God", "Matter", "Reason", "the Absolute", "Energy", are so many solving names. You can rest when you have them. You are at the end of your metaphysical quest. But if you follow the pragmatic method, you cannot look on any such word as closing your quest. You must bring out its practical cash value, set it at work within the stream of your experience. It appears less as a solution, then, than as a program for more work, and more particularly as an indication of the ways in which existing realities may be changed. Theories thus become instruments, not answers to enigmas, in which we can rest' (James 1987 [1907]: 509).

No culture is a closed book, a story finished. Variations of the Western welfare state are not the direct outflow of religiously derived conceptions, but of ferocious historical struggles and external forces shaped by the inescapable but by no means unalterable framework of culture. In short, neither *West* nor *East* denote geographical entities – and no religion is somehow territorially fixed once and for all times. This should help to acknowledge that other factors are relevant as well, most importantly, of course, those stemming from the pressures of a competitive international environment, from the needs of societies to adapt, and from the simple necessity to economize because of the scarcity of means. This does not deny a particular East Asian developmental path – but only acknowledges that it has a different cultural departure and reference point. In fact, as we tried to point out, East Asian development, too, is marked by the persistence of certain conceptions of the individual and of society which have inscribed themselves socially and institutionally in divergent forms and, just as in the West, in surprising inversions of earlier conceptions. It should not come as a surprise: counterforces emerge, asserting, not diminishing, local 'culture', since 'culture' is not a fixed entity but a mode of reaction to new challenges. Thus, as Huntington (1996: 69) pointed out, the West was the West before it was modern, and, as we would like to add, East Asia will stay East Asia after it has modernized. But this fact of persistency is explained by the functional adequacy of specific social policy solutions, by actual results deemed to be right by democratically empowered people, not by simply pointing to 'culture' or 'religion'. And when it comes to the actual results of social politics, the argument for Western forms of social policy may not be so strong as is often believed.

The doctrine of individualism underlying the social politics of Western welfare states has substantial potential as a socially disruptive force. There can be little doubt that the Western practice of clothing every conflict in terms of rights makes conflicts more, and not less, intense. For many, the actual states of social order achieved in Western societies challenge their sense of a rational and consistent social reality. The difference between *individual* acts – including the political attempts to use the law for large-scale social engineering – and *collective* outcomes is not only substantive, it is also *constitutive* for our Western sense of the *emergence* of social order. In fact, the birth of sociology is the discovery that social order as a result of the interaction of self-propelled individuals cannot be reduced to the intentions of these individuals. As the German lawyer Friedrich Karl von Savigny put it in the nineteenth century, 'the outcome of the general will is no one's will in particular' (cited in Weinstein 1987: 16).

One has to remember that not only the Confucian macro-region East Asia and mainland China, but, all in all, three-quarters of the members of the world's population define themselves in terms of kinship and primordial community rather than as free-standing bearers of rights. We may have seriously to entertain the notion that the very particular political, economic and social principles underlying the *project* of economic globalization will not only preclude the promise of material prosperity for all from becoming real, but will also intensify domestic strife and international conflicts. Considering the stakes in a world society awash in poverty, strengthening rather than dissolving social bonds – relying on Confucian notions of communitarian order rather than on the gamble of an emerging or spontaneous order brought about by some invisible hand behind the back of fundamentally disengaged individuals celebrating their difference – should not be neglected as an alternative.

In our *second* point we assert that it is predominantly social policy that will drive processes of divergence rather than convergence. After mapping the differences between Western and East Asian pathways of welfare state development, the question needs to be posed anew, and more urgently: to what extent is Confucian social policy driven by an independent dynamic? The answer is: presumably more so than one would believe at first sight, according to which a new standard culture of Western origin and Western in form is prevailing inexorably in East Asia as well. This is true above all because this Confucian social policy does not stand alone in the new international environment. Rather, East Asian countries' economies and societies are equally, each in their own way, shaped by Confucian ethics and culture. Just as in the West, forces are at work there that are not easily accessible to political intervention and socio-political manipulation or correction. In both cultures, the basic features of development become evident as individual decisions systematically accumulate and result in a particular political-institutional *drift*.

Moreover, in their influence on development, these basic features transcend the functional boundaries of societal sub-sectors. In East Asia, group-bound relationships based on trust and loyalty do not only shape the social and socio-political division of labour, but also economic and political action. This simultaneously simplifies and complicates the question of East Asian development. It becomes simplified in that we now see that in East Asia decisions on social policy are not made in isolation. Rather, social policy systematically interrelates with the other elements of economy and society, because they are shaped by the same cultural framework. It becomes complicated because our subject of enquiry now extends to the entire society's ability to adapt and survive. Thus despite superficial similarities in institutional and organizational form, fundamental Western political and economic ideas can have different meanings in East Asia. In the course of translation they develop different connotations and also have different institutional and political repercussions. Their cultural background, attendant habitus and the mentality resulting from both of these cannot be imported and implemented in an unmediated way. Taking culture seriously, we can see that it is social politics that continues to produce divergence.

The terms in which globalization and its meaning for the non-Western world are typically discussed are, in essence, the same as those articulated as 'natural laws of capitalist production' by Karl Marx in *Capital*, where he states that 'it is not a question of the higher or lower degree of development of the social antagonism that spring from the natural laws of capitalist development. It is a question of these laws working themselves out with iron necessity. The country that is more developed industrially only shows, to the less developed, the image of its own future' (1977 [1867]: 91). The 'iron law' of Marx became Francis Fukuyama's 'end of history': market-oriented economic order and liberal democracy are the only viable alternatives for modern societies (1992; 1999).

A closer look, however, reveals sociological experiences of *indigenous* globalization: the integration of globalization-technologies in indigenous sociologies and cosmologies. Unified by the deep integration of globalization that has occurred since the 1970s, the world is also being rediversified by indigenous adaptations to the global juggernaut. As Marshall Sahlins and other anthropologists noted, global homogeneity and local differentiation have developed together (1999: ix–x). This becomes most obvious when we look at social policy, since social policy seems to be the most important vehicle for both the resistance to globalization pressures and the cultural differentiation of globalization results. Curiously enough, when Karl Marx went on to discuss the economic situation on the European continent, noting that the situation is 'much worse than in England', he explained this difference not with reference to the levels of economic development, but, rather, he argued that it stemmed from the absence of the 'counterpoise of the Factory Acts', i.e. the early forms of social policy in England. 'We suffer', he elaborated, 'not only from the development of capitalist production, but also from the *incompleteness* of that development' (Marx 1977 [1867]: 91; emphasis added).

Then and now social policy is the process through which societies attempt to re-organize themselves in the face of the irresistible forces of the capitalist world system. They do so according to their own cosmology, depending on their culture and the mode of global integration. They try to benefit from new markets, technologies, organizations and social structures, and one of their basic means is the creation of their own versions of social policies. The fact that culture is as unavoidable as is the spread of global capitalism becomes the clearer the more we note the various ways religion makes itself felt in the East and the West, in the North as well as in the South. The people take whatever technology and organizational forms promise to work and shape them according to their own purposes and uses. Culture *includes* the economics of globalization, and the economics of globalization *include* culture. Culture *is* the medium by which economic as well as other forces become realized as structures, and the same is true for the allocation and organization of those needs not left to the mechanism of the market. Particularly with regard to social policy we should note the ongoing creation of new forms of public policy, in the East as well as in the West. The welfare state is not a finished tradition of public policy, a burdensome legacy, but, rather, an ongoing, creative project, and the more so the more that markets develop and spread. The welfare state is a set of projects, a living tradition, depending on the particular frame of culture – and thus neither in its Western nor in its Eastern forms does it have the last word. Social policy is an inexhaustible reservoir of *different* responses to the challenge of capitalist market economies.

Our *third* and last point suggests a paradoxical, but not altogether surprising renewal of social policy. When we take a broader look at East Asia, neither the 'modernization' in the past nor the 'globalization' of today constitute movements towards some predestined end. Instead, they consist, now and then, of a set of conflicts over political, economic and cultural goals framed in Confucian terms, and of different courses of change and its management in different Confucian societies. In all developed countries the strong blast of globalized capitalist competition rushes against an opposing, deeply entrenched social order – and it is therefore rising global capitalism itself which brings about a counter-current articulated in cultural terms and instituted through social policies broadly understood.

From the standpoint of *any* social order, dramatically increased levels of economic competition will bring about changes in social stratification which present themselves more often than not as unassimilable discrepancies between individual situations and legitimate expectations of social standing. In welfare societies, the typical way to address such discrepancies is corrective public intervention, or 'social policy'. Under conditions of diverse cultures, the new social differentiations caused by capitalism take on the character of a cultural contest over the legitimacy of the new social hierarchy.

This contest, however, is internal to societies; it is not a struggle in which societies or cultures *in toto* are pitted against global capitalism. Moreover, and that is often forgotten, it is not the first time that Confucian societies are changing so dramatically that culture must respond. But it will, as before, respond according to its logic, because the challenge too presents itself to these societies on their own terms, and not on some universal (or our) terms. As in the West, in the East Asian countries a highly politicized debate about globalization takes place. When we look at the substance of social policy, the difference is, however, that in the East Asian societies all the positions reflect a Confucian agenda, in the same way as in the West all the positions reflect an agenda informed by Judaeo-Christian values. For that reason, the policy outcomes of the conflicts over globalization, too, will in one form or another reflect distinct value orientations. In the West and in the Far East, the new technological and economic factors and the new forms of international governance influence economic and cultural development decisively, but in the countries of each macro-region they are articulated and channelled by indigenous elites, institutional orders and cultures. The new technological, economic and legal considerations inspire the human imagination and are articulated in terms of thinking and cultural vocabularies that have governed thought and social organization in the respective regions for millennia.

A priori, then, and to repeat the first point, there is no reason to believe that the now global capitalism and a globalized world economy will enforce a reformulation of social policies in sync with neoliberal lines. First of all, both companies and markets are much more bound to national regulatory contexts and thus to national legal cultures than much of the globalization discussion suggests. Second, and looking east, because of their fundamentally Confucian underpinnings, the East Asian countries are welfare democracies just like the Western countries, and that means that economic globalization will have to produce *superior* material results for all the politically significant groups in society compared with social policy outcomes. Social policies get instituted when, for some reason, collective goals of social welfare broadly understood are not achieved. Welfare democracy means that the results of the economic system are measured against the scales of values embodied in the cultural order and, in the case of incongruity, imperatively necessitate corrective measures. Confucianism, as well as the universalistic-egalitarian creed of Western welfare states, sets value scales that provide standards for legitimate political action and the substantive criteria of rational social policy.

The unassailable competitive advantage of the welfare state over the spontaneous order of markets lies in the fact that a social right as the typical vehicle of socio-political action is an *individuated* social aim. It calls for a specified opportunity or resource for particular individuals, something markets cannot provide with the same degree of certainty. There is no direct relationship between a capitalist system based on the profit motive and the consumption needs of social groups and societies: the profitability of enterprises has ‘nothing to do with an optimum use of the available productive resources for the provision of consumers’ goods for a given population’ (Weber 1978: 105). Of course, competitive capitalism can have – and often enough did in fact produce – results superior to those achieved by bureaucratic systems. And, of course, the promise of social rights very often remains just that: a promise.

Nevertheless, since the results of competitive markets emerge ‘spontaneously’, it cannot be a secure, guaranteed result for the *individual* market participant. For that reason, the more the impersonal mechanism of the market is given rein, the stronger the belief will grow 'that deliberate regulation of all social affairs must necessarily be more successful than the apparent haphazard interplay of independent individuals' (Hayek 1935: 119). In the welfare democracies of both the West and the Far East, economic globalization as such is not a sufficient justification for denying citizens what they wish as individuals and social beings, for imposing some loss or injury upon them. For that reason, and for better or worse, globalization will mean more rather than less social policy.

References

A Short Introduction to the Literature

The fundamental category of economic activity is *power*.

Frank H. Knight 1972 [1941]: 9; emphasis not in the original

The pervasiveness of globalization's impact on the state, economy and society is juxtaposed with a rather unseemly chaos prevailing in the social sciences. The literature is characterized by contradictory positioning: it is oriented more towards influencing public policy than towards enlightening the public with substantive insights. Viewed positively, the protagonists of the social sciences have become part of the modern *democratic* struggle over the limits of economic power. Yet at the same time, globalization – as an apparently immeasurable force of rapid social change – seems to have overwhelmed the analytical capacities of the social sciences. Here we offer a short guide to that part of the literature which, in our view, is of high analytical use value. This should provide students of the social politics of globalization with some of the analytical tools and empirical data necessary to reach more informed conclusions.

At the core of globalization are markets. Most studies of the structure and functioning of markets stem from the field of economics and are arcane and highly mathematical in nature; few introductions exist which are accessible and useful to social scientists. Sowell (2000), however, provides an easily digestible introduction to economics that discusses both its centrality to modern life and its use as an analytical technique. The best recent overview of the potential, limits and nature of social action in and shaped by the market is provided by Lindblom (2001). An excellent introduction to the comparative political economy of the OECD world, focusing on institutional-historical differences, is that of Hall and Soskice (2001). Krugman and Obstfeld (2002) introduce the reader in problem-oriented fashion to international economic and trade-policy theory. To gain orientation in the complex landscape of American trade policy, consult Destler (1995). For the most basic links to the trade policies of various governments and social science research, see http://www.uoregon.edu/~bruceb/adpage/html.

In a volume edited by Hilf and Petersmann (1993) the legal and constitutional features of trade policy in the USA, Germany and the European Union are presented in a manner highly relevant to an understanding of the social politics of globalization. John H. Jackson (1997a) provides a comprehensive, problem-oriented introduction to international economic law. The WTO treaties are available via http://www.wto.org.

Gilpin (2001) presents a problem-oriented analysis of the political dimensions of globalization, building on his classic contribution of 1987. The leading political science textbook is Keohane and Nye (2001). Held et al. (1999) provide a comprehensive, mainly descriptive account of global change. Myrdal (1957), Ruggie (1982), Milner (1988), Rogowski (1989), Rodrik (1997), Garrett (1998) as well as Scharpf and Schmidt (2000) provide landmark studies of the relationship of the international economy to national social policy in an increasingly interdependent world. Robbins (1937) still most clearly depicts how revolutionary the development of the welfare state was for the national and international economy. An annotated bibliography on 'Globalization and the Western Welfare State' provides an overview of the literature through the mid-1990s and may be accessed on the web at http://www.zes.uni-bremen.de/arbeitspapiere/D_abstract_95-01.html. A good starting point for research on the political economy of globalization is the website of the Institute for International Economics: http://www.iie.com/.

In exemplary fashion, T. H. Marshall (1964a) outlines the autonomous status and independent logic of social policy and its opposition to the basic principles of the market economy. Marmor et al. (1990) present a good introduction to the peculiarities of US social policy, now complemented by Hacker (2002), who contrasts the trajectories of pension versus health provision in their quite different public/private mixes. For an introduction to German social politics see Alber (2001a) and Manow (2001; for a German language basic teaching text and especially the accompanying broad internet outreach, see Bäcker et al. 2000 and htpp://www.sozialpolitik-lehrbuch.de/.). Pierson (2001) and also Huber and Stephens (2001) offer overviews of the comparative study of advanced welfare states in periods of austerity. A well-organized database on social policy reforms in OECD countries can be found at www.reformmonitor.org (the International Reform Monitor Project of the Bertelsmann Foundation, which provides information and statistics on social policy, labour market policy and industrial relations). For research on German economic and social policy, see the web resources of the Max Planck Institute for the Study of Societies at http://www.mpi-fg-koeln.mpg.de/. On recent developments in US social policy, see the websites of the Center on Budget and Policy Priorities (http://www.cbpp.org), the Brookings Institution (http://brook.edu/), the Economic Policy Institute (http://epinet.org/), the Urban Institute (http://www.urban.org/) and the Center for Law and Social Policy (http://www.clasp.org/). A good starting point for research on social policy in East and South East Asia is a compilation of web resources organized by the World Bank at http://worldbank.org/eapsocial/asemsocial/.

A list of links containing all of the addresses mentioned above and in the table below can also be obtained on the web at http://www.zes.uni-bremen.de/arbeitspapiere/D_abstract_95-01.html.

Journal Abbreviations

AER	American Economic Review
AERPP	American Economic Review. Papers and Proceedings
AmJIL	American Journal of International Law
AJS	American Journal of Sociology
APSR	American Political Science Review
ArizJICL	Arizona Journal of International and Comparative Law
ASS	Archiv für Sozialwissenschaft und Sozialpolitik
FAZ	Frankfurter Allgemeine Zeitung (German national newspaper)
IHT	International Herald Tribune
JEH	Journal of Economic History
JEL	Journal of Economic Literature
JEP	Journal of Economic Perspectives
JEPP	Journal of European Public Policy
JPE	Journal of Political Economy
JPuE	Journal of Public Economics
JSP	Journal of Social Policy
JWT	Journal of World Trade
MJIL	Michigan Journal of International Law
NBER	National Bureau of Economic Research (Cambridge, MA)
NYT	New York Times

Aaron, Henry 1989: 'Politics and the Professors Revisited', *AERPP* 79/2 (Jan): 1–15.
——1994a: 'Public Policy, Values, and Consciousness', *JEP* 8/2 (Spring): 3–21.
——1994b: 'Issues Every Health Care Financing Must Confront', *JEP* 8/3 (Summer): 31–43.
Aaronson, Susan Ariel 1996: *Trade and the American Dream: A Social History of Postwar Trade Policy.* Foreword by William V. Roth, Jr. and Robert T. Matsui (Lexington: University Press of Kentucky).
——2001: *Taking Trade to the Streets: The Lost History of Public Efforts to Shape Globalization.* Foreword by Pat Choate and I. M. Destler (Ann Arbor: University of Michigan Press).
Abbott, Kenneth W. 2001: 'Rule-Making in the WTO: Lessons from the Case of Bribery and Corruption', *Journal of International Economic Law* 4/2: 275–96.
Abramovitz, Moses 1986: 'Catching Up, Forging Ahead, and Falling Behind', *JEH* 46/2 (June): 385–406.
Abromeit, Heidrun 1992: *Der verkappte Einheitsstaat* (Leverkusen/Opladen: Leske and Budrich).
Achinger, Hans 1971 [1958]: *Sozialpolitik als Gesellschaftspolitik. Von der Arbeiterfrage zum Wohlfahrtsstaat* (Frankfurt am Main: Press of the Deutscher Verein für öffentliche und private Fürsorge).
Ackerman, Bruce 1992: 'Liberating Abstraction'. In Geoffrey R. Stone, Richard A. Epstein and Cass R. Sunstein, eds, *The Bill of Rights in the Modern State* (Chicago: University of Chicago Press), pp. 317–48.
Adams, Thomas McStay 1990: *Bureaucrats and Beggars. French Social Policy in the Age of Enlightenment* (Oxford: Oxford University Press).
Addison, John T. and Welfens, Paul J. J., eds 1998: *Labor Markets and Social Security. Wage Costs, Social Security Financing and Labor Market Reforms in Europe* (Berlin: Springer).
Aghion, Philippe 1998: 'Inequality and Economic Growth'. In Aghion and Williamson 1998, pp. 5–102.
——and Williamson, Jeffrey G. 1998: *Growth, Inequality and Globalization. Theory, History and Policy* (Cambridge: Cambridge University Press).
Ahmad, Ehtisham, Orize, Jean, Hills, John and Sen, Amartya, eds 1991: *Social Security in Developing Countries* (Oxford: Clarendon Press).
Aho, C. Michael 1985: 'US Labor Market Adjustment Policies in a Changing World Economy'. In Catherine Stirling and John N. Yochelson, eds, *Under Pressure. US Industry and the Challenge of Structural Adjustment* (Boulder, CO: Westview), pp. 219–60.
——and Bayard, Thomas O. 1980: 'American Trade Adjustment Assistance after Five Years', *World Economy* 3 (Oct): 359–76.
Alber, Jens 1984: 'Versorgungsklassen im Wohlfahrtsstaat. Überlegungen und Daten zur Situation in der Bundesrepublik', *Kölner Zeitschrift für Soziologie und Sozialpsychologie* 36/2: 225–51. (See also idem: 'Der Wohlfahrtsstaat als Motor sozialen Wandels: Zu Problemen der sozialen Integration und der Systemintegration'. In idem *Der Sozialstaat in der Bundesrepublik 1950–1983* (Frankfurt am Main: Campus Verlag, 1989), pp. 126–66.)
——1987 [1982]: *Vom Armenhaus zum Wohlfahrtsstaat. Analysen zur Entwicklung der Sozialversicherung in Westeuropa* (Frankfurt am Main: Campus Verlag).
——1988: 'Die Gesundheitssysteme der OECD-Länder im Vergleich'. In Manfred G. Schmidt, ed., *Staatstätigkeit: International und historisch vergleichende Analysen* (Opladen/Wiesbaden: Westdeutscher Verlag), pp. 116–50.
——1998: 'Der deutsche Sozialstaat im Licht international vergleichender Daten', *Leviathan* 26/2: 199–227.
——2001a: 'Recent Developments of the German Welfare State: Basic Continuity or a Para-

digm Shift', ZeS (Working paper 06/01). (Also forthcoming in Neil Gilbert and Rebecca A. van Voorhis, eds, *Changing Patterns of Social Protection* (New Brunswick, NJ: Transaction Publishers, forthcoming).

——ed. 2001b: *Sozialstaat und Arbeitsmarkt* (Wiesbaden: Chmierlorz). (*Sozialpolitik in Europa*, vol. 8, *Zeitschrift für Sozialreform* 47/4: 293–480.)

——2001c: 'Hat sich der Wohlfahrtsstaat als soziale Ordnung bewährt?'. In Mayer 2001a, pp. 59–111.

Albion, Robert G. 1932: 'The "Communication Revolution"', *American Historical Review* 37: 718–20.

Alchian, Armen A. and Demsetz, Harold 1972: 'Production, Information Cost, and Economic Organization', *AER* 62/5 (Dec): 777–95.

Alfino, Mark, Caputo, John S. and Wynyard, Robin, eds 1998: *McDonaldization Revisited: Critical Essays on Consumer Culture* (Westport, CT: Praeger).

Allmendinger, Jutta 1999: 'Bildungsarmut. Zur Verschränkung von Bildungs- und Sozialpolitik', *Soziale Welt* 50/1: 35–50.

——and Hinz, Thomas 1997: 'Mobilität und Lebensverlauf'. In Stefan Hradil and Stefan Immerfall, eds, *Die westeuropäischen Gesellschaften im Vergleich* (Leverkusen/Opladen: Leske and Budrich), pp. 247–85. (Trans. as: 'Occupational Careers Under Different Welfare Regimes: West Germany, Great Britain and Sweden'. In Leisering and Walker 1998, pp. 63–84.)

——and Leibfried, Stephan 2003: 'Education and the Welfare State: The Four Worlds of Competence Production', *Journal of European Social Policy* 13/1: 63–81.

Alt, James E., Frieden, Jeffrey, Gilligan, Michael J., Rodrik, Dani and Rogowski, Ronald 1996: 'The Political Economy of International Trade. Enduring Puzzles and Agenda for Inquiry', *Comparative Political Studies* 29/6: 689–717.

Amenta, Edwin 1998: *Bold Relief: Institutional Politics and the Origins of Modern American Social Policy* (Princeton, NJ: Princeton University Press).

Amenta, Edwin and Skocpol, Theda 1989: 'Taking Exception. Explaining the Distinctiveness of American Public Policies in the Last Century'. In Francis G. Castles, ed., *The Comparative History of Public Policy* (Cambridge: Polity), pp. 292–333.

Amsden, Alice H. 1979: 'Taiwan's Economic History: A Case of Etatisme and a Challenge to Dependency Theory', *Modern China. An Interdisciplinary Journal* 5: 341–79.

——1985: 'The State and Taiwan's Economic Development'. In Evans et al. 1985, pp. 78–106.

——1989: *Asia's Next Giant. South Korea and Late Industrialization* (Oxford: Oxford University Press).

——1991: 'Diffusion or Development: The Late-Industrializing Model and Greater East-Asia', *AERPP* 81: 282–86.

——1993: 'Structural Macroeconomic Underpinnings of Effective Industrial Policy: Fast Growth in the 1980s in Five Asian Countries', Geneva: UNCTAD (Discussion paper 57).

——1994: 'Why Isn't the Whole World Experimenting with the East Asian Model to Develop? Review of the *East Asian Miracle*', *World Development* 22: 627–33.

——1995: 'Like the Rest: South-East Asia's "Late Industrialization"', *Journal of International Development* 7: 791–99.

Anderson, James E. and Young, Leslie 2000: 'Trade Implies Law: The Power of the Weak', NBER (Working paper 7702).

Anderson, Kym, Hayami, Yujiro and Honma, Masayoshi 1986: 'The Growth of Agricultural Protection'. In Kym Anderson and Yujiro Hayami, eds, *The Political Economy of Agricultural Protection. East Asia in International Perspective* (Sydney: Allen and Unwin), pp. 17–30.

Andrew, Edward 1988: *Shylock's Rights. A Grammar of Lockian Claims* (Toronto: University of Toronto Press).
Anelauskas, Valdas 1999: *Discovering America As It Is* (Atlanta, GA: Clarity Press).
Aoki, Masahiko 1988: *Information, Incentives, and Bargaining in the Japanese Economy* (Cambridge: Cambridge University Press).
——1996: 'An Evolutionary Parable of the Gains from International Organizational Diversity'. In Ralph Landau, Timothy Taylor and Gavin Wright, eds, *The Mosaic of Economic Growth* (Stanford: Stanford University Press), pp. 247–63.
Arendt, Hannah 1967: 'Truth and Politics'. In Peter R. Baehr, ed., *The Portable Hannah Arendt* (New York: Penguin, 2000), pp. 545–75.
Arkes, Hadley 2000: 'Lochner v. New York and the Cast of Our Laws'. In Robert P. George, ed., *Great Cases in Constitutional Law* (Princeton, NJ: Princeton University Press), pp. 94–129.
Arrow, Kenneth J. 1994: 'Methodological Individualism and Social Knowledge', *AERPP* 84/2 (May): 1–9.
Asher, Mukul G. 1995: 'The Role of the Central Provident Fund in Singapore', *National Economic Review* (June): 40–9.
Ashford, Douglas 1986: *The Emergence of the Welfare State* (Oxford: Blackwell Publishing).
Ashton, David and Green, Francis 1996: *Education, Training and the Global Economy* (Cheltenham: Edward Elgar).
Aspalter, Christian, ed. 2002: *Discovering the Welfare State in East Asia* (London: Routledge).
Aspinall, Robert and Cave, Peter 2001: 'Lowering the Flag: Democracy, Authority and Rights at Tokorozawa High School', *Social Science Japan Journal* 4/1: 77–93.
Assmann, Jan 1998: *Moses der Ägypter. Entzifferung einer Gedächtnisspur* (München: Hanser).
Atkinson, Anthony B. 1999: *The Economic Consequences of Rolling Back the Welfare State* (Cambridge, MA: MIT Press).
——and Hills, John 1991: 'Social Security in Developed Countries: Are There Lessons for Developing Countries?'. In Ahmad et al. 1991, pp. 81–111.
Autor, David H. 2000: 'Outsourcing at Will: Unjust Dismissal Doctrine and the Growth of Temporary Help Employment', NBER (Working paper 7557).
Avi-Yonah, Reuven S. 2000: 'Globalization, Tax Competition, and the Fiscal Crisis of the Welfare State', *Harvard Law Review* 119/7 (May): 1573–676.
Axelrod, Robert and Keohane, Robert O. 1985: 'Achieving Cooperation under Anarchy: Strategies and Institutions'. In Kenneth A. Oye, ed., *Cooperation under Anarchy* (Princeton, NJ: Princeton University Press), pp. 226–54.
Ayres, B. Drummond Jr. 2000: 'High Gasoline Prices As a Campaign Issue', *NYT* (9 April): A-24.
Baack, Bennett D. and Ray, Edward John 1985: 'The Political Economy of the Origin and Development of the Federal Income Tax'. In Robert Higgs, ed., *Emergence of the Modern Political Economy* (Greenwich, CT: JAI Press), pp. 121–38.
Bäcker, Gerhard, Bispinck, Reinhard, Hofemann, Klaus and Nägele, Gerhard 2000: *Sozialpolitik und soziale Lage in Deutschland,* 2 vols (Opladen/Wiesbaden: Westdeutscher Verlag).
Badura, Peter 1999: 'Arbeitsrecht und Verfassungsrecht', *Recht der Arbeit* 52/1/2: 8–13.
Bagehot, Walter 1928 [1867]: *The English Constitution* (Oxford: Oxford University Press).
Baier, Horst 1999: 'Gesundheit als organisiertes Staatsziel oder persönliches Lebensschicksal? Zur Sozialgeschichte und Soziologie des Wohlfahrtsstaates'. In Häfner 1999, pp. 31–59.
Bairoch, Paul 1989: 'European Trade Policy, 1815–1914'. In Peter Mathias and Sidney Pollard, eds, *The Cambridge Economic History of Europe,* vol. 8 (Cambridge: Cambridge University Press), pp. 1–160.
——1993: *Economics and World History. Myth and Paradoxes* (Chicago: University of Chicago Press).

——1999: 'Brief History of the Social Clauses in Trade Policy'. In Mathias Dewatripont, André Sapir and Khalid Sekkat, eds, *Trade and Jobs in Europe. Much Ado about Nothing?* (Oxford: Oxford University Press), pp. 161–71.

Bak-Boychuk, Laura H. 1999: 'Internet Gambling: Is Avoiding Prosecution in the United States as Easy as Moving the Business Operations Offshore?', *Southwestern Journal of Law and Trade in the Americas* 6/2 (Fall): 363–83.

Baldwin, Peter 1990: *The Politics of Social Solidarity. Class Bases of the European Welfare State 1875–1975* (Cambridge: Cambridge University Press).

Baldwin, Robert E. 1985a: *The Political Economy of US Import Policy* (Cambridge, MA: MIT Press).

——1985b: 'Ineffectiveness of Protection in Promoting Social Goals', *World Economy* 8/2 (June): 109–18.

——and Magee, Christopher S. 2000: 'Congressional Trade Votes: From NAFTA Approval to Fast Track Defeat', Institute for International Economics (Policy Analysis in International Economics 59).

——Chen, Tain-Jy and Nelson, Douglas 1995: *Political Economy of US – Taiwan Trade* (Ann Arbor: University of Michigan Press).

Barnet, Richard J. and Müller, Ronald E. 1974: *Global Reach. The Power of the Multinational Corporations* (New York: Simon and Schuster).

Baron, David P. 1997: 'Integrated Strategy, Trade Policy, and Global Competition', *California Management Review* 39/2 (Winter): 145–69.

Barr, Nicholas A. 1993: *The Economics of the Welfare State,* 2nd edn (Oxford: Oxford University Press; 3rd edn 1998).

Bartlett, Will, Roberts, Jennifer A. and LeGrand, Julian 1998: *A Revolution in Social Policy. Quasi-Market Reforms in the 1990s* (Bristol: Policy Press).

Bary, William Theodore de 1988: *East Asian Civilizations. A Dialogue in Five Stages* (Cambridge, MA: Harvard University Press).

——1991: *The Trouble with Confucianism* (Cambridge, MA: Harvard University Press).

——1998: *Asian Values and Human Rights. A Confucian Communitarian Perspective* (Cambridge, MA: Harvard University Press).

Bary, William Theodore de and Weiming, Tu, eds 1998: *Confucianism and Human Rights* (New York: Columbia University Press).

Bates, Robert H. 1989: *Beyond the Miracle of the Market: The Political Economy of Agrarian Development in Kenya* (Cambridge: Cambridge University Press).

Bates, Robert H. and Anne O. Krueger, eds 1993: *Political and Economic Interactions in Economic Policy Reform: Evidence from Eight Countries* (Oxford: Blackwell Publishing).

Baucus, Max 2002: 'The Trade Act of 2002'. Keynote speech: 'Trade Policy in 2002', conference, presented at the Institute for International Economics, 26 February 2002 (http://www.iie.com/papers/baucus0202.htm – 29.03.02).

Bauman, Kurt J. 1999: *Extended Measures of Well-Being: Meeting Basic Needs* (Washington, DC: US Census Bureau; Current Population Reports, Household Economic Studies P70-67, June).

Baumol, William J., Panzar, John C. and Willig, Robert D. 1982: *Contestable Markets and the Theory of Industry Structure* (New York: Harcourt Brace Jovanovich) (rev. 1988).

Beard, Charles A. 2000 [1913]: *An Economic Interpretation of the Constitution of the United States* (Union, NJ: Lawbook Exchange).

Bebchuk, Lucian A. and Ferrell, Allen 1999: 'Federalism and Corporate Law: The Race to Protect Managers From Takeovers', *Columbia Law Review* 99/5 (June): 1168–99.

Beck, Ulrich 1997: *What is Globalization?* trans. Patrick Camiller (Cambridge: Polity). (Original ext. version: *Was ist Globalisierung? Irrtümer des Globalismus – Antworten auf Globalisierung* (Frankfurt am Main: Suhrkamp), 1999.)

——ed. 1998: *Politik der Globalisierung* (Frankfurt am Main: Suhrkamp).

Beckerman, Wilfred 1979: *Poverty and the Impact of Income Maintenance Programmes in Four Developed Countries: Case Studies of Australia, Belgium, Norway, and Great Britain* (Geneva: ILO).
Bederman, David J. 2001: 'Review of Anthony Clark Arend, *Constructivism, Positivism, and Empiricism in International Law: Legal Rules and International Society*', *Georgetown Law Journal* 89/2: 469–99.
Beisheim, Marianne, Dreher, Sabine, Walter, Gregor, Zangl, Bernhard and Zürn, Michael 1999: *Im Zeitalter der Globalisierung? Thesen und Daten zur gesellschaftlichen und politischen Denationalisierung* (Baden-Baden: Nomos Publishers).
Bellah, Robert 1985 [1957]: *Tokuwaga Religion. The Cultural Roots of Modern Japan* (New York: The Free Press).
Bello, Judith Hippler 1996: 'The WTO Dispute Settlement Mechanism: Less is More', *AmJIL* 90/3 (July): 416–18.
Bendix, Reinhard 1977 [1964]: *Nation-Building and Citizenship. Studies of Our Changing Social Order* (Berkeley/Los Angeles: University of California Press).
Benedek, Wolfgang 1998a: *Die Welthandelsorganization (WTO). Alle Texte einschließlich GATT (1994), GATS und TRIPS* (München: Beck).
——1998b: *Die Rechtsordnung des GATT aus völkerrechtlicher Sicht. Mit einer Zusammenfassung in englischer Sprache* (Berlin: Springer).
Beng-Huat, Chua 1994: 'Arrested Development: Democratization in Singapore', *Third World Quarterly* 15: 655–68.
Bennefield, Robert L. 1998: *Dynamics of Economic Well-Being: Health Insurance 1992–93. Who Loses Coverage and for How Long?* (Washington, DC: US Census Bureau; Current Population Reports, Household Economic Studies P70-54, May).
Bensel, Richard Franklin 1984: *Sectionalism and American Political Development, 1880–1980* (Madison: University of Wisconsin Press).
——1991: *Yankee Leviathan: The Origins of Central State Authority in America, 1859–1877* (Cambridge: Cambridge University Press).
——2000: *The Political Economy of American Industrialization, 1877–1900* (Cambridge: Cambridge University Press).
Bensen, Matthew 1999: 'The All New (International) "People's Court": The Future of the Direct Effect Clause After *Voest-Alpine Trading USA Corp.* v. *Bank of China*', *Minnesota Law Review* 83/4 (April): 997–1026.
Benvenisti, Eyal 1999: 'Exit and Voice in the Age of Globalization', *Michigan Law Review* 98/1 (Oct): 167–213.
Benz, Ernest 1959: 'On Understanding Non-Christian Religions'. In Mircea Eliade and Joseph M. Kitagawa, eds, *The History of Religions: Essays in Methodology* (Chicago: University of Chicago Press), pp. 120–35.
Bergeijk, Peter A. G. van and Mensink, Nico W. 1997: 'Measuring Globalization', *JWT* 31/3: 159–68.
Berger, Mark T. 1997: 'The Triumph of the East? The East Asian Miracle and Post-Cold War Capitalism'. In Berger and Borer 1997, pp. 260–87.
——and Borer, Douglas A., eds 1997: *The Rise of East Asia. Critical Visions of the Pacific Century* (London: Routledge).
Berger, Peter L. 1986: *The Capitalist Revolution. Fifty Propositions About Prosperity, Equality, and Liberty* (New York: Basic Books).
——and Hsiao, Hsin-Huang Michael, eds 1988: *In Search of an East Asian Development Model* (New Brunswick, NJ: Transaction Publishers).
Berkey, Judson Osterhoudt 1998: 'The European Court of Justice and Direct Effect for the GATT: A Question Worth Revisiting', Cambridge, MA: Harvard Law School Jean Monnet (Working paper 3/98).
Berlin, Isaiah 1998: 'Nationalism. Past Neglect and Present Power'. In idem, *The Proper Study*

of Mankind. An Anthology of Essays (New York: Farrar, Straus and Giroux), pp. 581–604.

Bernhard, Ludwig 1914: *Undesired Results of German Social Legislation*, trans. Herold G. Villard (New York: Workmen's Compensation Library; originally German edn Berlin: Julius Springer, 1912).

Bernstein, Jared 1999: *The Next Step: The New Minimum Wage Proposal and the Old Opposition* (Washington, DC: Economic Policy Institute, 27 April) (see also: http://www.epinet.org under *issue guides*, *minimum wage*, etc.).

——Brocht, Chauna and Spade-Aguilar, Maggie 2000: *How Much is Enough? Basic Family Budgets for Working Families* (Washington, DC: Economic Policy Institute).

Bernstein, Peter L. 1996: *Against the Gods: The Remarkable Story of Risk* (New York: John Wiley and Sons).

Berthold, Norbert 1997: *Der Sozialstaat im Zeitalter der Globalisierung* (Tübingen: J. C. B. Mohr).

Best, Michael H. 1990: *The New Competition: Institutions of Industrial Restructuring* (Cambridge: Polity/Cambridge, MA: Harvard University Press).

——2001: *The New Competitive Advantage: What Lies Behind the Renewal of American Industry* (Oxford: Oxford University Press).

Bhagwati, Jagdish N. 1982: 'Directly Unproductive, Profit-Seeking DUP Activities', *JPE* 90/5 (Sep/Oct): 988–1002.

——1988: *Protectionism* (Cambridge, MA: MIT Press).

——1998: *A Stream of Windows. Unsettling Reflections on Trade, Immigration, and Democracy* (Cambridge, MA: MIT Press).

——2001: *Free Trade Today* (Princeton, NJ: Princeton University Press).

Bhagwati, Jagdish N. and Dehejia, Vivek H. 1994: 'Freer Trade and the Wage of the Unskilled – Is Marx Striking Again?'. In Jagdish N. Bhagwati and Marvin H. Koster, eds, *Trade and Wages. Levelling Wages Down* (Washington, DC: American Enterprise Institute), pp. 36–75.

——and Hudec, Robert E., eds 1996: *Fair Trade and Harmonization. Prerequisites for Free Trade?* vol. I: *Economic Analyses*, vol. II: *Legal Analysis* (Cambridge, MA: MIT Press).

Bhala, Raj 2000: 'Enter the Dragon: An Essay on China's WTO Accession Saga', *American University International Law Review* 15/6: 1469–538.

Bhandari, Jagdeen S. and Sykes, Alan O. Jr., eds 1997: *Economic Dimensions of International Law: Comparative and Empirical Perspectives* (Cambridge: Cambridge University Press).

Birkinshaw, Patrick 1985: *Grievances, Remedies and the State* (London: Sweet and Maxwell).

Blackhurst, Richard 1998: 'The Capacity of the WTO to Fulfill Its Mandate'. In Anne O. Krueger, ed., *The WTO as an International Organization* (Chicago: University of Chicago Press), pp. 31–58.

——Marian, Nicolas and Tumlir, Jan 1977: 'Trade Liberalization, Protectionism and Interdependence', Geneva: GATT Secretariat (GATT Studies in International Trade 5; Nov).

Blank, Rebecca M. 1997: *It Takes a Nation: A New Agenda for Fighting Poverty* (New York: Russell Sage Foundation Press/Princeton, NJ: Princeton University Press).

——2000: 'Fighting Poverty: Lessons from Recent U.S. History', *JEP* 14/2 (Spring): 3–19.

Blank, Rebecca M. and Haskins, Ron, eds 2001: *The New World of Welfare Reform* (Washington, DC: Brookings Institution Press).

Blaug, Mark 1963: 'The Myth of the Old Poor Law and the Making of the New', *JEH* 23/2: 151–84.

BMA (Bundesminister für Arbeit und Sozialordnung) 1998: *Statistisches Taschenbuch 1998. Arbeits- und Sozialstatistik* (Bonn: BMA) (http://www.bma.de/index.cfm?D6015A3203A34E09B9D39D1DDF0811E1).

——2000: *Statistisches Taschenbuch 1999. Arbeits- und Sozialstatistik* (Bonn: BMA) (http://www.bma.de/index.cfm?D6015A3203A34E09B9D39D1DDF0811E1).

——2002: *Sozialbericht 2001* (Berlin: BMA) (http://www.bma.de/download/broschueren/A101.pdf) (Part B, pp. 367ff. contains the: 'Sozialbudget', the social budget statistics). *Materialband zum Sozialbudget 2001* (Berlin: BMA) (http://www.bma.de/download/broschueren/A102.pdf).

BMA and Bundesarchiv, eds 2001: *Geschichte der Sozialpolitik in Deutschland seit 1945* (Baden-Baden: Nomos Publishers), 12 vols (2 in print, of which vol. 1 *Grundlagen der Sozialpolitik*; rest in prep.).

Bogdandy, Armin von 2001: 'Verfassungsrechtliche Dimensionen der Welthandelsorganisation', *Kritische Justiz* 34: 3: 264–81; and 4: 425–41.

Böhm-Bawerk, Eugen von 1881: *Rechte und Verhältnisse vom Standpunkte der volkswirthschaftlichen Güterlehre. Kritische Studie von Dr. . . .* (Innsbruck: Wagner).

Bok, Derek 2001: *The Trouble with Government* (Cambridge, MA: Harvard University Press).

Boltho, Andrea and Toniolo, Gianni 1999: 'The Assessment: The Twentieth Century – Achievements, Failures, Lessons', *Oxford Review of Economic Policy* 15/4: 1–17.

Bonoli, Giuliano, George, Vic and Taylor-Gooby, Peter 2000: *European Welfare Futures: Towards a Theory of Retrenchment* (Cambridge: Polity).

Bonturi, Marcos and Fukasaku, Kiichiro 1993: 'Globalization and Intra-Firm Trade: An Empirical Note', *OECD Economic Studies* 20 (Spring): 145–59.

Bordo, Michael D. and James, Harold 2000: 'The International Monetary Fund: Its Present Role in Historical Perspective', NBER (Working paper 7724).

Bordo, Michael D., Eichengreen, Barry J. and Irwin, Douglas A. 1999: 'Is Globalization Today Really Different from Globalization a Hundred Years Ago?'. In Susan M. Collins and Robert Z. Lawrence, eds, *Brookings Trade Forum*, vol. 2 (Washington, DC: Brookings Institution Press), pp. 1–72 (also in NBER, Working paper 7195).

Borjas, George J. 1994: 'The Economics of Immigration', *JEL* 32/4 (Dec): 1667–717.

——1995: 'The Economic Benefits from Immigration', *JEP* 9/2 (Spring): 3–22.

Börsch-Supan, Axel 2000a: 'Rentabilitätsvergleiche im Umlage- und Kapitaldeckungsverfahren: Konzepte, empirische Ergebnisse, sozialpolitische Konsequenzen', Mannheim: Institut für Volkswirtschaftslehre und Statistik (Working paper 585–00).

——2000b: 'Pension Reform in Germany: To Fund or Not to Fund', *World Economics* 1/1: 81–101.

Boudon, Raymond and Bourricaud, François 1992: *Soziologische Stichwörter. Ein Handbuch* (Opladen/Wiesbaden: Westdeutscher Verlag).

Boulding, Kenneth E. 1950: 'Religious Perspectives in Economics'. In idem 1970, pp. 179–97.

——1952: 'Religious Foundations of Economic Progress'. In idem 1970, pp. 198–211.

——1957: 'Some Contributions of Economics to Theology and Religion'. In idem 1970, pp. 219–26.

——1970: *Beyond Economics. Essays in Society, Religion, and Ethics* (Ann Arbor: University of Michigan Press).

——1976: *Ökonomie als Wissenschaft* (München: Piper).

Bowles, Samuel and Gintis, Herbert 1986: *Democracy and Capitalism. Property, Community, and the Contradictions of Modern Social Thought* (New York: Basic Books).

Bowman, Karlyn 1999: 'Health Care Attitudes Today', American Enterprise Institute (Papers and Studies).

Boyd, Gavin and Dunning, John H., eds 1999: *Structural Change and Cooperation in the Global Economy* (Cheltenham: Edward Elgar).

Boyle, Francis Anthony 1985: *World Politics and International Law* (Durham, NC: Duke University Press).

——1999: *Foundations of World Order: The Legalistic Approach to International Relations (1898–1922)* (Durham, NC: Duke University Press).

Brainard, Lael and Litan, Robert E. 2002: *Globalization. What Now?* (Washington, DC: Brookings Institution Press).

Braithwaite, John and Drahos, Peter 2000: *Global Business Regulation* (Cambridge: Cambridge University Press).

Brand, Ronald A. 1996/97: 'Direct Effect of International Economic Law in the United States and the European Union', *Journal of International Law and Business* 17 (Winter/Spring): 556–608.

Brauner, Sarah and Loprest, Pamela 1999: *Where Are They Now? What States' Studies of People Who Left Welfare Tell Us* (Washington, DC: The Urban Institute; Series A, No. A-32, *Assessing the New Federalism*).

Bray, Francesca 1986: *The Rice Economies. Technology and Development in Asian Societies* (Berkeley/Los Angeles: University of California Press).

Brennan, Geoffrey and Buchanan, James M. 1985: *The Reason of Rules* (Cambridge: Cambridge University Press).

Brierly, James Leslie 1924: 'The Shortcomings of International Law'. In idem, *The Basis of Obligation in International Law and Other Papers* (Oxford: Clarendon Press, 1958), pp. 68–80.

Briggs, Asa 1968: 'The World Economy: Interdependence and Planning'. In C. L. Mowat ed., *The Shifting Balance of World Forces 1898–1945* (2nd edn of vol. XII, *The Era of Violence* in *The New Cambridge Modern History*) (Cambridge: Cambridge University Press), pp. 37–86.

Brimmer, Andrew F. 1983: 'Monetary Policy and Economic Activity: Benefits and Costs of Monetarism', *AERPP* 73/2 (May): 1–12.

Brody, Evelyn 1996: 'Agents Without Principals: The Economic Convergence of the Nonprofit and For-Profit Organizational Forms', *New York Law School Law Review* 40/3: 4457–536.

Brown, Benjamin H. 1943: *The Tariff Reform Movement in Great Britain, 1881–1895* (New York: Columbia University Press).

Brown, Charles C. and Oates, Wallace E. 1987: 'Assistance to the Poor in a Federal System', *JPuE* 32/3: 307–30.

Brown, Drusilla K., Deardorff, Alan V. and Stern, Robert M. 1996: 'International Labor Standards and Trade: A Theoretical Analysis'. In Bhagwati and Hudec 1996, vol. I, pp. 227–80.

Brown, H. Lowell 1999: 'The Extraterritorial Reach of the US Government's Campaign against International Bribery', *Hastings International and Comparative Law Review* 22/3 (Spring): 407–522.

Brown, Murray 1966: *On the Theory and Measurement of Technological Change* (Cambridge: Cambridge University Press).

Buchanan, James M. 1988: 'Contractarian Political Economy and Constitutional Interpretation', *AERPP* 78: 135–9.

——1989: 'The State of Economic Science'. In Werner Sichel, ed., *The State of Economic Science: Views of Six Nobel Laureates* (Kalamazoo, MI: W. E. Upjohn Institute for Employment Research), pp. 79–95.

Buffett, Warren E. 2000: 'The Billionaire's Buyout Plan', *NYT* (10 Sept): WK–17.

Bull, Hedley 1995 [1977]: *The Anarchical Society: A Study of Order in World Politics* (London: Macmillan; 1st edn, New York: Columbia University Press).

Burckhardt, Jacob 1982 [1905]: *Über das Studium der Geschichte. Der Text der: 'Weltgeschichtlichen Betrachtungen', auf Grund der Vorarbeiten von Ernst Ziegler nach den Handschriften*, Peter Ganz, ed. (München: Beck).

Büren, Herbert 1934: *Arbeitgeber und Sozialpolitik: Untersuchung über die grundsätzliche Haltung des deutschen Unternehmertums gegenüber der Sozialpolitik der Vorkriegs-, Kriegs- und Nachkriegszeit* (Köln: May).

Burke, Vincent J. and Burke, Vee 1974: *Nixon's Good Deed: Welfare Reform* (New York: Columbia University Press).

Burnett, Alan D. and Taylor, Peter J., eds 1981: *Political Studies from Spatial Perspectives. Anglo-American Essays on Political Geography* (Chichester: John Wiley and Sons).

Burtless, Gary and Litan, Robert E. 2001: *Globaphobia Revisited. Open Trade and Its Critics* (Washington, DC: Brookings Institution Press).
Burtless, Gary, Lawrence, Robert Z., Litan, Robert E. and Shapiro, Robert J. 1998: *Globaphobia. Confronting Fears about Open Trade* (Washington, DC: Brookings Institution Press/ Progressive Policy Institute/New York: Twentieth Century Fund).
Byers, Michael, ed., 2000: *The Role of International Law in International Politics. Essays in International Relations and International Law* (Oxford: Oxford University Press).
Cairnes, John Elliot 1874: *Some Leading Principles of Political Economy Newly Expounded* (London/New York: Macmillan/Harper and Bros).
Calhoun, Michael J. 1999: 'Tension on the High Seas of Transnational Securities Fraud: Broadening the Scope of United States Jurisdiction', *Loyola University Chicago Law Journal* 30/4 (Summer): 679–726.
Came, Barry 2000: 'Pumped on Anger', *Maclean's* 25 (Sept): 30.
Cameron, David 1978: 'The Expansion of the Public Economy: A Comparative Analysis', *APSR* 72/11 (Dec): 1243–61.
Cameron, Maxwell A. and Tomlin, Brian W. 2000: *The Making of NAFTA. How the Deal was Done* (Ithaca, NY: Cornell University Press).
Campbell, Duncan 2000: 'The Running Mate's Bottom Line', *Guardian* (7 Oct): 17.
Campos, Jose Edgardo and Root, Hilton L. 1996: *The Key to the Asian Miracle. Making Shared Growth Credible* (Washington, DC: Brookings Institution Press).
Card, David E. and Blank, Rebecca M., eds 2000: *Finding Jobs: Work and Welfare Reform* (New York: Russell Sage Foundation Press).
Carmody, Chi 1997: 'Third Parties Under GATT', *MJIL* 18/3: 615–57.
Carr, Edward Hallett 1945: *Nationalism and After* (New York/London: Macmillan; repr. 1968).
Cary, William L. 1974: 'Federalism and Corporate Law: Reflections Upon Delaware', *Yale Law Journal* 83/4 (March): 663–705.
Case, Anne C., Rosen, Harvey S. and Hines, James R. 1993: 'Budget Spillovers and Fiscal Policy Interdependence. Evidence From the States', *JPuE* 52/3: 285–307.
Cashin, Sheryll D. 1999: 'Federalism, Welfare Reform, and the Minority Poor: Accounting for the Tyranny of State Majorities', *Columbia Law Review* 99/3 (April): 552–627.
Cass, Deborah Z. 2001: 'The "Constitutionalization" of International Trade Law: Judicial Norm-Generation as the Engine of Constitutional Development in International Trade', *European Journal of International Trade* 12/1: 39–76.
Cass, Ronald A. 1991: 'Velvet Fist in an Iron Glove. The Omnibus Trade and Competitiveness Act of 1988', *Regulation* 14/1 (www.edition).
Castells, Manuel 1992: 'Four Asian Tigers With a Dragon Head. A Comparative Analysis of the State, Economy, and Society in the Asian Pacific Rim'. In Richard P. Appelbaum and Jeffrey Henderson, *States and Development in the Asian Pacific Rim* (London: Sage), pp. 33–70.
Castells, Manuel, Goh, L. and Kwok, R. Y.-W. 1990: *The Shek Kip Mei Syndrome. Economic Development and Public Housing in Hong Kong and Singapore* (London: Pion).
Castles, Francis G. 1978: *The Social Democratic Image of Society: A Study of the Achievements and Origins of Scandinavian Social Democracy in Comparative Perspective* (London: Routledge and Kegan Paul).
——ed. 1989: *The Comparative History of Public Policy* (Cambridge: Polity).
Chan, Gordon Hou-Sheng 1985: 'Taiwan'. In Dixon and Kim 1985, pp. 324–53.
Chan, Steve 1997: 'Democracy and Inequality: Tracking Welfare Spending in Singapure, Taiwan and South Korea'. In Midlarsky 1997, pp. 227–43.
Chang, In-Hyub 1985: 'Korea, South'. In Dixon and Kim 1985, pp. 176–213.
Charnovitz, Steve 1997: 'Two Centuries of Participation: NGOs and International Governance' *Michigan Journal of International Law* 18: 183–286.
Cheikbossian, Guillaume 2000: 'Federalism, Distributive Politics and Representative Democracy', *Economics of Governance* 1/2: 105–22.

Chiang, Tung-liang 1997: 'Taiwan's 1995 Health Reform', *Health Policy* 39: 225–39.
Chibundu, Maxwell O. 1999: 'Making Customary International Law through Municipal Adjudication: A Structural Inquiry', *Virginia Journal of International Law* 39/4 (Summer): 1069–149.
Cho, Lee-Jay and Lee, Chung-Hoon 1995: 'The Government-Business Relationship in Korea: Cultural Dimensions'. In Yu and Lee 1995, pp. 327–44.
Choi, Sung-Jae 1992: 'Ageing and Social Welfare in South Korea'. In David R. Phillips, ed., *Ageing in East and Southeast Asia* (London: Arnold), pp. 148–66.
Chow, Nelson 1998: 'The Making of Social Policy in Hong Kong: Social Welfare Development in the 1980s and 1990s'. In Goodman et al. 1998, pp. 159–74.
Clark, Anne Marie, Friedman, Elisabeth J. and Hochstetler, Kathryn 1998: 'The Sovereign Limits of Global Civil Society: A Comparison of NGO Participation in UN World Conferences on the Environment, Human Rights, and Women', *World Politics* 51: 1–35.
Clark, Peter 1997: 'Reforming Antidumping'. In Hart 1997, pp. 215–51.
Clasen, Peter Adolf 1913: *Der Salutismus. Eine sozialwissenschaftliche Monographie über General Booth und seine Heilsarmee* (Jena: Eugen Diederichs).
Claude, Inis L. Jr. 1958: 'Multilateralism – Diplomatic and Otherwise', *International Organization* 12/1 (Winter): 43–52.
——1981: 'Casual Commitment in International Relations', *PoSciQ* 96/3 (Fall): 367–79.
Clayton, Richard and Pontusson, Jonas 1998: 'Welfare State Retrenchment Revisited: Entitlement Cuts, Public Sector Restructuring, and Inegalitarian Trends in Advanced Capitalist Societies', *World Politics* 51/1 (Oct): 67–98.
Cline, William R. 1997: *Trade and Income Distribution* (Washington, DC: Institute for International Economics).
Clymer, Adam 2000: 'The 2000 Campaign: The Republican Running Mate. Cheney More Generous by His Own Numbers', *NYT* (6 Sept): *A*–22.
Coase, R. H. 1988: *The Firm, the Market, and the Law* (Chicago: University of Chicago Press).
Cohen, Stephen D. 2000 [1977]: *The Making of United States International Economic Policy. Principles, Problems, and Proposals for Reform* (Westport, CT: Praeger).
Cohn, Gustav 1889: 'Income and Property Taxes in Switzerland', *PoSciQ* 4/1 (March): 37–65.
Coldwell, Daniel III and Reid, John 1998: 'An Inquiry into the Effects of US Multinationals on US Intraindustry Trade', *Journal of Global Marketing* 12/1: 81–104.
Coleman, James Samuel 1992 [1982] *The Asymmetric Society* (Syracuse, NY: Syracuse University Press).
Congressional Budget Office 1998: *Antidumping Action in the United States and Around the World: An Analysis of International Data* (Washington, DC) (http://www.cbo.gov).
——2000: *Historical Budget Data* (Washington, DC: US Government Printing Office) (http://www.cbo.gov).
Conybeare, John A. C. 1980: 'International Organization and the Theory of Property Rights', *International Organization* 34/3 (Summer): 307–34.
Conybeare, John A. C. and Zinkula, Mark 1996: 'Who Voted Against the NAFTA? Trade Unions Versus Free Trade', *World Economy* 19/1 (Jan): 1–12.
Cooper, Richard N. 1968: *The Economics of Interdependence: Economic Policy in the Atlantic Community* (New York: McGraw Hill/Council on Foreign Relations).
Cooter, Robert C. 2000: *The Strategic Constitution* (Princeton, NJ: Princeton University Press).
Corden, Warner Max 1997 [1974] *Trade Policy and Economic Welfare* (Oxford: Clarendon Press).
Coser, Lewis 1956: *The Functions of Social Conflict* (New York: Free Press; repr. 1996).
Council of Economic Advisers, USA 1996: *Economic Report of the President transmitted to the Congress* (Washington, DC: US Government Printing Office).
Cowles, Maria Green, Caporaso, James and Risse, Thomas, eds 2001: *Transforming Europe. Europeanization and Domestic Change* (Ithaca, NY: Cornell University Press).

Crafts, Nicholas F. R. 2000: 'Globalization and Growth in the Twentieth Century', Washington, DC: IMF (Working paper 00–44).

Cranston, Ross 1985: *Legal Foundations of the Welfare State* (London: Weidenfeld and Nicolson).

Croley, Steven P. and Jackson, John H. 1996: 'WTO Dispute Procedures, Standard of Review, and Deference to National Governments', *AmJIL* 90/2 (April): 193–213.

Croome, John 1995: *Reshaping the World Trading System: A History of the Uruguay Round* (Geneva: WTO).

Currie, Janet and Yelowitz, Aaron 2000: 'Health Insurance and Less Skilled Workers'. In Card and Blank 2000, pp. 233–61.

Dahrendorf, Ralf 1959: *Class and Class Conflict in Industrial Society* (London: Routledge and Kegan Paul).

——1988: *The Modern Social Conflict. An Essay on the Politics of Liberty* (New York: Weidenfeld and Nicolson).

——1999: *Ein neuer Dritter Weg? Reformpolitik am Ende des 20. Jahrhunderts* (Tübingen: J. C. B. Mohr).

——2002: 'Was von Dauer ist. Klassen ohne Kampf, Kampf ohne Klassen', *FAZ* (9 March): 8.

Dalaker, Joseph 1999: *Poverty in the United States: 1998* (Washington, DC: US Census Bureau; Current Population Reports P60–207).

Dam, Kenneth W. 1970: *The GATT. Law and International Economic Organization* (Chicago: University of Chicago Press).

Davey, William J. 2000: 'Supporting the World Trade Organization Dispute Settlement System', *JWT* 34/1: 167–70.

Davis, Steven J., Haltiwanger, John C. and Schuh, Scott 1996: *Job Creation and Destruction* (Cambridge, MA: MIT Press).

Deacon, Bob 2000a: *Globalization and Social Policy: The Threat to Equitable Welfare* (Geneva: UNRISD).

——2000b: 'Globalisation: A Threat to Equitable Provision', *Social Policy Review* 12: 250–71.

Deacon, Bob (with Michelle Hulse and Paul Stubbs) 1997: *Global Social Policy. International Organizations and the Future of Welfare* (London: Sage).

Deardorff, Alan V. 1987: 'Safeguard Policy and the Conservative Welfare Function'. In Henryk Kierzkowksi, ed., *Protection and Competition in International Trade. Essays in Honor of W. M. Corden* (Oxford: Blackwell Publishing), pp. 22–40.

Deardorff, Alan V. and Stern, Robert M., eds 1998: *Constituent Interests and US Trade Policies* (Ann Arbor: University of Michigan Press).

——eds 2000: *Social Dimensions of U.S. Trade Policies* (Ann Arbor: University of Michigan Press).

Decker, Paul T. and Corson, Walter 1995: 'International Trade and Worker Displacement: Evaluation of the Trade Adjustment Assistance Program', *Industrial and Labour Relations Review* 48/4 (July): 758–74.

De Long, J. Bradford 1996: 'Keynesianism, Pennsylvania Avenue Style: Some Economic Consequences of the Employment Act of 1946', *JEP* 10/3 (Summer): 41–53.

De Nardi, Mariacristina, Ren, Liqian and Wei, Chao 2000: 'On the Distribution of Income in Five Countries', Luxembourg: Luxembourg Income Study (Working paper 227).

Destler, Irving M. 1986: *American Trade Politics: System Under Stress* (Washington, DC: Institute for International Economics/New York: Twentieth Century Fund; 3rd edn 1995).

——1997: *Renewing Fast-Track Legislation* (Washington, DC: Institute for International Economics).

——1998: 'Congress, Constituencies, and US Trade Policy'. In Deardorff and Stern 1998, pp. 93–108.

Destler, I. M. and Odell, John S. (with Kimberly Ann Elliott) 1987: *Anti-Protection. Changing Forces in United States Trade Politics* (Washington, DC: Institute for International Economics).

Deuchler, Martina 1992: *The Confucian Transformation of Korea. A Study of Society and Ideology* (Cambridge, MA/London: Council on East Asian Studies, Harvard University Press).

Deutsch, Karl W. 1979: *Tides among Nations* (New York: Free Press). (Orig. *Nationenbildung – Nationalstaat – Integration* (Düsseldorf: Bertelsmann Universitätsverlag, 1972).)

Deutsch, Karl W. and Alexander Eckstein 1961: 'National Industrialization and the Declining Share of the International Economic Sector, 1890–1959', *World Politics* 13/2 (Jan): 267–99.

Deyo, Frederic C., ed. 1987: *The Political Economy of the New Asian Industrialism* (Ithaca, NY: Cornell University Press).

——1989: *Beneath the Miracle. Labor Subordination in the New Asian Industrialism* (Berkeley/Los Angeles: University of California Press).

——1990: 'Economic Policy and the Popular Sector'. In Gereffi and Wyman 1990, pp. 179–204.

——1991: 'Singapore: Developmental Paternalism'. In Steven M. Goldstein, ed., *Mini Dragons. Fragile Economic Miracles in the Pacific* (New York/Boulder CO: Ambrose Video Publ./ Westview Press), pp. 64–103, 186–7.

——1992: 'The Political Economy of Social Policy Formation. East Asia's Newly Industrialized Countries'. In Richard P. Applebaum and Jeffrey Henderson, *States and Development in the Asian Pacific Rim* (London: Sage), pp. 289–305.

Diebold, William Jr. 1952: *The End of the ITO* (Princeton, NJ: Internal Finance Sect., Dept. of Economic and Social Institutions, Princeton University; Essays in Internal Finance 16).

Dixon, John and Kim, Hyung Shik, eds 1985: *Social Welfare in Asia* (London: Croom Helm).

Dobbin, Frank, Sutton, John R., Meyer, John W. and Scott, W. Richard 1993: 'Equal Opportunity Law and the Construction of Internal Labor Markets', *AJS* 99/2 (Sept): 396–427.

Dodd, Peter and Leftwich, Richard 1980: 'The Market for Corporate Charters: "Unhealthy Competition" Versus Federal Regulation', *Journal of Business* 53/3 (July, part I): 259–83.

Domenach, Jean-Luc 1998: *L'Asie en danger* (Paris: Fayard).

Donahue, John D. and Nye, Joseph S. Jr., eds 2001: *Governance Amid Bigger, Better Markets* (Washington, DC: Brookings Institution Press).

——eds 2002: *Market-based Governance: Supply Side, Demand Side, Upside and Downside* (Washington, DC: Brookings Institution Press).

Doremus, Paul N., Keller, William W., Pauly, Louis W. and Reich, Simon 1998: *The Myth of the Global Corporation* (Princeton, NJ: Princeton University Press).

Dorner, Peter and Thiesenhusen, William C. 1990: 'Selected Land Reforms in East and Southeast Asia: Their Origins and Impacts', *Asia-Pacific Economic Journal* 4: 65–95.

Dowty, Alan 1987: *Closed Borders. The Contemporary Assault on Freedom of Movement* (New Haven, CT: Yale University Press).

Drèze, Jean and Sen, Amartya 1991: 'Public Action for Social Security: Foundations and Strategy'. In Ahmad et al. 1991, pp. 1–40.

Drezner, Daniel W. 2000: 'Bottom Feeders'. *Foreign Policy* 171 (Nov/Dec): 64–70.

Dunning, John H. 1993: *The Globalization of Business. The Challenge of the 1990s* (London: Routledge).

——1997a: *Alliance Capitalism and Global Business* (London: Routledge).

——ed. 1997b: *Governments, Globalization, and International Business* (Oxford: Oxford University Press).

——ed. 1998: *Globalization, Trade, and Foreign Direct Investment* (Amsterdam: Elsevier).

Durkheim, Emile 1964 [1902]: *The Division of Labor in Society* (New York: Free Press).

Duus, Peter 1996: 'Introduction'. In Duus et al. 1996, pp. xi–xlvii.

Duus, Peter and Schreiner, Irwin 1998: 'Socialism, Liberalism, and Marxism, 1901–31'. In Bob Tadashi Wakabayashi, ed., *Modern Japanese Thought* (Cambridge: Cambridge University Press), pp. 147–206.

Duus, Peter, Myers, Ramon and Peattie, Mark R., eds 1996: *The Japanese Wartime Empire 1931–1945* (Princeton, NJ: Princeton University Press).

Dworkin, Ronald 1978: *Taking Rights Seriously* (Cambridge, MA: Harvard University Press).

Easterbrook, Frank H. 1984: 'Managers' Discretion and Investors' Welfare: Theories and Evidence', *Delaware Journal of Corporate Law* 9/3: 540–71.

——1992: 'Abstraction and Authority'. In Geoffrey R. Stone, Richard A. Epstein and Cass R. Sunstein, eds, *The Bill of Rights in the Modern State* (Chicago: University of Chicago Press), pp. 349–80.

Eaton, Jonathan and Grossman, Gene H. 1985: 'Tariffs as Insurance. Optimal Commercial Policy when Domestic Markets are Incomplete', *Canadian Journal of Economics* 18/2 (May): 258–72.

Eatwell, John, Milgate, Murray and Newman, Peter, eds 1989: *The Invisible Hand* (New York and London: Norton; The New Palgrave).

Ebbinghaus, Bernhard and Visser, Jelle 2000: *Trade Unions in Western Europe since 1945* (London, UK: Macmillan Reference/New York: Grove's Dictionaries).

Eckes, Alfred E., Jr. 1995: *Opening America's Market: US Foreign Trade Policy Since 1776* (Chapel Hill: University of North Carolina Press).

——ed. 2000: *Revisiting US Trade Policy: Decisions in Perspective* (Athens, OH: Ohio University Press).

Edwards, Richard C. 1970: 'Economic Sophistication in Nineteenth Century Congressional Tariff Debates', *JEH* 30/4 (Dec): 802–38.

Eichengreen, Barry J. 1996a: *Globalizing Capital. A History of the International Monetary System* (Princeton, NJ: Princeton University Press).

——1996b: 'Institutions and Economic Growth after World War II'. In Nicholas Crafts and Gianni Toniolo, eds, *Economic Growth in Europe since 1945* (Cambridge: Cambridge University Press), pp. 38–72.

——2001: 'A Review of Robert Gilpin, The Challenge of Global Capitalism: The World Economy in the 21st Century', *Labour* 47: 217–18.

Eichenhofer, Eberhard 1990: *Recht der sozialen Sicherheit in den USA* (Baden-Baden: Nomos Publishers).

Eisenstadt, Shmuel Noah 1973: *Tradition, Change, and Modernity* (New York: John Wiley and Sons).

——1990: 'Über die Beziehung zwischen Konfuzianismus, Entwicklung und Modernisierung'. In Krieger and Trauzettel 1990, pp. 444–50.

El-Agraa, Ali M. 1995: 'Japan's Trade Policy: A Minisymposium' (Editorial Introduction), *World Economy* 18: 182–90.

Elazar, Daniel Judah 1998: *Constitutionalizing Globalization. The Post Modern Revival of Confederal Arrangements* (Lanham, MD/Oxford: Rowman and Littlefield).

——1999: 'Political Science, Geography, and the Spatial Dimension of Politics', *Political Geography* 18: 875–86.

Eliot, T. S. 1940: 'East Cooker'. In idem, *Collected Poems 1909–1962* (New York: Harcourt, Brace and Co., 1963), pp. 182–90.

Elliott, Kimberly Ann 2000: 'Getting Beyond No . . . ! Rights and Trade'. In Schott 2000, pp. 187–204.

Ellwood, David T. 1988: *Poor Support. Poverty in the American Family* (New York: Basic Books).

——2000: *A Working Nation: Workers, Work, and Government in the New Economy* (New York: Russell Sage Foundation Press).

Epping, Volker 1998: *Die Außenwirtschaftsfreiheit* (Tübingen: J. C. B. Mohr).

Epstein, Richard Allen 1985: *Takings: Private Property and the Power of the Eminent Domain* (Cambridge, MA: Harvard University Press).

Esping-Andersen, Gøsta 1985: *Politics Against Markets. The Social Democratic Road to Power* (Princeton, NJ: Princeton University Press).

——1990: *The Three Worlds of Welfare Capitalism* (Cambridge: Polity/Princeton, NJ: Princeton University Press).
——1999: *Social Foundations of Postindustrial Economies* (Oxford: Oxford University Press).
——ed. 2002: *Why We Need a New Welfare State* (Oxford: Oxford University Press).
Esping-Andersen, Gøsta and Regini, Marino, eds 2000: *Why Deregulate Labour Markets?* (Oxford: Oxford University Press).
Esty, Daniel C. 1998: 'Non-Governmental Organizations at the World Trade Organization: Cooperation, Competition, or Exclusion', *JEL* 1/1 (March): 123–47.
Etges, Andreas 1999: *Wirtschaftsnationalismus: USA und Deutschland im Vergleich (1815–1914)* (Frankfurt am Main: Campus Verlag).
Eto, Mikiko 2001: 'Public Involvement in Social Policy Reforms: Lessons from Japan's Elderly Care Insurance Scheme', *JSP* 30/1: 17–36.
Eulenburg, Franz 1929: *Außenhandel und Außenhandelspolitik (Die internationalen Wirtschaftsbeziehungen*) (Tübingen: J. C. B. Mohr).
EUROSTAT 1968: *National Accounts 1958–1967* (Luxembourg: OOPEU, Statistical Office of the European Communities).
——1983: *National Accounts (Aggregates), 1960–1982* (Luxembourg: OOPEU).
——1997: *Volkswirtschaftliche Gesamtrechnungen (Aggregate), 1970–1995* (Luxembourg: OOPEU).
——1999: *Social Protection: Expenditure and Receipts 1980–1996* (Luxembourg: OOPEU).
Evans, G. E. 2000: *Lawmaking Under the Trade Constitution: A Study in Legislating by the World Trade Organization* (London: Kluwer International Law).
Evans, John W. 1971: *The Kennedy Round in American Trade Policy: The Twilight of the GATT?* (Cambridge, MA: Harvard University Press).
Evans, Peter, Rueschemeyer, Dietrich and Skocpol, Theda, eds, 1985: *Bringing the State Back In* (Cambridge: Cambridge University Press).
Falkner, Gerda 1998: *EU Social Policy in the 1990s: Towards a Corporatist Policy Community* (London: Routledge).
——2000: 'EG-Sozialpolitik nach Verflechtungsfalle und Entscheidungslücke: Bewertungsmaßstäbe und Entwicklungstrends', *Politsche Vierteljahresschrift* 41/2: 279–301.
Farinelli, Franco 2000: 'Friedrich Ratzel and the Nature of (Political) Geography', *Political Geography* 19/8 (Winter): 943–55.
Feenstra, Robert C., ed. 2000: *The Impact of International Trade on Wages* (Chicago: University of Chicago Press).
Feher, Michel 2000: *Powerless by Design. The Age of the International Community* (Durham, NC: Duke University Press).
Fei, John C. H. 1995: 'Chinese Cultural Values and Industrial Capitalism'. In Yu and Lee 1995, pp. 183–204.
Feiler, Arthur 1937: 'Current Tendencies in Commercial Policy', *AERPP* 27/1 (Suppl.): 29–42.
Feinman, Jay M. 1976: 'The Development of the Employment at Will Rule', *American Journal of Legal History* 20/2: 118–35.
Feinstein, Charles H., Termin, Peter and Tonioli, Gianni 1997: *The European Economy Between the Wars* (Oxford: Oxford University Press).
Fenwick, Charles R. 1982: 'Crime and Justice in Japan: Implications for the United States', *International Journal of Comparative and Applied Criminal Justice* 6/1: 61–71.
Fernandez, Rachel and Rodrik, Dani 1991: 'Resistance to Reform: Status-quo Bias in the Presence of Individual-specific Uncertainty', *AER* 81/5 (Dec): 1146–55.
Feynman, Richard P. 1999: *The Pleasure of Finding Things Out* (Cambridge, MA: Perseus).
Fields, Gary S. 1984: 'Employment, Income Distribution and Economic Distribution in Seven Small Open Economies', *The Economic Journal* 94: 74–83.
——1985: 'Industrialization and Employment in Hong Kong, Korea, Singapore, and Taiwan'.

In Walter Galenson, ed., *Foreign Trade and Investment* (Madison, WI: University of Wisconsin Press), pp. 333–75.
——1994: 'Changing Labor Market Conditions and Economic Development in Hong Kong, the Republic of Korea, Singapore, and Taiwan, China', *The World Bank Economic Review* 8: 395–414.
Finer, Samuel E. 1999: *The History of Government*, vol. 1: *Ancient Monarchs and Empires;* vol. 2: *The Intermediate Ages*; vol. 3: *Empires, Monarchies, and the Modern State* (Oxford: Oxford University Press).
Finger, J. Michael 1982: 'Incorporating the Gains from Trade into Policy', *World Economy* 5/4: 367–78.
——1983: 'The Political Economy of Trade Policy', *Cato Journal* 3/3: 743–50.
——1991: 'The Meaning of "Unfair" in US Import Policy', Washington, DC: World Bank (Working paper 745).
——1992: 'Dumping and Antidumping: The Rhetoric and the Reality of Protection in Industrial Countries', *World Bank Research Observer* 7/2 (July): 121–43.
——1996: 'Legalized Backsliding: Safeguard Provisions in GATT'. In Will Martin, ed., *The Uruguay Round and Developing Countries* (Cambridge: Cambridge University Press), pp. 316–40.
——1998: 'GATT Experience with Safeguards: Making Economic and Political Sense of the Possibilities that the GATT Allows to Restrict Imports', Washington, DC: World Bank (Working paper 2000).
Finger, J. Michael and Dhar, Sumana 1992: 'Do Rules Control Power?', GATT Articles and Arrangements in the Uruguay Round, World Bank (Working paper 818).
Finger, J. Michael and Murray, Tracy 1990: 'Policing Unfair Imports. The US Example', Washington, DC: World Bank (Working paper 401).
Finger, J. Michael, Hall, Keith and Nelson, Douglas R. 1982: 'The Political Economy of Administered Protection', *AER* 72/3 (June): 452–66.
Finger, J. Michael, Ng, Francis and Wangchuk, Sonam 2001: 'Antidumping as Safeguard Policy', World Bank (Working paper 2730).
Finlayson, John and Zacher, Mark W. 1981: 'The GATT and the Regulation of Trade Barriers: Regime Dynamics and Functions', *International Organization* 35/4 (Fall): 561–602.
Fishlow, Albert and Parker, Karen, eds 1999: *Growing Apart. The Causes and Consequences of Global Wage Inequality* (New York: Council on Foreign Relations Press).
Flora, Peter 1974: *Modernisierungsforschung. Zur empirischen Analyse der gesellschaftlichen Entwicklung* (Opladen/Wiesbaden: Westdeutscher Verlag).
——1975: *Quantitative Historical Sociology* (The Hague/Paris: Mouton) (*Current Sociology* XXIII).
——1981: 'Solution or Source of Crisis? The Welfare State in Historical Perspective'. In Wolfgang Mommsen, ed., *The Emergence of the Welfare State in Britain and Germany 1850–1950* (London: Croom Helm), pp. 343–89.
——1983: *State, Economy, and Society in Western Europe 1814–1975. A Data Handbook*; vol. 1: *The Growth of Mass Democracies and Welfare States* (Frankfurt am Main: Campus Verlag).
——1986–1987: *Growth to Limits. The Western European Welfare States since World War II*, vol. 1: *Sweden, Norway, Finland, Denmark*; vol. 2: *Germany, United Kingdom, Ireland, Italy*; vol. 4: *Appendix: Synopses, Bibliographies* (Berlin: Walter de Gruyter).
——1989: 'From Industrial to Postindustrial Welfare State?', *Annals of the Institute of Social Science* (Tokyo: Institute of Social Science; focus issue *The Advanced Industrial Societies in Disarray: What Are the Available Choices?*), pp. 149–62.
Flora, Peter and Alber, Jens 1981: 'Modernization, Democratization and the Development of Welfare States in Western Europe'. In Flora and Heidenheimer 1981, pp. 27–80.
Flora, Peter and Heidenheimer, Arnold J., eds 1981: *The Development of Welfare States in Europe and America* (New Brunswick, NJ: Transaction Publishers).

Flora, Peter, Alber, Jens and Kohl, Jürgen 1977: 'Zur Entwicklung der westeuropäischen Wohlfahrtsstaaten', *Politische Vierteljahresschrift* 18: 707–72.

Flora, Peter, Kraus, Franz and Pfenning, Winfried 1987: *State, Economy, and Society in Western Europe 1815–1975. A Data Handbook*; vol. 2: *The Growth of Industrial Societies and Capitalist Economies* (Frankfurt am Main: Campus Verlag).

Fogel, Robert William 2000: *The Fourth Great Awakening and the Future of Egalitarianism* (Chicago: University of Chicago Press).

Foreign Policy 2000: 'The FP Interview. Lori's War', *Foreign Policy* 118 (Spring): 29–55.

Foreign Press Center 1995: *Social Security in Japan (1995)* (Tokyo: Foreign Press Center/Japan; About Japan Series No. 17).

Forsthoff, Ernst 1971: *Der Staat der Industriegesellschaft, dargestellt am Beispiel der Bundesrepublik Deutschland* (München: Beck).

Franck, Thomas M. 1999: *The Empowered Self. Law and Society in the Age of Individualism* (Oxford: Oxford University Press).

——ed. 2000: *Delegating State Powers: The Effect of Treaty Regimes on Democracy and Sovereignty* (Ardsley, NY: Transnational Publishers).

Franck, Thomas M. and Weisband, Edward 1979: *Foreign Policy by Congress* (Oxford: Oxford University Press).

Frank, Dana 1999: *Buy American. The Untold Story of Economic Nationalism* (Boston, MA: Beacon Press).

Freeman, Richard Barry and Gottschalk, Peter, eds 1998: *Generating Jobs. How to Increase Demand for Less-Skilled Workers* (New York: Russell Sage Foundation Press).

Freeman, Richard Barry and Medoff, James L. 1984: *What Do Unions Do?* (New York: Basic Books).

Freeman, Richard Barry and Rogers, Joel 1999: *What Workers Want* (Ithaca, NY: ILR Press; Cornell University Press/New York: Russell Sage Foundation Press).

Freudenheim, Milt 2000: 'HMO. Costs Spur Employers to Shift Plans', *NYT* (6 Sept): A-1, 22.

Frey, Bruno S., Pommerehne, Werner, Schneider, Friedrich and Gilbert, Guy 1984: 'Consensus and Dissension Among Economists: An Empirical Inquiry', *AER* 74/5 (Dec): 986–94.

Freytag, Andreas 1995: *Die strategische Handels- und Industriepolitik der EG. Eine politikökonomische Analyse* (Köln: Institut für Wirtschaftspolitik an der Universität zu Köln).

Fried, Barbara H. 1998: *The Progressive Assault on Laissez Faire. Robert Hale and the First Law and Economics Movement* (Cambridge, MA: Harvard University Press).

Fried, Charles 1984: 'Individual and Collective Rights in Work Relations: Reflections on the Current State of Labor Law and its Prospects', *University of Chicago Law Review* 51/4 (Fall): 1012–40.

Frieden, Jeffry A. and Lake, David A. 2000: *International Political Economy: Perspectives on Global Power* (Boston, MA: Bedford/St Martin's).

Frieden, Jeffry A. and Rogowski, Ronald 1996: 'The Impact of the International Economy on National Policies: An Analytical Overview'. In Keohane and Milner 1996, pp. 25–47.

Friedman, Kathi V. 1981: *Legitimation of Social Rights and the Western Welfare State. A Weberian Perspective* (Chapel Hill: University of North Carolina Press).

Friedman, Lawrence M. 1996: 'Borders: On the Emerging Sociology of Transnational Law', *Stanford Journal of International Law* 32/1 (Winter): 65–90.

Friedman, Milton 1982: 'Monetary Policy: Theory and Practice', *Journal of Money, Credit and Banking* 14/1 (Feb): 98–118.

Friedman, Thomas L. 1997: 'Plotting Politics on the New Globalization Graph', *IHT* (14 Nov): 8.

——1999: *The Lexus and the Olive Tree* (New York: Farrar Straus and Giroux).

Fröhlich, Hans-Peter 1994: 'EU Trade Policy: Special Interests versus Social Welfare'. In Franz Waldenberger, ed., *The Political Economy of Trade Conflicts. The Management of Trade Relations in the US-EU-Japan Triad* (Berlin: Springer), pp. 17–31.

Frost, Robert 1916: 'Christmas Trees'. In idem, *The Poetry of Robert Frost. The Collected Poems, Complete and Unabridged,* ed. Edward Connery Lathem (New York: Henry Holt and Co., 1975), pp. 105–7.
Fukui, Haruhiro 1970: *Party in Power: The Japanese Liberal-Democrats and Policy-Making* (Berkeley/Los Angeles: University of California Press).
Fukuyama, Francis 1992: *The End of History and the Last Man* (New York: Free Press).
——1999: 'Second Thoughts: The End of History 10 Years Later', *New Perspectives Quarterly* 16/4: 40–2.
Fuller, Thomas 1998: 'Asian Crisis: More Than Just Crony Capitalism', *IHT* (14 Aug): 1, 17.
Fuller, Thomas and Pfanner, Eric 2002: 'In Imposing Steel Tariffs, US Hits Allies Hardest. EU Lodges Formal Complaints in the WTO', *IHT* (8 March): 1, 8.
Galenson, Walter 1959: 'Introduction'. In idem, ed., *Labor and Economic Development* (New York: Wiley), pp. 1–123.
——1992: *Labor and Economic Growth in Five Asian Countries. South Korea, Malaysia, Taiwan, Thailand, and the Philippines* (New York: Praeger).
Galligan, Denis J. 1986: *Discretionary Powers. A Legal Study of Official Discretion* (Oxford: Clarendon Press).
Gal-Or, Noemi 1998: 'Labor Mobility Under NAFTA: Regulatory Policy Spearheading the Social Supplement to the International Trade Regime', *ArizJICL* 15/2 (Spring): 365–414.
Ganssmann, Heiner 2000: *Politische Ökonomie des Sozialstaats* (Münster: Westfälisches Dampfboot).
Gantz, David A. 2000: 'Failed Efforts to Initiate the Millennium Round in Seattle: Lessons for Future Global Trade Negotiations', *ArizJICL* 17/2 (Spring): 349–69.
Garon, Sheldon 1987: *The State and Labor in Modern Japan* (Berkeley/Los Angeles: University of California Press).
Garrett, Geoffrey 1997: *Partisan Politics in the Global Economy* (Cambridge: Cambridge University Press).
——1998: 'Global Markets and National Politics: Collision Course or Virtuous Circle', *International Organization* 52/4 (Fall): 787–824 (also in Held and McGrew 2000, pp. 301–18).
Garrison, Roger W. and Kirzer, Israel M. 1989: 'Friedrich August von Hayek'. In Eatwell et al. 1989, pp. 119–30.
Gayle, Curtis Anderson 2001: 'Progressive Representations of the Nation: Early Post-war Japan and Beyond', *Social Science Japan Journal* 4/1: 1–19.
Gebhardt, Thomas 1997: 'Ending Welfare as We Know It. Die US-amerikanische Sozialhilfereform 1993–1996', Centre for Social Policy Research, Bremen University (Working paper 2/97).
——1998: *Arbeit gegen Armut. Die Reform der Sozialhilfe in den USA* (Opladen/Wiesbaden: Westdeutscher Verlag).
——1999: 'Von Welfare zu Workfare. Der Fall der Sozialhilfe in Deutschland und in den USA', *WeltTrends. Zeitschrift für internationale Politik und vergleichende Studien* 7/24: 95–116.
Gebhardt, Thomas and Jacobs, Herbert 1997: 'Amerikanische Verhältnisse? Sozialhilfe in den USA und Deutschland: Ein Vergleich aus historischer, institutioneller und rechtlicher Perspektive', *Zeitschrift für Sozialreform* 43/8 (Aug): 597–633.
Geertz, Clifford 1995: *After the Fact. Two Countries, Four Decades, One Anthropologist* (Cambridge, MA: Harvard University Press).
——2000: *Available Light. Anthropological Reflections on Philosophical Topics* (Princeton, NJ: Princeton University Press).
Geldsetzer, Lutz and Han-ding, Hong 1998: *Grundlagen der chinesischen Philosophie* (Stuttgart: Reclam).
Genschel, Philipp 2000: 'Der Wohlfahrtsstaat im Steuerwettbewerb', *Zeitschrift für internationale Beziehungen* 7/2: 267–96.
Gentz, Manfred 1999: 'Das Arbeitskampfrecht in Deutschland und der internationale

Wettbewerb'. In Thomas Klebe, Peter Wedde and Martin Wolmerath, eds, *Recht und soziale Arbeitswelt. Festschrift für Wolfgang Däubler zum 60. Geburtstag* (Frankfurt am Main: Bund-Verlag), pp. 421–30.

Gereffi, Gary and Wyman, Donald L., eds 1990: *Manufacturing Miracles. Paths of Industrialization in Latin America and East Asia* (Princeton, NJ: Princeton University Press).

Gerloff, Wilhelm 1913: *Die Finanz- und Zollpolitik des Deutschen Reiches nebst ihren Beziehungen zu Landes- und Gemeindefinanzen von der Gründung des Norddeutschen Bundes bis zur Gegenwart* (Jena: Gustav Fischer).

German Council of Economic Experts (Sachverständigenrat zur Begutachtung der gesamtwirtschaftlichen Entwicklung) 1998: *Vor weitreichenden Entscheidungen. Jahresgutachten 1998/99* (Stuttgart: Metzler-Poeschel).

——1999: *Wirtschaftspolitik unter Reformdruck. Jahresgutachten 1999/2000* (Stuttgart: Metzler-Poeschel).

Gerschenkron, Alexander 1943: *Bread and Democracy in Germany* (Berkeley/Los Angeles: University of California Press; Ithaca, NY: Cornell University Press, 1989, Intr. Charles S. Maier).

Gerth, Hans H. and Mills, C. Wright 1946: 'The Man and the Work'. In idem, eds, *From Max Weber. Essays in Sociology* (Oxford: Oxford University Press), pp. 1–74.

Geyer, Robert R. 2000: *Exploring European Social Policy* (Cambridge: Polity).

Giddens, Anthony 1981: *A Contemporary Critique of Historical Materialism* (London: Macmillan).

Gilbert, Neil, ed. 2001: *Targeting Social Benefits: International Perspectives and Trends* (New Brunswick, NJ: Transaction Publishers).

——2002: *Transformation of the Welfare State. The Silent Surrender of Public Responsibility* (Oxford: Oxford University Press).

Gilcher-Holtey, Ingrid 1998: 'Plädoyer für eine dynamische Mentalitätsgeschichte', *Geschichte und Gesellschaft* 24: 476–97.

Gilens, Martin 1999: *Why Americans Hate Welfare. Race, Media, and the Politics of Antipoverty Policy* (Chicago: University of Chicago Press).

Gillon, Steven M. 2000: *'That's Not What We Meant to Do'. Reform and Its Unintended Consequences in Twentieth-Century America* (New York and London: Norton).

Gilpin, Robert 1975: *US Power and the Multinational Corporation: The Political Economy of Foreign Investment* (New York: Basic Books).

——1984: 'The Richness of the Tradition of Political Realism', *International Organization* 38/2 (Spring): 287–304.

——(with Jean Millis Gilpin) 1987: *The Political Economy of International Relations* (Princeton, NJ: Princeton University Press).

——(with Jean Millis Gilpin) 2000: *The Challenge of Global Capitalism: The World Economy in the 21st Century* (Princeton, NJ: Princeton University Press).

——(with Jean Millis Gilpin) 2001: *Global Political Economy: Understanding the International Economic Order* (Princeton, NJ: Princeton University Press).

Girgenzer, Gerd 2000: *Adaptive Thinking. Rationality in the Real World* (Oxford: Oxford University Press).

Glassman, James K. 1997: 'Know-Nothing Congress Can't Even Grasp a No-Brainer', *IHT* (12 Nov): 8.

Glassman, Jim 1999: 'State Power beyond the "Territorial Gap": The Internationalization of the State', *Political Geography* 18: 669–96.

Glazer, Nathan 1988: *The Limits of Social Policy* (Cambridge, MA: Harvard University Press).

——1998: 'The American Welfare State: Exceptional No Longer?'. In Henry Cavanna, ed., *Challenge to the Welfare State: Internal and External Dynamics for Change* (Cheltenham: Edward Elgar), pp. 7–20.

Goldin, Claudia 1994: 'The Political Economy of Immigration Restriction in the United States, 1890–1921'. In Claudia Goldin and Gary D. Libecap, eds, *The Regulated Economy: A Historical Approach to Political Economy* (Chicago: University of Chicago Press), pp. 223–57.

Goldin, Claudia and Katz, Lawrence F. 2000: 'Decreasing (and then Increasing) Inequality in America: A Tale of Two Half Centuries'. In Finis Welch, ed., *The Causes and Consequences of Increasing Inequality* (Chicago: University of Chicago Press), pp. 37–82.

Goldman, Alvin I. 1999: *Knowledge in a Social World* (Oxford: Clarendon Press).

Goldstein, Judith L. 1988: 'Ideas, Institutions, and American Trade Policy', *International Organization* 42/1 (Winter): 179–217.

——1993: *Ideas, Interests, and American Trade Policy* (Ithaca, NY: Cornell University Press).

Goldstein, Judith L. and Martin, Lisa L. 2000: 'Legalization, Trade Liberalization, and Domestic Politics: A Cautionary Note', *International Organization* 54/3 (Summer): 603–32 (also in Goldstein et al. 2001, pp. 219–48).

Goldstein, Judith L., Kahler, Miles, Keohane, Robert O. and Slaughter, Anne-Marie, eds 2001: *Legalization and World Politics* (Cambridge, MA: MIT Press).

Goodhart, Charles 1989: 'The Conduct of Monetary Policy', *Economic Journal* 99/396 (June): 293–346.

Goodin, Robert E. 1985: *Protecting the Vulnerable. A Reanalysis of Our Social Responsibilities* (Chicago: University of Chicago Press).

Goodin, Robert E. and Dryzek, John 1987: 'Risk-Sharing and Social Justice: The Motivational Foundations of the Post-War Welfare State'. In Goodin and LeGrand 1987, pp. 37–73.

Goodin, Robert E. and LeGrand, Julian, eds 1987: *Not Only the Poor. The Middle Classes and the Welfare State* (London: Allen and Unwin).

Goodin, Robert E., Heady, Bruce, Muffels, Ruud and Dirven, Henk-Jan 1999: *The Real Worlds of Welfare Capitalism* (Cambridge: Cambridge University Press).

Goodman, Robert 1998: 'The "Japanese-style Welfare State" and the Delivery of Personal Social Services'. In Goodman et al. 1998, pp. 139–58.

Goodman, Robert, White, Gordon and Kwon, Huck-ju, eds 1998: *The East Asian Welfare Model. Welfare Orientalism and the State* (London: Routledge).

Gordon, Andrew 1985: *The Evolution of Labor Relations in Japan: Heavy Industry, 1853–1955* (Cambridge, MA: Harvard University Press).

Gordon, Michael E. and Turner, Lowell, eds 2000: *Transnational Cooperation Among Labor Unions* (ILR Press at Ithaca, NY: Cornell University Press).

Gordon, Scott 1999: *Controlling the State. Constitutionalism from Ancient Athens to Today* (Cambridge, MA: Harvard University Press).

Gottschalk, Marie 2000: *The Shadow Welfare State: Labor, Business, and the Politics of Health Care in the United States* (ILR Press at Ithaca, NY: Cornell University Press).

Gough, Leo 1998: *Asia Meltdown. The End of the Miracle?* (Oxford: Capstone).

Gourevitch, Peter Alexis 1977: 'International Trade, Domestic Coalitions, and Liberty: Comparative Responses to the International Economic Crisis of 1873–1896', *Journal of Interdisciplinary History* 8/2: 281–313.

——1978: 'The Second Image Reversed: The International Sources of Domestic Politics', *International Organization* 32/4 (Fall): 881–912.

——1986: *Politics in Hard Times. Comparative Responses to International Economic Crisis* (Ithaca, NY: Cornell University Press).

Goyder, Daniel George 1993: *EC Competition Law,* 2nd edn (Oxford: Clarendon Press).

Graebner, William 1977: 'Federalism in the Progressive Era: A Structural Interpretation of Reform', *Journal of American History* 64/2 (Sept): 331–57.

Grafers, Hans Wilfried 1999: *Einführung in die betriebliche Außenwirtschaft* (Stuttgart: Schäffer-Poeschel).

Graham, Carol 1994: *Safety Nets, Politics, and the Poor. Transition to Market Economies* (Washington, DC: Brookings Institution Press).

Graham, Edward M. 2000: 'Fighting the Wrong Enemy. Antiglobal Activists and Multinational Enterprises', (Washington, DC: Institute for International Economics).

Granet, Marcel 1985: *Das chinesische Denken. Inhalt, Form, Charakter* (Frankfurt am Main: Suhrkamp). (Orig. pub. in French, 1934).

Graser, Bernd 2001: *Dezentrale Wohlfahrtsstaatlichkeit im föderalen Binnenmarkt? Eine verfassungs- und sozialrechtliche Untersuchung am Beispiel der Vereinigten Staaten von Amerika* (Berlin: Duncker and Humblot).

Gray, John 1998: *False Dawn. The Delusions of Global Capitalism* (New York: The New Press/Free Press; London, UK: Granta Books; also in Held and McGrew 2000, pp. 328–31).

Green Book 1996 ff.: see House of Representatives 2000.

Green-Pedersen, Christoffer and Haverland, Markus 2002: 'The New Politics and Scholarship of the Welfare State', *Journal of European Social Policy* 12/1: 43–51.

Greenspan, Alan 2001: 'Globalization', Speech at the Institute for International Economics', First Annual Stavros S. Niarchos Lecture, 24 October (http://www.iie.com/papers/greenspan1001.htm–29.03.02).

Greider, William 1997: *One World, Ready or Not: The Manic Logic of Global Capitalism* (New York: Simon and Schuster).

Grodzins, Morton 1966: *The American System. A New View of the Government in the United States,* ed. Daniel J. Elazar (Chicago, IL: Rand McNally).

Grossman, Gene M. and Helpman, Elhanan 1994: 'Protection for Sale', *AER* 84/4 (Sept): 833–50.

Grotius, Hugo 1950 [1625]: *De jure belli ac pacis. Libri tres*, new German text and intr. by Walter Schätzel (Tübingen: J. C. B. Mohr).

Gruber, Lloyd 2000: *Ruling the World. Power Politics and the Rise of Supranational Institutions* (Princeton, NJ: Princeton University Press).

Gylfason, Thorvaldur 2000: 'Growing Apart', *JWT* 34/4: 37–62.

Habermas, Jürgen 1989: 'The New Obscurity: The Crisis of the Welfare State and the Exhaustion of Utopian Energies'. In idem, *The New Conservatism* (Cambridge, MA: MIT Press), pp. 48–70.

Hacker, Jacob S. 1997: *The Road to Nowhere: The Genesis of President Clinton's Plan for Health Security* (Princeton, NJ: Princeton University Press).

——1998: 'The Historical Logic of National Health Insurance: Structure and Sequence in the Development of British, Canadian and US Medical Policy', *Studies in American Political Development* 12 (Spring): 57–130.

——2002: *The Divided American Welfare State: Public and Private Benefits* (Cambridge, MA: Harvard University Press).

Häfner, Heinz, ed. 1999: *Gesundheit unser höchstes Gut?* (Berlin: Springer).

Haggard, Stephan 1990: *Pathways From the Periphery. The Polititics of Growth in the Newly Industrializing Countries* (Ithaca, NY: Cornell University Press).

Haggard, Stephan and Kaufman, Robert R. 1995: *The Political Economy of Democratic Transitions* (Princeton, NJ: Princeton University Press).

Haggard, Stephan and Moon, Chung-In 1983: 'The South Korean State in the International Economy: Liberal, Dependent, or Mercantile?'. In John Gerard Ruggie, ed., *The Antinomies of Interdependence. National Welfare and the International Division of Labor* (New York: Columbia University Press), pp. 131–89.

Halaby, Charles N. 1986: 'Worker Attachment and Workplace Authority', *American Sociological Review* 51/5 (Oct): 634–49.

Haley, John Owen 1991: *Authority Without Power. Law and the Japanese Paradox* (Oxford: Oxford University Press).

Hall, Peter A. 1997: 'The Political Economy of Adjustment in Germany'. In Frieder Naschold, David Soskice and Bob Hancké, eds, *Ökonomische Leistungsfähigkeit und institutionelle Innovation. Das deutsche Produktions- und Politikregime im globalen Wettbewerb* (Berlin: Sigma), pp. 293–317 (WZB Yearbook).

Hall, Peter A. and Soskice, David, eds 2001: *Varieties of Capitalism: The Institutional Foundations of Comparative Advantage* (Oxford: Oxford University Press).

Hallstein, Walter 1962: *United Europe: Challenge and Opportunity* (Cambridge, MA: Harvard University Press).

Hamilton, Alexander 1817: *The Soundness of the policy of protecting domestic manufactures: fully established by Alexander Hamilton in his report to Congress on the subject, and by Thomas Jefferson, in his letter to Benjamin Austin: to which were added, Extracts from the address of the American Society for Promoting Domestic Manufactures, established in New York* (Philadelphia, PA: Printed by J. R. A. Skerrett for the Philadelphia Society for the Promotion of American Manufactures).
——1928: *Industrial and Commercial Correspondence of Alexander Hamilton, anticipating his report on manufactures*, ed. Arthur Harrison Cole (Chicago, IL: A. W. Shaw).
Hamilton, Alexander, Madison, James and Jay, John 1999 [1787–8]: *The Federalist Papers* (New York: Mentor).
Handler, Joel F. 1986: *The Conditions of Discretion. Autonomy, Community, Bureaucracy* (New York: Russell Sage Foundation Press).
Hansen, Alvin H. and Viner, Jacob 1947: 'Two Discussions of the Employment Act of 1946 and Its Early Operation', *Review of Economic Statistics* 29/2 (May): 69–79.
Hansen, John Mark 1990: 'Taxation and the Political Economy of the Tariff', *International Organization* 44/4 (Fall): 527–51.
Hardt, Michael and Negri, Antonio 2000: *Empire* (Cambridge, MA: Harvard University Press).
Harrison, J. Richard and March, James G. 1984: 'Decision-Making and Postdecision Surprises', *Administrative Science Quarterly* 29/1 (March): 26–42.
Hart, Michael, ed., 1997: *Finding Middle Ground: Reforming the Antidumping Laws in North America* (Ottawa: Centre for Trade Policy and Law).
Harvey, David 1985: *Studies in the History and Theory of Capitalist Urbanization* (Baltimore, MA: Johns Hopkins University Press).
Hatton, Timothy J. and Williamson, Jeffrey G. 1994: *Migration and the International Labor Market 1850–1939* (London: Routledge).
——1998: *The Age of Mass Migration: Causes and Economic Impact* (Oxford: Oxford University Press).
Haveman, Robert H. and Wolfe, Barbara L. 1998: 'Welfare to Work in the US: A Model for Other Nations?', Madison, WI: Institute for Research on Poverty (Discussion paper 1158–98).
Haverkate, Görg and Huster, Stefan 1999: *Europäisches Sozialrecht* (Baden-Baden: Nomos Publishers).
Hayek, Friedrich August von 1935: 'Socialist Calculation I: The Nature and History of the Problem'. In idem 1980, pp. 119–48.
——1945: 'Individualism: True and False'. In idem. 1980, pp. 1–32.
——1946: 'The Meaning of Competition'. In idem 1980, pp. 92–106.
——1947: '"Free" Enterprise and Competitive Order'. In idem 1980, pp. 107–18.
——1969: *Freiburger Studien* (Tübingen: Mohr).
——1980: *Individualism and Economic Order* (Chicago: University of Chicago Press).
Heckscher, Eli Filip 1994 [1935]: *Mercantilism*, 2 vols (London: Routledge).
Heclo, Hugh 1994: 'Poverty Politics'. In Sheldon H. Danziger, Gary D. Sandefur and Daniel H. Weinberg, eds, *Confronting Poverty. Prescriptions for Change* (New York: Russell Sage Foundation Press/Cambridge, MA: Harvard University Press), pp. 396–436.
——1995: 'The Social Question'. In Katherine McFate, Roger Lawson and William Julius Wilson, eds, *Poverty, Inequality, and the Future of Social Policy* (New York: Russell Sage Foundation Press), pp. 665–91.
——1998: 'A Political Science Perspective on Social Security Reform'. In R. Douglas Arnold, Michael Graetz and Alicia H. Munnell, eds, *Framing the Social Security Debate. Values, Politics and Economics* (Washington, DC: Brookings Institution Press), pp. 65–89.
——2001: 'The Politics of the New Welfare System'. In Blank and Haskins 2001, pp. 169–200.
Hegel, Georg Wilhelm Friedrich 1961 [1840]: *Vorlesungen über die Philosophie der Geschichte* (Stuttgart: Reclam).

Heidenheimer, Arnold J. 1981: 'Education and Social Security Entitlements in Europe and America'. In Flora and Heidenheimer 1981, pp. 269–306.

——1983: 'Secularization Patterns and the Westward Spread of the Welfare State, 1883–1983. Two Dialogues About How and Why Britain, the Netherlands, and the United States Have Differed', *Comparative Social Research* 6: 3–65.

Heinemann, Frederick Henry 1948: 'Truths of Reason and Truths of Fact', *The Philosophical Review* 57/5 (Sept): 458–80.

Heinz, Walter R., ed. 1991: *Theoretical Advances in Life Course Research* (Weinheim: Deutscher Studien Verlag).

Heinze, Meinhard 1984: *Möglichkeiten der Fortentwicklung des Rechts der Sozialen Sicherheit zwischen Anpassungszwang und Bestandsschutz* (München: Beck; Gutachten E zum 55. Deutschen Juristentag).

Held, David and McGrew, Anthony, eds, 2000: *The Global Transformation Reader* (Cambridge: Polity).

Held, David, McGrew, Anthony, Goldblatt, David and Perraton, Jonathan 1999: *Global Transformations: Politics, Economics and Culture* (Cambridge: Polity/Stanford: Stanford University Press).

Helleiner, Eric 1994: *States and the Reemergence of Global Finance. From Bretton Woods to the 1990s* (Ithaca, NY: Cornell University Press).

Heller, Hermann 1983 [1934]: *Staatslehre,* revised edn (Tübingen: J. C. B. Mohr) (See also idem, *Gesammelte Schriften,* vol. 3: *Staatslehre als politische Wissenschaft* (Leiden: Sijthoff, 1971).

Henderson, David 1998: 'International Agencies and Cross-Border Liberalization: The WTO in Context'. In Krueger 1998, pp. 97–130.

Hennis, Wilhelm 2000 [1963]: *Politik und praktische Philosophie. Eine Studie zur Rekonstruktion der politischen Wissenschaft.* In idem, *Politikwissenschaft und politisches Denken. Politikwissenschaftliche Abhandlungen,* vol. 2 (Tübingen: J. C. B. Mohr), pp. 1–126.

Hennock, E. P. 1987: *British Social Reform and German Precedents. The Case of Social Insurance 1880–1914* (Oxford: Oxford University Press).

Henrekson, Magnus 2001: 'Swedish Economic Growth and Scholarly Objectivity. An Objective Sociologist vs. Subjective Economists or the Other Way Around?', *Challenge* 44/4: 38–58.

Henrekson, Magnus and Jakobsson, Ulf 2001: 'Where Schumpeter was nearly Right – the Swedish Model and Capitalism, Socialism and Democracy'. *Journal of Evolutionary Economics* 11/3: 331–58.

Henry, John F. 1983: 'John Bates Clark and the Marginal Product: An Historical Inquiry into the Origins of Value-free Economic Theory', *History of Political Economy* 15/3: 375–89.

Herz, Elicia J., Parizek Baumrucker, Evelyne and Gillespie, Jennifer 2000: 'Reaching Low-Income, Uninsured Children: Are Medicaid and SCHIP Doing the Job', Washington, DC: Congressional Research Service, 1 May (Order code RL 30556).

Hicks, Alexander M. 1999: *Social Democracy and Welfare Capitalism. A Century of Income Security Politics* (Ithaca, NY: Cornell University Press).

Higgott, Richard and Payne, Anthony, eds 2000: *The New Political Economy of Globalisation,* 2 vols (Cheltenham: Edward Elgar).

Higgs, Robert 1987: *Crisis and Leviathan. Critical Episodes in the Growth of American Government* (Oxford: Oxford University Press).

Hikino, Takashi and Amsden, Alice H. 1994: 'Staying Behind, Stumbling Back, Sneaking Up, Soaring Ahead: Late Industrialization in Historical Perspective'. In William J. Baumol, Richard R. Nelson and Edward N. Wolff, eds, *Convergence of Productivity. Cross-National Studies and Historical Evidence* (Oxford: Oxford University Press), pp. 281–315.

Hilf, Meinhard 1997: 'New Frontiers in International Trade: The Role of National Courts in International Trade Relations', *MJIL* 18 (Winter): 321–56.

Hilf, Meinhard and Petersmann, Ernst-Ulrich, eds 1993: *National Constitutions and International Economic Law* (Deventer, NL/Boston, MA: Kluwer Law and Taxation Publishers).

Hillman, Arye L. 1982: 'Declining Industries and Political-Support. Protectionist Motives', *AER* 72/5 (Dec): 1180–7.
——1989: *The Political Economy of Protection* (Chur, Switzerland Harwood Academic Publishers).
Hinrichs, Karl 2001: 'Elephants on the Move: Patterns of Public Pension Reform in OECD Countries'. In Leibfried 2001, pp. 77–102.
Hirschman, Albert O. 1970 *Exit, Voice, and Loyalty. Responses to Decline in Firms, Organizations, and States* (Cambridge, MA: Harvard University Press).
——1980 [1945]: *National Power and the Structure of Foreign Trade* (Berkeley/Los Angeles: University of California Press).
Hizon, Ernesto M. 1994: 'The Safeguard Measure/VER Dilemma: The Jekyll and Hyde of Trade Protection', *Northwestern Journal of International Law and Business* 15/1 (Fall): 105–38.
Hobson, John A. 1907: *The Fruit of American Protection. The Effects of the Dingley Tariff upon the Industries of the Country, and Especially upon the Well-being of the People* (London, UK: Cassell).
Hockerts, Hans Günter 1980: *Sozialpolitische Entscheidungen im Nachkriegsdeutschland. Alliierte und deutsche Sozialversicherungspolitik 1945 bis 1959* (Stuttgart: Klett-Cotta).
Hodge, Peter 1973: 'Social Policy: An Historical Perspective as Seen in Colonial Policy', *Journal of Oriental Studies* XI: 207–19.
Hody, Cynthia A. 1996: *The Politics of Trade. American Political Development and Foreign Economic Policy* (Hanover, NH/London: University Press of New England).
Hoekman, Bernard M. and Kostecki, Michel M. 2001: *The Political Economy of the World Trading System. The WTO and Beyond*, 2nd edn (Oxford: Oxford University Press).
Hoffmann, Walther (with Franz Grumbach and Helmut Hesse) 1965: *Das Wachstum der deutschen Wirtschaft seit der Mitte des 19. Jahrhunderts* (Berlin: Springer).
Hofstadter, Richard 1972 [1955]: *The Age of Reform: From Bryan to FDR* (New York: Knopf/Vintage Books).
Holla, Alaka 2001: 'Social Safety Nets and the IMF: The Socialization of an International Financial Institution', Providence RI: Brown University (Honors Thesis in the International Relations Program, on file with the authors).
Homann, Karl 1988: *Rationalität und Demokratie* (Tübingen: J. C. B. Mohr).
Homann, Karl and Pies, Ingo 1996: 'Sozialpolitik für den Markt. Theoretische Perspektiven konstitutioneller Ökonomik'. In Ingo Pies and Martin Leschke, eds, *James Buchanans konstitutionelle Ökonomie* (Tübingen: J. C. B. Mohr), pp. 203–23.
Hoover, Calvin Bryce 1945: *International Trade and Domestic Employment* (New York: McGraw-Hill).
Horlick, Gary N. and Clarke, Peggy A. 1997: 'Adjustments to the Administration of Antidumping Laws among NAFTA Members: Proposals and Suggestions'. In Hart 1997, pp. 143–220.
House of Commons 1999: 'Millennium Trade Talks and the "Battle in Seattle"', London, UK: House of Commons Library (Research Paper 99/107).
House of Representatives 2000: Committee on Ways and Means, *The 2000 Green Book. Background Material and Data on Programs within the Jurisdiction of the Committee on Ways and Means* (Washington, DC: US Government Printing Office; earlier version 1998) (http://www.access.gpo.gov/congress/wm001.html).
Howard, Christopher 1993: 'The Hidden Side of the American Welfare State', *Political Science Quarterly* 108/3 (Fall): 403–36.
——1997: *The Hidden Welfare State: Tax Expenditures and Social Policy in the United States* (Princeton, NJ: Princeton University Press).
Howenstine, Ned G. and Troia, Rosaria 2000: 'Foreign Direct Investment in the United States: New Investments in 1999', *Survey of Current Business* 80/6: 55–63.
Huber, Evelyne and Stephens, John D. 2001: *Political Choice in Global Markets: Development and Crisis of Advanced Welfare States* (Chicago: University of Chicago Press).

Huber, Max 1910: 'Beiträge zur Kenntnis der soziologischen Grundlagen des Völkerrechts und der Staatengesellschaft', *Jahrbuch des öffentlichen Rechts* 4: 56–134.

Hudec, Robert E. 1987: '"Transcending the Ostensible": Some Reflections on the Nature of Litigation between Governments', *Minnesota Law Review* 72/2 (Dec): 211–26.

——1993: *Enforcing International Trade Law: The Evolution of the Modern GATT Legal System* (Salem, NH: Butterworth).

——1996: 'International Economic Law: The Political Theatre Dimension', *University of Pennsylvania Journal of International Economic Law* 17/1 (Spring): 9–15.

——1999a: *Essays on the Nature of International Trade Law* (London, UK: Cameron May).

——1999b: 'The New Dispute Settlement Procedure: An Overview of the First Three Years', *Minnesota Journal of Global Trade* 8/1: 1–53.

——2000: 'Comment on Jackson [2000d]', *Brookings Trade Forum:* 220–31.

Hufbauer, Gary Clyde and Elliott, Kimberly A. 1994: *Measuring the Costs of Protection in the United States* (Institute for International Economics).

Huff, W. G. 1995: 'The Developmental State, Government, and Singapore's Economic Development Since 1960', *World Development* 23: 1421–38.

Hull, Cordell 1948: *The Memoirs of Cordell Hull*, 2 vols (New York: Macmillan).

Hume, David 1953: *Political Essays* (New York: Liberal Arts Press).

——1912 [1788]: *Essays Moral, Political, and Literary*, vol. I (London: Longmans, Green).

——1788a: 'Of Commerce'. In idem 1912, pp. 287–99.

——1788b: 'Of the Jealousie of Trade'. In idem 1912, pp. 345–48.

Hunger, Uwe 2001: 'Globalisierung auf dem Bau', *Leviathan* 29/1 (March): 70–82.

Huntington, Samuel P. 1968: *Political Order in Changing Societies* (New Haven, CT: Yale University Press).

——1996: *The Clash of Civilizations and the Remaking of World Order* (New York: Simon and Schuster).

Huntington, Samuel P. and Dominguez, Jorge I. 1975: 'Political Development'. In Fred I. Greenstein and Nelson W. Polsby, eds, *Handbook of Political Science*, vol. 3 (Reading MA: Addison-Wesley), pp. 1–114.

Hurwicz, Leonid 1973: 'The Design of Mechanisms for Resource Allocation', *AERPP* 63: 1–30.

Huston, James L. 1983: 'A Political Response to Industrialism: The Republican Embrace of Protectionist Labor Doctrines', *Journal of American History* 70/1 (June): 35–57.

Hüther, Michael 1997: 'Umbau der Sozialen Sicherungssysteme im Zeichen der Globalisierung?', *Zeitschrift für Wirtschaftspolitik* 46/2: 193–214.

Ignatius, David 2002: 'So Much For Backing Free Trade. Bush Caves on Steel Tariffs', *IHT* (9–10 March): 10.

Ikegami, Eiko 1995: *The Taming of the Samurai. Honorific Individualism and the Making of Modern Japan* (Cambridge, MA: Harvard University Press).

ILO (International Labour Office) 1997: *World Labour Report 1997–98* (Geneva: ILO Publications).

——2001: *World Employment Report 2001* (Geneva: ILO Publications).

IMF 1994: *World Economic Outlook* (Washington, DC: IMF).

——1997: *International Financial Statistics* (Washington, DC: IMF; monthly).

——1999a: *International Financial Statistics Yearbook* (Washington, DC: IMF; annually).

——1999b: *Government Finance Statistics Yearbook* (Washington, DC: IMF; annually).

Inman, Robert P. and Rubinfeld, Daniel L. 1997a: 'The Political Economy of Federalism'. In David Mueller, ed., *Perspectives on Public Choice: A Handbook* (Cambridge: Cambridge University Press), pp. 73–105.

——1997b: 'Rethinking Federalism', *JEP* 11/4 (Fall): 43–64.

Irwin, Douglas A. 1994: *Managed Trade. The Case Against Import Targets* (American Enterprise Institute).

——1996a: *Against the Tide. An Intellectual History of Free Trade* (Princeton, NJ: Princeton University Press).

——1996b: 'The United States in a New Global Economy? A Century's Perspective', *AERPP* 86/2 (May): 41–6.

Irwin, Douglas A. and Kroszner, Randall S. 1999: 'Interests, Institutions, and Ideology in Securing Policy Change: The Republican Conversion to Trade Liberalization after Smoot Hawley', *The Journal of Law and Economics* 42/2 (Fall): 643–73.

Iversen, Torben 2001: 'The Dynamics of Welfare State Expansion: Trade Openness, Deindustrialization, and Partisan Politics'. In Pierson 2001, pp. 45–79.

Iversen, Torben and Cusack, Thomas R. 2000: 'The Causes of Welfare State Expansion: Deindustrialization or Globalization?', *World Politics* 52/3 (Summer): 313–49.

Iversen, Torben and Soskice, David 2001: 'An Asset Theory of Social Policy Preferences', *APSR* 95/4 (Dec): 875–93.

Iversen, Torben and Wren, Anne 1998: 'Equality, Employment, and Budgetary Restraint – The Trilemma of the Service Economy', *World Politics* 50/4: 507–46.

Jackson, John Howard 1990: *Restructuring the GATT System* (London: Royal Institute of International Affairs).

——1992: 'Status of Treaties in Domestic Legal Systems: A Policy Analysis', *AmJIL* 86/2 (April): 310–40.

——1997a [1989]: *The World Trading System. Law and Policy of International Economic Relations* (Cambridge, MA: MIT Press).

——1997b: 'The Great 1994 Sovereignty Debate: United States Acceptance and Implementation of the Uruguay Round Results', *Columbia Journal of Transnational Law* 36/1/2: 157–88.

——2000a: *The Jurisprudence of GATT and the WTO: Insights on Treaty Law and Economic Relations* (Cambridge: Cambridge University Press).

——2000b: 'International Economic Law in Times That are Interesting', *JEL* 3/1 (March): 3–14.

——2000c: 'Dispute Settlement and a New Trade Round'. In Schott 2000, 269–82.

——2000d: 'The Role and Effectiveness of the WTO Dispute Settlement Mechanism', *Brookings Trade Forum:* 179–210.

Jackson, John Howard and Sykes, Alan O. Jr. 1997: *Implementing the Uruguay Round* (Oxford: Clarendon Press).

Jackson, John Howard, Davey, William J. and Sykes, Alan O. Jr. 2002 [1977]: *Legal Problems of International Economic Relations: Cases, Materials, and Texts on the National and International Regulation of Transnational Economic Relations* (St Paul, MN: West).

Jackson, Vicki C. 1998: 'Federalism and the Uses and Limits of Law: Printz and Principle?', *Harvard Law Review* 111/8 (June): 2180–259.

——2000: 'Seductions of Coherence, State Sovereign Immunity, and the Denationalization of Federal Law', *Rutgers Law Journal* 31/3 (Spring): 691–739.

Jacobs, Didier 1998: 'Social Welfare Systems in East Asia: A Comparative Analysis Including Private Welfare', London: LSE, Centre for Analysis of Social Exclusion (CASE Paper 10).

Jacoby, Sanford M. 1995: *The Workers of Nations: Industrial Relations in a Global Economy* (Oxford: Oxford University Press).

——1997: *Modern Manors. Welfare Capitalism Since the New Deal* (Princeton, NJ: Princeton University Press).

James, Harold 1996: *International Monetary Cooperation Since Bretton Woods* (Washington, DC: IMF/Oxford: Oxford University Press).

——2001: *End of Globalization: Lessons from the Great Depression* (Cambridge, MA: Harvard University Press).

James, William 1987 [1901–2]: 'The Varieties of Religious Experience'. In idem, *Writings 1902–1910* (New York: Library of America), pp. 1–477.

——1987 [1907]: 'Pragmatism. A New Way for Some Old Ways of Thinking. Popular Lectures on Philosophy'. In idem, *Writings 1902–1910* (New York: Library of America), pp. 479–624.

Janelli, Roger (with Dawhee Yim) 1993: *Making Capitalism. The Social and Cultural Construction of a South Korean Conglomerate* (Stanford: Stanford University Press).

Jänicke, Martin 1990: *State Failure. The Impotence of Politics in Industrial Society* (University Park, PA: Penn State Press).

Janowitz, Morris 1976: *Social Control of the Welfare State* (New York: Elsevier).

Jaspers, Karl 1957: *Die großen Philosophen* (München: Piper).

Jay, Peter 2000: *The Wealth of Man* (New York: Public Affairs).

Jellinek, Georg 1927 [1895]: *Die Erklärung der Menschen- und Bürgerrechte* (Berlin: Duncker and Humblot).

Jenkins, Rhys 1991: 'The Political Economy of Industrialization: A Comparison of Latin American and East Asian Newly Industrializing Countries', *Development and Change* 22: 197–231.

Jenks, Clarence Wilfred 1963: *Law, Freedom and Welfare* (New York/London, UK: Oceana/ Stevens).

Jensen, Merrill 1940: *The Articles of Confederation. An Interpretation of the Social-Constitutional History of the American Revolution 1774–1781* (Madison: University of Wisconsin Press).

Jensen, Michael C. and Meckling, William H. 1976: 'Theory of the Firm: Managerial Behavior, Agency Costs and Ownership Structure', *Journal of Financial Economics* 3/4: 305–60.

Jerger, Jürgen and Spermann, Alexander 1998: 'Alternative Subsidies for Low-Wage Employment'. In Addison and Welfens 1998, pp. 49–68.

Johnson, Nicholas and Lazere, Ed 1998: 'Rising Number of States Offer Earned Income Tax Credit', Washington, DC: Center on Budget and Social Priorities (http://www.cbpp.org/9-14-98sfp.htm).

Jones, Catherine 1990a: *Promoting Prosperity. The Hong Kong Way of Social Policy* (Hong Kong: The Chinese University Press).

——1990b: 'Hong Kong, Singapore, South Korea, and Taiwan: Oikonomic Welfare States', *Government and Opposition* 25: 446–62.

——1993: 'The Pacific Challenge'. In idem, ed., *New Perspectives on the Welfare State in Europe* (London: Routledge), pp. 198–217.

——ed. 2001: *Comparing the Social Policy Experience of Britain and Taiwan* (Aldershot: Ashgate).

Jones, Maldwyn Allen 1992 [1960]: *American Immigration* (Chicago: University of Chicago Press).

Jordan, Lisa and van Tuijl, Peter 2000: 'Political Responsibility in Transnational NGO Advocacy', *World Development* 28/12: 2051–65.

Josey, Stan 2000: 'Truckers Threaten to Park Rigs', *Toronto Star* (21 Nov): 1.

Kahler, Miles 1985: 'European Protectionism in Theory and Practice', *World Politics* 37/4 (July): 475–502.

——1995: *International Institutions and the Political Economy of Integration* (Washington, DC: Brookings Institution Press).

——2000: 'Conclusion: The Causes and Consequences of Legalization', *International Organization* 54/3 (Summer): 661–83 (also in Goldstein et al. 2001, pp. 277–99).

Kahn, Herman 1979: *World Economic Development: 1979 and Beyond* (Boulder CO: Westview Press).

Kahneman, David and Tversky, Amos 1979: 'Prospect Theory: An Analysis of Decisions under Risk', *Econometrica* 47/2 (March): 263–91.

Kamerman, Sheila B. and Kahn, Alfred J., eds 1997: 'Confronting the New Politics of Child and Family Policy in the United States, Report VI – Final Report: P. L. 104–93: Challenges and Opportunities' (New York: Cross-National Studies Research Program, Columbia University School of Social Work).

Kang, C. S. Eliot 1997: 'US. Politics and Greater Regulation of Inward Foreign Direct Investment', *International Organization* 51/2 (Spring): 301–33.

Kangas, Olli 1991: *The Politics of Social Rights. Studies on the Dimension of Sickness Insurance in OECD Countries* (Stockholm: Stockholm University, Swedish Institute for Social Research).

Kapstein, Ethan B. 1994: *Governing the Global Economy: International Finance and the State* (Cambridge, MA: Harvard University Press).

——1998: 'A Global Third Way: Social Justice and the World Economy', *World Policy Journal* 15/4: 23–34.

——1999: *Sharing the Wealth: Workers and the World Economy* (New York: W. W. Norton).

——2000: 'Winners and Losers in the Global Economy', *International Organization* 54/2 (Spring): 359–84.

Katz, Michael B. 1983: *Poverty and Policy in American History* (New York: Academic Press).

Katzenstein, Peter J., ed. 1978: *Between Power and Plenty: Foreign Economic Policies of Advanced Industrial States* (Madison: University of Wisconsin Press).

——1980: 'Capitalism in one Country? Switzerland in the International Economy', *International Organization* 34/4 (Fall): 507–40.

——1984: *Corporatism and Change. Austria, Switzerland, and the Politics of Industry* (Ithaca, NY: Cornell University Press).

——1985: *Small States in World Markets: Industrial Policy in Europe* (Ithaca, NY: Cornell University Press).

Katzenstein, Peter J., Keohane, Robert O. and Krasner, Stephen D., eds 1999: *Exploration and Contestation in the Study of World Politics* (Cambridge, MA: MIT Press).

Katznelson, Ira and Weir, Margaret 1985: *Schooling for All: Class, Race and the Decline of the Democratic Ideal* (New York: Basic Books).

Kauffman, Stuart 2000: *Investigations* (Oxford: Oxford University Press).

Kaufmann, Franz-Xaver 1997a: *Herausforderungen des Sozialstaates* (Frankfurt am Main: Suhrkamp).

——1997b: 'Verschwindet die integrative Funktion des Sozialstaates?', *Berliner Journal für Soziologie* 7/1: 5–22.

——2001a: 'Towards a Theory of the Welfare State'. In Leibfried 2001, pp. 15–36.

——2001b: 'Der Begriff Sozialpolitik und seine wissenschaftliche Deutung'. In BMA and Bundesarchiv 2001, vol. 1, pp. 3–101.

——2001c: 'Der deutsche Sozialstaat im internationalen Vergleich'. In BMA and Bundesarchiv 2001, vol. 1, pp. 799–989.

——2002: *Sozialpolitik und Sozialstaat. Soziologische Analysen* (Leverkusen/Opladen: Leske and Budrich).

Keck, Margaret E. and Sikkin, Kathryn 1998: *Activists Beyond Borders: Advocacy Networks in International Politics* (Ithaca, NY: Cornell University Press).

Keller, Bruce P. 1999: 'The Game's the Same: Why Gambling in Cyberspace Violates Federal Law', *Yale Law Journal* 108/7 (May): 1569–609.

Kennedy, David 1995: 'The International Style in Postwar Law and Policy. John Jackson and the Field of International Economic Law', *American University Journal of International Law and Policy* 10/X: 671–716.

Kennedy, David M. 1999: *Freedom From Fear: The American People in Depression and War, 1929–1945* (Oxford: Oxford University Press).

Kennedy, Paul Michael 1998 [1980]: *The Rise of the Anglo-German Antagonism, 1860–1914* (London: Allen and Unwin).

Keohane, Robert Owen 1982: 'The Demand for International Regimes', *International Organization* 36/2 (Spring): 325–55.

——1989: *International Institutions and State Power. Essays in International Relations Theory* (Boulder, CO: Westview).

——2002: *Power and Governance in a Partially Globalized World* (London: Routledge).

Keohane, Robert Owen and Milner, Helen V., eds 1996: *Internationalization and Domestic Politics* (Cambridge: Cambridge University Press).

Keohane, Robert Owen and Nye, Joseph S. Jr., 1974: 'Transgovernmental Relations and International Organizations', *World Politics* 27/1 (Oct): 39–62.
——1989: *Power and Interdependence*, 2nd edn (Glenview, IL: Scott and Foresman).
——2000: 'Globalization: What's New? What's Not? (And So What?)', *Foreign Policy* 118 (Spring): 104–19.
——2001: *Power and Interdependence*, 3rd edn (New York: Longman).
Kerr, William 2001: 'Dumping – One of Those Economic Myths', *Estey Centre Journal of International Law and Trade Policy* 2/2: 211–20.
Kersbergen, Kees van 1995: *Social Capitalism. A Study of Christian Democracy and the Welfare State* (London: Routledge).
Kessie, Edwini 2000: 'Enhancing Security and Predictability for Private Business Operators under the Dispute Settlement System of the WTO', *JWT* 34/6: 1–17.
Keynes, John Maynard 1933: 'National Self-Sufficiency'. In Donald Moggridge, ed., *The Collected Writings of John Maynard Keynes*, vol. XXI: *Activities 1931–1939. World Crises and Policies in Britain and North America* (Cambridge: Cambridge University Press, 1982), pp. 233–46.
——1988 [1920]: *The Economic Consequences of the Peace* (New York: Harcourt, Brace and Howe).
Keyssar, Alexander 2000: *The Right to Vote: The Contested History of Democracy in the United States* (New York: Basic Books).
Kieser, Alfred 1998: 'Über die allmähliche Verfertigung der Organisation beim Reden. Organisieren als Kommunizieren', *Industrielle Beziehungen* 5: 45–75.
Kieserman, Brad J. 1999: 'Profits and Principles: Promoting Multinational Corporate Responsibility by Amending the Alien Tort Claims Act', *Catholic University Law Review* 48/3 (Spring): 881–937.
Kim, Hwanjoon 2000: 'Anti-Poverty Effectiveness of Taxes and Income Transfers in Welfare States', Luxembourg Income Study (Working Paper 228).
Kindleberger, Charles Poor 1951: 'Group Behavior and International Trade', *JPE* 59/1 (Feb): 30–47.
——1975: 'The Rise of Free Trade in Western Europe, 1820–1875', *JEH* 35/1 (March): 20–55.
——1986a [1973]: *The World in Depression: 1929–1939* (Berkeley/Los Angeles: University of California Press).
——1986b: 'International Public Goods without International Government', *AER* 76/1 (March): 1–13.
——1996: *World Economic Primacy, 1500–1990* (Oxford: Oxford University Press).
——2000: *Comparative Political Economy: A Retrospective* (Cambridge, MA: MIT Press).
Kinsley, Michael 2000: 'Lies the Press Likes', *The Washington Post* (10 Oct): A25.
Kirsch, Guy, ed. 1977: *Föderalismus* (Stuttgart: Fischer; Wirtschaftswiss. Seminar 5).
Kitschelt, Herbert 2001: 'Partisan Competition and Welfare State Retrenchment: When Do Politicians Choose Unpopular Policies?'. In Pierson 2001, pp. 265–302.
Kitschelt, Herbert, Lange, Peter M., Marks, Gary W. and Stephens, John D., eds 1999: *Continuity and Change in Contemporary Capitalism* (Cambridge: Cambridge University Press).
Klein, Rudolf 1983: *The Politics of the National Health Service* (London: Longman).
Kletzer, Lori G. and Litan, Robert E. 2001: 'A Prescription to Relieve Worker Anxiety', *International Economic Policy Briefs* 01–2 (Washington, DC: Institute for International Economics).
Knight, Frank H. 1947: 'Liberalism and Christianity'. In idem and Thornton W. Merriam, eds, *The Economic Order and Religion* (London: Kegan Paul, Trench, Trubner and Co.), pp. 9–101.
——1951: 'The Role of Principles in Economics and Politics', *AER* 41/1 (March): 1–29.
——1966: 'Abstract Economics as Absolute Ethics', *Ethics* 76: 163–77.
——1972 [1941]: 'Social Science', *Ethics* 83/1 (Oct): 1–12.
Knorr, Klaus Eugen 1947a: 'The Bretton Woods Institutions in Transition', *International Organization* 2/1 (Feb): 19–38.

——1947b: 'Economics and International Relations: A Problem in Teaching', *Political Science Quarterly* 62/4 (Dec): 552–68.
——1951a: 'The European Welfare State in the Atlantic System', *World Politics* 3/4 (July): 417–49.
——1951b: 'Welfare State Measures and the Free Market in International Trade', *AERPP* 41/2 (May): 431–44.
Kobayashi, Hideo 1996: 'The Postwar Economic Legacy of Japan's Wartime Empire'. In Duus et al. 1996, pp. 324–4.
Kohli, Atul 1994: 'Where Do High Growth Political Economies Come From? The Japanese Lineage of Korea's "Developmental State"', *World Development* 22: 1269–93.
——1997: 'Japanese Colonialism and Korean Development: A Reply', *World Development* 25: 883–8.
Kohli, Martin 2000: 'Arbeit im Lebenslauf: Alte und neue Paradoxien'. In Jürgen Kocka and Claus Offe (with Beate Redslob), eds, *Geschichte und Zukunft der Arbeit* (Frankfurt am Main: Campus Verlag), pp. 362–82.
Konfuzius 1998: *Gespräche (Lun-yu)*, trans. and ed. Ralf Moritz (Stuttgart: Reclam).
Kono, Makoto 2000: 'The Impact of Modernization and Social Policy on Family Care for Older People in Japan', *JSP* 29/2: 181–203.
Koo, Hagen 1993: 'Strong State and Contentious Society'. In idem, ed., *State and Society in Contemporary Korea* (Ithaca, NY: Cornell University Press), pp. 231–49.
Kornai, Janos, Haggard, Stephan and Kaufman, Robert R., eds 2001: *Reforming the State: Fiscal and Welfare Reform in Post-Socialist Countries* (Cambridge: Cambridge University Press).
Korpi, Walter 1996: 'Eurosclerosis and the Sclerosis of Objectivity: On the Role of Values Among Economic Policy Experts', *Economic Journal* 106/439 (Nov): 1727–46.
——2000: 'Welfare States, Economic Growth and Scholarly Objectivity', *Challenge* 43/2 (March/April): 49–66.
Korpi, Walter and Palme, Joakim 1998: 'The Strategy of Equality and the Paradox of Redistribution', *American Sociological Review* 63/5: 661–87.
Koschman, J. Victor 1996: *Revolution and Subjectivity in Postwar Japan* (Chicago: University of Chicago Press).
Koslowski, Peter 1988: *Prinzipien ethischer Ökonomie. Grundlegung der Wirtschaftsethik und der auf die Ökonomie bezogenen Ethik* (Tübingen: J. C. B. Mohr).
Kostel, Mary E. 1993: 'A Public Choice Perspective on the Debate over Federal Versus State Corporate Law', *Virginia Law Review* 79/8 (Nov): 2129–54.
Koulen, Mark 1995: 'The New Antidumping Code Through Its Negotiation History'. In Jacques H. J. Bourgeois, Frederique Berrod and Eric Gippini Fournier, eds, *The Uruguay Round Results: An European Lawyers' Perspective* (Brussels: European Interuniversity Press), pp. 151–246.
Kramer, Larry D. 2000: 'Putting the Politics Back into the Political Safeguards of Federalism', *Columbia Law Review* 100/1 (Jan): 215–93.
Krasner, Stephen D., ed. 1983: *International Regimes* (Ithaca, NY: Cornell University Press).
——1999: 'Globalization and Sovereignty'. In David Smith, Dorothy Solinger and Steven Topik, eds, *States and Sovereignty in the Global Economy* (London: Routledge), pp. 34–52.
——2001: 'Abiding Sovereignty', *International Political Science Review* 22/3: 229–51.
Krause, Lawrence B. 1989: 'Changes in the International System: The Pacific Basin', *Annals* 505: 105–16.
Krauss, Melvyn B. 1997: *How Nations Grow Rich: The Case for Free Trade* (Oxford: Oxford University Press).
Kreider, Carl 1940: 'International Affairs: Democratic Processes in the Trade Agreements Program', *APSR* 34/2 (April): 317–32.
——1943: *The Anglo-American Trade Agreement. A Study of British and American Commercial Policies, 1934–1939* (Princeton, NJ: Princeton University Press).

Krieger, Silke and Trauzettel, Rolf, eds. 1990: *Konfuzianismus und die Modernisierung Chinas* (Mainz: v. Haase and Koehler).

Kristof, Nicholas D. and WuDunn, Sheryl 2000: *Thunder from the East: Portrait of a Rising Asia* (New York: Alfred A. Knopf).

Kroeber, Alfred Louis and Kluckhohn, Clyde 1952: *Culture: A Critical Review of Concepts and Definitions* (Cambridge, MA: Papers of the Peabody Museum, Harvard University, vol. 47, no. 1).

Krongkaew, Medhi 1994: 'Income Distribution in East Asian Developing Countries: An Update', *Asian-Pacific Economic Literature* 8: 58–73.

Krueger, Alan B. 1991: 'The Evolution of Unjust Dismissal Legislation in the United States', *Industrial and Labour Relations Review* 44/4 (July): 644–60.

Krueger, Anne O. 1974: 'The Political Economy of the Rent-Seeking Society', *AER* 64/3 (June): 291–303.

——1995: *American Trade Policy: A Tragedy in the Making* (Washington, DC: American Enterprise Institute Press).

——1997: 'Trade Policy and Economic Development: How we Learn', *AER* 87/1 (March): 1–22.

——(with Chouira Aturupane), ed. 1998: *The WTO as an International Organization* (Chicago: University of Chicago Press).

Krugman, Paul R. 1987: 'Is Free Trade Passé?', *JEP* 1/2 (Fall): 131–44.

——1990: *Rethinking International Trade* (Cambridge, MA: MIT Press).

——1993: 'The Narrow and the Broad Arguments for Free Trade', *AERPP* 83/2 (May): 362–66.

——1995: *Growing World Trade: Causes and Consequences* (Washington, DC: Brookings Institution Press), *Papers on Economic Activity*, vol. l, pp. 327–77.

——1996: *Pop Internationalism* (Cambridge, MA: MIT Press).

——1997: 'What Should Trade Negotiators Negotiate About?', *JEL* 35/1 (March): 113–20.

——2001: 'Going Fiscal', *NYT* (10 Jan): A-23.

Krugman, Paul R. and Lawrence, Robert Z. 1994: 'Trade, Jobs, and Wages', *Scientific American* 270/4: 44–9. (An extended version can be found in NBER 1993, Working paper 4478.)

Krugman, Paul R. and Obstfeld, Maurice 2002: *International Economics: Theory and Policy*, 6th edn (Boston, MA: Addison-Wesley).

Ku, Yeun-wen 1997: *Welfare Capitalism in Taiwan. State, Economy and Social Policy* (Houndmills, Basingstoke: Macmillan/New York: St Martin's Press).

——1998: 'Can We Afford It? The Development of National Health Insurance in Taiwan'. In Goodman et al. 1998, pp. 119–38.

Kuper, Adam 1999: *Culture. The Anthropologists' Account* (Cambridge, MA: Harvard University Press).

Kuznets, Paul W. 1988: 'An East Asian Model of Economic Development: Japan, Taiwan, and South Korea', *Economic Development and Cultural Change* 36: S11–43.

Kwok, D. W. Y. 1998: 'On the Rites and Rights of Being Human'. In Bary and Weiming 1998, pp. 83–93.

Kwon, Huck-ju 1997: 'Beyond European Welfare Regimes. Comparative Perspectives on East Asian Welfare Regimes', *JSP* 26: 467–84.

——1998a: 'Democracy and the Politics of Social Welfare: A Comparative Analysis of Welfare Systems in East Asia'. In Goodman et al. 1998, pp. 27–74.

——1998b: 'The South Korean National Pension Programme: Fulfilling its Promise?' In Goodman et al. 1998, pp. 106–18.

——1999a: *The Welfare State in Korea: The Politics of Legitimation* (London: Macmillan).

——1999b: 'Inadequate Policy or Operational Failure? The Potential Crisis of the Korean National Pension Programme', *Social Policy and Administration* 33/1: 20–38.

——2001: 'Income Transfers to the Elderly in Korea and Taiwan', *JSP* 30/1: 81–93.

Lake, David A. 1988a: 'The State and American Trade Strategy in the Pre-Hegemonic Era', *International Organization* 42/1 (Winter): 33–58.
——1988b: *Power, Protection, and Free Trade. International Sources of U.S. Commercial Strategy, 1887–1939* (Ithaca, NY: Cornell University Press).
Lampert, Heinz 1994: *Lehrbuch der Sozialpolitik*, 3rd edn (Berlin: Springer; 5th edn 1998).
——1995: 'Voraussetzungen einer Sozialstaatsreform – Kritische Anmerkungen zur aktuellen Diskussion über den Umbau des Sozialstaates', *Jahrbücher für Nationalökonomie und Statistik* 214/5: 513–31.
——1999: 'Der Sozialstaat: Auslaufmodell oder Leitbild der Zukunft?' In Gerhard Kleinhenz, ed., *Mehr Beschäftigung für Deutschland: Ordnungs- und wirtschaftspolitische Ansätze* (Nürnberg: Institut für Arbeitsmarkt- und Berufsforschung der Bundesanstalt für Arbeit, pp. 11–42 (*Beiträge zur Arbeitsmarkt- und Berufsforschung* 224).
Langille, Brian Alexander 1996: 'General Reflections on the Relationship of Trade and Labor (Or: Fair Trade is Free Trade's Destiny)'. In Bhagwati and Hudec 1996, vol. II, pp. 231–66.
Larkin, John Day 1937: 'The Trade Agreement Act in Court and in Congress', *ASR* 31/3 (June): 498–507.
Laski, Harold J. 1933: *Democracy in Crisis* (Chapel Hill: University of North Carolina Press).
Lastra, Rosa Maria 2000: 'The International Monetary Fund in Historical Perspective', *JEL* 3/3 (Sept): 507–23.
Lavery, Brian 2001: 'Trade Feud on Bananas Not as Clear as It looks', *NYT* (7 Feb).
Lawrence, Robert Z. 1997: 'Current Economic Policies: Social Implications over the Long Term'. In OECD 1997, pp. 27–38.
Lazear, Edward P. 1990: 'Job Security Provisions and Employment', *Quarterly Journal of Economics* 105/3 (Aug): 699–726.
Leamer, Edward E. 2000: 'Foreigners and Robots: Assistants of Some, Competitors of Others'. In Deardorff and Stern 2000, pp. 19–58.
Leary, Virginia A. 1996: 'Workers' Rights and International Trade: The Social Clause (GATT, ILO; NAFTA, U.S. Laws)'. In Bhagwati and Hudec 1996, vol. II, pp. 177–230.
Ledyard, John O. 1989: 'Incentive Compatibility'. In John Eatwell, Murray Milgate and Peter Newman, eds, *Allocation, Information, and Markets* (New York and London: Norton), pp. 141–51.
Lee, Frances E. and Oppenheimer, Bruce I. 1999: *Sizing Up the Senate. The Unequal Consequences of Equal Representation* (Chicago: University of Chicago Press).
Lee, Hye Kyung 1992: 'Development of the Welfare State in an Authoritarian Capitalist Society: The Korean Experience'. Unpublished paper, prepared for the International Conference on Social Welfare: 'Welfare State: Present and Future', organized by the Korean Academy of Social Welfare, 25–6 Sept.
——1994: 'Social Security in South Korea: Programs and Policy Issues', Yonsei University, Seoul, unpublished paper.
Lee, Maw-Lin, Liu, Ben-Chieh and Wang, Ping 1994: 'Education, Human Capital Enhancement and Economic Development: Comparison Between Korea and Taiwan', *Economics of Education Review* 13: 275–88.
Leibfried, Stephan 1994: '"Sozialstaat" oder "Wohlfahrtsgesellschaft"? Thesen zu einem japanisch-deutschen Sozialpolitikvergleich', *Soziale Welt* 45: 389–410.
——ed. 2001: *Welfare State Futures* (Cambridge: Cambridge University Press).
Leibfried, Stephan and Obinger, Herbert 2001: 'Welfare State Futures. An Introduction'. In Leibfried 2001, pp. 1–13.
Leibfried, Stephan and Pierson, Paul, eds 1995: *European Social Policy: Between Fragmentation and Integration* (Washington, DC: Brookings Institution Press).
Leibfried, Stephan and Pierson, Paul 2000: 'Social Policy. Left to Courts and Markets?'. In Wallace and Wallace 2000, pp. 267–92.

Leibfried, Stephan and Wagschal, Uwe, eds 2000: *Der deutsche Sozialstaat. Bilanzen – Reformen – Perspektiven* (Frankfurt am Main: Campus Verlag).

Leibfried, Stephan, Müller, Rainer, Schmähl, Winfried and Schmidt, Manfred G. 1998: 'Thesen zur Sozialpolitik in Deutschland', *Zeitschrift für Sozialreform* 44/8 (Aug): 525–69.

Leipziger, Danny and Dollar, David 1992: *The Distribution of Income and Wealth in Korea* (Washington DC: World Bank; EDI Development Studies).

Leisering, Lutz 1992: *Sozialstaat und demographischer Wandel. Wechselwirkungen, Generationenverhältnisse, politisch-institutionelle Steuerung* (Frankfurt am Main: Campus Verlag).

——1995: 'Grenzen des Sozialversicherungsstaats? Sozialer Wandel als Herausforderung staatlicher Einkommenssicherung', *Zeitschrift für Sozialreform* 41/11/12 (Nov/Dec): 860–80.

Leisering, Lutz and Leibfried, Stephan 1999: *Time and Poverty in Western Welfare States. United Germany in Perspective* (Cambridge: Cambridge University Press).

Leisering, Lutz and Walker, Robert, eds 1998: *The Dynamics of Modern Society. Poverty, Policy and Welfare* (Bristol: The Policy Press).

Lenski, Gerhard E. 1966: *Power and Privilege: A Theory of Social Stratification* (New York: McGraw-Hill; 2nd edn, Chapel Hill: University of North Carolina Press, 1984).

Lepsius, M. Rainer 1979: 'Soziale Ungleichheit und Klassenstruktur in der Bundesrepublik Deutschland'. In Hans-Ulrich Wehler, ed., *Klassen in der europäischen Sozialgeschichte* (Göttingen: Vandenhoeck and Ruprecht), pp. 166–209.

——1986: 'Interessen und Ideen. Die Zurechnungsproblematik bei Max Weber'. In Friedhelm Neidhardt, M. Rainer Lepsius and Johannes Weiß, eds, *Kultur und Gesellschaft* (Opladen/Wiesbaden: Westdeutscher Verlag; *Kölner Zeitschrift für Soziologie und Sozialpsychologie* special issue 27), pp. 20–31.

Lerman, Robert I. 1999: 'Retreat or Reform? New US Strategies for Dealing with Poverty?', *Social Policy Review* 11: 224–43.

Lessenich, Stephan and Ostner, Ilona, eds 1998: *Welten des Wohlfahrtskapitalismus. Der Sozialstaat in vergleichender Perspektive* (Frankfurt am Main: Campus Verlag).

Levy, Frank 1998: *The New Dollars and Dreams. American Incomes and Economic Change* (New York: Russell Sage Foundation Press).

Levy, Hermann 1905: 'Die Entwicklungsgeschichte einer amerikanischen Industrie. Studien über den Einfluß der Zolltarife und Trusts auf die Weissblechindustrie der Vereinigten Staaten', *Jahrbücher für Nationalökonomie und Statistik* 84 (NF III 29): 145–81.

Levy, Marion J. 1995: 'Confucianism and Modernization'. In Yu and Lee 1995, pp. 205–14.

Lewin, Tamara 2000: 'Suit Asks Coverage for the Pill. Company's Insurance Plan is Called Sexually Biased', *IHT* (21 July): 3

Lewis, Verne B. 1952: 'Towards a Theory of Budgeting', *Public Administration Review* 12/1 (Winter): 42–54.

Lichtblau, Eric 2000: 'Cheney's Standard of Living Soars in Private Sector', *Los Angeles Times* (19 Oct): A22.

Liefmann, Robert 1897: *Die Unternehmerverbände (Konventionen, Kartelle), ihr Wesen und ihre Bedeutung* (Tübingen: J. C. B. Mohr).

Lindauer, David L., Kim, Jong-Gie, Lee, Joung-Woo and Vogel, Ezra F. 1997: *The Strains of Economic Growth: Labor Unrest and Social Dissatisfaction in Korea* (Cambridge MA: Harvard Institute for International Development and Korea Development Institute/ Cambridge, MA: Harvard University Press).

Lindbeck, Assar 1997: 'The Swedish Experiment', *JEL* 35/3 (Sept): 1273–319.

——2001: 'Changing Tides for the Welfare State – An Essay', Stockholm: The Research Institute of Industrial Economics (Working paper 550).

Lindbeck, Assar and Snower, Dennis J. 1996: 'Reorganization of Firms and Labor-Market Inequality', *AERPP* 86/2 (May): 315–21.

Lindblom, Charles Edward 1959: 'The Science of "Muddling Through"', *Public Administration Review* 19/2 (Autumn): 79–88.

——1982: 'The Market As Prison', *The Journal of Politics* 44: 324–36.
——2001: *The Market System: What It Is, How It Works, and What To Make of It* (New Haven, CT: Yale University Press).
Lindert, Peter H. and Williamson, Jeffrey G. 2002: 'Does Globalization Make the World More Unequal?'. In Michael D. Bordo, Alan Taylor and Jeffrey G. Williamson, eds, *Globalization in Historical Perspective* (Chicago: University of Chicago Press).
Lindlar, Ludger 1995: 'Internationale Wettbewerbsfähigkeit der südostasiatischen Schwellen- und Entwicklungsländer', *Vierteljahreshefte zur Wirtschaftsforschung* 64: 303–22.
Lippmann, Walter 1937: *The Good Society* (Boston: Little, Brown).
Lipset, Seymour Martin 1959: 'Some Social Requisites of Democracy', *APSR* 53: 69–105.
Lipset, Seymour Martin and Salman Lenz, Gabriel 2000: 'Corruption, Culture, and Markets'. In Samuel P. Huntington and Lawrence E. Harrison, eds, *Culture Matters. How Values Shape Human Progress* (New York: Basic Books), pp. 112–24.
List, Friedrich 1930 [1841]: *Das nationale System der politischen Ökonomie* (Berlin: Hobbing).
Litan, Robert E. 2000: 'US Trade Policy and the World Trade Organization. Interview with Robert E. Litan', *Georgetown Public Policy Review* 5/X: 127–34.
Little, Steven R. 1999: 'Corporate Welfare Wars: The Insufficiency of Current Constraints on State Action and the Desirability of a Federal Legislative Response', *Hamline Law Review* 22/3 (Spring): 849–96.
Livingston, James 1997: *Pragmatism and the Political Economy of Cultural Revolution, 1850–1940* (Chapel Hill: University of North Carolina Press).
Locke, John 1996 [1689]: *Ein Brief über Toleranz* (Hamburg: Meiner).
Lødemel, Ivar (with Heather Trickey), eds 2001: *'An Offer You Can't Refuse'. Workfare in International Perspective* (Bristol: Policy Press).
Long, William J. 1989: *US Export Control Policy: Executive Autonomy vs. Congressional Reform* (New York: Columbia University Press).
Lotz, Walther 1902: 'Wirkung der gegenwärtigen und Ziele der zukünftigen Handelspolitik, insbesondere in socialpolitischer Hinsicht'. In *Schriften des Vereins für Socialpolitik*, vol. XCVIII (Verhandlungen der Generalversammlung des Vereins für Socialpolitik über die Wohnungsfrage und die Handelspolitik in München, 23, 24 and 25 Sept 1901) (Leipzig/Berlin: Duncker and Humblot), pp. 121–52.
Lovett, William Anthony 1999: 'Rebalancing US Trade'. In idem, Alfred E. Eckes, Jr. and Richard L. Brinkman, eds, *US Trade Policy: History, Theory, and the WTO* (Armonk, NY: M. E. Sharpe), pp. 136–82.
Lowenfeld, Andreas F. 1994: 'Remedies Along with Rights: Institutional Reform in the New GATT', *AmJIL* 88/3 (July): 477–88.
Luck, Edward C. 1999: *Mixed Messages. American Politics and International Organization 1919–1999* (Washington, DC: Brookings Institution Press).
Luhmann, Niklas 1981: 'Subjektive Rechte: Zum Umbau des Rechtsbewußtseins für die moderne Gesellschaft'. In idem, *Gesellschaftsstruktur und Semantik. Studien zur Wissenssoziologie der modernen Gesellschaft,* vol. 2 (Frankfurt am Main: Suhrkamp), pp. 45–104.
——1989: 'Individuum, Individualität, Individualismus'. In idem, *Gesellschaftsstruktur und Semantik. Studien zur Wissenssoziologie der modernen Gesellschaft,* vol. 3 (Frankfurt am Main: Suhrkamp), pp. 149–258.
——1990: *Political Theory in the Welfare State* (Berlin and New York: Walter de Gruyter).
Lukes, Steven 1971: 'The Meaning of "Individualism"', *Journal of the History of Ideas* 32/1 (Jan/March): 45–66.
——1973: *Individualism* (New York/Oxford: Harper and Row/Blackwell).
——1992: 'On Trade-Off Between Values', Florence: European University Institute (EUI, Working paper in Political and Social Science 92/24).
Lunch, William M. 1987: *The Nationalization of American Politics* (Berkeley/Los Angeles: University of California Press).

Lusardi, Annamaria 2001: 'Explaining Why So Many People Do Not Save', Boston: Boston College (Center for Retirement Research at Boston College, Working paper 2001–05).

Lusztig, Michael 1996: *Risking Free Trade. The Politics of Trade in Britain, Canada, Mexico, and the United States* (Pittsburgh, PA: University of Pittsburgh Press).

Luttwag, Edward 1999: *Turbo Capitalism: Winners and Losers in the Global Economy* (London: Oriel Publishers; New York: The Free Press).

MacLeod, W. Bentley 1995: 'Incentives in Organizations: An Overview of Some of the Evidence and Theory'. In Horst Siebert, ed., *Trends in Business Organization: Do Participation and Cooperation Increase Competitiveness?* (Kiel Institute for World Economics, Tübingen: J. C. B. Mohr), pp. 3–42.

Macpherson, C. B. 1964: *The Political Theory of Possessive Individualism* (Oxford: Clarendon Press).

Maddison, Angus 1991: *Dynamic Forces in Capitalist Development. A Long-run Comparative View* (Oxford: Oxford University Press).

——1995: *Monitoring the World Economy, 1820–1992* (Paris: OECD).

Madison, James 1987 [1787]: *Notes of Debates in the Federal Convention of 1787* (New York/London: Norton).

Madrick, Jeff 2002: 'For Most in US, No Pension Windfalls', *IHT* (22 Feb): 13.

Magee, Stephen P. and Young, Leslie 1987: 'Endogenous Protection in the United States, 1900–1984'. In Robert Mitchell Stern, ed., *U.S. Trade Policies in a Changing World Economy* (Cambridge, MA: MIT Press), pp. 145–95.

Magee, Stephen P., Brock, William A. and Young, Leslie 1989: *Black Hole Tariffs and Endogenous Policy Theory: Political Economy in General Equilibrium* (Cambridge: Cambridge University Press).

Magnusson, Lars 1994: *Mercantilism. The Shaping of an Economic Language* (London: Routledge).

Maier, Harold G. 1982: 'Extraterritorial Jurisdiction at a Crossroads: An Intersection between Public and Private Interest International Law', *AmJIL* 76/2 (Apr): 280–320.

Mandeville, Bernard 1988 [1724]: *The Fable of the Bees. Or Private Vices, Publick Benefits* (Indianapolis, IN: Liberty Press).

Mann, Michael 1988: *States, War and Capitalism* (Oxford: Blackwell).

Manne, Henry G. 1965: 'Mergers and the Market for Corporate Control', *JPE* 73/2 (April): 110–20.

Manow, Philip 2001: 'Social Protection, Capitalist Production: The Bismarckian Welfare State and the German Political Economy from the 1880s to the 1990s', Konstanz: University (Habilitation, 17 July).

Manow, Philip and Seils, Eric 2000: 'Adjusting Badly: The German Welfare State, Structural Change, and the Open Economy'. In Scharpf and Schmidt 2000, pp. 264–307.

Margulis-Ohnuma, Zachary 1999: 'The Unavoidable Correlative: Extraterritorial Power and the United States Constitution', *New York University Journal of International Law and Politics* 32/1 (Fall): 147–203.

Marin, Bernd, Meulders, Daniele and Snower, Dennis J., eds 2000: *Innovative Employment Initiatives* (Aldershot, UK/Brookfield, VT: Ashgate).

Markusen, James R. 1995: 'The Boundaries of Multinational Enterprises and the Theory of International Trade', *JEP* 9/2 (Spring): 169–89.

Marmor, Theodore R. 2000 [1970]: *Politics of Medicare*, 2nd edn (New York: de Gruyter).

Marmor, Theodore R., Mashaw, Jerry L. and Harvey, Philip L. 1990: *America's Misunderstood Welfare State. Persistent Myths, Enduring Realities* (New York: Basic Books).

Marsh, Robert M. 1996: *The Great Transformation. Social Change in Taipei, Taiwan Since the 1960s* (Armonk, NY/London: M. E. Sharpe).

Marshall, T. H. 1938: 'The Nature of Class Conflict'. In idem 1964a, pp. 164–73.

——1945: 'Work and Wealth'. In idem 1964a, pp. 209–25.

——1949: 'Citizenship and Social Class'. In idem 1964a, pp. 65–122.
——1953: 'Social Selection in the Welfare State'. In idem 1964a, pp. 235–55.
——1961a: 'The Welfare State – a Comparative Study'. In idem 1964a, pp. 277–95.
——1961b: 'The Welfare State and the Affluent Society'. In idem 1964a, pp. 256–76.
——1962: 'International Comprehension in and through Social Science'. In idem 1964a, pp. 42–61.
——1964a: *Class, Citizenship, and Social Development. Essays* (Garden City, NY: Doubleday).
——1964b: 'Changing Ideas about Poverty'. In idem 1981, pp. 29–49.
——1965: 'The Right to Welfare'. In idem 1981, pp. 83–94.
——1969: 'Reflections on Power'. In idem 1981, pp. 137–53.
——1972: 'Value Problems of Welfare Capitalism'. In idem 1981, pp. 104–22.
——1981: *The Right to Welfare and Other Essays* (New York: Free Press).
——1985 [1965]: *Social Policy in the 20th Century*, ed. A. M. Rees (London, UK: Hutchinson).
Martin, Mitchell 2002: 'A Cost Crunch for Pension Plans', *IHT* (24 April): 11.
Marx, Karl 1848: 'Rede über die Frage des Freihandels'. In idem and Friedrich Engels *Werke*, vol. 4 (Berlin: Dietz, 1959), pp. 444–58.
——1977 [1867]: *Capital. A Critique of Political Economy*, vol. 1 (New York: Random House).
Marx, Karl and Engels, Friedrich 1998 [1848]: *Manifesto of the Communist Party* (London: Verso).
Maskus, Keith E. 2000: 'Regulatory Standards in the WTO. Comparing Intellectual Property Rights with Competition Policy, Environmental Protection and Core Labor Standards', Washington, DC: Institute for International Economics (Working paper 00–1).
Mason, Alpheus Thomas 1969 [1925]: *Organized Labor and the Law, with Especial Reference to the Sherman and Clayton Acts* (New York: Arno).
Mason, Timothy 1978: *Sozialpolitik im Dritten Reich* (Opladen/Wiesbaden: Westdeutscher Verlag).
Mataloni, Raymond J. Jr. 2000: 'An Examination of the Low Rates of Return of Foreign-Owned US Companies', *Survey of Current Business* 80/3: 55–73.
Matthes, Joachim 1993: 'Was ist anders an anderen Religionen? Anmerkungen zur zentristischen Organisation des religionssoziologischen Denkens'. In Jörg Bergmann, Alois Hahn and Thomas Luckmann, eds, *Religion und Kultur* (Opladen/Wiesbaden: Westdeutscher Verlag), pp. 16–30.
Matthews, Jessica Tuchman 1997: 'Power Shift', *Foreign Affairs* 76/1 (Jan/Feb): 50–66.
Mayer, Karl-Ulrich ed. 2001a: *Die beste aller Welten? Marktliberalismus versus Wohlfahrtsstaat. Eine Kontroverse* (Frankfurt am Main: Campus Verlag).
——2001b: 'The Paradox of Global Social Change and National Path Dependencies. Life Course Patterns in Advanced Societies'. In Alison E. Woodward and Martin Kohli, eds, *Inclusions/Exclusions* (London: Routledge), pp. 89–110.
Mayer, Karl-Ulrich and Müller, Walter 1986: 'The State and the Structure of the Life Course'. In Aage B. Sørensen, Franz E. Weinert and Lonnie R. Sherrod, eds, *Human Development and the Life Course: Multidisciplinary Perspectives* (Hillsdale, NJ: Erlbaum), pp. 217–45.
——and Müller, Walter 1989: 'Lebensverläufe im Wohlfahrtsstaat'. In Ansgar Weymann, ed., *Handlungsspielräume. Untersuchungen zur Individualisierung und Institutionalisierung von Lebensverläufen in der Moderne* (Stuttgart: Enke), pp. 41–60.
McCloskey, Donald N. 1985: *The Rhetoric of Economics* (Madison: University of Wisconsin Press).
McClure, Matthew Thompson 1918: 'Pragmatism and Democracy', *The Journal of Philosophy* 15/18 (29 Aug): 481–8.
McCraw, Thomas K. 1984: *Prophets of Regulation. Charles Francis Adams, Louis D. Brandeis, James M. Landis, Alfred E. Kahn* (Cambridge, MA: Harvard University Press).

McCulloch, Rachel 1993: 'The Optimality of Free Trade: Science or Religion?', *AERPP* 83/2 (May): 367–71.
McGinnis, John O. and Movsesian, Mark L. 2000: 'The World Trade Constitution', *Harvard Law Review* 114/2 (Dec): 512–605.
McGuiness, Michael Joseph 2000: 'The Politics of Labor Regulation in North America: A Reconsideration of Labor Law Enforcement in Mexico', *University of Pennsylvania Journal of International Economic Law* 21/1 (Spring): 1–40.
McKay, David 1999: *Federalism and the European Union: A Political Economy Perspective* (Oxford: Oxford University Press).
McKeown, Timothy J. 1984: 'Firms and Tariff Regime Change: Explaining the Demand for Protection', *World Politics* 36/2 (Jan): 215–33.
McLaughlin, Eugene 1993: 'Hong Kong: A Residual Welfare Regime'. In Allan Chochran and John Clarke, eds, *Comparing Welfare States. Britain in International Context* (London: Sage), pp. 105–40.
McLeod, Ross H. and Garnaut, Ross 1998: *East Asia in Crisis. From Being a Miracle to Needing One?* (London: Routledge).
Meier, Christian 1980: *Die Entstehung des Politischen bei den Griechen* (Frankfurt am Main: Suhrkamp).
Merton, Robert K. 1968: *Social Theory and Social Structure* (New York: Free Press).
——1987: 'Three Fragments from a Sociologist's Notebook: Establishing the Phenomenon, Specified Ignorance, and Strategic Research Materials', *Annual Review of Sociology* 13: 1–28.
Mesa-Lago, Carmelo 1978: *Social Security in Latin America: Pressure Groups, Stratification and Inequality* (Pittsburgh PA: Pittsburgh University Press).
——1990: *Ascent to Bankruptcy: Financing Social Security in Latin America* (Pittsburgh PA: Pittsburgh University Press).
——1991: 'Social Security and Prospects for Equity in Latin America', Washington, DC: World Bank (Discussion paper 140).
Messerlin, Patrick A. 2000: 'Antidumping and Safeguards'. In Schott 2000, pp. 159–83.
Meyer, Bruce D. and Rosenbaum, Dan T. 1999: 'Welfare, the Earned Income Tax Credit, and the Labor Supply of Single Mothers', NBER (Working paper 7363).
Midlarsky, Manus I., ed. 1997: *Inequality, Democracy, and Economic Development* (Cambridge: Cambridge University Press).
Miegel, Meinhard 1983: *Die verkannte Revolution (I)* (Stuttgart: Verlag Bonn Aktuell).
Miles, Thomas J. 2000: 'Common Law Exceptions to Employment at Will and US Labor Markets', *Journal of Law, Economics, and Organization* 16/1 (April): 74–101.
Milgrom, Paul and Roberts, John 1990: 'The Economics of Modern Manufacturing: Technology, Strategy, and Organization', *AER* 80/3 (June): 511–28.
Milner, Helen V. 1988: *Resisting Protectionism: Global Industries and the Politics of International Trade* (Princeton, NJ: Princeton University Press).
Mishel, Lawrence, Bernstein, Jared and Schmitt, John 1999: *The State of Working America 1998–1999* (ILR Press at Ithaca, NY: Cornell University Press).
——2001: *The State of Working America 2000–2001* (ILR Press at Ithaca, NY: Cornell University Press).
Mitchell, Brian R. 1993: *International Historical Statistics: The Americas 1750–1988*, 2nd edn (Basingstoke: Macmillan).
——1995: *International Historical Statistics: Africa, Asia and Oceania 1750–1988*, 2nd rev. edn (New York: Stockton).
——1998: *International Historical Statistics: Europe 1750–1988*, 4th edn (Basingstoke: Macmillan).
Mock, Wolfgang 1982: *Imperiale Herrschaft und nationales Interesse: 'Constructive Imperialism' oder Freihandel in Großbritannien vor dem ersten Weltkrieg* (Stuttgart: Klett-Cotta).
Moffat, James E. 1928: 'Nationalism and Economic Theory', *JPE* 36/4 (Aug): 417–46.

Moffit, Robert 1992: 'Incentive Effects of the US Welfare System: A Review', *JEL* 30/1 (March): 1–61.

Molyneux, Candido Tomas Garcia 2001: *Domestic Structures and International Trade. The Unfair Trade Instruments of the United States and the European Union* (Oxford/Portland, OR: Hart Publishers).

Mommsen, Wolfgang J. 1974: *Max Weber und die deutsche Politik 1890–1920*, 2nd rev. edn (Tübingen: J. C. B. Mohr).

——1989: 'The Antinomical Structure of Max Weber's Political Thought'. In idem *The Political and Social Theory of Max Weber* (Chicago: University of Chicago Press), pp. 24–43.

Montgomery, David 1987: *The Fall of the House of Labor: The Workplace, the State, and American Labor Activism, 1865–1925* (Cambridge: Cambridge University Press).

Moran, Theodore H. 2000: 'Investment Issues'. In Schott 2000, pp. 223–41.

Moravcsik, Andrew M. 1993a: 'Preferences and Power in the European Community: A Liberal Intergovernmentalist Approach', *Journal of Common Market Studies* 31/4 (Dec): 473–524.

——1993b: 'Integrating International and Domestic Theories of International Bargaining'. In Peter B. Evans, Harold K. Jacobson and Robert D. Putnam, eds, *Double-Edged Diplomacy. International Bargaining and Domestic Politics* (Berkeley/Los Angeles: University of California Press), pp. 3–42.

——1998a: *The Choice for Europe. Social Purpose and State Power from Messina to Maastricht* (Ithaca, NY: Cornell University Press).

——1998b: 'Informal Influence: What Can We Learn from the Failures of International Entrepreneurs?', Cambridge, MA: Weatherhead Center for International Affairs (Working paper series).

Moravcsik, Andrew M. and Nicolaïdis, Kalypso 1998: 'Federal Ideals and Constitutional Realities in the Treaty of Amsterdam', *Journal of Common Market Studies. Annual Review* 36: 13–38.

——1999: 'Explaining the Treaty of Amsterdam: Interests, Influence, Institutions', *Journal of Common Market Studies* 37/1 (March): 59–85.

Moreno, Sara 2000: 'Steel Needs to Get Real' (http://www.dismal.com/todaysecon/te1102002.asp – 3 Nov).

Morgenson, Gretchen 2000: 'Why a Soft Landing Could be Worse This Time', *NYT* (10 Sept): 3.1.

Moritz, Ralf 1998: 'Nachwort'. In Konfuzius 1998, pp. 161–215.

Morrison, Fred L. and Hudec, Robert E. 1993: 'Judicial Protection of Individual Rights under the Foreign Trade Laws of the United States'. In Hilf and Petersmann 1993, pp. 91–133.

Morton, Peter 2000: 'Clinton Promises Relief From High Fuel Prices: Truckers Want Tax Lifted: Administration Worries Prices Will Trigger Inflation', *Financial Post* (17 March): C-10.

Moynihan, Daniel P. 1973: *The Politics of a Guaranteed Income: The Nixon Administration and the Family Assistance Plan* (New York: Random House).

——1990: *On the Law of Nations* (Cambridge, MA: Harvard University Press).

Mullainathan, Sendhil and Thaler, Richard H. 2000: 'Behavioral Economics', NBER (Working paper 7948).

Murakami, Yasusuke 1996: *An Anticlassical Political-Economic Analysis. A Vision for the Next Century* (Stanford: Stanford University Press).

Murray, Charles A. 1994: *Losing Ground. American Social Policy, 1950–1980,* 2nd edn (New York: Basic Books).

——1999: 'The Underclass Revisited', American Enterprise Institute Papers and Studies (http://www.aei.org/ps/psmurray.htm – 4 Feb).

Mussa, Michael L. 1993: 'Making the Practical Case for Freer Trade', *AERPP* 83/2 (May): 372–6.

Mussler, Werner 1998: *Die Wirtschaftsverfassung der Europäischen Gemeinschaft im Wandel: Von Rom nach Maastricht* (Baden-Baden: Nomos Publishers).

Myerson, Roger B. 1989: 'Mechanism Design'. In John Eatwell, Murray Milgate and Peter Newman, eds, *Allocation, Information, and Markets* (New York/London: Norton/The New Palgrave), pp. 191–206.

Myles, John and Pierson, Paul 1997: 'Friedman's Revenge: The Reform of "Liberal" Welfare States in Canada and the United States', *Politics and Society* 25/4 (Sept): 443–72.

——2001: 'The Comparative Political Economy of Pension Reform'. In Pierson 2001, pp. 305–33.

Myrdal, Gunnar 1957: 'Economic Nationalism and Internationalism', *Australian Outlook* 11/1: 3–50.

Nader, Ralph 2000: *Cutting Corporate Welfare* (New York: Seven Stories Press).

——2002: *Crashing the Party: Taking on Corporate Government in an Age of Surrender* (New York: St. Martin's Press).

Naifeh, Mary 1998: *Dynamics of Economic Well-Being, Poverty 1993–94: Trap Door? Revolving Door? Or Both?* (Washington, DC: US Census Bureau; Current Population Reports, Household Economic Studies P70–63, July).

Nakane, Chie 1970: *Japanese Society* (Berkeley/Los Angeles: University of California Press).

Nathan, Richard P. and Gais, Thomas L. 1999: *Implementing the Personal Responsibility Act of 1996: A First Look* (Albany, NY: Nelson A. Rockefeller Institute of Government).

Nelson, Joan M. 1990: *Economic Crisis and Political Choice: The Politics of Adjustment in the Third World* (Princeton, NJ: Princeton University Press).

Neumann, Franz Leopold 1963 [1942]: *Behemoth. The Structure and Practice of National Socialism* (London: V. Gollancz and Toronto/New York: Oxford University Press).

Neumann, John von and Morgenstern, Oskar 1990 [1944]: *Theory of Games and Economic Behavior* (Princeton, NJ: Princeton University Press).

Neumann, Sigmund 1949: 'The International Civil War', *World Politics* 1/3 (April): 333–50.

Newhouse, Joseph P. 1996: 'Policy Watch: Medicare', *JEP* 10/3 (Summer): 159–67.

Nickell, Stephen J. 1998: 'The Collapse in the Demand for the Unskilled: What Can be Done?'. In Freeman and Gottschalk 1998, pp. 297–319.

Niebuhr, H. Richard 1954: *The Social Sources of Denominationalism* (Hamden, CT: The Shoe String Press).

——1964 [1951]: 'Christ Against Culture'. In Louis Schneider, ed., *Religion, Culture and Society. A Reader in the Sociology of Religion* (New York: John Wiley and Sons), pp. 203–19.

Nitschke, August 1996: 'Naturwissenschaftliche Erklärungen innerhalb der Kulturgeschichte'. In Wolfgang Hardtwig and Hans-Ulrich Wehler, eds, *Kulturgeschichte Heute* (Göttingen: Vandenhoeck und Ruprecht), pp. 316–33.

Nivola, Pietro S. 1997: 'American Social Regulation Meets the Global Economy'. In idem, ed., *Comparative Disadvantages. Social Regulations and the Global Economy* (Washington, DC: Brookings Institution Press), pp. 16–65.

Noble, Charles 1997: *Welfare As We Knew It: A Political History of the American Welfare State* (Oxford: Oxford University Press).

Noelle-Neumann, Elisabeth 1998: 'Ein Riß teilt das Land. Abschied vom sozialen Klima der Nachkriegszeit', *FAZ* (18 Nov): 5.

Noland, Marcus 1997: 'Chasing Phantoms: The Political Economy of USTR', Washington, DC: Institute for International Economics (Working paper 97-1).

Nullmeier, Frank and Rüb, Friedbert W. 1993: *Die Transformation der Sozialpolitik. Vom Sozialstaat zum Sicherungsstaat* (Frankfurt am Main: Campus Verlag).

Nunnenkamp, Peter, Gundlach, Erich and Agarwal, Jamuna P. 1994: *Globalisation of Production and Markets* (Tübingen: J. C. B. Mohr; Kieler Studien 262).

Nye, Joseph S. Jr. and Donahue, John D. eds 2000: *Governance in a Globalizing World* (Washington, DC: Brookings Institution Press).

Oates, Wallace E. 1999: 'An Essay on Fiscal Federalism', *JEL* 37/3 (Sept): 1120–49.

Obinger, Herbert 1998: 'Federalism, Direct Democracy, and Welfare State Development in Switzerland', *Journal of Public Policy* 18: 241–63.
——and Wagschal, Uwe, eds 2000: *Der gezügelte Wohlfahrtsstaat: Sozialpolitik in reichen Industrienationen* (Frankfurt am Main: Campus Verlag).
O'Brien, Robert, Goetz, Anne Marie, Scholte, Jan Aart and Williams, Marc 2000: *Contesting Global Governance. Multilateral Economic Institutions and Global Social Movements* (Cambridge: Cambridge University Press).
Obstfeld, Maurice and Rogoff, Kenneth 2000: 'The Six Major Puzzles in International Macroeconomics: Is There a Common Cause?', NBER (Working paper 7777).
O'Connell, Mary Ellen 1999: 'New International Legal Process', *AmJIL* 93/2: 334–51.
Odell, John S. 1990: 'Understanding International Trade Policies: An Emerging Synthesis', *World Politics* 43/1 (Oct): 139–67.
——2000: *Negotiating the World Economy* (Ithaca, NY: Cornell University Press).
OECD 1983: *National Accounts: Main Aggregates 1952–1981* (Paris: OECD).
——1995: *National Accounts: Main Aggregates 1960–1993* (Paris: OECD).
——1996: 'Trade and Competition. Frictions After the Uruguay Round (Note by the Secreteriat)', Paris: OECD, Economics Department.
——ed. 1997: *Societal Cohesion and the Globalising Economy. What Does the Future Hold* (Paris: OECD).
——1999a: *Historical Statistics 1960–1997* (Paris: OECD).
——1999b: *OECD Health Data* (Paris: OECD, CD-Rom).
——2000a: *Private Pension Systems and Policy Issues* (Washington DC: Brookings Institution Press).
——2000b: *Education at a Glance* (Paris: OECD).
——2001: *Economic Survey Sweden* (Paris: OECD, March).
Offe, Claus 1997: 'Towards a New Equilibrium of Citizen's Rights and Economic Resources?'. In OECD 1997, pp. 81–108.
O'Halloran, Sharyn 1994: *Politics, Process, and American Trade Policy* (Ann Arbor: University of Michigan Press).
Ohlin, Bertil 1931: 'Protection and Non-Competing Groups', *Weltwirtschaftliches Archiv* 33: 30–45.
Ohmae, Kenichi 1995: *End of the Nation State. The Rise of Regional Economies* (New York: The Free Press/London: HarperCollins).
O'Leary, Christopher J. O. and Wandner, Stephen A., eds 1997: *Unemployment Insurance in the United States. Analysis of Policy Issues* (Kalamazoo, MI: W. E. Upjohn; Institute for Employment Research).
Olson, Mancur Jr. 1963: 'Rapid Growth as a Destabilizing Force', *JEH* 23/4 (Dec): 529–52.
——1971: *The Logic of Collective Action: Public Goods and the Theory of Groups* (Cambridge, MA: Harvard University Press).
——1982: *The Rise and Decline of Nations. Economic Growth, Stagflation, and Social Rigidities* (New Haven, CT: Yale University Press).
——1987: 'Economic Nationalism and Economic Progress', *World Economy* 10/3: 241–64.
——2000: *Power and Prosperity: Outgrowing Communist and Capitalist Dictatorships* (New York: Basic Books).
O'Rourke, Kevin H. and Williamson, Jeffrey G., eds 1999: *Globalization and History: The Evolution of a 19th Century Atlantic Economy* (Cambridge, MA: MIT Press).
Osberg, Lars 2000: 'Long Run Trends in Economic Inequality in Five Countries: A Birth Cohort View', Luxembourg Income Study (Working paper 222).
Osborne, David E. 1988: *Laboratories of Democracy* (Boston, MA: Harvard Business School Press).
Osterloh, Margit and Weibel, Antoinette 1996: 'Handlungsspielräume eines multinationalen Unternehmens – Das Beispiel ABB'. In Pamela Meil, ed., *Globalisierung industrieller Pro-*

duktion. Strategien und Strukturen. Ergebnisse des Expertenkreises: 'Zukunftsstrategien', vol. II (Frankfurt am Main: Campus Verlag), pp. 123–48.

Oye, Kenneth A. 1992: *Economic Discrimination and Political Change. World Political Economy in the 1930s and 1980s* (Princeton, NJ: Princeton University Press).

Paqué, Karl-Heinz 1998: 'Structural Unemployment in Europe: A Bird's Eye View'. In Addison and Welfens 1998, pp. 17–43.

——1999a: 'Beschäftigung für Arbeitskräfte mit geringer Produktivität: Ein Beitrag zum Umbau des Sozialstaats', *Jahrbücher für Nationalökonomie und Statistik* 219/1/2: 194–215.

——1999b: *Structural Employment and Real Wage Rigidity in Germany* (Tübingen: J. C. B. Mohr).

Park, Young Duk 2000: 'WTO Dispute Settlement, 1995–2000: A Statistical Analysis', *Brookings Trade Forum*: 211–19.

Parker, Geoffrey 2000: 'Ratzel, the French School and the Birth of Alternative Geopolitics', *Political Geography* 19/8: 957–69.

Parsons, Talcott 1938: 'The Role of Ideas in Social Action'. In idem, *Essays in Sociological Theory* (New York: Free Press, 1954), pp. 19–33.

Patten, Christopher 1998: *East and West. China, Power, and the Future of Asia* (New York: Times Books/Random House).

Patterson, James T. 1994: *America's Struggle Against Poverty, 1900–1994* (Cambridge, MA: Harvard University Press).

——1996: *Grand Expectations: The United States, 1945–1974* (Oxford: Oxford University Press; 2nd edn 2000).

Pauly, Louis W. 1997: *Who Elects the Bankers? Surveillance and Control in the World Economy* (Ithaca, NY: Cornell University Press).

Pauly, Mark V. 1997: *Health Benefits at Work. An Economic and Political Analysis of Employment-Based Health Insurance* (Ann Arbor: University of Michigan Press).

Pear, Robert 2000: 'Number of Insured Americans Up for the First Time Since '87', *NYT* (29 Sept): *A*-15.

Pei, Minxin 1998: 'Constructing the Political Foundations of an Economic Miracle'. In Henry S. Rowan, ed., *Behind East Asian Growth. The Political Foundations of Prosperity* (London: Routledge), pp. 39–59.

Peng, Shin-yi 2000: 'The WTO Legalistic Approach and East Asia: From the Legal Culture Perspective', *Asian-Pacific Law and Policy Journal* 1/2 article 13, 35 pp. (http://www.hawaii-edu/aplpj).

Perrez, Franz-Xaver 1998: 'The Efficiency of Cooperation: A Functional Analysis of Sovereignty', *ArizJICL* 15/2 (Spring): 515–82.

Petersmann, Ernst-Ulrich 1993: 'National Constitutions and International Economic Law'. In Hilf and Petersmann 1993, pp. 3–52.

——1997: *The GATT/WTO Dispute Settlement System: International Law, International Organization and Dispute Settlement* (The Hague/Boston/London: Graham Trotham Limited).

Peterson, Paul E. 1995: *The Price of Federalism* (Washington, DC: Brookings Institution Press).

Peterson, Paul E. and Rom, Mark C. 1989: 'American Federalism, Welfare Policy, and Residential Choices', *APSR* 83/3 (Sept): 711–28.

——1990: *Welfare Magnets. A New Case for a National Standard* (Washington, DC: Brookings Institution Press).

Pfaff, William 1997: 'Don't Forget That Globalization Creates Losers, Too', *IHT* (13 Nov): 8.

Pfanner, Eric 2002: 'US Unveils Steep Levies on Foreign Steelmakers. European and Asian Officials Warn of Challenge in WTO', *IHT* (6 March): 1, 5.

Phelps, Edmund S. 1994: 'Low-wage Employment Subsidies versus the Welfare State', *AERPP* 84/2 (May): 54–8.

Picot, Arnold and Reichwald, Ralf 1994: 'Auflösung der Unternehmung? Vom Einfluß der IuK-

Technik auf Organisationsstrukturen und Kooperationsformen', *Zeitschrift für Betriebswirtschaft* 64/5 (May): 547–70.

Picot, Arnold, Ripperger, Tanja and Wolff, Birgitta 1996: 'The Fading Boundaries of the Firm: The Role of Information and Communication Technology', *Journal of Institutional and Theoretical Economics* 152/1: 65–79.

Pierson, Paul 1993: 'When Effect Becomes Cause: Policy Feedback and Political Change', *World Politics* 45/4 (July): 595–628.

——1994: *Dismantling the Welfare State? Reagan, Thatcher and the Politics of Retrenchment* (Cambridge: Cambridge University Press).

——1995: 'Fragmented Welfare States: Federal Institutions and the Development of Social Policy', *Governance* 8/4: 449–78.

——1996: 'The New Politics of the Welfare State', *World Politics* 48/2 (Jan): 143–79.

——1998: 'Irresistible Forces, Immovable Objects: Post-Industrial Welfare States Confront Permanent Austerity', *JEPP* 5/4 (Dec): 539–60.

——ed. 2001: *The New Politics of the Welfare State* (Oxford: Oxford University Press).

Pies, Ingo 1993: *Normative Institutionenökonomik. Zur Rationalisierung des politischen Liberalismus* (Tübingen: J. C. B. Mohr).

Pincus, Jonathan J. 1977: *Pressure Groups and Politics in Antebellum Tariffs* (New York: Columbia University Press).

Polanyi, Karl 1957 [1944]: *The Great Transformation. The Political and Economic Origins of Our Time* (Boston, MA: Beacon Press).

Polanyi, Michael 1945: *Full Employment and Free Trade* (Cambridge: Cambridge University Press).

Pollack, Mark 2000: 'International Relations Theory and European Integration', Florence: European University Institute (Schumann Centre; Working paper 55).

Pollack, Mark and Shaffer, Gregory C., ed. 2001: *Transatlantic Governance in the Global Economy* (Lanham, MD: Rowman and Littlefield).

Power, Paul E. 1968: 'American Employer Behavior in the International Labor Organization', *Midwest Journal of Political Science* 12/2: 259–78.

Prasad, Eswar S. 2000: 'The Unbearable Stability of the German Wage Structure: Evidence and Interpretation', Washington, DC: IMF (Working paper 00/22).

Prechal, Sacha 2000: 'Does Direct Effect Still Matter?', *Common Market Law Review* 37/5 (Oct): 1047–69.

Preeg, Ernest H. 1995: *Traders in a Brave New World. The Uruguay Round and the Future of the International Trading System* (Chicago: University of Chicago Press).

——1999: *Feeling Good or Doing Good with Sanctions: Unilateral Economic Sanctions and the US National Interest,* foreword by Lee H. Hamilton (Washington DC: Center for Strategic and International Studies).

——2000: *The Trade Deficit, the Dollar, and the US National Interest* (Indianapolis, IN: Hudson Institute).

Preston, Holly Hubbard 2002: 'Walking Papers: How to Make the Best of Losing a Job', *IHT* (16–17 March): 13.

Proff, Heike 1997: 'Bedeutung der zunehmenden Regionalisierung der Weltwirtschaft für die Gesamtunternehmensstrategien international diversifizierter Unternehmen', *Zeitschrift für Betriebswirtschaft* 67/5/6 (May/June): 601–25.

Pryor, Frederic L. and Schaffer, David L. 1999: *Who's Not Working and Why? Employment, Cognitive Skills, Wages, and the Changing U.S. Labor Market* (Cambridge: Cambridge University Press).

Przeworski, Adam 1985: *Capitalism and Social Democracy* (Cambridge: Cambridge University Press).

Przeworski, Adam and Limongi, Fernando 1997: 'Modernization. Theories and Facts', *World Politics* 49: 155–83.

Przeworski, Adam and Sprague, John 1986: *Paper Stones. A History of Electoral Socialism* (Chicago: University of Chicago Press).

Putnam, Robert D. 1988: 'Diplomacy and Domestic Politics. The Logic of Two-Level Games', *International Organization* 42/X: 427–60.

Putnam, Robert D. and Bayne, Nicholas 1987: *Hanging Together. Cooperation and Conflict in the Seven-Power Summits,* rev. edn (Cambridge, MA: Harvard University Press).

Puurunen, Tapio 2000: 'The Legislative Jurisdiction of States over Transactions in International Electronic Commerce', *John Marshall Journal of Computer and Information Law* 18/3 (Spring): 689–753.

Pye, Lucian W. 1985: *Asian Power and Politics. The Cultural Dimensions of Authority* (Cambridge, MA: Harvard University Press).

——1988: 'The New Asian Capitalism: A Political Portrait'. In Berger and Hsiao 1988, pp. 81–98.

Quadagno, Jill S. 1994: *The Color of Welfare. How Racism Undermined the War on Poverty* (Oxford: Oxford University Press).

Quian, Yingyi and Weingast, Barry R. 1997: 'Federalism as a Commitment to Preserving Market Incentives', *JEP* 11/4 (Fall): 83–92.

Ragosta, John A. and Magnus, John R. 1997: 'Antidumping and Antitrust Reform in the NAFTA: Beyond Rhetoric and Mischief'. In Hart 1997, pp. 86–142.

Rainwater, Lee 1974: *What Money Buys: Inequality and the Social Meanings of Income* (New York: Basic Books).

Ramaswamy, Ramana 1994: 'The Structural Crisis in the Swedish Economy', *IMF Staff Papers* 41/2: 367–79.

Ramesh, Mishra and Holliday, Ian 2001: 'The Health Care Miracle in East and Southeast Asia: Activist State Provision in Hong Kong, Malaysia and Singapore', *JSP* 30/4: 637–51.

Ranis, Gustav 1993: 'Labor Markets, Human Capital, and Development Performance in East Asia', New Haven CT: Yale University (Economic Growth Center: Working paper 697).

Ratzel, Friedrich 1923: *Politische Geographie,* rev. by Eugen Oberhummer (München/Berlin: Oldenbourg).

——1940: 'Raumverhältnisse und Raumbewältigung'. In idem, *Erdenmacht und Völkerschicksal* (Stuttgart: Kröner), pp. 137–48.

Reagan, Michael D. 1999: *The Accidental System: Health Care Policy in America* (Boulder, CO: Westview).

Reich, Arie 1996/7: 'From Diplomacy to Law: The Juridification of International Trade Relations', *Journal of International Law and Business* 17/2–3 (Winter/Spring): 775–849.

Reich, Charles A. 1964: 'The New Property', *Yale Law Journal* 73/X: 733–87.

Reinicke, Wolfgang J. 1998: *Global Public Policy: Governing Without Government?* (Washington DC: Brookings Institution Press).

Reischauer, Edwin Oldfather and Jansen, Maris B. 1995: *The Japanese Today. Change and Continuity* (Cambridge, MA: Harvard University Press).

Renzsch, Wolfgang 1997: 'Einheitlichkeit der Lebensverhältnisse oder Wettbewerb der Regionen?', *Staatswissenschaften und Staatspraxis* 8/1: 87–109.

Republic of China 1997: *Statistical Yearbook of the Republic of China* (Taipeh: Republic of China).

Reynolds, Glenn Harlan 1995: 'Is Democracy Like Sex?', *Vanderbilt Law Review* 48/6 (Nov): 1635–61.

Ricardo, David 1973 [1817]: *Principles of Political Economy and Taxation* (London/Dent, VE: Dutton; Everyman's Library).

Ricci, David Morgenstein 1970: 'Democracy Attenuated: Schumpeter, the Process Theory, and American Democratic Thought', *Journal of Politics* 32/2 (May): 239–67.

Rieger, Elmar 1992a: *Die Institutionalisierung des Wohlfahrtsstaates* (Opladen/Wiesbaden: Westdeutscher Verlag).

——1992b: 'Strategien der Institutionenbildung. Über die Bedeutung von Wahlverwandtschaften im Prozeß der Entstehung des Wohlfahrtsstaates', *Journal für Sozialforschung* 32: 157–76.
——1995a: 'The Common Agricultural Policy'. In Wallace and Wallace 1995, pp. 194–230.
——1995b: 'Protective Shelter or Straitjacket: An Institutional Analysis of the Common Agricultural Policy of the European Community'. In Leibfried and Pierson 1995, pp. 194–230.
——1997: 'Amerikanische Sozialpolitik und die Theorie des Wohlfahrtsstaates (Besprechungsessay)', *Kölner Zeitschrift für Soziologie und Sozialpsychologie* 49/2: 327–34.
——1998: 'Soziologische Theorie und Sozialpolitik im entwickelten Wohlfahrtsstaat'. In Lessenich and Ostner 1998, pp. 59–90.
——1999a: 'Global Capitalism and the Politics of Social Policy Reform in Germany and in the United States'. In Carl Lankowski, ed., *Responses to Globalization in Germany and in the United States. Seven Sectors Compared* (Washington DC: American Institute for Contemporary German Studies; Research Report 10), pp. 101–29.
——1999b: *Auf dem Holzweg. Die Gemeinsame Agrarpolitik der Europäischen Union in institutionentheoretischer Perspektive* (Universität Mannheim, Fakultät für Sozialwissenschaften; Habilitation).
——2000: 'The Common Agricultural Policy'. In Wallace and Wallace 2000, pp. 179–210.
——2001: 'Eine Regierung für Regierungen. Territoriale Organization und Sozialpolitik in der Europäischen Union und in den Vereinigten Staaten'. In Walter Müller, Oliver Fromm and Bernd Hansjürgens, eds, *Regeln für den europäischen Systemwettbewerb* (Marburg: Metropolis), pp. 307–35.
Rieger, Elmar and Leibfried, Stephan 1995: *Globalization and the Western Welfare State, An Annotated Bibliography* (Bremen/Mannheim/Berlin/New York: GAAC/SSRC/Wissenschaftskolleg zu Berlin and ZeS and Mannheimer Zentrum für Europäische Sozialforschung; ZeS Working paper 1/95). (http://www.zes.uni-bremen.de/D_arbeitspapiere1995.html).
——1997: 'Die sozialpolitischen Grenzen der Globalisierung', *Politische Vierteljahresschrift* 38/4: 771–96.
——1998a: 'Welfare State Limits to Globalization', *Politics and Society* 26/4 (Sept): 363–90.
——1998b: 'Wirtschaftliche Globalisierung und Sozialpolitik – Zur Analyse einer Wechselbeziehung am Beispiel der USA', sfb 186 report (7 July): 1–10; also in Holger Backhaus-Maul, ed., *Von der Sozialhilfe in die Erwerbsarbeit: Die Welfare Reform in den USA* (Frankfurt am Main: Press of the Deutscher Verein für öffentl. und priv. Fürsorge, 1999), pp. 232–52.
——1999: 'Wohlfahrtsstaat und Sozialpolitik in Ostasien. Der Einfluß von Religion im Kulturvergleich'. In Gert Schmidt and Rainer Trinczek, eds, *Globalisierung. Ökonomische und soziale Herausforderungen am Ende des 20. Jahrhunderts* (Baden-Baden: Nomos Publishers), pp. 407–93.
——2000: 'Wohlfahrtsmerkantilismus. Wechselwirkungen zwischen demokratischer Sozialpolitik und Welthandelsordnung', *Aus Politik und Zeitgeschichte* B 48 (24 Nov): 12–22.
Rifkin, Jeremy 1995: *The End of Work: The Decline of the Global Labor Force and the Dawn of the Post-Market Era* (New York: G. P. Putnam).
Riley, Trish and Herz, Elicia J. 2000: 'Reaching Uninsured Children: Are Medicaid and SCHIP Doing the Job?' Proceedings of a CRS Seminar, Washington, DC: Congressional Research Service, 25 July (Order Code RL 30632).
Rimlinger, Gaston 1974: *Welfare Policy and Industrialization in Europe, America, and Russia* (New York: John Wiley and Sons).
——1977: 'Labor and the Government: A Comparative Historical Perspective', *JEH* 37/1 (March): 210–25.
Ringlstetter, Max and Skrobarczyk, Peter 1994: 'Die Entwicklung internationaler Strategien. Ein integrierter Bezugsrahmen', *Zeitschrift für Betriebswirtschaft* 64/3 (March): 333–57.

Riphahn, Regina T., Snower, Dennis J. and Zimmermann, Klaus F., eds 2001: *Employment Policy in Transition: The Lessons of German Integration for the Labor Market* (Berlin: Springer).

Rittberger, Volker, with the asssistance of Bernhard Zangl 1995: *Internationale Organisationen. Politik und Geschichte: Europäische und weltweite zwischenstaatliche Zusammenschlüsse* (Leverkusen/Opladen: Leske and Budrich); forthcoming as *International Organizations. Polity, Politics, Policies* (Basingstoke: Palgrave).

Ritter, Gerhard A. 1983: *Sozialversicherung in Deutschland und England. Entstehung und Grundzüge im Vergleich* (München: Beck).

Ritter, Lennart, Braun, W. David and Rawlinson, Francis 2000: *EC Competition Law: A Practioner's Guide*, 2nd edn (Den Haag and Boston, MA: Kluwer Law International).

Ritzer, George 2000: *The McDonaldization of Society: An Investigation into the Changing Character of Contemporary Social Life*, 2nd rev. edn (Thousand Oaks, CA: Pine Forge Press).

Robbins, Lionel C. 1937: *Economic Planning and International Order* (London: Macmillan).

Robson, William A. 1976: *Welfare State and Welfare Society: Illusions and Reality* (London: Allen and Unwin).

Rodrik, Dani 1995: 'Political Economy of Trade Policy'. In Gene M. Grossman and Kenneth Rogoff, eds, *Handbook of International Economics*, vol. 3 (Oxford: North Holland), pp. 1457–94.

——1996: 'Why do More Open Economies Have Bigger Governments?' NBER (Working paper 5537).

——1997: 'Has Globalization Gone Too Far?', *California Management Review* 39/3 (Spring): 29–53.

——1998: *Has Globalization Gone Too Far?* (Washington DC: Institute for International Economics).

——2000a: 'How Far Will International Economic Integration Go?', *JEP* 14/1 (Winter): 177–86.

——2000b: 'Governance of Economic Globalization'. In Nye and Donahue 2000, pp. 347–65.

——2001: 'Trading in Illusions', *Foreign Policy* (March/April): 55–62.

Roessler, Frieder 1993: 'The Constitutional Function of the Multilateral Trade Order'. In Hilf and Petersmann 1993, pp. 53–62.

Roetz, Heiner 1992: *Die chinesische Ethik der Achsenzeit. Eine Rekonstruktion unter dem Aspekt des Durchbruchs zu postkonventionellem Denken* (Frankfurt am Main: Suhrkamp).

——1995: *Konfuzius* (München: Beck).

Rogers, Joel 1990: 'Divide and Conquer: Further "Reflections on the Distinctive Character of American Labor Laws"', *Wisconsin Law Review* 1990/1 (Jan/Feb): 1–147.

Rogowski, Ronald 1987: 'Political Cleavages and Changing Exposure to Trade', *APSR* 81/4 (Dec): 1121–37.

——1989: *Commerce and Coalitions. How Trade Affects Domestic Political Alignments* (Princeton, NJ: Princeton University Press).

——ed. 1998: *Comparative Politics in the International Political Economy* (Cheltenham: Edward Elgar).

Romano, Roberta 1987: 'The State Competition Debate in Corporate Law', *Cardozo Law Review* 8/4: 709–57.

Romero, Alicia Cebada 1999: 'Antidumping, Countervailing Duties, and Safeguard Measures: Comparison Between the Agreements of the European Community and Eastern European Countries and NAFTA', *ArizJICL* 16/2 (Spring): 437–79.

Root, Hilton L. 1996: *Small Countries, Small Lessons. Governance and the Rise of East Asia* (Hong Kong/Oxford/New York: Oxford University Press/Asian Development Bank).

Root, Hilton L. and Weingast, Barry R. 1996: 'The State's Role in East Asian Development'. In Root 1996, pp. 139–44.

Röpke, Wilhelm Theodor 1942: *International Economic Disintegration. With an Appendix by*

Alexander Rüstow (London, UK: William Hodge; US repr. Philadelphia, PA: Porcupine Press 1978).

Rose, Richard and Shiratori, Rei, eds 1986: *The Welfare State in East and West* (Oxford: Oxford University Press).

Rose-Ackerman, Susan 1981: 'Does Federalism Matter? Political Choice in a Federal Republic', *JPE* 89/1 (Feb): 152–65.

Rosemont, Henry Jr. 1998: 'Human Rights: A Bill of Worries'. In Bary and Weiming 1998, pp. 54–66.

Rosenberg, Hans 1976 [1967]: *Große Depression und Bismarckzeit. Wirtschaftsablauf, Gesellschaft und Politik in Mitteleuropa* (Frankfurt am Main: Ullstein/Berlin: Walter de Gruyter).

Rosencranz, Armin and Campbell, Richard 1999: 'Foreign Environmental and Human Rights Suits Against US Corporations in US Courts', *Stanford Environmental Law Journal* 18/2: 145–208.

Ross, Jan 1999: 'Die Rückkehr der Gleichheit', *DIE ZEIT* 3 (14 Jan): 3.

Rostow, Walter W. 1971: *Politics and the Stages of Growth* (Cambridge: Cambridge University Press).

Roth, Philip 2000: *The Human Stain* (London: Vintage).

Rothfels, Hans 1927: *Theodor Lohmann und die Kampfjahre der staatlichen Sozialpolitik, 1871–1905* (Berlin: C. S. Mittler).

Rothgang, Heinz 1997: *Ziele und Wirkungen der Pflegeversicherung. Eine ökonomische Analyse* (Frankfurt am Main: Campus Verlag).

——2001: 'Providing Long-Term Care for the Elderly in Germany. Projections on Public Long-Term Care Insurance Financing'. In Gert Hullen, ed., *Living Arrangements and Households* (Wiesbaden: Kohlhammer), pp. 95–112.

Rothschild, Kurt W. 1947: 'Price Theory and Oligopoly', *Economic Journal* 57/227 (Sept): 299–320.

——1992: *Ethik und Wirtschaftstheorie* (Tübingen: J. C. B. Mohr).

Rueschemeyer, Dietrich, Stephens, Evelyne Huber and Stephens, John D., eds 1992: *Capitalist Development and Democracy* (Cambridge: Polity).

Ruggie, John Gerald 1982: 'International Regimes, Transactions, and Change: Embedded Liberalism in the Postwar Economic Order', *International Organization* 36/2 (Spring): 379–415.

——1993: 'Territoriality and Beyond: Problematizing Modernity in International Relations', *International Organization* 47/1: 139–74.

——1994: 'Trade, Protectionism and the Future of Welfare Capitalism', *Journal of International Affairs* 48/1 (Summer): 1–11.

Ruggiero, Renato 2000: 'Reflections from Seattle'. In Schott 2000, pp. xiii–xvii.

Rugman, Alan M. and Anderson, Andrew D. M. 1987: *Administered Protection in America* (London: Croom Helm).

Rüthers, Bernd 1996: *Beschäftigungskrise und Arbeitsrecht: Zur Arbeitsmarktpolitik der Arbeitsgerichtsbarkeit* (Bad Homburg: Frankfurter Institut – Stiftung Marktwirtschaft und Politik).

——1998: 'Arbeitsrecht und ideologische Kontinuitäten?', *Neue Juristische Wochenschrift* 51/20: 1433–40.

——2000: *Die Arbeitsgesellschaft im Umbruch – Krise auf Zeit oder Zerfall eines Leitbildes?* (Köln: Wirtschaftsverlag Bachem).

Sack, Robert 1986: *Human Territoriality. Its Theory and History* (Cambridge: Cambridge University Press).

Sahlins, Marshall 1999: 'What Is Anthropological Enlightenment? Some Lessons of the Twentieth Century', *Annual Review of Anthropology* 28: i–xxiii.

Salvatore, Dominick, ed. 1993: *Protectionism and World Welfare* (Cambridge: Cambridge University Press).

Sandefur, Gary D. and Tienda, Marta, eds 1988: *Divided Opportunities. Minorities, Poverty, and Social Policy* (New York: Plenum Press).
Sanger, David E. and Kahn, Joseph 2002: 'Promise of Steel-Industry Aid Bedevils Bush. Market Ideals Conflict with Political Realities', *IHT* (5 March): 1, 7.
Sato, Kazuo 1995: 'Economic Growth, Foreign Trade, and Trade Policy in Japan', *World Economy* 18: 193–217.
Sawhill, Isabel V. 1995: 'The Economist vs. Madmen in Authority', *JEP* 9/3 (Summer): 3–13.
Schaefer, Matthew 1998: 'Sovereignty Revisited: The "Grey Areas" and "Yellow Zones" of Split Sovereignty Exposed by Globalization: Choosing among Strategies of Avoidance, Cooperation, and Intrusion to Escape an Era of Misguided "New Federalism"', *Canada-United States Law Journal* 24: 35–72.
Schak, David C. 1991: 'Assistance to Poor Relatives: Chinese Kinship Reconsidered'. In E. K. Y. Chen, Jack F. Williams and Joseph Wong, eds, *Taiwan. Economy, Society and History* (Hong Kong: Centre of Asian Studies, University of Hong Kong), pp. 206–34.
Schanz, Kai-Uwe 1995: *Export, Lizenzvergabe oder Direktinvestition? Eine wirtschaftstheoretische Analyse unternehmerischer Internationalisierungsstrategien vor dem Hintergrund der neuen WTO-Welthandelsordnung* (Chur/Zürich: Rüegger).
Scharpf, Fritz W. 1995: 'Subventionierte Niedriglohnbeschäftigung statt bezahlter Arbeitslosigkeit?', *Zeitschrift für Sozialreform* 41/2 (Feb): 65–82.
——1997: 'Economic Integration, Democracy and the Welfare State', *JEPP* 4/1 (March) 18–36.
——2000a: 'The Viability of Advanced Welfare States in the International Economy: Vulnerabilities and Options', *JEPP* 7/2 (June): 190–228 (also in Leibfried 2001, pp. 123–50).
——2000b: 'Economic Changes, Vulnerabilities, and Institutional Capabilities'. In Scharpf and Schmidt 2000, vol. 1, pp. 21–124.
Scharpf, Fritz W. and Schmidt, Vivian A., eds 2000: *Welfare and Work in the Open Economy*, vol. 1: *From Vulnerability to Competitiveness*, vol. 2: *Diverse Responses to Common Challenges* (Oxford: Oxford University Press).
Schattschneider, Elmer E. 1935: *Politics, Pressures and the Tariff: A Study of Free Enterprise in Pressure Politics, as Shown in the 1929–1930 Revision of the Tariff* (New York: Prentice-Hall; reprint University Microfilms 1975).
——1975 [1960]: *The Semisovereign People. A Realist's View of Democracy in America* (Hinsdale, IL: Dryden Press).
Schein, Edgar H. 1996: *Strategic Pragmatism. The Culture of Singapore's Economic Development Board* (Cambridge, MA: MIT Press).
Schelkle, Waltraud 1999: 'Welfare Reform in the United States: Lessons for a Future Social Federation of the EMU', Washington DC: American Institute for Contemporary German Studies (Policy paper 9).
Schiller, Wendy J. 2000: *Partners and Rivals. Representation in US Senate Delegations* (Princeton, NJ: Princeton University Press).
Schindler, Dietrich 1948: 'Gedanken zum Wiederaufbau des Völkerrechts'. In idem, *Recht – Staat – Völkergemeinschaft. Ausgewählte Schriften aus dem Nachlaß* (Zürich: Schulthess and Co.), pp. 233–61.
Schluchter, Wolfgang, ed. 1983: *Max Webers Studie über Konfuzianismus und Taoismus. Interpretation und Kritik* (Frankfurt am Main: Suhrkamp).
Schmähl, Winfried 1999a: 'Pension Reforms in Germany: Major Topics, Decisions and Developments'. In Katharina Müller, Andreas Ryll and Hans-Jürgen Wagener, eds, *Transformation of Social Security: Pensions in Central-Eastern Europe* (Heidelberg: Physica), pp. 91–120.
——1999b: 'Grundlegende Entscheidungen für Reformen im Bereich der Alterssicherung', *Zeitschrift für Sozialreform* 45/3 (March): 189–98.
——2000: 'Alterssicherung in Deutschland: Weichenstellungen für die Zukunft – Konzeptionen, Maßnahmen und Wirkungen'. In Leibfried and Wagschal 2000, pp. 381–417.
Schmähl, Winfried and Rothgang, Heinz 1996: 'The Long Term Costs of Public Long-term Care

Insurance in Germany. Some Guesstimates'. In Roland Eisen and Frank A. Sloan, eds, *Long-Term Care: Economic Issues and Policy Solutions* (Norwell, MA: Kluwer), pp. 181–222.

Schmid, Günther and Grazier, Bernard, eds 2002: *The Dynamics of Full Employment. Social Integration through Transitional Labour Markets* (Cheltenham: Edward Elgar).

Schmid, Günther, O'Reilly, Jacqueline and Schomann, Klaus, eds 1996: *International Handbook on Labour Market Policy and Evaluation* (Cheltenham: Edward Elgar).

Schmid, Günther, Reissert, Bernd and Bruche, Gert 1992: *Unemployment Insurance and Active Labor Market Policy. An International Comparison of Financing Systems* (Detroit, MI: Wayne State University Press).

Schmidt, Manfred G. 1982: *Wohlfahrtsstaatliche Politik unter bürgerlichen und sozialdemokratischen Regierungen* (Frankfurt am Main: Campus Verlag).

——1996: 'When Parties Matter. A Review of the Possibilities and Limits of Partisan Influence on Public Policy', *European Journal of Political Research* 30/2: 155–83.

——1998: *Sozialpolitik in Deutschland. Historische Entwicklung und internationaler Vergleich*, 2nd edn (Leverkusen/Opladen: Leske and Budrich).

——ed. 2001a: *Wohlfahrtsstaatliche Politik – Institutionen – Prozesse – Leistungsprofil* (Leverkusen/Opladen: Leske and Budrich).

——2001b: 'Sozialpolitik in der Ära Kohl. Die Jahre von 1982 bis 1989/90. Finanzielle Konsolidierung und institutionelle Reform'. In BMA and Bundesarchiv 2001, vol. 7 (in prep.).

Schmidt, Vivian A. 2002: *The Futures of European Capitalism* (Oxford: Oxford University Press).

Schneider, Franz 2000: 'The Shadow Economy Around the World: Sizes, Causes, and Consequences', *JEL* 38/1: 77–144.

Schneider, Louis 1987: *Paradox and Society. The Work of Bernard Mandeville* (New Brunswick, NJ: Transaction Publishers).

Schnur, Roman, ed. 1964: *Zur Geschichte der Erklärung der Menschen- und Bürgerrechte* (Darmstadt: Wissenschaftliche Buchgesellschaft).

Schoeni, Robert F. and Blank, Rebecca M. 2000: 'The Effects of Welfare Reform and Welfare Waivers on Welfare Participation, Employment, Income, Poverty, and Family Structure', NBER (Working paper 7627).

Schoepfle, Gregory K. 2000: 'US Trade Adjustment Assistance Policies for Workers'. In Deardorff and Stern 2000, pp. 95–122.

Schott, Jeffrey J., ed. 2000: *The WTO After Seattle* (Washington, DC: Institute for International Economics).

Schott, Jeffrey J. and Watal, Jayashree 2000: 'Decision Making in the WTO'. In Schott 2000, pp. 283–9.

Schroeder, Wolfgang 2000: *Das Modell Deutschland auf dem Prüfstand. Zur Entwicklung der industriellen Beziehungen in Ostdeutschland* (Opladen/Wiesbaden: Westdeutscher Verlag).

Schröter, Harm G. 1996: 'Cartelization and Decartelization in Europe, 1870–1995: Rise and Decline of an Economic Institution', *Journal of European Economic History* 25/1: 129–53.

Schulin, Bertram and Igl, Gerhard 2002: *Sozialrecht*, 7th edn (Düsseldorf: Werner).

Schultze, Charles L. 1996: 'The CEA: An Inside Voice for Mainstream Economics', *JEP* 10/3 (Summer): 23–39.

Schumpeter, Joseph A. 1918: 'Die Krise des Steuerstaates', *Zeitfragen aus dem Gebiet der Soziologie* 4: 1–71. Trans. as 'The Crisis of the Tax State?'. In Alan T. Peacock, Ralph Turvey, Wolfgang F. Stolper and Elizabeth Henderson, eds, *International Economic Papers*, 4 (London: Macmillan 1954) pp. 5–38; also in Richard Abel Musgrave and Alan Turner Peacock, eds, *Classics in the Theory of Public Finance* (New York/London: Macmillan, 1994).

——1927: 'Die goldene Bremse an der Kreditmaschine. Die Goldwährung und der Bankkredit'. In idem. *Aufsätze zur ökonomischen Theorie* (Tübingen: J. C. B. Mohr, 1952) pp. 158–84.

——1940: 'The Influence of Protective Tariffs on the Industrial Development of the United States'. In idem *Essays: On Entrepreneurs, Innovations, Business Cycles, and the Evolution of Capitalism* (New Brunswick, NJ: Transaction Publishers, 1991), pp. 169–74.

——1946: Review of Friedrich A. Hayek, *The Road to Serfdom*, *JPE* 54/3 (June): 269–70.

——1950 [1942]: *Capitalism, Socialism and Democracy* (New York: Harper and Row).

Schuster, Thomas 2000: 'Die Entwicklung von Sozialstandards am Beispiel des Mutterschaftsurlaubes und Mutterschaftsgeldes: Ein europäischer Vergleich'. In Hilmar Schneider, ed., *Europas Zukunft als Sozialstaat: Herausforderungen der Integration* (Baden-Baden: Nomos Publishers), pp. 125–45.

Schwartz, Herman 2000: 'Internationalization and Two Liberal Welfare States: Australia and New Zealand'. In Scharpf and Schmidt 2000, vol. 2, 69–130.

Schweinitz, Karl de, Jr. 1958/9: 'Industrialization, Labor Controls and Democracy', *Economic Development and Cultural Change* 7: 385–404.

Scott, Robert E. 1997: 'Pay Attention to Workers Before Taking the Fast Track', *IHT* (5 Nov): 8.

Seeleib-Kaiser, Martin 1996: 'Historische Entwicklung und Struktur der Sozialhilfe- und Arbeitsmarktpolitik in Japan und der Bundesrepublik Deutschland'. In Dietrich Thränhardt, ed., *Japan und Deutschland in der Welt nach dem Kalten Krieg* (Münster: LIT), pp. 117–64.

——1999: 'Wohlfahrtssysteme unter Bedingungen der Globalisierung: Divergenz, Konvergenz oder divergente Konvergenz?', *Zeitschrift für Sozialreform* 45/1: 3–23.

——2002: *Globalisierung und Sozialpolitik. Ein Vergleich der Diskurse und Wohlfahrtssysteme in Deutschland, Japan und den USA* (Frankfurt am Main: Campus Verlag).

Segal, Philip 1998: 'Risk of Social Crisis Rising In Asia, UN Agency Finds', *IHT* (2 December): 1, 4.

Senti, Richard 1986: *GATT: Allgemeines Zoll- und Handelsabkommen als System der Welthandelsordnung* (Zürich: Schulthess).

——2000: *WTO – System und Funktionsweise der Welthandelsordnung* (Zürich: Schulthess/Wien: Verlag Österreich).

Shanks, Cheryl, Jacobson, Harald K. and Kaplan, Jeffrey H. 1996: 'Inertia and Change in the Constellation of International Governmental Organizations, 1981-1992', *International Organization* 50/4 (Fall): 593–629.

Shell, G. Richard 1995: 'Trade Legalism and International Relations Theory: An Analysis of the World Trade Organization', *Duke Law Journal* 44/5: 829–927.

Sherwin, Richard K. 2000: *When Law Goes Pop. The Vanishing Line Between Law and Popular Culture* (Chicago: University of Chicago Press).

Shin, Wookhee 1994: 'Geopolitical Determinants of Political Economy: The Cold War and South Korean Political Economy', *Asian Perspective* 18: 119–40.

Shklar, Judith N. 1986: *Legalism, Law, Morals, and Political Trials* (Cambridge, MA: Harvard University Press).

——1991: *American Citizenship. The Quest for Inclusion* (Cambridge, MA: Harvard University Press).

Shlaes, Amity 1994: 'Germany's Chained Economy', *Foreign Affairs* 73/5: 109–24.

Siebert, Horst 1996a: 'On the Concept of Locational Competition', Kiel Institute for World Economics (Working paper 731).

——ed. 1996b: *Sozialpolitik auf dem Prüfstand: Leitlinien für Reformen* (Tübingen: J. C. B. Mohr).

——1999a: *The World Economy* (London: Routledge).

——ed. 1999b: *Globalization and Labor* (Tübingen: J. C. B. Mohr).

——2000a: 'What Does Globalization Mean for the World Trade System?'. In The WTO Secretariate, ed., *From GATT to the WTO: The Multilateral Trading System in the New Millennium* (The Hague: Kluwer Law International), pp. 137–65.

——2000b: 'The Paradigm of Locational Competition', Kiel: Institute for World Economics (Discussion paper 367).

Siegel, Nico 2002: *Baustelle Sozialpolitik. Konsolidierung und Rückbau im internationalen Vergleich* (Frankfurt am Main: Campus Verlag).

Simmel, Georg 1984 [1957]: *Das Individuum und die Freiheit. Essays* (Berlin: Wagenbach).
——1992 [1908]: *Soziologie. Untersuchungen über die Formen der Vergesellschaftung* (Frankfurt am Main: Suhrkamp).
Simmons, Beth A. 1994: *Who Adjusts? Domestic Sources of Foreign Economic Policy During the Interwar Years* (Princeton, NJ: Princeton University Press).
Sinn, Hans-Werner 1995: 'A Theory of the Welfare State', *Scandinavian Journal of Economics* 97/4: 495–526.
——1996: 'Social Insurance Incentives and Risk Taking', München: Center for Economic Studies (Working paper 102).
——2000a: 'Eine Quarantäne-Station auf dem Weg in die Union. Die Osterweiterung wird für den westlichen Sozialstaat zur Zerreißprobe. Für eine zumindest temporäre Einführung des Heimatlandprinzips im Sozialwesen', *FAZ* (12 Aug): 13.
——2000b: 'Die Osterweiterung der EU und die Zukunft des Sozialstaates'. In Leibfried/Wagschal 2000, pp. 474–89.
Sinn, Stefan 1992: 'The Taming of Leviathan: Competition Among Governments', *Constitutional Political Economy* 3/2: 177–96.
Skocpol, Theda 1991: 'Targeting within Universalism: Politically Viable Policies to Combat Poverty in the United States'. In Christopher Jencks and Paul E. Peterson, eds, *The Urban Underclass* (Washington, DC: Brookings Institution Press), pp. 411–36. (Also in Skocpol 1995, pp. 250–74.)
——1992: *Protecting Mothers and Soldiers. The Political Origins of Social Policy in the United States* (Cambridge, MA: Harvard University Press).
——1995: *Social Policy in the United States. Future Possibilities in Historical Perspective* (Princeton, NJ: Princeton University Press).
——1997: *Boomerang: Health Care Reform and the Turn against Government* (New York: W. W. Norton).
Skocpol, Theda and Fiorina, Morris P., eds 1999: *Civic Engagement in American Democracy* (Washington, DC: Brookings Institution Press/New York: Russell Sage Foundation Press).
Skocpol, Theda and Ikenberry, John 1983: 'The Political Formation of the American Welfare State in Historical and Comparative Perspective', *Comparative Social Research* 6: 87–148. (Also in Richard F. Thomasson, ed., *The Welfare State, 1883–1983* (Greenwich, CT: JAI Press).)
Slaughter, Anne-Marie 2000a: 'Virtual Visibility. Secretive Global Technocrats Become Accountable on the World Wide Web', *Foreign Policy* 121 (Nov/Dec): 84–5.
——2000b: 'Governing the Global Economy through Government Networks'. In Byers 2000, pp. 177–205.
——2000c: 'A Liberal Theory of International Law', *Proceedings of 94th Annual Meeting of the International Law Society*, pp. 240–9.
Small, Albion W. 1900: 'The Scope of Sociology II.: The Development of Sociological Method', *AJS* 5/5 (March): 617–47.
Smart, Barry, ed. 1999: *Resisting McDonaldization* (London, UK: Sage).
Smith, Adam 1981 [1778]: *An Inquiry Into the Nature and Causes of the Wealth of Nations* (Indianapolis, IN: Liberty Fund). (See also 1937 [1776] edn, New York: Modern Library.)
Snower, Dennis J. 1994: 'Converting Unemployment Benefits into Employment Subsidies', *AERPP* 84/2 (May): 65–70.
——1997: 'Challenges to Social Cohesion and Approaches to Policy Reform'. In OECD 1997, pp. 39–60.
Social Security Administration (Office of Research, Evaluation and Statistics) 1999 (and earlier): *Social Security Throughout the World* (US Government Printing Office; SSA Publ. 13–11805) (http://www.ssa.gov/statistics/ores_home.html).

Somary, Felix 1929: *Wandlungen der Weltwirtschaft seit dem Kriege* (Tübingen: J. C. B. Mohr).

Sombart, Werner 1976 [1906]: *Why is there no Socialism in the United States?* trans. Patricia M. Hocking and C. H. Husbands; intr. C. H. Husbands, foreword by Michael Harrington (London: Macmillan and White Plains/NY: M. E. Sharpe).

Sørenson, Max 1952: 'Federal States and the International Protection of Human Rights', *AmJIL* 46/2 (April): 195–218.

Soros, George 1998: *The Crisis of Global Capitalism: Open Society Endangered* (London: Little, Brown/New York: Public Affairs).

Soskice, David 1990: 'Reinterpreting Corporatism and Explaining Unemployment: Co-ordinated and Non-co-ordinated Market Economies'. In Renato Brunetta and Carlo Dell'Aringa, eds, *Labour Relations and Economic Performance* (London: Macmillan, in association with the International Economic Association), pp. 170–211.

—— 1999: 'Divergent Production Regimes: Coordinated and Uncoordinated Market Economies in the 1980s and 1990s'. In Kitschelt et al. 1999, pp. 101–34.

Soto, Hernando de 2000: *The Mystery of Capitalism. Why Capitalism Triumphs in the West and Fails Everywhere Else* (New York: Basic Books).

Sowell, Thomas 2000: *Basic Economics. A Citizen's Guide to the Economy* (New York: Basic Books).

Spengel, Christoph and Schmidt, Frank 1997: *Betriebliche Altersversorgung, Besteuerung und Kapitalmarkt. Ein Vergleich der Verhältnisse in Deutschland, Großbritannien, den Niederlanden und den USA* (Baden-Baden: Nomos Publishers).

Spiro, Peter S. 2000: 'Globalization, International Law, and the Academy', *New York University Journal of International Law and Politics* 32/2: 567–90.

Staderman, Hans-Joachim 1995: *Arbeitslosigkeit im Wohlfahrtsstaat. Eine Bestimmung ihres Ausmaßes und ihrer Ursachen illustriert mit Daten aus dem deutschen Arbeitsmarkt* (Tübingen: J. C. B. Mohr).

Staley, Eugene 1939: *World Economy in Transition: Technology vs. Politics, Laissez Faire vs. Planning, Power vs. Welfare* (New York: Council on Foreign Relation).

Statistisches Bundesamt 2000 (and earlier): *Statistisches Jahrbuch für die Bundesrepublik Deutschland 1999* (Stuttgart: Metzler-Poeschel).

Steel, Ronald 1981: *Walter Lippmann and the American Century* (New York: Vintage Books).

Stege, Dieter 1999: 'Arbeitsrecht am Standort Deutschland – Kritische Anmerkungen eines Praktikers aus Anlaß einer wissenschaftlichen Auseinandersetzung'. In Udo Isenhardt and Ulrich Preis in cooperation with the Deutscher Arbeitsgerichtsverband e.V., eds, *Arbeitsrecht und Sozialpartnerschaft. Festschrift für Peter Hanau* (Köln: OUS Verlag Dr Otto Schmidt), pp. 107–35.

Steiner, George 2001: *Grammars of Creation* (New Haven, CT: Yale University Press).

Stephens, John D., Huber, Evelyne and Ray, Leonard 1999: 'The Welfare State in Hard Times'. In Kitschelt et al. 1999, pp. 164–93.

Stevens, Beth 1988: 'Blurring the Boundaries: How the Federal Government Has Influenced Welfare Benefits in the Private Sector'. In Margaret Weir, Ann Shola Orloff and Theda Skocpol, eds, *The Politics of Social Policy in the United States* (Princeton, NJ: Princeton University Press), pp. 123–48.

Stevenson, Richard W. 2000: 'Veto of Estate-Tax Repeal Survives Vote in the House', *NYT* (8 Sept): *A*–14.

Stiglitz, Joseph E. 1996: 'Some Lessons From the East Asian Miracle', *The World Bank Research Observer* 11: 151–77.

Stinchcombe, Arthur L. 1968: *Constructing Social Theories* (New York: Harcourt, Brace and World).

Stone, Deborah 1984: *The Disabled State* (Houndmills, Basingstoke: Macmillan).

——1997: *Policy Paradox. The Art of Political Decision Making* (New York/London: Norton).
Strange, Susan 1996: *The Retreat of the State: The Diffusion of Power in the World Economy* (Cambridge: Cambridge University Press).
Streeck, Wolfgang 1989: 'Skills and the Limits of Neo-Liberalism: The Enterprise of the Future as a Place of Learning', *Work, Employment and Society* 3: 89–104.
——1992: 'Revisiting Status and Contract: Pluralism, Corporatism and Flexibility'. In idem, *Social Institutions and Economic Performance. Studies of Industrial Relations in Advanced Capitalist Economies* (London/Newbury Park, CA: Sage), pp. 41–75.
——1999: *Korporatismus in Deutschland: Zwischen Nationalstaat und Europäischer Union* (Frankfurt am Main: Campus Verlag).
Streeck, Wolfgang and Yamamura, Kozo, eds 2001: *The Origins of Nonliberal Capitalism: Germany and Japan in Comparison* (Ithaca, NY: Cornell University Press).
Sunstein, Cass R. 1990: *After the Rights Revolution: Reconceiving the Regulatory State* (Cambridge, MA: Harvard University Press).
Suttles, Gerald 1985: 'A Tribute to Morris Janowitz'. In idem and Mayer N. Zald, eds, *The Challenge of Social Control. Citizenship and Institution Building in Modern Societies. Essays in Honor of Morris Janowitz* (Norwood, NJ: Ablex), pp. 3–12.
Sutton, John Raymond, Dobbin, Frank, Meyer, John W. and Scott, W. Richard 1994: 'The Legalization of the Workplace', *AJS* 99/4 (Jan): 944–71.
Swaan, Abram de 1988: *In Care of the State. Health Care, Education and Welfare in Europe and the USA in the Modern Era* (Cambridge: Polity).
Swoboda, Frank 2000: 'Big 3 Carmakers Give Health Benefits to Gay Partners', *IHT* (10/11 June): 3.
Sykes, Alan O. Jr. 1998: 'Comparative Advantage and the Normative Economics of International Trade Policy', *Journal of International Economics* 1/1: 49–82.
——1999: 'Regulatory Protectionism and the Law of International Trade', *University of Chicago Law Review* 66/1 (Winter): 1–46.
Sykes, Robert, Palier, Bruno and Prior, Pauline, eds 2000: *Globalization and European Welfare States: Challenges and Changes* (London: Macmillan).
Tandy, David W. 1997: *Warriors into Traders. The Power of the Market in Early Greece* (Berkeley/Los Angeles: University of California Press).
Tang, Wen-hui Anna 1997: 'State, Politics, and National Health Insurance in Taiwan', *American Asian Review* 15: 59–103.
Tanikawa, Miki 2002: 'Tough Times? Take a Test. In Japan, Schools and Subsidies Help Redirect the Jobless', *IHT* (16–17 March): 13.
Tanzi, Vito 2000: 'Globalization and the Future of the Welfare State', Washington DC: IMF (Working paper 00/12).
Taussig, Frank W. 1888: 'The Early Protective Movement and the Tariff of 1828', *Political Science Quarterly* 3/1 (March): 17–45.
——1966 [1931]: *The Tariff History of the United States* (New York: Johnson Reprint Corp.).
Taussig, Frank W. and White, Harry Dexter 1931: *Some Aspects of the Tariff Question* (Cambridge, MA: Harvard University Press).
Taylor, Alan and Williamson, Jeffrey G. 1997: 'Convergence in the Age of Mass Migration', *European Review of Economic History* 1/1 (April): 27–63 (NBER 4711).
Taylor, Charles 1989: *Sources of the Self. The Making of the Modern Identity* (Cambridge, MA: Harvard University Press).
Taylor, Peter James, ed. 1993: *Political Geography of the Twentieth Century. A Global Analysis* (London/New York: Belhaven Press/Halstad Press).
Teixeira, Ruy A. and Rogers, Joel 2000: *America's Forgotten Majority: Why the Working Class Still Matters* (New York: Basic Books).
Teles, Steven M. 1996: *Whose Welfare? AFDC and Elite Politics* (Lawrence, KA: University of Kansas Press).

Tennstedt, Florian 1988: 'Geschichte des Sozialrechts'. In Bernd von Maydell and Franz Ruland, eds, *Handbuch des Sozialrechts (SRH)* (Neuwied: Luchterhand), pp. 66–113.

Terrill, Tom E. 1969: 'David A. Wells, the Democracy, and Tariff Reduction, 1877–1894' *Journal of American History* 56/3 (Dec): 540–55.

Thelen, Kathleen and Kume, Ikuo 1999: 'The Effects of Globalization on Labor Revisited: Lessons from Germany and Japan', *Politics and Society* 27/4: 477–505.

Thibout, Charles M. 1956: 'A Pure Theory of Local Expenditures', *JPE* 64/5 (Oct): 416–24.

Thomson, Janice E. and Krasner, Stephen D. 1989: 'Global Transactions and the Consolidation of Sovereignty'. In Ernst-Otto Czempiel and James N. Rosenau, eds, *Global Changes and Theoretical Challenges. Approaches to World Politics for the 1990s* (Lexington, MA: Lexington Books), pp. 195–219.

Thränhardt, Anna Maria 1995: 'Soziale Sicherheit in Japan'. In Hans Jürgen Mayer and Manfred Pohl, eds, *Länderbericht Japan. Geographie, Geschichte, Politik, Wirtschaft, Gesellschaft, Kultur* (Darmstadt: Wissenschaftliche Buchgesellschaft), pp. 426–41.

——1996: 'Kreativer Konservatismus im "Japanischen Modell der Wohlfahrtsgesellschaft"'. In Paul Levenhörster and Dietrich Thränhardt, eds, *Herausforderungen an den Wohlfahrtsstaat. Internationalisierung, Individualisierung und gesellschaftlicher Wandel* (Münster: LIT), pp. 47–68.

Thurow, Lester C. 1992: *Head to Head: The Coming Economic Battle among Japan, Europe and America* (New York: Morrow).

——1996: *The Future of Capitalism: How Today's Economic Forces Shape Tomorrow's World* (New York: Morrow).

Tiefenbrunner, Susan 2000: 'Free Trade and Protectionism: The Semiotics of Seattle', *ArizJICL* 7/2 (Spring): 257–82.

Tillman, Hoyt Cleveland 1982: *Utilitarian Confucianism. Ch'en Liang's Challenge to Chu Hsi* (Cambridge MA: Council on East Asian Studies, Harvard University; Cambridge, MA: Harvard University Press).

Tilly, Richard and Welfens, Paul J. J., eds 1999: *Economic Globalization, International Organizations and Crisis Management. Contemporary and Historical Perspectives on Growth, Impact and Evolution of Major Organizations in an Interdependent World* (Heidelberg: Springer).

Timmer, Ashley S. and Williamson, Jeffrey G. 1998: 'Immigration Policy Prior to the 1930s: Labor Markets, Policy Interaction, and Globalization Backlash', *Population and Development Review* 24/4 (Dec): 739–71.

Titmuss, Richard M. 1956: 'The Social Division of Welfare'. In idem, *Essays on 'The Welfare State'* (London: Allen and Unwin), pp. 34–55.

Tocqueville, Alexis de 1835: 'Memoir on Pauperism'. In Seymour Drescher, ed., *Tocqueville and Beaumont on Social Reform* (New York/Evanston, IL/London: Harper and Row, 1968), 1–27.

——1994 [1835–45]: *Democracy in America*, 2 vols (New York and Toronto: Everyman's Library).

Tonelson, Alan 1994: 'Beating Back Predatory Trade', *Foreign Affairs* 73/4: 123–35.

Toner, Robin 2001: 'Before Leaving Health Agency, Shalala Offers a Little Advice on a Big Job', *NYT* (16 Jan): A-16.

Tönnies, Ferdinand 1926: *Die Entwicklung der sozialen Frage bis zum Weltkriege* (Berlin and Leipzig: de Gruyter).

Torres, Raymond 2000: *Towards a Socially Sustainable World Economy. An Analysis of the Social Pillars of Globalization* (Geneva: ILO).

Tremewan, Christopher 1998: 'Welfare and Governance: Public Housing under Singapore's Party State'. In Goodman et al. 1998, pp. 77–105.

Troeltsch, Ernst 1931: 'Sect-Type and Church-Type Contrasted'. In Louis Schneider, ed., *Religion, Culture and Society. A Reader in the Sociology of Religion* (New York: John Wiley and Sons, 1964), pp. 557–65.

——1994 [1912]: *Die Soziallehren der christlichen Kirchen und Gruppen* (Tübingen: J. C. B. Mohr).
Tschierschky, Siegfried 1924: *Wirtschaftsverfassung* (Breslau: F. Hirt).
Tsurumi, E. Patricia 1996: 'Colonial Education in Korea and Taiwan'. In Duus et al. 1996, pp. 275–311.
Tullock, Gordon 1988: *Wealth, Poverty, and Politics* (Oxford: Blackwell).
Tversky, Amos and Kahneman, Daniel 1981: 'The Framing of Decisions and the Psychology of Choice', *Science* 211: 453–58.
Tyabij, Amina 1993: 'Social Security in the Asian-Pacific Region', *Asian-Pacific Economic Literature* 7: 53–72.
Tynes, Sheryl R. 1996: *Turning Points in Social Security. From 'Cruel Hoax' to 'Sacred Entitlement'* (Stanford: Stanford University Press).
UNCTAD 2000: *World Investment Report 2000: Cross-border Mergers and Acquisitions and Development* (New York: United Nations).
UNDP 1999: *Human Development Report 1999* (New York: UNDP).
US Census Bureau, US Department of Commerce 1976: *The Statistical History of the United States. From Colonial Times to the Present* (New York: Basic Books).
——2001 (and earlier): *Statistical Abstract of the United States. The National Data Book* (US Government Printing Office) (http://www.census.gov/statab/www).
US Department of Commerce 1986 (and earlier): *Statistical Abstract of the United States* (US Government Printing Office).
US Department of Health and Human Services (DHHS), National Center for Health Statistics (NCHS) 2000: *Health United States, 2000. With Adolescent Health Chart Book* (Hyattsville, MD: NCHS) (http://www.cdc-gov/nchs/data/hus00.pdf).
US International Trade Commission 2000: *Value of US Imports for Consumption, Duties Collected, and Ratio of Duties to Values 1891–1999* (Washington DC: USITC, Statistical and Editorial Services Division).
Vaugh, Karen I. 1989: 'Invisible Hand'. In Eatwell et al. 1989, pp. 168–72.
VDR (Verband Deutscher Rentenversicherungsträger) 2000: *Rentenversicherung in Zeitreihen, VDR-Statistik Aktiv Versicherte* (Frankfurt am Main: VDR).
Verdier, Daniel 1994: *Democracy and International Trade. Britain, France, and the United States 1860–1990* (Princeton, NJ: Princeton University Press).
Verhovek, Sam Howe 2000: 'Frustration Grows With Cost of Health Insurance', *NYT* (18 Sept): A-1, 20.
Vernon, Raymond 1971: *Sovereignty at Bay: The Multinational Spread of U.S. Enterprises* (New York: Basic Books).
——1977: *Storm Over the Multinationals: The Real Issues* (Cambridge, MA: Harvard University Press).
Viner, Jacob 1949: 'Power versus Plenty as Objectives of Foreign Policy in the Seventeenth and Eighteenth Centuries', *World Politics* 1/1 (Oct): 1–29.
——1966: *Dumping. A Problem in International Trade* (New York: Augustus M. Kelley).
Visser, Jelle and Hemerijck, Anton 1997: *A Dutch Miracle. Job Growth, Welfare Reform and Corporatism in the Netherlands* (Amsterdam: Amsterdam University Press).
Vogel, David 1997: *Barriers or Benefits? Regulation in Transatlantic Trade* (Washington DC: Brookings Institution Press).
Vogel, Ezra 1967: 'Kinship Structure, Migration to the City, and Modernization'. In Ronald P. Dore, ed., *Aspects of Social Change in Modern Japan* (Princeton, NJ: Princeton University Press), pp. 91–111.
——1991: *The Four Little Dragons. The Spread of Industrialization in East Asia* (Cambridge, MA: Harvard University Press).
Voigt, Stefan 1992: *Die Welthandelsordnung zwischen Konflikt und Stabilität. Konfliktpotentiale und Konfliktlösungsmechanismen* (Freiburg im Breisgau: R. Haufe).

Völker, E. L. M. 1993: 'Community Trade Regulations on Foreign Trade'. In Hilf and Petersmann 1993, pp. 137–73.
Wade, Robert 1989: 'What Can Economics Learn from East Asian Success?', *Annals* 505: 68–79.
——1990a: 'Industrial Policy in East Asia: Does it Lead or Follow the Market?'. In Gereffi and Wyman 1990, pp. 231–66.
——1990b: *Governing the Market. Economic Theory and the Role of Government in East Asian Industrialization* (Princeton, NJ: Princeton University Press).
——1998: 'The Asian Crisis: The High Debt Model Versus the Wall-Street-Treasury-IMF Complex', *New Left Review* 228: 3–23.
Wahl, Adalbert 1909: 'Zur Geschichte der Menschenrechte', *Historische Zeitschrift* 103: 79–85.
Walker, Alan and Wong, Chack-Kie 1996: 'Rethinking the Western Construction of the Welfare State', *International Journal of Health Sciences* 26/1: 67–92.
Walker, Robert and Wiseman, Michael 1997: 'The Possibilities of a British Earned Income Tax Credit', *Fiscal Studies* 18/4: 401–25.
Wallace, Helen S. and Wallace, William, eds 2000: *Policy-Making in the European Union*, 4th edn (Oxford: Oxford University Press; 3rd edn 1995).
Wallace, Michael and Singer, J. David 1970: 'Intergovernmental Organization in the Global System, 1815–1964: A Quantitative Description', *International Organization* 24/2 (Spring): 239–87.
Wallerstein, Michael 1987: 'Unemployment, Collective Bargaining, and the Demand for Protection', *APSR* 31/4 (Nov): 729–52.
Wallis, John Joseph 1984: 'The Birth of the Old Federalism: Financing the New Deal, 1932–1940', *JEH* 44/1 (March): 139–59.
Walter, Gregor, Dreher, Sabine and Beisheim, Marianne 1999: 'Globalization Processes in the OECD World', *Global Society* 13/3: 229–50.
Waltz, Kenneth N. 1959: *Man, the State and War* (New York: Columbia University Press).
——1962: 'Kant, Liberalism, and War', *APSR* 56/2 (June): 331–40.
——1970: 'The Myth of National Interdependence'. In Charles P. Kindleberger, ed., *The International Corporation. A Symposium* (Cambridge, MA: MIT Press), pp. 205–23.
Walzer, Michael 1983: *Spheres of Justice. A Defense of Pluralism and Equality* (New York: Basic Books).
Wang, Ching Dao 1913: 'Die Staatsidee des Konfuzius und ihre Beziehung zur konstitutionellen Verfassung', *Mitteilungen des Seminars für Orientalische Sprachen zu Berlin, Ostasiatische Studien* 16: 1–49.
Waters, Malcolm 1995: *Globalization* (London: Routledge).
Weaver, R. Kent 1988: *Automatic Government. The Politics of Indexation* (Washington DC: Brookings Institution Press).
——1997: 'Ending Welfare as We Know it: Policy Making for Low Income Families in the Clinton/Gingrich Era'. In Weir 1997, pp. 361–416.
——2000: *Ending Welfare as We Know it* (Washington DC: Brookings Institution Press).
Weber, Alfred 1913: 'Neuorientierung in der Sozialpolitik?', *ASS* 36/1: 1–13.
Weber, Max 1895: 'The Nation State and Economic Policy'. In idem 1994, pp. 1–28.
——1894: 'Argentinische Kolonistenwirthschaften'. In idem, *Landarbeiterfrage, Nationalstaat und Volkswirtschaftspolitik. Schriften und Reden 1892–1899* (Tübingen: J. C. B. Mohr, 1993), pp. 286–303.
——1896: 'The Social Causes of the Decay of Ancient Civilization'. In idem 1999, pp. 138–53.
——1904: '"Objectivity" in Social Science and Social Policy'. In idem 1949, pp. 49–112.
——1906: 'On the Situation of Constitutional Government in Russia'. In idem 1994, pp. 29–74.
——1908: 'Marginal Utility Analysis and "The Fundamental Law of Psychophysics"'. In idem 1999, pp. 249–60.
——1917a: 'The Meaning of "Ethical Neutrality" in Sociology and Economics'. In idem 1949, pp. 1–47.

——1917b: 'Suffrage and Democracy in Germany'. In idem 1994, pp. 80–129.
——1918a: 'Parliament and Government in Germany'. In idem 1994, pp. 130–271.
——1918b: 'Socialism'. In idem 1994, pp. 272–303.
——1919: 'The Profession and the Vocation of Politics'. In idem 1994, pp. 309–69.
——1920: 'The Social Psychology of the World Religions'. In idem, *From Max Weber. Essays in Sociology* (New York: Oxford: Oxford University Press, 1946), pp. 267–301.
——1949: *The Methodology of the Social Sciences*, trans. and ed. Edward A. Shils and Henry A. Finch, foreword by Edward A. Shils (Glencoe, IL/New York: The Free Press).
——1951 [1915]: *The Religion of China* (New York: Macmillan).
——1958 [1921]: *The City* (Glencoe, IL: Free Press).
——1978: *Economy and Society*, 2 vols, ed. Guenther Roth and Claus Wittlich, trans. Ephraim Fischoff (Berkeley/Los Angeles: University of California Press).
——1981 [1923]: *General Economic History*, trans. Frank H. Knight, with a new intr. by Ira J. Cohen (New Brunswick, NJ: Transaction Publishers).
——1989 [1915]: *Die Wirtschaftsethik der Weltreligionen. Konfuzianismus und Taoismus (Schriften 1915–1920)* (Tübingen: J. C. B. Mohr).
——1994: *Political Writings*, ed. Peter Lassman (Cambridge: Cambridge University Press).
——1999: *Essays in Economic Sociology,* intr. Richard Swedberg (Princeton, NJ: Princeton University Press).
Weber, Steven 1997: 'The End of the Business Cycle?', *Foreign Affairs* 76/4 (July/Aug): 65–82.
Weggel, Oskar 1991: *Die Geschichte Taiwans* (Köln/Weimar/Wien: Böhlau).
Weide, Ursula 1998: 'A Comparison of American and German Cost Containment in Health Care: Tort Liability of US Managed Care Organizations vs. German Health Care Reform Legislation', *The Tulane European and Civil Law Forum* 13 (Winter): 47–110.
Weigert, Hans Werner 1942a: *German Geopolitics* (Oxford: Oxford University Press).
——1942b: *Generals and Geographers: The Twilight of Geopolitics* (Oxford: Oxford University Press).
Weiler, Joseph H. H. 1999: *The Constitution of Europe: 'Do the New Clothes Have an Emperor?' and Other Essays on European Integration* (Cambridge: Cambridge University Press).
——2000: 'The Rule of Lawyers and the Ethos of Diplomats: Reflections on the Internal and External Legitimacy of WTO Dispute Settlement', Cambridge MA: Harvard Law School/Jean Monnet Chair (Harvard Jean Monnet Working paper 09/00).
Wei-Ming, Tu 1988: 'Confucius and Confucianism', *Encyclopedia Britannica, Macropedia*, vol. 16, pp. 653–62.
——ed. 1996: *Confucian Traditions in East Asian Modernity. Moral Education and Economic Culture in Japan and the Four Mini Dragons* (Cambridge: Cambridge University Press).
Weiner, Tim and Gori, Graham 2000: 'Can Mexico's New Leader Really Work Wonders?', *NYT* (29 Oct): 3.1, 12.
Weingast, Barry R. 1993: 'Constitutions as Governance Structures: The Political Foundations of Secure Markets', *Journal of Institutional and Theoretical Economics* 149: 286–311.
——1995: 'The Economic Role of Political Institutions: Market-Preserving Federalism and Economic Development', *Journal of Law, Economics, and Organization* 11/1 (April): 1–31.
Weinstein, Jay 1987: 'Editorial Foreword'. In Louis Schneider, ed., *Paradox and Society. The Work of Bernard Mandeville* (New Brunswick, NJ: Transaction Publishers), pp. 1–22.
Weir, Margaret 1992: *Politics and Jobs. The Boundaries of Employment Policy in the United States* (Princeton, NJ: Princeton University Press).
——ed. 1997: *The Social Divide. Political Parties and the Future of Activist Government* (Washington DC: Brookings Institution Press/New York: Russell Sage Foundation Press).
Weisbrod, Carol 1999/2000: 'Insurance and the Utopian World', *Connecticut Insurance Law Journal* 6/2: 381–422.

Weiss, Linda 1993: 'War, the State, and the Origins of the Japanese Employment System', *Politics and Society* 21/3: 325–54.
——1998: *The Myth of the Powerless State* (Ithaca, NY: Cornell University Press).
Welch, Lawrence Stephenson 1993: 'Outward Foreign Licensing by Australian Companies'. In Peter J. Buckley and Pervez N. Ghauri, eds, *The Internationalisation of the Firm. A Reader* (London: Academic Press), pp. 64–90.
Wellisch, Dietmar and Walz, Uwe 1998: 'Why Do Rich Countries Prefer Free Trade Over Free Migration? The Role of the Welfare State', *European Economic Review* 42/8: 1595–612.
Western, Bruce 1997: *Between Class and Market. Postwar Unionization in the Capitalist Democracies* (Princeton, NJ: Princeton University Press).
White, Gordon, Goodman, Roger and Kwon, Huck-ju 1998: 'The Politics of Welfare in East Asia'. In Richard Maidment, David Goldblatt and Jeremy Mitchell, eds, *Governance in the Asia-Pacific* (London: Routledge), pp. 195–220.
Wiebe, Robert H. 1967: *The Search for Order 1877–1920* (New York: Hill and Wang).
Wildawsky, Aaron 1987: 'Choosing Preferences by Constructing Institutions. A Cultural Theory of Preference Formation', *APSR* 81: 3–21.
Wilensky, Harold 1975: *The Welfare State and Equality* (Berkeley/Los Angeles: University of California Press).
——2002: *Rich Democracies: Political Economy, Public Policy, and Performance* (Berkeley/Los Angeles: University of California Press).
Wilkins, Mira and Schroeter, Harm G., eds, 1998: *The Free Standing Company in the World Economy, 1830–1996* (Oxford: Oxford University Press).
Wilkinson, Barry 1994: *Labour and Industry in the Asia-Pacific. Lessons from the Newly Industrialized Countries* (Berlin: de Gruyter).
Will, George F. 2002: 'Bush Plays Politics with Trade', *IHT* (8 March): 4.
Williams, Bernard 1973: *Problems of the Self* (Cambridge: Cambridge University Press).
Williams, William Carlos 1986 [1927]: *The Collected Poems of William Carlos Williams, vol. I: 1909–1939* (New York: New Directions).
Williamson, Jeffrey G. 1964: *American Growth and the Balance of Payments, 1820–1913. A Study of the Long Swing* (UNCP).
——1974: *Late Nineteenth Century American Development: A General Equilibrium History* (Cambridge: Cambridge University Press).
——1995: 'The Evolution of Global Labor Markets Since 1830: Background Evidence and Hypothesis', *Explorations in Economic History* 32/2 (April): 141–96.
——1996: 'Globalization, Convergence, and History', *JEH* 56/2 (June): 1–30.
——1997: 'Globalization and Inequality. Past and Present', *World Bank Research Observer* 12/2 (Aug): 117–35.
——1998a: 'Globalization and the Labor Market: Using History to Inform Policy'. In Aghion and Williamson 1998, pp. 103–200.
——1998b: 'Globalization, Labor Markets and Policy Backlash in the Past', *JEP* 12/4 (Fall): 51–72.
Williamson, Oliver E. 1985: *The Economic Institutions of Capitalism: Firms, Markets, Relational Contracting* (New York: Free Press).
——1993: 'Transaction Cost Economics and Organization Theory'. In idem, *The Mechanisms of Governance* (Oxford: Oxford University Press, 1996), pp. 219–49.
Wilson, Woodrow 1911: 'Inaugural Address as Governor of New Jersey'. In idem, *The Public Papers of Woodrow Wilson,* vol. 2 (New York: Harper and Row, 1925), pp. 270–82.
Winer, Stanley J. 1983: 'Some Evidence on the Effects of the Separation of Spending and Taxing Decisions', *JPE* 91: 126–40.
Winham, Gilbert R. 1986: *International Trade and the Tokyo Round Negotiation* (Princeton, NJ: Princeton University Press).

Wiseman, Michael 1997: 'Welfare Reform in the United States: A Background Paper', *Housing Policy Debate* 7/3: 1–54.
Wittfogel, Karl 1931: *Wirtschaft und Gesellschaft Chinas. Versuch der wissenschaftlichen Analyse einer großen asiatischen Agrargesellschaft* (Leipzig: Hirschfeld).
——1957: *Oriental Despotism: A Study in Total Power* (New Haven, CT: Yale University Press).
Wolferen, Karel van 1989: *The Enigma of Japanese Power* (New York: Knopf).
Wolff, Birgitta 1995: *Organisation durch Verträge. Koordination und Motivation in Unternehmen* (Wiesbaden: Deutscher Universitätsverlag).
——1996: 'Incentive-Compatible Change Management in a Welfare State: Asking the Right Questions in the German Standort-Debate', Cambridge, MA: Harvard University, Center for European Studies (Working paper Series 6.4).
——1999: *Anreizkompatible Reorganisation von Unternehmen* (Stuttgart: Schaeffer-Pöschel).
Wolff, Birgitta and Lazear, Edward P. 2001: *Einführung in die Personalökonomik* (Stuttgart: Schäffer-Poeschel).
Wollheim, Richard 1958: 'Democracy', *Journal of the History of Ideas* 19/2 (April): 225–42.
Wong, John and Wong, Aline 1995: 'Confucian Values as a Social Framework for Singapore's Economic Development'. In Yu and Lee 1995, pp. 293–326.
Woo, Jenny Hay 1991: 'Education and Economic Growth in Taiwan: A Case of Successful Planning', *World Development* 19: 1029–44.
Woo, Wing Thye, Sachs, Jeffrey D. and Schwab, Klaus, eds 2000: *The Asian Financial Crisis. Lessons for a Resilient Asia* (Cambridge, MA: MIT Press).
Wood, Adrian 1995: *North–South Trade, Employment and Inequality. Changing Fortunes in a Skill-Driven World* (Oxford: Clarendon Press).
——1997: 'Openness and Wage Inequality in Developing Countries: The Latin American Challenge to East Asian Conventional Wisdom', *World Bank Economic Review* 11/1 (Jan): 33–57.
——1998: 'Globalization and the Rise in Labour Market Inequalities', *Economic Journal* 108 (Sept): 1463–82.
Wood, Diane P. 1989: 'International Jurisdiction in National Legal Systems: The Case of Antitrust', *Northwestern Journal of International Law and Business* 10/1 (Spring): 56–74.
——1994: 'United States Antitrust Law in the Global Market', *Indiana Journal of Global Legal Studies* 1/2 (Spring): 409–29.
——1996: 'Regulation in the Single Global Market: From Anarchy to World Federalism', *Ohio Northern University Law Review* 23/2: 297–307.
——1999: 'International Law and Federalism: What is the Reach of Regulation?', *Harvard Journal of Law and Public Policy* 23/1 (Fall): 97–110.
——2000: 'Diffusion and Focus in International Law Scholarship (What's Wrong with International Law Scholarship?)', *Chicago Journal of International Law* 1/1 (Spring): 141–8.
Wood, Stewart 2001a: 'Labour Market Regimes Under Threat? Sources of Continuity in Germany, Britain and Sweden'. In Pierson 2001, pp. 368–407.
——2001b: 'Business, Government and the Patterns of Labor Market Policy in Germany, Britain and France'. In Hall and Soskice 2001, pp. 247–74.
Woodiwiss, Anthony 1998: *Globalization, Human Rights and Labour Law in Pacific Asia* (Cambridge: Cambridge University Press).
Woolcock, Stephen 2000: 'European Trade Policy. Global Pressures and Domestic Constraints'. In Wallace and Wallace 2000, pp. 373–99.
World Bank 1993: *The East Asian Miracle: Economic Growth and Public Policy* (Oxford: Oxford University Press).
——1998: *World Development Indicators* (Washington DC: World Bank, CD ROM).
Wright, Gordon 1964: *Rural Revolution in France. The Peasantry in the Twentieth Century* (Stanford: Stanford University Press/Oxford: Oxford University Press).

Wright, Quincy 1944: 'The United States and International Agreements', *AmJIL* 38/3 (July): 341–55.
WTO 2001: *Annual Report* (Geneva: WTO).
Yamamura, Kozo, ed. 1997: *A Vision of a New Liberalism? Critical Essays on Murakami's Anticlassical Analysis* (Stanford: Stanford University Press).
You, Jong-Il 1995: 'Changing Capital-Labor Relations in South Korea'. In Juliet Schorr and Jong-Il You, eds, *Capital, the State and Labour. A Global Perspective (*Aldershot: Edward Elgar), pp. 111–51.
Young, Oran R. 1994: *International Governance. Protecting the Environment in a Stateless Society* (Ithaca, NY: Cornell University Press).
Yu, Tzong-shian 1989: 'Taiwan's Economic Development: A Case of Growth with Equity'. In Y. C. Jao, Victor Mok and Lok-sang Ho, eds, *Economic Development in Chinese Societies: Models and Experiences* (Hong Kong: Hong Kong University Press), pp. 207–20.
Yu, Tzong-shian and Lee, Joseph S. 1995: *Confucianism and Economic Development* (Taipeh: Chung-Hua Institution for Economic Research).
Zamagni, Stephano 1989: 'Economic Laws'. In Eatwell et al. 1989, pp. 99–104.
Zebel, Sydney H. 1940: 'Fair Trade: An English Reaction to the Breakdown of the Cobden Treaty System', *Journal of Modern History* 12/2 (June): 161–85.
Zeile, William J. 1997: 'US Intrafirm Trade in Goods', *Survey of Current Business* (Feb): 23–38.
——2000: 'US Affililates of Foreign Companies Operations in 1998', *Survey of Current Business* (Aug): 141–58.
Zilsel, Edgar 1942: 'The Genesis of the Concept of Physical Law', *Philosophical Review* 51/3 (May): 245–79.
Zöllner, Wolfgang and Loritz, Karl-Georg 1998: *Arbeitsrecht*, 5th edn (München: Beck).
Zolo, Danilo 1991: *Democracy and Complexity: A Realist Approach*, trans. David McKie (University Park, PA: Pennsylvania State University Press).
Zürn, Michael 1992: 'Jenseits der Staatlichkeit. Über die Folgen der ungleichzeitigen Denationalisierung', *Leviathan* 20/4: 490–513.
——1998: *Regieren jenseits des Nationalstaates. Globalisierung und Denationalisierung als Chance* (Frankfurt am Main: Suhrkamp).
Zukunftskommission der Friedrich-Ebert-Stiftung 1998: *Wirtschaftliche Leistungsfähigkeit, sozialer Zusammenhalt, ökologische Nachhaltigkeit. Drei Ziele – ein Weg* (Bonn: Dietz Verlag).
Zwiedineck-Südenhorst, Otto von 1911: *Sozialpolitik* (Leipzig: Teubner).
——1924: 'Zum Schicksal der Sozialpolitik in Deutschland', *Schmollers Jahrbuch* 47: 77–142.
——1925: *Macht und ökonomisches Gesetz* (München: Haeber).

Index